CARMELITE MONASTERY
BARRE, VERMONT

W9-ADV-650

THE DEVELOPMENT OF CHRISTIAN
DOCTRINE BEFORE THE COUNCIL OF NICAEA

VOLUME ONE

THE DEVELOPMENT OF CHRISTIAN DOCTRINE BEFORE THE COUNCIL OF NICAEA

VOLUME ONE

THE THEOLOGY OF

JEWISH CHRISTIANITY

JEAN DANIÉLOU

Translated and edited by

JOHN A. BAKER

LONDON

DARTON, LONGMAN & TODD

CHICAGO

THE HENRY REGNERY COMPANY

HENRY REGNERY COMPANY
114 West Illinois Street
Chicago, Illinois 60610

First published 1964

© *1964, Darton, Longman & Todd Ltd*

© *1964 Henry Regnery Company*

230

Manufactured in the United States of America
Library of Congress Catalog Card No. 64-25658

CONTENTS

NOTE ON THE FIRST ENGLISH LANGUAGE EDITION

This edition is far from being merely a translation of the French edition of 1958. With the needs of students particularly in mind, the author has, in conjunction with the translator, taken the opportunity to make important alterations both in content and arrangement, with the purpose of enhancing the usefulness of the work.

As regards arrangement, the most notable feature is that a great quantity of reference material and of discussion of secondary points has been transferred to footnotes in order to allow a freer and clearer reading of the main argument. The order of chapters has also been revised to give a more satisfying logical sequence, and the bibliography has been re-arranged in a more convenient form.

The not inconsiderable additions and expansions include: the insertion of several new pages into the account of New Testament Apocrypha in Chapter 1 and extensive revision of the discussion; the addition of some fifty new references to the patristic texts and to more recent literature; the enlarging and rewriting of the Introduction and Conclusion to bring out the wider implications of the study and to clarify certain points raised in comment on the French edition; the expansion of the Bibliography to include all the literature to which reference is made in the course of the work; and the addition of a Glossary to ease the path of students unfamiliar with the field.

Finally it may be mentioned that the patristic references have been corrected where necessary; and, not least, that the author has in numerous places revised and clarified details in the argument.

GLOSSARY

(a) General

AGRAPHON (Gk.: 'unwritten'). A Dominical saying derived from a source other than the received text of the canonical Gospels.

ALLEGORICAL SENSE *vide* SENSE.

ANAGOGICAL SENSE *vide* SENSE.

ANAPHORA (Gk.: 'offering'). The central section of the Eucharistic liturgy from the Sursum Corda up to and including the Communion.

ANTHROPOS, androgynous. According to an ancient myth the human race was descended from a primal being who was both male and female in one, the androgynous Anthropos. A well-known, and not wholly serious, presentation of this myth is to be found in Plato, *Symposium* 189–192, but its origins go far back into the history of the Ancient Near East, in particular that of Babylonia and Sumeria.

APOCRYPHON (Gk.: 'hidden'). A name traditionally given to those Jewish works found in the LXX but not in the Hebrew canon of Scripture, and by modern critical scholarship to early Christian works outside the N.T. Canon but belonging to one of the genres of writing found within it. The term is also applied loosely to some pseudepigrapha or agrapha.

COSMOCRATOR (Gk.: 'world-ruler'). A term, found in the N.T. (*Eph.* 6:12) and borrowed from Hellenistic religion, in which it denoted the spiritual powers (often identified, under the influence of Babylonian astrological theories, with the planets) who were thought to exercise a baleful tyranny over Nature and human destinies. A considerable element in the joy of the early Christian was his sense that Christ by His victory had released the believer from their domination.

ENCRATISM. (Gk: ἐγκράτεια, self-control). Extreme severity in ascetic teaching and practice. Those, both Christian and Gnostic, who followed this way of life in the early centuries of the Church are known as Encratites.

EPICLESIS (Gk.: 'invocation'). The term can have the general sense of 'petition', but most commonly refers to the invocation of the Holy Spirit on the Eucharistic elements or the worshippers during the ANAPHORA (q.v.), or of the Trinity in Baptism.

HAGGADA (Heb.: 'narration'). One of the two classes into which the traditions of Jewish piety were divided in the Rabbinic period. It comprised material, e.g. legends, anecdotes, etc., other than the HALAKHA (q.v.), the legal prescriptions. Cf. also MIDRASH.

HALAKHA (subst. from Heb. verb 'to walk': cf. *I Thess.* 4:1). Regulations formulated by the Rabbinic schools to cover situations not dealt with in the O.T. Law. Cf. also MIDRASH.

HEBDOMAD. In the system of Valentinian gnosis the world of seven heavens inhabited by the seven planetary powers (or alternatively their principal, the Demiurge, who ruled over it), and situated immediately below the OGDOAD (q.v.).

HYPOSTASIS. A Greek term meaning 'basis' or 'foundation', and so the 'substance' of a thing, that by virtue of which it is a real existent. During the fourth century A.D. it came to be used for an individual instance of such a substantial reality, a particular existent being, notably the Persons of the Trinity. In modern scholarship it is still used in this sense, as e.g. in discussion whether the figure of Wisdom in the O.T. and Apocrypha is intended as a hypostasis, or simply as a personified attribute of God.

KABBALA. A late Hebrew term used as the name of a body of esoteric Jewish mystical speculation of a Gnostic type, probably dating from the first centuries A.D. In mediaeval and early modern times it attracted and influenced many thinkers outside Judaism.

KENOMA. In the system of Valentinian gnosis the temporal realm, the created flux of phenomenal existence, into which men are born, and from which the gnosis enables its adepts to escape.

LITERAL SENSE *vide* SENSE.

LOGION. A term which may be used generally to denote any Dominical saying. In a more restricted sense it is applied to non-canonical sayings, such as those in the *Oxyrhynchus Papyri* (nos. 1 and 654), the *Gospel of Thomas*, etc.

LULAB (Heb.: 'palm-branch'). One of the four festal branches, consisting of a palm-shoot bound up together with three myrtle twigs and two willow branches, in obedience to the prescription in *Lev.* 23:40 for the ceremonial at the Feast of Tabernacles. During the chanting of the Hallel (*Ps.* 118) the branches are waved toward the four winds, the heaven and the earth. Representations of them have been found on a coin of Bar-Kokhba, and on glassware from the Jewish catacombs in Rome.

MAZDAISM. An early and relatively non-syncretistic form of the Zoroastrian religion. It was Zoroaster who added the epithet *mazda* ('wise') to the ancient divine name *Ahura* ('Lord') to denote the Supreme Creator God; and consequently his religion was known as the 'worship of Mazda' to differentiate it from the 'worship of Ahura', a description which might equally well have been applied to the pagan cults he was attempting to supersede.

MERKABA (Heb.: 'chariot'). The throne-chariot of Yahweh. Beginning from the visions of Ezekiel (chh. 1 and 10) Judaism developed a considerable mystical speculation around the *merkaba*. The first intimation of such teaching, which was always strictly esoteric, may be as early as *Ecclus* 49:8.

MIDRASH. A corpus of Jewish exegesis, including both HAGGADA (q.v.) and HALAKHA (q.v.), designed to extract religious value from every detail of the OT text, even the most trifling incidentals. Some of the material may date from as early as the second century B.C. Its methods are akin to those of Christian allegory and typology, which may indeed be considerably indebted to it.

MISHNAH. The authoritative written version of the oral Law of Judaism, asserted by the Pharisaic party to have been delivered to Moses on Sinai.

MORAL SENSE *vide* SENSE.

NOACHIC PRECEPTS. According to the O.T. (*Gn.* 9:1-17, esp. vv. 4-7) the fundamental law of all human society, laid down by God in His everlasting covenant with the whole human race in the person of Noah. The commands are to abstain from eating the blood with the meat, and from murder, and to multiply the human race. Cf. the rules of the Apostolic Council for the guidance of Gentile Christians, *Acts* 15:29.

OGDOAD. In the developed Valentinian gnosis (though possibly not in the original teaching of Valentinus himself) the four highest syzygies (q.v.) of the Pleroma (q.v.), constituting an eightfold Godhead, or a Godhead with eight principal attributes or aspects, the source of all other being. In the system, however, the term is also applied to the highest of the four Places outside the Pleroma, probably because it comes immediately above the sevenfold system of heavens, the Hebdomad (q.v.), ruled by the Demiurge. This ogdoad is the dwelling-place of Sophia and Jesus. In both cases the ogdoad represents the divine realm, the perfect order to which the Gnostic seeks to escape, as opposed to the Hebdomad, the imperfect and tyrannous order in which he is embroiled.

PLEROMA. In the system of Valentinian gnosis the eternal realm, the world of unchanging spiritual existence beyond all the heavens, to which the initiate attains by virtue of the gnosis.

PROTOCTIST (Gk.: 'first-created'). An epithet applied to the great angels, the first works of the divine Creator.

PSYCHICS. Valentinian Gnosticism divided mankind into three classes, corresponding to the three levels of existence—spirit (*pneuma*), soul (*psyche*) and matter (*hyle*). Salvation consisted in escaping from the phenomenal world of matter and passion, the *kenoma* (q.v.). 'Hylics' were those, viz. the pagans, who never escaped but were eternally lost. 'Pneumatics' were the Valentinians who escaped fully, attaining the *pleroma* (q.v.) through their esoteric knowledge (*gnosis*). 'Psychics' were ordinary Christians (also referred to, e.g. in the *Gospel of Philip*, as 'Catholics' or 'apostolics') who made a partial escape to the lowest heaven, that of the Demiurge, by virtue of faith (*pistis*—inferior to *gnosis*) and good works.

SENSE. In Scholastic exegesis Scripture is understood in two main senses, the Literal and the Typical. By the *Literal* sense is denoted that meaning which the author consciously, deliberately and directly intended; the *Typical* sense (sometimes called 'spiritual' or 'mystical') is that by which some person, object or event in the text (the 'type') has reference to a truth revealed literally at a later period (the 'antitype'). The Typical sense has three subdivisions: the *allegorical*, where the reference of the type is to an antitypal belief, the *moral*, relating to an antitypal virtue, and the *anagogical*, relating to an antitypal blessing or promise.

SYZYGY (Gk.: 'couple'). A term used in Valentinian gnosis for the pairs of Aeons emanating in series from the Pleroma (q.v.), and linking it with the Demiurge, and so with the Kenoma (q.v.).

TARGUM. An officially accepted translation of the Hebrew OT into Aramaic, made in Later Judaism for the benefit of synagogue congregations for whom Hebrew was a dead language. Such translations were to a great extent paraphrases, incorporating explanatory expansions; the term may therefore loosely be applied to the products of similar processes in Christianity.

TESTIMONIA. The term used to denote those OT passages held by the Early Church to be particularly prophetic of Christ, and which, in the view of some scholars, were at one time collated in handbooks for the benefit of the preaching, teaching and apologetic ministries, though no such books are extant.

(b) Proper names

AXIONICUS. A disciple of Valentinus, active at Antioch *c*. A.D. 180. According to Hippolytus one of the leading exponents of Valentinianism in the East, he nevertheless added little or nothing to his master's system

BAR-DAISAN. A Syrian heretical teacher from Edessa, who flourished at the end of the second century A.D. His system, which may perhaps best be described as para-Gnostic, was strongly fatalistic.

BARDESANES *vide* BAR-DAISAN.

BASILIDES. A Gnostic leader, active at Alexandria *c*. A.D. 140. His teaching offered men escape from the world of matter and from the tyranny of the Creator God of the O.T. through the gnosis revealed for the benefit of the initiate by the divine Mind present in Jesus. His system is characterised by the immense number of heavens (365) and powers interposed between the Supreme God and the world.

CERDO. A Syrian Gnostic leader, active in Rome *c*. A.D. 140. He distinguished the God of the O.T. from the true God, the Father of Jesus Christ, and denied the resurrection of the body.

HERACLEON. A Valentinian Gnostic teacher, active *c*. A.D. 160, the author of the *Hypomnemata*, an allegorising commentary on the Fourth Gospel, of which some fragments are extant.

HERODIANS. A party within Judaism at the time of Our Lord, and hostile to Him (*Mt.* 22:16; *Mk.* 3:6, 12:13).

PISTIS SOPHIA. A third-century Egyptian text, the work of a writer greatly influenced by Valentinian Gnosticism. It is cast in the form of post-Resurrection teaching given by Jesus.

PNEUMATOMACHI. A heretical sect active in the East, A.D. 370–400, who denied the divinity of the Holy Ghost. From a probably false tradition that they were founded by Macedonius, the Semi-Arian bishop of Constantinople (deposed A.D. 360), they were also known as 'Macedonians'.

PTOLEMAEUS. The leading disciple of Valentinus in Italy (*fl. c.* A.D. 180), author of the *Letter to Flora*, a document, preserved in Epiphanius, *Haer.* 33, which seeks to define those portions of the Mosaic Law still valid since Christ, and which is of great importance for the study of Gnosticism.

THERAPEUTAE. A sect of Egyptian Jews (*fl.* first century B.C.), both men and women, who lived by a severe ascetic rule in monastic communities. Their practice and teaching are described by Philo in the *De Vita contemplativa*. A feature of their spirituality was the allegorical interpretation of the O.T.

VALENTINUS. The greatest of the Gnostic teachers, active at Rome *c.* A.D. 150. His disciples included Theodotus, elements of whose teachings have been preserved by Clement of Alexandria in the *Excerpta ex Theodoto*, Heracleon (q.v.) and Mark the Magician, founder of the Marcosian sect. For the elements of the Valentinian system, cf. KENOMA, OGDOAD, PLEROMA, PSYCHICS, SYZYGY.

LIST OF ABBREVIATIONS

ACW	Ancient Christian Writers
A.T.	Altes Testament; Ancien Testament
ATR	Anglican Theological Review
BJRL	Bulletin of the John Rylands Library
BWANT	Beiträge zur Wissenschaft vom Alten und Neuen Testament
BZ	Byzantinische Zeitschrift
BZNW	Beihefte zur Zeitschrift für die neutestamentliche Wissenschaft
CA	Cahiers archéologiques
CDC	Damascus Document
CSEL	Corpus Scriptorum Ecclesiasticorum Latinorum
DSD	Dead Sea Rule of the Community ('Manual of Discipline')
DSH	Dead Sea Midrash of Habakkuk
DSS	Dead Sea Scrolls
DST	Dead Sea Psalms of Thanksgiving ('Hodayoth')
DSW	Dead Sea War Scroll ('War of the Sons of Light and the Sons of Darkness')
EE	Estudios Ecclesiasticos
EL	Études Liturgiques
Eph L	Ephemerides Liturgicae
E.T.	English Translation
ET	Evangelische Theologie
ETL	Ephemerides Theologicae Lovanienses
EVV	English Versions
GCS	Griechische christliche Schriftsteller (cf. Bibliography s.v.)
HNT	Handbuch zum Neuen Testament
HTR	Harvard Theological Review
JA	Journal Asiatique
JBL	Journal of Biblical Literature
JEH	Journal of Ecclesiastical History
JJS	Journal of Jewish Studies
JTS	Journal of Theological Studies
LXX	Septuagint
MSR	Mélanges des Sciences Religieuses
MT	Massoretic text
N.F.	Neue Folge
NRT	Nouvelle Revue Théologique
N.S.	New series
N.T.	New Testament; Neues Testament; Nouveau Testament
NTS	New Testament Studies
OCP	Orientalia Christiana Periodica
OS	Ostkirchliche Studien
O.T.	Old Testament
PG	Patrologiae graecae cursus completus (cf. Bibliography, 'Migne, J.P.')
PO	Patrologie Orientale (cf. Bibliography s.v.)
RAC	Reallexikon für Antike und Christentum
RB	Revue Biblique
RBen	Revue Bénédictine

REG	Revue des Études Grecques
REJ	Revue des Études Juives
Rev SR	Revue des Sciences Religieuses
Rev T	Revista de Teologia
RHR	Revue de l'Histoire des Religions
Riv AC	Rivista di Archeologia Cristiana
ROC	Revue de l'Orient Chrétien
RP	Revue Philologique
RQ	Römische Quartalschrift
RQH	Revue des Questions Historiques
RSPT	Revue des Sciences Philosophiques et Théologiques
RSR	Recherches de Science Religieuse
RT	Recherches théologiques
RV (mg)	Revised Version (margin)
SJT	Scottish Journal of Theology
ST	Studia Theologica
Stud Patr	Studia Patristica
TL	Theologische Literaturzeitung
TR	Theologische Rundschau
TS	Theological Studies
TWNT	Theologisches Wörterbuch zum Neuen Testament
TZ	Theologische Zeitschrift
VC	Vigiliae Christianae
VS	Vie Spirituelle
VT	Vetus Testamentum
WW	Wissenschaft und Wahrheit
ZAW	Zeitschrift für die alttestamentliche Wissenschaft
ZKG	Zeitschrift für Kirchengeschichte
ZKT	Zeitschrift für katholische Theologie
ZNW	Zeitschrift für die neutestamentliche Wissenschaft
ZRGG	Zeitschrift für Religions- und Geistesgeschichte
ZTK	Zeitschrift für Theologie und Kirche

INTRODUCTION

THREE worlds went to the making of the Christian Church, three cultures, three visions and expressions of truth—the Jewish, the Hellenistic and the Latin; and each of them produced its own distinctive Theology. By Theology is here meant the attempt to construct a systematic world-view on the basis of the data provided by the divine events of the Incarnation and Resurrection of the Word. It is not Revelation, but the product of reflection on the Revelation, at once exploring and expounding the meaning of the latter at ever deeper levels, and bringing to light its power and value for the individual soul, for the Church, for society, for history and for the whole created order. It is not suggested that Theology is the product of a phase which begins after Revelation is complete; nor that Revelation is to be identified simply with the Scriptures, and Theology with non-canonical writings. As soon as Revelation began there was bound to be Theology; for successful Revelation—which God's must surely be—implies response, and response involves reflection on the fact and in the power of the divine grace in the very Revelation itself. Revelation must indeed be logically prior to Theology, but chronologically, for practical purposes, it is possible for us to treat them as contemporary.

Theology, thus strictly understood, is already present in the New Testament itself, most noticeably perhaps in the writings of St. Paul and St. John, but no less certainly in all the canonical books, from *Matthew* to *Revelation*; and this Biblical Theology (though not all scholars who use the term do so to denote the same thing) has for Christians the force of a Rule of Faith. It is a distinctive and inspired creation. Nevertheless, it naturally and inevitably has its points of contact and affinities with extra-canonical theology—and what is more, with theology of both Hellenistic and Jewish Christian type. Indeed, as regards the latter, there are good grounds, as the reader of the present work will discover, for considering the Jewish Christian theologising within the New Testament not as a more elementary stage of that found elsewhere, but as in fact a profounder form of a teaching which has survived in more archaic and primitive versions in other and later writings.

It may be asked, however, even today what evidence there is that such a distinctive, specifically Jewish Christian theology existed? Conventional courses of instruction on the history of Christian Doctrine begin with the Apostolic Fathers and the Apologists, and trace the progess of dogmatic thought by the steady increase in the infiltration of Greek philosophical terms and concepts. Harnack, for example, regarded Theology as born from the union of the Gospel message and Greek philosophy; and in his *History of Dogma* a Jewish Christian theology finds no place, simply because he never suspected its existence.

The reasons for this mistake, for such it must now be counted, were twofold. First, the fact that our own civilisation derived its manner of expressing metaphysical things entirely from the Greek conceptual system blinded scholars to the possibility that the classic documents of their faith might contain other quite different terms and images for the same realities. Theology and Greek thought being thus equated, the emergence of the one was deduced from the incidence of the other; and the level of Trinitarian orthodoxy in, say, the *Shepherd of Hermas*, or the *Didache* was assessed by the occurrence or otherwise of particular words and illustrations current in later times. Not the least damaging consequence of this method was the view, still current among many students, that either the full Catholic faith did not develop until the fourth or fifth century or else that it must be assumed *a priori* to have been present in the earliest period in default of documentary evidence.

The second, and complementary, reason for this false picture of Christian history was something which could not be helped: the paucity of material from which this earliest theology could be reconstructed. Indeed, the literary evidence can still hardly be described as plentiful; but it is at last sufficient in quantity to make practicable an attempt at a comprehensive survey such as the present volume. The phases in this advance were three. First, in the closing years of the nineteenth century, after two generations of unprecedentedly intense critical study of the central texts, scholars were free to turn their attention to more exotic works, with the result that for the first time a whole range of fragments, apocalypses, Old and New Testament apocrypha and pseudepigrapha became available in critical editions. Between the years 1890 and 1914 the publications of such scholars as Lipsius, Violet, Charles, Lightfoot, Resch, Preuschen, Tisserant and Rendel Harris opened up for inspection a whole mass of material in a variety of languages, much of which had come to light only in comparatively recent times as a result of the more systematic and expert exploration of libraries and MS collections. This new material, however, presented baffling problems. The second phase, from 1914 to 1946, was a time of activity, but little progress; and in spite of the pioneer work of such men as Hilgenfeld, Hoennicke and Kittel recognition of Jewish Christianity as an entity was slow to come. No hypothesis seemed to propose a satisfactory *Sitz im Leben* for this literature so laboriously collected; it was not truly at home either with the writings of the New Testament, or with those of Hellenistic Gnosticism, or with Rabbinic Judaism—the only three candidates. The trouble was, though no one then fully realised it, that there was a great void in our knowledge of the religious world of the first and second centuries after Christ.

The breakthrough came when, in the years following 1946, this void was at least partly filled by the almost simultaneous discovery of the Dead Sea Scrolls and of the twelve volumes of Gnostic texts from Nag Hammadi, north of Luxor in Egypt. Since these texts became available the whole picture of the world of the Early Church has changed, as is well known, and not least a coherent setting has been found which makes it possible in large measure to identify a great many elements in writings already familiar as belonging to a homogeneous body of thought which we may call the theology of Jewish Christianity.

The forms in which this theology is embodied are of considerable diversity. There are the traditions of the Elders to which Papias, Irenaeus and Clement of Alexandria refer, and which they claim to have come down to them from Apostolic times, though distinguishing them from the Rule of Faith; there is the 'gnosis of the mysteries' into which the author of the *Epistle of Barnabas* proposes to initiate the more advanced Christians; and there are the special teachings, which purport to have been given in private by Christ to His followers after the Resurrection, and to have been preserved in oral tradition, and which have been transmitted to us in such works as the *Epistle of the Apostles* and the *Apocalypse of Peter*. Nevertheless, for all the variety of form, there is a similarity in the content of these works which suggests a common basis; and it is to help delineate this basis, Jewish Christian theology, that they are relevant to the present study.

For it should not be forgotten that our concern is not to describe and analyse theologians, but a theology. None of the great writers of the Early Church belongs wholly to one tradition, to one alone of the three worlds mentioned earlier. Consequently, when a fierce light is focussed on only those details in Ignatius or Justin or Tertullian, for example, which add to our knowledge of the Jewish Christian tradition, these figures are apt to appear strange and distorted. There may, indeed be advantages in this; they may seem more exciting than they did, and needed attention may be drawn to features of their work once all too cavalierly glossed over in the search for conventional formulas. At the same time it may not be out of place to warn the reader that a complete portrait of any particular Christian theologian of the first two, or even three, centuries will not be found either in this volume or in the second, each taken by itself; though the two in combination may have something of value to convey in suggesting how in other days Christian thinkers achieved the translation of the Gospel from the language of one world to that of another.

For all this, however, the principal subject remains the world of belief, and not its outstanding exponents. In so far as the conceptions of individuals are represented here, it is rather those of the nameless thousands of believers who did not move between the worlds, but worshipped God through the eyes, and served Him through the ordinances of their Jewish forefathers. These are they who pressed on to perfection, ceasing to speak of the first principles of Christ and rejoicing in the solid theological food of full-grown men (*Heb.* 5:14–6:1), who 'no longer babes' desired to hear of 'heavenly things' (IGNATIUS, *Trall.* V, 1–2). This food, these heavenly things, were the earliest Christian theology, a doctrinal system that was Semitic in structure and expression.

The distinguishing marks of this theology will become clearer in the following chapters. Fundamentally it is characterised by the fact that its imagery is that of the dominant Jewish thought-form of the time, namely apocalyptic. It is conceived in terms of the revelation of cosmic secrets; of the dwelling-places of angels and demons and the souls of men; of the secrets of history written beforehand in the book of God; of the mystery of the Cross of glory, and of the pre-existent Church, at once old and yet young and beautiful. The heart of its faith is the affirmation that Christ alone has penetrated beyond the veil, and opened the seals of the heavenly scroll, achieving Paradise for those who bear the Name of the Son of God.

This theology suffered from serious limitations in its terminology and in some of its conclusions; and these defects exposed it to heresies and misinterpretations which vitiated its usefulness as a vehicle of salvation, and led to its supersession by a more adequate instrument. It survived in some measure, however, in Syriac Christianity, which is startlingly marked both in its liturgical and other remains by a strongly visionary and apocalyptic character. But the reconstruction of Jewish Christian theology is far from being of merely academic historical interest; it is of vital service to us, both because the Jewish Christian interpretation of the Faith is that of a tradition still in living continuity with the world of Scripture, and because it preserved emphases in the wholeness of Christ which we very much need to re-learn.

Such a work as this must inevitably draw heavily on a multitude of specialist contributions. A glance at the Bibliography will show both the author's indebtedness to many scholars, among whom the names of Schoeps, Cullmann, Goppelt and Dix should be especially acknowledged, and also how marvellously it has become possible in the last ten years, after seventeen centuries of obscurity, to begin to discern once again the features of the unknown face of the Primitive Church.

JEAN DANIÉLOU

CHAPTER ONE

THE LITERARY HERITAGE OF JEWISH CHRISTIANITY

B ETWEEN the Incarnation and the emergence of Hellenistic theology in the works of the Apologists there was a phase of Christian thought of which the character is little known, because the works in which it expressed itself have largely disappeared.

The reasons for this disappearance are twofold. First, the works in question represented an incomplete expression of Christian truth, and gave place to a more comprehensive understanding. Secondly, they were the product of a particular environment, Christianity of a Semitic or (as Dix[1] has called it) Syriac structure; and when this environment had completely disappeared, no further interest was taken in the works which had characterised it. The labours of the last fifty years have, however, made it possible to reconstruct part of this lost literary heritage; and this chapter must, therefore, be devoted to the preliminary task of identifying and describing such of these sources as research has made available.

It will be best to begin by defining exactly what is meant by the term 'Jewish Christianity', for it has three possible references. First, it may designate those *Jews who acknowledged Christ as a prophet or a Messiah, but not as the Son of God,* and thus form a separate class, half-way between Jews and Christians. Perhaps the best known of this group are the Ebionites,[2] but they are by no means alone. Between the years A.D. 40 and 70 the Jewish world was disturbed by a wave of political and messianic excitement, and the propaganda associated with this movement exerted a strong influence on the young Christian communities,[3] which may possibly have been responsible for the various groups with which Saint Paul

1. Cf. G. DIX, *Jew and Greek*, London, 1953.
2. This sect forms the subject of H. J. SCHOEPS' great work, *Theologie und Geschichte des Judenchristentums.*
3. This is the view of Bo REICKE, *Diakonie, Festfreude und Zelos*, Uppsala, 1951, pp. 233–368.

clashed in Corinth, Colossae and Galatia. The effects of a Jewish messianism of this kind can certainly be detected in the materialistic millenarianism of Cerinthus.[4]

In addition to groups of the kinds mentioned so far, this first general class includes those Jewish Christian syncretists among whom Gnostic dualism seems to have made its earliest appearance. Before reaching its hellenised form in Basilides and Valentinus[5] this dualism had taken shape in Jewish Christian communities, probably under the influence of Iran. Examples of this earlier phase are the sects of Cerdo at Antioch, and Carpocrates at Alexandria[6]; Simon Magus,[7] the predecessor of Mark the Magician,[8] probably had a similar background. There was also a sect, the Elkesaites, or disciples of Elkesai, in which Ebionism and Gnosticism were mixed[9] and which appeared in the reign of Trajan.

The second possible reference for the term 'Jewish Christianity' is *the Christian community of Jerusalem*, dominated by James and the tendencies for which he stood. This community was perfectly orthodox in its Christianity but remained attached to certain Jewish ways of life, without, however, imposing them on proselytes from paganism.[10] Until A.D. 70 the church of Jerusalem enjoyed considerable prestige, so that Paul had to struggle to get his views accepted; and indeed, it was only after the fall of the city that the Pauline position definitely gained the upper hand.[11] Nevertheless, in spite of their differences there was always a basic unity underlying their different attitudes.[12]

After the fall of Jerusalem these Jewish Christians, sometimes given the name of Nazarenes, gradually disappeared. As regards their literary remains it is possible that the New Testament *Epistle of Jude* is theirs[13]; and they composed an Aramaic *Gospel according to the Hebrews*. In theology they remain faithful to an archaic tradition, restricted to monotheism and belief in the messianic role of Jesus—though, in contrast to the messianism of the Ebionites, theirs implied the divinity of Christ, and therefore entitles the

---

4. Cf. pp. 68 ff. below.   5. Cf. Glossary s.v.; also pp. 76 f. below.
6. For Cerdo cf. Glossary s.v.; on Carpocrates, pp. 84 f. below.
7. Cf. pp. 72 ff. below.   8. Cf. p. 76 below.   9. Cf. pp. 64 ff. below.
10. The Tübingen school were the first to recognise the opposition between this trend in Christianity and that led by Paul. They made the mistake, however, of linking Peter with the Jerusalem circle, whereas he was in fact much closer to the Christianity of the missionary type.
11. Cf. S. G. F. BRANDON, *The Fall of Jerusalem and the Christian Church*, pp. 126–154.
12. As DIX (*Jew and Greek*, p. 66) has pointed out in correction of Brandon's thesis.
13. So DIX, *op. cit.*, p. 65.

Jerusalem church to the description 'orthodox' given it above. When obliged to quit Jerusalem with the rest of the Jews the group lost its vitality. Some may have joined the Ebionites; others, no doubt, were assimilated by the Hellenistic communities. Justin met some of them as late as the middle of the second century, and it is possible that their congregation survived even longer in eastern Syria.

Finally, a third possible reference of the term 'Jewish Christianity' is a type of *Christian thought expressing itself in forms borrowed from Judaism.* In this sense the term covers a much wider field. It does not necessarily involve any connection with the Jewish community, but includes, in addition to the groups already mentioned, men who had broken completely with the Jewish world, but who continued to think in its terms.[14] Thus the Apostle Paul, though by no means a Jewish Christian in the second of these three senses, was certainly one in this third sense. Nor was this kind of Jewish Christianity confined to Christians coming from Judaism. It was also found among pagan converts, for it is a universal fact of missionary experience that there is a considerable time-lag between the planting of the Gospel in a new people and its expression in the thought-forms of that people's culture.[15]

Jewish Christianity in this third sense is of the highest importance for the historical study of Christian doctrine.[16] Though spread over the whole Mediterranean basin, Christianity nevertheless remained until the middle of the second century in character a Judaistic religion. This statement, however, requires more exact definition, for the name 'Judaism' may in this period be given to three different phenomena.[17] First, it may connote no more than the continuing use of the Old Testament, which forms in any case an indispensable part of the Christian heritage. Secondly, it may refer to the Judaism contemporary with Christ, that of the Pharisees, Essenes and Zealots, to which the name Later Judaism (*Spätjudentum*) is commonly given; it was this Judaism whose thought-forms Christianity used at the first as its medium of expression, and was still using during the period studied in this volume. Finally, there was the rabbinical, legalistic Judaism

14. Cf. DIX, *op. cit.*, pp. 55–59.
15. Thus there have been Christians in India and Indian Christians now for three centuries, but there is still no Christian theology that is specifically Indian in character.
16. The credit for demonstrating this must go first and foremost to LEONHARD GOPPELT's classic study, *Christentum und Judentum.*
17. The following analysis is that of GOPPELT, *op. cit.*

developed after the Fall of Jerusalem; between this Judaism and Christianity there was continual and open war.

In this work Jewish Christianity should be understood to refer to *the expression of Christianity in the thought-forms of Later Judaism.* The latter was itself, however, an amalgam of various types, and these reappear in the varieties of Jewish Christianity. Thus we find Palestinian Jewish Christians of a somewhat Pharisaic and legalist tendency; apocalyptist and messianist groups in Asia Minor with Zealot characteristics; Christians under Essene influence, responsible at Rome for the *Shepherd of Hermas,* and at Edessa for the *Odes of Solomon*; and even a rabbinical type in the Aramaic-speaking church of eastern Syria.[18]

For the sake of completeness other Jewish influences on Christianity ought perhaps to be mentioned. Judaism remained a live and active force right down into the fourth century.[19] In the new forms which it took on in this period, especially in the Haggadic literature,[20] it continued to influence Christian writers. Justin was in contact with the Jew Trypho; Origen consulted rabbis, and borrowed exegeses from them; Syriac literature in particular absorbed Jewish *haggada*, notably in Eusebius of Emesa and Ephraem. But these were only secondary contributions, Jewish traditions incorporated in a whole that was no longer Jewish, and in any case fall outside the period under review.

If attention is confined to the earlier period, it will be found that in spite of the variety of constituent elements there was a common outlook. The thesis of this volume is that *there was a first form of Christian theology expressed in Jewish-Semitic terms,* and it is this theology which is the real object of the present study. Chronologically this theology overlaps with the period generally known as that of the Apostolic Fathers, but its forms of thought and expression are not necessarily contemporary with theirs. Are there then any means of arriving at this theology? any documents from which it can be known? or have they not in fact as good as disappeared? It is the conviction of the present writer that they have not, and that a reconstruction is possible[21]; and the first step in any such reconstruction

18. The influence of Philo is not included here, since it belongs to a type of Judaism expressed in the forms of Greek philosophy, and will therefore be of more direct concern in the study of Hellenistic Christianity.
19. Cf. MARCEL SIMON, *Verus Israel*, Paris, 1948, p. 14.
20. Cf. Glossary s.v. 'Haggada'.
21. The purpose of the present work might be expressed another way by saying that it is the author's ambition to do for orthodox what Schoeps has already done for heterodox Jewish Christianity.

must therefore clearly be to identify the literary heritage of Jewish Christianity.

This source material falls into three classes. First of all, there are the extant works which are the direct product of Jewish Christian thinking. These works present a number of problems which will have to be studied in the following pages. Secondly, there is the direct testimony of other writers, that is to say, the explicit attribution of certain doctrines to the primitive community by authors of a later date. This class of evidence raises the question of the traditions of the Elders, to be found in Irenaeus and Clement of Alexandria. Finally, there is indirect testimony, namely the presence in writers who are not Jewish Christians of doctrines which can be ascribed to Jewish Christianity. These writers may be orthodox—as, for instance, in the case of Justin, Irenaeus, Hippolytus and Methodius—but equally they may not; and this therefore raises the problem of those elements of archaic Jewish Christian theology which were taken over for their own use by the Gnostics, a question which will also have to be examined with some care.[22]

Old Testament Pseudepigrapha

The first problem then is to decide what works can be classed as the direct product of Jewish Christian thought. What criteria are available for their identification? First, there is the chronological one. The Jewish Christian period extends from the beginnings of Christianity to approximately the middle of the second century; hence evidence for the dating of a particular work becomes extremely relevant. A second criterion is that of literary genre. In this connection the discoveries at Qumran in particular, by enlarging our knowledge of the literature of Later Judaism, have made it much easier to distinguish which Christian works are constructed to the same pattern. Finally, there is the doctrinal criterion. Jewish Christianity expresses itself in certain characteristic categories of ideas, notably those of apocalyptic, and themes originating in these categories can be identified in Christian works. It should, of course, go without saying that all three criteria will not necessarily be applicable to each and every work.

The first group of works to be considered consists of a number of writings regarding which the main question is not whether they are of

22. The main documents involved under this head are listed in the closing pages of this chapter, but a full discussion of them will be found in chapter II.

Jewish origin, as it is quite obvious that they are, but whether they are Christian, and if so to what extent? They comprise certain Old Testament apocrypha in which it is hardly possible not to notice Christian features, and in particular three: the *Ascension of Isaiah*, *II Enoch* and the *Testaments of the Twelve Patriarchs*. These works certainly have a Jewish background, and are typical of Later Judaism in their literary forms—visions, ascensions, testaments. Moreover, they have a literary relationship to known Jewish works: *II Enoch* is related to *I Enoch*, the *Testaments* to the *Book of Jubilees*, the *Ascension* to the accounts of the martyrdoms of the prophets.[23]

The first problem posed by these works is to distinguish what comes from Judaism and what is Christian—an important question, since the answer is obviously of vital relevance to any study of the Christian contribution by itself. But an answer is not easily arrived at. It is true, as was remarked earlier, that the discoveries at Qumran have shown even more clearly than before the relationship between certain primitive Christian forms of presentation and those of the Jewish apocalypses. But even when with this help the Christian contributions have been identified and agreed, there remains the further question—secondary, but none the less real—whether the documents under discussion are Jewish works interpolated by Christians, or Christian works using Jewish material. Only the latter conclusion would make them genuinely Jewish Christian writings, the creation of Christians still deeply involved with Judaism.

The case admitting of the clearest solution is that of the *Ascension of Isaiah*. This work, which has survived in its entirety only in Ethiopic, consists of three parts: the Martyrdom of Isaiah, in the tradition of the Jewish *haggada* and in particular of the accounts of the martyrdoms of the prophets; the Testament of Hezekiah, a prophecy about Christ, the Church and the end of time; and the Vision of Isaiah, a revelation made to Isaiah by an angel concerning the heavenly world and the passage through it of the 'Beloved' in his descent and ascension. This last part belongs to the literary genre of visions, typical of apocalyptic, in which the heavenly world and its secrets are shown to a seer in the course of an ascension to heaven in which he is assisted by an angel. It is one of the most characteristic features of Jewish Christian literature.

The archaic character of the text is shown by numerous details. The presence of prophets is mentioned side by side with that of pastors and

23. Cf. CHARLES, *Apocrypha and Pseudepigrapha of the Old Testament, ad loc.*

presbyters (III, 27), a Jewish Christian characteristic that reappears in the *Didache* and the *Shepherd*. The trinitarian theology is expressed in terms of angelic beings.[24] The resurrection is described in terms very close to those of the *Gospel of Peter* (III, 15–17). Certain other details provide even more definite indications: the work records that the descent and nativity of the 'Beloved' were hidden from 'the heavens and all the princes and all the gods of this world' (XI, 16). Now this certainly looks like an earlier form of a passage in Ignatius of Antioch: 'And hidden from the prince of this world were the virginity of Mary and her childbearing' (*Eph*. XIX, 1). Since the *Epistles* of Ignatius come from the beginning of the second century, in this case the *Ascension of Isaiah* would belong to the end of the first.

Another detail suggests a similar dating. The author considers the end of the world to be near. It must be preceded by the coming of Antichrist (IV, 2). But this Antichrist is expected in the form of a reincarnation of Nero: 'Beliar will descend from his firmament in the likeness of a man, a lawless king, the slayer of his mother' (IV, 2). The same idea appears in the *Sibylline Oracles* (IV, 121), and probably also in the New Testament (*Rev*. 13:3 and 17:8).[25] Nero died in the year 68, and this belief in his return could probably only occur for a short time afterwards. Furthermore *Revelation* itself can hardly be very much later than the death of Nero, so that the *Ascension of Isaiah* must be placed in roughly the same period, probably between the years 80 and 90.

There remains the question of the geographical and religious background of the work. It is quite typical of Palestinian Jewish Christian apocalyptic. On the other hand it does not exhibit the characteristics of the Asiatic community, its millenarianism being only a very attenuated form[26] (IV, 16). This suggests the centre where Palestinian Jewish Christians seem mostly to have gathered after the year 70, namely Antioch.[27] The work in fact derives from those speculations on the celestial world to which Ignatius of Antioch alludes when he writes: 'I . . . also . . . can comprehend heavenly things, and the arrays ($\tau o\pi o\theta\epsilon o i\alpha s$) of the angels and the musterings of the principalities' (*Trall*. V, 2). The doctrine of the seven heavens, which is

24. Cf. chap. v below for a discussion of this feature of Jewish Christian texts.
25. Cf. S. GIET, 'La guerre des Juifs de Flavius Josèphe et quelques énigmes de l'Apocalypse', *RevSR*, XXVI, 1952, pp. 18–22.
26. On the subject of millenarianism cf. chap. II below.
27. Cf. GOPPELT, *loc. cit.*, p. 177.

foreign to the Jewish Christian apocalyptic, seems to be a Syriac influence, and reappears in the *Testaments*.

With regard to the religious background, there is no ground for assuming that there were especially marked Essene influences. The use of the term Beliar (IV, 2) was common in Judaism. The setting is therefore that of ordinary Judaism, or more exactly of Jewish gnosis, the distinguishing feature of which is the claim to a knowledge of heavenly mysteries. This does not imply any kind of heterodoxy: there is not a trace of Gnosticism in the book, and its theology of the Trinity and of the Incarnation are archaic but not heretical. The work is interesting because it represents an original form of gnosis, an early example of Christian theology, borrowing its modes of expression from the Jewish apocalyptic. It is therefore a source of outstanding importance for our purpose.

The *Testaments of the Twelve Patriarchs* pose a more delicate problem. On the one hand the Christian allusions are less explicit, so much so in fact that it frequently requires considerable discussion to decide whether any given passage is Jewish or Christian. But above all the general character of the work is difficult to ascertain. Most scholars have seen it as a Jewish work with Christian interpolations,[28] dating its original form in the first century B.C. The presence of certain specific doctrines, for example those of the Two Spirits, the two Messiahs descended from the tribes of Judah and Levi respectively, and the visitation ($\dot{\epsilon}\pi\iota\sigma\kappa\sigma\pi\dot{\eta}$) of the Lord, have led others[29] to see a connection with the Qumran sect. Whether this be so or not, it is certainly true that the work has characteristic features linking it with the Essenes.

It is possible, however, to reverse this view,[30] and to hold that the author used previous Jewish documents, but that in its present form[31] it is a Jewish Christian text. On this hypothesis isolated Jewish *Testaments* must have existed, but the grouping of them together in a single book was the work of a Jewish Christian.[32] This view seems to be supported by the discoveries at Qumran, for there fragments of an Aramaic *Testament of Levi* have been discovered different from the one in the *Testaments*, but evidently

---

28. Notably CHARLES; the same view has been urged more recently by G. MOLIN, 'Qumran, Apocalyptic, Essenism' in *Saeculum*, VI, 1955, pp. 244–281.
29. So A. DUPONT-SOMMER, *The Jewish Sect of Qumran and the Essenes*.
30. So R. DE JONGE, *The Testaments of the Twelve Patriarchs*, Assen, 1953.
31. Especially in recension B.
32. R. DE JONGE, *The Testaments of the Twelve Patriarchs*, pp. 117–128.

its inspiration.[33] There is also a Hebrew *Testament of Naphtali*, different from the one in the *Testaments* and purely Jewish in character. In any case, however, the Christian sections of the *Testaments* form part of the documentary sources for Jewish Christian theology.[34]

The strongly marked Jewish character of the work would of itself suggest an early date but there is one episode in particular by which this can perhaps be determined more precisely. The author speaks of the Angel of the Presence abandoning the Temple of Jerusalem,[35] a feature which seems to be dependent on the account Josephus gives of the fall of Jerusalem in the year 70 (*Bell.* VI, 5:3), an account borrowed by Tacitus (*Hist.* V, 13). The compilation therefore cannot be much later than Josephus' report of the fall of the Temple.[36]

As with the *Ascension*, the geographical setting seems to be Syria. The grounds for this conclusion are twofold. First, there is a doctrine of seven heavens,[37] a cosmology which seems to have been a Syriac modification of the more archaic system of three heavens. This would suggest that there must have been a version earlier than our present one, already Jewish Christian in character, and originating from Palestinian circles before A.D. 70. It is clear from other evidence that the text has in any case passed through several stages. Secondly, the *Testament of Levi* contains a description of the baptismal initiation in which the anointing with oil precedes the actual baptism.[38] This, which was the normal order in Jewish Christian liturgy,[39] reappears in the later liturgy of the Syrian church.[40]

The religious background seems still to be one of an orthodox Jewish Christianity, but one composed in the main of convert Essenes. Some characteristics pointing to this have already been noted, in particular the large part played by the doctrine of the Two Spirits, a doctrine which

33. J. T. MILIK, 'Le Testament de Lévi en araméen', *RB*, LXII, 1955, pp. 398–407.
34. Cf. F. M. BRAUN, 'Les Testaments des Douze Patriarches et le problème de leur origine', *RB*, LXVII, 1960, pp. 516–550.
35. DE JONGE, *op. cit.*, pp. 123–124.
36. This is borne out by the fact that the theme is not presented in the form which it was to take in Melito (*Hom. Pasch.*, 98), who depended on the *Testaments*, but in accordance with *Mt.* 27:51 explicitly links the incident with the Passion of Christ.
37. At least in certain recensions; cf. DE JONGE, *op. cit.*, pp. 47–51. On the subject of the differing numbers of heavens in the various cosmologies cf. below, pp. 174 ff.
38. Cf. T. W. MANSON, 'Miscellanea Apocalyptica', III, *JTS*, XLVIII, 1947, pp. 59–61; also pp. 324 f. below.
39. Cf. DIX, 'The Seal in the Second Century' in *Theology*, LI, 1948, p. 7.
40. Cf. DE JONGE, *op. cit.*, p. 128.

reappears in other Jewish Christian works influenced by Essenism, notably the *Didache* and the *Shepherd of Hermas*. One more feature may be stressed. The author of the *Testaments* borrows *testimonia*[41] which seem to be of Essene provenance in order to apply them to Christ—in particular *Num.* 24:17, 'There shall come forth a star out of Jacob', which occurs several times in the Qumran texts.[42] Though very closely related to the group which produced the *Ascension of Isaiah*, the community from which the *Testaments* came seems to have been of slightly different orientation, less Gnostic in tendency and more faithful to classic Essenism.

It has recently been suggested that *II Enoch* may also be a product of this same community.[43] Certainly a number of details point to the Jewish Christian character of the work. The first is the concept of the corporeal ascension of the just to Paradise before the Judgment. This feature is not found in the old Jewish apocalyptic, where the ascensions are only temporary heavenly journeys; in *II Enoch*, however, the doctrine takes on the same form as in the *Ascension of Isaiah* (cf. *II Enoch* XXXVI, 2 and *Asc. Isa.* IX, 7 ff).[44] The representation of the Word and the Holy Ghost by the figures of higher angels is another Jewish Christian trait. Thus, as in the *Ascension*, the figure of Gabriel takes the part of the Holy Spirit (cf. *Asc. Isa.* VII, 23; IX, 35 f.; XI, 33 with *II Enoch* XXII, 6; XXIV, 1).

It may reasonably be assumed, therefore, that *II Enoch* is a Jewish Christian work, though of a later date than the *Ascension of Isaiah*, probably somewhere toward the end of the first century. The geographical setting is once again quite certainly Syria. In particular the reappearance of the doctrine of the seven heavens—a characteristic of Syrian Jewish Christian apocalyptic—confirms the connection with the *Ascension* and the *Testaments*.

Another work which must be associated with the same group is the *Prayer of Joseph*,[45] quoted on several occasions by Origen.[46] The two major

41. Cf. Glossary s.v.   42. Cf. especially the *Damascus Document*, VIII, 19.

43. Cf. A. VAILLANT, *Le Livre des secrets d'Hénoch*, Paris, 1952. Not all Vaillant's arguments may strike the reader as of equal value, but his case in general is strong. Cf. also CHARLES, *Apocrypha and Pseudepigrapha*, II, from which all *II Enoch* references in the present work are taken.

44. The same doctrine reappears in *Rec. clem.* I, 52, and in the traditions of the Elders in Irenaeus (*Adv. haer.* V, 5:1) where its Christian character is clear.

45. SCHÜRER regarded this work as a Jewish apocryphon, but RESCH (*Agrapha*, pp. 296 f.) has conclusively demonstrated its Jewish Christian character.

46. *Comm. Joh.* I, 31; II, 31; *Comm. Gen.*, PG, pp. 12, 73b, 81b; *Hom. Num.* XVII, 4.

fragments which survive will call for detailed study at a later stage. For the moment let it suffice to mention the system of seven heavens, already noted in the *Ascension* and *II Enoch*, and the expression κατέβην ἐπὶ τὴν γῆν, which recalls the doctrine of the descent of the Beloved in the *Ascension*. Other resemblances will become apparent on further examination, and there can be little doubt that both the *Ascension* and the *Prayer* are archaic works cherished by the same group of Jewish Christians. The latter document is of outstanding importance for Jewish Christian trinitarian theology.[47]

The works just discussed are related to another collection, that of the Jewish Christian *Sibylline Oracles*. There is here an exact parallel in one respect, namely that this is another instance either of Christian remodelling of Jewish works or of Christian compositions directly inspired by Jewish prototypes. But with the *Oracles* it is possible to go further, and in fact to trace the development of this genre through the various strata of the extant collection. Thus Books III and IV are Jewish, Book V is a Jewish work remodelled by a Christian, and Books VI and VII are Jewish Christian works of the period with which we are concerned.[48] The other Books, which date from a later period, may be left aside. The genre is similar to that of the apocalypses, but in place of Enoch or Noah it is the Sibyls who are regarded as announcing the eschatological events.

Book V is very markedly Jewish, but several passages are clearly Christian, especially those relating to the birth of Christ (256–259). In its present form it is therefore a Jewish Christian work, whether through interpolations or through composition done by a Christian. The principal mark of the work is its violent hostility to Rome, a very different note from that of previous apocalypses. It is probably the product of Jewish Christians who were fairly close to the Jews, and shared their resentment against Rome after the fall of Jerusalem. The work cannot therefore date from very long after that event[49]; it might perhaps be placed during the reigns of Domitian or Nerva.

47. Another point raised by RESCH, which links the *Prayer* with the *Ascension*, may perhaps be stressed here. The *Prayer* applies to the seventh angel the title πνεῦμα ἀρχικόν. Epiphanius mentions a sect of Jewish Christian heretics called the 'Αρχοντικοί who possessed a sacred book, the Συμφωνία, dealing with the seven heavens and their angels, and who also—at least according to Epiphanius—made use of the *Ascension of Isaiah* (*Pan.* XL, 2).

48. The analysis here given is that of GEFFCKEN, *Komposition und Entstehungszeit der Oracula Sibyllina*, Leipzig, 1902.

49. So GEFFCKEN, *op. cit.*, p. 25.

Its place of origin seems to have been Egypt.[50] This involves an important conclusion concerning the origins of the Jewish Christian church of Egypt, which are still very obscure. The violent anti-Roman tone, which is to be found neither in Syrian nor in Asian Jewish Christianity, seems to show that the Jewish Christians of Egypt, like the Jews, had been especially persecuted by the Roman authorities at this time. This precarious situation would explain why so little information on early Egyptian Christianity has survived. It will be observed how markedly hellenised the work is—a characteristic in keeping with an Alexandrian background, though an Alexandria strongly influenced by Palestinian apocalyptic and far removed from the tendencies of Philo.

Book VI is a typical Jewish Christian work.[51] It begins with an account of the baptism of Christ (1–8), an archaic characteristic that is found also in the New Testament in *Mark*, was to persist among the more archaising heretics, the Ebionites and Cerinthus, and was to be taken up again by the Gnostics. Furthermore, this account speaks of the fire in the Jordan, a point that reappears in several archaic texts, but is interpreted here in the same sense as in the *Gospel of the Ebionites*.[52] The book concludes with a heavenly ascension of the cross, which recalls the *Gospel of Peter*,[53] a work which it also resembles in its polemical anti-Jewish character. Rather than an apocalypse it is an archaic poem inspired by early *targumim*[54] of the Gospel. The work may belong to the beginning of the second century. Certain features that it has in common with the other books suggest that this also originates from Egypt.

The chief interest of Book VII is a long description of the eschatological plagues: cosmic chaos with the consuming of the world by fire, social chaos with confusion of nations, moral chaos with illicit unions. These times are to be followed by the messianic age which has, however, a less materialistic tinge than that of Asiatic millenarianism.[55] All this is close to later Jewish apocalyptic. The cosmic conflagration appears in the *Apocalypse of Peter* and in the New Testament *Second Epistle of Peter*.[56] The episodes from the life of Christ are typical of Jewish Christian theology—notably the setting

---

50. As Geffcken shows by certain geographical indications (*op. cit.*, p. 26).
51. Geffcken, *op. cit.*, p. 31.
52. On the subject of this imagery and its use, cf. chap. 7, pp. 227 ff. below; for the *Gospel of the Ebionites*, cf. further, pp. 58 f.   53. Cf. pp. 20 ff. below.
54. Cf. Glossary s.v.   55. Cf. chap. 14 below.
56. As indeed it does also in the Qumran *Psalms of Thanksgiving*.

on fire of the Jordan at the Baptism, and the raising up of the angels at the Ascension.

This book may belong to the middle of the second century. Once again, several details suggest Egyptian origin. Christ is exalted above the angels (32–35), without any reference to the seven heavens of Syrian writing. The treatment of the Baptism and not the Nativity as the beginning of the account of the life of Christ recalls the connection of *Mark* with Alexandria, and the emergence of the feast of the Baptism in that city as attested by Clement of Alexandria. In contrast, the Syrian Apocalypses stress the Nativity. The allusion to the ogdoad[57] (139) as the final period of history is found at the same period at Alexandria in the *Epistle of Barnabas*. The work may therefore be assigned to Egypt, and regarded as the Egyptian form of Jewish Christian apocalyptic.

The clearest evidence we have about the environment from which the work came is its relationship to the *Gospel of the Ebionites*, but at the same time there is no trace of heterodox christology. It has been observed that the eschatological descriptions are related to those of the Qumran documents, where fire also plays an important part. All this would seem to point to Essene converts, but without the heterodox tendencies of the Ebionites.[58] Books VI and VII would thus be evidence of the presence in Egypt of Christians of Essene origin, and this would fit in with the strong solidarity with the Jews that is shown in Book V.[59]

NEW TESTAMENT APOCRYPHA

A second source of material for our knowledge of Jewish Christian theology is the pseudepigraphical literature of the New Testament. This consists first of all of Gospels and kindred matter which have survived in whole or in part from the earliest times in addition to the canonical Gospels. Of full-scale Gospels may be mentioned the *Gospel of Peter*, the *Gospel of James*, the *Gospel of the Nazarenes*, the *Gospel of the Hebrews*, the *Gospel of the Egyptians* and the *Gospel of Thomas*. The papyri have also bequeathed to us non-canonical accounts of incidents in the life of Jesus; and a certain

57. Cf. p. 34, n. 123 below.
58. A different view is taken by GEFFCKEN, *op. cit.*, p. 31.
59. This would confirm Brandon's thesis of the exile to Egypt after A.D. 70 of a part of the Jewish Christian community of Palestine (*op. cit.*, pp. 178–226) or Dupont-Sommer's theory of the previous existence of Essenes in Egypt, a certain number of whom would have been converted.

number of λόγια of Jesus, additional to those in the canonical Gospels, have been handed down by the papyri and by ancient authors.[60]

To decide what portions of this literature derive from orthodox Jewish Christianity is a difficult matter. Some texts can be excluded at once on account of their patently heterodox character—such, for example, as the *Gospel of the Ebionites*, quoted by Epiphanius, of which more will be said later when dealing with that sect. Yet other documents are—at any rate in their final form—of late date. Such is the case, for instance, with the *Gospel of James*. Such works may well contain archaic elements, but they cannot be associated as they stand with the Jewish Christianity of the first two centuries. Nevertheless, when all such inadmissible material has been excluded, there still remain a number of texts which can be regarded as genuine expressions of Jewish Christianity, and which bear witness to the variety of its thought.

The first of these is the *Gospel of Peter*.[61] Its existence was known from the references of ancient writers, in particular Origen (*Comm. Mt.* X, 17) before considerable fragments of it were discovered at Akhmim. Objection might be raised to deriving the work from Jewish Christianity on the grounds that it displays a very marked anti-Jewish polemical character. This would, however, be an argument against connecting it with judaising circles within Jewish Christianity, rather than with Jewish Christian literature as such. Furthermore, in view of the fact that this polemical tone appears in other works which are generally accepted as Jewish Christian, such as the *Epistle of Barnabas* or the *Didache*, it may be considered justifiable to place it in this category.[62]

That the *Gospel of Peter* derives from the culture of Later Judaism is beyond question. Its characteristic feature is to make use of apocalyptic symbolism in presenting the events of the life of Christ with a view to bringing out their theological import. It is interesting therefore not for the traditions which it records, but for the character of its doctrine. Its purpose

60. It is hardly possible to decide today whether these fragmentary episodes and sayings existed as isolated units of tradition, or once formed part of complete Gospels. On the whole mass of material, cf. E. HENNECKE, *Neutestamentliche Apokryphen in deutscher Übersetzung*, 3rd edn. by W. SCHNEEMELCHER, Tübingen, 1959.

61. Text and translation by VAGANAY, Paris, 1930; Cf. JAMES, *Apocryphal N.T.*, pp. 90 ff.

62. So, e.g. GOPPELT (*op. cit.*, p. 187) considers that the anti-Jewish character of this text is no bar to its being Jewish Christian. There are, after all, two Judaisms to be taken into account; a work might belong to the cultural setting of Later Judaism and still be opposed to the rabbinising Judaism of the years after A.D. 70.

is 'to throw into bold relief the divine character of the person of Christ'.[63]
Thus in the account of Christ's resurrection there are a number of details
of an apocalyptic colouring: the heavens opened, the great noise in the
sky, the raiment of light worn by the angels. A typical feature is the use of
immense size to indicate the divinity of Jesus, and the importance of the
angels (40). The same feature is to be found in *Test. Reub.* V, 7 and *II
Enoch* I, 4. It derives from Jewish apocalyptic, and may be seen also in
the *Damascus Document* (II, 19). The *Gospel of Peter* is a work from the
same environment.

Certain other points may be noted which are, as will become clear in
later chapters, characteristic of Jewish Christian theology. Thus the Resurrection is identified with the Ascension, a consequence of the early understanding according to which the Ascension denoted the exaltation of Jesus'
humanity above all created things.[64] The Descent into Hell has as its
purpose the salvation of the saints of the Old Testament, another judaising
and archaic feature.[65] Equally characteristic is the theme, which appears here
for the first time, of the living Cross of light, conferring on the instrument
of Jesus' execution a symbolic meaning, and transforming it into a sign of
glory. This *theologia gloriae* is one of the marks of Jewish Christian theology.

This archaic character of the theological data implies a fairly early date,
the beginning of the second century at the latest. The place of origin is
certainly Syria. External evidence on this point is decisive,[66] all the ancient
witnesses—in particular Serapion[67] (end of second century) and the
Didascalia—being Syrian. As far as internal evidence is concerned, attention may be drawn to the marked resemblance between the account of the
Resurrection in the *Gospel of Peter* and in the *Ascension of Isaiah*. The
religious environment, likewise, must be that of the Jewish Christian
church of Antioch. Together with the *Ascension* the *Gospel* represents an
echo of the gnosis, that is to say, the theology of this particular community,
the way in which it expressed Christian doctrines through the symbolism
of Jewish apocalyptic.[68]

63. VAGANAY, *L'Évangile de Pierre*, p. 119.
64. So BENOIT, 'L'Ascension', *RB*, LVI, 1949, p. 168.
65. Cf. W. BIEDER, *Die Vorstellung von der Höllenfahrt Jesu Christi*, Zurich, 1949, pp.
129–135.
66. As VAGANAY has shown (*op. cit.*, p. 179).   67. Cf. EUSEBIUS, *HE* VI, 12:2.
68. RESCH (*Agrapha*, pp. 381–383) has equally well demonstrated the derivation of this
work by reference to the *Apocryphon of Jeremiah*, an example of very early Jewish
Christian *midrash* (cf. below pp. 102 ff.).

The *Gospel of the Nazarenes* directs our attention to quite a different quarter. Care must be taken to distinguish this work from two others: first, the *Gospel of the Ebionites*, which is in fact a reshaping of the *Gospel of the Nazarenes* in the interests of heterodoxy; and secondly, a *Gospel of the Hebrews*, quoted by Clement of Alexandria and Origen, which also exhibits heterodox features.[69] The *Gospel of the Nazarenes* is first mentioned by Hegesippus,[70] but the principal witness to it is saint Jerome. Both Hegesippus and Jerome record that it was written in the Syrian dialect, that is to say, in Aramaic, but it has only survived in the Latin translation which Jerome gives of certain passages. Its date must be early. The reference of Hegesippus pushes its publication back into the first half of the second century; and the presence in Ignatius of Antioch of a quotation which, according to Jerome (*De vir. ill.* 16), comes from this Gospel might suggest an even earlier date. Nevertheless, Jerome's statement has been disputed,[71] and the evidence may in any case prove no more than a common source.[72]

Epiphanius and Jerome believed that this work was the Aramaic original of the New Testament *Matthew*, but the quotations given by Jerome prove this to have been impossible. Nevertheless, the text does bear some relation to *Matthew*, the only canonical Gospel accepted by this community, and various views have been put forward as to what this relationship is. To see in the *Gospel of the Nazarenes* simply 'a re-arrangement in Aramaic of the Greek *Matthew*'[73] is, however, to go too far; and the same may be said of the view that those Nazarenes who were in communion with the Gentile churches 'received from them the *Gospel of Matthew*, and composed their Aramaic Gospel along the same lines in the style of a *targum*'.[74] Whatever the answer may be, the environment with which the *Gospel of the Nazarenes* should be associated is that of the Jewish Christians of Syria, who spoke Aramaic and who were the most direct heirs of the Palestinian Jewish Christian community, from whom they may have received certain traditions.

The *Gospel of the Hebrews* and the *Gospel of the Egyptians* are very different in character from the *Gospel of the Nazarenes*. There is no question here of a simple reworking of *Matthew*. The *Gospel of the Hebrews* is known to us

69. Cf. P. VIELHAUER in HENNECKE-SCHNEEMELCHER, *op. cit.*, pp. 89 f.
70. EUSEBIUS, *HE* IV, 22:8.   71. VIELHAUER, *op. cit.*, pp. 82 f.
72. So KÖSTER, *Synoptische Überlieferung bei den Apostolischen Vätern*, Berlin, 1957, pp. 45–56.
73. So SCHOEPS, *Theologie*, p. 26.   74. So DIX, *op. cit.*

from Clement of Alexandria and Origen. The fact that it may have been one of the sources of the *Gospel of Thomas* would place it at the beginning of the second century; and it ought probably to be associated with the Jewish Christian community in Egypt.[75] Certainly its Jewish Christian character is very marked. The Spirit is called Mother, a usage which presupposes the feminine Hebrew noun *ruaḥ* rather than the Greek neuter (ORIGEN, *Comm. Joh.* II, 12). It is to James that Christ first appears after his Resurrection (JEROME, *De vir. ill.* II). The account of Christ's Baptism also exhibits Jewish Christian features (JEROME, *Comm. Is.* XI, 2).

The principal source of our knowledge of the *Gospel of the Egyptians* is Clement of Alexandria, but it seems to have been used as early as the time of the pseudo-Clementine *Homilies*. This again suggests a date in the first half of the second century. As the title indicates, it is of Egyptian origin, but derives from a different community from that of the *Gospel of the Hebrews*.[76] It is marked chiefly by a pronounced encratism,[77] for which it was criticised by Clement of Alexandria, though he did not in fact regard it as heterodox. Certain features derive from Jewish Christian gnosis, notably the role of Salome. These different elements are typical of a stream of Jewish Christianity which was to manifest itself later in the apocryphal *Acts*, and they bear striking testimony to the variety of background present in Egyptian Christianity in the first half of the second century.

A lineal descendant of this group of texts is the *Gospel of Thomas*.[78] The discovery at Nag Hammadi of this collection of sayings of Jesus has already given rise to a considerable literature. The fact that the work includes a number of λόγια found elsewhere, either in the papyri or in citations by various authors, suggests that the writer drew on a variety of sources in compiling his text.[79] Some passages are related to sayings of Christ as these have been preserved in the New Testament, but seem to have come down by way of a different tradition closer to the original Aramaic.[80] In this connection the work is of interest for the exegesis of the New Testament.

75. So VIELHAUER in HENNECKE-SCHNEEMELCHER, p. 107.
76. Cf. HENNECKE-SCHNEEMELCHER, p. 117.   77. Cf. Glossary s.v.
78. Text and translation by A. GUILLAUMONT, H.-CH. PUECH, G. QUISPEL, W. TILL and Y. ABD EL MASIH, Paris, 1959; cf. also WILSON, *Studies*, London, 1960.
79. Cf. H.-CH. PUECH in HENNECKE-SCHNEEMELCHER, pp. 199-223; JEAN DORESSE, *L'Évangile selon Thomas et les Paroles de Jésus*, Paris, 1959; R. M. GRANT, *The Secret Sayings of Jesus according to the Gospel of Thomas*, London, 1960.
80. Cf. A. GUILLAUMONT, 'Sémitismes dans les Logia de Jésus retrouvés à Nag

In addition, however, the author seems to have made use of the *Gospel of the Hebrews* and the *Gospel of the Egyptians*. Certain features are typical of Jewish Christianity. Thus James is given a prominent role; it is he 'for whose sake the heaven and the earth were brought forth' (12). There are allusions to the apocryphal accounts of the childhood of Christ (4). Logion 22 on 'the height which becomes the depth' is paralleled in the *Odes of Solomon*, the pseudo-Clementine *Homilies*, the *Acts of Peter* and the *Gospel of the Egyptians*, and will call for further attention at a later stage. The symbolism of the lion (7), and of the wood and the stone (77), have Jewish Christian parallels.[81]

The work then is substantially Jewish Christian. It does nevertheless exhibit traces of fairly pronounced dualism, which seem to indicate that at least in its final recension as attested by the Coptic text it has been retouched by the Gnostics who used it. The condemnation of marriage would not of itself be decisive, for the same feature appears in the *Gospel of the Egyptians*. But other points are more conclusive.[82] Thus there is emphasis on esoteric doctrine, on the completely interior nature of the Kingdom of God, on the final condemnation of the material world and of the Old Testament.[83] The *Gospel* may therefore be said to occupy a position halfway between Jewish Christian gnosis and heterodox gnosticism.

As regards its place of provenance the text itself affords one clue. Memories of the apostle Thomas are especially connected with the region of Edessa,[84] and there is extant an *Acts of Thomas* written in Syriac at Edessa in the third century. This document states that Thomas 'was initiated into the secret teaching of Christ', a comment which may well be an allusion to the *Gospel*. Adiabene had been converted to Judaism *c.* A.D. 30, and it is likely that the *Gospel of Thomas* was originally the work of the Jewish Christians of Adiabene, fulfilling here the part played by the *Gospel of the Egyptians* and the *Gospel of the Hebrews* in Egypt. It is best

81. As Doresse has rightly pointed out (*op. cit.*, pp. 134, 188).
82. Cf. R. M. Grant, *op. cit.*, pp. 180–191.
83. W. R. Schoedel has noted various points of contact between the *Gospel of Thomas* and the Naassenian gnosis, as this is known to us from Hippolytus: 'Naassene Themes in the Coptic Gospel of Thomas', *VC*, xiv, 1960, pp. 223–235.
84. Cf. Doresse, *op. cit.*, pp. 40–48.

Hammadi', *JA*, 1958, pp. 113–120; G. Quispel, 'The Gospel of Thomas and the New Testament', *VC*, xi, 1957, pp. 189–207, and 'L'Évangile selon Thomas et le texte occidental du Nouveau Testament', *VC*, xiv, 1960, pp. 204–216.

dated in the first half of the second century, and associated with the *Odes of Solomon*, another document for which Edessa is the likeliest place of origin.

Some examples of Christian remodelling of Jewish apocalypses have already been considered in dealing with the *Ascension of Isaiah* and *II Enoch*. But Christian apocalypses also existed—notably, of course, the canonical *Revelation* of John, though this is in fact only one privileged case among many. Some examples of these Christian apocalypses have survived, representing types as various as those of Jewish apocalyptic itself.[85]

The first to be considered is the *Apocalypse of Peter*, which survives in an Ethiopic translation and Greek fragments. It is an amplification of the scene of the Transfiguration, comprising revelations made by Christ to his chosen Apostles concerning the end of time and the punishments of the damned, after which the Apostles behold Christ ascend into heaven. The Jewish character of the various elements is very apparent. The description of the End recalls certain of the *Psalms of Thanksgiving* from Qumran, and anticipates the Christian *Sibyllines*. In particular the 'cataracts of fire' are characteristic of later Jewish apocalyptic; and the theme of ascension, in the sense which the word has here, that is to say, the temporary exaltation of a man so that he may contemplate heavenly realities, is the central theme of all Jewish apocalyptic. Another instance is Paul's ascension to the third heaven (*II Cor.* 12:2).

There is one detail in this apocalypse which is of capital importance: the idea of a special instruction reserved by Christ for his chosen apostles, and constituting a kind of higher enlightenment, a gnosis. The theme occurs again in the *Epistle of the Apostles*, and was to be taken up and used for their own ends by the Gnostics, who claimed in this way to have authority for their teaching.[86] Clement of Alexandria, however, also shared this idea of an esoteric enlightenment by Christ, distinct from the one transmitted by the canonical works. It seems likely that this is in fact a Jewish Christian gnosis fictitiously attributed to Christ by Jewish Christian authors according to a practice that was then current, and which misled Greeks like Clement. Nevertheless, this self-styled esoteric gnosis is of the

85. In one sense all Jewish Christian literature may be termed 'apocalyptic', if its theological method is of the kind associated with this genre. In the present context, however, the term 'apocalypse' will be confined to those works whose total presentation is in this form, and will not be extended to cover any which may contain elements borrowed from apocalyptic proper.
86. Thus Basilides claims to be the disciple of Glaucias, Peter's interpreter, Valentinus of Theodas, an intimate friend of Paul (CLEM. ALEX., *Strom.* VII, 17).

highest importance since it constitutes one of the sources of Jewish Christian theology, which it is the object of the present work to discover.

Jewish apocalyptic was, in other words, a gnosis. It was made up of information about the hidden realities of the heavenly world and the ultimate secrets of the future. These revelations on the fringe of the canonical scripture were put under the patronage of the ancient sages, Noah, Enoch or Abraham. The Christians adopted the same method.[87] They too developed speculations on the fringe of, and enlarging upon, the canonical scriptures of the New Testament, and placed these teachings likewise under a patronage that would give them authority, that of Christ himself.

There are several witnesses to the antiquity of the *Apocalypse of Peter*. The Muratorian Canon mentions it side by side with the *Revelation* of John, which indicates the great authority it must have enjoyed at the end of the second century. Clement of Alexandria quotes it twice in the *Eclogae Propheticae* (41, 48). The archaic character of its theology gives grounds for supposing that the work dates from the end of the first century. The place of origin is, however, not so easy to determine. The work was known to Clement of Alexandria and was found in Egypt, but neither of these pieces of evidence is decisive. More important is its association with the *Gospel of Peter*, the Syrian origin of which has already been demonstrated. It is therefore probable that it should be assigned to Syria.[88]

With regard to the background from which it came, it is typical of the Jewish Christianity of the Great Church, without, however, any marked features that would attach it to any particular sect. In this connection the fact of its being placed under the patronage of Peter is of some importance. Its eschatological imagery is similar to that of the New Testament *II Peter*, and the Akhmim fragments link it with the *Gospel of Peter*. Peter seems in fact to be the typical figure of a central Jewish Christianity, standing in opposition both to the Jewish particularism of James and the Hellenising tendencies of Paul, and writings linked with him[89] appear to be expressions of this classic current of Jewish Christianity of which Syria was the centre.[90]

87. Cf. e.g. A. MARMORSTEIN, 'Jüdische Parallelen zur Petrusapocalypse', *ZNW*, x, 1909, pp. 297–300.
88. This is also the conclusion reached by GOPPELT, *op. cit.*, p. 208.
89. With these ought perhaps to be included the most ancient form of the *Acts of Peter*, which we possess only in an Ebionite form in the pseudo-Clementines, or in a Gnostic form in the *Acta Vercellensia*.
90. GOPPELT, *op. cit.*, p. 178.

The *Epistle of the Apostles* also belongs to this genre of apocalypses. It takes the form of a letter addressed to the Churches by the Twelve, the contents of which consist of an account of revelations made to them by Christ during the period between the Resurrection and the Ascension. Here again the theme is the same as that of the *Apocalypse of Peter*: revelations aiming at giving instruction about the most secret mysteries and at throwing light on matters which the Gospel left in darkness—a work typical of orthodox Jewish Christian gnosis. Furthermore, the choice of the period immediately following the Resurrection for the setting of the work is precisely that found in a number of Gnostic texts, notably the *Pistis Sophia*.[91]

The work is certainly Jewish Christian in character. The descent into hell, as in the *Gospel of Peter*, is concerned to secure the salvation of the saints of the Old Testament. As in the *Ascension of Isaiah*, Christ passes through the seven heavens at his Descent, and puts on the form of the angels (13). The Parousia is preceded by cosmic signs that are part of the common stock of apocalyptic, and is accompanied by the glorious Cross, a detail deriving from the theology of the Cross already observed in the *Gospel of Peter*. The designation of the highest heaven as the ogdoad, like that of the seven heavens, is a detail from the Judaism of the Diaspora, and was to be taken up by the Gnostics.[92]

The date must certainly be before A.D. 180, since Christ predicts his return in 150 years. Seeing that he is supposed to be speaking somewhere about A.D. 30, the year 180 is yet to come. One cannot go far wrong, therefore, in placing the work in the first half of the second century.[93] Some points of contact with the *Ascension of Isaiah* and the *Gospel of Peter* might suggest Syria as its place of origin; but the important part played by the Apostle John argues more strongly for Asia Minor. Indeed, it is possible that the very conception of secret information given by Christ between the Resurrection and the Ascension has a Johannine origin, in view of the suggestion[94] that Christ's discourses, which in the canonical *Gospel according to St. John* occur after the Supper, were originally placed between the Resurrection and the Ascension, and may have been moved in reaction

91. Cf. Glossary s.v. *Epistle refs. are to* JAMES (*Apoc. N.T.*, pp. 485–503).
92. It comes, however, from an orthodox gnosis, as Carl SCHMIDT has pointed out: *Gespräche Jesu mit seinen Jüngern*, Leipzig, 1919, pp. 175 ff. Cf. Glossary s.v. OGDOAD.
93. Cf. SCHMIDT, *op. cit.*, pp. 285, 302, 501.
94. Cf. V. BRETON, *Jésus au Cénacle. Une hypothèse exégétique, EL*, 1953, pp. 263–278.

against the abuse that the Gnostics made of the concept of esoteric information imparted after the Resurrection.

Other features point to a setting in Asia Minor. The place of rest, the ogdoad, is called κυριακή (17), a term found in Asia from the time of the New Testament (*Rev.* 1:10) onward; Easter is celebrated on the 14 Nisan, the normal Asiatic practice. The fact that the text makes no reference to millenarianism, however, seems to suggest that, even if it is to be placed in Asia Minor, it must derive from another group than that of Papias and the Elders of Irenaeus, for the latter were characterised by a messianism still strongly marked by the spirit of the Palestinian zealots. The *Epistle* is akin to the more speculative stream of Jewish Christian gnosis, and in this respect comes close to the Syrian school already encountered in several works. If, nevertheless, the Asiatic setting is correct, this would prove that tendencies of the Syrian type were also present in Asia Minor.[95]

LITURGICAL TEXTS

The works just discussed represented the theological reflection, the gnosis, of Jewish Christians on the data of the Gospels. The next group to be considered consists of works that are the product of the life of the Jewish Christian church. Their interest lies in the fact that their Jewish Christian character shows itself not only in theological thought-forms but also in the concrete forms of the life of the church, worship, morality and asceticism, catechetical instruction. Furthermore, these documents provide evidence of how the specifically Jewish forms of expression of the first Christian community in Palestine endured among the Jewish Christian communities of the Diaspora.

The first of these works is the *Didache*. The discussion which there has been—and still is—about this work, the type of community from which it came, its date and place of origin is well known. Even if, however, the text in its present form has undergone some revision,[96] it is now plain that the basis of it is quite definitely Jewish Christian.[97] This is clear enough as

95. Cf. pp. 176 f. below. The *Apocryphon Jacobi*, a non-Gnostic work discovered at Nag Hammadi, ought also to be classed with this group. Cf. W. C. VAN UNNIK, 'The Origin of the recently discovered Apocryphon Jacobi', *VC*, x, 1956, pp. 149–156, and H.-CH. PUECH in HENNECKE-SCHNEEMELCHER, p. 249.

96. As PETERSON has shown: 'Über einige Probleme der Didache-Überlieferung', *RAC*, XXVII, 1952, pp. 37 ff.

97. This has been firmly established by the work of J.-P. AUDET, *La Didachè, Instruc-*

regards the moral section, the *Treatise on the Two Ways*, the Judaistic character of which has been apparent for a long time, and has been confirmed in a striking manner by the discovery of the Qumran *Rule of the Community*, embodying very similar teaching. Indeed, the literary genre of the *Didache* as a whole is akin to that of the Essene *Rule*.

However, the liturgical section of the *Didache* also presents a number of Jewish Christian features. These are to be found, for example, in the ritual of baptism, especially in the rule requiring the use of living water.[98] The practice of prayer thrice daily (VIII, 3) should be compared with that of the Essenes, also attested by the *Rule of the Community*.[99] The typically Jewish Christian character of the prayers of blessing (IX, X) is quite certain in view of such elements as the allusion to the Vine of David, the use of the expression παῖς for Jesus, and the tabernacling of the Name. These blessings must surely derive from old epicleses, even if their use in this particular text cannot be shown conclusively to be eucharistic.[100] The *Marana tha* which concludes the last blessing (X) is the most precious relic of the primitive Aramaic liturgy of Jerusalem.[101]

The passages concerning the structure of the hierarchy exhibit similar characteristics. Especially noteworthy is the place assigned to the prophets, a specifically Jewish Christian institution, as is indicated by the fact that the *Ascension of Isaiah* (III, 27) at a slightly later date but in the same type of community laments their becoming so rare, and by their presence in the *Shepherd of Hermas* (*Mand.* XI, 7-9).

The provenance of the text can only be Syrian. It was in the Syrian liturgy, alongside the *Didascalia* and the *Apostolic Constitutions* that it was preserved down to the fourth century; it is in Syria that the Aramaic phrases in the text—*Hosanna, Marana tha, Amen*—are most appropriate, and from Syria that they must have spread to other areas; and it is Syria that is indicated by the many points of contact with the *Ascension of Isaiah*.

98. BENOIT (*Le baptême chrétien au Second Siècle*, Paris, 1953, p. 31) has gone so far as to call this 'a Jewish rite tinged with Christianity'.

99. Cf. JUNGMANN, 'Altchristliche Gebetsordnung im Lichte des Regelbuches von En-Feschka', *ZKT*, LXXV, 1953, pp. 214 f.

100. Cf. PETERSON, 'Didachè cap. 9 e 10', *EL*, LVIII, 1944, pp. 3-13. Similar conclusions have been reached by Audet.

101. Cf. O. CULLMANN, *Early Christian Worship*, London, 1953, pp. 13-14.

tions des Apôtres, Paris, 1958. The older view of VOKES (*The Riddle of the Didache*, London, 1938, pp. 129-146) who saw in it a Montanist work, the archaisms of which were of a purely literary character, can no longer be regarded as tenable.

This does not exclude the possibility of an ultimate origin in Palestine[102] with the basic stratum of the document going back behind A.D. 70.

The spirituality of the *Didache* exhibits striking affinities with Essene texts. Attention has already been drawn to the common ground of the Two Ways, the three hours of prayer, baptism with living water, and the prophets. According to Josephus, the Essenes were the only group in Judaism among whom prophetism still survived in the first century A.D. However, it is possible to distinguish two stages in the relations between Essenism and Christianity. At the very beginning there was borrowing of a purely external kind by the primitive community in Jerusalem; then, after A.D. 70, Essenism influenced certain Jewish Christians in a more specific manner, a feature which has already been remarked in the *Testaments* and the *Sibylline Oracles*. The *Didache* seems to be an example of the former influence; it is stamped with Essenism in the same sense as was all early Christianity.[103]

This leads to important conclusions regarding the date of the work. It seems that in its original form it dates back to the first community at Jerusalem, though it was no doubt developed after A.D. 70 in a Syrian community. Finally, the extant version has undergone some touching up later than the second century. Nevertheless, it is possibly the most venerable surviving document of Jewish Christian literature.[104]

After the *Didache*, the most precious document still in existence relating to the Jewish Christian liturgy is the *Odes of Solomon*. They are so markedly Semitic in character that it has proved possible to make out a case for their Jewish origin. But it is impossible not to recognise that they come from a Christian background: everything in them speaks of Jewish Christianity. There are features typical of apocalyptic, especially the symbolism of the Book of Life (VIII, IX). The main themes are those of Jewish Christian theology, in particular the Descent into Hell (XVII, XXIII) which here appears at a more developed stage than in the *Gospel of Peter*.[105] The symbolism of the Cross also plays an important part (XXIII, XXVII,

102. So PETERSON, *op. cit.*, p. 9.

103. Cf. J. DANIÉLOU, 'La Communauté de Qumran et l'organisation de l'Église ancienne', in *La Bible et l'Orient*, Congrès d'archéologie et d'orientalisme biblique de Saint-Cloud, 1954, pp. 104–117.

104. In a recent lecture to the Berliner Theologentag 1956, Alfred ADAM reaches similar conclusions regarding the origins of the work in Jerusalem and its development in Syria: 'Erwägungen zur Herkunft der Didache', *ZKG*, LXVIII, 1957, pp. 33–47.

105. Cf. BIEDER, *op. cit.*, pp. 172–182.

XXXVII). The allusions to the sacraments point in the same direction; the frequent mention of living water recalls the baptismal regulation of the *Didache* on this subject, while that of the crowns (I, 1–2; V, 10) also refers to a Jewish Christian practice of coronation at baptism. The feminine character of the Spirit as in the *Gospel of the Hebrews* is also worth noting.[106]

The work is certainly of Syrian origin.[107] The fact that it has been preserved in Syriac, although the original was certainly in Greek, is an argument in favour of this, and in fact everything about the work suggests Syria. Thus great importance is attached to the virginal motherhood of Mary (XIX, 6–10) as in the *Ascension of Isaiah*. This seems to have been a particular characteristic of the Syrian school, whereas at Alexandria and in the West the accent was on the Baptism. It is a curious fact that the same distinction has been explicitly affirmed by Hippolytus in the case of the Gnostics: 'The Italian school to which Heracleon and Ptolomaeus belong, say that the body of Jesus was born animal ($\psi\upsilon\chi\iota\kappa\acute{o}\nu$), and that this was why at his Baptism the Holy Spirit came down as a dove. . . . The Eastern school, on the other hand, such as Axionicus and Ardesianes[108] assert that the body of the Saviour was spiritual ($\pi\nu\epsilon\upsilon\mu\alpha\tau\iota\kappa\acute{o}\nu$); for the Holy Spirit came upon Mary' (*Elench*. VI, 35).

The value of this observation has been disputed, but it is in fact considerable. The important point is not that of the opposition between the Valentinians of Rome and of Alexandria, but the reference to Bardaisan. He was a typical representative of the Eastern Syrian school in the second century, and some have even thought of attributing the *Odes of Solomon* to him. Hippolytus' remark should therefore be interpreted to mean that an emphasis on the divine motherhood of Mary was a characteristic of Syrian thought; and if this characteristic is also found in the Eastern Gnostics, it is only because it was already esteemed by the school as a whole. By contrast the Alexandrians, without denying the virginal motherhood, saw the inauguration of the mystery of Christ in the baptism, and the Gnostics of Italy drew from this the heretical conclusion that the Baptism was also the beginning of Christ's divinity.

106. The *Odes* are quoted by *Pistis Sophia* in the third century; they themselves must come from the middle of the second.
107. Cf. R. M. GRANT, 'The Odes of Solomon and the Church of Antioch', *JBL*, LXIII, 1944, pp. 363–377; J. DE ZWAAN, 'The Edessene Origin of the Odes of Solomon' in *Quantulacumque (Studies presented to Kirsopp Lake)*, pp. 285–302.
108. I.e., Bardesanes, or Bar-Daisan; for brief details of the figures mentioned in this passage, cf. Glossary s.vv.

There are other features which point to Syria. The *Odes* attach great importance to descriptions of Paradise, but on the other hand make no allusion to the heavens. Now this theology of Paradise was to remain a characteristic of Eastern Syria; it recurs in Ephraem. More especially the Church is considered as Paradise (XI, 15–16). This continued to be a favourite theme of the Syrian catechesis, as this is found, for example, in Theodore of Mopsuestia. The importance of nuptial imagery will also be noted (VII, 7–9, 20). This recurs in the baptismal catechesis of Cyril of Jerusalem, which is connected with the Syrian liturgy. Finally, there are points of contact between the *Odes* and the *Epistles* of Ignatius,[109] in particular the resemblance between 'the speaking water' of *Ode* XI and the 'living and speaking water' of Ignatius (*Rom.* VII, 2).

It is more difficult to determine the exact environment from which the book came, for it contains verse elements. Certain details recall the Qumran manuscripts. Emphasis is placed on the praise of the lips (VIII, XII, XIV), and furthermore the *Odes* belong to the same literary genre as the *Psalms of Thanksgiving* of Qumran, in the same way as the *Didache* was related to the *Rule*. They are an expression of the liturgical prophetism characteristic of Jewish Christianity of an Essene type. The element of gnosis is also fairly marked. A typical example is the mysterious *Ode* XXIII in which the Cross is symbolised by a wheel, and it is said that 'the head went down to the feet'.[110] This should probably be compared with a strange passage in the *Acts of Peter* (38) in which the crucifixion of Peter upside down is a symbol of the descent of the Word.[111]

One last characteristic feature is the presence of traces of asceticism.[112] The *Odes* seem to regard marriage with suspicion[113]; it is the 'bitter herb of Paradise' (XI, 18). Wine is never mentioned. It will be recalled that Tatian, who also comes from the school of Eastern Syria, exhibits the same tendencies in an exaggerated form (IRENAEUS, *Adv. haer.* I, 28:1). It has,

---

109. Cf. GOPPELT, *op. cit.*, pp. 194–201.
110. ORBE interprets the text in a Valentinian sense, but it is more likely to be a speculation on the Cross, characteristic of Jewish Christian gnosis and without any suggestion of heresy; cf. *Los primeros herejes ante la persecución*, pp. 167–213.
111. This would also serve to confirm the association of the *Acts of Peter* with the Syrian community, and to incorporate it in the Petrine literature which is characteristic of that group.
112. Cf. PETERSON, *L'origine dell' ascesi cristiana*, *Euntes docete* (1948), pp. 195–204.
113. Cf. RENDEL HARRIS, *The Psalms and Odes of Solomon*, pp. 70 f.

moreover, been established[114] that in Syria in the early period the baptised used to choose at the moment of baptism between marriage and celibacy, and that those who chose virginity were baptised first. All this seems to be in keeping with a setting marked by asceticism of the type prevalent in certain Jewish communities, but not carried to heretical excess.

Taken as a whole, the evidence of the *Odes* agrees with the picture of the Syrian version of the main tradition of Christianity, and has points of contact with both the *Ascension of Isaiah* and the *Epistles of Ignatius*. Nevertheless, the group from which they came seems to have been one in which Essene influence had remained particularly active, while certain details suggest Eastern Syria rather than Antioch itself.[115] It would be reasonable, therefore, to conclude that the *Odes* are the work of Jewish Christians in the tradition of the Great Church, who came from Eastern Syria, the home of Bar-Daisan, and among whom ascetic tendencies of an Essene type remained especially strong.[116]

BARNABAS AND HERMAS

With the *Epistle of Barnabas* we are still dealing with direct evidence of the Jewish Christian church. The book is a catechetical manual in two parts, dogmatic and moral. The second part is a treatise on the Two Ways analogous to the one in the *Didache*; the first is a collection of *testimonia* accompanied by a commentary, and grouped according to a catechetical plan.[117]

The work has not been generally admitted to be Jewish Christian in character, principally because of its anti-Jewish tone. Thus, for example, the *Epistle* stresses that it was the Jews who put Christ to death. But no more than with the *Gospel of Peter*, where the same charge is found (11–12), does this prevent the Epistle from being Jewish Christian.[118] Similarly, criticism of the sacrifices of the Old Law, and polemic against official

---

114. Cf. Vööbus, *Celibacy, a Requirement for Admission to Baptism in the Early Christian Church*, Stockholm, 1951, pp. 20–34.

115. Cf. DE ZWAAN, *op. cit.*

116. To the same environment belongs the *Song of the Pearl*, an ancient Jewish Christian liturgical composition preserved in the Gnostic *Acts of Thomas* (108–113). Cf. A. ADAM, *Die Psalmen des Thomas und das Perlenlied*, pp. 55–75.

117. Cf. G. SCHILLE, 'Zur urchristlichen Tauflehre. Stylistische Beobachtungen am Barnabasbrief', *ZNW*, XLIX, 1958, pp. 31–52; L. W. BANNARD, 'The Epistle of Barnabas and the Tannaitic Catechism', *ATR*, XLI, 1959, pp. 177–190.

118. Cf. BRANDON, *op. cit.*, p. 236.

Judaism already existed among the Essenes; *a fortiori*, therefore, it is hardly surprising to discover it also among Jewish Christians.

On the positive side, the Jewish Christian characteristics of the work are quite clear. First, there is the question of literary genre. Here the Qumran manuscripts again provide the decisive touchstone. For not only is it now known that the Jews had collections of messianic *testimonia*, and that the Christians used them, but above all the discovery of the *Midrash of Habakkuk*, and of fragments of *midrashim*[119] of the other minor prophets, proves that there existed among the Essenes a literary genre which is precisely that of which the *Epistle of Barnabas* gives us the first Christian example. In such works the prophecies are applied to contemporary events regarded as fulfilling the eschatological promises. The only difference is that the *Epistle* applies the method not to one continuous text, but to a collection of *testimonia*.

The emphasis placed by the *Epistle* on γνῶσις (II, 3) points to the same conclusion. This γνῶσις is the knowledge of eschatological realities.[120] In the case of the *Midrash of Habakkuk* the purpose is to impart knowledge of *the* mystery, the hidden meaning of the prophecies—that is to say, their fulfilment in the Teacher of Righteousness and in the other contemporary events which are also events of the End (*DSH* VII, 1–8).[121] To this the sense of γνῶσις in the Epistle of Barnabas is exactly parallel.

This is not to say, however, that the *Epistle* employs only that kind of exegesis which may be called figurative or typological. Other kinds are also present, and these too are of Jewish origin. First there are moral allegories in the rabbinic manner, notably in the interpretation of the OT dietary prohibitions (X).[122] Secondly, there is the speculative interpretation of the Creation of the world in seven days as a figure of the cosmic week[123] (XV).

119. Cf. Glossary s.v.
120. Cf. J. Dupont, *Gnosis. La connaissance religieuse dans les Épîtres de Saint Paul*, Louvain, 1949, p. 198. It will have become clear by now that gnosis in this sense cannot be regarded, as once it was, as the result of Hellenistic influence, but must have been a characteristic of Later Judaism.
121. Cf. J. Daniélou, 'Eschatologie chrétienne et eschatologie sadocite' in *Les Manuscrits de la Mer Morte* (*Colloque de Strasbourg*, 25–27 May, 1955), 1957, pp. 118–125.
122. This kind of allegorical exegesis occurs also in the *Letter of Aristeas* and in Philo; in the latter, however, it is a method he has inherited from the tradition, and should be carefully distinguished from his hellenising use of allegory, which of course is not found in the *Epistle*.
123. I.e., six thousand years, then the millennium (Sabbath), and the new Creation (ogdoad).

This derives from Jewish speculations on the opening chapters of *Genesis*, and was to play a vital role in Jewish Christian theology, appearing not only in the Epistle, but also in Papias, Theophilus of Antioch, and the *Shepherd of Hermas.*[124]

The exegesis in the Epistle is thus of a Jewish Christian type, as numerous other features confirm. Among these may be mentioned: the references to the Jewish apocalypses, *I Enoch* (IV, 3) and *II* (4) *Esdras* (XII, 1); the application to Christ of the term the 'Beloved' (III, 6), as in the *Ascension of Isaiah*; the specifically Jewish expression δικαιώματα (I, 2; II, 1); the prominence of speculations about the Cross (XI–XII); and statements of millenarian doctrine (XV). The allusion to milk and honey (VI, 8–13)[125] recalls the *Odes of Solomon*. The author's attitude to the Sabbath, to sacrifices and to the Temple also show that he belonged to a Jewish environment. The whole *Epistle* expresses the efforts of a Jewish Christian to induce Jews to forsake ritual observances, and to show them that Judaism finds its true realisation in Christianity. Hence it is clear that the author did not belong to the group of which James was the head, for they kept up Jewish practices; but, as has already been remarked, that group was not truly representative of Jewish Christianity in the sense in which the term is here being used.

When the *Epistle* is studied more closely, it will be found that many of its elements recall an Essene setting and seem to have persisted from the earliest days of Jewish Christianity. This is plain in the case of *Barnabas'* treatise of the Two Ways, in which the Essene characteristics are more prominent than in the *Didache*. The two ways are the way of light and the way of darkness; the former is under the control of God and his 'light-giving angels', the latter that of Satan, the archon of the present age, and his angels (XVIII, 1–2). Satan is also referred to as 'the Black One' (XX, 1), an expression which was to reappear among the Ebionites, a group among whom there was certainly an Essene ascendancy. The holding of goods in common (XIX, 8) was a characteristic of the primitive Jewish Christian community, again taken over from Essene practice. In the same way, the polemic against bloody sacrifices as opposed to the worship of the lips, and against the Temple of Jerusalem as opposed to the cosmic temple

124. For further discussion of this topic, cf. pp. 107–115 below.
125. Cf. N. A. DAHL, 'La terre où coulent le lait et le miel' in *Aux sources de la tradition chrétienne* (*Mél. Goguel*), pp. 62–70.

and God's dwelling in the heart (XVI, 7) has certain precedents in Essenism.[126] It is interesting that there is no trace of the purely Christian theme of Christ as the New Temple.

There is certainly then an Essene influence in the *Epistle*, but it is analogous to the one found in the *Testaments*, the *Didache* and the *Odes*. It is simply an expression of the fact that the liturgical and ascetic structure of primitive Christianity was inspired by Essene Judaism. This is not a question of a local group, but of a general character which has been observed in a Syrian setting, will be found again at Rome, and belongs in this case to Egypt, for the *Epistle* does in fact come from Egypt, as is indicated by the witness of Clement[127] and Origen.[128] Some of the features already noted also provide points of comparison with the Jewish Christian *Sibylline Oracles*, especially the theme of the ogdoad as the consummation of the cosmic week (XV).

The *Epistle* may well be of great antiquity in view of the importance Clement attaches to it, for this presupposes that he dates it back to Apostolic times, as with the *Apocalypse of Peter*. But the question may be settled more precisely by another detail. The *Epistle* was composed after the fall of the Temple, since it contains an allusion to this event, but it comes soon enough afterwards for there still to be a possibility of the Temple's being rebuilt (XVI, 7). This can only apply to the reign of Hadrian, and the text ought therefore to be placed somewhere about the year 120. It reflects a moment in the history of Jewish Christianity in Egypt at which the Roman persecution of Trajan's day seemed to have died down, and the conflict was chiefly with the Jews. From this point of view it is contemporary with the *Preaching of Peter*,[129] also quoted by Clement of Alexandria.[130]

In the opinion of the present writer the *Shepherd of Hermas* ought also to be included among those works that contribute to our knowledge of the gnosis of the Jewish Christian Church. Its precise subject is the discipline of penance, and its context the church congregation. Here again the Jewish Christian origin of the work has been disputed in favour of a derivation from the vision-literature of Hellenism, and more particularly the *Hermetic*

J. H. BAUMGARTNER, 'Sacrifice and Worship among the Jewish sectarians of DSS', *HTR*, XLVI, 1953, pp. 141–161.

127. *Strom.* II, 7:35.
128. *Contra Celsum* I, 63.   129. Cf. H. KÖSTER, *Synoptische Überlieferung*, p. 158.
130. *Strom.* VI, 5:42.

writings.[131] Quite apart, however, from the fact that the latter books may themselves have been subject to Jewish influences, the Jewish Christian characteristics of the *Shepherd* are much more marked than has been allowed.[132] There are indeed Hellenistic literary influences as well, but the basis of the work is Jewish Christian.

This verdict is supported first of all by the literary genres of the various fragments that make up the book. The *Visions* are closely parallel to those in the apocalypses, where the heavens are opened and revelations are made through an angelic intermediary. The only difference is that here the visionary is a contemporary, and the visions concern the life of the Church. In this the work is close to the New Testament *Revelation* of John. Hermas was in fact one of that class of prophets whose existence is attested by the *Didache*, and whose disappearance was regretted by the *Ascension of Isaiah*.

The other sections of the book equally bear the stamp of Jewish Christianity. The *Mandates* are largely a treatise on the discernment of spirits, developing the doctrine of the Two Ways as this is found in the *Didache* and the *Epistle of Barnabas*. There are numerous points of contact with these two works and with the *Testaments*; and together they constitute a summary of Jewish Christian moral and ascetical theology. The *Similitudes* belong to the type of symbolical visions that are found in large numbers in Jewish apocalyptic literature, especially in *I Enoch* and *II* (4) *Esdras*. The comparison with this last work, which is contemporaneous with the *Shepherd*, is especially important.

A number of details show the *Shepherd's* dependence on Jewish apocalyptic, notably the angelology. The angel of repentance had already figured in *I Enoch* (XL, 9) under the name of Phanuel. Angels are given the task of creation (*Vis.* III, 4:1); there is a doctrine of a good and a bad angel set over human life (*Mand.* VI, 2:1), which corresponds to some extent to the doctrine of the Two Ways which, as has already been noted, was of Jewish origin. Mention should also be made of the enormous stature of the angels (*Sim.* VIII, 1:2), and the theme of the angels bearing the central figure in an ascension (*Vis.* III, 10:1), which is also found in the

---

131. So REITZENSTEIN, *Poimandres*, Leipzig, 1904 and PETERSON, 'Beiträge zur Interpretation der Vision in Pastor Hermae', *OCP*, XIII, 1947, pp. 624 ff.
132. Cf. AUDET, 'Affinités littéraires et doctrinales du Manuel de discipline', in *RB*, LX, 1953, pp. 41–82.

Gospel of Peter. Angelology of this kind comes directly from Jewish apocalyptic and Essene spirituality.

The *Shepherd* exhibits in addition numerous characteristics of Jewish Christian theology. The purpose of the Descent into Hell (*Sim.* IX, 16:2) is again the salvation of the saints of the Old Testament, as in the *Gospel of Peter* and the *Epistle of the Apostles*. For its theology of the Trinity the *Shepherd* borrowed its symbolism from angelology, but in a different form from that found in the *Ascension of Isaiah*: the Word appears as the chief of the six archangels, being himself the seventh. This angelomorphic theology which is, as will appear later, perfectly orthodox, is typically Jewish Christian.[133] The same applies to the use of the expression 'the Name' for the Word, which occurs also in the *Gospel of Truth*, where it is a borrowing from Jewish Christian theology.[134]

The ecclesiastical discipline in the *Shepherd* is equally characteristic of Jewish Christianity, and shows once more the strong impression made upon early Christianity in this domain by Essenism. Two examples may be quoted. First of all the discipline of penance, which is in fact the subject of the book; excommunication, whether temporary or for life, appears as the expression of the apostolic power to remit or to retain sins, as exercised in a Jewish Christian community. Secondly, there is the passage in which Hermas tells how he passed a night with holy virgins (*Sim.* IX, 11). In the context this is given an allegorical interpretation, but the passage may well be inspired by a religious practice akin to that alluded to in Tatian (XV, 1) and the *Didache* (XI, 11).[135] This again seems to belong to the context of the Essene ideal as described by Philo in the *De vita contemplativa*; but as in the case of a number of other Christian continuations of Essene practice—for example, combining the Eucharist with a meal—the custom presupposed the Jewish mentality, and there could be no question of continuing it in a Christian community that consisted of former pagans.

The *Shepherd*, then, is one of the essential works for a knowledge of the theological and spiritual life of Jewish Christianity. The problem of dating is complex, though the data are well enough known. On the one hand,

133. Cf. chap. 4 below.
134. AUDET (*op. cit.*) rightly urged the Jewish Christian character of the theology of the *Shepherd*, but he unfortunately failed to recognise its trinitarian nature.
135. Cf. A. ADAM, 'Erwägungen zur Herkunft der Didache', *ZKG*, LXVIII, 1957, pp. 21–23. It is possible that there is an allusion to these spiritual unions in Saint Paul (*I Cor.* 7:36–38).

Hermas says that he received an order from Pope Clement to write the book, which would place it in the year 90; on the other, the Muratorian Canon records that the *Shepherd* was written at Rome under Pope Pius about A.D. 140. The solution seems to be that the work is the product of several editions, of which the first would go back to about the year 90. From this it can be seen that the text is all the more important, giving as it does in its first form information on a very early state of the Roman community. The indications concerning the hierarchy, which fit in with those in the *Didache*, seem to confirm this solution. It is supported also by the state of the text which shows variants that are evidence of remodelling. The most important of these is the substitution of the expression 'the Name of the Lord' for the typically Jewish Christian expression 'the Name' which was no longer understood.[136]

The text itself gives Rome as its place of origin, and there is no reason to doubt this statement. There remains the question of the type of community from which it came. The fact that Essene influences are so marked raises the question whether, as in the case of the last three works examined, this is an instance of the Essene imprint which is to be found on all early Jewish Christianity in the spheres of morality and religious institutions, or whether there is a more precise influence, and Hermas should be seen as the son of an Essene convert, who came to Rome from Jerusalem after A.D. 70. The different climate of the *Shepherd* compared with that of the contemporary *I Clement* gives grounds for believing that there is more in Hermas than the mere survival of primitive Essene characteristics, and it ought probably to be concluded that the *Shepherd* shows signs of Essene influences dating from after A.D. 70.[137] The work is comparable in this respect with the *Odes of Solomon*, with which its mystical asceticism has a certain kinship.

IGNATIUS AND CLEMENT

It now remains to discuss two works, the *Epistles* of Ignatius of Antioch and *I Clement*, which belong to a special genre, namely letters of an official nature composed by bishops. They are, however, very different from one

136. Cf. pp. 147 ff. below. It may be added that the authority which Origen accords to the *Shepherd* is an argument in favour of its origin in the Apostolic age; and it is at least interesting that it should be appended to the New Testament in the *Codex Sinaiticus*.

137. So AUDET, *op. cit.*

another in character. The *Epistles* of Ignatius are the most important work of our period, and in many aspects lie outside the scope of the present enquiry. On the one hand they contain no theological speculations or private traditions, but the very faith of the Church, handed on through a succession of bishops; on the other, they are the work of a great saint enlightened by the Spirit, in whom the ideal of primitive Christianity was expressed with unequalled splendour.

The only aspect of Ignatius of concern here, however, is his importance as a witness to Jewish Christianity. At first sight there might be some doubt about placing him in the same environment as the authors so far studied. In the first place his work shows markedly anti-Judaising tendencies: 'It is monstrous to talk of Jesus Christ and to practise Judaism' (*Magn.* X, 3). However, it has already been remarked several times, as for example in the case of the *Epistle of Barnabas*, that the struggle against Judaising tendencies was typical of Jewish Christians. The adversaries whom he accuses of corrupting the community, and whom he combats unceasingly, are Christians who are under the influence of Gnostic Judaism of the heterodox type, who deny the reality of the incarnation, and who claim that in this they are supported by the Old Testament.[138]

Moreover, the theological developments in Ignatius unquestionably show resemblances to some of the works already mentioned, especially the *Ascension of Isaiah* and the *Odes of Solomon*. The soundest conclusion with regard to these works seemed to be that they were a product of Syrian Christianity. Now Ignatius was Bishop of Antioch, and his work does in fact show traces of the influence of this Syriac theology which borrowed its modes of expression from Jewish gnosis.[139]

Among features typical of Jewish Christianity the following may be mentioned here. The expression 'the Beloved' ($\dot{\eta}\gamma\alpha\pi\eta\mu\acute{\epsilon}\nu o s$) is applied to Christ (*Smyrn.* Inscr.); this is the usual expression in the *Ascension of Isaiah* and is archaic in character. The imagery of the Father as a gardener, and of the Church as his 'planting' ($\varphi\upsilon\tau\epsilon\acute{\iota}\alpha$: *Phil.* III, 1; *Trall.* XI, 1), is also typical of Jewish Christianity, and may be compared with the following phrase in the *Ascension of Isaiah* (IV, 3): '(The Church) is the garden

138. Cf. E. MOLLAND, 'The Heretics combated by Ignatius of Antioch', *JEH*, V, 1952 pp. 1–6.
139. H. SCHLIER has the credit for having established this point in most convincing detail: *Religionsgeschichtliche Untersuchungen zu den Ignatiusbriefen*, Giessen, 1929, pp. 175–186.

which the twelve Apostles of the Beloved have planted', and with the *Odes of Solomon* (XXXVIII, 18–21).[140]

In Ignatius is again found the Descent into Hell in its archaic form, in which it was an attempt to deal with the problem of the salvation of the saints of the Old Testament: 'For even the prophets, being disciples in the Spirit, were expecting Him as their teacher; for which cause He whom they awaited in righteousness, when He came, raised them from the dead' (*Magn.* IX, 3).[141]

Ignatius has a curious passage on the heavenly hierarchy. 'Am I not able to write to you of heavenly things? But I fear lest I should cause you harm being babes ($\nu\dot\eta\pi\iota\iota$) . . . I . . . can comprehend heavenly things, and the arrays ($\tau\iota\pi\iota\theta\epsilon\sigma\dot\iota\alpha\varsigma$) of the angels and the musterings of the principalities. . . . I am not yet by reason of this a disciple' (*Trall.* V, 2). This may be compared with *Hebr.* 5:11–12: 'of whom we have many things to say . . . but ye have need again that some one teach you the rudiments ($\sigma\tau\iota\iota\chi\epsilon\hat\iota\alpha$) of the first principles of the oracles of God; and are become such as have need of milk, and not of solid food.' These two texts are closely parallel; in each a distinction is drawn between the elementary catechesis which provides nourishment for the neophytes (cf. *I Pet.* 2:2) who were traditionally compared to $\nu\dot\eta\pi\iota\iota$, and a higher teaching. This higher teaching is the gnosis. In this passage Ignatius states his intention of keeping to the elementary teaching; and for this reason only allusions to the gnosis are to be found in his work, although he claims to be acquainted with it.

One of these allusions is especially remarkable, namely the famous passage in *Eph.* XIX to which reference will frequently be made in later chapters:

And hidden from the Prince of this world were the virginity of Mary and her child-bearing—and likewise also the death of the Lord—three mysteries to be cried aloud—the which were wrought in the silence of God. How then were they made manifest to the ages? A star shone forth in the heaven above all the stars; and its light was unutterable and its strangeness caused amazement; and all the rest of the

140. Cf. SCHLIER, *op. cit.*, p. 50. The expression was familiar to the Qumran community (cf. *DSD* VIII, 5).

141. BIEDER (*Die Vorstellung von der Höllenfahrt Jesu Christi*, p. 142) observes that this theme is not integral to Ignatius' thought, and seems therefore to be a fragment which he has received from the Jewish Christian tradition. It is likely that he is here dependent on a *midrash* of *Jeremiah* to which further reference will be made, cf. pp. 102 ff. below.

constellations with the sun and moon formed themselves into a chorus about the star; but the star itself far outshone them all; and there was perplexity to know whence came this strange appearance which was so unlike them. From that time forward every sorcery and every spell dissolved (1–3).

This remarkable text, which will have to be studied in detail, is certainly related to the *Ascension of Isaiah*.[142] It is concerned with a *descensus* of the Word, hidden from the angels. The allusion to the silence of God should be noted: 'There is one God, who manifested himself through Jesus Christ His Son, who is His Word that proceeded from silence' (*Magn.* VIII, 2). But this silence is also that of the bishop, God's representative: 'In proportion as a man seeth that his bishop is silent, let him fear the more. For everyone whom the Master of the household sendeth to be steward over His own house we ought so to receive as Him that sent him. Plainly therefore we ought to regard the bishop as the Lord Himself' (*Eph.* VI, 1).[143]

In this passage may be seen the essentially Syrian, Antiochene character of this type of Jewish Christianity, with its sense of the mystery of God, its emphasis on his transcendence. These motifs were given heterodox expression in the negative theology of Gnosticism, but were also to endure more fruitfully in orthodox Syrian thought, and in the work of another great Antiochene, John Chrysostom, to inspire his great Homilies *On the Incomprehensible Nature of God*. They were also to be found in the Syriac liturgy, which emphasised the separation of the holy mysteries from the profane world. The hierarch officiating in the sanctuary is the visible image of the hidden God. This is a constant feature of the Antiochene religious genius under its superficial Hellenistic veneer.

Another feature of the *Letters* of Ignatius is the hierarchical organisation of the community in three degrees: 'Be ye zealous to do all things in godly concord, the bishop presiding after the likeness of God and the presbyters after the likeness of the council ($\sigma\upsilon\nu\acute{\epsilon}\delta\rho\iota o\nu$) of the Apostles, with the deacons also who are most dear to me, having been entrusted with the diaconate of Jesus Christ' (*Magn.* VI, 1). This distinct triple division recalls the structure of the Essene community, and must therefore be rooted in

142. So SCHLIER, *Untersuchungen*.
143. Cf. H. CHADWICK, 'The Silence of Bishops in Ignatius', *HTR*, XLIII, 1950, pp. 169–172; P. MEINHOLD, 'Schweigende Bischöfe', *Festgabe Lortz*, Baden-Baden, 1957, pp. 467–490.

Jewish Christianity. It seems to be constructed on the model of the first monarchical community at Jerusalem, to which Antioch is very close.

The echoes of the liturgical life to be found in Ignatius call to mind the *Odes of Solomon*. The celebrated passage: 'There is . . . in me only living water . . . saying within me, Come to the Father' (Rom. VII, 2) recalls *Ode* XI, 6: 'Waters that speak have touched my lips springing from the fountain of the Lord'. Both passages suggest the living water of Jewish Christian baptism. The many references to perfumed ointment, for example: 'the Lord received ointment on His head, that he might breathe incorruption upon the Church' (*Eph.* XVII, 1) are also found in the Odes: 'My nostrils enjoyed the pleasant odour of the Lord' (XI, 13), and they emphasise the importance of this baptismal anointing in Syria.

Finally there is one more feature which is especially characteristic of Ignatius, and has a remarkable Jewish parallel. The *Epistles* are full of the thought of martyrdom, and a familiar expression in them is the idea of offering his life as a 'ransom' (ἀντίψυχον) for his brethren (*Eph.* XXI, 1; *Smyr.* X, 2). Now there happens to be extant a Jewish homily, written in Greek, which was actually composed at Antioch in the time of Ignatius, the work known as the *Fourth Book of Maccabees*, which is a eulogy of the heroes of the Jewish revolt against Antiochus. In it is found the same expression as in Ignatius[144]: 'Take my soul to ransom (ἀντίψυχον) their souls', says the aged Eleazer (VI, 29) and again: 'They having as it were become a ransom for our nation's sin' (XVII, 22).

The *Epistle of Clement* of Rome raises a similar problem to that of Ignatius. It clearly contains hellenistic elements, particularly the use of typically Stoic expressions.[145] Especially noteworthy are: σύγκρασις ('mixing') and συμπνεῖν ('breathing together') to express the unity of the members of the Church, διοίκησις ('direction') to designate the ordering of the κόσμος ('universe'). Some hellenistic allusions may also be noted; the story of the Phoenix as a symbol of the resurrection (XXV, 2–3), or of the alternation of day and night (XX, 2) which appears in Seneca.[146]

---

144. Cf. DUPONT-SOMMER, *Le quatrième Livre des Macchabées*, Paris, 1939, pp. 67–85.
145. Cf. SANDERS, *L'hellénisme de Clément de Rome et le paulinisme*, Louvain, 1943, pp. 109–140; also G. BARDY, 'Vocabulaire Stoïcien dans la Prima Clementis'. *RSR*, XII, 1922, pp. 73 ff.
146. *Epist.* XXXVI, 10–11. It should be remembered, however, that the allusion to the Danaids and to Dirce, which used to be regarded as the most striking of all, is probably the result of a faulty reading: cf. DAIN, 'Note sur le texte de Clément de Rome', in *Mél. Lebreton*, I, pp. 353–362.

In spite of all this, however, Clement's theological setting is Jewish Christian,[147] though it is a very different Jewish Christianity from that of Antioch. It has no connection with any esoteric or Gnostic Judaism.[148] The work belongs to the class of edifying Jewish literature with a moral purpose, such as is to be found in Palestinian Judaism, and was continued in the *midrashim*.[149] *I Clement* was created against a Jewish–Stoic background.

Attention may be drawn first of all to some features of archaic theology. Christ in his role as the Father's agent in creation is called 'the Name' (LIX, 3).[150] The expression 'the Beloved' appears several times (LIX, 2–3). The long final prayer, which is a kind of liturgical anaphora,[151] is made up almost entirely of Old Testament allusions (LIX–LXI). The *Epistle* also makes use of *targumim*, in particular of a *midrash* of *Jeremiah*, which was noted above in connection with the *Epistles* of Ignatius, and was in circulation among the community at Rome. Again, the reflections in chapter XX on the created order as an expression of the will of God may be paralleled in *II Enoch* and the *Testaments*.[152] In all these respects Clement appears to be in touch with the archaic literature of Christianity, though himself belonging to a later phase.

Most important of all, however, is the fact that *I Clement* provides several examples[153] of another typically Jewish genre, the homiletic *haggada*, in which a succession of characters from the Old Testament are presented as object-lessons for the practice of various virtues.[154] This genre is already to be found in the Wisdom literature with its eulogies of the Fathers[155]; it appears in the New Testament *Epistle to the Hebrews* in the

---

147. As was seen by HARNACK and WREDE; on this point SANDERS' book is open to question. PETERSON ('Das praescriptum des I Clemens-Briefes', in *Pro Regno Pro Sanctuario*, pp. 351–354) has demonstrated that the literary genre of the Epistle is Jewish, more so in fact than that of the Pauline letters.

148. GOPPELT has rightly remarked on the total absence of any speculation of this kind (*op. cit.*, p. 224).

149. GOPPELT is again surely right in suggesting that this type of literature was more in keeping with Latin moralising tendencies (*op. cit.*, p. 240).

150. Cf. pp. 147 ff. below.

151. Cf. Glossary s.v.

152. Cf. VAN UNNIK, 'Is I Clement XX purely Stoic?', *VC*, IV, 1950, pp. 181–190.

153. Cf. e.g., IV, VII, IX–XII, XVII, XXXI.

154. Cf. H. THYEN, *Der Stil der jüdisch-hellenistischen Homilie*, Göttingen, 1955, pp. 11–39.

155. Cf. *Ecclus.* 44–50; *Wis.* 10–19.

praises of Faith,[156] and again in *IV Maccabees* (XVI, 20 f.), while the *Testaments* also derive from the same class of writing. Further examples, connected beyond dispute with Jewish sources, may be seen in the liturgy of the *Apostolic Constitutions* (VIII, 5–14). Finally, Jewish iconography, both at Doura Europos and in the paintings from the catacombs, provides examples of similar series of personages which must go back to early prototypes.[157]

The examples of this genre in *I Clement* exhibit a number of interesting features. There is a *haggada* of the effects of jealousy (IV, 1–12), which uses as its examples Cain, Esau, the brothers of Joseph, Aaron and Miriam, Dathan and Abiram, and the enemies of David. Later follows a eulogy of the saints of the Old Testament: Enoch, the model of obedience (IX, 3), Noah of fidelity (IX, 4), Abraham of faith (X, 1–7), Lot of hospitality (XI, 1–3), Rahab also of hospitality (XII, 1–7). The choice of these examples might seem curious. It was certainly traditional, for these characters recur frequently in old texts and monuments. Particularly interesting is the prominence accorded in these lists to non-Jews such as Enoch, Noah, Lot and Rahab, a feature which may well, as in *II Enoch*, be motivated by an apologetic intention.

Later there is a eulogy of humility. The penitents are the first to be mentioned (XVII, 1), Elisha, Elijah and Ezekiel, clothed in goat-skins, a detail which recalls *Heb.* 11:37. Abraham acknowledges that he is dust and ashes (XVII, 2). To Moses are attributed the following words, which must come from some apocryphon: 'I am smoke ($\dot{\alpha}\tau\mu\dot{\iota}s$) from the pot' (XVII, 6). David recites the *Miserere* (XVIII, 1). In another chapter Abraham, Isaac and Jacob are shown as models of those who walk in the ways of God (XXXI, 2–4).

TRADITIONS OF THE ELDERS

The chief surviving monuments of the Jewish Christian period of the history of theology have now been assembled. In addition, however, to the study of the written documents there remains the question whether any

156. Cf. *Heb.* 11; the same form is modified to serve a rather different intention in Stephen's speech in *Acts* 7.
157. Cf. A. G. MARTIMORT, 'L'iconographie des catacombes et la catéchèse antique *RAC*, xxv, 1949, pp. 1–12.

oral tradition coming from the same type of community survived and was later committed to writing. On this point there are two vital witnesses: Papias and Clement of Alexandria. Both claim to have recorded traditions which have come down to them from the Apostles. This should be understood to mean not the Apostles themselves, but rather the apostolic circle, the primitive Jewish Christian community. The study of these traditions leads by a different route to the same doctrines already seen to be present in the written texts, and therefore confirms their Jewish Christian character.

Papias is known to us chiefly through Irenaeus and Eusebius. The evidence of the former is all the more valuable because he belongs to the same circle as Papias, and is only a little later than him in time. He writes: 'And these things Papias, who was a hearer of John and a companion of Polycarp, witnesseth in writing in the fourth of his books; for there are five books composed by him' (*Adv. haer.* V, 33:4). Irenaeus knew Polycarp, and therefore his first-hand information about Papias,[158] who, he asserts, belonged to a generation that could still be said to be contemporaries of the Apostles.[159] He also affirms his Asiatic origin. Moreover, Irenaeus also knew the work of Papias; and it was his well-known feeling for the Apostolic tradition which made him prize this work so highly, for he regarded it as putting him in contact with Apostolic times.

This at once poses a question central to the present study. Tradition may be taken in two ways with reference to the time of Irenaeus. On the one hand, there existed an official handing on of the faith, as expressed in the rule of faith, and the instrument for this was the succession of bishops. This tradition was both oral and written, and was concerned with the fundamental truths. On the other hand, the period was also marked by oral traditions bearing on very varied aspects of theology, which went back not indeed to the Apostles themselves, but to the Apostolic generation, the primitive community, and for this reason enjoyed great authority in the second century. They do not, however, put us in touch with tradition in the sense of official, basic dogma, but only with ancient 'traditions'. The immediate importance of these traditions is that their content is precisely the object of this present study, namely, the theology of the Jewish Christian community in Apostolic times.

This is confirmed by the second witness to Papias, Eusebius. He has

158. Indeed Jerome calls him a disciple of Papias himself (*Ad Theodoram* 75, c. 3).
159. Cf. E. GUTWENGER, 'Papias, Eine chronologische Studie'. *ZKT*, LXIX, 1947, p. 416.

preserved the preface to Papias' work, and also its title *Exegesis of the Sayings of the Lord*:

> I will not hesitate to set down for thy benefit, along with the interpretations (ἑρμηνείας), all that I ever carefully learnt and carefully recalled from the Elders, guaranteeing its truth. . . . If anyone chanced to come who had actually been a follower of the Elders, I would enquire as to the discourses of the Elders, what Andrew or what Peter said, or what Philip, or what Thomas or James or what John or Matthew or any other of the Lord's disciples. . . . For I did not think that things out of books could profit me so much as the utterances of a voice which liveth and abideth (*HE* III, 39:3-4).

This text is quite explicit. By 'Elders' Papias seems to connote the primitive community as a whole, both Apostles and others. He is not therefore concerned with the teaching of the Apostles as such. He distinguishes clearly between books, the canonical scriptures, and oral traditions, which are quite a different matter and one in which he is especially interested. It could hardly be possible to define more precisely what he is handing on: doctrines from the Jewish Christian community, but not belonging to the official traditions of the Church, in other words the theology of the first community. Papias moreover makes his own contribution: he has made ἑρμηνείαι, that is to say, he has been both exegete and theologian. From this point of view he represents a distinct and later source, but none the less one still belonging to Jewish Christian theology.

Leaving aside traditions of a purely historical nature, several other points are of importance. Andrew of Caesarea[160] tells us that Papias taught that God had conferred on certain angels the task of administering the Earth, and that they betrayed this trust.[161] This doctrine is manifestly of Jewish origin, and moreover reappears in Athenagoras, Irenaeus and Gregory of Nyssa, who classify it as a παράδοσις.[162] It belongs to that type of Jewish Christian speculation which had come to be considered as venerable tradition because of its archaic character. Furthermore, the importance attributed to angelology has already been noted several times as a typical characteristic of Jewish Christian theology.

The second, and most important, doctrine that Papias claims to have

160. *In Apocalypsin*, c. 34, serm. 12.
161. Cf. PREUSCHEN, *Antilegomena*, 2nd edn. Giessen, 1905, p. 96.
162. Cf. J. DANIÉLOU, *Les Anges et leur mission*, 2nd edn. Chevetogne, 1953, pp. 62-67.

received from tradition is that of millenarianism. This doctrine is already found in the New Testament *Revelation* of John, but with Papias it undergoes developments inspired by Jewish apocalyptic and especially by the *Apocalypse of Baruch*. These developments are recorded by Irenaeus, who adopted them out of respect for the tradition (*Adv. haer.* V, 33:3). Eusebius, while he is equally explicit, is more severe. He speaks of ξένας τε τινας παραβολὰς τοῦ Σωτῆρος, 'strange teachings of the Saviour' taught by Papias 'as having come down to him from unwritten tradition', and of τινα μυθικώτερα, 'statements of a rather mythical character' (III, 39:11). Once again it was the authority of their antiquity which secured for these Jewish Christian speculations the good fortune to survive so late as the fourth century.

Irenaeus records other interesting data attributed to 'the Elders who were disciples of the Apostles', a description which clearly refers to the same environment as the one from which Papias drew his traditions. One is concerned with the corporal translation to Paradise of Enoch and Elijah after their death 'as first fruits of the resurrection' (V, 5:1). This detail has already been noted in *II Enoch*. It is related to the Jewish Christian doctrine that the resurrection of the Old Testament saints had already taken place. Another tradition refers to the variety of mansions in Paradise—'heavens, paradise and city'—and connects this with *Mat.* 13:8, the verse about the seed which bears fruit 'some a hundredfold, some sixty, some thirty' (V, 36:1). Now this text from *Matthew* is the subject of similar speculations in the pseudo-Cyprianic treatise *De centesima sexagesima tricesima*, which contains many Jewish Christian elements.[163]

Thus internal evidence confirms the external data pointing to the traditions reported by Papias as a form of Jewish Christian theology. These traditions obviously go back to a very early date; some may come from the Palestinian community before A.D. 70, while others date from *c.* 80, and are connected with an Asiatic environment, since it was here that millenarianism reached its full development in the church founded by John. As will be seen later this particular stream in Jewish Christianity had a strong Messianist flavour, probably deriving from Zealot elements in the congregation; for the greater degree of toleration obtaining in Asia Minor resulted in the continuance of a more active Jewish nationalism there than elsewhere. It is therefore an entirely new side of Jewish Christianity which is disclosed in Papias.

163. Edited by REITZENSTEIN, in *ZNW*, XV, 1914, pp. 74–88.

It is also possible that there is an echo of the traditions of the Asiatic Elders in the interpretations given to several of the Gospel parables by Origen. Concerning the parable of the Good Samaritan, for instance, he writes: 'One of the Elders said that the man who was going down to Jericho is Adam, Jerusalem is Paradise, Jericho the world, the thieves the evil powers, the Samaritan Christ' (*Hom. Luc.* 34). The same exegesis had already appeared in Irenaeus,[164] but since it is hardly likely that Origen would call Irenaeus 'one of the Elders', the common source of both passages must be the tradition in question.[165]

Some traditions that Irenaeus attributes to the 'Elders' or 'predecessors' may belong to the same environment, though he does not associate them directly with Papias and the Apostolic community, and they must therefore constitute a different source. One of them certainly goes back to an anti-Marcionite work attributed to an Elder. It speaks of the Descent into Hell as bringing salvation to the saints of the Old Testament (IV, 27:2)—a doctrine already remarked as Jewish Christian. Another, which refers to a 'predecessor', speaks of Christ's extending his arms on the cross as a symbol of the reconciliation of Jews and Gentiles (V, 17:4). This is part of a theology of the Cross in which some Jewish Christian characteristics can be detected, and which will be discussed in more detail in a later chapter.[166]

Up to now the oral traditions considered have been those handed on from Asiatic presbyters through Papias and Irenaeus. But there is another author, in another type of community, who also claims to have recorded ancient oral traditions. This author is Clement of Alexandria, who relates at the beginning of the *Stromateis* how he collected from the oral tradition some mysterious information which, after some hesitation, he decided to commit to writing (I, : 1 13–14). Two questions immediately suggest themselves: from whom did Clement receive these oral traditions? and what was their content?

The first of these two questions, that of sources, must at present remain open[167]; but it is incontestable that certain passages in Clement's work,

---

164. Cf. J. DANIÉLOU, 'Le Bon Samaritain', in *Mél. Robert*, Paris-Tournai, 1957, pp. 457–465.
165. If this were so, it might be that the analogous exegeses in Origen's *Commentary on Matthew* come from the same source, possibly Papias. Perhaps it is these exegeses that Eusebius calls ξένας παραβολάς.
166. Cf. ORBE, *Los primeros herejes ante la persecución*, p. 228; also chap. 9 below.
167. BOUSSET (*Jüdisch-christlicher Schulbetrieb in Alexandria und Rom*, Göttingen, 1915)

3—T.J.C.

notably in the *Eclogae Propheticae*, the *Adumbrationes* and part of the *Stromateis*, contain doctrines too distinctive in character to be entirely Clement's own—the more so since they do not follow his usual train of thought.

However, certain by now familiar features make it possible to place these doctrines. Thus there is a developed angelology, characteristic of Jewish apocalyptic; in particular the doctrine of the firstborn angels is connected with Jewish tradition.[168] The concept of the soul on its journey through the heavens putting on the forms of the successive angelic hierarchies is found in the *Ascension of Isaiah*. Other curious speculations include the theory of the successive covenants, and their relation with various angels; the concept of God's having a body—which is in flat contradiction with the rest of Clement's thought; the opposition between the masculine element, which is the source of whatever is strong in the world, and the feminine, the source of all weakness. However, all these doctrines are to be found in the pseudo-Clementines, which are Jewish Christian heterodox writings, and contain numerous elements of Jewish theology.[169]

All this compels one to recognise that the most striking feature of the passages in question is their Judaistic colouring, deriving not from the oral instruction of the Alexandrian school as this already existed among the Hellenised Jews with Philo,[170] and which represents quite a different stream of thought, but from Palestinian Jewish teaching. It has been suggested that it may be regarded as the fruit of Clement's journey in Palestine, where he would have met Jewish rabbis; but another piece of evidence suggests quite a different interpretation. It should be noticed that in regard to this teaching Clement insists on its character as 'tradition'. What he

---

168. Cf. F. SAGNARD, *Clément d'Alexandrie, Extraits de Théodote*, Paris, 1948, p. 77.

169. As COLLOMP long ago observed: 'Une source de Clément d'Alexandrie et des Homélies pseudo-clémentines', *RP*, XXXVII, 1913, pp. 19 ff. On the subject of the pseudo-Clementines, cf. further pp. 59 ff. below; on the angels and the hierarchies etc., pp. 181 ff.

170. The view put forward by BOUSSET, *op. cit.*

---

attempted to prove that Clement received the traditions principally from Pantaenus, to whom he refers on several occasions as his teacher (cf. also EUSEBIUS, *HE* VI, 13:2). However, CASEY (*The Excerpta ex Theodoto*, London, 1934, pp. 11–14) and MUNCK (*Untersuchungen über Klemens von Alexandrie*, Stuttgart, 1933, pp. 151–205) have both since demonstrated that this hypothesis, though attractive, is not really justified by the evidence of the text.

intended was to put the oral traditions in writing lest they should perish, and oral traditions mean for him those that go back to Apostolic times.

After briefly mentioning his teachers Clement continues in the following words:

> They, preserving the tradition (παράδοσις) of the blessed doctrine derived directly from the holy apostles Peter, James, John and Paul, the son receiving it from the father (but few were like their fathers), came—thanks be to God!—to us also to sow these fertile and apostolic seeds. And well I know that what will please my readers will not be the literary form in which they are now presented, but simply the traditions which these notes preserve. This sketch, then, is the work of a soul whose only desire is to guard intact the blessed instruction (*Strom.* I, 11:3–12:1).

Eusebius comments: 'In the first book of the *Stromateis* Clement shows us that he himself was very close to the tradition of the Apostles. In the same work he promises also to write a commentary on *Genesis*. And in his treatise *On the Pasch* he professes that he was compelled . . . to commit to writing traditions that he had heard from the elders of olden time' (*HE* VI, 13:8–9).

Here, therefore, is a situation parallel to the one in Irenaeus. Clement of Alexandria also knew oral traditions coming, not from the Apostles themselves, but from the Apostolic community, and consequently a part of Jewish Christian theology. In other passages he recalls the oral character of this teaching: 'The presbyters did not write' (*Eclog.* 27); 'This gnosis came down from the Apostles through their successors to a few (of us), being handed on unwritten (ἀγράφως)' (*Strom.* VI, 7:61). The intermediate link in the tradition between him and Apostolic times had been the elders of Alexandria, perhaps especially Pantaenus, but only as an intermediary. It is therefore a Jewish Christian tradition, but one distinct from the Asiatic tradition of the presbyters of Papias, and linking the community of Alexandria with the end of the Apostolic epoch.

This conclusion is confirmed by the content of the traditions. It will be observed that they include principally exegeses of *Genesis*—a characteristic topic of Jewish Christianity on which a great deal will have to be said later.[171] At Alexandria itself the *Epistle of Barnabas* showed traces of this

171. Cf. pp. 107 ff. below.

kind of exegesis. Moreover, in Jewish and Jewish Christian circles the exegesis of *Genesis* provided the occasion for esoteric speculations, and could not therefore be put in writing lest they should be imprudently divulged; and Clement writes down only a few of them, and these with some hesitation. These exegeses of *Genesis* played a large part in Alexandrian Gnostic theology, especially that of the Ophites and Valentinians; and since the Gnostics depended largely on the Jewish Christians for their material, it may therefore be said that in Jewish Christianity in general, and at Alexandria in particular, the theology of the learned, the gnosis, must have consisted to a great extent of commentaries on *Genesis*, of which some outstanding fragments are to be found in the *Eclogae*.

It remains to decide to what type of community Clement's Elders belonged. It seems to have been very different from that of the Asiatic Elders. There is no trace of millenarianism among them, but on the other hand, there is certain common ground with Ebionism. At the end of the *Paedagogus* Clement gives a version of the Two Ways, a pattern that originated in the Essene catechesis. It will be remembered that the two works already recognised as belonging to Egyptian Christianity, the *Sibylline Oracles* and the *Epistle of Barnabas*, also show pronounced Essene characteristics, the former also exhibiting a marked Ebionite tendency.

This suggests some possible conclusions regarding the very obscure origins of the Church of Alexandria. It must have been founded, in part at least, by Essene Christians who came from Palestine after A.D. 70.[172] This would explain the special character of their theology, which is closer to Ebionism than that of the Jewish Christians in Syria or at Rome. Immersed in the Jewish colony, having little contact with the more hellenised circles of the Herodians[173] or the disciples of Philo, persecuted along with the Jews of Alexandria, they must have led a precarious and clandestine existence. It was only when more peaceful times came that Christianity was able to spread to the more hellenised groups, and that Alexandrianism properly so called came into being with Pantaenus and Clement.

The traditions of the Elders conclude this survey of the direct sources of Jewish Christian theology. Its chief characteristics have been determined,

172. Cf. pp. 18, 36 above.   173. Cf. Glossary s.v.

its various currents discerned. Before passing on, however, to a detailed study of its doctrines, there are some indirect sources which must be added to the direct ones so far studied; that is to say, it is possible to recognise Jewish Christian doctrines in later authors thanks to the clear definitions which it has already been possible to make. Nevertheless, this is obviously a much more delicate matter and the available data must be used with caution. However, they do provide useful information in cases where the Jewish Christian origin of a doctrine is already assured.

These indirect sources are of three principal kinds. First of all, Jewish Christian theology has obviously left many traces in the Fathers of the Church of the second and third centuries. This is especially true of the second century, which has a certain continuity with Apostolic times, and a living contact with Jewish Christianity. Theophilus of Antioch, Justin, Irenaeus and Clement of Alexandria are valuable sources in this regard.[174] With Origen[175] the oral tradition loses its prestige, but it is none the less true that authors like Hippolytus of Rome and Methodius of Olympus, not to mention Origen himself, still incorporate many elements borrowed from it.

The second kind of indirect source is that of the late apocrypha of the New Testament. Hitherto only those have been accepted as Jewish Christian whose date can be placed very early, and whose forms fit the Jewish Christian literary genres; and this has meant, for example, entirely excluding the apocryphal books of *Acts*, which no more than the canonical *Acts of the Apostles* belong to a Jewish Christian literary type. Similarly the *Protevangelium Jacobi* and the *Gospel of Nicodemus* have been omitted on account of the late date at which they were edited. Nevertheless, all this literature obviously contains important elements derived from Jewish Christianity, all the more that its popular character has many affinities with the style of Jewish Christian works with their richness of imagery. The oldest of these documents, the *Acts of Andrew* and the *Acts of John*, will prove a source of valuable data.

The last type of indirect source is that of the heterodox archaic literature. This includes in the first place the Ebionite texts, in which many elements derive from the common heritage of Jewish Christianity. Secondly, however, there are the Gnostic teachings, the affinities of which with the

174. KRETSCHMAR has recently shown this in the case of Theophilus: *Studien zur früh-christlichen Trinitätstheologie*, pp. 27–52.
175. As HANSON has proved: *Origen's Doctrine of Tradition*, London, 1954, p. 192.

works discussed in this chapter have often been remarked, with the result that many doctrines found in the latter, such as the descent of Christ through the seven heavens, or the cosmic symbolism of the Cross, have been treated as Gnostic conceptions in the strict sense of the word. In fact, however, the relationship runs in the reverse direction. The original gnosis is the theology of Jewish Christianity, and is found in the works so far examined. The Gnostic dualists borrowed the symbolism of this Jewish Christian gnosis, and that is why the Christian elements in their writings have such a marked archaic character. They also drew inspiration from Jewish Christian ritual; but they adapted their borrowings to the demands of their own dualist system, and it is this system which constitutes Gnosticism properly so-called.

Thus it is that, at least so far as the second century is concerned, Gnostic literature, as a result of the discoveries at Nag Hammadi, has become one of the principal sources for our knowledge of Jewish Christian gnosis. It is true that to distinguish the various ingredients is a delicate task; the Gnostics were eclectics, and borrowed from Hellenistic philosophies and cults as well. Nevertheless the Jewish Christian share in the material they used is still considerable; and it is therefore of some importance to describe in outline the body of this heterodox literature before going on in the rest of the book to study it not for its own sake, but for the sake of the elements which it borrowed from the Jewish Christianity of the Great Church.

CHAPTER TWO

HETERODOX JEWISH CHRISTIANITY

B ESIDES the orthodox Jewish Christian gnosis, the literary heritage of which has just been surveyed, early documents reveal the existence of heretical Jewish Christian sects.[1]
However, the question of what constitutes heterodoxy is rather different at this stage from what it was to be later. The background common to both orthodoxy and heterodoxy is the Judaism of the apocalypses, which itself includes both an orthodox tradition and various heresies. The forms of expression which characterise this apocalyptic were also employed in its speculations by Jewish Christianity; but this in its turn took on various forms with the passage of time. There was orthodox Jewish Christianity, which has already been considered; but, in continuation of heterodoxies in Judaism, various streams of heterodox Jewish Christian thought also developed. Since the object of this volume is to present the history of archaic Christian theology, there is no need to give a detailed account of these systems. Nevertheless, in so far as they preserve certain elements which they had in common with Jewish Christianity, they can be of service, and therefore it is necessary to give a brief sketch of them.

THE EBIONITES

The first group to be discussed is the sect of the Ebionites. The name is not derived from a man named Ebion as Epiphanius believed, but from the Hebrew *ebyon* meaning 'poor'. The group is mentioned by Irenaeus

1. The relationship between these two groups has been the subject of various hypotheses. SCHOEPS identifies Jewish Christianity with Ebionism and claims the primacy for the heterodox sect; *Theologie und Geschichte des Judenchristentums*, pp. 5-13. Recently WOLFSON has also taken up this thesis. BAUER is inclined to see rather a burgeoning of of tendencies from which orthodoxy gradually emerged as the dominant one: *Recht-gläubigkeit und Ketzerei im ältesten Christentum*, 1934, pp. 6-48. TURNER has recently reviewed the question from an angle which to the present writer's way of thinking gives

(*Adv. haer.* I, 26:2), and by Origen (*Contra Celsum* II, 1). It consisted of Jews who rallied to Christ but saw in him only the greatest of the prophets and not the Son of God. This is the position of Moslems today, and it is possible that they came into contact with Ebionites in Transjordan.

The Ebionites, therefore, were a clearly defined group in primitive Christianity. It is important to understand the precise reference of the name, for it is often used incorrectly. They should not be confused purely and simply with the heirs of the first, Aramaic-speaking, Christians who fled to Transjordan after the fall of Jerusalem in A.D. 70,[2] and who were perfectly orthodox. Nor should they be confused with another neighbouring group, the Nazarenes, mentioned by Epiphanius (*Panarion* XXIX), who separated from the rest of the Church because they regarded the Jewish observances of sabbath and circumcision as still of obligation. St. Jerome came across these Nazarenes in Beroea, a city in Syria in the fourth century (*De Viris ill.* 3). As already noted in the previous chapter, he made a copy of a version of *Matthew* written in Aramaic but in Hebrew characters, which was the only Gospel they had. It showed some original developments, but they were in no way heretical.

The primary and most precise source of information about the Ebionites is the notice devoted to them by Epiphanius:

> Besides the daily ritual bath they have a baptism of initiation and each year they celebrate certain mysteries in imitation of the Church of the Christians. In these mysteries they use unleavened bread and, for the other part, pure water. They say that God has established two beings, Christ and the Devil. To the former has been committed the power of the world to come, and to the other the power of this world. They say that Jesus was begotten of human seed, and chosen, and thus called by election Son of God, Christ having come upon him from on high in the form of a dove. They say that he was not begotten by God the Father, but that he was created, like the archangels, but greater than they. He came into the world and he taught, as it is written in their gospel: I have come into the world to destroy sacrifices, and if

2. This identification is maintained by H. J. SCHOEPS, cf. e.g. *Aus Frühchristlicher Zeit*, p. 282.

---

a juster account, namely that from the beginning there was the tradition of the Great Church around which the various heterodox sects sprang up in abundance: *The Pattern of Christian Truth*, 1954, pp. 97–143.

you do not give up sacrificing the anger of God shall not cease (*Panarion* XXX, 16).

Many features in this passage recall Essenism.[3] It is known, for instance, that the ritual bath was an essential Essene rite. It will be observed, however, that Epiphanius adds that the Ebionites also had a baptism of initiation. This is a Christian feature.[4] The reference to mysteries is evidently concerned with the Eucharist, and one detail in particular should be noticed, the exclusion of the wine. This is not Essene but is connected with Encratite tendencies, which were a characteristic of certain Jewish circles, and were to pass from them into a number of Christian groups.

The second part of the passage exhibits pure Essene doctrine. God has established from the beginning a good and an evil principle (cf. *DSD* III, 18). The opposition between the two worlds, the present world which belongs to the devil, and the future world which belongs to Christ is also Essene (*DSD* IV, 16–23). It occurs again in the Essene part of the *Epistle of Barnabas* (XVIII, 2). Jesus is a man like other men, born of an ordinary marriage. But Christ, who is the good principle existing from the beginning, rested on him at the moment of baptism, in the form of a dove. Nor is this Christ the Son of God, but a higher archangel, the one whom the *Rule of the Community* calls the Prince of Light (*DSD* III, 20). Thus Jesus is a prophet who is assisted by the Angel of Good.[5]

The last point mentioned by Epiphanius in his notice is especially significant. It speaks of a condemnation of sacrifices. This might seem strange coming from a Jew, but it will be remembered that one of the features of Essenism, a consequence of their break with the official priesthood, was in fact the condemnation of the bloody sacrifices of the Temple, for which they substituted the praise of the lips (*DSD* IX, 5). The Ebionites exaggerate this attitude. This feature should be compared with another that Epiphanius mentions later: 'They do not accept the entire Pentateuch of Moses, but suppress certain passages', that Abraham, for example, offered

3. Cf. CULLMANN, 'Die neuentdeckten Qumrantexte und das Judenchristentum der Pseudo-Klementinen', in *Neut. Stud. Bultmann*, pp. 35–51; TEICHER, 'The Dead Sea Scrolls, Documents of the Jewish Christian sect of Ebionites', *Journal of Jewish Studies*, 1951, p. 96 ff.; SCHOEPS, 'Handelt es sich wirklich um ebionitische Dokumente?', *ZRGG*, 1951, p. 232 ff.
4. It is an important detail as it confirms that Christian baptism cannot be identified with the lustrations of the Essenes, but is essentially different in character.
5. This angel also rested on Adam (*Panarion* XXX, 3), and on Moses and the other prophets. Cf. below, p. 65.

a calf with milk to the angels, or that Noah, Isaac, Jacob or Moses made sacrifice (XXX, 18). Here again is the condemnation of sacrifices. But there is another point also, the rejection of everything in the Pentateuch connected with this aspect of the Law.[6]

The question arises, are there any Ebionite works which provide first-hand information about their teaching? Epiphanius has some interesting remarks on this point: 'They accept the *Gospel of Matthew* and use only that, calling it the *Gospel according to the Hebrews*. But the *Gospel of Matthew* which they possess is not complete, but falsified and mutilated' (XXX, 3 and 13). Now in his account of the Nazarenes he states that the *Gospel according to Matthew* which they kept was a very full version. The other then must be a different text, but it is probably not quite correct to speak of a different gospel.[7] More likely the Ebionites had the same text as the Nazarenes and also a version of the text altered in a heterodox sense, perhaps simply a commentary on certain parts. This is the text known as the *Gospel of the Ebionites*.

Epiphanius has preserved some fragments of this Gospel in his account,[8] and they contain some typical Ebionite features. Of John the Baptist it is said that 'his food was wild honey, which had the taste of manna, like that of an oil-cake ($\dot{\epsilon}\gamma\kappa\rho\acute{\iota}s$ $\dot{\epsilon}\nu$ $\dot{\epsilon}\lambda\alpha\acute{\iota}\omega$)' (XXX, 13). The point of this alteration is to rule out locusts ($\dot{\alpha}\kappa\rho\acute{\iota}s$), and is connected with the Ebionite rejection of all meat.[9] The account of the baptism of John contains some note-worthy details. The Holy Ghost who comes down in the form of a dove is said 'to descend and enter into Jesus'. This is appropriate to an adoptionist theology and is in keeping with Essene theories about the action of the Holy Ghost on the prophets. There is also the mention of 'a great light' which 'shone about the place'. This is not Ebionite, but occurs in Tatian's *Diatessaron*.

The story of the call of the Apostles, which seems to have been placed before the Baptism, is told as follows: 'Jesus, having come to Capernaum, entered the house of Simon, and opened his mouth and said: When I had drawn near to the Lake of Tiberias, I chose John and James, the sons of Zebedee, and Simon and Andrew' (XXX, 13:2). A Jewish Christian feature of this narrative is the primacy given to John and James instead of

6. For the grounds on which the Ebionites justified such a rejection, cf. below, p. 60.
7. SCHOEPS, *Theologie und Geschichte des Judenchristentums*, pp. 25–33.
8. These have been edited by PREUSCHEN (*Antilegomena*, 10–12).
9. This is possibly of Essene origin (SCHOEPS, *op. cit.*, p. 253).

to Peter. Another curiosity is the distortion of the Lord's reply, when the Apostles ask him: 'Where do you wish that we prepare the Passover?' (*Mat.* 26:17). Jesus answers: 'Do you think that I have desired to eat meat for Passover with you?' (XXX, 22:4)—an alteration designed to exclude any suggestion that Christ could have eaten the paschal Lamb.

Epiphanius also included among the sacred books of the Ebionites the Περίοδοι Πέτρου, or *Journeys of Peter*, said to have been written by Clement; and it is interesting that his quotations from the Ebionite Gospel have been shown to accord with the text of the pseudo-Clementine *Homilies* and *Recognitions*,[10] which describe Peter's journeys in the course of his missionary work. From this and many other indications it is possible to establish a relationship between the Clementines and Ebionism, a fact which opens up a very important source of information on the sect, and one in entire agreement with the description of it given by Epiphanius. With some variation in detail, all scholars now recognise it.[11]

The final version of both the works in question dates from the fourth century and it is difficult to decide which is the older. But from an analysis it can be seen that they are the result of a fusion of composite elements; and it has proved possible to separate these without difficulty. One of these elements, and the most ancient, is the *Preaching of Peter*, an Ebionite work of the second century which preserves the theology of Ebionism.[12]

This *Preaching of Peter* was combined at some time during the third century with other documents[13] to form the basic stratum common to both the *Recognitions* and the *Homilies*, and it is this compound stratum which is to be identified with the *Journeys of Peter*. The work is quoted in two passages of Origen.[14] Moreover, it is under the same title, Περίοδοι, that Epiphanius lists the work among the sacred books of the Ebionites.

The *Preaching of Peter* includes in the first place Peter's Epistle to

10. These writings have enjoyed a considerable reputation thanks to their fictitious ascription to Clement. They were translated into Latin by Rufinus in the fourth century.
11. So H. WAITZ, *Die Pseudo-Klementinen*, 1904, pp. 161 f.; H. J. SCHOEPS, *op. cit.*, pp. 37–61; O. CULLMANN, *Le problème littéraire et historique du roman pseudo-clémentin*, 1940, pp. 220–257; E. MOLLAND, 'La circoncision, le baptême et l'autorité du décret apostolique dans les milieux judéo-chrétiens des Pseudo-clémentines', *ST*, IX, 1955, pp. 1–9.
12. This is an entirely different work from a *Kerygma of Peter* quoted by Clement of Alexandria which is the first orthodox treatise of apologetics (cf. REAGAN, *The Preaching of Peter*, Chicago, 1923).
13. Cf. G. STRECKER, *Das Judenchristentum in den Pseudoclementinen*, pp. 140–256.
14. Cf. CULLMANN, *op. cit.*, pp. 32 f.

James. Peter explains to James that he is sending him an exposition of his doctrine to be used in the training of 'those who wish to take up the work of teaching' in order to ensure the orthodoxy of their ideas. For, he says, 'Some from among the Gentiles have rejected my teaching which is in accordance with the Law, and attached themselves to certain lawless and trifling doctrines of the man who is my enemy' (II). Peter thus emphasises that his teaching is faithful to the Jewish Law. The 'enemy' designates Paul, who was regarded as responsible for the rejection of the observance of the Jewish Law. It may be remembered that Irenaeus and Epiphanius spoke of this rejection of Paul as one of the characteristics of Ebionism.

As regards that part of the material which may properly be called the *Preaching*, this is distributed among the various sermons of Peter which fill the *Homilies* and the *Recognitions*. It would have been a problem to reconstruct the plan of them had not Peter, in chapter 75 of Book III, having decided to send James the summary of his teaching just mentioned, given a table of contents! Thus, while distributing the earlier composition throughout the whole of his work, the author has taken care to leave us a guide by means of which it can be restored.[15]

The first book treats of the true prophet and the true understanding of the Law in conformity with the teaching of the tradition of Moses. This is one of the most important parts of the work. In the first place comes the conception of Christ as the true Prophet (*Hom.* I, 19), then that of Adam as the first incarnation of the true Prophet, and free from sin (*Hom.* III, 17–28). This is a direct echo of the Essene doctrine of the succession of the prophets.

But the second part of the book is equally important, for it contains the doctrine of the 'false pericopes'. The passage in question reads: 'A great many falsehoods against God have been added to the Scriptures, and in the following way. The prophet Moses, in accordance with the will of God, had passed on the Law, together with the necessary commentary, to seventy chosen men, in order that they should enable such of the people as wished to do so to profit by it. But shortly afterwards, when the Law had been put into writing, it received a certain number of additions containing falsehoods against the only God' (*Hom.* II, 38). In the *Letter to Flora* by the Gnostic Ptolemaeus this theory reappears, and it would seem that he must have borrowed it from Jewish Christianity. It corresponds to a preoccupation, already evident in Essene writings like the *Book of Jubilees*, with removing

15. Cf. SCHOEPS, *op. cit.*, pp. 40–52.

from the Old Testament anything that might give offence. Epiphanius gives the same information: 'They do not accept the whole of the Pentateuch of Moses, but suppress certain passages. If in regard to the eating of meat you raise the objection that Abraham offered a calf to the angels . . . they say that they do not believe that' (XXX, 18).[16]

The sixth book presents the fundamental doctrine of the two spirits, which was mentioned by Epiphanius:

> God, having appointed two kingdoms, established also two ages, decreeing that the present world should be given to the Evil One, and the world to come to the Good. Wherefore also Two Ways have been set before Man—that of Law and that of Lawlessness; and two kingdoms have been established, the one called the kingdom of heaven, and the other the kingdom of those who are now kings upon earth. Also two kings have been lawfully appointed; the one has been chosen as legitimate ruler of the present transitory world, the other is also king, but of the age to come. Each of these two seeks to dispossess the other. Every man has power to obey whichever of them he pleases (*Hom.* XX, 2–3).

The conception of the two kingdoms is introduced throughout the Old Testament story by the theory of the syzygies, or pairs, according to which every true prophet is preceded by a corresponding false one. This doctrine is characteristic of Ebionism:

> To teach men the truth of things God, who Himself is One, divided all extremes into pairs of opposites. On the same system he arranged the great figures of prophecy. Thus it was that immediately after Adam, who had been made in the image of God, the first to be born was an unrighteous man, Cain, and the second a righteous, Abel. It was the same later in the case of the two birds released by him whom you call Deucalion; the first was the black raven, the second the white dove. Again it was the same with the two eldest sons of Abraham, the father of our race; the first to be born was Ishmael, the second Isaac, the one beloved of God. Likewise the High Priest came first in time; only afterwards was the Lawgiver born (*Hom.* II, 15–16).

16. This conception appears also in the *Didascalia* (*Apost. Const.* VI, 20); cf. SCHOEPS, *op. cit.*, pp. 179–187.

This last point, of course, implies a criticism of the priesthood and of worship.

The series of opposites is continued in the New Testament: 'Wherefore, also, he who was among those born of woman came first (John the Baptist); then he who was among the sons of men came second (Jesus). It were possible, following this order, to perceive to which series Simon belongs (Paul), who came before me to the Gentiles, and to which I myself, who came in second place succeeding him as light succeeds darkness. . . . After this, also, as the End approaches, Antichrist must first come; and only then will the true Christ, Jesus, be manifested' (II, 17). The polemic against John the Baptist will be noticed. This had its roots in the conflict between the disciples of John and the disciples of Jesus in the Jewish Christian community.[17] Paul, 'the man who is my enemy', here called 'Simon' as being a false deceiver like Simon Magus, is once again opposed to Peter.

There is a striking resemblance between this doctrine and that of the *Rule of the Community*. Once again two princes have been instituted by God from the beginning. One corresponds to the present world, the other to the world to come. The conflict between them is carried throughout the whole of history. In each generation it is expressed in the opposition between a good and a false prophet. This idea is also found in the *Zadokite Document* (V, 17–21). Furthermore, this conflict exists in the soul of every man, for each is a mixture of good and bad dispositions,[18] and with two ways open to him. The Ebionite doctrine is therefore pure Essenism with only a colouring of Christianity, Christ becoming the latest of the true prophets.

A third source of knowledge of Ebionite theology is the translation of the Old Testament into Greek by Symmachus. Origen used this translation in the *Hexapla*, and Jerome was especially appreciative of it. He praises Symmachus 'for not having simply translated literally, like Aquila, but also for having attempted to express the movement of thought' (*Com. Amos* III, 11). In this respect Symmachus has had some influence on the Vulgate. However, it is Eusebius who supplies the information that he was an Ebionite[19]:

---

17. Cf. O. CULLMANN, Ὁ ὀπίσω μου ἐρχόμενος, *Conj. Neot.*, XI, 1947, pp. 26–32.
18. This, as SCHOEPS has rightly observed (*Aus frühchristlicher Zeit*, pp. 48 f.), is the doctrine of the two *yeṣerim*, which was evolved to deal with two types of problem, the cosmological and the psychological.
19. The Ebionites are sometimes called Symmachaeans (AMBROSIASTER, *Com. Gal. Prol.* in *PL*, XVII, 337).

Now as regards these same translators it is to be noted that Symmachus was an Ebionite. Those who belong to the heresy of the Ebionites, as it is called, affirm that the Christ was born of Joseph and Mary, and suppose Him to be a mere man, and strongly maintain that the Law ought to be kept in a more strictly Jewish fashion. And commentaries by Symmachus are still extant today in which he tries his hardest to support the said heresy from the Gospel of Matthew. Origen mentions that he acquired these works, together with others of Symmachus' comments on the Scriptures, from a certain Juliana, who had received them from Symmachus himself (*HE* VI, 17).[20]

By combining the evidence from the Fathers and from the Ebionite documents it is possible to form some idea of Ebionite theology. The first point so far established is their Christology. They believe in Jesus, and that distinguishes them radically from the Jews. But they regard Jesus simply as a man chosen by God. They deny his virgin birth—a point they make very clear. It was at his baptism that a power from God descended on him.[21] The Ebionites are radically anti-trinitarian.

They also reject any aspect of Christianity which makes it a religion of salvation. For them Christ's mission is simply one of teaching. In the expression used by the *Preaching*, he is the 'true prophet'. The general Ebionite view now emerges: there is a succession of prophets who maintain the tradition of the true religion, of whom Moses and Jesus are the chief. In this sense the conception of Adam as a prophet and impeccable is typical, as is also the importance of Moses. Jesus is seen as coming after them to reform Judaism and to lead it back to its true purity. Only the importance accorded to Jesus distinguishes this from pure Essenism.

Finally, the Ebionites are faithful observers of the Law. They observe circumcision and the sabbath. They hold that Jesus did not wish to suppress the Law—this was the work of Paul, their great adversary, 'the man that is our enemy' of the *Preaching*. They claim to defend the true thought of Jesus against the deformation to which Paulinism subjected it. But on the other hand they see Jesus as a reformer of the Law who brings it back to the true ideas of Moses. As it exists in Judaism the Law seems to them to be

20. H. J. SCHOEPS has made this question the object of a special study: *Theologie und Geschichte der Judenchristentums*, pp. 350–366; *Aus frühchristlicher Zeit*, pp. 82–119.
21. Related to this point are the emphasis in the *Preaching of Peter* on monotheism, and the elimination of passages from the Old Testament which might suggest a plurality in God, and which the Christians used in a trinitarian sense.

mixed with elements of diabolical origin which are of a later date than Moses. The elements to be rejected are primarily the Temple worship and, in particular, bloody sacrifices. This seem to derive from a Jewish heterodoxy which pushes to its logical conclusion the Essene break with the official cultus.[22]

ELKESAI AND HIS DISCIPLES

Elkesaism, one of the most interesting heterodox Jewish Christian groups, is fairly closely related to Ebionism. The sect is known from notices in Origen, Hippolytus and Epiphanius. The first two were acquainted with it at first-hand in Alexandria and Rome, where it was spreading at the beginning of the third century. According to information given by Hippolytus, however, the revelation made to Elkesai took place in the third year of the reign of Trajan (*Elench* IX, 16), and this date is fully confirmed by the archaic character of the doctrine. Epiphanius gives the further detail that Elkesai 'came from Judaism and thought as a Jew' (XIX, 1:5). Finally, the Christian elements are certainly primitive.

In the first place there are numerous points of contact between the Elkesaites and the Ebionites. Both remain faithful to Jewish customs. Hippolytus writes: 'Elkesai puts forward a way of life in accordance with the Law, alleging once again that believers are under an obligation to be circumcised and to live according to the Law' (*Elench*. IX, 14). According to Epiphanius (*Pan.* XIX, 3:5–6), he obliged his disciples to pray facing toward Jerusalem, but in addition he proscribed sacrifices and forbade the use of meat (*ib.*). This all indicates a schismatic Jewish group, closely related to the Essenes.

Other features show a resemblance to the Ebionites: '(The sect), writes Origen, rejects certain portions of Scripture; but for the rest makes use of texts drawn from every part of the Old Testament and the Gospels; the Apostle it rejects entirely' (*HE* VI, 38). This is strictly in accordance with the Ebionite method and its theory of the false pericopes, while its Judaising

22. It seems that with Cullmann we may regard the Ebionites as Essenes who rallied to the person of Christ after the fall of the Temple. Cf. CULLMANN, 'Die neuentdeckten Qumrantexte und das Judenchristentum der Pseudoklementinen', in *Neutestamentliche Studien für R. Bultmann*, pp. 35–51; cf. also TEICHER, 'The Dead Sea Scrolls, Documents of the Jewish-Christian sect of the Ebionites', *JJS*, II, 1951, pp. 65 ff.: SCHOEPS, 'Handelt es sich wirklich um ebionitische Dokumente?', *ZRGG*, III, 1951, pp. 322 ff.

character is clearly seen in the rejection of Saint Paul. In Christology the sect is equally Ebionite. 'According to Elkesai, Christ was a man like every other man, nor was this the first occasion on which he was born of a virgin. This event had already happened in the past, for Christ has been born, and continues to be born, many times' (*Elench*. IX, 14). Here, once more, are the two doctrines of Christ as a simple prophet and of the re-incarnations of the true prophet as in Ebionism. According to Epiphanius, they regard Adam as the first of these incarnations (*Pan*. LIII, 1:8).

But built upon this basis which the sect has in common with Ebionism there is also the special revelation of Elkesai, the essential feature of the sect. Hippolytus describes the circumstances and the content of the revelation thus. In a vision Elkesai received a book, which had been given him by an angel. This angel was immense, 96 miles high, and 'was accompanied by a feminine being whose dimensions were of the same scale. The masculine being was the Son of God, the feminine was called the Holy Spirit' (*Elench*. IX, 13). The contents of the book were the joyful announcement of a remission of sins committed after baptism, given 'in the name of the Great and Most High God', calling to witness 'those seven witnesses that have been described in this book: the heaven, and the water, and the holy spirits, and the angels of prayer, and the oil, and the salt and the earth' (*Elench*. IX, 15).[23]

All this material comes directly from the context of Jewish Christian theology, and is closely akin to the *Gospel of Peter* or the *Shepherd*. Most of the features mentioned here have already been encountered: the gigantic stature of the angels, the Son of God and the Holy Ghost considered under the form of two angels, the feminine character of the Spirit. Moreover, the setting of the vision is typical of the end of the first century: the appearance of an angel, the communication of a book by the angel, both being directly reminiscent of the visions of Hermas. Elkesai appears, like Hermas, as a prophet, but a heterodox prophet. There is no ground for regarding these Christian themes as superimposed.[24] They are the very stuff of the original vision.

But the resemblance to Hermas goes deeper than this, extending not only to the form of the revelation, but also to its content. It is concerned with the announcement of a remission of sins committed after baptism, a second

23. Before Ebionite baptism the candidate called the four elements to witness that he would not betray the mysteries: *Hom. clem., Diamart*. I.
24. Cf. THOMAS, *Le Mouvement baptiste en Palestine et en Syrie*, p. 155.

repentance. Now this was precisely the content of the book given to Hermas by the aged woman who appeared to him. If the first part of Hermas dates from the end of the first century and from the beginning of the second, then it was contemporary with Elkesai's vision. Both were dealing with a problem which was especially important in the Jewish Christian community at that time. Hermas seems to have come from Essenism and Elkesai from Ebionism, but both had a trinitarian theology. In this regard Elkesai was nearer to orthodox Christianity than the Ebionites.

At the same time this conclusion justifies the consideration of Elkesaite rites of the second repentance as borrowed from the practices of the Jewish Christian Church. At this point two observations may usefully be made. The first concerns the seven witnesses who were invoked. The first and the last of them are the heaven and the earth. This may be an echo of *Isaiah* 1:2: 'Hear, O heaven, and hearken, O earth',[25] the text quoted by the *Epistle of Barnabas* with the addition of ὅτι ὁ κύριος ἐλάλησεν ταῦτα εἰς μαρτύριον (IX, 3). It also recalls the confession of God the Creator before baptism. The elements that were invoked were probably those which were used in baptism. From this it would seem that besides water there was an anointing with oil and an eating of salt. The former concurs with what is already known of the Jewish Christian ritual.

The two other witnesses provide still more precise information. The 'holy spirits' are invoked after the water. This is clearly an allusion to baptism in water and the Spirit. But the plural reflects the fact that in Jewish Christianity there is perpetually a transition from the Spirit to spirits, whether it be the seven spirits, as in the *Revelation* of John, who are an expression of the outpouring of the Spirit, or whether it be, as in Hermas, the 'holy spirits' which are the supernatural virtues communicated at baptism. However, in Hermas it is generally the Holy Spirit who is opposed to the 'evil spirits'. In this case Elkesai's text would preserve a more archaic formula.

With regard to the presence of 'angels of prayer', these too provide a link with Jewish Christian speculative theology. 'Speculations on the Name and the Angel of Baptism have a very ancient Christian basis'.[26] The Angel of Baptism occurs in Tertullian's *De Baptismo* (6), and it is the angels who build the Church upon the water, that is, preside over baptism, in Hermas

25. This text of *Isaiah* is frequently quoted in the Gnostics (*Elench.* V, 27; VI, 13). A similar invocation occurs in Philo, *Adv. Flaccum*, 123.
26. QUISPEL, 'L'inscription de Flavia Sophè', *Mél. de Ghellinck* I, p. 214.

(*Vis.* III, 3–4).[27] The doctrine was to reappear in Origen and in the fourth century as an inheritance from the old theology.[28]

The second important aspect from the sacramental point of view is the use of baptismal rites and of anointings apart from the first baptism. Elkesai attests this as a ritual of reconciliation; elsewhere there is mention of baptisms for the deliverance of the possessed (*Elench.* IX, 16).[29] Similar features are to be found in the Gnostics. There was among the Valentinians a kind of baptism in preparation for death.[30] Epiphanius also notes that the Elkesaites 'had a veneration for water' (LIII, 1:7). It should perhaps be concluded from this that in Jewish Christianity, under the influence of Essene baptism, baptismal rites might have various uses, as did anointings and laying-on of hands. Thus re-baptism may have been simply a rite of reconciliation, but it was finally abolished because of the ambiguity to which it gave rise in relation to the initial baptism.

Thus the pattern of Elkesaism begins to emerge. It is a kind of Ebionism influenced by the theology of the Great Church. The Gnostic elements are those drawn from Jewish Christian theology: the theme of the descent through the heavens, the doctrine of the Son and the Spirit as angels. It seems to be very close to the *Ascension of Isaiah* or the *Gospel of Peter*. It is furthermore of vital importance for our knowledge of Jewish Christian theology and liturgy. Its heresy lies in the fact that it regarded Jesus as a mere prophet.

CHRISTIAN ZEALOTISM

Many writers have recently pointed out the importance of the Zealot movement in the Jewish world between the years A.D. 30 and 70, with its

27. There may also be an allusion to the presence of angels at baptism in the *Odes of Solomon* IV, 8; cf. BERNARD, *The Odes of Solomon*, pp. 51–52.
28. Cf. DANIÉLOU, *Les Anges et leur mission*, pp. 79–83. KRETSCHMAR notes in regard to this text that 'the conception of angels as witnesses of baptism was widespread from the earliest times' (*Studien zur frühchristlichen Trinitätstheologie*, p. 213). It may go back to the Essenes, for the Slavonic Josephus mentions that the oath taken on entry into the community includes a calling of the angels to witness. Cf. H. PHILONENKO, 'La notice du Josèphe Slave sur les Esséniens', *Semitica*, VI, 1956, p. 71. The text also mentions an invocation of 'the divine Spirit'.
29. Cf. PETERSON, 'Le traitement de la rage par les Elkasaïtes', *RSR*, 1947, pp. 232 ff.; also *Frühkirche, Judentum und Gnosis*, pp. 227 f.
30. A. ORBE, *Los primeros herejes ante la persecución*, p. 134. Among the Ebionites baptism was also used as an ordination rite, accompanied by the invocation of the four elements (cf. *Diamart.* 1).

messianism that was both political and religious; and they have shown that there is no mistaking the fact that such tendencies also came to light in Jewish Christian communities.[31] The question must now be asked whether there was any other branch, besides Ebionite Jewish Christianity, which appears to have been drawn into this Jewish nationalist current with its this-worldly aspirations? A study of the catalogues given by the ancient historians of heresy shows that such groups did exist.

The most typical representative of this tendency is Cerinthus.[32] He has certain points in common with the views already studied. Like the Ebionites he sees Jesus as an ordinary man on whom Christ descended at Baptism. Moreover, Cerinthus is related to Jewish heterodoxy when he affirms that the world was created by angels.[33] It was quite definitely this heterodox Jewish Christianity in Asia which St. John was concerned to combat.

It appears from Eusebius that Cerinthus was in fact a partisan of a very markedly materialistic millenarianism: 'This was the doctrine which he taught, that the kingdom of Christ would be on earth; and he dreamed that it would consist in those things which formed the object of his own desires (for he was a lover of the body and altogether carnal) in the full satisfaction of the belly and lower lusts' (*HE* III, 28:4). Furthermore, Cerinthus believed in the material restoration of the Temple of Jerusalem and of the sacrifices. All this is a continuation of political Judaism, a temporal Messianism, but with a Christian flavour. The Judaising character of Cerinthus can also be seen in the fact that he kept circumcision and the sabbath and only recognised the *Gospel of Matthew*.[34]

It has been noted that this carnal Messianism seems to have developed mainly in Asia Minor.[35] It was not simply a matter of sins of gluttony and drunkenness, but of manifestations of religious messianism.[36] Several of the features to be found in Cerinthus, in particular the rejection of the

31. BRANDON, *The Fall of Jerusalem and the Christian Church*, pp. 88–154; REICKE, *Diakonie, Festfreude und Zelos*, pp. 233–397.
32. Cf. G. BARDY, 'Cérinthe', *RB*, xxx, 1921, p. 371.
33. This is mentioned as a Jewish heresy by Justin (*Dialogue*, LXII, 3) and by the *Treatise on the Three Natures* (cf. G. QUISPEL, 'Christliche Gnosis und jüdische Heterodoxie' in *Evang. Theol.*, XIV, 1954, p. 2). Cf. also R. McL. WILSON, 'The Early Exegesis of Gen. 1:26', in *St. Patr.*, I, pp. 420–432.
34. EPIPHANIUS, *Pan.* XXVIII, 5: 1–3.
35. There may be an echo of it in Paul's condemnations of orgies: cf. *I Cor.* 11:20 ff., 33 f.
36. REICKE, *Diakonie, Festfreude und Zelos*, pp. 283–287.

resurrection of Christ and of the practice of baptism for the dead,[37] are similar to those condemned by Paul in *I Corinthians*.

These various features begin to reveal the character of this group. They are men of strictly Jewish origin, which explains their association with the Ebionites and the early Gnostics. Their thoughts are centred on the Parousia, the coming of the Messianic age, which they conceive as being essentially earthly. In this they are profoundly opposed to the Ebionites. Their expectation of the Messiah crystallises in a millenarian doctrine, and in this way they are representative of whole current of heterodox views in Asia, which may be seen in the *Apocalypse* and in Papias. Their hope is centred on this earth. For some of them the Messianic times have already arrived—an idea that is expressed in the orgiastic character of their feasts, an expression of Messianic festivity.[38]

SAMARITO–CHRISTIAN GNOSIS

By now it will have become apparent that the same complexity in the Jewish world and its sects at the time of Christ which is reflected in the various currents of Jewish Christianity in the Great Church, also finds a counterpart in the various forms of heterodox Jewish Christianity. If Ebionism is a continuation of the Essene community, and the Cerinthians a development of zealot Messianism, the sects which have now to be considered are still more closely connected with heterodox Jewish sects, and in particular with the Samaritans.

According to the testimony of all ancient writers, the origins of the Gnostic movement in Christianity must be connected with a Jewish gnosis[39]; and therefore it may be as well to state clearly once again what is meant by 'gnosis'. The Jewish pre-Christian gnosis had two main characteristics. On the one hand it included cosmological and theological speculations, based for the most part on an esoteric exegesis of *Genesis*[40]; but this is proper to gnosis rather as an attitude than as a system, and is a characteristic which persists in orthodox as well as heretical writers.[41] The

37. *I Cor.* 15:4, 12 ff., 29 ff.   38. Cf. REICKE, *op. cit.*, p. 281.
39. This was pointed out by FRIEDLÄNDER (*Der vorchristliche jüdische Gnosticismus*, 1898, pp. 62–75) and is confirmed today by advances that have been made in the history of Gnosticism (QUISPEL, 'Christliche Gnosis und jüdische Heterodoxie', *Evang. Theol.*, 1954, pp. 1–11).
40. SCHOEPS, *Urgemeinde, Judenchristentum, Gnosis*, pp. 44–61.
41. This point is well taken by R. McL. WILSON, 'Gnostic Origins again', *Vigil. Christ.*, II, 1957, pp. 93–110.

Ascension of Isaiah or the *Epistle of the Apostles* belong just as much to the Jewish gnosis as do the speculations of Simon or of Carpocrates, both of which are concerned with similar topics. From this point of view, heterodox writers provide evidence of a fund of speculations deriving from a common Jewish Christian outlook, and it is quite justifiable to use them for our present purpose.

But it seems clear that by this time certain Jewish sects were exhibiting a development of some of the characteristics of Jewish gnosis, especially of its dualism, which was heretical even from the point of view of Jewish orthodoxy. This has naturally raised the question, what was the origin of those heterodox tendencies which constitute Gnosticism as a system? Are they a development within Judaism itself? Were they the result of the influence of Iranian dualism on Judaism, or was there contamination by Hellenism? It is, however, hardly possible to give a detailed answer to this question of the origins of Gnosticism here; it must suffice to state the general conclusions that, in the first place, Gnosticism as a system is fundamentally foreign both to Judaism and to Christianity, and secondly, that this system became a Christian heresy through the intermediate influence of heterodox Jewish groups.

This derivation is attested by numerous witnesses. The oldest evidence is that of Hegesippus reported by Eusebius (*HE* IV, 22:4–7). It is of exceptional interest because of the fact that Hegesippus, according to Eusebius, 'was himself a believer of Hebrew origin' (IV, 22:8). He knew, therefore, the unwritten Jewish tradition, while on the other hand he had at his disposal valuable sources of information regarding the Church of Jerusalem. It was he who recorded certain details about James, and a list of the latter's successors as head of the Jewish Christian Church (IV, 22:4). There is no witness better qualified to speak of Palestinian Jewish Christianity.

Hegesippus writes that under the episcopate of Simeon, the successor of James, the Church 'had not yet been corrupted by vain teachings. But Thebuthis, because he had not been made bishop, made use of the seven sects which then existed among the (Jewish) people, and to which he himself belonged, to begin the process of corruption. From these same sects came Simon, founder of the Simonians, and Cleobius, founder of the Cleobienes, and Dositheus, founder of the Dositheans, and Gorthaeus, founder of the Gorathenes, and the Masbotheans. From the last-named sprang the Menandrianists and Marcianists and Carpocratians and Valentinians and Basilideans and Satornilians' (IV, 22:5).

The importance of this notice of Hegesippus does not appear to have been generally recognised. In the first place the author affirms that Thebuthis, Simon and other heretics come from the 'seven Jewish sects'. What were these sects? Fortunately, Eusebius happens to have preserved another fragment of Hegesippus which enumerates them: 'These were the different opinions in the circumcision among the children of Israel against the tribe of Judah and against the Christ: Essenes, Galileans, Hemerobaptists, Masbotheans, Samaritans, Sadducees and Pharisees' (IV, 22:7).

This list calls for a few remarks. In the first place there are the three great sects mentioned by Philo and Josephus, Pharisees, Sadducees and Essenes. Galileans, who are mentioned also in Justin's list (*Dial.* LXXX, 4), could here be another name for the Zealots[42]; Galilee seems to have been one of the chief centres of Zealotism, and one of the leaders of the movement was Judas the Galilean. The Samaritans constituted a schism within the community of Israel. These, therefore, comprise the five principal groups in existence at the time of Christ. Of the remaining two, a certain amount is also known about the Hemerobaptists—Epiphanius mentions them in his own list of the seven Jewish heresies, which, incidentally, differs from that of Hegesippus (*Pan.* XVII, 1–2). They appear to be distinct from the rest of the Jews only in the obligation of daily ablutions.[43] The Masbotheans likewise are a baptist sect, but of a very different type. They are almost certainly a Transjordan group of syncretistic character originating from Mandaism.[44]

a. *Dositheans*

Two of the names quoted in the first text from Hegesippus above are known from other sources: those of Simon and Dositheus. Dositheus is connected by Epiphanius with the heresies originating from the Samaritans (*Pan.* XIII, 1:1).[45] On the other hand, the *Clementine Recognitions* (I, 54) make Dositheus a Sadducee, though the word in this context probably

---

42. CULLMANN observes that 'the Galileans mentioned in *Lk.* 13:1 must be identified with the Zealots': *Dieu et César*, p. 17. We may note also the mention of 'Galileans' in one of the letters of Bar Kokhba found at Wadi Murabba'at.

43. On the Hemerobaptists cf. THOMAS, *Le mouvement baptiste*, pp. 34–37.

44. Cf. K. RUDOLF, *Die Mandäer*, 1960, I, pp. 228 f.

45. SCHOEPS has shown what grounds Epiphanius had for this assertion: *Theologie und Geschichte des Judenchristentums*, pp. 392–395.

means a Zadokite, that is to say, an Essene.[46] Origen writes (*Contra Cels.* I, 57) that Dositheus applied to himself the prophecy of *Deut.* 18:18—a prophecy dear to the Essenes (4Q *Testimonia*). He kept the Sabbath (*De Princ.* IV, 3:2), was an ascetic,[47] and seems to represent a Samaritan Messianism combined with ascetic ideals, a sort of Samaritan Essenism. Thus he does not present any genuinely Christian features. Epiphanius counts him among the founders of Jewish sects. The only feature that connects him with Christianity seems to be that he began preaching his doctrine after the death of John the Baptist, in competition with the preaching of Jesus.[48]

b. *Simonians*

Simon, on the other hand, affords the first instance of specifically Gnostic speculation. According to the *Clementines* he had some connection with Dositheus,[49] and this is confirmed by an *Apocalypse of Dositheus* discovered at Nag Hammadi. But his teaching also contains dualistic speculations which indicate influences from outside Judaism, in particular Iranian, as his name of Magus suggests. Moreover, he was acquainted with Christianity, as can be seen from a passage in the *Acts of the Apostles* (8:10). Epiphanius, therefore, following Hegesippus, is quite right in calling him a Christian heretic.

The name of Hellenians given by Origen to the disciples of Simon (*Contr. Cels.* V, 62) should perhaps be associated with the Hellenists, who are mentioned in the immediately preceding section of *Acts*,[50] and who may have been Essene converts to Christianity.[51] Simon would, in this case, have been one of them for some time before founding his own sect. It should be noted that Justin, who was from Samaria, gives the name of Hellenians to a Jewish sect which might well be that of the Essenes (*Dial.* LXXX, 4).[52] If the Hellenians were the Samaritan branch of the Essenes, then the same name will have clung to both the Essene Christians or Hellenists, and the Essene Gnostics or Hellenians.

---

46. Cf. R. McL. WILSON, 'Simon Dositheus and the DSS', *ZRGG*, IX, 1957, pp. 21–30. On the contacts between Dositheus and the Zadokite community of Damascus, cf. LURIE, 'Histoire de la communauté juive de Damas', *Eretz Israel*, IV, 1956, pp. 111–118.
47. *Contr. Cels.* VI, 11; cf. Epiphanius, *Pan.* XIII, 2.
48. *Rec. clem.* II, 8:11; *Hom. Clem.* II, 23–24.
49. Cf. GOPPELT, *Christentum und Judentum*, pp. 132–134.   50. 6:1, 8, 9 ff.
51. Cf. CULLMANN, 'The Significance of the Qumran texts for Research into the Beginnings of Christianity', *JBL*, LXXIV, 1955, pp. 220–223.
52. Cf. M. SIMON, 'Les sectes juives chez les Pères', *St. Patr.*, I, pp. 526–540.

It is difficult to decide whether the other Jewish sects mentioned by Hegesippus belong to the same stream. Cleobius probably did, coming between Simon and Dositheus. On the other hand, Epiphanius associates the Gorathenes with the Dositheans, while Thebuthis remains an enigma. One thing is clear, however, that the first Christian heresies were on the borderline between heterodox Judaism and Christianity. This environment seems to have been the original home of Gnosticism, and when Hegesippus associates with it Basilides, Satornil, Menander, Carpocrates and Valentinus, he is tracing the genealogy which runs from the pre-Christian Jewish-Samaritan gnosis through Simon to Christian Gnosticism.

This genealogy is confirmed by the study of the extant notices appertaining to these early forms of Christian Gnosticism, for it shows the latter to have been a development of pre-Christian Jewish Gnosticism. This is the case with the Simonian gnosis, which contained the following speculative account of creation and salvation.

The history of the creation falls into three stages, of which the first two are the production of Ennoia, and the creation of this world by the angels, who also inspired the Old Testament prophets. But the angels governed the world badly because of their rivalries for the primacy; and that is why the Power came, 'making himself like to the Virtues, Powers and Angels' in order to set men free (*Adv. haer.* I, 23:3).

This version includes a certain number of elements derived from contemporary Judaism which have already been encountered in orthodox writers: the creation of the angels before the world; the role of the angels in the government of the cosmos and the economy of history; the struggle between the angels for possession of the primacy; the designation of angels by the words Powers, Virtues; the Saviour's putting on the appearance of the angelic orders in the course of his descent through the heavens. All this belongs to a conception of the world that was common to the Jewish gnosis, the orthodox Christian gnosis, and to Gnosticism. But the last-mentioned introduced its own vision: a radical opposition between the world of the angels and the world of the Saviour, the fall of the Ennoia that had issued from the Father, and the deliverance of Ennoia by gnosis.

It is this radical dualism, therefore, which is the properly Gnostic element, not the various images through which it is expressed. This ontological dualism is foreign both to Judaism and to Jewish Christianity. But even of this it may be asked whether it did not have a Jewish origin, for dualism is a common feature of thought in later Judaism. In the *Rule of the Community* it is expressed in the doctrine of the two spirits, a doctrine which left a deep impression on Jewish Christianity, as may be seen in the *Didache* or Hermas. This is not, however, as significant as it might seem at first sight, for the problem of evil is at the heart of most theological speculation in the middle of the first century. It is the central point of discussion in the *Epistle to the Romans* as much as in *II* (4) *Esdras*. The peculiarity of Gnosticism was to push this tendency to the extreme of an ontological, substantial dualism by which the world of the angels, of the cosmos, and of the Old Testament is not only secondary but also alien to the Father. This may in fact have come about through non-Jewish influences, but it does also appear to be a development of tendencies characteristic of later Judaism, and to be found in the other movements connected with it.

c. *Satornilians*

Satornil is connected with Simon by being a follower of the Samaritan Menander, who was himself one of Simon's disciples.[53] Satornil was an Antiochene, nor is this surprising, since at the end of the first century, after the fall of Jerusalem, Syria was the great centre for speculative thought. He presents some of the features of Simonian Gnosticism, being, according to Irenaeus, the first to have taught the existence of two races of men, one good and the other evil (I, 24:2). Moreover, the Jewish basis of his teaching is very apparent in, for example, his doctrine of the seven angels, or his mention of the archangels and of evil demons. Especially significant is his commentary on the account of creation given in *Genesis* and on the words 'Let us make man in our image', which he attributes to the angels. The comparison which he makes of man before the spirit was breathed into him to a worm may come from *Psalm* 21 (EVV 22). It reappears among the Naassenians[54] (Hippolytus, *Elench.* V, 8:18) and the psalm was much used in the Jewish Christian community.[55]

Furthermore, the Satornilians exhibit encratite tendencies which relate them both to Jewish sects of the time and to Jewish Christianity. Thus, they taught that 'marriage and generation are from Satan' (I, 24:2)—an idea which recurs later in Tatian and Julius Cassian and reflects the views of the Jewish Christian communities in Syria. Many of them also ab-

53. Cf. Irenaeus, *Adv. haer.* I, 23:5   54. Cf. below, p. 84.
55. Cf. Daniélou, 'Le Psaume XXI dans la catéchèse pascale', *Maison-Dieu*, xlix, 1957, pp. 17–23.

stained from the flesh of animals. Irenaeus attributes this to a false asceticism (*continentes*). It is clear how largely this is in keeping with a rigorous interpretation of Jewish precepts. This same abstinence from meat reappears among the orthodox Jewish Christian followers of James, among the Ebionites of the *Clementines* and elsewhere.

Basilides, who, like Satornil, was a disciple of Menander, introduced the latter's teaching into Alexandria, where he developed it into a much fuller system of doctrine. It will not be necessary to give a complete account of that system here, but only to note those features which betray Jewish influence.[56] Basilides taught that the lowest heaven, that is, the one which can be seen by men, was the dwelling of angels. These angels made the Earth, and divided the dominion of it between them, one of them securing the government of the Jewish people. His desire to subject the rest of the nations to his own led to a clash with the other archons.[57] This is the familiar doctrine of the angels of the nations, found both in the Jewish apocrypha, among the Jewish Christians, and among the Ebionites.

Another feature of the Basilidean gnosis is the hierarchy of three hundred and sixty-five heavens, each with its corresponding angelic order. Knowledge of the names of the heavens and of their angels is an essential part of the gnosis, because it is this which allows the soul to pass through the heavens without being seen. This again would seem to be a development of standard elements in Jewish, and especially Jewish Christian, gnosis, such as have already been encountered on several occasions. As early as Josephus, knowledge of the names of the angels was a topic of primary importance in the esoteric teaching of the Essenes. It is hardly surprising then to learn from Irenaeus (*Adv. haer.* I, 24:6) that the Basilideans declared themselves to occupy a position half-way between the Jews and the Christians. Such a statement is as much a claim to a share in a common stock of imagery with Jews and Jewish Christians as to a doctrinal originality of their own.

There is one more aspect of Basilides' teaching which betrays his relationship with Jewish Christianity, and that is his conception of the vices as personal demons dwelling in the soul: 'For him', writes Clement of

56. It is interesting that Basilides mentions two prophets, Barcabbas and Barcoph, who may be Jewish Christian (Eusebius, *HE* IV, 7:7).
57. Cf. Irenaeus, *Adv. haer.* I, 24:4; also J. DANIÉLOU, *Les sources juives de la doctrine des anges des nations chez Origène* in *RSR*, XXXVIII, 1951, pp. 131–137. The special importance of the presiding angel of Israel should be noted.

Alexandria, 'the passions have an individual existence, as if they were a kind of spirits ($\pi\nu\epsilon\acute{u}\mu\alpha\tau\alpha$) which cleave to the rational soul' (*Strom.* II, 20:112). Now this is a characteristic doctrine of Jewish Christianity. It plays an important part in the *Testaments of the Twelve Patriarchs* (cf. *Test. Reuben* III, 3–6); and it is by way of this work that it reaches Origen. It is also found in the pseudo-Clementine *Homilies* (IX, 10) and in *Hermas* (*Mand.* II, 3; V, 2). Here again is the background common to Ebionism, to Jewish Christianity and to Gnosticism, namely the Jewish speculations of the period of apocalyptic.[58]

It was through Basilides, who came from Antioch, that the Simonian gnosis took root in Alexandria, where, during the first half of the second century, it was to undergo a remarkable process of development. The master of the school was Valentinus, knowledge of whose ideas need, since the discovery of the *Gospel of Truth* at Nag Hammadi,[59] no longer be confined to the accounts by the Church's historians of heresy. He was to have disciples no less important than himself, notably, in the East Theodotus and Mark the Magician, and in the West Heracleon and Ptolemaeus. To Heracleon should certainly be ascribed the *Treatise on the Three Natures*, discovered at Nag Hammadi.[60]

It would seem, therefore, that the whole of the Jung Codex is the work of this school. All these works exhibit the same system, that of Valentinus. Strictly speaking, however, they go beyond the limits of the material proper to this volume, being in fact a Hellenistic elaboration of Jewish Christian Gnosticism. Nevertheless, it is easy to demonstrate the continuing influence in their thought of Judaism and of Jewish Christianity; and much valuable information concerning the latter may be gained from them, if allowance is made for Gnostic distortions.

SETHIANS AND OPHITES

There is one other sect which must be included under the heading of heterodox Jewish Christianity, namely the Egyptian Gnostics. It would be truer in this case to speak of a swarm of sects. Irenaeus records that 'they have sprung up . . . like mushrooms' (I, 29:1). They include such groups

58. Cf. DANIÉLOU, art. 'Démons', in *Dict. Spir.*, III, cols. 168–174.
59. *Evangelium veritatis*, Coptic text and translation, by MALININE, PUECH and QUISPEL, Zurich, 1956.
60. PUECH and QUISPEL, 'Le quatrième écrit du Codex Jung', *Vig. Christ.*, IX, 1955, pp. 65–102.

as the Naassenians, the Sethians, the Ophites, the Barbelognostics, the followers of Justin and the Peratae. But all these sects have so many features in common, that they may be regarded as various ramifications of the same movement. Hitherto, the only information concerning them has come from the notices in the ancient historians of heresy, and especially from chapters 29 and 30 in Book I of the *Adversus haereses* of Irenaeus. Now, thanks to the discoveries of Coptic manuscripts, especially those of Nag Hammadi, it is possible to study the texts themselves.

The oldest extant texts, like the *Apocryphon of John*, must date from the middle of the second century. But there are good grounds for seeing in them the handing down of older doctrines. Several of these works purport to contain esoteric doctrines dating back to the time of the Apostles, a feature common to Jewish Christian literature in general. In these texts there must indeed be a good deal of fiction, but this may well rest on a basis of older speculations. Their works may therefore be regarded as the expression of an ancient Jewish Christian gnosis, albeit in somewhat altered form.

This form of Gnosticism has some features in common with Valentinus and his school, of which, it was formerly believed, it represented a secondary and degraded form. The facts, however, seem to indicate otherwise. The Egyptian Gnostics are in the line of descent from an old Jewish Christian Gnosticism. From these sometimes rather confused doctrines Valentinus later extracted the essential outline. He also borrowed from orthodox Jewish Christian theology, and out of these elements he built the powerful system which characterises him and his disciples. But although Valentinus supplies precious material for a knowledge of Jewish Christianity and of older Gnosticism, he no longer belongs to that sphere, but, like Justin or Irenaeus, to the world of Hellenistic theology. It is proposed, therefore, to leave the discussion of his ideas to another volume.

The first example to be considered here is, therefore, the *Apocryphon of John*. The importance of this book for the group at present in question is shown by the fact that three copies of it have been found at Nag Hammadi.[61] The comparison of the text with Irenaeus' account of it has shown that chapter 29 of Book I, devoted to the Barbelognostics, is a very faithful summary of the first part of the *Apocryphon*. The work summarised by Irenaeus in chapter 30, in which he gives us the teaching of the Ophites, is in its second half influenced by the *Apocryphon*. Irenaeus may, therefore,

61. A copy was already extant in the Papyrus Berolinensis 8502, recently edited by TILL: *Texte und Untersuchungen*, LX, Berlin, 1955.

have omitted to summarise the conclusion of the *Apocryphon* in order to avoid repetitions. All this suggests that the work was a writing of fundamental importance to Egyptian Gnosticism. Certain points in common with the *Letter of Eugnostus* suggest that the work ought perhaps to be attributed to that writer, who would thus be the founder of the movement in Egypt. He would seem to belong to the first half of the second century.[62]

Its literary genre proclaims the work as belonging to Jewish Christianity. It claims to be a revelation made by the risen Christ to Saint John on the Mount of Olives (20, 5–6). Thus the work is fictitiously represented as belonging to those esoteric apostolic traditions which constitute Jewish Christian theology. Moreover, its content points to the same conclusion. It is specifically Gnostic, but its Gnosticism is expressed in the form of a commentary on *Genesis* as in other works to be considered. It will be recalled that the speculative exegesis of *Genesis* was one of the features of Judaism of the time of Christ which was inherited by Jewish Christianity. The work therefore belongs to the general class of such commentaries, though it is distinguished from those of the Great Church by its characteristically Gnostic content.

The first part (20, 7–45, 5) summarised by Irenaeus may be passed over, since it contains a genealogy of the aeons of the Pleroma which has no direct relation to the text of *Genesis*. But from 45, 5 onwards there are many important references. First, there is mention of the Mother ($\sigma o \varphi i \alpha$) who begins to move ($\dot{\epsilon} \pi \iota \varphi \acute{\epsilon} \rho \epsilon \sigma \theta \alpha \iota$) in the darkness above the waters (45, 5–19: Cf. *Gen.* 1:2). Further on, the seven archons say to one another: 'Let us make a man in the image and likeness of God', then by their powers they produce ($\pi \lambda \acute{\alpha} \sigma \sigma \epsilon \iota \nu$) a form ($\pi \lambda \acute{\alpha} \sigma \mu \alpha$) (48, 10–17). This is a heterodox Jewish Christian theme of the formation of man by the angels, which was appropriated by the Gnostics, and has already been observed in Cerinthus and Satornil, though in the last-named cases the allusion was not, as it is here, to the archons, the angels of the planets. Also present is the idea that Man is incapable of motion (50, 15), and must be animated by Sophia— another conception to be found in Satornil.

On the other hand, because he has received power from Sophia, Adam is more intelligent than the archons (52, 14), and thus incurs their jealousy, and especially that of their chief Ialdabaoth (52, 1). This again is one of the themes of Jewish Christian theology—the angels of the cosmos jealous of Man (Irenaeus, *Dem.* 11–16)—but obviously it is altered to fit in with

62. So H. C. PUECH in HENNECKE-SCHNEEMELCHER.

the Gnostic perspective. Later, there are some curious exegeses: the sleep sent to Adam by God signified the hardening of his heart, with a reference to *Is.* 6:10 (58, 17–59, 5); the rib from which Eve is formed is a symbol of the image of herself which the ἐπίνοια of light raises up for Adam (59, 17–60, 12).[63]

After this the *Apocryphon* continues its commentary on the biblical story: first the birth of Cain and of Abel, then that of Seth; the deluge that was provoked by Ialdabaoth; the episode of the angels who contract unions with the daughters of men, and reveal to them the use of metals (74, 1–75, 3). This comes from *I Enoch* and is part of the Jewish Christian tradition inherited from apocalyptic Judaism. Finally, the work ends with the sending of the Saviour (77, 5). It is therefore a commentary on *Genesis* based on a Jewish or Jewish Christian commentary, and given a distinctly Gnostic flavour. The points of contact with Satornil should be noted. The whole seems to be a development of Syriac Jewish Christian Gnosticism[64] which had migrated to Egypt, and which ran parallel to the more learned tradition that began with Basilides and finally produced Valentinus.

The *Apocryphon of John* and the 29th chapter of Irenaeus should be compared with the document summarised by Irenaeus in chapter 30 as being the teaching of the Sethians and the Ophites. The second part of this exposition shows several points of contact with the second part of the *Apocryphon of John*. It too is a commentary on the account of Paradise, the Fall and the later history of the human race after *Genesis*, which, as remarked earlier, may explain Irenaeus' omission to analyse the second part of the *Apocryphon*. What distinguishes this second document is a strongly marked Jewish Christian character which may be seen in the initial description of the Pleroma and in the development given to the story of Christ. The interesting point of a comparison with the *Apocryphon* is that it demonstrates the progressive christianisation of a Gnosticism that was at first almost purely Jewish.

Irenaeus' account begins by mentioning speculation on the aeons of the Pleroma. The latter includes first of all the Father, then the pair, Son and Holy Ghost, and finally the pair, Christ and the Church. Obviously there is here a Gnostic transposition of speculations to be found also in orthodox Jewish Christianity. Especially noteworthy are the feminine character of

63. Also noteworthy are the commentaries on the two trees of Paradise and on the Serpent.
64. Cf. Goppelt, *op. cit.*, pp. 193–194.

the Spirit and the theme of Christ and the Church regarded as pre-existent aeons.

The continuation of the passage also belongs in the context of the *Hexaemeron*. The aeons of the Pleroma produce Sophia, who descends to to the world below (I, 30:3-4). She receives a body from the lower waters; but the light from on high which is present in her is always striving to return to the Pleroma, and this results in a dilation which produces the sky from her body. Moreover by her union with the lower waters she begets seven sons. 'Thus was the hebdomad . . . brought into being.' The names of the seven are Ialdabaoth, Iao, Sabaoth, Adonai, Elohim, Astaphaios and Horaios (I, 30:5; *Apocryph.* 41, 18 *et seq.*). These sons are the seven heavens and their seven angels. It is quite clear that this is the theme of the creation of heaven, and of the seven days from *Genesis*. Having been transposed into the Jewish Christian cosmology of the seven heavens, it is now interpreted from a Gnostic standpoint.

The commentary now proceeds to the next chapters of *Genesis*. Ialda-baoth's brothers are jealous of him and struggle with him for the primacy. This idea appears in the *Ascension of Isaiah* and also in Simon. Ialdabaoth begets a new son, the Serpent, from whom proceed breath and the soul (*Gn.* 2:7). Then he says: 'Let us make man in our image.' Six powers answer this appeal, and they form a man of immense length and breadth (I, 30:6). Then Ialdabaoth creates Eve. The powers admire her beauty, form unions with her and beget the angels. Adam and Eve are tempted by the Serpent and violate the precept of Ialdabaoth, whereupon he expels them from Paradise (I, 30:8).

The analysis given by Irenaeus then goes on to describe the birth of Cain, the Deluge, the history of the prophets and the descent of Christ from on high (I, 30:11), the last being to the amazement of the powers and without the knowledge of Ialdabaoth. Christ descends through the seven heavens, taking the form of the angels of each heaven. All light becomes concentrated in him and first of all he puts on Sophia. He descends united to Sophia. All this latter part derives from the major themes of Jewish Christian theology: the descent through the seven heavens, and the fact that this descent is unknown to the angels. In particular, the idea that Christ puts on in his descent the gifts of the Spirit, and first of all the gift of Wisdom, is found in the *Epistle of the Apostles* and in the *Demonstratio* of Irenaeus.

A consideration of the two chapters of Irenaeus and of the *Apocryphon of John* as a whole, leads to the conclusion that the more developed form of teaching presented by chapter 30 depends on two main sources. On the one hand, the middle of the chapter is inspired by the *Apocryphon of John*, i.e. the part concerning Ialdabaoth; its basic material is a Jewish commentary on *Genesis* 1–3 which was of a speculative nature and was taken up by Jewish Christianity. The *Apocryphon* gives this a Gnostic twist. On the other hand, the beginning and the end of the chapter constitute an exposition of the essential themes of Jewish Christian theology, such as we find developed in the *Ascension of Isaiah* or the *Epistle of the Apostles*. These also are interpreted in a Gnostic sense.

Justin

The *Book of Baruch* was analysed by Hippolytus (V, 23–28), and attributed by him to a Gnostic named Justin. It is very close to the Sethians of Irenaeus and the *Apocryphon of John*. Hippolytus is the only source of information about this work. First of all it describes a Trinity; the Father, a second, masculine principle, Elohim, and a feminine principle called Eden and Israel. Elohim is seized with desire for Eden, and they beget twenty-four angels, whose names are given: paternal angels like Michael, Amen, Baruch, Gabriel, or maternal angels like Babel, Achamoth, Naas, Bel, Satan, Adonai. Together they form Paradise (V, 26).

Eden and Elohim form man, Eden giving him the soul and Elohim the spirit. But Elohim returns to the Father and forgets Eden. She, in order to be revenged, orders the angel Naas to persecute the Spirit of Elohim which is in men. Elohim then sends his angel Baruch, who comes to find Jesus, 'a young lad of twelve, keeping the sheep'. Jesus agrees to preach the Father and Elohim. He is persecuted by Naas, who has him crucified. When he dies, Jesus leaves his body to Eden and returns to the Father. Here is another speculation on the beginning of *Genesis* on exactly the same lines as that in the *Apocryphon of John*. Its Jewish character is quite evident, and the Christian element only appears in the latter part, as in the *Apocryphon*.

Naassenians

A fourth example of Jewish Christian gnosticism occurs in the notice which Hippolytus devotes to the Naassenians (*Elench.* V, 1–11). Here again the teaching described by Hippolytus is certainly in a fairly advanced stage of development. In his day the Naassenians were established at Rome,[65] at which time various elements gave their system a markedly syncretist character. But the archaic Jewish Christian origin of the sect is none the less apparent for that, and makes it of special interest for the present study.

In the first place, attention should be drawn to the kind of ancestry the sect claims for itself. It regards itself as presenting the teaching of James, the brother of the Lord (V, 7). These associations with James are always a sign of a Jewish Christian origin.[66] The Naassenians also took their inspiration from the *Gospel according to the Egyptians* (V, 7). At Nag Hammadi two copies of this Gnostic Gospel have been found, different from the one quoted by Clement of Alexandria. The sect also draws on the *Gospel according to Thomas*, another work discovered at Nag Hammadi.

The interesting point is that this proves that the Naassenian teaching, as expounded to us by Hippolytus at the beginning of the third century, is based on earlier works which must go back at least to the second half of the second century. From this same older source may also come certain liturgical pieces of the sect, especially the hymn with which Hippolytus ends his notice: 'On this account, O Father, send me; bearing the seals I shall descend; I shall discover all aeons, reveal all mysteries' (V, 10). Here, once more, is the old Jewish Christian theme, noted on so many occasions already, the descent of the Saviour through the angelic spheres.

It is only necessary to point out a few features of the Naassenian doctrine which are of special interest. First of all, the name of the sect is related to the Hebrew *nāḥāš*, serpent, indicating a link with the Sethians, whose speculations on the serpent in *Genesis* have already been mentioned. This feature was to reappear among the Peratae (*Elench.* V, 16) with a plainer reference still to the *Genesis* story. The original context, therefore, is again the Jewish gnosis on *Genesis*, the importance of which is so strikingly clear. It was the ultimate common source of both Jewish Christian and Gnostic presentations of this subject.

There are two noteworthy features about the Naassenians. In the first

---

65. M. Carcopino has shown that the cemetery discovered at the Viale Manzoni must have been theirs: *De Pythagore aux Apôtres*, pp. 99–132.

66. Among the still unpublished Nag Hammadi manuscripts are two *Apocalypses of James* which are probably connected with this sect. These should be distinguished from another *Apocalypse of James* which forms part of the *Jung Codex*. Cf. VAN UNNIK, 'The Origin of the recently discovered Apocryphon Jacobi', *VC*, x, 1956, pp. 149–156, who regards it as an orthodox Jewish Christian work.

place, continuing the important part played by speculations on *Genesis*, attention should be drawn to their account of the creation of Man, which recalls Carpocrates and the Sethians:

> Adam is the only man whom the earth brought forth; he lay without breath, life or movement, like a statue; an image of that heavenly man hymned under the name of Adamas, he is the work of many powers. The Naassenians seek to discover also what is the soul, so that it may be able, when it comes to give life to man, to correct and bring into subjection the work of the perfect man (V, 7).

There are also speculations on the four rivers of Paradise, which are regarded as the powers of man (V, 9).

As well as making use of this Jewish gnosis on *Genesis*, the Naassenians are dependent on Jewish Christianity. But the most striking thing about them is not that they use the setting of Jewish Christian theology, like the Sethians, but that they use Old Testament figures in the same way as the Christians, and the collections of *Testimonies*. First, similarities to Christian usage appear in the speculations on the passage of the Red Sea, a figure of deliverance from matter, and on the Great Jordan in which Jesus-Joshua gives spiritual birth by introducing men through it into the Promised Land. This is a new use of the old themes of the Christian typology of baptism, and supplies valuable evidence of them. Clement of Alexandria connects this speculation on the passage of the Red Sea as a deliverance from matter with the traditions of the Elders (*Eclog. Proph.* VI, 1). The same speculation is found among the Peratae (*Elench.* V, 16).

Secondly, the Naassenians use the collections of *Testimonies*. Among the texts which they employ are some of the classic examples from this source, but now given an esoteric, heterodox sense, as for instance in the case of the stone: Adamas is the corner stone that is become the head of the corner (*Ps.* 118:22); from this heavenly man has fallen the earthly man, 'cut out without hands' (*Dan.* 2:34). These two texts form a classic complex of testimonies in archaic theology.[67]

Another remarkable grouping of two of the most frequently used psalms in the *Testimonies*, *Pss.* 21 and 23 (EVV: 22 and 24), reads as follows: 'These words of Scripture: Open, ye eternal gates (24:7), apply to the ascension of the perfect man. For, says the Naassenian, Who is the king of

67. Cf. DANIÉLOU, *Sacramentum futuri*, pp. 210–211; RENDEL HARRIS, *Testimonies*, I, pp. 18–31.

glory? (24:10). A worm and no man (22:7). Such is the king of glory, the king powerful in war' (24:8).

Thus the examination of this notice leads to the same conclusion as in the case of Irenaeus' account of the Sethians. Two aspects of it may be distinguished: first, an old stratum of Jewish Gnosticism related to the Simonian gnosis, and like it having some Christian touches. This is the aspect that really concerns the present study. Secondly, this stream of Gnosticism uses themes from Jewish Christian theology, exegesis and liturgy. This is characteristic of a second stage in Gnosticism illustrated by Valentinus. In this stage the Gnostic documents are valuable because of the material which they have borrowed from the Great Church and which it is possible to rediscover in them; but there is no indebtedness in the reverse direction. The Church owes nothing to the Gnostics.

CARPOCRATES

Hegesippus, Irenaeus and Eusebius all mention Carpocrates, who seems to have been a contemporary of Satornil and Basilides, as the founder of a distinct sect. He does not evince the specific characteristics of the Gnosticism of Simon and his disciples. What is present, however, is the idea that 'the world and the things which are therein were created by angels greatly inferior to the uncreated Father' (*Adv. haer.* I, 25:1). This is a conception to be found frequently in this period amongst all the Gnostics, but it also appears prior to Gnosticism in Jewish heterodoxy.[68] There is evidence of this in Justin (*Dial.* LXII, 1) and also in the *Treatise of the Three Natures* (col. 112).

On the other hand, Carpocrates shows himself to be a Jewish Christian with a tinge of Ebionism when he affirms that Jesus was born of Joseph and is in everything like other men. But 'a power was sent upon him . . . that by means of it he might escape from the creators of the world, and pass through them all and come to the Father' (I, 25:1). Here again is the classic theme from Jewish Christianity, the ascension of the soul through the angelic spheres and the possibility of its escaping them in its passage, thanks to a power which is bestowed upon it. This idea, however, as already remarked, is in no way Gnostic and was commonly held in Jewish Christianity.

Jesus, therefore, is in no way a Saviour. What he received and what he

68. Cf. QUISPEL, 'Christliche Gnosis und jüdische Heterodoxie', *Evang. Theol.*, 1954 pp. 2–4.

accomplished, others could have done equally well. This point is especially emphasised by Irenaeus:

> 'The soul which is able, like that of Christ, to despise the archons who were the creators of the world, receives the same powers as he to accomplish the like results. This is why they are raised to such a pitch of pride that they declare themselves comparable to Jesus, some of them indeed maintaining that in some respects they are his betters' (I, 25:2).

They place Peter and Paul on the same plane as Jesus. Thus they see Jesus as a model—an idea very different from that of Gnosticism. In Carpocrates there is no trace of the descent of a Christ from on high to save men held captive by the archons.

One last feature of the Carpocratians is their moral indifferentism (I, 25:4; I, 28:2). This may possibly be related to the carnal messianism of the millenarian Jewish Christians, but in Carpocrates it adopts a special justification. Man can only be freed from the archons after having been the slave of all the vices over which they preside and thus having paid his debt; otherwise he would have to be reincarnated after death in order to carry out this payment. There seems to be here a trace of Pythagorean or Indian syncretism, and it should be remembered that the disciples of Carpocrates venerated the image of Pythagoras side by side with that of Jesus (I, 25:6). The idea may however have existed already in Jewish heterodoxy. Origen records that some Jews believed in reincarnation.[69]

The case of Carpocrates is a remarkable one. He seems to be essentially dependent on a heterodox Jewish gnosis which accepts that the angels created the world, and believes in metempsychosis. On the other hand he shows no trace of Samaritan Gnosticism; his Gnosticism is strictly Jewish. Moreover, Carpocrates is a heterodox Jew who accepts Christ, but only in the manner of the Ebionites, seeing in him no more than a prophet and a model. Finally, he seems to have been affected by Zealot Messianism. All this makes him a rather unusual figure in heterodox Jewish Christianity. His son Epiphanius was to hellenise Jewish Gnosticism just as Valentinus did Samaritan Gnosticism and Justin the orthodox gnosis of the same period.

69. Cf. *Com. Jn.* VI, 7.

CHAPTER THREE

JEWISH CHRISTIAN EXEGESIS

T HE whole conceptual system of Judaism is controlled and shaped by the Old Testament; and while Christianity is indeed a new event and a new revelation, it remains true, none the less, that it appeared in a Jewish environment and expressed itself in the concepts of that environment. Hence it inevitably emerged as an interpretation of the Jewish Scriptures. Moreover, because primitive Christianity did in this way declare itself to be a new revelation and at the same time regard the Old Testament as the Word of God, the starting-point of its exegesis was the need to demonstrate the fulfilment of the Old Testament types and figures in Christ.

Hence the Christian attitude to the Old Testament is an essential topic in the study of primitive Christianity; but since it must primarily be a question of New Testament exegesis, it lies beyond the scope of the present work, which will concern itself with a more particular and limited subject, namely, to try to discover *whether, in interpreting the Old Testament, Jewish Christianity made use of the methods of the Judaism of its day.*

In Judaism at the time of Christ there were several types of exegesis. Of these the work of Philo exhibits the first attempt to apply to Scripture the exegetical methods of Hellenism, and this too is, therefore, outside the present field. But it is now known that there also existed a Palestinian exegesis of a different type, samples of which have been found at Qumran, and which included *pešārîm*, or commentaries, like those on Habakkuk, Nahum, Hosea and Micah.[1] This kind of exegesis normally made use of typology, especially with regard to the figures of Adam and Moses.[2] There

1. Cf. J. VERMÈS, 'A propos des commentaires bibliques découverts à Qumran' in *La Bible et l'Orient*, 1955, pp. 95–104; J. T. MILIK, 'Fragments d'un midrash de Michée dans les manuscrits de Qumrân', *RB*, LIX, 1952, pp. 412–419; J. M. ALLEGRO, 'Further Light on the History of the Qumran Sect', *JBL*, LXXIV, 1956, pp. 89–96; 'Further Messianic references in Qumran Literature', *JBL*, LXXVI, 1957, pp. 174–188.
2. Cf. J. DANIÉLOU, *Sacramentum futuri*, pp. 3–25; 135–170.

was also a moral *haggada*, such as that for instance in *Jubilees* or the *Testaments of the Twelve Patriarchs*.[3] Only two aspects are of direct concern for Jewish Christian theology: first, the existence of Targums, or of *midrashim*, which constitute one of the sources of our knowledge of this theology; and secondly, the existence of commentaries on *Genesis* forming one of the principal fields in which this theology was applied.

JEWISH CHRISTIAN TARGUMS

The Hebrew text of the Old Testament had, in the years immediately preceding and following the arrival of the Christian era, been translated into both Aramaic and Greek. It is not, however, the Aramaic versions, the Targums properly so called, which are relevant to our present concern, but the Greek translations. The history of the latter is well known, and has recently been the subject of a fresh presentation.[4] The most important of these versions is, of course, the Septuagint, but fragments also survive of translations by Aquila, Theodotion and Symmachus—the latter apparently the work of a Jewish Christian, perhaps an Ebionite.[5] Other fragments have been found, in particular in the Cairo Geniza and the Judaean desert,[6] which have raised the question whether there may not have been many translations, of which the Septuagint represents only one type.[7]

The point of immediate interest, however, is that these translations are at the same time interpretations. This is already true of the LXX, in which the doctrine of resurrection is made explicit (*Is.* 26:19; *Dan.* 12:2; *Job* 42:17), and in which angelology has an important place. Thus, in *Deut.* 32:8, 'the angels of the nations' replace 'the children of Israel'. In *Ps.* 8:5, 'Thou madest him a little lower than God' is interpreted as 'Thou madest him a little lower than the angels'. Other such cases are quite a normal occurrence. In the same way the translation of Symmachus corresponds to Ebionite theology.[8] In *Is.* 7:14, νεᾶνις replaces the παρθένος of the LXX; in *Jer.* 4:4, 'Purify your hearts' replaces the metaphor of circumcising the foreskin of the heart. Similar comments might be made about Theodotion and Aquila.

---

3. Cf. H. THYEN, *Der Stil der Judisch-hellenistischen Homilie*, p. 25.
4. Cf. B. J. ROBERTS, *The Old Testament, Text and Versions*, pp. 101–188.
5. Cf. chap. 2, pp. 62 above.
6. Cf. D. BARTHÉLEMY, 'Redécouverte d'un chaînon manquant de l'Histoire des LXX', *RB*, LX, 1953, pp. 18–30.
7. Cf. P. KAHLE, *Die hebräischen Handschriften aus der Höhle*, Stuttgart, 1951, pp. 30 ff.
8. Cf. H. J. SCHOEPS, *Theologie und Geschichte des Judenchristentums*, pp. 350–366.

The next question is whether there were any Jewish Christian translations of the Old Testament. It looks as though the text of the LXX was ordinarily used, but there are exceptions to this. The best-known instance is that of the quotations from Isaiah and the Minor Prophets in the first part of *Matthew*. The text is quite different from the LXX. To see this it is only necessary to compare *Mt.* 4:15 ff. with *Is.* 9:1 ff. (MT 8:23 ff.), or still more, *Mt.* 12:18 ff. and *Is.* 42:1 ff. Various interpretations have been put upon the matter.[9] The most convincing view, however, is that which sees these translations as the expression of the theology of a group of Jewish Christian teachers.[10]

This should not be taken to imply that the Christians felt a need for a complete Greek translation of the Old Testament of their own. They used the LXX, which they held in great veneration and regarded as inspired by the Holy Ghost. But on the other hand they did not hesitate to refashion certain texts which had for them particular theological importance. These alterations were more than a translation; they are genuine pieces of exegesis, taking the various forms of fusion, modification, addition or suppression of passages. They may have been influenced by apologetic considerations, but possibly also by liturgical ones, and are characteristic of a very archaic period of Christianity[11]; moreover the method itself derives from a Judaistic environment to which Hellenistic literary methods were completely foreign.[12]

The procedure is not unknown in the New Testament,[13] in which texts from the Old undergo some elaboration. There is an example of fusion, for instance, in the complex of several *testimonia*, all relating to Christ as the Stone, which is to be found in *I Pet.* 2:6 ff.; *Eph.* 2:20; *Mt.* 21:42; *Lk.* 20:17-18; *Acts* 4:11 and *Rom.* 9:32. In these passages an amalgamation of *Is.* 28:16; *Ps.* 117:21 (EVV 118: 22) and *Is.* 8:14 results in a homogeneous text. *Barnabas* (VI, 2) alludes to the same complex in the following

9. Thus KILPATRICK is content simply with pointing it out (*The Origin of the Gospel according to Matthew*, Oxford, 1946, p. 56). KAHLE sees in it the proof of the existence of a Greek translation independent of the LXX (*op. cit.*, p. 32). BAUMSTARK comes to the same conclusion ('Die Zitate des Mt.-Evangeliums aus dem Zwölfprophetenbuch', *Biblica*, XXXVII, 1956, pp. 296–313).
10. Cf. STENDAHL, *The School of St. Matthew*, Uppsala, 1954.
11. Cf. B. FISHER, 'Le Christ dans les Psaumes', *Maison-Dieu*, XXVII, 1951, p. 100.
12. It is to be found in particular in the DSS: cf. ALLEGRO, *The Dead Sea Scrolls*, London, 1956, pp. 138–139. Thus, e.g., 4*Q Testimonia* fuses *Deut.* 5:28 and 18:18.
13. For St. Paul's writings, cf. E. E. ELLIS, *Paul's Use of the Old Testament*, Edinburgh, 1957, pp. 59–61.

words: 'The prophet speaks of the time when he is to be set as a hard stone, ordained for crushing (εἰς συντριβήν): Behold, I will set in the foundations of Zion a stone elect, a precious corner-stone' (*Is.* 28:16). The expression εἰς συντριβήν is a clear allusion to *Is.* 8:14, which speaks of 'a stumbling stone' and was associated in the writer's mind with 'the corner-stone'.[14] Barnabas enriches this group with a new text, *Is.* 50:7, which will call for comment later.

The New Testament also contains instances of texts being altered. One of the most remarkable of these is the change in the quotation from *Ps.* 67:19 (EVV 68:18): 'Ascending on high, he led captivity captive, he gave (ἔδωκε) gifts to men' which occurs in *Eph.* 4:8. The LXX text has: thou receivedst (ἔλαβες) gifts'. The first translation may be of Jewish origin,[15] but it is also possible that Paul himself—or liturgical practice applying this text to Christ's Ascension even before his time[16]—has adapted it to the mystery to which it has been applied. This kind of procedure, which will be the main subject of the present discussion, results in an expression of Christian theology by means of the rearrangement and re-casting of Old Testament texts in such a way that they in fact present new data.

The *Epistle of Barnabas* affords numerous examples of this kind of exegesis. 'Thus (God) speaketh to us: The sacrifice unto God is a broken heart, the smell of a sweet savour unto the Lord is a heart that glorifies its Maker' (II, 10). The first part of this quotation comes from *Ps.* 50:19 (LXX: EVV—51:17), with the substitution of καρδία συντετριμμένη for the LXX πνεῦμα συντετριμμένον; but what of the second part? It has sometimes been regarded as a quotation from an apocryphon, but it will be observed that, unlike the second member of the LXX verse, it is in strict parallelism with the first, τῷ κυρίῳ καρδία echoing τῷ θεῷ καρδία and ὀσμὴ εὐωδίας balancing θυσία. Since in other texts (*Eph.* 5:2; *Test. Levi.* III, 5 f.) ὀσμὴ εὐωδίας is a Jewish Christian term for the Eucharistic sacrifice, the conclusion which suggests itself is that the second member in *Barnabas* is a paraphrase of the first of a liturgical character.

It is worth noting that *Ps.* 50, 19 occurs elsewhere, coupled with other

14. Cf. RENDEL HARRIS, *Testimonies*, pp. 26–32; V. TAYLOR, *The Names of Jesus*, pp. 93–100; R. A. KRAFT, 'Barnabas' Isaiah text and the Testimony Book hypothesis', *JBL*, LXXIX, 1960, pp. 344 f.
15. Cf. KRETSCHMAR, 'Himmelfahrt und Pfingsten', *ZKG*, LXV, 1956, pp. 216 ff.
16. This would seem to be supported by the fact that the same modification is found in *Test. Dan.* V, 11.

verses of Scripture, which suggests that it may belong to the *testimonia* of Jewish Christianity and its liturgical practice. Thus it is quoted in *I Clement* (LII, 4)—this time in the strict LXX form with $\pi\nu\epsilon\hat{v}\mu\alpha$—only preceded now by *Ps.* 49 (EVV 50), 14 f.[17] which ought also to be included among the primitive *testimonia* (cf. JUSTIN, *Dial.* XXII, 9; CYPRIAN, *Ad Quir.* I, 16). This type of exegesis, consisting of a juxtaposition and welding together of biblical texts to form a new whole, will also be encountered again.

Another noteworthy case appears in *Barnabas* (V, 13), where the writer is speaking of *testimonia* of the Passion: 'He that prophesied said concerning Him, Spare my soul from the sword; and, Pierce My flesh with nails, for the congregations of evil-doers have risen up against Me.' In this complex the first component comes from *Ps.* 21:21 (LXX: EVV 22:20), the second from *Ps.* 118:120 (EVV 119) and the third from *Ps.* 21:17 (EVV22:16).[18] Now the same complex is found in Irenaeus (*Dem.* 79), where, however, it is given as forming a single long quotation: 'Deliver my soul from the sword and spare my body from the nails, for a troop of wicked men is risen against me.' This is, therefore, an instance of a complex which has become traditional, and whose composite character is no longer apparent —a not uncommon occurrence in the Jewish Christian use of the Old Testament.

These are not, however, the only points of interest in this particular example. The second component, for instance, is not quoted exactly, the LXX text being: 'Pierce my flesh with thy fear ($\dot{\epsilon}\kappa$ $\tau o\hat{v}$ $\varphi\acute{o}\beta ov$ σov)' in a metaphorical and moral sense. But the Jewish Christians kept the text because of the allusion to the nails ($\kappa\alpha\theta\acute{\eta}\lambda\omega\sigma ov$), at the same time suppressing the allusion to 'fear', thus radically modifying the sense so that it takes on another meaning.[19] It will be observed that in the *Testimonies* of Cyprian *Ps.* 118:120 is quoted side by side with *Ps.* 21:7-10, but in the correct form: 'Confige clavis de metu tuo carnes meas.'[20]

17. 'Sacrifice to God a sacrifice of praise ($\theta v\sigma\acute{\iota}\alpha$ $\alpha\dot{\iota}v\acute{\epsilon}\sigma\epsilon\omega s$) and pay thy vows to the Most High: and call upon me in the day of thine affliction, and I will deliver thee, and thou shalt glorify me.'

18. The first component in *Barnabas* has $\varphi\epsilon\hat{\iota}\sigma\alpha\iota$ for the LXX $\dot{\rho}\hat{v}\sigma\alpha\iota$, and the third appears to have been affected by reminiscence of other similar passages, possibly *Pss.* 85:14 or 91:12 (LXX: EVV 86: 14; 92:11).

19. The other modification in Irenaeus—'Spare my body from the nails' instead of 'Pierce my flesh with nails'—seems to be the result of an error by the Armenian translator: cf. L. FROIDEVAUX, 'Sur trois textes cités par Saint Irénée', *RSR*, XLIV, 1956, pp. 408-414.

20. Cf. R. HARRIS, *Testimonies*, I, p. 74.

Equally significant modifications are found later in the work. *Barnabas* first quotes *Is.* 50:7 in the correct form: 'My face did I set as a hard rock (V, 14), but later on he links the text to a collection of *testimonia* about Christ as the Rock and quotes thus: 'And He set Me as a hard rock', suppressing πρόσωπον (VI, 3). This second form of the text is found in *Odes of Solomon* XXXI, 9, where it is linked with *Ps.* 21:18. In the same chapter *Barnabas* quotes as a prophecy: 'This is the great and wonderful (θαυμαστή) day, which the Lord made' (VI, 4). The commentators quite rightly quote *Ps.* 117:24 (EVV 118), but that only speaks of the Day. There is in fact contamination with another text, *Mal.* 3:22, which speaks of 'the great and glorious (ἐπιφανῆ) day of the Lord', only with the variant θαυμαστή. Justin (*Dial.* XLIX, 2) quotes the text of Malachi with a third variant, φοβερά, which is in fact the sense of the MT. This evidence makes it possible to conjecture the process underlying the present texts, namely that there was a collection of *testimonia* on the theme of Christ as the Day, to which in particular *Ps.* 117:24 and *Mal.* 3:22 belonged, and these texts have tended to fuse one with another.

The association of the brazen serpent with the prayer of Moses is a very ancient complex, and is connected with *testimonia* relating to the Cross. But in itself it seems certainly to be older than Christianity, a fact which underlines its Jewish character.[21] The *Epistle of Barnabas* (XII, 7) provides the earliest Christian instance. What is of interest, however, in the passage from *Barnabas* is the discourse which he puts into the mouth of Moses: 'Whensoever . . . one of you shall be bitten, let him come to the serpent which is placed on the tree (ξύλον), and let him believe and hope that the serpent being himself dead can make alive; and forthwith he shall be saved' (XII, 7). Now this is a paraphrase of *Num.* 21:8. It will be noted that in the text in *Num.* the word used is σημεῖον not ξύλον; the application to Christ crucified is stressed by the choice of word. Again, *Num.* says simply: 'Everyone that looks upon it shall live'; the commentary on the death that can give life is a gloss that emphasises the vivifying power of the death of Christ.

But *Barnabas* was not responsible for this complex. A parallel text in Justin makes Moses say: 'If ye look to this figure, and believe, ye shall be saved thereby' (*I Apol.* LX, 3). Here again is the same allusion as in *Barnabas* to the necessary faith, and the expression 'be saved'. Moreover,

21. Cf. T. W. MANSON, 'The Argument from Prophecy', *JTS*, XLVI, 1945, pp. 135 ff.; also J. DANIÉLOU, *Sacramentum futuri*, pp. 144–151.

the brazen serpent is designated by the word τύπος as in *Barnabas* XII, 6. It is remarkable to find once more a parallel development in two authors. It is possible of course that Justin was influenced by *Barnabas*, but it seems more probable that there was a full account of the episode with a Christian colouring in the *testimonia*.

In the same chapter XII, *Barnabas* quotes *Exod.* 17:14: 'Moses therefore saith to Jesus the son of Nun . . .: Write what the Lord saith, how that the Son of God shall cut up by the roots all the house of Amalek in the last days' (XII, 9). Now the text of *Exodus* is quite different: 'The Lord said to Moses . . . Speak this in the ears of Jesus (Joshua), that I will utterly blot out the memorial of Amalek from under heaven, . . . for with a secret hand the Lord wages war on Amalek to all generations.' The procedure is very much the same as the one discernible in the case of *Num.* 21:8, namely, a summary which introduces Christian features into the text. Thus there is no mention of the Son of God in Exodus, nor the expression 'in the last days'. On the other hand, this paraphrase is not the work of *Barnabas*; he only quotes it, as is proved by the fact that he regards this text as an evidence that Jesus is the Son of God. Moreover, the text from *Exodus* is one of the ancient *testimonia*; it is quoted with only one variant from the LXX form by Justin (*Dial.* XLIX, 8).

Farther on in the same chapter of *Barnabas*, *Is.* 45:1: 'Thus saith the Lord God to my anointed Cyrus' is changed to: 'The Lord said unto my Christ the Lord' (XII, 11). The change from Κύρῳ to Κυρίῳ was an easy one.[22] The text is associated with *Ps.* 109:1 (EVV 110) and serves to show that Christ is Kyrios, that is, God. This alteration may be compared with another in the LXX of *Lam.* 4:20. The Hebrew text reads: 'The breath of our nostrils, the anointed of Yahweh (= Χριστὸς Κυρίου)'; but all the LXX MSS have Χριστὸς Κύριος. The confusion may arise from the fact that both Κύριος and Κυρίου were abbreviated in the form Κυ[23]; nevertheless the preference given to Κύριος is still remarkable. Since this text is one of the most ancient *testimonia* (JUSTIN, *I Apol.* LV, 5; IRENAEUS, *Dem.* 71), it seems very likely that the choice of Κύριος is of Christian origin. It was almost certainly from some such consideration that Luke wrote Χριστὸς Κύριος in 2:11 instead of the classic expression Χριστὸς Κυρίου 'the Lord's anointed'.[24]

22. Cf. R. HARRIS, *Testimonies*, I, p. 37; KRAFT, *op. cit.*, p. 341.
23. Cf. RAHLFS, *ad loc.*
24. Cf. J. DANIÉLOU, 'Christos Kyrios, Un texte des Lamentations dans le recueil des Testimonia', *RSR*, XXXIX, 1951, pp. 338–352.

Chapter XIII contains a quotation from *Gn.* 17:5: 'Behold I have made thee, Abraham, a father of nations that believe in God in uncircumcision' (XIII, 7). *Gn.* 17:5, however, speaks simply of 'father of many nations'. The precise reference to the conversion of the uncircumcised and to the necessity of faith is clearly of Christian origin. Chapter XIV mentions that 'Moses received from the Lord the two tables which were written by the finger of the hand of the Lord in spirit (ἐν πνεύματι)' (XIV, 2). This is clearly a reference to *Exod.* 31:18 but in that text there is no mention of the Spirit. However, the use of the phrase, . . . the 'finger of God', to mean the Spirit, which occurs in *Lk.* 11:20 (cf. *Mt.* 12:28), allows us to see in the words ἐν πνεύματι a Christian gloss alluding to the concept of the 'spiritual law' written on the heart.[25]

The *Epistle of Barnabas* in particular contains a considerable number of texts thus adapted for Christian use. But the other Jewish Christian writings have them also. Thus in *I Clement* we read: 'For he saith in a certain place, The Spirit of the Lord (Πνεῦμα Κυρίου) is a lamp searching the closets of the belly' (XXI, 2).[26] The LXX text (*Prov.* 20:27) gives: 'The spirit of man is a light of the Lord (φῶς Κυρίου πνοὴ ἀνθρώπων).' There is certainly some translation other than the LXX behind this quotation, for πνοή is replaced by πνεῦμα and φῶς by λυχνός. But the attaching of πνεῦμα to Κυρίου, which permits the text to be referred to the Holy Ghost, certainly seems to be a Christian modification. *I Clem.* XLII, 5 is still more characteristic: 'For thus saith Scripture in a certain place: I will appoint their bishops (ἐπισκόπους) in righteousness and their deacons (διακόνους) in faith.' *Isaiah*, from which this quotation is taken, has the two halves in reverse order, and in place of the clause about deacons 'thy princes (ἄρχοντας) in peace' (60:17). The deacons are a Christian retouching, injecting incidentally quite a new sense into ἐπισκόπους.[27]

But the most remarkable feature of *I Clem.* is the presence of a dossier of

25. The same quotation occurs in the *Demonstratio* of Irenaeus. The text is obscure: 'In the desert Moses received from God the Law, ten commandments written with the finger of God on tables of stone; by "finger of God" we are to understand that which is put forth by the Father in the Holy Spirit (ἐν πνεύματι)' (26; *PO*, XII, 769). In the long note which he devotes to this text, BARTHOULOT does not refer to *Barnabas*. Nevertheless it seems fairly clear that in both cases we are dealing with the same modified quotation. This does not necessarily mean that Irenaeus borrowed it from Barnabas: it is more probably a christianised text incorporated in the *testimonia*.

26. Cf. also CLEMENT, *Strom.* IV, 16–107, 5.

7. Cf. RESCH, *Agrapha*, p. 315.

texts in which the resurrection is suggested by the introduction of the verb ἀνίσταναι. Thus Clement writes: 'For he saith in a certain place; And Thou shalt raise (ἐξαναστήσεις) me up and I will praise thee' (XXVI, 2). This is usually held to be a quotation from *Ps.* 27:7 (EVV 28:7): 'My flesh has flourished (ἀνέθαλεν) and willingly will I give praise to him', but the allusion to the resurrection certainly appears to be Jewish Christian.[28] Another example of this class of alteration occurs in the very next verse quoted by Clement, *Ps.* 3:6 (EVV 5). This time it is given in the LXX form—'I went to rest and slept, I was awaked (ἐξηγέρθην), for Thou art with me', except that the last phrase is not that in *Ps.* 3, but comes from *Ps.* 22:4 (EVV 23), a *locus classicus* for the doctrine of the resurrection.[29]

I Clement next (XXVI, 3) cites *Job* 19:26. Here, of course, the verb ἀνίσταναι and the idea of resurrection had already been introduced by the LXX translator; but the instance does at least illustrate the way in which the Jewish Christians stood in the tradition of the Jewish translators. Clement has another curious quotation: 'It is written, Enter into the closet (ταμιεῖα) for a very little while, until Mine anger and My wrath shall pass away, and I will remember a good day and will raise you from your tombs' (L, 4). The first part, down to 'pass away', comes from *Is.* 26:20, and the final phrase, 'and will raise you from your tombs', from *Ezek.* 37:12. A major shift in the sense has, however, been achieved by the substitution of ἀναστήσω for Ezekiel's ἀνάξω, and by the rearrangement of the whole in order to make the ταμιεῖα denote the dwelling-places of the dead until the resurrection—all ideas quite foreign to the original texts.

Nevertheless, the use of *Is.* 26:20 in this connection becomes a good deal less surprising when attention is turned to the immediately preceding verse: 'The dead shall rise (ἀναστήσονται) and they that are in the tombs shall awake.' This text, in which ἀναστήσονται is already present in the LXX, is a classic *testimonium* of the resurrection, and appears also in a curious passage in Justin (*I Apol.* XLVIII, 2) which is a complex of *Is.*

28. *Ibid.*, p. 307.
29. JUSTIN (*I Apol.* XXXVIII, 5) also quotes *Ps.* 3:6: 'He saith again, I laid me down and slept, and I rose up (ἀνέστην), because the Lord took care (ἀντελάβετο) of me.' Here the LXX text of *Ps.* 3:6 is closely followed without contamination, and with the sole substitution of ἀνέστην for ἐξηγέρθην. It is also worth noting that in Justin the text is linked with *Ps.* 21:17–19, only in an inverted and abbreviated form: 'They cast lots upon my vesture, and pierced my hands and feet.' *Ps.* 3:6 is also quoted in IRENAEUS, *Dem.* 73 (*PO* XII, 791), and CLEMENT ALEX. *Strom.* V, 14:105. It is likely that underlying these instances is a complex of *testimonia* on the Passion and Resurrection of considerable elaboration.

35:5 f., 61:1 and 26:19: 'It was predicted. . . . At His coming (παρουσία) the lame shall leap as an hart, and the tongue of the dumb shall be eloquent, the lepers shall be cleansed, and the dead shall rise (ἀναστήσονται) and walk about.' This passage has, moreover, certain affinities with *Mt.* 11:5 and *Lk.* 7:22, which are also composite texts, and from which the allusion to the lepers has been borrowed. Justin's tradition, however, is an independent one,[30] in particular reading ἀναστήσονται in place of the ἐγείρονται of *Matthew* and *Luke*.

That this substitution of ἀναστήσονται is in fact an allusion to *Is.* 26:19 is confirmed by Irenaeus, for in *Dem.* 67 instead of giving a composite text, as the authors so far cited have done, he quotes two prophecies separately, namely *Is.* 35:3-6 and 26:19. Moreover, the latter is given entire, including the phrase '. . . and they in the tombs shall be raised up'. It seems, therefore, that all these writers were dealing with a complex of texts from Isaiah which had already been fused into an established group by the time of the New Testament, though also being susceptible of a variety of arrangements,[31] and that this is the real explanation of the application of *Is.* 26:20 to the resurrection in *I Clement*.

It would be easy to quote other examples of this kind,[32] but it will be sufficient to conclude with a text which shows decisively that these Christian *targumim* are not the work of the authors who quote them, but represent a previous exegesis of an archaic kind. In controversy with the Jews the authenticity of these *testimonia* was bound to arise; Trypho, for instance, puts this challenge to Justin, but Justin rather surprisingly retorts that it is the Jews who have falsified Scripture. He is, therefore, firmly convinced that the *testimonia* he quotes represent the authentic text; and this is only explicable if these manipulations of Scriptural passages were fully traditional by his time.

He quotes an example which is in fact one of the most remarkable instances of the adaptation of a text in the interests of Christology: 'From the ninety-fifth Psalm . . . they (sc. the Jews) have removed this short phrase, "from the tree" (ἀπὸ τοῦ ξύλου) . . . for it was said, Tell it among the Gentiles that the Lord reigned from the tree' (*Dial.* LXXIII, 1). Now

---

30. Cf. E. MASSAUX, *Influence de l'Évangile de St. Matthieu*, Louvain, 1950, pp. 498 f.
31. Cf. RENDEL HARRIS, *Testimonies*, I, pp. 8-10.
32. Cf. R. M. GRANT, 'The Bible of Theophilus of Antioch', *JBL*, LXVI, 1947, pp. 178 f.; T. SCHNEIDER, 'Das prophetische Agraphon der Epistola Apostolorum', *ZNW*, XXVI, 1925, pp. 151-154.

no ancient MS of *Ps.* 95:10 (EVV 96) gives the words ἀπὸ τοῦ ξύλου, but they do appear in other Christian texts. Thus Justin himself refers to them (*I Apol.* XLII, 4) and Tertullian mentions them in *Adv. Marc.* III, 19. They are clearly a Christian interpolation, and belong to an important group of testimonia, those embodying the word ξύλον. Several instances of the intrusion of this word have already been noted; an example exactly parallel to the present one occurs in certain manuscripts from Upper Egypt in the fourth century, where the text of *Ps.* 50:9 (EVV 51:7) has been expanded to read: 'Thou shalt sprinkle me with hyssop by the blood of the tree.'[33]

ANCIENT CHRISTIAN MIDRASHIM

The texts so far considered have exhibited passages from the Old Testament slightly modified to adapt them the better for Christian use. It is now time to turn to a second type of exegesis. The oldest Christian works, the *Epistle of Barnabas* and *I Clement* especially, contain passages quoted as belonging to the Scriptures, and attributed to Old Testament authors, which do not appear in the canonical writings. They are paraphrases of the Old Testament, a sort of *midrash* palpably Christian in tone, and providing fragments of Jewish Christian theology of great antiquity.

The interpretation of these texts poses some difficult problems. They are clearly *midrashim* of the Old Testament, but are they Jewish or Christian glosses? Attention will here be restricted to those the Christian character of which seems to be safely established. Again, since they are indicated by a variety of lemmas, it is difficult to be certain from which Old Testament passage they derive. There seem to be some grounds for recognising *midrashim* of *Leviticus*, *Ezra*, *Jeremiah* and *Ezekiel*, but any such attributions must remain largely matter for conjecture. It seems, however, that they can at least be classified in a certain number of groups, and it is the nature of these groups which we must now try to determine.

The *Epistle of Barnabas* contains a series of quotations which seem to come from a Christian *midrash* of *Leviticus* and *Numbers*.[34] The Jewish rites are described in such a way as to throw into relief their points of contact with Christianity. One of the first of these passages refers to the

33. Cf. B. FISHER, 'Le Christ dans les Psaumes', *Maison-Dieu*, XXVII, 1951, p. 100. For a similar interpolation into *Deut.* 28:66 cf. J. DANIÉLOU, 'Das Leben das am Holze hängt' in *Kirche und Überlieferung (Festgabe Geiselmann)*, Freiburg, 1960, pp. 22–34.
34. On these passages cf. H. KÖSTER, *Synoptische Überlieferung*, pp. 148–156.

sacrifice of a he-goat on the Day of Atonement: '. . . there is a commandment in Scripture, Whosoever shall not observe the fast (νήστεια) shall
surely die' (VII, 3). A little farther on the text reads as follows: 'What then
saith He in the prophet? And let them eat of the goat (τράγου) that is
offered at the fast for all their sins (πασῶν τῶν ἁμαρτιῶν). Attend carefully: And let all the priests alone eat the entrails unwashed with vinegar
(ὄξος)' (VII, 4).

These texts develop what is said in *Lev.* 23:29 and *Num.* 29:11. But the
translation is different from the LXX, which speaks of χίμαρος and not of
τράγος (*Num.* 29:11), and the fast (νηστεύειν) replaces humiliation
(ταπεινοῦσθαι) (*Lev.* 23:29). Moreover, the expression 'for all their sins'
gives a more universal validity to the offering than *Num.* 29, which says
simply 'for sin'. Finally, the last part of the quotation contains details not
found in Scripture. It seems likely that it refers to the Mishnah,[35] the ritual
traditions. Nevertheless it may be noticed that the allusion to vinegar (ὄξος)
is found in Scripture in *Ps.* 68, 22 (EVV 69:21), implied by *Mt.* 27:48.[36]

If these elements are taken as a whole, the context which suggests itself
is the New Testament *Epistle to the Hebrews*, in which the same comparison
of the sacrifices of the Old and the New Testaments is to be found. Furthermore, the word τράγος is peculiar in the New Testament to *Hebrews*, and
found there no fewer than four times (9:12, 13, 19; 10:4) in the section
relating to this topic (9:11–10:18). The description of the worship of the
Old Testament in *Hebrews* draws freely for its inspiration on both Scripture
and tradition, and the same appears to be true of *Barnabas*. Again *Barnabas*
comes from the same Alexandrian background as *Hebrews*. This passage
then may reasonably be taken to represent a remnant of a Christian *midrash* on the Day of Atonement (10 Tishri) deriving from the Elders of
Alexandria.

The Christian character of this *midrash* appears more clearly in a second
fragment, relating this time not to the goat actually sacrificed on the Day
of Atonement, but to the scapegoat driven off into the desert on the same
day.[37] Moreover, it seems as if the author confuses the two:

Attend ye to the commandments which He gave. Take two goats
(τράγους) fair and alike, and offer them, and let the priest take one
for a whole burnt-offering for sins. But the other one—what must

35. Cf. Glossary s.v.   36. Cf. KÖSTER, *op. cit.*, pp. 148–152.
37. Cf. KÖSTER, *op. cit.*, pp. 152–156.

they do with it? Accursed (ἐπικατάρατος), saith He (φησίν), is the one . . . And do ye all spit (ἐμπτύσατε) upon it and goad it (κατα-κεντήσατε), and place scarlet wool about its head, and so let it be cast into the wilderness (VII, 6–8).

Here again *Barnabas* quotes a more ancient text which is a midrash on *Lev.* 16:7–8.

The rites mentioned at the end of the quotation may still be traditional but the manner in which they are presented and the choice of words certainly indicate a Christian origin.[38] It has already been remarked that τράγος replaces χίμαρος in the *Epistle to the Hebrews*. The word ἐπι-κατάρατος echoes *Gal.* 3:10. The detail of the 'spitting' (ἐμπτύσατε) recalls the scene of the mocking in the praetorium, where *Matthew* uses the same verb (ἐνέπτυσαν, 26:67); the goading (κατακεντήσατε) reminds us of *Jn.* 19:37 which has ἐξεκέντησαν; finally, the scarlet wool (κόκκινος) crowning the head is a clear allusion to the bloody crown which surrounds the head of Jesus. Behind the scapegoat stands the figure of Jesus in the praetorium.

Barnabas is still quoting the same source when it adds: 'And when it is so done, he that taketh the goat into the wilderness leadeth it, and taketh off the wool, and putteth it upon the branch which is called Rachia' (VII, 8). The juxtaposition of the scarlet (κόκκινος) and the thorns certainly seems to be related to the mention of the scarlet (κοκκίνην) tunic and the crown of thorns in the praetorium scene (*Matt.* 27:28 f.). The text speaks here only of ῥαχή (brambles), but a little later (VII, 11) replaces the word by ἀκάνθη, which—both in *Barnabas* and *Mt.* (27:28–29)—is closely linked with κόκκινος. The same association is found in Melito's *Paschal Homily*: 'Thou hast placed scarlet (κόκκινος) on his body and thorns (ἄκανθαν) on his head' (XIII, 3–4). Moreover, it will not be forgotten that the sacrifice of Isaac forms a part of the complex of ideas attached to the Day of Atonement,[39] that *Barnabas* compares the sacrifice of the goat with that of Isaac (VII, 3), and that in the latter episode the ram is immolated in place of Isaac, hanging from a bush of thorns—an incident regarded as a figure of Christ at a very early date.[40]

---

38. Cf. RESCH, *Agrapha*, p. 299.
39. Cf. H. RIESENFELD, *Jésus transfiguré*, Copenhagen, 1947, pp. 86.
40. TERTULLIAN, *Adv. Jud.* XIII, 21; cf. DANIÉLOU, *Sacramentum futuri*, pp. 106–108. In the following chapter (*Adv. Jud.* XIV, 9) Tertullian uses for the scapegoat the same source as *Barnabas*.

The passage concludes with a precise statement of the spiritual significance of this figure:

> But what meaneth it, that they place the wool in the midst of the thorns? It is a type of Jesus set forth for the Church, since whosoever should desire to take away the scarlet wool it behoveth him to suffer many things owing to the terrible nature of the thorn, and through affliction to win the mastery over it. Thus, he saith ($\varphi\eta\sigma\acute{\iota}\nu$), they that desire to see Me and to attain unto My kingdom, must lay hold on me through tribulation and affliction (VII, 11).

The scarlet wool therefore represents the benefits of Christ's Passion which cannot be won save by passing through the bush of thorns, whose fruit, however, is then sweeter than any other (VII, 8). This is an archaic echo of a symbolism of the thorn ($\H{\alpha}\kappa\alpha\nu\theta\alpha\iota$), resting principally on such passages as *Gn.* 3:18, the Burning Bush,[41] and the Crowning with Thorns. The thorns represent either the punishment of the Jews, the sins of the world or the trials of the spiritual life.

Barnabas finally turns to a third incident, that of the Red Heifer in *Num.* 19. The Old Testament passage is not, strictly speaking, quoted, but dealt with in a manner analogous to that of the previous instances, and quite certainly deriving from the same source:

> The commandment was given ($\grave{\epsilon}\nu\tau\acute{\epsilon}\tau\alpha\lambda\tau\alpha\iota$) to Israel that men who have committed great sins should offer a heifer ($\delta\acute{\alpha}\mu\alpha\lambda\iota\varsigma$), slaughter it and burn it; next that servants ($\pi\alpha\acute{\iota}\delta\iota\alpha$) should collect the ashes and pour them into vessels; that they should twine scarlet wool ($\kappa\acute{o}\kappa\kappa\iota\nu o\varsigma$) and hyssop round a piece of wood—behold once more the figure ($\tau\acute{\upsilon}\pi o\varsigma$) of the Cross and the scarlet wool!—and finally, that these servants should sprinkle all the people, one by one, to purify them from their sins (VIII, 1).

The text goes on to speak first of twelve servants (VIII, 3), then of three (VIII, 4).

Several of these elements are taken from the biblical text, in particular the wood wound round with scarlet wool (*Num.* 19:6). The occurrence of the wool in this passage and the preceding one gives grounds for believing that there was a collection of canonical and apocryphal *testimonia* containing

41. This, according to Clement of Alexandria (*Paed.* II, 8:75) was a thorn bush ($\grave{\alpha}\kappa\alpha\nu\theta\grave{\omega}\delta\epsilon\varsigma$ $\phi\upsilon\tau\acute{o}\nu$).

the word κόκκινος. It included, beside the two texts already mentioned, *Gn.* 38:28, the scarlet thread used to identify Zerah the son of Tamar, *Jos.* 2:18, the scarlet cord which Rahab placed as a σημεῖον in her window, and *Cant.* 4:3, the lips of the bride which are like two scarlet ribbons. The antiquity of these *testimonia* is seen by the fact that *I Clement* already saw in Rahab's scarlet cord 'the blood of the Lord' (XII, 7).

But the text also includes an elaboration of the passage from *Numbers*. First, the heifer is said to be offered by great sinners; *Barnabas* explains that these are they who put Christ to death (VIII, 2). *Numbers*, however, only speaks of the priest, and of legal defilement. There is thus a transition from the Jewish rite to the Christian reality. Nor does *Numbers* mention the παιδια, but only the priest. These servants, numbering twelve or three, whom *Barnabas* regards as a symbol of the Apostles, are also a Christian gloss. The sprinkling is performed not with blood but with the ashes mixed with water, and, what is more, over each of the people in turn. All this is quite foreign to *Numbers* and suggests baptism. It seems, therefore, that this is another instance of a Jewish Christian elaboration, this time based on *Num.* 19, a passage which formed part of two sets of *testimonia*, those on ξύλον and those on κόκκινος. This would suggest that the *midrashim* were built up around the *testimonia*.

A second group of Jewish Christian *midrashim* is linked with *II Esdras*.[42] The first example is of special interest. It concerns a passage where Justin reproaches the Jews with having cut out of the Old Testament passages containing Christian allusions. These passages are in fact Christian. The first is the addition of ἀπὸ τοῦ ξύλου to *Ps.* 95 which has already been mentioned; the second is a *midrash* on *II Esdras*. Justin states the case thus:

> From the expositions (ἐξηγήσεις) which Esdras gave of the law of the Passover, they have removed this: And Esdras said to the people: This Passover is our Saviour (σωτήρ) and our refuge. And if you reflect, and the thought arise in your heart that we are to humble Him on a cross (σημεῖον), and afterwards put our hope in Him, this place will never be laid desolate, saith the Lord of Hosts. But if you do not believe in Him nor hearken to His preaching (κήρυγμα) you shall be a laughing stock to the Gentiles (*Dial.* LXXII, 1).

42. I.e., the LXX ᾿Εσδρας β΄, corresponding to the MT *Ezra*, not the apocalyptic *II Esdras* of the Apocrypha, which is referred to throughout as *II (4) Esdras*.

Lactantius[43] gives the same text with variants which prove that he did not take it from Justin. The passage is an elaboration of *II Esd.* 6: 19 ff. Its Christian character is quite obvious.[44] The expression 'This Passover is our Saviour' recalls *I Cor.* 5:7: 'For our passover also hath been sacrificed, even Christ.' The word ταπεινοῦν appears in the Christian vocabulary of the Passion (*Phil.* 2:8), while the term σημεῖον in particular is a normal usage for the Cross, and replaces σταυρός. The context seems to show that this *midrash* was part of a group of testimonia on the Cross. More will have to be said about this group later, for it is the most important of them all.

It is a remarkable fact that the second *midrash* on *II Esdras* also refers to the Cross. It occurs in the *Blessings of Moses* by Hippolytus. After other prophecies about the Cross he continues: 'Blessed is the Lord who has stretched forth his hands and made Israel live again',[45] a saying which is an elaboration of *II Esdras* 7:27, and therefore belongs to the same context as the previous example. Its Christian character is equally certain. The Jewish Christians had picked out passages which mentioned 'the stretching out of the hands', such as *Is.* 65:2, or Moses' praying with outstretched arms. The verb ἐκτείνειν has thus an almost technical meaning in Jewish Christian language as connoting the Crucifixion. It must therefore have been introduced by a Christian, and as in the previous instance, the text belongs to the *testimonia* of the Cross. One would be very much inclined to assign a Palestinian origin to the *midrashim* of *II Esdras*.

Side by side with the *midrash* of *II Esdras* Justin quotes as coming from *Jeremiah* a passage which is not in the canonical *Jeremiah*, and is certainly a Christian *midrash*:

> From the words of the same Jeremiah have they likewise excised the following: And the Lord God remembered His dead which were of Israel (ἀπὸ Ἰσραὴλ τῶν νεκρῶν αὐτοῦ), those that had fallen asleep (κεκοιμημένων) in the earth of the tomb, and He went down (κατέβη) unto them to preach to them the good news (εὐαγγελίσα-σθαι) of His salvation (*Dial.* LXXII, 4).

This same text is quoted five times by Irenaeus who attributes it once to Isaiah (*Adv. haer.* III, 20:4), once to Jeremiah (IV, 22:1), and three times to Scripture in general (IV, 33:1; 33:12; V, 31:1). The Christian character of the text is certain, especially with its theme of the 'gospel'.

43. *Div. Inst.* IV, 18.   44. Cf. RESCH, *Agrapha*, p. 305.
45. Cf. *PO* XXVII, 131.

This passage is of the greatest importance, for it is probably the oldest extant attestation of the belief in the Descent into Hell. The words ἀπὸ Ἰσραήλ underline its Jewish Christian character,[46] and it witnesses to that same pre-occupation with the fate of the Old Testament saints which has already been shown to underlie this doctrine. It seems to be earlier than the *Gospel of Peter* of which it is probably the source, and which presents the doctrine with the same expression, 'those who sleep'.[47]

Probably to be associated with the same *midrash* of *Jeremiah* is another valuable text which is attributed in general terms to 'a prophet' in the *Epistle of Barnabas*: 'Again, He defineth concerning the Cross in another prophet, who saith; And when shall these things be accomplished? saith the Lord. Whensoever a tree (ξύλον) shall be bended and stand upright (ἀναστῇ), and whensoever blood shall drop (σταξῇ) from a tree (ξύλου)' (XII, 1). The same text, however, is quoted in the *Testimonia adversus Judaeos* of Gregory of Nyssa, and there attributed to Jeremiah, and it has therefore been argued[48] that it should be assigned to the *midrash* on *Jeremiah*; but while this may be valid as regards the first part of the passage, it must be contested for the second.

The text is in fact made up of two quotations. The first, which speaks of the tree bending down and standing upright, is one of the *testimonia* of the Cross. This alone would emphasise the Christian character of the passage, but the actual word used, ἀναστῇ, is also of great importance.[49] It has already been remarked that this verb is almost a Christian technical term connoting the resurrection, and was frequently intruded into the *testimonia*; and here it is applied to the Cross itself. The idea of the Cross coming back to life may seem a strange conception, but it is in fact precisely the one found in the *Gospel of Peter*, in which (39–42) the Cross comes out of the tomb, and rises with Christ, after having been buried with him.[50]

46. Cf. BIEDER, *Die Vorstellung von der Höllenfahrt, J.-C.*, pp. 135-153.

47. On the relation between this text and the *Gospel of Peter*, cf. below, pp. 235 ff. The passage calls for special study in connection with the Descent into Hell, but it was necessary to indicate in the present context its doctrinal importance for archaic Jewish Christian theology. It will be observed that Irenaeus gives 'sanctus Israel', which supposes ἅγιος Ἰσραήλ in place of ἀπὸ Ἰσραήλ; but this seems to be a later correction intended to remove the narrowly Jewish Christian perspective of the primitive text.

48. Cf. RESCH, *Agrapha*, p. 320.

49. Cf. RESCH, *ibid*.

50. When it is remembered that the previous passage from the *midrash* on *Jeremiah* also exhibited parallels to the *Gospel of Peter*, it seems likely that the *Apocryphon of Jeremiah* must also have derived from the same environment.

Two final comments on this part of the quotation are called for.[51] The first is that Irenaeus in recounting this doctrine of the risen Cross associates it with a 'certain Elder' (*Adv. haer.* IV, 27:1–2), which would seem to imply an identification of the Elder with the author of this *midrash*. If so, then it would not be rash to conclude that the *midrashim* under consideration go back to the Elders, and form part of their tradition—it was after all they who were the theologians of primitive Jewish Christianity. Secondly, there appears to be a relationship between this passage and *Mt.* 27:52, where the words κεκοιμημένων ἁγίων occur.[52] It is perfectly possible that it is *Matthew* which is dependent on the *midrash* here, and not the other way round, since it is known that the New Testament writers made use of the *testimonia*. If this were indeed so, it would be yet another indication of the great antiquity of the *midrash*.

The second part of the passage, however, poses a different question. It will be observed in the first place that the words occur independently in a Christian interpolation in *II* (4) *Esd.* V, 5. Furthermore, the expression αἷμα στάζειν appears in a variant reading from the *Life of Moses* by Gregory of Nyssa in connection with the bunch of grapes hanging from a pole in *Num.* 13:23. Gregory speaks of the cluster 'hanging (κρεμασθέντα)[53] and dripping blood (αἷμα στάξαντα)' (II, 270).[54] But the most interesting point of all is the link established by the *Life of Moses* between the expression 'dripping blood' and *Num.* 13:23. It may well be asked whether this is not also the true context for the second half of the quotation from *Barnabas*.

The bunch of grapes hanging from the wood, and with the juice dropping from it, was in fact an ancient symbol of Christ on the Cross. The *Blessings of Isaac* by Hippolytus, which contains so many Jewish Christian elements, reads at one point: 'Since he himself, hanging (= κρεμασθείς) from the wood,[55] was grape and bunch, he who, pierced in the side, made blood and water gush forth (αἷμα στάξας)' (18; *PO* XXVII, 83). This is related to

51. Reference to RESCH, *op. cit.*, will indicate the indebtedness of the present writer for the remarks in this paragraph.
52. Cf. p. 234 below.
53. The connotation of the Crucifixion in the use of this particular verb will at once be apparent: cf. *Lk.* 23:39; *Acts* 5:30; 10:39; *Gal.* 3:13.
54. It will be observed that both expressions occur also in the *Testimonia adversus Judaeos*, which would incline one to accept the authenticity of that work.
55. The linking of κρεμάννυμι and ξύλον will have been noted in the passages from *Acts* and *Galatians* cited in n. 53 above.

a group of *testimonia* in which wine is a symbol of the blood of Christ, and of which the principal texts are *Gn.* 49:11, quoted by Justin (*Dial.* LIII, 1; LIV, 1; LXIII, 2; LXXVI, 2) and by Hippolytus (*Ben. Isaac*, 18), *Deut.* 32:14: 'they drank wine, the blood of the grape', and *Is.* 25:6.[56] Without, therefore, ruling out the possibility that the fragment belongs to the *midrash* of *Jeremiah* it may be said that it does nevertheless at the same time contain an allusion to *Num.* 13:23.[57]

The most important *midrash* apart from that of *Jeremiah* is that of *Ezekiel. I Clement* offers a certain number of *agrapha*[58] which, it seems, should be referred to this. The first example reads:

The Master of the Universe Himself spake concerning repentance with an oath: For as I live, saith the Lord, I desire not the death of the sinner so much as his repentance (*Ezek.* 33:11); and He added also a merciful judgment: Repent ye, O house of Israel, of your iniquity; say unto the sons of My people, Though your sins reach from the earth even unto the heaven, and though they be redder than scarlet and blacker than sackcloth, and ye turn (ἐπιστραφῆτε) unto Me with your whole heart and say Father, I will give ear unto you as unto a holy people (VIII, 2-3).

This certainly belongs to a *midrash* of Ezekiel, and may well be described as added (προστιθείς) to a quotation from the prophet! Moreover, Clement of Alexandria when he quotes it attributes the last phrase to Ezekiel (*Paed.* I, 10:91). Its Christian character, without being marked, is nevertheless apparent. The term πατήρ, applied to God, though it occurs in the Old Testament (cf. e.g. *Jer.* 3:19; *Is.* 63:16; 64:7), has a Christian

56. Cf. C. Leonardi, *Ampelos*, Rome, 1947, pp. 25-51.
57. It is possible that certain *agrapha* ascribed to Jeremiah may also belong to this *midrash*. Thus Barnabas after quoting *Jer.* 4:4 continues: 'And again He saith, Hear, O Israel, for thus saith the Lord thy God. Who is he that desireth to live for ever (εἰς τον αἰῶνα)? Let him hear with his ears the voice of My servant (παιδός)' (IX, 2). παῖς is, of course, one of the particular designations of Christ in the primitive community (cf. L. Cerfaux, 'La première communauté chrétienne à Jérusalem' in *Rec. L. Cerfaux*, II, p. 141), but as the term derives from the Servant of Yahweh in *Isaiah* (52:13 f.) it might be better to think of a *midrash* of the latter prophet. This particular *agraphon* recalls another, also in *Barnabas* (VI, 3): 'Then again what saith He? And whosoever shall set his hope on Him shall live for ever (εἰς τὸν αἰῶνα)', which Resch (*op. cit.*, p. 313) connects with *Is.* 28:16. Both these passages therefore are more probably to be ascribed to the *midrashim* of *Isaiah*.
58. Cf. Glossary s.v.

ring about it; the expression 'blacker than sack cloth' is the general language of apocalyptic, but it brings to mind in particular *Rev.* 6:12. The text also contains allusions to other prophets, notably *Is.* 1:18: 'Though your sins be as scarlet.' It is in fact an agglomeration of various Old Testament elements, but it certainly seems to be the work of a Christian hand.

I Clement presents other *agrapha* related to the same *midrash*, as, for example:

Wretched are the double-minded ($\delta\acute{\iota}\psi\upsilon\chi o\iota$), which doubt ($\delta\iota\sigma\tau\acute{\alpha}$-$\zeta o\nu\tau\epsilon s$) in their soul and say, These things we did hear in the days of our fathers also, and behold we have grown old, and none of these things have befallen us. Ye fools, compare yourselves unto a tree; take a vine. First it sheddeth its leaves, then a shoot cometh, then a leaf then a flower, and after these a sour berry, then a full ripe grape. Ye see that in a little time the fruit of the tree attaineth unto mellowness (XXIII, 3).

The same text, save for a few slight variants, is also found in *II Clem.* (XI, 2-4) with the added ending: 'So likewise my people had tumults and afflictions: but afterwards they shall receive gifts' (XI, 4).

This text presents certain points of contact with the canonical *Ezekiel*,[59] but more probably it belongs to the collection of *logia*.[60] The term $\delta\acute{\iota}\psi\chi o s$ especially is typical of archaic Christian spirituality, appearing in the *Didache, Barnabas* and *Hermas*,[61] while there is a very clear association with *James* 4:8: 'Woe to those of a double soul.' The verb $\delta\iota\sigma\tau\acute{\alpha}\zeta\epsilon\iota\nu$ also appears in *Hermas* (*Mand.* IX, 5). On the other hand, the theme bears a close resemblance to *II Pet.* 3:4, with the same allusion to the 'brethren'; there the $\delta\acute{\iota}\psi\upsilon\chi o\iota$ are called $\dot{\epsilon}\mu\pi\alpha\hat{\iota}\kappa\tau\alpha\iota$. Finally the growth of a tree was a common symbol in the Synoptics.

The contacts between this text and *Hermas*, and its presence in *Clement* will be noted. All this indicates a Roman setting. Moreover, it has been noted earlier that *Hermas* has Essene antecedents, and this text exhibits similar characteristics. The concept of $\delta\acute{\iota}\psi\upsilon\chi\acute{\iota}\alpha$ is related to the doctrine of the Two Ways, and the tree is a frequent theme of the *Psalms of Thanksgiving*. It is therefore likely that the passage is connected with an Essene

59. Cf. RESCH, *op. cit.*, p. 326.   60. Cf. Glossary s.v.
61. Cf. O. J. SEITZ, 'Antecedents and Signification of the term $\delta\acute{\iota}\psi\upsilon\chi o s$', in *JBL*, LXVI, 1947, pp. 211-219: cf. also chap. 13, pp. 362 ff. below.

Christian environment, which would explain the very Jewish nature of the language and the eschatological slant. In this respect it is clearly very different from the *midrash* of *Jeremiah*, which comes from a more Alexandrian background.

Such are the chief Jewish Christian *midrashim* that have been preserved. An examination of the text of the *agrapha* reveals a number of other passages quoted as Scripture which do not appear as they stand in the Old Testament, but for the most part it is simply a question of straight quotation with the alteration of one of two expressions.[62]

Nevertheless the texts quoted in this section form an important group, both because they display the workings of Jewish Christian exegesis and because of their doctrinal content.

THE INTERPRETATION OF GENESIS

Another field in which Jewish Christian exegesis seems to depend on that of Judaism is the interpretation of the first chapters of Genesis, and there is a good deal of evidence that this esoteric exegesis occupied an important place in later Judaism.[63]

The first source of information is the writings of Philo. It is not proposed to make use of them in this book in view of the fact that they belong to Hellenised Judaism, and are dependent upon Greek philosophy. But it is nevertheless true that Philo had some contact with Palestinian Judaism, and frequently records exegeses that date from before his time. The exposition of the first chapters of *Genesis* has an important place in his work, and this is an indication of the significance attached to such exegesis by contemporary Jewish speculation.

A second source of evidence is to be found in Later Judaism. The speculations of the Cabbala consist largely of a sacred cosmology arrived at by way of elaborations on the opening chapters of *Genesis*; and various elements in this material, such as the immense importance attached to the *bereshith*,[64] suggest that its background must stretch even to the early days

62. This applies, for instance, in the case of *I Clement* XXIX, 3; L, 4. RESCH associates these texts with an *Apocryphon of Ezekiel*, but in fact they belong to the category of *targumim* studied above, rather than to that of *midrashim*.
63. Cf. especially G. LINDESKOG, *Studien zum neutestamentlichen Schöpfungsgedanken*, Uppsala, 1952, pp. 85-159.
64. Cf. pp. 166 ff. below.

with which we are immediately concerned.[65] Finally, there is a third source of information in the *Hermetic Writings*, especially the *Poimandres*, pagan speculations on *Genesis*, but with a Jewish basis having some points of contact with Philo.[66]

This interest in speculations on *Genesis* seems to have been a feature of early Christianity as well.[67] 'The First Book of Moses played an immense role in the first centuries of the Church's history.'[68] Eusebius records that several authors such as Rhodo (*HE* V, 13:8), Apion and Candidus (V, 27) wrote commentaries on the Hexaemeron[69]; and the subject seems to have had a special importance among the Gnostics. The *Apophasis*, attributed by Hippolytus (*Elench.* VI, 12–18) to Simon, is largely an exposition of *Gn.* 1–3, while Irenaeus devotes a whole chapter to the exegesis which Mark the Magician gave to the Hexaemeron (*Adv. haer.* I, 18:1). But above all, the writings of the earliest Church authors contain numerous passages which constitute speculative exegeses of *Genesis*, and in which Jewish influences are easily discernible.

It is noteworthy that the New Testament authors already provide evidence of the existence of these speculations. The Prologue of *John* is manifestly based upon the opening of Genesis, as the words ἐν ἀρχῇ indicate. Furthermore, in *Ephesians* Paul presents the union of man and woman as a figure of Christ and the Church, and designates this creation as a μυστήριον, that is, a hidden secret only revealed in recent times. These two examples introduce us to two types of speculation on *Genesis*, the one concerned with pre-existent realities, the other with the proclamation of eschatological events. Both these types will be met with again in the writing of Jewish Christians.

The first witnesses come from the traditions of the Elders. 'Papias', records Anastasius Sinaiticus, 'interpreted the entire Hexaemeron as

---

65. The Old Testament apocrypha, *Jubilees* and *II* (4) *Esdras*, provide a certain amount of material: cf. L. Gry, 'La création en sept jours d'après les Apocryphes de l'Ancien Testament', *RSPT*, vi, 1908, pp. 276–293.
66. As C. H. Dodd has shown: *The Bible and the Greeks*, London, 1935, pp. 99–147. Grant ('Theophilus of Antioch to Autolycus', *HTR*, XL, 1947, p. 234) remarks, 'In Imperial times interest in cosmogony was widespread, and the book of Genesis was much admired and discussed', quoting in support Numenius, Galienus and Longinus.
67. For the Ebionites cf. Schoeps, *Urgemeinde, Judenchristentum, Gnosis*, pp. 44–61.
68. Cf. Kretschmar, *op. cit.*, p. 31.
69. I.e., the account of the Creation of the world in six days; the word is a patristic technologism.

applying to Christ and the Church', just as did Pantaenus.[70] There may be an echo of these speculations of Pantaenus in the *Eclogae Propheticae* of Clement of Alexandria, which represent Jewish Christian exegetic traditions transmitted orally. The first sections are largely devoted to *Genesis*. 'In the beginning God created the heaven and the earth, the earthly things and the heavenly things' (III, 1); here 'heaven' and 'earth' refer not to material realities, but, as the sequel shows, to two categories of spirits. Again, 'The Scriptures use the words "heavens" and "waters" to designate pure powers, as we see also in Genesis' (I, 2). Thus 'the heavens' and 'the waters above the firmament' designate the creation of the angels.

It will be observed that the creation of the angels is prior to the creation of the material world. This was not the conception of traditional Judaism, in which the angels had bodies of fire, and were created after the fire, just as the fish were created after the sea, and four-footed things after the land. The same conception occurs again in *II Enoch*, in which the creation of the angels, of the animals and of the fish comes after that of their material setting (XXIX, 3). According to this view the angels were created only on the fourth day of creation,[71] but Clement's text gives evidence of another view which interpreted the words of *Genesis* in an allegorical manner—a tendency which seems indeed to have been already present in Judaism itself.[72] The same statement is to be found in Theophilus of Antioch (II, 13) and in the *Clementine Recognitions*.

Another exegesis given by Clement in the *Eclogae* (VII, 1) shows a different approach to this topic: 'Regeneration is wrought by water and the Spirit, likewise all generation, for: the Spirit of God moved upon the face of the water' (*Gn.* 1:2). This verse is the object of very varied commentaries. Theophilus interprets the passage in a literal sense: 'And by the Spirit which is borne above the waters, he means that which God gave as the principle of life of the whole creation' (II, 13; cf. I, 5). But the exegesis of which Clement gives evidence is also found elsewhere. In the *De baptismo* Tertullian takes up this theme of the parallel between the first creation and baptism: 'Water was the first to produce that which had life, that it might be no wonder in baptism if waters know how to give life' (III,

70. Cf. PREUSCHEN, *op. cit.*, p. 96.
71. Cf. H. B. KUHN, 'The Angelology of the Non-canonical Jewish Apocalypses'. *JBL*, LXVII, 1948, p. 214.
72. The LXX translation suggests such a sense for *Gn.* 1:1; cf. GRANT, 'Theophilus of Antioch to Autolycus', *HTR*, XL, 1947, p. 237, which also cites parallels from the Tannaite rabbis.

4). And later he says: 'Baptism . . . was even then prefigured by the very attitude which the Spirit assumed . . . who hovered over the waters' (IV, 1).

Speaking of the 'water which was above the firmament' (*Gn.* 1:7) Clement continues this exegesis:

> Since baptism is produced by water and the Spirit, being a remedy against the double fire, that which affects visible things and that which affects invisible things, there must be in water both the spiritual and the sensible element, the remedy against the double nature of fire. And the water which is on earth washes the body, whereas the water which is above the heaven, because it is spiritual and invisible, signifies the Holy Spirit, the purifier of invisible things (VIII, 1–2).

Here the waters above heaven are a symbol of the Holy Spirit. The references to the divine Persons of the Godhead in the exegesis of these verses of *Genesis* should be noted.

Something has already been said of Theophilus of Antioch and his exegesis of *Genesis*, which is both literal and speculative. In both these aspects it is marked by Jewish influences,[73] though only the speculative aspects, which are numerous and strange, will be considered here. Apart from his interpretation of ἐν ἀρχῇ and of the spiritual heaven mentioned above, he sees the life spread over the earth (*Gn.* 1:11) as a prefiguring of the resurrection—a theme that occurs frequently in archaic texts. It is already present in *I Cor.* 15:42 f. and *Jn.* 12:24, and reappears in *I Clem.* XXIV, 4–5. The sea (*Gn.* 1:10) represents the world: just as the sea would dry up without the rivers, so would the world without the Law of God[74]— a strictly prophetic exegesis, in which the realities described in *Genesis* are interpreted figuratively.

In this connection there is a curious elaboration on the subject of the islands:

> As in the sea there are islands . . . so God has given to the world which is driven and tempest-tossed by sins, assemblies (συναγωγαί)—we mean holy churches (ἐκκλησίαι)—in which are found the doctrines

73. Cf. KRETSCHMAR, *Studien zur frühchristlichen Trinitätsteologie*, pp. 58–59: also R. M. GRANT, 'The Problem of Theophilus of Antioch', *HTR*, XLIII, 1950, pp. 188–196, and especially 'Theophilus of Antioch to Autolycus', *HTR*, XL, 1947, pp. 234–242.
74. Cf. H. RAHNER, 'Das Meer der Welt', *ZKT*, LXVI, 1949, pp. 89–118; E. PETERSON, 'Das Schiff als Symbol der Kirche', *TZ*, VI, 1950, pp. 77–79.

of truth as in island-harbours of good anchorage. . . . And as again
there are other islands, rocky and without water, . . . on which ships
are wrecked—so there are erroneous teachings (αἱ διδασκαλίαι τῆς
πλάνης)—I mean heresies (II, 14).

This whole passage belongs to 'the setting of the Wisdom literature of
later Judaism'.[75] The transposition of 'synagogues' into 'churches' and
of 'erroneous teachings' into 'heresies' will be observed, giving the impression as it does of the adaptation of a Jewish commentary. The comparison of the Law to a river belongs to the same context (cf. Ecclus.
24:23–31).

What follows is still more surprising: '(The luminaries) contain the
pattern and type of a great mystery. For the sun is a type of God, and the
moon of Man' (II, 15). And Theophilus goes on to develop this idea; the
sun, like God, is immutable, the moon diminishes and increases like Man.
Its growing is a figure of the resurrection.[76] It will be remembered that in
Rev. 21:23 'the glory of God' occupies in the new creation the place that
was filled by the sun in the old. Again, in Ecclus. 27:11 the moon is the
figure of changeable Man. The context is still therefore that of the Wisdom
literature.

Theophilus then continues. 'In like manner also the three days which
were before the luminaries are types of the Trinity (τῆς τριάδος): of God,
and His Word, and His Wisdom. And the fourth is the type of Man who
needs light' (II, 15).[77]

75. Cf. KRETSCHMAR, op. cit., p. 36.
76. This is an archaic form of exegesis of Gn. 1:14. Later the sun and the moon are
taken as symbols of Christ and the Church (H. RAHNER, Griechische Mythen in christlicher
Deutung, pp. 200–215), as we find in Anastasius of Sinai (PG, LXXXIX, 513 C–D). We
may ask whether the latter has not also collected some elements of Jewish Christian
symbolism, since he recalls that Papias and Pantaenus interpreted the Hexaemeron with
reference to Christ and the Church. But the exegesis of Theophilus is different.
77. This exegesis in which the Days denote the Persons of the Godhead is of great
importance for Jewish Christian trinitarian theology. One aspect will call for detailed
study (cf. pp. 168 ff. below). For the moment it will be sufficient to recall that side by
side with this assimilation of the Three Days to the Three Persons which characterises
the Antiochene exegesis of Theophilus, there is the assimilation of the seven Days to the
seven protoctist archangels, the first of whom is the Son of God: this was the exegesis of
Hermas. Furthermore, 'Day' is one of the names of the Word in Justin, Hippolytus and
Marcellus of Ancyra, who quotes an ancient agraphon: 'I am the Day.' One of the sources
of this designation seems to be Gn. 1:5: 'God called the light Day.'
    It is interesting to note that a similar exegesis of the Three Days is found elsewhere:
firstly among the Gnostics for, according to Hippolytus, the Sethians teach that 'the

The assimilation of the Third Person to Wisdom should be observed. This was a special feature of Theophilus' trinitarian theology and was to be taken up by Irenaeus. But the remarkable thing is that this detail once more recalls the context of the Wisdom literature; the theme of the pre-existence of Wisdom is a central one with the Sapiential writers.[78]

On the fourth day were created the luminaries:

> The disposition of the stars, too, contains a type of the arrangements and order of the righteous and the pious and of those who keep the Law (τηρούντων τὸν νόμον) and the commandments of God. For the brilliant and bright stars are an imitation of the prophets; and therefore they remain fixed, not declining, nor passing from place to place. And those which hold the second place in brightness are types of the people of the righteous. And those again which change their position . . . which also are called planets, they too are a type of the men who have wandered from God, abandoning His Law (νόμον) and his prophets (II, 15).

It should be noted that the context of this passage contains no Christian allusion: it is concerned with the Law, and the Prophets of the Old Testament.[79]

The fifth day reverts to a theme already encountered, the waters of

78 It seems as though Christ affirmed himself to be the eschatological incarnation of this pre-existing Wisdom; cf. A. FEUILLET, *L'Église plérôme du Christ d'après Eph.* 1:23, in *NRT*, LXXVIII, 1956, pp. 462–466. But Theophilus represents another tradition connected with Jewish speculations centred on the exegesis of the creation. Kretschmar (*op. cit.*, pp. 27–62) is therefore right in seeing here an echo of a sapiential exegesis of the Hexaemeron in later Judaism. The three days also appear in the fragment preserved in the Egerton Papyrus (89–90; IDRIS BELL and SKEAT, *Fragments of an Unknown Gospel*, p. 47; cf. H. CHADWICK, 'The Authorship of Papyrus Egerton 3', *HTR*, LIX, 1956, p. 150). Cf. also CLEM. ALEX., *Strom.* V, 11:73, for whom the three days signify 'the mystery of the sphragis, that is, of the Trinity'.

79. Cf. R. M. GRANT, *The Problem of Theophilus*, pp. 188–189.

three days before the sun and the moon' are the three words that constitute all reality (V, 20). The text of the *Great Apophasis* attributed to Simon by Hippolytus is still more curious: 'When therefore (the Simonians) affirm that there are three days begotten before the sun and moon, they speak enigmatically of Mind and Intelligence, that is Heaven and Earth, and of the seventh Power, the indefinite one, for these Three Powers are produced antecedent to all the rest' (VI, 14). In a totally different connection Origen was to call the three divine Persons 'the Three Days eternally subsisting together' (*Com. Mt.* XII, 20). He also made an express reference to the paschal triduum, but behind all this he probably wishes to suggest the three primordial days.

baptism: 'Moreover, the things proceeding from the waters were blessed by God, that this also might be a sign of men's being destined to receive repentance and remission of sins, through the water and laver of regeneration' (II, 16). The text of Theophilus adds the allusion to things born of water, that is to fish. Soon Tertullian was to write: 'But we, little fish, who get our name from our ἰχθύς, Jesus Christ, we are born in water' (De Bapt. I, 2). This theme is very ancient, going back to Judaism[80] and appearing in the oldest sculptured monuments.[81] It is connected with a figurative exegesis of Gn. 1:20, with which Ambrose was to associate it explicitly (De Sacr. III, 3).

Finally Theophilus makes a long comparison of the different species of animals with the various categories of men: sea-monsters and flesh-eating birds are like the ambitious (πλεονεκτῶν) and the transgressors (παραβατῶν): four-footed and wild beasts are 'a type of some men, who neither know nor worship God: . . . but those who turn from their iniquities . . . in spirit fly upwards like birds' (II, 17). This type of allegory reaches far back into Judaism. It is found in the Letter of Aristeas concerning prohibitions in the matter of food (145–152), and is also developed in the Epistle of Barnabas (X, 1–12).

This passage from Theophilus has been studied in some detail, because it is the longest exegesis of the Hexaemeron to be found in this period. It is not the only one, but the most characteristic. The conclusion to be drawn from it is clearly its Jewish Christian character. 'There is a strong note of literalism and a clear reliance on Jewish exegesis. For this exegesis Theophilus usually turns to his Jewish and Jewish Christian masters. Almost everything in it has its parallel in Jewish haggadic exegesis.'[82]

Clement of Alexandria and Theophilus of Antioch have thus preserved precious data relating to Jewish Christian speculations about the Hexaemeron. But elements of these speculations are also to be found in a good many other authors. Since there will be occasion to consider them again during the course of this book,[83] it will be sufficient just to mention them here. Hermas has preserved elements of a speculation on the pre-existent Church in relation to the account of creation (Vis. I, 3:4). The theme of the

---

80. Cf. E. GOODENOUGH, Jewish Symbols in the Greco-Roman Period, v, 1956, pp. 30–61; A. ALLGEIER, 'Vidi aquam', RQ, XXXIX, 1931, pp. 23–43.
81. Cf. F. J. DÖLGER, ΙΧΘΥΣ, Das Fischsymbol in frühchristlicher Zeit, pp. 3–19.
82. GRANT, Theophilus of Antioch to Autolycus, pp. 235 ff.
83. Cf. pp. 294 ff., 396 ff. below.

seven days has also been the object of very varied speculations; apart from the tradition already mentioned which sees in them the seven archangels, there is another, attested by *Barnabas*, which gives the passage an eschatological meaning, seeing the seven days as the seven periods of the cosmic week: '(God) ended (his work) in six days. He meaneth this, that in six thousand years the Lord shall bring all things to an end' (XV, 4).

So far no reference has been made to the question of the creation of man and woman. Philo affords some idea of the speculations which took the two accounts of this creation for their subject. They occur again in *Poimandres*, and have an important place in Gnosticism. The most interesting element is the theme of the comparison of Adam and Eve to Christ and the Church,[84] which appears also in Paul (*Eph.* 5:23–25) and in John the Divine (*Rev.* 21:1–3). Some writers find a typological significance, but others speak of the creation of the pre-existent Church, especially *II Clement*. Once again it is a question of Jewish Christian speculations which Gnosticism took over and twisted to its own purposes.[85] In Ebionism they acquire a special character by which the masculine and feminine elements are in opposition as principles of good and evil.[86]

As with the speculations on the Creation, those on Paradise are of great variety, but all deeply indebted to the Jewish gnosis. Beside the purely literal exegeses, such as are to be found in Theophilus of Antioch (II, 24), there are again two types of speculation. One presents Paradise as the expression of pre-existent spiritual realities, and is reflected particularly in certain Gnostics, such as the Justin mentioned by Hippolytus who taught: 'The multitude of all these angels together is Paradise, concerning which Moses speaks: God planted a garden in Eden. It is by an allegory that the angels are styled trees of Paradise' (*Elench.* V, 26).

But the majority of these speculations are of the second type, and refer principally to the Church, as in the case of Papias, of whom Anastasius Sinaiticus says: 'He interpreted Paradise spiritually as referring to the Church of Christ.'[87] Papias certainly represents an Asiatic tradition attested by, among others, the *Revelation* of John, in which the images of the Bride, the City and Paradise, stand for the eschatological Church

---

84. Cf. pp. 301 ff. below.
85. Cf. A. Orbe, 'Cristo y la Iglesia en su matrimonio anterior á los siglos', *EE*, xxix, 1955, pp. 299–344.
86. Cf. H. J. Schoeps, *Urgemeinde, Judenchristentum, Gnosis*, pp. 56–59.
87. Cf. Preuschen, *op. cit.*, p. 96.

(*Rev.* 21, 22). For Irenaeus Paradise sometimes means the Church as at present existing: 'Men, if they do truly progress by faith . . . and receive the Spirit of God . . . shall be spiritual, as being planted in the Paradise of God' (*Adv. haer.* V, 10:1). The same interpretation is attested for Alexandria, Anastasius ascribing it to Pantaenus; it occurs also in the *Epistle to Diognetus* (XII, 2). Its presence in Syria is indicated by the *Odes of Solomon* (XI, 14), and in North Africa it is found in Tertullian (*Adv. Marc.* II, 4). Such a widespread distribution was made possible only by derivation from a common heritage of Jewish Christian tradition.

CHAPTER FOUR

THE TRINITY AND ANGELOLOGY

ONE of the characteristics of theology which is genuinely archaic and Jewish Christian is the use of terms borrowed from the vocabulary of angelology to designate the Word and the Holy Spirit.[1] 'Angel' is one of the names given to Christ up to the fourth century. After that the practice tends to disappear because of the ambiguity of the expression and of the use made of it by the Arians. But in the second century the word was used in a restricted sense which constituted the ordinary form in which the Jewish Christian theology of the Trinity was cast.

The practice can be traced to several sources. Of these the chief is the expression *mal 'ak Yahweh*, 'Angel of Yahweh', by which the Old Testament often refers to the manifestations of God under the old dispensation. The Christians appropriated these theophanies to the Word. The expression in no way implied that God himself was not involved, and indeed in such passages as that of the Burning Bush he quite plainly was. The application of the term Angel to the Word in such passages was therefore perfectly correct. But this conception, dear to the Apologists, is not specifically Jewish Christian.

A second source is the development of angelology in the true sense of the word in later Judaism. Here the angels constitute a supernatural world of intermediaries between God and men. Many of the functions attributed by Judaism to God were now conceded to them. Eminent figures begin to stand out among them: Raphael who appears in *Tobit*, Michael who is mentioned in *Daniel*, Uriel who guides Enoch in his ascension. Altogether there is a group of seven archangels, but Michael, the leader of the heavenly hosts, is the most important. According to Josephus the Essenes also had speculations on the angels. The most important of these

1. The history of this form of trinitarian theology has been written by J. BARBEL (*Christos Angelos*, Bonn, 1941) and G. KRETSCHMAR (*Studien zur frühchristlichen Trinitätstheologie*, Tübingen, 1956).

is the doctrine of the Angel of Light to whom God gave in charge the conduct of all history, and to whom is opposed the Prince of Darkness.

Finally Hellenistic Judaism had developed its own angelology parallel to that of Palestinian Judaism. The translation of the LXX is already a witness to this trend, which was to reach full development in Philo. For him the angels are the ministers of God in the administration of the cosmos and in the communication of revelations. Philo does not develop a hierarchy of them, but he assigns the Logos as their chief, 'the oldest of the angels, such that he is called an archangel' (*Conf.* 146). The Logos is also the *mal 'ak Yahweh*, who manifests himself in the theophanies. Thus in Philo is developed the idea of a certain relationship between the Logos, who is the $\pi\rho\hat{\omega}\tau$os $\mathring{\alpha}\gamma\gamma\epsilon\lambda$os, and the angels who are $\lambda\acute{o}\gamma$o.[2] The consequences of this will be seen especially in Origen and the Arians, but it also played a part in the formation of primitive theology.

How is this theology expressed in terms of angels to be interpreted?[3] It seems fairly certain that the use of such terms in no way implies that Christ is by nature an angel. The Semitic categories which underlie this expression are not Hellenistic concepts. In fact the word angel has an essentially concrete force; it connotes a supernatural being manifesting itself. The nature of this supernatural being is not determined by the expression but by the context. The word represents the Semitic form of the designation of the Word and the Spirit as spiritual substances, as 'persons', though the latter terminology was not to be introduced into theology until a good deal later. 'Angel' is its old-fashioned equivalent.

The use in this domain of expressions borrowed from apocalyptic speculations was, as will be seen plainly enough, to a high degree ambiguous. It is sometimes impossible to decide whether it is divine persons or angels

2. Gregory Dix ('The Seven Archangels and the Seven Spirits', *JTS*, XXVIII, 1926, pp. 233–285) has convincingly shown how 'the Angel of the Presence' was identified with one of the seven archangels, now Uriel, now Michael, without ceasing to be regarded as superior to the others.

3. This question has given rise to lively discussion. In a work compiled on a plan similar to this, MARTIN WERNER (*Die Entstehung des christlichen Dogmas*, Leipzig, 1941, pp. 302–389) held that for the Jewish Christian theologians Christ was an angel in the strict sense of the word, that is, a heavenly creature sent by God into the world. This thesis has been strongly opposed by WILHELM MICHAELIS (*Zur Engelchristologie im Urchristentum*, Basle, 1942, cf. also KRETSCHMAR, *op. cit.*, pp. 220–223) who has shown conclusively that the application of the term 'angel' to Christ in no way implied that he was regarded as a creature. He has also set aside Werner's views on the Son of Man as obscuring the question by mixing two distinct problems.

that are spoken of, while on the other hand there is no denying that in many cases a subordinationist tendency is implied by this terminology. In certain heterodox writers the Word and the Spirit are frankly likened to angels in the full sense of the term. All these reasons must be held responsible for the very rapid decline of this first form of the theology of the Trinity.

THE GLORIOUS ANGEL

A characteristic feature of the theology of *Hermas* is to call the Word 'glorious (ἔνδοξος) angel' or 'most venerable (σεμνότατος) angel'. He distinguishes very clearly the angel who visits him, whom he calls variously 'shepherd' and 'angel of repentance' from the supreme being, whom he also calls an angel, but who is quite different from the other since it is he who sends that other. His attributes also are quite different. As this point has been the subject of frequent discussion, the most important texts will be given here.

In the *Fifth Vision*, the Shepherd appears to Hermas and says: 'I was sent by the most venerable (σεμνότατος) angel' (V, 2). The latter is then the one who sends (ἀποστέλλειν) the angels. In the *Fifth Mandate* another characteristic appears: it is still the Shepherd speaking and he tells of those who do penance: 'For I will be with them and will preserve them; for they all were justified by the most venerable angel' (V, 1:7). This text is still more decisive, for justification is a strictly divine work. To attribute it to the most venerable angel is a clear affirmation of the divinity of the latter. In the *Fifth Similitude* the Shepherd says: 'thou who hast been strengthened by the holy (ἅγιος) angel, and hast received from him such (powers of) intercession . . . wherefore dost thou not ask understanding of the Lord? (Κύριος)' (V, 4:4). The holy angel and the Kyrios are placed on the same footing. The Shepherd on the other hand belongs to another sphere as is shown by what follows.

It should be noted that the expression 'holy' angel is equivalent to 'venerable' angel. In the *Seventh Similitude* the same being is called 'glorious' (ἔνδοξος) angel. Hermas complains of having been delivered to the angel of chastisement, and the Shepherd answers: 'It is necessary for thee to be afflicted; for so the glorious angel ordered concerning thee' (VII, 1). The same expression comes again in the same context in VII, 2 and VII, 3. But in VII, 5 he is called 'angel of the Lord': 'Thou must be afflicted as the angel of the Lord commanded, even he that delivered thee unto me.' This expression recurs several times but under various forms in the same chapter. The expression 'glorious angel' reappears again in IX, 1:3.

Finally the following passage occurs in the *Eighth Similitude*: '(The Shepherd) showed me a great willow, overshadowing plains and mountain. . . . And by the willow there stood an angel of the Lord, glorious (ἔνδοξος) and very tall, having a great sickle, and he was lopping branches from the willow, and giving them to the people that sheltered beneath the willow; and he gave them little rods about a cubit long' (VIII, 1:1–2). The angel next asks the people to return their branches, which he takes and examines. Then,

> the angel of the Lord commanded crowns to be brought. And crowns were brought, made as it were of palm-branches; and he crowned the men that had given up rods which had shoots and some fruit, and sent them away into the tower. And the others also he sent into the tower, even those who had given up rods green and with shoots, but the shoots were without fruit; and he set a seal (σφραγίς) upon them. And all they that went into the tower had the same raiment, white as snow (VIII, 2:1–3).

This text is of considerable interest for Jewish Christian liturgy. It is without a doubt concerned with the discipline of penance. This seems to be carried out on the occasion of an assembly of the community, and recalls the annual ceremony of the regrouping of members at Qumran, in accordance with the *Rule of the Community* (V, 20–24). Furthermore the imagery presents the same sacramental context as that of Jewish Christian baptism in the *Odes of Solomon*, with the crown, the white garment and the seal.[4] There appears to be also a biblical context, that of the Feast of Tabernacles, in the allusion to the branches of willow and palm. In rabbinic tradition these branches, which must be presented and examined on the first day of the Feast, are indeed, as in *Hermas*, the symbol of good works.[5]

Two points are of immediate interest. The first is the function attributed to the 'glorious angel of the Lord'. He distributes the branches; he distinguishes between the just and sinners; he crowns the just; he confers the seal; he introduces the people into the Tower, which is the Church of the Saints. These are divine functions: the judgment of souls, the rewarding

4. Cf. LAMPE, *The Seal of the Spirit*, 1951, p. 112.
5. The same conception is found in Methodius of Olympus: *Conv.* IX, 3.

of the just, the bestowal of grace, the incorporation into the Church of the Saints. For the Jewish Christian tradition they form part of the peculiar mission of the Son of God to whom judgment has been committed. The scene is a developed application of the imagery of apocalyptic and in particular of *Revelation* in which are found the crown (2:10), the seal (7:3), the white robe (7:9) and the palms (7:9). Hermas applies all this to the anticipation of the judgment which he sees in penance.

The second point to consider is the colossal stature of the 'glorious angel'. This again is specifically characteristic of Jewish Christian teaching,[6] being a peculiarity of their representation of angels. It serves precisely to establish the transcendence of the 'glorious angel' by showing that he surpasses the angels infinitely. The same detail appears in the *Gospel of Peter*: 'The head of the first two (the angels who support Christ in his Ascension) touched the sky; but the head of him whom they were escorting reached above the sky' (41). It is also found in other apocrypha,[7] the Elkesaites making extravagant speculations about it (*Hippolytus, Elench.* IX, 13:2). Above all it appears again in *Hermas* with reference to the Son of God: 'I see . . . a man of such lofty stature that he overtopped the tower' (*Sim.* IX, 6:1). This manner of representation passed into primitive iconography in which Christ is often shown as taller than the persons who surround him.[8]

The Word and Michael

It appears certain then that the 'glorious angel' of Hermas represents the Word himself, and most critics would agree on this point. However, a certain number of other Jewish Christian texts reveal stranger representations. There is first of all the one which presents the Word in the context of the seven archangels.[9] It introduces a new problem, for it is not now merely a question of a simple analogy of terms by which ἄγγελος was used to denote the Word. The Word is here expressly designated in a particular relationship to the angels. This is a transformation of the theme of the seven archangels as this appeared in later Judaism (*Tobit*), which now becomes the theme of the six archangels who surround the Word of God.

6. Cf. pp. 21, 65 above.
7. E.g., 'Acts of Peter, James and Andrew', *PG*, CIII, 389; cf. also *Acts of Perpetua and Felicity*, 4 and 10.
8. Cf. GRILLMEIER, *Der Logos am Kreuz*, Munich, 1956, pp. 56–62.
9. This theme has been extensively studied by BARBEL: *Christos Angelos*, pp. 192–223.

Hermas again provides the best starting point. He writes in the *Ninth Similitude*:

> Didst thou see the six men and the glorious (ἔνδοξος) and mighty man in the midst of them, him that walked about the tower and rejected the stones from the building? . . . The glorious man is the Son of God, and those six are the glorious angels who guard him on the right and on the left. Of these glorious angels not one shall enter in unto God without him; whosoever shall not receive His Name, shall not enter into the Kingdom of God[10] (IX, 12:7–8).

Here the glorious and colossal being already mentioned is explicitly identified with the Son of God, and his transcendence in relation to the angels is equally clearly indicated. He is the sole mediator. The text seems even to be an attack upon the cult of angels, and there could therefore be no question of the Word's being considered here as an angel.

That this was an habitual conception with Hermas is proved by the fact that with him, contrary to the general practice, there are never more than six archangels. So in the *Third Vision*, the aged woman who is the Church, is accompanied by six young men (III, 1:6); they are the holy angels, created before all other creatures (πρῶτοι κτισθέντες), 'to whom the Lord delivered all His creation to increase and to build it, and to be masters of all creation' (III, 4:1–2), a feature which occurs again later (III, 10:1). Now in Clement of Alexandria the first-created angels are *seven* in number, and the Logos is not counted amongst them. The representation we find in Hermas is therefore rigorously Jewish Christian.[11]

Subsequent traces of this development are found in various forms. An amethyst is extant on which is engraved the inscription: 'Raphael, Renel, Uriel, Ichtys, Michael, Gabriel, Azael.'[12] This amethyst represents Christ by the ☧; hence it is obviously he that is designated by 'Ichtys' and surrounded on either side by three angels, those of the right hand and those of the left, as in Hermas. But the most ancient document is the pseudo-

10. Cf. also IX, 6:1–2.
11. It should, moreover, be noted that in *Ezek.* 9:2 the being clothed in linen, who marks the elect with the sign of the *tau*, is distinguished from the six archangels. Hippolytus (*Comm. Dan.* IV, 57) identifies him with the Word. It would seem that Hermas was also inspired by *Ezekiel*. Cf. PETERSON, 'Das Amulet von Akra,' *Aegyptus*, XXXIII (1953), pp. 172–178.
12. Cf. LECLERQ, art. 'Anges', *DACL*, I, 2088.

Cyprianic Treatise *De Centesima sexagesima tricesima*.[13] In this the same representation occurs in a heterodox context and in relation to the theme of the six days and the seventh.

The following is the relevant passage: 'When the Lord created the angels from fire to the number of seven, he determined to make one of them his Son. He it is whom Isaiah declares to be the Lord Sabaoth. We see that there remained then six angels who had been created with the Son' (216, p. 82). The author then recalls the story of creation, how God ceased to create on the sixth day, and blessed the seventh, and he continues: 'This day the ascetic imitates without knowing it, when he sets a term to malicious deeds.'

This text is plainly of Jewish Christian inspiration. There are however several intrusive themes. There is first of all the one already encountered in Hermas, but with a subordinationist character which it does not have in his work. Then there is the Jewish tradition in which Sabaoth is the name of an angel, and of which there is evidence in particular in the magic papyri.[14] The anonymous author identifies this angel with the Word. Finally there is the interesting parallel drawn between the creation of the first six days and that of the six archangels, and between that of the seventh day and that of the Son of God. The basis for this may be those texts in which Christ calls himself the Sabbath, the repose of the soul.[15] It should also be remembered that Day is one of Justin's names for Christ.[16] This exegesis of the story of creation was to be continued in Byzantine iconography.[17]

This designation of Christ as the seventh day may be compared to another, which comes in *Hermas*, in which Christ is identified with the archangel Michael. In the parable of the willow-tree it was said that 'by the willow there stood an angel of the Lord, glorious (ἔνδοξος) and very tall' (*Sim.* VIII, 1), and it has been shown that this angel is clearly the Word. Hermas

13. Edited by REITZENSTEIN, 'Eine Frühchristliche Schrift von der dreierlei Früchten', *ZNW*, xv, 1914, pp. 74–88.
14. Cf. BARBEL, *op. cit.*, p. 193. Origen (*Com. Joh.* 1, 31) records hearing from a Jew that Sabaoth is a name of God.
15. Cf. *Bible et Liturgie*, pp. 304–314.
16. *Dial.* C, 4. Marcellus of Ancyra quotes a logion in which Christ says of himself: 'I am the Day' (Eusebius, *Adv. Marcel.* I, 2; cf. W. BAUER, *Das Leben Jesu*, p. 384). Clement of Alexandria writes, 'Christ is frequently called Day' (*Eclog. Proph.* LIII, 1); cf. pp. 169 ff. below.
17. Cf. M. TH. D'ALVERNY, 'Les Anges et les Jours', *Cah. Arch.*, IX, 1957, pp. 271–300.

explains the parable as follows: 'the great and glorious (ἔνδοξος) angel is
Michael, who hath the power over this people and is their captain. For this
is he that putteth the Law into the hearts of the believers. Therefore he
himself inspecteth them to whom he gave it' (VIII, 3:3). The comparison
of the two texts shows that it is really the Word who is called Michael.[18]
This is not surprising, for Michael in Jewish tradition is the chief of the
archangels and the prince of all the heavenly hosts. Once the archangels
came to be considered as only six in number with the Word as their chief,
it was natural that the name of Michael, which is the title of this chief,
should be attributed to the Word. To this may be added the fact that the
title ἀρχιστράτηγος, given to Michael in a number of texts,[19] is applied
to the Word by Christians. While, however, the name Michael, which
tended to confuse the issue, was only given to the Word in primitive
theology, the title of ἀρχιστράτηγος was to endure in tradition, particularly
in Methodius and Eusebius.[20]

It is interesting to observe the two attributes ascribed to Michael in
the text just quoted. First, it is he who governs the people. Such was indeed
Michael's function as regards the people of Israel (*Dan.* 10:13); but with
the coming of the New Covenant the Word of God replaces the angels,
whose mission was only a preparatory one.[21] It is he who now becomes the
chief of the people of God. This stands out more clearly if we consider the
second characteristic given by Hermas. Judaism believed that the Old
Testament law had been given by the angels.[22] The *Book of Jubilees* in
particular attributes its promulgation to Michael (I, 27). But Paul contrasts
with this the new Law communicated by the Word himself (*Gal.* 3:20;
Heb. 2:3). In Hermas this function is performed by Michael. This name
must therefore be regarded as a name of the Word.

The assimilation of Michael to the Word is not, however, peculiar to
Hermas. It occurs in other Jewish Christian texts which show up still
more clearly the unskilful christianisation of the Jewish theme, as in the
following passage from *II Enoch*:

> The Lord called me by his own mouth: Take courage, Enoch, be not
> afraid, and stand for ever before my face. And Michael, the great

18. As HARNACK, SEEBERG and the majority of critics have recognised; BARBEL, *op. cit.*,
pp. 230–231. Cf. also BAKKER, 'Christ an Angel?', *ZNW*, XXXII, 1933, p. 257.
19. Cf. BARBEL, *op. cit.*, p. 227.
20. *Ibid.*, p. 236.
21. Cf. J. DANIÉLOU, *Les anges et leur mission*, 2nd edn., p. 19.
22. JOSEPHUS, *Ant.* XV, 136; *Gal.* 3:19; *Acts* 7:53; *Heb.* 2:2

archangel of the Lord lifted me and brought me before the face of the Lord. And the glorious ones bowed down and said: Let him go up. And the Lord said to Michael: Take Enoch and strip him of his earthly garments; and anoint him with good oil; and clothe him again in vesture of glory (XXII, 4–9).
•

Two details in this passage indicate an allusion to the Word. The first is the resemblance to the *Ascension of Isaiah*, in which there is a similar scene. But in the latter work it is 'the Lord', that is, the Son of God who takes the role played by Michael in *II Enoch*, namely that of comforting the visionary and of bringing him before the face of God (XXII, 6).[23] Furthermore, the description of Michael in *II Enoch* is remarkably reminiscent of that of the Son of God in *Hermas*; he is again called 'angel of the Lord', 'mighty angel', 'Michael'; his functions consist in the same way in introducing people into the holy place, which is the Church of Paradise, of giving vestments of glory, of anointing or giving the seal. The chief difference is that in *II Enoch* the christianisation of the theme is a degree less advanced.

There is an analogous example in the *Testament of Dan*. The Christian author writes: 'Draw near unto God and unto the angel that intercedeth for you, for he is a mediator between God and men' (VI, 2). This theme of the angel who intercedes for Israel is to be found elsewhere in the Testaments (*Test. Levi* V, 6),[24] and this angel is clearly Michael. But now the angel does not intercede for Israel only; he is 'the mediator between God and men'—a Christian expression to be found in *I Tim.* 2:5. Furthermore, the angel does not defend Israel against its enemies; his combat is 'against the Kingdom of the Enemy' (VI, 2). It certainly looks as if there is here another transposition from the Jewish theme of Michael to the Christian theme of the Word.[25]

There is a similar conception in the heterodox Jewish Christianity of the Ebionites. Tertullian says of them: 'They make of him a mere man, though more glorious than the prophets, in that they say that an angel was in him' (*De Carn. Christ* XIV, 5). Epiphanius goes further: 'They do not say that the Word was begotten of the Father, but that he was created as one of the archangels, and that he rules over the angels and over everything that has

23. Cf. also IX, 4–5.
24. Cf. DE JONGE, *The Testaments of the Twelve Patriarchs*, p. 93.
25. The germ of the idea is, however, already present in a text from Qumran (*DSW*, XVII, 5–7).

been made by the Almighty' (*Pan.* XXX, 16:4).[26] This is the same teaching as in the pseudo-Cyprianic treatise cited earlier. The thought is cast in heretical mould, reducing Christ to the first of the archangels, that is to say, identifying him with Michael. Hermas' conception was quite different. He defined Christ in terms borrowed from Jewish speculations on Michael.

The Ebionite conception, however, is concerned not with the theme of the seven archangels, but with that of the seventy angels of the nations,[27] as is proved by the Clementines. The following passage occurs in the *Recognitions*:

> Every nation has an angel, to whom God has committed the government of that nation, . . . for God . . . has divided the nations of the earth into seventy two parts and over these He hath appointed angels as princes. But to the one among the archangels who is greatest was committed the government of those who, before all others, received the worship and knowledge of the Most High God. . . . The princes of the several nations are called gods. But Christ is God of princes who is judge of all (II, 42).

Moreover the author explains that in all these cases the word 'god' is not to be taken in its strict sense.[28]

In the *Homilies* the identification of Michael the angel protector of Israel with the Son of God is expressed even more positively:

> (The Father), when he had marked out the limits of the nations by seventy different languages, according to the number of the sons of Israel, who went into Egypt and who were seventy persons, gave to his Son, who is called 'Lord', and who made heaven and earth, the Hebrews as his portion, and appointed him to be god of gods—by gods I mean those who received the rest of the nations for their portion. Laws therefore went forth from all those called gods to their portions (that is to say, all the rest of the nations); and in like manner from the Son of the Lord of all went forth the law which is found among the Hebrews (XVIII, 4).

26. Cf. H. J. Schoeps, *Theologie and Geschichte des Judenchristentums*, pp. 80–82.
27. Cf. J. Daniélou, 'Les sources juives de la doctrine des anges des nations chez Origène', *RSR*, XXXVIII, 1950, pp. 132–137.
28. This usage may be compared with that of *DSW* XVII, 7–8, where it is said that 'God will exalt the empire of Michael among the gods, and the dominion of Israel over all flesh'.

A comparison of this text with the previous one shows that the author considers the Son of God to be Michael, the chief of the angels, as Epiphanius observed.

This is a development of the Jewish tradition[29] according to which, at the time of the division of languages, Michael was placed over the people of Israel and the other angels over the other peoples. The way in which this tradition was developed by the Ebionites and by the main body of the Church respectively shows clearly the different point of view of each. For the former, Christ is simply a new manifestation of the Angel of Israel; but for the Great Church Christ is the Word of God who dispossesses all the angels of their functions and unites all the nations under his sole sovereignty.[30] Whereas in the *Homilies* the angel who gave the Law to Israel, Michael, is the same who reappears in Christ, the New Testament contrasts the Law given by angels with the Gospel given by the Word.[31]

THE SPIRIT AND GABRIEL

Assimilation of Michael to the Word is confirmed by, and finds a counterpart in that of Gabriel to the Holy Ghost. The crucial text is the *Ascension of Isaiah*. 'The Angel of the Holy Spirit' is frequently mentioned here, and he is identical with Gabriel. Is this simply a title given to Gabriel, or is the Holy Ghost in fact represented in the form of the angel Gabriel? The question is still under discussion. 'The author of the *Ascension* makes free use of the expression "angel of the Holy Spirit" and we cannot be sure whether he means the third person of the Trinity or an angel.'[32] It is also possible that the author himself is not altogether sure. He is christianising earlier apocalyptic themes, and this process, as was observed in the case of the Word and Michael in *II Enoch*, may be more or less thoroughly carried out.

One of the first passages to be considered concerns the Resurrection of Christ. Among the attendant circumstances of this event the author lists the following: 'the descent of the angel of the Christian Church, he who will summon (sc. the elect) at the last days', and the opening of the tomb on the third day by 'the angel of the Holy Spirit and Michael, the prince

29. Cf. W. LUECKEN, *Michael*, 1898, pp. 13–14.
30. Cf. J. DANIÉLOU, *Les anges et leur mission*, pp. 11–50.
31. *Gal.* 3:19 f.; *Acts* 7:53; *Heb.* 2:2–3. In *Rev.* 12:7, 10 Michael defeats the dragon, but the dominion is given to Christ.
32. So Cardinal Tisserant in the preface to his translation (p. 14)

of the holy angels' (III, 15–16). This text recalls the *Gospel of Peter* (39), in which two angels—and there the beings involved quite definitely are angels—bear up the Christ as he comes forth from the tomb. But it is clear that there are very real differences between the two texts, the first of which is, of course, that in the *Ascension* allusion is made to three angels, not two. If, however, as is possible, the angel of the Christian Church really belongs to an earlier episode, and has nothing to do with the opening of the tomb, then the latter incident, as in the *Gospel of Peter*, would in fact be attended by only two angels.[33] Secondly, in the *Ascension* these two angels do not bear up the Risen Christ. This immediately suggests that it may be a matter here of more than angelic beings, and that as in *Hermas*, where Michael, the prince of the people of God, is one of the titles of the Son of God, this passage ought to be added to those in which the Word is called Michael.

This suggestion would be strengthened if it were possible to consider the angel of the Holy Ghost as the Holy Ghost himself, and in fact such a conclusion is irresistible in the light of other uses of the expression in the work. Thus chapter VII, 23 reads: 'I rejoiced with great joy, that those who love the Most High and His Beloved will afterwards ascend thither (into the seventh heaven) to their last end by the Angel of the Holy Spirit.' The function of introducing people into the celestial world is often given to Michael, in Jewish apocalyptic,[34] but it belongs also to Gabriel. Here, however, it is a question of entry not merely into heaven, but into the very sanctuary of the Trinity. The author has just said that 'the throne, the garments and the crowns' which symbolise this divine vocation of man are 'above all the heavens and their angels' (VII, 22). It must therefore be the Holy Ghost himself who is represented by this angel.[35]

Two final texts afford definite proof. Isaiah is admitted to the contemplation of the seventh heaven:

And I saw One standing, whose glory surpassed that of all, and His glory was great and wonderful. And . . . all the angels drew nigh and worshipped and sang praise. . . . And the angel said unto me: This is the Lord of all the splendours which thou hast seen. And whilst he was still speaking, I saw another Glorious One who was like Him, and the righteous drew nigh and worshipped and sang praise. . . . And I saw the Lord and a second angel, and they were standing. But the

33. As KRETSCHMAR (*op. cit.*, p. 94) would allow.
34. Cf. *II Enoch* XXII, 6.
35. TISSERANT (*op. cit.*, p. 156) admits the possibility of this.

second whom I saw was on the left of the Lord. And I asked: Who is this? and he said unto me: Worship him, for he is the Angel of the Holy Spirit, who rests upon thee, and who spake also in the rest of the righteous (IX, 27-36).

The Lord is the Word, and the Angel of the Holy Spirit is like him. There can be no doubt that this refers to the Third person of the Trinity. The first seat is on the right hand of God, the second is on the left hand— a detail borrowed in fact from the Jewish figure of Gabriel. They both transcend all the angels and are the object of the adoration of all creatures. Furthermore it is the angel of the Holy Spirit who spoke through the prophets. Nevertheless there is one detail which, while not casting any doubt on what has been said, indicates a certain subordinationism; the Lord and the Angel of the Spirit adore and praise God (IX, 40). This is one of the particulars in which the angelomorphic theology of the Jewish Christians was to exert an unfortunate influence on the theology of Origen and the Arians.

In a parallel text Isaiah contemplates the glorious ascension of Christ:

And I saw how he ascended into the seventh heaven, and all the righteous and all the angels praised Him. And then I saw him sit down on the right hand of that Great Glory, whose brightness I told you that I was not able to look upon. And also the angel of the Holy Spirit I saw sitting on the left hand. And this angel said unto me: Isaiah, son of Amoz, I now dismiss thee. . . . Return into thy earthly vesture until thy days are fulfilled. Then thou shalt return hither (XI, 32-35).

There is a strict parallelism here between the Beloved and the Holy Spirit; they share the same divine glory. These are among the most ancient Christian trinitarian texts, but in them the Second and Third Persons are presented in angelomorphic terms.

The *Ascension of Isaiah* makes it possible to throw light on another Jewish Christian text, *II Enoch*, which affords a complete parallel with it, and at the same time to show more explicitly that the angel of the Holy Spirit really is an adaptation of the Jewish theme of Gabriel. In it Gabriel is seen carrying out all the functions which in the *Ascension of Isaiah* belong to the Angel of the Holy Spirit. From this it may be concluded that the Angel of the Holy Spirit in the *Ascension* is a christianisation of the Jewish Gabriel theme, and conversely that the Holy Ghost should be recognised in the Gabriel of *II Enoch* just as the Word was recognised in Michael.

In an early passage Gabriel presents Enoch before the face of God:

> The Lord sent one of his Glorious Ones, Gabriel, who said to m
> Take courage, Enoch, be not afraid, arise and come with me and stand
> before the face of the Lord for ever. And I answered him: Alas, my
> Lord, my soul is gone out of me for fear. Call to me the men who
> brought me to this place. And Gabriel took me and placed me before
> the face of the Lord. And I saw the Lord, his face glorious and
> terrible. . . . And the Lord called me with his own mouth and said to
> me: Take courage, Enoch, be not afraid, arise and stand before my
> face for ever (XXI, 3–XXII, 5).

In this passage Gabriel performs the same functions of comforting and presenting as does the angel of the Holy Spirit in the *Ascension*, that is to say, he fulfils the role of a Paraclete. It will be observed that, again as in the *Ascension*, the angels who had till then accompanied Enoch can now do no more for him. Also, the words of Gabriel are repeated verbatim by the Lord, a feature which recalls the authoritative tone of the angel of the Holy Spirit in the final passage quoted above from the *Ascension*: 'He dismisses the prophet with the same authority as God.'[36]

The second passage is still more striking. It will be remembered that in the *Ascension of Isaiah*, the angel of the Holy Spirit sits at the left hand of the Lord. Now *II Enoch* reads: 'The Lord called me and placed me at his left hand, next to Gabriel, and I adored the Lord' (XXIV, 1).[37] Gabriel, then, is the Angel sitting on the left. There is thus a complete parallel here, which makes it quite certain that the angel of the Holy Spirit in the *Ascension* is an adaptation of Gabriel.

There is one last text which will introduce a new aspect of the assimilation of the Holy Spirit and Gabriel. In connection with the events following the Annunciation *Asc.* XI, 4 comments: 'But the angel of the Spirit appeared in this world, and after that Joseph did not put her away but kept Mary.' This is clearly a reference to the Angel Gabriel, the ordinary messenger for everything concerned with the Incarnation, and implies the equation of the Angel of the Holy Spirit with Gabriel. But since it has

36. TISSERANT, *op. cit.*, p. 211.
37. VAILLANT quotes the variant 'nearer than Gabriel' and prefers it (p. 29). But it seems less probable in every respect.

already been established that the Angel of the Holy Spirit is God the Holy Spirit, this indicates an assimilation of the angel Gabriel to the Holy Ghost in the episodes of the birth of Christ.

The Word and Gabriel

With this theme may be compared another Jewish Christian tradition which identifies the angel Gabriel in the scene of the Annunciation not with the Holy Ghost, but with the Second Person of the Trinity.[38] But this is not really an instance of the same conception. The Word is not defined in terms of an angel, he simply manifests himself in the form of an angel. This stems from another, more traditional line of thought which sees in the angels of the Old and New Testaments manifestations of the Logos, in the sense of the *mal'ak Yahweh*. This was the general interpretation of the Old Testament theophanies at the beginning of the Christian era, and it is now extended to the New Testament.

There are two Jewish Christian texts which are of the first importance on this point. The first is the *Epistle of the Apostles*. In it Christ is represented as saying:

I took the form of the Angel Gabriel, I appeared unto Mary and spake with her; her heart accepted me; she believed and laughed. I, the Word, entered into her and became flesh. And I myself became a minister unto myself. . . . It was in the appearance of an angel that I acted thus. Thereafter did I return to my Father (14; *PO* IX, 198).

The meaning of the text is quite clear. It was the Word himself who appeared to Mary, to announce to her the Incarnation before accomplishing it. But to do so he took on the form of an angel, the angel Gabriel.

There is a parallel passage in the Jewish Christian *Sibylline Oracles*:

'In the last times (the Word) came upon earth, and having abased himself, he arose a new light from the womb of the Virgin Mary. Having descended from heaven he put on a mortal shape. First of all he showed himself as Gabriel in pure and mighty form; then, as an archangel he spoke these words to the young maiden: Receive God in your spotless womb, O Virgin (VIII, 456–461).

38. Cf. BARBEL, *op. cit.*, pp. 235–262.

It is again the Word himself who appears to Mary in the guise of the archangel, to announce his Incarnation to her before accomplishing it; and this is still the traditional theme of the manifestation of God in the form of an angel, not that of the presentation of a Person of the Godhead in angelological imagery.[39]

THE ANGEL ISRAEL

In Jewish Christian teaching there are traces of the application of other angelic titles to the Word beside those of Michael and Gabriel. In the list of names of the Word, which Justin gives more than once, there occurs the following statement: 'He (sc. the Word) was also called Israel, and he bestowed this name on Jacob' (*Dial.* LXXV, 2; cf. CXIV, 2: also CXXX, 3; CXXXIV, 6; CXXXV, 1, 3).[40] Justin adds various comments on this: 'I would like you to teach me, asked Trypho, the virtue ($\delta\acute{v}\nu\alpha\mu\iota s$) of the name Israel' (CXXV, 1); Justin replies that the angel who appeared to Jacob 'inasmuch as he was the firstborn of all creation was God. . . . Israel had been a name of his from of old, and with it he surnamed the blessed Jacob' (CXXV, 3-5).

Thus the angel who appeared to Jacob was called Israel.[41] Furthermore, he was not an angel, but the firstborn, that is to say, the Word himself. This is an instance of the classic motif of Justin's theology, which sees the Logos in the angelic appearances in the Old Testament. Israel is simply a

---

39. This theme was also borrowed by the Gnostics, and twisted to suit their own teaching. Gabriel is no longer the Word, for the latter belongs to the Pleroma (cf. Glossary s.v.) on high, but an archon, the projection of the Word in the world below, who raises up the man Jesus in the womb of Mary. Irenaeus describes the teaching of Mark the Magician in the following terms: 'There were in the Tetrad Anthropos, Ecclesia, Logos and Zoe. From these emanated the powers which engendered the earthly, visible Jesus. The place of the Logos was taken by the angel Gabriel, that of Zoe by the Holy Spirit, that of Anthropos by the power of the Highest, that of Ecclesia by Mary' (*Adv. haer.* I, 15:3; cf. also *Pistis Sophia* VII, 12; LXII, 124). This is another clear example of the use of Jewish Christian concepts by the Gnostics who adapted them to their own systems. On the later forms of these perversions cf. F. J. DÖLGER, 'Die eigenartige Marienverehrung der Philomarianiten oder Kollyridianer in Arabien' in *Antike und Christentum*, I, pp. 112–118.

40. Cf. also HIPPOLYTUS, *Contra Noetum*, 5; *Ben. Moys.*, PO, XXVII, p. 132.

41. Israel as the name of an angel is found in the magical papyri (cf. J. BARBEL, *op. cit.*, pp. 207, 263), and in the Cabbala (cf. G. SCHOLEM, *Major Trends in Jewish Mysticism*, p. 62).

name of the Logos.[42] Justin seems to be indebted to Philo here to judge from the following passage: 'The firstborn Logos is the eldest ($\pi\rho\epsilon\sigma$-$\beta\upsilon\tau\alpha\tau\sigma$) among the angels; he is archangel, and bears many names, being called indeed "Beginning", "Name of God", "Word" . . . "He that seeth", "Israel" ' (*Conf.* 146–147).[43] In Philo then, as in Justin, Israel is one of the names of the firstborn, the Logos; but for Philo Israel does not denote the angel whom Jacob encounters, but Jacob himself who is an allegory of the Logos.

This idea reappears in a curious apocryphal work, the *Prayer of Joseph*, known to us through Origen.[44] In it Jacob says: 'I, Jacob and Israel, who speak to you am an angel of God and one of the principal ($\dot\alpha\rho\chi\iota\kappa\dot\sigma\nu$) spirits. I, Jacob, am called Jacob by men, but my name is Israel, for by God was I called Israel, "the man who sees God",[45] because I am firstborn ($\pi\rho\omega\tau\dot\sigma\gamma\sigma\nu\sigma s$) of all living things that receive their life from God' (*Comm. Jn.* II, 31). It is noteworthy that the same expressions, Firstborn, Beginning, He that sees God, are found here as occur in Philo and Justin, and it is difficult to avoid understanding by them something more than an angel. Israel has the same attributes as the Philonian Logos.

The continuation of the quotation in Origen confirms this:

'When', said Jacob, 'I arrived from Syrian Mesopotamia, Uriel the angel of God came out and said: I have come down upon earth, and I have set up my tabernacle among men, and: I am called by the name of Jacob. He became my rival and made war upon me. He fought against me saying that his name, which is the name of him that is before all the angels, would prevail over mine. I told him his name, and what his rank was amongst the sons of God: Are you not Uriel, the eighth after me, and I Israel, the archangel of the power of the Lord and the archistrategos among the sons of God? Am I not Israel the first of those who serve before the face of the Lord? And I will call upon my God by his eternal name' (*ibid.*).

42. It is in this sense that Justin interprets the expression $\theta\epsilon\dot\sigma s$ '$I\sigma\rho\alpha\dot\eta\lambda$ in *Ps.* 71:18 (EVV 72).
43. In an anonymous text from Nag Hammadi (no. 40) Israel designates the firstborn who dwells with Sabaoth: cf. DORESSE, *Les Livres secrets des gnostiques d'Égypte*, Paris, 1959, p. 189.
44. *Comm. Jn.* I, 31; II, 31; *Comm. Gen.* (*PG*) XII, 73B, 81B; *Hom. Num.* XVII, 4.
45. This derivation of the name Israel from '*ish rā'āh 'ēl* is of great antiquity, and occurs also in Philo.

There is no need to insist on the strangeness of this passage.[46] Each of the characters present claims the name of Jacob, but it is not the true name of either. The name of the angel who fights against Jacob is Uriel. Jacob's true name is Israel. But what are important are the qualifying epithets applied to him. He is the archangel of the power of the Lord[47]; and the fact that this title is parallel in construction to the title 'angel of the Holy Spirit' in the *Ascension*, and that the latter is used to designate God the Holy Spirit in person, suggests that this expression too may in effect be equivalent in meaning to 'the power of the Lord'. Again, the expression 'first ($\pi\rho\tilde{\omega}\tau o\varsigma$) angel' is used of the Word in a Novatianist inscription.[48] Above all, however, if Uriel is eighth in order after Israel, then the latter does not fall within the series of seven archangels. The schematisation is that of Clement of Alexandria, not of Hermas.

THE TWO SERAPHIM

In the symbolism considered hitherto there were two different systems. The first was concerned with the Logos, who was then regarded either as surrounded by six archangels and himself taking the place of the seventh, or as outside the number of the seven archangels and regarded as an eighth, as was the case with the angel Israel. But there was also another scheme, according to which the Son and Spirit were considered as the two Angels of the Presence transcending all others—as, for example, in the *Ascension of Isaiah*. In this text and *II Enoch* they appear as an adaptation of the figures of Michael and Gabriel, and it frequently happens that these two archangels are separated from the rest and treated on a common higher level.[49]

But other representations of this type exist which refer neither to Michael nor to Gabriel. The first is one which Origen says that he had from a Hebrew, and which identifies the Seraphim of *Isaiah* 6 with the Son and the Holy Ghost: 'The Hebrew said that the two Seraphim with six wings

46. For its influence at a later period cf. T. SCHNEIDER, 'Der Engel Jakob bei Mani', *ZNW*, XXXIII, 1934, pp. 218–220.
47. The parallel expression 'archistrategos of the power of the Lord', is regularly applied to the Word in Eusebius (*HE* I, 2:11; *Dem. Ev.* V, 19:3; *Praep. Ev.* VII, 15:2).
48. Cf. W. M. CALDER, 'Epigraphy of Anatolian Heresies' in *Anatolian studies*, 1923, pp. 76 f.; also H. GRÉGOIRE, 'Un nom mystique du Christ', *Byzantion*, II, 1925, pp. 449–453.
49. Cf. BARBEL, *op. cit.*, pp. 262–269.

in Isaiah who cry to one another and say: Holy Holy Holy is the Lord Sabaoth, are the only Son of God and the Holy Spirit. For our part we believe that the expression in the *Psalm of Habakkuk*: "In the midst of the two living creatures", refers to Christ and the Holy Spirit.'[50] In his *Homilies on Isaiah* Origen repeats this trinitarian interpretation of the Seraphim twice on his own account and seeks to justify it.[51]

This interpretation was to arouse the indignation of Saint Jerome. 'A certain one wickedly interprets the two Seraphim as the Son and the Holy Ghost.'[52] Even before Saint Jerome's time, however, this view had called forth a refutation, the *Tractatus contra Origenem de visione Isaiae*[53]—a rebuttal all the more necessary in that Origen's exegesis was being used by the Arians and the Pneumatomachi[54] to support the thesis that the Son and the Holy Spirit were creatures.

What is of particular interest with regard to this exegesis is that Origen claims to have received it from a Hebrew. It is certainly an interpretation of a Jewish Christian type. Nevertheless, the question is whether the 'hebraeus doctor' (*Princ.* IV, 3:14) was a Jew, and whether the Christian modification of the theme comes from Origen or from some earlier Jewish Christian. In support of the first hypothesis can be urged the proximity of this view to that of Philo. In the *de Deo* Philo quotes *Isaiah* 6 and then goes on to say that the name Seraphim 'applies directly to the powers ($\delta v v \acute{a} \mu \epsilon \iota s$)' (9). Moreover, the context shows that the powers in question are 'the creative power to which is rightly assigned the name of God, and the hegemonic or royal power, that of the Lord' (6).[55]

There are nevertheless serious objections against making Philo Origen's source in this matter. First of all, although he often uses Philo, he never describes him by the word 'Hebrew', which is a term he generally reserves for Jews or Jewish Christians contemporary with himself. Secondly Origen says explicitly that the Hebrew assimilated the two Seraphim to the

50. *Princ.* I, 3:4; cf. also IV, 3, 14. The words in question are not found in the MT, but occur in the LXX of *Hab.* 3:2.
51. *Hom. Is.* I, 2; IV, 1.   52. *Comm. Is.* III, 6:2.
53. Published by AMELLI in 1901, and wrongly attributed by him to Jerome; the text was re-edited by Dom MORIN in *Anecdota Maredsolana* III, 3, Oxford, 1903, pp. 103–121. Wilhelm DIETSCHE has suggested that it is in fact a Latin translation of a work by Didymus the Blind: *Didymus von Alexandrien als Verfasser der Schrift über die Seraphenvision*, Fribourg, 1942. This view has been contested by B. ALTANER, *Theol. Rev.*, XLII, 1943, pp. 147–151; and L. CHAVOURIER ('Querelles origénistes et controverses trinitaires', *VC*, XIV, 1960, pp. 9–14) attributes the work to Theophilus of Alexandria.
54. Cf. Glossary s.v.   55. Cf. BARBEL, *op. cit.*, p. 273.

Only-begotten and the Holy Spirit, but Philo's interpretation is quite different. In his opinion the two Seraphim are two divine powers which surround the only-begotten Logos. It would seem therefore that Origen's source is a Jewish Christian who made use of the same Jewish speculations on the Seraphim as Philo, but independently of him.[56]

Origen interpreted 'the two living creatures' of the *Psalm of Habakkuk* in a similar manner to his interpretation of the two Seraphim in Isaiah. But there is another more interesting case in which he gives the same exegesis, and raises once again the question of Philonian origins, namely that of the two Cherubim of the Tabernacle (*Exod.* 25:22), which he similarly identifies with the Son and the Holy Ghost in his *Commentary on the Epistle to the Romans*. He begins, following *Rom.* 3:25, by explaining the mercy-seat ($\iota\lambda\alpha\sigma\tau\eta\rho\iota\sigma\nu$) as the humanity of Christ. Then he comes to the Cherubim:

> What are we to think of them as a symbol? Cherubim means fullness of knowledge. Where do we find fullness of knowledge if not in him of whom the Apostle says 'in whom are all the treasures of wisdom and knowledge' (*Col.* 2:3)? And the Apostle says that of the Word. He also writes the same things of the Holy Spirit when he says: 'The spirit scrutinises all things, even the deep things of God' (*I Cor.* 2:10).[57]

In the continuation of the passage Origen explains that the presence of the two Cherubim over the mercy-seat symbolises the indwelling of the Word and the Holy Ghost in the soul of Christ, and in this connection quotes the *Psalm of Habakkuk* in which the 'two living creatures' are mentioned.[58] As regards the Ark beneath the mercy-seat 'it may signify the body of Christ, or on the other hand the angelic powers, which are also capable of receiving the Word and the Spirit, though only through the mediation of Christ's humanity'. Thus the transcendence of the Word and the Spirit over the angels is emphasised.[59]

56. KRETSCHMAR (*op. cit.*, p. 65) comes to the same conclusion.
57. *Comm. Rom.* III, 8.   58. Cf. KRETSCHMAR, *op. cit.*, pp. 91 f.
59. The Greek text of this passage was among the papyrus fragments of the work discovered at Toura, near Cairo, in 1941, and has been published by SCHERER. In substance it is the same as Rufinus' translation, but there are differences of detail: 'The translation of Cherubim is fullness of knowledge. And these Cherubim are engraved in order to represent by this fine ornamentation the divine nature. What then may the Ark be, placed beneath the mercy-seat and the Cherubim, if not, as I think, the holy and blessed powers which, like bodies, are capable of receiving the divinity of the Son and the Holy Spirit and also the soul of Jesus, which is the mercy-seat and contains the two Cherubim, and is set above that which is figuratively called Ark?' (160, 15–161, 1).

Did Origen have some source for this exegesis ? The problem is different from that of the two Seraphim. The exegesis of the Cherubim forms part of an exegesis of the Tabernacle—a theme frequently dealt with by Philo, whereas there is only one allusion in his works to the two Seraphim.[60] In the *Life of Moses* (II, 99) the two Cherubim are the creative power and the royal power. In the *Questions on the Exodus* the same interpretation is found (II, 62), while later in the same work (II, 68) the voice of God sounding forth between the Cherubim is the Logos. The *De Cherubim* is concerned with the Paradise story, but the exegesis is the same in principle; the flaming sword borne by the Cherubim is the Logos. The *De Deo* returns to the conception of the creative and royal powers (4–9).

Now these passages, particularly those from the *Questions on the Exodus*, display numerous points at which Origen is dependent on Philo. The name Cherubim is interpreted in a similar way as meaning ἐπιστήμη πολλή[61]; the fact that the two Cherubim are face to face signifies the full communication existing between them[62]; the gold of which the Cherubim are made is in both writers likened to the divine nature.[63] There can be no doubt that in these respects Origen is drawing on Philo. The difference is that for Philo the 'powers' are not the Logos and the Spirit, which suggests that what in fact has happened is that Origen has applied an allegory of Philo's to the subject of the Trinity. This conclusion is borne out by another detail, namely that whereas Origen ascribed his previous exegesis of the two Seraphim to a Hebrew who interpreted them in a trinitarian manner,

60. Dom LANNE has listed the principal relevant texts on both topics in Philo: 'Cherubim et Seraphim', *RSR*, XLIII, 1955, pp. 527–530; cf. also GOODENOUGH, *By Light Light*, London, 1935, pp. 25–28.
61. *Vit. Mos.* III, 8; cf. *Comm. Rom.* III, 8.
62. *Quaest. Ex.* II, 68; cf. *Comm. Rom.* III, 8.
63. *Quaest. Ex.* II, 67; cf. *Comm. Rom.* 160, 15 f. (SCHERER).

It is hard to decide which is the better text. Scherer believes, rightly in my opinion, that the identification of the Ark with the body of Christ, which is found only in Rufinus, has been added by the latter (*Le Commentaire d'Origène sur Romains*, p. 54). Moreover, Rufinus has omitted the important detail of the engraving of the cherubim, a symbol of Christ, which is certainly original. But Scherer notes that the Greek compiler of these excerpts has definitely abridged Origen's commentary on the Cherubim, and that therefore Rufinus' text is more complete on this point, which is why it has here been quoted first. The passage about the powers able to receive (χωρητικαί) the Word and the Holy Spirit is quoted by Saint Basil (*Treatise on the Holy Spirit*, 29), which shows that the passage could be interpreted in an entirely orthodox sense. (In *Hom. Num.* X, 3, Origen interprets the cherubim and the mercy-seat as the 'Knowledge of the Trinity'. This may well be a correction by Rufinus, inspired by Didymus and anticipating Evagrius.)

here he does nothing of the kind. The Trinitarian application is his own, though he may very probably have been led to it by the Jewish Christian precedent of a similar interpretation of the two Seraphim.

On the other hand it should be observed that in a parallel case Origen does not make the same adaptation of the Philonian theme. In the *De Deo* Philo likens the appearance of the three angels to Abraham (*Gn.* 18:1–2) to that of the Logos surrounded by the two principal powers. This theme recurs often in his work (*Abr.* 121–122; *Sacr.* 59). Now when Origen has to treat of this theme in the *Homilies on Genesis* he sees it as an appearance of the Word accompanied by two angels (IV, 1–2). That there was a Christian tradition which interpreted the theme in this way is attested in particular by Justin (*Dial.* LVI, 10; LVIII, 3; CXXVI, 4); it is simply in accord with the principle of attributing to the Logos those passages in the Old Testament in which the Angel of Yahweh is mentioned.

What has been said so far justifies the interpretation in the same sense of another, more difficult text in which the Seraphim and the Cherubim are mentioned simultaneously as designations of the Word and the Spirit. This is from the *Demonstratio* of Irenaeus, and was at one time rendered as follows: 'Now this God is glorified by His Word, who is His eternal Son, and by the Holy Spirit, who is Wisdom and the Father of all. And these two, the Word and Wisdom, have at their service a host (*sc.* of angelic spirits) called Cherubim and Seraphim, who glorify God with their unceasing song' (10).[64] But it appears that a more accurate translation would yield the following: 'And their powers (*lit.* their power), that of the Word and Wisdom, who are called Cherubim and Seraphim, with unceasing voice glorified God.'[65] The import of the new version is clear:

> There can be no question of various angelic powers, dependent on the Word and the Holy Spirit, and called Cherubim and Seraphim, which is the way in which the French version understands it. The passage must be taken to mean that the Word and Wisdom, which are powers of the Father, and are also called Cherubim and Seraphim, give glory to God with their unceasing voice.[66]

64. In this translation from the Armenian by J. Barthoulot the Cherubim and Seraphim denote the angelic choirs, and do not refer to the divine Persons; this interpretation was upheld by Lebreton (*Histoire du Dogme de la Trinité*, II, p. 632); cf. also Barbel, *op. cit.*, p. 275.
65. So Smith, 'Proof of the Apostolic Preaching' (*ACW*), London, 1952, p. 54.
66. Dom Lanne, *op. cit.*, p. 530.

In this text, therefore, the two Cherubim and the two Seraphim signify the powers of the Son and of the Spirit, that is to say, the Son and the Spirit in person. The passage is earlier than Origen; does it make it possible to determine the origin of these concepts? The arguments in favour of a Philonian source are not inconsiderable.[67] In Philo the Cherubim represent the two higher powers, the creative and the royal; Irenaeus also speaks of powers. The Cherubim and the Seraphim in Irenaeus would represent the Son and the Spirit in their action in the world; and they are also associated in this sense in the text from the *De Deo* quoted above. Finally in several texts in Philo the allegory of the Cherubim is associated with that of the seven-branched candlestick which was a figure of the seven heavens; and in Irenaeus the passage is in fact preceded by one on the seven heavens.

Nevertheless this case comes up against numerous difficulties. First of all, the speculations on the seven heavens and the angels of the Presence, as well as on the allegorical significance of the objects in the Tabernacle, must have been much developed by the Judaism of the period, to judge from the importance which they retained in later Jewish mysticism. It is only the absence of documents that prevents greater precision on this point. It is therefore quite possible that Philo and Irenaeus were referring to common sources, as were Philo and Origen in the case of the Seraphim.[68] Furthermore, Philo's system and that of Irenaeus are differently constructed; in one case the Logos is above the Seraphim and Cherubim, in the other the Logos and the Spirit are identified with the two Cherubim or the two Seraphim.

Moreover, the passage from Irenaeus suggests another comparison just as striking as that with Philo, namely with the *Ascension of Isaiah*.[69] In this work the theme of the seven heavens and that of the two higher angels, the angel of the Lord and the angel of the Spirit, are constantly appearing. The schematisation is much closer to Irenaeus than to Philo. The only difficulty is that the angel of the Lord and the angel of the Spirit are not explicitly identified with the Cherubim and Seraphim. But the Seraphim are not mentioned anywhere else in the *Demonstratio* either, their functions being fulfilled exactly by the two Angels. The most natural

---

67. This is the view of Dom LANNE, *op. cit.*, p. 533, q.v.
68. Cf. KRETSCHMAR, *op. cit.*, p. 93.
69. As LEBRETON and BARBEL have remarked.

conclusion is that in addition to the identification already made of the two Angels with Michael and Gabriel they are also to be equated with the two Seraphim.

Now that Irenaeus should have been influenced by the *Ascension* is far more likely than an influence from Philo, of which this would be the only example. The only other likely hypothesis would be the adoption and adaptation of a Gnostic theme, since the opposition between the seven heavens, the hebdomad, and the eighth, the ogdoad, is certainly a notion dear to this school. The connection with the *Ascension of Isaiah* is, however, the more plausible; and since the latter is a Jewish Christian work, it seems that Irenaeus must have received the tradition used in this passage from Jewish Christian circles, and that it is therefore right to include it in the corpus of Jewish Christian theology.

The Jewish Christian origin of this theme in its general form is further confirmed by the important evidence of Elkesaism. Hippolytus puts the alleged revelation of Elkesai in the reign of Trajan, and there is no reason for doubting this evidence. It is a Gnostic form of Jewish Christianity, plainly under apocalyptic influence. Mention has already been made of the gigantic stature attributed to the Son represented in the form of an angel. But Hippolytus speaks also of the Holy Spirit: 'Elkesai alleged that his message had been revealed by an angel whose height was 24 schoenoi, which makes 96 miles. This angel was accompanied by a female being, whose size was equal to that already mentioned. The male being was the Son of God, and the female was called the Holy Spirit' (*Elench.* IX, 13).

Everything in this text bears a Semitic stamp. The Spirit is regarded as a feminine being, because *ruah* in Hebrew is feminine, a feature which recurs in the *Gospel of the Hebrews*, also a Jewish Christian work[70]; the angels are described as human beings of gigantic stature; and the last characteristic, the assimilation of the Son and the Spirit to two huge angels, is palpably Jewish Christian. There is no reference here to any particular one of the symbolic schemes discussed in this chapter, the presentation of divine Persons in terms of Michael, Gabriel, the two Seraphim and the two Cherubim. But these different schemes are all only variations on the same basic theme, of which this Elkesaite teaching is probably the oldest surviving evidence.[71]

70. Quoted by ORIGEN, *Com. Jn.* II, 12; cf. also Valentinus according to HIPPOLYTUS, *Elench.* VI, 31.
71. Cf. KRETSCHMAR, *op. cit.*, p. 99.

The Holy Spirit and The Prince of Light

The next type of symbolism to be considered is entirely different from those so far examined; it consists in an expression of the theology of the Holy Spirit by means of the Essene doctrine of the Two Spirits. The discovery of the *Rule of the Community* has revealed the importance of this doctrine in the Qumran sect; and it plays an equally prominent part in the literature of Jewish Christianity, in *Barnabas*, *Hermas* and the Ebionite texts. In this context the affinity between the two groups is certain.[72] The question to be discussed here is in what way this doctrine was used in trinitarian theology; whether, in fact, the figure of the Essene 'prince of Light' was used to denote the Third Person of the Holy Trinity.

This would, of course, call for a transformation of the Essenian scheme, for in the perspective of this system, the two Spirits are on the same plane and are both created by God. Clearly, from a Christian standpoint the Spirit of Evil is a fallen creature, and the problem is therefore to decide whether the Spirit of Good who opposes him is kept on the same plane of creaturehood or whether he becomes a divine person. In this connection it should be remembered that Christians have often spoken of the struggle between Christ and Satan as if it were a conflict between equals without in fact implying that they were on the same plane.

It will be best to begin by recalling certain features of the *Rule of the Community*. '(God) . . . made for man two spirits, . . . the spirits of truth and wickedness' (III, 18–19). 'In the hand of the Prince of Light is dominion over all the sons of righteousness. . . . And in the hand of the Angel of Darkness is dominion over the sons of wickedness' (III, 20–21). The Prince of Light is called 'Angel of truth' (III, 24), 'Holy Spirit' (IV, 21). 'He is the source of all understanding and of all goodness' (IV, 2–6). At the end of time the Spirit of malice will be destroyed and the Spirit of truth will reign alone in the future life. This Spirit was created by God in the beginning.

This doctrine passed into Jewish Christian theology as may be seen from numerous examples. The *Testament of Judah* says that 'Two spirits wait upon man, the spirit of truth and the spirit of deceit' (XX, 1). The *Epistle of Barnabas* speaks of angels in the plural: 'There are two ways of teaching and of power. . . . On the one are stationed the light-giving angels of God,

---

72. Cf. J. Danélou, 'Une source de la spiritualité judéo-chrétienne: la doctrine des deux esprits', *Dieu Vivant*, xxv, 1953, pp. 127–136.

on the other the angels of Satan' (XVIII, 1). The Greek text of the *Didache* speaks of the Two Ways without mentioning the two angels; but the *Treatise of the Two Ways* reads: 'There are two ways in the world, over which are placed two angels, one of righteousness and the other of iniquity.'[73] In all these passages it is obviously a question of two angels; there is no adaptation of the Essene doctrine to trinitarian use.

With *Hermas* the case is quite different. His doctrine of the Two Spirits is developed in the *Mandates*. First, it is the duty of a servant of God to ensure that in himself 'no complicity with evil should abide with the Spirit of truth, nor bring grief to the Spirit which is holy and true' (III, 4). The expression 'spirit of truth' occurs in the *Rule of the Community*, but in addition it is used in *Jn.* 16:13 of the Third Person of the Trinity, while the phrase 'bring grief to the Spirit which is holy' recalls *Eph.* 4:30.

This impression is confirmed by the expressions referring to 'the angel of righteousness'. Men are to 'trust in the angel of righteousness' (VI, 2:6). Still more important is the expression: 'It is good to follow ($\dot{\alpha}\kappa o\lambda o\upsilon\theta\epsilon\hat{\imath}\nu$) the angel of righteousness and renounce ($\dot{\alpha}\pi o\tau\dot{\alpha}\xi\alpha\sigma\theta\alpha\iota$) the angel of wickedness' (VI, 2:10). The second phrase is the one used in the renunciation of Satan in baptism, and the complement to this renunciation was adherence to Christ, just as in Hermas it was adherence to the Spirit. Now the Essene initiation ceremony included an oath to break with the world of sin and to commit oneself to the community, oaths springing from the doctrine of the two Spirits. In this as in many other points, the Christian rite seems to be dependent upon the Essene one,[74] and this would be an indication in the liturgy itself of the transference of the Essene concept of the Prince of Light to the Word or the Spirit.

One more text is important to show the distinction made by Hermas between the Holy Spirit as a divine person and the 'spirits', that is to say, the interior motions which the Holy Spirit himself produces in the soul. Hermas speaks of those whom 'the devil filleth with his own spirit ($\pi\nu\epsilon\hat{\upsilon}\mu\alpha$)' (XI, 3). On the other hand

> (a) spirit ($\pi\nu\epsilon\hat{\upsilon}\mu\alpha$) given of God . . . having the power of the deity, speaketh all things of itself because it is from above, even from the power of the divine spirit ($\tau\dot{o}\ \theta\epsilon\hat{\iota}o\nu\ \pi\nu\epsilon\hat{\upsilon}\mu\alpha$). . . . When then the man who hath the divine spirit cometh into an assembly . . . then the angel

73. *De duabus viis*, ed. SCHECHT, Freiburg, 1900, p. 8.
74. Cf. J. DANIÉLOU, 'La communauté de Qumran et l'Église ancienne', *La Bible et l'Orient*, 1955, p. 105.

of the prophetic spirit who is attached to him, filleth the man, and the man, being filled with the Holy Spirit, speaketh to the multitude, according as the Lord willeth. In this way then the Spirit of the deity shall be manifest. This then is the greatness of the power as touching the Spirit of the deity of the Lord (XI, 5–10).

This text makes a clear distinction between two levels of reality. On the one hand there is the movement of the soul 'given of God', 'having the power of the deity', 'coming from above, from the power of the divine Spirit'; it is 'the Spirit of the deity' whose 'divine character' can be discerned by its fruits. On the other hand there is the one who gives this motion, who is variously called 'God', 'Spirit of the deity', 'Angel of the prophetic Spirit', 'Lord'. This spirit then is a divine being, since he is called Kyrios and God, and he is also a distinct person, else he would not be called an Angel. Once again the word 'Angel' appears as the technical term borrowed from Judaism to designate the divine Persons.

Moreover, the expression 'angel of the Spirit', is already familiar, for in the *Ascension of Isaiah* it was certainly used of the Third Person of the Trinity.[75] It seems therefore that in *Hermas* the Essene doctrine of the two angels has been taken up from a Christian standpoint as the opposition between the Holy Spirit and the Devil. In addition there are some expressions in the *Rule of the Community* in which the Prince of Light is called the Holy Spirit, which may have facilitated this adaptation.[76] But this does not mean that Hermas shares the same view.

This is a matter of some importance for the trinitarian theology of Hermas, which seems to be characterised by the fact that he borrowed his theology of the Word and his theology of the Spirit from two different systems. That of the Word is in the same line of development as the figure of the seventh Angel of apocalyptic, surrounded by six archangels. That of the Spirit is in the same tradition as the Prince of Light opposed to the Angel of Darkness, and comes from the *Rule of the Community*. This is the explanation of the apparent lack of coherence in his theology. There is one theology of the Word and another theology of the Spirit, both Jewish

75. AUDET'S objection ('Affinités littéraires et doctrinales du Manuel de Discipline', *RB*, LX, 1953) that Hermas tells us that the Holy Spirit 'serves' (λειτουργεῖ) God (V, 1:2) is hardly valid, for exactly the same idea is to be found in the *Ascension of Isaiah*; and elsewhere in Jewish Christian literature 'God' is constantly used to designate the Father.

76. As AUDET, *op. cit.*, has pointed out; cf. *DSD* IX, 3.

Christian, but no unified theology of the Word and the Spirit together; and when he does speak of them both at the same time his thought is confused, as in the *Fifth Similitude*.

It is interesting to observe that the theme of the Two Angels and the Two Ways was taken up and adapted in another current of Jewish Christian thought, namely that of the Ebionites. But the course of development was quite different. In the first place the 'Prince of Light' was not identified with the Holy Spirit but with Christ, and furthermore it was not a question of a trinitarian doctrine, but on the contrary of a conception of Christ as an angel.[77] Epiphanius describes the Ebionite doctrine as follows: 'They say that Christ has obtained as his lot the future world and the devil the present world' (*Pan.* XXX, 16:2), while in a text already quoted, he adds that for them Christ 'is not begotten of God the Father, but is created, and that he is one of the archangels reigning over the angels and all the work of the Almighty' (*Pan.* XXX, 16:4).

This doctrine reappears in a different form in the pseudo-Clementines. God, foreseeing that men would fall into two categories, 'has allotted to each both a place and a king: . . . the good King has as his portion the good, and the wicked one the evil' (*Rec.* III, 52). The first is the king of things to come, the second of things present (*Hom.* XX, 2). The world is thus divided into 'two states whose kings are at variance with one another' (*Rec.* II, 24), and the meeting of Christ and Satan is the meeting of 'the King of piety and the king of the present moment' (*Hom.* VIII, 21). But for all this Christ is only an angel (*Hom.* VIII, 42); the *Epistle to the Hebrews* was already replying to this doctrine when it said 'not to the angels hath he made subject the world to come' (2:5).

The Ebionite doctrine is thus a fusion of the apocalyptic and the Essene traditions. It regards Christ as the 'first of the archangels' (*Rec.* II, 42), that is to say, he is identified with Michael; he is also 'the King of righteousness' and identified with the 'Prince of Light'. Ebionism uses the same conceptual system as orthodox Jewish Christianity, but its theology is different. Its doctrine remains purely and simply Jewish with a simple Christian colouring; it is in no way trinitarian, and in it Christ is not God. The teaching of *Hermas* and of the *Ascension of Isaiah* on the other hand is a Christian doctrine which makes use of Jewish concepts. The problem was no different from that which in a Greek environment was to set Arians and Orthodox at odds, for Eunomius was a Neo-Platonist using Christian

77. Cf. H. J. SCHOEPS, *Urgemeinde, Judenchristentum, Gnosis*, p. 24.

terms, while Gregory of Nyssa was a Christian using Neo-Platonist concepts. In both cases, if one does no more than compare the language used by each side, the question is thrown completely out of focus.

THE GUARDIAN OF THE TEMPLE

The Essene 'Prince of Light' and Gabriel are not the only angelic figures that the Jewish Christians used to denote the Holy Spirit. There is a well-known later Jewish tradition according to which an angel guarded the Temple and abandoned it at its destruction by Titus.[78] The Christians took up this tradition and associated it with the theme of the rending of the veil of the Temple at the death of Christ; according to them it was then that the angel or angels abandoned the Temple.[79] The presence of the angel was linked with that of Yahweh, with the *shekinah*. When the sacred function of the Temple came to an end, the angels departed from it.

The *Testaments of the Twelve Patriarchs* gives a version of this tradition in which the angel is replaced by the Holy Spirit. This appears in the *Testament of Benjamin*: 'The veil ($\H{\alpha}\pi\lambda\omega\mu\alpha$) of the Temple shall be rent, and the Holy Spirit shall descend on the Gentiles like a spreading fire' (IX, 4).[80] The expression here used proves conclusively that the Christian conception of the Holy Spirit is meant, for the idea of the Holy Spirit's abandoning the Jerusalem Temple to spread himself like fire over the nations is an obvious allusion to Pentecost.[81] Here is yet another instance of a motif in the angelology of Later Judaism which has already been remarked, namely that of the angelic protection of Israel. Just as Michael gave Israel the Law, so an angel—perhaps also Michael—dwelt in the Temple.[82] In each case Jewish Christianity adapted the doctrine to its own uses.

78. *Apoc. Bar.* VI, 7; VIII, 1; JOSEPHUS, *Bell. Jud.* VI, 5:3; TACITUS, *Hist.* V, 13.
79. Cf. J. DANIÉLOU, *Les anges et leur mission*, pp. 18–19.
80. M. PHILONENKO (*Les interpolations chrétiennes des Testaments des XII Patriarches et les manuscrits de Qumran*, Paris, 1960, p. 18) has adduced another instance of the use of $\H{\alpha}\pi\lambda\omega\mu\alpha$ to denote the veil of the Temple in *Vit. Proph. Habac.* I, 2; the identification of $\H{\alpha}\pi\lambda\omega\mu\alpha$ with $\kappa\alpha\tau\alpha\pi\acute{\epsilon}\tau\alpha\sigma\mu\alpha$ in Asterius the Sophist, *Comm. Ps.* XXI (ed. RICHARD, p. 163) should also be noted. The word was later used of an altar-cloth, and even of the oratory of a monastery (cf. O. PREISIGKE, *Wörterbuch der greich. Pap.* s.v.).
81. This is in fact one of the passages which indicates the Christian character of the *Testaments*.
82. Certain fragmentary pieces of evidence corroborate this by suggesting that the Veil was sometimes regarded as the vesture of this angel. Thus $\dot{\epsilon}\nu\delta\upsilon\tau\acute{\eta}$ is a synonym for $\H{\alpha}\pi\lambda\omega\mu\alpha$ in the sense of 'altar-cloth'; and a passage in the Clementine *Recognitions* (I, 41)

The *Testament of Benjamin* is now, however, the only work in which this conception appears. Another instance occurs in a work soaked in Jewish imagery, the *Didascalia of the Apostles* (XXIII, 5:7)[83]:

> When he abandoned the people, he left their Temple desolate; He rent the veil, He withdrew his Holy Spirit, and shed Him upon them that believed from among the Gentiles, as He said by Joel: 'I will pour out my Spirit upon all flesh.' For he took away from that people His Holy Spirit, and the power of His Word, and all the ministry, and established it in His Church.

The same theme appears in Tertullian.[84]

These then are the strictly Jewish Christian conceptions of angelomorphic Christology, those which have been borrowed from the angelology of later Judaism, and in which Christ and the Holy Spirit are represented in their eternal nature, and not simply in their mission, by means of the imagery of various angelic beings. The question of the application to Christ of the term ἄγγελος in so far as he is the envoy of the Father may be left aside; this usage, based on the Old Testament, reappears frequently until the fifth century. It involved dangers of subordinationism, and was in fact misused in this way by the Arians, which was the cause of its eventual disappearance. But this lies outside the present subject.[85]

---

83. Also quoted by DE JONGE, *op. cit.*, p. 124.
84. *Adv. Jud.* XIII, 26. Other texts are cited by CAMPBELL BONNER ('Two Problems in Melito's Homily', *HTR*, XXXI, 1938, pp. 182–190) and M. RIST (*Additional Parallels to the Rending of the Veil in Melito's* 'Homily on the Passion', *HTR*, XXXI, 1938, pp. 249–250).
85. The long history of the term has been told by BARBEL, *op. cit.*

---

reads: 'The veil of the Temple was rent, as if it were lamenting over the imminent disaster.' Less ambiguous is the strange saying of Melito: 'The people not being rent, the angel was rent (περιεσχίσατο)' (*Hom. Pasch.* 98). DE JONGE (*The Testaments of the Twelve Patriarchs*, p. 124) rightly comments, 'Melito sees in the veil of the Temple the vesture of the angel who dwells there', and he goes on to remark that 'this parallel explains the use of ἔνδυμα in *Test. Levi.* X, 3, where the author of the *Testaments* alludes either to the vesture of the angel, or of the personified Temple' (*ibid.*).

CHAPTER FIVE

THE SON OF GOD

O NE of the more striking features of Jewish Christian theology is the great variety of expressions used to designate Christ.[1] Justin several times gives lists of these titles, and in this he is heir to the *testimonia* which date back to the Jewish Christian community. Many of the titles relate to Christ only in respect of his earthly mission. These will be disregarded and only those considered which designate the pre-existent Word. Of the latter several were already in use in the New Testament: Son of God, Word, Wisdom. These were indeed adopted by the Jewish Christians, but will also have to be left aside as belonging more properly to New Testament theology. The present chapter will deal only with a few strictly Semitic expressions which were later abandoned, but which reveal the richness of the Jewish Christian theology of the Word.

THE NAME

The first of these expressions, and one of the first to be given up, since it was unintelligible and dangerous in a Greek milieu, is that which designates Christ as the 'Name of God'.[2]

The origins of this Christology clearly lie in the Old Testament. There, the Name (*šem*) is frequently used of Jahweh's self-manifestation. The term is especially associated with God's revelation of himself (*Ex.* 23:21),

1. The New Testament contains as many as forty-two names or titles; cf. VINCENT TAYLOR, *The Names of Jesus*, 1953.
2. The importance of this in the primitive Jewish Christian community has been pointed out by CERFAUX ('La première communauté chrétienne', in *Rec. L. Cerfaux*, II, pp. 148–149) and PETERSON ('Didachè cap. 9 e 10', *EL*, LVIII, 1944, pp. 4–5, 11), though contested by AUDET in respect of *Hermas*. But the discovery of the Gnostic manuscripts of Nag Hammadi, and especially of the *Gospel of Truth* has confirmed its importance in a striking manner (cf. QUISPEL, *The Jung Codex*, pp. 68–78). Henceforth it must be regarded as one of the essential aspects of Jewish Christian theology.

and with his dwelling in the Temple (*Deut.* 12:11). It has the same attributes as Yahweh, holiness and glory (*Tob.* 8:5).[3] But this Old Testament background does not suffice to account for the Christological use of the word, which is based on the developed theology of the Name in Later Judaism. This development appears in the first instance to be related to the sacred character conferred on the tetragrammaton (YHWH).[4] The Name is used to designate Yahweh in his ineffable reality, and is therefore a Semitic equivalent of what the divine οὐσία was to be for the Greeks.

There is, however, more to the question than this. By extension from the Old Testament theological conception of the Name as the manifestation of Yahweh, the expression came to mean the power by which God accomplishes his works. There is a passage of *I Enoch* which speaks of 'the secret Name enunciated in the Oath' (LXIX, 14). Now the 'secrets of the Oath' are that 'by it the heaven was suspended before the world was created and to all eternity. And by this Oath the deeps were established' (LXIX, 16–19); and again: 'This Oath is established in power over the spirits' (LXIX, 25). Certainly the Name and the Oath appear here as the instruments of God in creation.[5] The Name plays the same role as the λόγος in Philo, and Philo does in fact use ὄνομα as one of the names of the Logos.[6] The indications are, therefore, that there was another line of theological thought, parallel to that of Philo, but with the Name not the Logos, as its focal concept.

This development is connected with the stream of Jewish apocalyptic, but it is important to notice that the documents in which the Name assumes the character of a true hypostasis[7] are fairly late, the most notable examples being *III Enoch* and the *Apocalypse of Abraham.*[8]

The Qumran texts give an important place to the Name as an expression of the power of Yahweh, but without the speculations of the later apocalypses.[9] There would seem therefore to be some difficulty in maintaining that the Jewish gnosis accounts for the Jewish Christian theology of the Name as a designation of Christ. This theology appears to have been

3. Cf. P. VAN IMSCHOOT, *Théologie de l'Ancien Testament*, I, Paris, 1954, pp. 207–212.
4. Cf. BIETENHARD, art. ὄνομα, in *TWNT*, V, pp. 242–269; *Rec. Luc. Cerfaux*, I, pp. 112, 172.
5. *Jubilees* speaks of the 'Oath by the glorious, great and mighty Name that made heaven and earth' (XXXVI, 7).
6. *Conf.* 146.   7. Cf. Glossary s.v.
8. Cf. QUISPEL, *The Jung Codex*, pp. 69–71.
9. Cf. *CDC* XV, 3; *DSW* XI, 2, 3; XVIII, 6, 8; *DST* XI, 6; XII, 3.

an original development which, starting from Old Testament data already taken up and elaborated in apocalyptic and Essene circles, constituted a Christology in which the Name is a person distinct from the Father. Its context, however, remains the Judaism of the time.

The beginnings of this Christology of the Name are already to be found in the New Testament. On the one hand Old Testament texts mentioning the Name are frequently quoted in the New Testament.[10] Thus *Acts* 15:17, quoting *Amos*. 9:12, reads: 'All the Gentiles, upon whom my Name is called (ἐπικέκληται).' Paul (*Rom.* 2:24) mentions *Is.* 52:5: 'The Name of God is blasphemed among the Gentiles because of you.' The same Epistle quotes *Ex.* 9:16: 'that my Name might be published abroad in all the earth' (*Rom.* 9:17). 'It looks very much as if in the messianic passages all the parts where the Name is given prominence had been carefully noted. . . . We may ask whether in these passages the Name is not a faint echo of the hypostasis of the Word.'[11]

In these various quotations the Name can in fact only mean Yahweh, but it is hard to see why these texts should have been collected in messianic dossiers unless the Name had appeared to have some relation to Christ. There are, moreover, some passages in which this relationship is explicitly stated. Thus *Joel* 3:5: 'Whosoever shall call on the Name of the Lord shall be saved' is quoted in *Acts* 2:21 and 4:12 in a somewhat indeterminate sense. But the same text is repeated in *Rom.* 10:12, as follows: '(Christ) is the same Lord (Κύριος) of all, and is rich unto all that call upon him: for, Whosoever shall call upon the Name of the Lord shall be saved.' Here the Name is clearly that of Christ; and in the *Epistle of Polycarp* the quotation from *Is.* 52:5 is used in a similar way: 'Follow the example of the Lord. . . . Woe to him through whom the Name of the Lord is blasphemed' (*Phil.* X, 10:1–3).

In the Gospel of *John* we are presented with a theological elaboration in which the Name has come to designate Christ. Christ manifests the Name of the Father (*Jn.* 17:6),[12] but this manifestation is his own person. 'If the Name of God is the symbol of his true nature, then the revelation of the Name which Christ gives is that unity of Father and Son to which He bears witness.'[13] Consequently when the Father glorifies the Son, he

10. Cf. *Rec. L. Cerfaux*, II, pp. 148 f.
11. Cf. CERFAUX, *op. cit.*, pp. 148–149.
12. Cf. C. H. DODD, *The Interpretation of the Fourth Gospel*, pp. 95–96.
13. DODD, *op. cit.*, p. 96.

glorifies his Name. Thus we have two equivalent formulas: 'Father, glorify thy Name' (12:28) and: 'And now, O Father, glorify thou me' (17:5). What is affirmed here is essentially the unity of nature between the Father and the Son, but also the fact that the Person of the Son is the revelation, that is to say, the Name of the Father.[14] John however preferred the term λόγος to ὄνομα since it was more accessible to Greek minds. For him the Name is an archaic usage.[15]

Finally 'the Name' in an absolute sense occurs in a text in the New Testament whose Jewish Christian character is quite certain, namely the *Epistle of James*. First, there is the expression: 'Do not they blaspheme the honourable Name which was called upon you?' (2:7: RV mg). Here again the Name is found in conjunction with terms already encountered in quotations from the *testimonia*: ἐπικαλεῖν, βλασφημεῖν. There seems also to be an allusion to baptism and the invocation (epiclesis) of the Three Persons.[16] The Name, therefore, does not stand here for the Person of the Word only; the passage is important nevertheless as evidence of the baptismal context in which the Name is involved. The second quotation, from the Epistle also, has a cultic context, namely that of the anointing with oil 'in the Name' (5:14).[17]

Thus even from the New Testament stage it is already possible to draw certain conclusions. On the one hand the Name, or the Name of the Lord, is used in a cultic context, beginning with a number of Old Testament expressions belonging to the *testimonia*. On the other, the term is applied to the Son, in a way that provides an incentive to theological speculation along these lines. In the texts from Paul and John the Name seems to designate Christ's divine nature, that which He has in common with the Father and the Holy Ghost, rather than the Person of the Word in himself. It was the latter aspect, however, that was to be developed in Jewish Christian theology, and is therefore relevant here. It seems to have been a continuation of an archaic Jewish Christian theology, earlier than Paul and John.

14. DODD observes that a similar theology underlies the quotation in *Heb.* 2:12 of *Ps.* 21:23 (EVV 22:22): 'I will publish thy Name to my brethren.'
15. Is it not possible that the expression: 'The Word ... dwelt among us' may be based on an older form: 'The Name ... dwelt among us'? In the Old Testament such dwelling is in fact the property of the Name, and not of the Word.
16. For the Jewish origin of the epiclesis see W. O. E. OESTERLEY, *The Jewish Background to the Christian Liturgy*, pp. 220 ff.; for the meanings of the term, cf. Glossary s.v.
17. This is the reading of a number of MSS; its archaic character makes it preferable to the alternative 'in the Name of the Lord'.

The first text to be considered is *I Clement*. The allusions to the Name only appear in the later part, which has a liturgical character. This is important because liturgical formulas are extremely conservative, and they serve to show how important was the doctrine of the Name. First, men are to 'be obedient unto His most holy (παναγίῳ) and glorious (ἐνδόξῳ) Name' (LVIII, 1), an expression which recurs in the final liturgical prayer: 'While we render obedience to Thine almighty (παντοκρατορι) and most excellent (παναρέτῳ) Name' (LX, 4). The prayer is addressed to the Father, and the Name designates the Son.

The text goes on to speak of 'trusting (πεποιθότες) in the most holy Name of his majesty' (LVIII, 1), probably a quotation from *Is*. 50:10. The next section acknowledges how God has 'called us . . . from ignorance to the full knowledge of the glory of his Name' (LIX, 2), and then, changing to direct speech, goes on immediately to say, 'that we may set our hope on Thy Name, which is the primal source (ἀρχέγονον) of all creation' (LIX, 3). Up to this point there may have been grounds for hesitating to consider the Name as the hypostasis of the Son, but this ὄνομα ἀρχέγονον, this Name which is the ἀρχή of creation, certainly appears to be the λόγος which according to John is in the beginning (ἀρχή).

On the other hand Clement makes no mention of the λόγος as a term for the divine person of Christ.[18] This suggests that there was a certain resistance to the Johannine λόγος in Jewish Christian circles, or, more exactly, that they represented a more archaic stage in theology in which the divine person of Christ was more naturally called by the Hebraic term ὄνομα. The development of this expression in contemporary Judaism cleared the way for the new use to which it was to be put, and which seems to have been the peculiar characteristic of Jewish Christian authors. Their theology of the Name does not merely continue the tradition of the Old Testament, in which the Name stands for the divine reality as a whole; it is also in sympathy with Later Judaism, in which the term takes on a quasi-hypostatic sense.

This conception of the Name as the personal power of God sustaining the Creation reappears in the *Shepherd of Hermas*. 'The Tower (i.e., the Church) has for its foundation (θεμέλιος) the word ('ῆμα) of the Almighty and Glorious (ἔνδοξος) Name, and is strengthened by the invisible power

18. This should be compared with the *Didache* X, 3: 'Thou . . . didst create all things for the sake of (ἔνεκεν) Thy Name', an expression which Peterson considers refers here to Christ (*op. cit.*, p. 6).

of the Master' (*Vis*. III, 3:5). The similarity of the expressions used in this text to those quoted from *I Clement* is striking; the Name is ἔνδοξος, παντοκράτωρ. However, from the expression 'word of the Name' it might seem that the Name represents no more than the Deity as such acting through its word.

Nevertheless, a comparison of this text with two others in *Hermas* tends to suggest that this hypothesis is inadequate, and that instead the Name ought to be regarded as a designation of the Word. Thus *Sim*. IX, 14:5 reads:

> The Name of the Son of God is great and infinite (ἀχώρητον), and sustaineth (βαστάζει) the whole world. If then all creation is sustained by the Son of God, what thinkest thou of those that bear (φοροῦντας) the Name of the Son of God? . . . Sees thou what manner of men He sustaineth (βαστάζει)? Even those that bear (φοροῦντας) His Name with their whole heart. He himself then is become their foundation (θεμέλιος), and He sustaineth them gladly, because they are not ashamed to bear His Name.

That this text is clearly parallel to the previous one is indicated by such a characteristic element as the term θεμέλιος. But the passage exhibits some surprising features. The greater part of it is straightforward enough: the Son of God sustains the whole Creation, how much more will He sustain and be a sure foundation to those who willingly bear his Name? But this neat piece of exhortation is quite tangled up by the opening sentence, which ought properly to lead into quite a different line of thought, a conceit on the principle: Christians 'bear the Name' of the Son of God, but it is this Name which in turn bears the whole world. As the passage now stands, therefore, the Name of the Son of God is equated with the person of the Son of God.

It is hard to resist the impression that what lies behind the present text is a train of thought in which not the 'Name of the Son of God', but the 'Name of God' sustained the Creation, and was equated with the 'Son of God', who in turn 'sustained' those who bear his own name, and that later this hypostatic use of the phrase 'the Name of God' was not understood, and the words 'Name of the Son of God' were substituted in the opening sentence to try to regularise the passage. This conjecture is supported by the fact that only in the *Ninth Similitude* does the expression 'the Name of the Son of God' occur, and that this section forms part of the most recent stratum of the *Shepherd*. But clearly, if this hypothesis is sound, then in the original quotation considered above (LIX, 3) 'the Name' is in all probability a designation of the Word.[19]

The investigation of this passage in *Hermas* may make it possible to suggest the proper line of interpretation of a whole series of texts which speak of those who 'bear' the Name. This significant expression occurs on several other occasions in *Hermas*. Thus *Sim.* IX, 14:5 speaks of those 'who bear ($\varphi o \rho \epsilon \hat{\iota} v$) the Name', and in *Sim.* IX, 13:2 f. the same phrase appears to be synonymous with 'receive' the Name. *Sim.* VIII establishes a connection between 'bearing the Name' and 'confessing the Name': 'They never denied God, but bore ($\dot{\epsilon} \beta \dot{\alpha} \sigma \tau \alpha \sigma \alpha v$) the Name gladly' (*Sim.* VIII, 10:3). *Sim.* IX identifies 'bearing the Name' with 'being baptised': 'If thou bear ($\varphi o \rho \epsilon \hat{\iota} v$) the Name, and bear not his power, thou shalt bear His Name to none effect. And the stones which thou didst see cast away, these bear the Name, but clothed not themselves with the raiment of virgins' (IX, 13:2 f.).

It is interesting to compare these passages with another text in which the Name appears, and of which the subject is baptism. Clement of Alexandria writes in the *Excerpta ex Theodoto*: 'When the coin was brought to him, the Lord did not say "Whose is this thing?", but "Whose is the image and superscription? Caesar's"; so that whose they are, to him it was given. So it is with the believer: he has as a superscription through Christ the Name of God, and the Spirit as an image' (86, 2). In this parable of baptism Clement is inspired by Theodotus. The simile is of a coin; the believer is marked by an imprint ($\sigma \varphi \rho \alpha \gamma \acute{\iota} s$) consisting of two elements, the $\dot{\epsilon} \pi \iota \gamma \rho \alpha \varphi \acute{\eta}$ and the $\dot{\epsilon} \iota \kappa \acute{\omega} v$. The fact that these two parts of the imprint are on a par in the illustration suggests that the corresponding elements in the reality illustrated are also on a par, that is to say, the Name of God and the Spirit. Hence the most probable antecedent for this simile is a passage to which further reference will have to be made later,[20] in which Theodotus contrasts the visible part of Jesus, with 'the invisible part, the Name, which is the Only-Begotten Son' (26, 1). The conclusion that the 'Name' in the simile of the coin designates the eternal 'Word' is almost irresistible; and is confirmed by the continuation of the passage, in which Clement says

19. AUDET (*op. cit.*, p. 54) is right in regarding the expression 'the Name of the Son of God' as secondary, but he fails to see that the 'Name' or 'Name of God' must denote the hypostasis of the Son.
20. Cf. pp. 161 f. below.

that 'he who has received the sealing (σφράγισμα) with the Truth bears the marks (στίγματα) of Christ' (86, 2).

In all these passages the use of the term 'the Name' seems to be closely connected with ritual matters, which suggests that liturgical history may perhaps be able to confirm the evidence of the literary data on the designation of the Word as the 'Name'. In fact a comparable situation does arise with regard to the expression 'to bear the Cross'.[21] Even though *Matthew* and *Mark* use λαμβάνειν and αἴρειν for 'to bear', *Luke* changes this to βαστάζειν (14:27), a term with a decidedly liturgical ring about it, which may refer to the *signatio* on the forehead with the sign + or ×. This practice is certainly attested for a very early date,[22] and it will be valuable to review its probable history in rather more detail.

The *tau*, the last letter of the Hebrew alphabet, also in its archaic form an ×, was, according to *Ezekiel* (9:4), the mark of Yahweh placed upon the forehead of the elect[23]; and as such is referred to in *Rev.* 7:2. That this mark was thought of as representing the name of God is clear from *Rev.* 14:1 and 22:4. But once the move had been made to Greek territory, the X, the sign of the divine Name, was no longer thought of as standing for Yahweh, but for Christ, and regarded as the first letter of Χριστός.[24]

Thus there is a shift from the divine Name, signified by the letter X, to the Name of Christ regarded as a divine Name. The *signatio* with the Name is more ancient than the *signatio* with the Cross, the sign of the cross in the form of T or X having at first signified the Name. It may be recalled that with regard to the symbolism of the letter *tau*, Origen[25] reports the opinion of a Jew who said that *tau* took its power from the fact that it was the last letter of the alphabet, and so was equivalent to the Greek Ω, the sacred letter *par excellence*. This seems to touch the very oldest stratum of the rite of the *signatio* in Jewish Christian circles, where the Jewish X comes to represent Christ as God.[26]

21. Cf. DINKLER, 'Jesus Wort vom Kreuztragen', *Neutest. Studien für Rudolf Bultmann*, 1954, pp. 110–128.
22. Cf. J. DANIÉLOU, *Bible et Liturgie*, pp. 76–96.
23. Cf. J. L. TEICHER, 'Christian Interpretation of the Sign X in the Isaiah Scroll', *VT*, V, 1955, pp. 196–198; and H. RAHNER, 'Das mystische Tau', *ZKT*, LXXV, 1955, p. 238.
24. Cf. TEICHER, *op. cit.*, p. 58.   25. *Hom. Ezek.* 9.
26. It should not be forgotten that 'Christ' is a name of God for the Gnostics, and even for Gregory of Nyssa. On the subject of χριστός as a divine name in Clement of Rome and Justin, cf. A. HOUSSIAU, *La christologie de Saint Irénée*, Louvain, 1955, pp. 165–172.

It will be remembered that in the texts from *Hermas* the central concept was that of 'bearing the Name'. This might suggest that he is concerned simply with a *signatio* with the sign which had represented the Name for the Jews, namely the *tau*. But henceforward this sign denoted Christ who was designated by the term, the Name. When the meaning of the *tau*, which was only comprehensible to Semites, was lost in Greek circles, it was interpreted either as representing $X(\rho\iota\sigma\tau\acuteo\varsigma)$ in the form of X, or as a symbol of the cross in the form of T.

It may seem strange that, when the formula is one of baptism in the 'Name of Jesus', it should have been the sign X and not the sign I or IH which was marked on the forehead; for there is no trace of a *signatio* with the latter. But this is precisely because the X was not originally marked on the forehead in allusion to the word $X\rho\iota\sigma\tau\acuteo\varsigma$—this was a secondary interpretation, occurring only in Greek circles.[27] Similarly, it is a later interpretation—this time by Jewish Christians—which sees the *tau*, in the form of T or +, as a symbol of the Cross. This development was all the easier because in the Jewish Christian community the Cross was itself a symbol of the Logos in his cosmic extension,[28] and therefore the Name and the Cross could be regarded as synonymous expressions since they both signified the Son of God. Nevertheless the interpretation of the + as a symbol of the Cross seems to be the secondary one; the sign placed on the forehead of the baptised person is still in fact the sign with which the true Israelites were marked in Ezekiel, though now it represents the true Name who is the Son.

There are other allusions to the Name in *Hermas* in a baptismal context, but in this case they are related to the epiclesis. The writer speaks, for example, 'of renegades that . . . were ashamed of the Name of the Lord which was invoked ($\dot{\epsilon}\pi\iota\kappa\lambda\eta\theta\acute{\epsilon}\nu$) upon them' (*Sim.* VIII, 6:4), and later of those 'who are called ($\dot{\epsilon}\pi\iota\kappa\alpha\lambda o\acute{\nu}\mu\epsilon\nu o\iota$) by the Name of the Lord' (IX, 14:3; cf. $\kappa\epsilon\kappa\lambda\eta\mu\acute{\epsilon}\nu o\iota$. VIII, 1:1). These formulas are probably borrowed from the Old Testament, for *Isaiah* (43:7) speaks of 'all who are called ($\dot{\epsilon}\pi\iota\kappa\alpha\lambda o\acute{\nu}\mu\epsilon\nu o\iota$) by my Name (sc. of the Lord)', and *Jeremiah* (14:9) has 'Thou art among us, O Lord, and thy Name is called ($\dot{\epsilon}\pi\iota\kappa\acute{\epsilon}\kappa\lambda\eta\tau\alpha\iota$) upon us'.[29]

The Name is linked not only with baptismal formulas but also with the

---

27. It may well be from the importance of X in Christian symbolism, interpreted by the Greeks with reference to $\chi\rho\iota\sigma\tau\acute o\varsigma$, that the appellation $\chi\rho\iota\sigma\tau\iota\alpha\nu o\acute{\iota}$ is derived. One would have expected rather to find the expression 'disciples of Jesus'

28. Cf. pp. 279 ff. below.   29. Cf. AUDET, *op. cit.*, p. 51.

Eucharistic liturgy. The vital text on this point comes from the Didache,[30] and forms part of the Eucharistic prayer: 'We give thee thanks, O Holy Father, for thy holy Name which thou hast made to tabernacle (κατε-σκήνωσας) in our hearts' (X, 2–3). The linking of the Name with the tabernacle (σκηνή) is in conformity with the Old Testament, as, for example, in *Jeremiah*: 'Shiloh, where I caused my Name to dwell (κατε-σκήνωσα) before' (7:12; cf. also *Ezek.* 43:7; *Ezra* 6:12). This is another case of a Jewish Christian adaptation to Christ of a formula applied by the Old Testament to Yahweh. 'The Name of God is an expression eminently suitable for a Jewish Christian hymn on the mystery of Christ.'[31]

It is in fact difficult not to connect the expression with a liturgical invocation of the Name; indeed it seems reasonable to conclude that 'the mention of the Name probably served the function of an epiclesis in the most ancient *fractio panis*'.[32] It should also be noted that dwelling is the Semitic category best suited to express the Incarnation. Thus the Fourth Evangelist writes: '(He) dwelt (ἐσκήνωσεν) amongst (ἐν) us' (1:14), where the resemblance to the expression in the *Didache* shows that the term 'in (ἐν) our hearts' could very effectively express Eucharistic dwelling.

The *Excerpta ex Theodoto* provide a parallel example: 'The bread and the oil are sanctified (ἁγιάζεται) by the power (δύναμις) of the Name' (82:1). Here the bread is the Eucharistic bread, and it is the invocation of the power of the Name which consecrates it—another instance of the epiclesis.[33] Attention should be drawn to the mention of oil, which is probably the oil of the baptismal anointing.[34] The connection of the Name with oil occurs also in the New Testament *Epistle of James*.[35] In all these texts the use of the Name seems to be linked with the epiclesis, as it was also with the *signatio*.

There is a final group of texts connected with persecution in which 'the Name' stands for Christ in so far as he is 'confessed'. *Acts* already speaks of the Apostles 'rejoicing that they were counted worthy to suffer dis-

30. Eric PETERSON has shown that the part played by the Name in this text is a sign of the Didache's Jewish Christian character ('Didachè cap. 9 e 10', p. 5) cf. also A. GRAFF, *Das älteste pascharituale der Kirche, Did. 1–10 und das Johannesevangelium*, Paderborn, 1929, pp. 90–104).
31. PETERSON, *op. cit.*, p. 11.   32. Cf. PETERSON, *op. cit.*, p. 5.
33. Cf. Gregory DIX, *The Shape of the Liturgy*, pp. 218–224).
34. Cf. SAGNARD, *Extraits de Théodote*, Paris, 1948, p. 207.
35. 5:14; cf. p. 150 above.

honour for the Name' (5:41); and Ignatius writes: 'Ye heard that I was on my way from Syria in bonds for the sake of the common Name' (*Eph.* I, 2) and later: 'I am in bonds for the Name's sake' (III, 1). The Name is also the subject of the Gospel message: Ignatius speaks of those 'who carry the Name to every part'.[36]

Analogous expressions may be found in the *Shepherd of Hermas. Vision III* speaks of 'those who have already been well-pleasing to God, and have suffered for the Name's sake' (1:9).[37] Its christological significance is again evident here from the fact that in *Similitude* IX it is found concurrently with the reading 'the Name of the Son of God'. Thus *Sim.* IX, 28 speaks first of 'they that suffered for the Name of the Son of God' (IX, 28:2); the next verse speaks of 'as many as ever suffered for the Name's sake', but the Latin versions give 'for the Name of the Lord (*domini*)' (IX, 28:3); the same paragraph again speaks of those who have 'suffered for the Name of the Son of God' (IX, 28:3) and finally a little later the alternative expressions: 'suffer for the Name's sake' (IX, 28:5) and 'suffered for the Name of the Lord' (IX, 28:6). In these expressions, $K\acute{v}\rho\iota o\varsigma$ stands for God the Father, the 'Name' designates the Son.[38]

There is further evidence for this theology of the Name as the divine Person of Christ in the various forms it assumes in those heterodox currents of thought which presuppose the Jewish Christian doctrine. Perhaps the item of most exceptional interest occurs in the *Gospel of Truth*, discovered at Nag Hammadi. It contains a christology of the Name more explicit and more fully developed than any other, while its Gnostic character is so little discernible that it provides evidence of a very pure Jewish Christian theology. 'It would seem possible . . . to prove that these speculations about the Name go back ultimately to more, or less heterodox Jewish conceptions, which were taken over into Gnosis as early as the beginning of the second century.'[39] If, as the present writer believes, it was through the medium of an earlier Jewish Christian elaboration that Valentinus was able to make use of these Jewish speculations, this would place this elaboration as far back as the end of the first century.

36. VII, 1; cf. POLYCARP, *Epist.* VI, 3.
37. The expression recurs twice more (2:1). For the latter passage AUDET opts for the reading $\tau o\hat{v}$ $\acute{o}\nu\acute{o}\mu a\tau o\varsigma$ $\tau o\hat{v}$ $\theta\epsilon o\hat{v}$ instead of $\tau o\hat{v}$ $\acute{o}\nu\acute{o}\mu a\tau o\varsigma$ (*op. cit.*, pp. 50–58). But the latter, which is the *lectio difficilior*, seems preferable (cf. WHITTAKER, *GCS*, p. 8, l. 24).
38. As AUDET (*op. cit.*, p. 54) has rightly observed.
39. QUISPEL, *The Jung Codex*, p. 72.

Because of its importance it will be necessary to translate and comment upon the whole passage in spite of its length. It begins:

Now the end is the taking cognizance ($\gamma\nu\tilde{\omega}\sigma\iota\varsigma$) of Him who is hidden. And this is the Father, from whom came forth the Beginning (and) towards whom are to return all those who came forth from Him and who became manifest for the Glory and the Joy of His Name. Now the Name of the Father is the Son. It is He (sc. the Father) who in the beginning, gave a Name to Him who came forth from Him and who was Himself, and whom He engendered as a Son. He gave him His Name which belonged to Himself—He, the Father, to whom belong all things which exist around Him. He possesses the Name, He has the Son. It is possible for them (sc. the Aeons) to see Him. But the Name on the contrary is invisible, for it alone is the Mystery of the Invisible, destined to penetrate to the ears which are completely filled with it. For, indeed, one does not pronounce the Name of the Father; but He reveals Himself through a Son. Thus, then, the Name is great.[40]

It is clear that this passage is rich in doctrinal content. The Name designates the divine Essence, which is invisible and ineffable. That this originally referred to the Jewish doctrine of the secret character of the divine Name, which must not be pronounced, is extremely probable,[41] but it has now developed into an apophatic theology of the divine incomprehensibility.[42] The Name of the Father is inaccessible—a doctrine which has possible points of contact with *Jn.* 1:18, 'No man hath seen God at any time.'

This ineffable Essence of the Father is however manifested to men through the Son. The Father has given him the Name. This means that the Son has the same nature as the Father. It is also stated that he has 'proceeded from the Father' and that 'he is the Father', so that there is no difference in nature between the Father and the Son. The Son not only has the Name, he is the Name. Hence the Name means God not only in himself, but also as manifesting himself, the sense which the expression has in the

---

40. *Évangile de Vérité*, 37:37–38:24; Fr. trans. H.-Ch. PUECH, pp. 37–39.
41. So QUISPEL, *ad loc.*
42. This is a point of the greatest interest, for the importance of the doctrine of the unknowable God in Gnosticism is familiar enough. Attempts have been made to discover its origins either in Platonism or in Mazdaism (cf. Glossary s.v.); but this text links the doctrine directly with the Jewish speculations of the early days of Christianity.

Old Testament. Moreover, this Name is a person; it stands for the Son, and is identical with him. Thus the Name refers to the Son under three aspects at once: as having the divine nature; as the one in whom the divine nature manifests itself; and as a person distinct from the Father.

An interesting point to notice here is the opposition between the invisible Father, and the visible Son. This is a characteristic of archaic theology. It is the basis of the teaching of Justin: 'To the Father of all . . . there is no name given', he writes (*II Apol.* VI).[43] It is also the reason why Irenaeus attributes all the theophanies of the Old Testament to the Son. Here then Valentinus' text is an exact reflection of the theology of his time, and it helps in tracing the origins of that theology in Jewish Christianity, since the designation of the Son by the Name gives it an archaic character. In Justin the same theology is much more Hellenised, which makes it reasonable to ask whether Gnosticism was not ultimately an archaic theology of Jewish Christian character, influenced by Jewish speculation.

The passage continues, developing the same views:

Since the Father is unengendered, it is He alone who engendered him for Himself, as a Name, before He had produced the Aeons, in order that the Name of the Father should be over their heads as a Lord, he who is the authentic Name, firm in his authority, in his power perfect. For this Name does not belong to the (category of) words (λέξεις), nor to the (category of) appellations (does) His Name (belong); but it is invisible. To him alone did He give the Name, being the only one able to see it (and) being alone capable of giving him the Name. For, indeed, the Unengendered has no Name. For what Name could one give to Him, who did not come into existence? On the contrary, he who did come into existence came into existence with his Name. And he is the only one who knows it, and it was to him alone that the Father was to give a Name. The Son is his Name. He did not, therefore, hide it secretly, but the Son existed: (to him) alone He gave the Name. The Name, then, is that of the Father just as the Name of the Father is the Son.[44]

First of all, there is a careful distinction between names in the ordinary sense of the word—appellations given by men—and the Name which is here in question, which is a hidden reality. Secondly, Valentinus remarks

43. Cf. also *I Apol.* LXI, 11: 'It is not possible to name the ineffable Name.'
44. *Évangile de Vérité*, 38:32–39:26; *op. cit.*, pp. 39–41.

that properly speaking the Father has no Name. It is strictly speaking the Son who is his Name, and what follows makes this point more clear:

> What is the Name? It is the authentic Name; it is, indeed, the Name which came from the Father for He is the proper Name. . . . There is no other person to whom He has given it. But it was unnameable, ineffable till the moment when He, He who is perfect, alone pronounced it. . . . When, therefore, it pleased Him that His well-beloved Son should be His Name, and (when) He gave the Name to Him, He who came forth from the depths spoke of His secrets.[45]

There is in this passage an extraordinarily elaborate development of the theology of the Name. The Name is that of the Father: it is the Name proper to Him ($\kappa\acute{u}\rho\iota os$), and is therefore of a different order from all the Aeons. It expresses the Father perfectly. It is, however, distinct from him, for the Father is ineffable. Once uttered, this expression, the Name, is a subsistent hypostasis.[46] Nevertheless the thought in this text is characterised by the fact that the Name does not appear as an instrument of creation, but as the mediator of revelation. This is in the true tradition of the Gnosis, but a gnosis in no way heterodox, since parallel expressions may be found in Justin and even in the Gospel of John.

Although, therefore, the theology of the Name in the *Gospel of Truth* presents peculiar features of its own, which spring from Judaism and Jewish esoteric speculations of the second century, it rests on an already elaborated Jewish Christian theology, echoes of which have been noted in *Hermas* and *I Clement*. This was to be developed in various directions by Valentinus' disciples. With Mark the Magician it takes the strange form of a symbolism of letters: the letters ($\sigma\tau o\iota\chi\epsilon\hat{\iota}\alpha$) are identical with the elements ($\sigma\tau o\iota\chi\epsilon\hat{\iota}\alpha$) of the whole; consequently the names formed by the letters come to signify the nature of things. The generation of the Word is the 'uttering of the name' ($\dot{\epsilon}\kappa\phi\acute{\omega}\nu\eta\sigma\iota s$ $\tau o\hat{u}$ $\dot{o}\nu\acute{o}\mu\alpha\tau os$) (*Adv. haer.* I, 14:1). This name is itself made up of letters which constitute other names, and in this way the pleroma[47] of beings unfolds itself. The Name of the Logos, which contains the pleroma of beings, must necessarily be the Name which contains the

---

45. *Évangile de Vérité*, 40:4–28.
46. 'In this text the Name is a manifestation of God, a subsistent hypostasis which plays the part of a mediator of the revelation' (QUISPEL, 'Christliche Gnosis und jüdische Heterodoxie', *Ev. Theol.*, XIV, 1954, p. 11).
47. Cf. Glossary s.v.

pleroma of letters. It is designated either by A and Ω, the first and last letters, or by περιστερά, which gives the numerical total 801, i.e. the number designated by A plus the number designated by Ω. As for the name of Jesus, it is the inexpressible name of the Saviour. It is formed of six letters, which is obviously symbolic,[48] and it denotes the earthly Jesus (I, 15:2). He, however, is the manifestation of the Logos at the earthly level, and this is expressed by the descent of the dove, the περιστερά, the expression of the Logos, upon Jesus at his baptism.[49]

There are several stages of thought in this teaching that must be distinguished. To begin with there are the Jewish Christian data, and in particular the doctrine of Christ as the Name in his reality as the Logos pronounced by the Father,[50] as well as views on the use of the name of Jesus to designate the Word clothed in flesh. Secondly, there is the speculation on letters and numbers, one of the technical devices of the period found also in other writings.[51] There are more Jewish Christian details here, but they appear to be only stray ones. All this is adapted by Mark to a Gnostic doctrine in which the letters represent the structure of the world on the Valentinian system: the pleroma, the genesis of the world below, the descent of the Saviour, and the distinction between the Logos and the earthly Jesus. This last aspect is not relevant here, but the others come within the scope of the present study, and serve as a complement to it.

Similar considerations apply to the *Excerpta ex Theodoto* in which the same doctrine appears, as in the following passage: 'In the beginning the angels were baptised in the redemption of the Name which descended upon Jesus in the form of a dove and redeemed him. For redemption was necessary even for Jesus' (22:6–7). The identification of the Name and the Dove is already familiar, and in this instance the Name is plainly the Son himself. Previous to this it was said that 'we possess the Name' necessary to entering into the Pleroma (22:4). Once again there is a baptismal context and the same expressions as in Mark: 'The visible part of Jesus was Wisdom and the Church . . . and he put it on through the flesh . . . but the invisible part is the Name, which is the Only-Begotten Son'

48. Cf. DUPONT-SOMMER, *La doctrine mystique de la lettre waw*, Paris, 1946, pp. 40–55.
49. Cf. SAGNARD's analysis in *Extraits de Théodote*, pp. 217–219, though this oversimplifies the data from Mark.
50. Cf. also the formula of 'redemption': 'The Name, hidden from all gods and lords, which Jesus of Nazareth put on in the circles of light' (*Adv. haer.* I, 21:3).
51. It was to persist in the Cabbala, which SCHOLEM has shown to be connected with Jewish apocalyptic.

(26:1). It will be noted that here Jesus is again the name of the Son in his self-manifestation outside the Pleroma.

The passage immediately following is also important: 'The High Priest on entering within the second veil removed the golden plate by the altar of incense, then entered himself in silence with the Name engraved upon his heart' (27:1). Clement is here inspired by Theodotus. The name is the sacred tetragrammaton, i.e. Yahweh or Iao, and in view of the previous quotation implies an identification of the Name in the Old Testament with the Person of the Son. The theology of the Name is here fully explicit and it is Clement who makes it so. This is not Gnosticism but an orthodox Jewish Christian development. Clement continues '(By that) indicating the laying aside of the body, which like the golden plate has become pure and light, of that body on which was engraved the lustre of piety, thanks to which he (the High Priest) was known to the Principalities and Powers as having put on the Name' (27:1). Here the Name is the power of the Logos in which the High Priest, who in Clement's allegory represents the soul of the spirit-filled Christian, is enrobed. The baptismal context is never far away.

A new element is now brought in: 'Having transcended the angelic teaching and the Name taught in Scripture, it comes to the knowledge and possession of realities' (27:5). There is thus a relationship between the Name in its material aspect and the reality which it signifies, which is the Son, which is paralleled by a link between the physical utterance of the Name and the knowledge of the Name in himself. This now rounds off what was said above about the Name in a cultic context; the utterance of the Name has an efficacy in the sacrament, for the Name is both knowledge and power. But this power of the Name is simply the reflection of the real Name which is the Son himself. As can be seen, the Name lent itself to denoting a rich complex of associations. This doctrine reappears elsewhere in Clement. Especially important is the passage about the tetragrammaton of the high-priest:

> The name engraven on the plate (of gold) has been judged worthy to be 'above every power and principality' (*Phil.* 2:9) and it is graven because of . . . His visible coming. It is called the Name of God because it is in contemplating the goodness of the Father that the Son acts, who is called God the Saviour, image of the invisible God before all ages, who has set his mark upon all that has been made after him (*Strom.* V, 38:6).

Here the Name is clearly the Son, the perfect expression of the Father, who is imprinted on all things.

To return to Theodotus and the Gnostic conception:

> They (the Aeons) knew that they are what they are by the grace of the Father: an unnameable Name (ὄνομα ἀνονόμαστον), Form and Knowledge. But the Aeon which wished to grasp that which is beyond knowledge . . . effected an abstraction of knowledge which is a shadow of the Name, that is the Son, the form of the Aeons. Thus the distribution of the Name among the Aeons is the loss of the Name (31:3-4).

In this passage, which recalls Mark, the Name is the Son, the form of the Pleroma. But the Name (the A–Ω) is broken up into the multitude of letters which are the various Aeons. It is fascinating to see Clement himself selecting in his study of Theodotus the elements of the traditional theology, the Jewish Christian doctrine of the Name, and making use of it on his own account, though he does also use the specifically Gnostic doctrine of the fall of the Pleroma and the breaking up of the Name into the various Aeons.[52]

THE LAW AND THE COVENANT

The Name was not the only expression of Semitic origin to be applied to the Word by Jewish Christian teaching. Another is νόμος, the Law, a translation of the Hebrew *torah*. Judaism at the time of Christ regarded the Torah as a divine reality existing before the world[53]; and the roll which contained it was to become in the Synagogue the object of a genuine cultus: the Law is so to speak the visible sacrament of the presence of the divine Word. For the Jew the Torah is the true incarnation, as the Koran was to be for the Moslem.[54]

In addition the identity of the Logos and Nomos had already been affirmed before Christianity by Philo. 'The identification of the Law with the Logos is complete.'[55] Thus in the *De Josepho*: 'The inquisitor is no

---

52. The 'Name' appears as one of the Aeons in the *Apophasis* (HIPPOLYTUS, *Elench.* VI, 9, 12, 13).

53. *Jub.* III, 10; *Test. Ash.* II, 10 (rec. β). Cf. BONSIRVEN, *Judaisme palestinien*, I, p. 250; STRACK-BILLERBECK, II, 353-356.

54. Cf. GOODENOUGH, *Jewish Symbols in the Greco-Roman Period*, IV, New York, 1954, pp. 99-144.

55. GOODENOUGH, *By Light Light*, p. 58.

man but God, Word or divine Law (θεῖος νόμος)' (174); and in another
place, divine Law and divine Word are identified as the real presence of
God (*Quaest. Gn.* IV, 140).[56]

It is not surprising therefore that νόμος is used to designate the Son of
God in Jewish Christian theology.[57] This is not due however to any
dependence on Philo, but is a parallel development, starting from the
speculations of the apocalypses on the Torah,[58] and clearly Jewish Christian
in character. One of the first passages to be considered occurs in *Hermas* and
treats of the vision of an immense willow-tree: 'This great tree which
over-shadows plains and mountains and all the earth is the Law of God
(νόμος Θεοῦ) which was given to the whole world; and this Law is the
Son of God preached unto the ends of the earth' (*Sim.* VIII, 3:2). The text
could hardly be more explicit. The Law is the name of the Son of God.
This is clearly an archaic expression in which νόμος takes the place of
λόγος, which never occurs in the *Shepherd*.

Another text of archaic character makes the same identification. Quoting
the *Preaching of Peter* Clement of Alexandria writes: 'In the *Preaching of
Peter* you will find the Lord called Law and Word (νόμος καὶ λόγος)'
(*Strom.* I, 182:3). Finally a passage from the *Eclogae Propheticae* adds an
interesting point: 'The Lord is himself called Law and Word according to
Peter in the *Kerygma*, and also according to the Prophet who writes: the
Law (νόμος) shall go out from Sion and the Word of God from Jerusalem
(*Is.* 2:3)' (*Ecl. Proph.* 58). The mention of the text from Isaiah is the more
interesting, since it occurs also in the primitive *testimonia*.

In Justin the Lord is called νόμος with reference to the same text.[59]
Thus in the *Dial.* XXIV, 1 he writes 'There is now another Covenant;
another Law has gone forth from Sion, Jesus Christ'.[60] Justin again refers

56. The *De plant.* 8 is of special interest. The accepted text reads: 'the Word (λόγος) of
the eternal God is the very sure and staunch prop of the Universe.' This text is given in
a quotation by Eusebius (*Praep. Ev.* VII, 13). But all the manuscripts give νόμος in
place of λόγος, and Goodenough prefers this reading, with good reason (*By Light Light*,
p. 57). The very fact that there is any doubt indicates how synonymous the expressions
must be in a context that is otherwise quite clear; and the probability is that Eusebius
emended the archaism νόμος with λόγος.
57. According to W. D. DAVIES (*Paul and Rabbinic Judaism*, p. 149) the idea is already
present in St. Paul.
58. Jules LEBRETON has collected some of the passages in which this identification is to
be found (*Origines du Dogme de la Trinité*, II, pp. 648–650).
59. Cf. C. ANDRESEN, *Logos und Nomos*, Berlin, 1955, pp. 325–329.
60. Here the punctuation of MS C is followed. Others attach 'Jesus Christ' to the
following phrase, but this seems to be a *lectio facilior*.

to Isaiah, though not to the same passage, a little further on: 'The Son of God ... Christ ... was proclaimed as about to come as an everlasting Law (νόμος) and new Covenant for the whole world' (*Dial.* XLIII, 1). It will be noticed that Christ is here called at the same time both Law and Covenant (διαθήκη). This conjunction had already been made in *Dial.* XI, 2: 'As an external and final (τελευταῖος) Law was Christ given, and this Covenant is sure, after which there is no law, or ordinance, or command.'[61]

This conception of Christ as the Covenant is found several times in Justin: 'The new Covenant (καινὴ διαθήκη) which had long since been proclaimed by God was now already present, that is to say, the Christ himself' (*Dial.* LI, 3). It is interesting to note that the expression had already been applied to the person of Christ by the *Epistle of Barnabas*, which quotes *Is.* 42:6: 'I have given thee to be a covenant of the peoples' (XIV, 7). The text of Isaiah applying the word Covenant to the Servant justified its application to Christ. In connection with this same text of Isaiah Justin writes: 'What is the covenant of God? Is it not Christ?' (*Dial.* CXXII, 5; cf. also CXVIII, 3; CXII, 4).

The conception of Christ as introducing a new covenant and bringing in the definitive Law was current in the New Testament.[62] But the interest of the texts quoted here lies in the fact that they add a new element, the personal identification of the Son of God with the Law and the Covenant. This could hardly be explained without some other influence than that of the Old Testament, that namely of apocalyptic Judaism in which the Law became a quasi-hypostasis. This does not mean to say that the texts from *Isaiah* are not the basis of these quotations, but the latter are in fact Christian speculations on the Bible taking as their starting-point the concepts of post-biblical Judaism.[63]

The designation of Christ as the Law was to continue in the later writers of the second century who drew their material from the same sources. Thus Irenaeus applied *Ps.* 77:5 (EVV 78): 'He established a testimony (μαρτύριον) in Jacob, and appointed a law (νόμος) in Israel' to the generation of the Word (*Adv. haer.* III, 16:3; cf. III, 10:5); and he too refers to *Is.* 2:3,[64] and shows the Law to be 'the Word of God, preached throughout

---

61. Cf. also XI, 4: 'He is the new Law, and the new Covenant.' Philo sees in διαθήκη a name of the Logos (*Somn.* II, 237).
62. C. A. BUGGE, 'Das Gesetz und Christus', *ZNW*, IV, 1903, pp. 89–110.
63. This is indeed the very definition of Jewish Christian theology.
64. This is further evidence of the importance of this chapter of *Isaiah* in the *testimonia* of the Early Church.

all the earth' (*Adv. haer.* IV, 34:4).[65] Finally, Clement of Alexandria was to write in the *Stromateis*: 'He who governs all things, and is truly Law (νόμος), Destiny (θεσμός) and Eternal Word, he it is who is in truth the Only-Begotten Son' (VII, 3:16).[66]

'ΑΡΧΗ AND 'ΗΜΕΡΑ

Other titles of the Word used in Jewish Christian theology are connected with speculations on the Hexaemeron, the importance of which for our period has already been noted on several occasions, and of these expressions two are of special interest in relation to the theology of the Word. The first is the designation ἀρχή. The study of its use may conveniently begin with the writings of Clement of Alexandria, who in the *Eclogae propheticae* undertakes to show that 'the Son is ἀρχή' (IV, 1). The interesting point about this demonstration is not Clement's complicated argument based on a text in *Hosea*, but the fact that the beginning of the *Eclogae* contains fragments of exegeses of the Hexaemeron, and that this is therefore almost certainly the correct context for the interpretation of the text.[67]

This is confirmed, moreover by another passage in Clement: 'One, in truth, is God, who established a beginning (ἀρχή) of all things as Peter writes, meaning the first-begotten Son and clearly referring to the words: In the beginning (ἐν ἀρχῇ) God made the heaven and the earth' (*Strom.* VI, 58:1). An earlier passage (VI, 39:1) indicates that Clement is again referring to the *Preaching of Peter*—a Jewish Christian work of the beginning of the second century, in which, as already mentioned, the title νόμος is applied to the Son.

Another text in which the Word is called ἀρχή, and which seems definitely to derive from Jewish Christian sources, comes from Theophilus of Antioch: 'God . . . begat (his Word) emitting Him along with His own Wisdom before all things. . . . He is called "Governing principle" (ἀρχή) because he rules and is Lord of all things fashioned by him' (II, 10). The sense here is very close to that of Clement, in whom ἀρχή suggests the idea of principate.

65. This last passage of Irenaeus is particularly interesting because the theme of the Law as applied to the Word is combined with that of the plough as a figure of the Cross, following *Is.* 2:4; cf. further pp. 274 ff. below, and J. Danièlou, 'La charrue figure de la Croix', *RSR*, XLII, 1954, pp. 193–204.
66. Cf. also *Protrept.* I, 3.
67. It will be remembered that Christ is called ἀρχὴ τῆς κτίσεως in *Rev.* 3:14.

Theophilus appeals to *Gn.* 1:1:

> Moses, who lived many years before Solomon, or, rather, the Word of God by him as by an instrument, says 'In the Beginning (ἐν ἀρχῇ) God created the heaven and the earth'. His first words were of 'beginning' and 'creation' . . . and that the true God might be known by his works, and that it might be known that by His Word God created the heavens and the earth, . . . he said: 'In the Beginning God created the heavens and the earth' (II, 10; cf. also I, 3).

This indicates that the tradition is in fact earlier than Clement, and comes from Syriac Jewish Christianity, in which this exegesis of the beginning of *Genesis* is already to be found. It reappears throughout the whole course of Greek patristic writing, affecting also the interpretation of *Prov.* 8:22: 'The LORD created me in the beginning (ἀρχή) of his way' to which Justin refers (*Dial.* LXI, 1; LXII, 4).

The Gnostics in their turn took up these speculations, claiming to find by means of this exegesis the data of their own system. Irenaeus records a specimen of Marcosian[68] exegesis of the opening verse of *Genesis*, the interpretation of which by Clement and by Theophilus has already been examined: 'Moses, then, they declare, by his mode of beginning the account of creation, at once shows the Principle (ἀρχή) to be the Mother of all things when he says "In the beginning God created the heaven and the earth"; for, as they maintain by naming these four—God, beginning, heaven and earth—he set forth their tetrad' (*Adv. haer.* I, 18:1). Here too ἀρχή is regarded as a personal concept, in accordance with the tradition of Jewish and Jewish Christian exegesis.[69]

This interpretation of ἐν ἀρχῇ (Heb. *bereshith*) as representing a divine hypostasis is clearly of Jewish origin. It is already to be found in the LXX of *Prov.* 8:22, where Wisdom is called ἀρχή. The Jerusalem Targum similarly relates *bereshith* to *Hokma*, pre-existent Wisdom. But there is a still more curious fact. According to St. Jerome,[70] Aristo of Pella states in the *Dialogue of Jason and Papiscos* that in Hebrew the first verse of Genesis reads: 'In filio Deus fecit coelum et terram'; and according to Origen Aristo was a Jewish Christian.[71] Again Irenaeus translates the verse: 'The

---

68. The Marcosians were the followers of Mark the Magician.
69. Cf. also the account given by HIPPOLYTUS (*Elench.* VI, 13) of the teaching of Simon.
70. *Quaest. heb. Gen.* I, 1.   71. *Contra Celsum* IV, 52.

son in the beginning; then God created heaven and earth' (*Dem.* 43)[72]; while according to Tertullian: 'Some say that in Hebrew the book of Genesis begins thus, "In the beginning God made unto Himself a son"' (*Adv. Prax.* 5).[73] Finally Hilary writes: 'Bresith verbum hebraicum est. Id tres significantias habet, id est, in principio, in capite, et in filio' (*Tract. Psalm.* II, 2).

What is the origin of this translation of *reshith* by 'son'? It is interesting to compare Hilary's text with one possible interpretation of *Col.* 1:15–18,[74] which sees St. Paul's text as an exegesis of the various meanings of *reshith*, namely beginning (πρὸ πάντων), head (κεφαλή), firstborn (πρωτότοκος) the same three meanings as those given by Hilary. What is more, in this same passage from *Colossians* Christ is also called ἀρχή. The only possible explanation is that the same rabbinical tradition is behind both passages. This also explains the equation of ἀρχή and Son; Son is here equivalent to firstborn, which is one of the meanings of *reshith*.

This interpretation of ἀρχή as designating the first-born son appears as a derivation from Jewish Christianity throughout the later patristic period. Confining ourselves, however, to the early period, it may be noted that it appears in Justin: 'God has begotten as a Beginning (ἀρχή) before all His creatures a kind of Reasonable (λογική) Power from Himself, which is also called by the Holy Spirit the Glory of the Lord, and sometimes Son, and sometimes Wisdom' (*Dial.* XLI, 1). Similarly Tatian has: 'The beginning (ἀρχή) . . . is the power of the Logos' (*Disc.* V). Origen was to sum up this teaching thus: 'In the beginning, God made heaven and earth. What is the beginning (ἀρχή) of all, if not our Saviour and Lord Jesus Christ, the first-born of all creatures? It is then in this principle, that is, in the Word that God has made heaven and earth' (*Hom. Gen.* I, 1). With this may be compared the following: 'He is called the beginning (ἀρχή) in so far as he is Wisdom' (*Com. Joh.* I, 19).

With ἀρχή may be associated another, less common title which also seems to originate in the Hexaemeron, namely the Day (ἡμέρα). Justin lists it together with Son and Wisdom (*Dial.* C, 4); Clement of Alexandria

72. Recently SMITH has suggested the reading: 'In the beginning God created a Son, then heaven and earth' ('Hebrew Christian Midrash in Irenaeus', *Biblica*, XXXVIII, 1957).
73. Cf. E. EVANS, *Tertullian's Treatise Adv. Praxean*, p. 209.
74. Cf. BURNEY, 'Christ as the 'APXH of the Creation', *JTS*, XXVII, 1926, pp. 175 f.; interest in this view has recently been revived by DAVIES, *Paul and Rabbinic Judaism*, pp. 150–153.

states that 'Christ is often called Day' (*Ecl. Proph.* LIII, 1); and Hippolytus writes that 'Day, Sun and Year were Christ' (*Ben. Mos.*, *PO*, XVII, 171).[75] What is the origin of this curious title?

All the terms quoted in Justin's lists are borrowed from Scripture; likewise, when Clement of Alexandria says that 'Christ is often called the Day', he clearly means that Christ is often given that title in Scripture. The context of this title therefore, as of the others, must be a collection of *testimonia* in which the word 'Day' was mentioned and which accordingly justified the application of the word to Christ.[76]

To what scriptural context, if any, does this appellation belong? The expression is not to be found in the New Testament, but it does appear in a very curious *logion* attributed to Christ by Marcellus of Ancyra, quoted by Eusebius:

> (Marcellus), continuing his exposition affirms that the Saviour said: I am the Day ('Εγώ εἰμι ἡ ἡμέρα), expressing himself thus: Formerly when darkness (σκότος) existed because of the ignorance of the wicked, and when the day was on the point of appearing—for he says 'I am the Day'—he rightly names him the morning star (ἑωσφόρον); and in another place he says: After he had put on flesh, he was proclaimed Christ and Jesus, Life, Way and Day (ἡμέρα) (*Contra Marcell.* I, 2).[77]

There is no reason for supposing that Marcellus forged this saying, and he must therefore have received it from an old tradition. There are several possible hypotheses as to its origin. It may be an independent *logion*, but there is a clear analogy between this formula and the words in the *Gospel of John*, 'I am the light of the world' (*Jn.* 8:12; 9:5).[78] It seems, however, to be carrying things too far to see in it no more than an error in quotation.[79] Since there is other evidence that the Day was a title of the Word in the primitive community, it is more plausible to regard the formula as archaic, and related to those in *John*.[80]

75. At a later period AMBROSE was to write: 'In the mystical sense the Day denotes the Christ' (*Exp. Luc.* VII, 222).
76. It will be remembered that a similar situation obtained in the case of that other remarkable title, the 'Name' (cf. *Recueil Lucien Cerfaux*, II, 149).
77. Cf. *Die Fragmente Marcells*, 32 and 43 in the appendix to 'Contra Marcellum', *GCS*, 189–190, 192.
78. Cf. T. ZAHN, *Marcellus von Ancyra*, p. 112.
79. So W. BAUER, *Das Leben Jesu im Zeitalter der neutestamentlichen Apocryphen*, p. 384.
80. The allusion to the morning star recalls *II Pet.* 1:19, which Marcellus may have

Nevertheless, the context from which the *logion* derives is most likely to have been the Old Testament. There the expression 'the Day' had at first a technical sense, denoting the eschatological era of the Lord's coming; and this may have been the original source of its application to Christ.[81] Marcellus understands the term along these lines, seeing in 'Day' the name of the Word in his manifestation on earth.[82] Secondly, the equation of φῶς and ἡμέρα clearly recalls *Gn.* 1:5: 'God called the light day.' In either case the *logion* quoted by Marcellus presupposes an Old Testament background and points to the *testimonia* as its likeliest source.

This is confirmed by the patristic references, and in particular by Clement's allusions to various Scriptural passages in support of his statement that Day is a title of Christ. Thus, in one passage he refers to Saint Paul—'The night is far spent, the day is at hand' (*Rom.* 13:11)—and comments: 'By Day and Light he designates figuratively (ἀλληγορεῖ) the Son' (*Strom.* IV, 141:3). This text is important both as evidence of the designation of the Son by the word Day, and because of the association of φῶς and ἡμέρα; and it would also seem to echo texts in the Old Testament in which 'the Day' has an eschatological force.[83]

This does not, however, seem to be the most important context, which is rather to be found in another passage of the *Stromateis* where Clement is commenting on *Gn.* 2:4: 'This is the book (βίβλος) of the generation (sc. of heaven and earth), and of the things in them when they were created; in the day in which (ᾗ ἡμέρᾳ) God made heaven and earth.' He continues:

> The expression: 'in the day in which God made', that is: in and by which God made 'all things', and 'without which not even one thing was made' (*Jn.* 1:3), denotes the operation of the Son, as David says, 'This is the day which the Lord hath made; let us rejoice and be glad in it' (*Ps.* 117:24: EVV 118); that is, in consequence of the

81. Cf. G. DELLINK, art. Ἡμέρα in *TWNT*, II, pp. 945–956.
82. Frag. 42 (*GCS* 190).
83. Cf. also *Barn.* XXI, 3: 'The day is at hand (ἐγγὺς ἡ ἡμέρα) in which everything shall be destroyed together with the Evil One. The Lord is at hand (ἐγγὺς ὁ κύριος) and His reward'; JUSTIN, *Dial.* XLIX, 2, which quotes *Mal.* 3:23 (EVV 4:5); and CLEM. ALEX., *Strom.* VII, 43:6: 'For those wrapped in ignorance has arisen a Day of knowledge of truth' (ἀνέτειλεν γνώσεως ἀληθείας ἡμέρα).

regarded as containing a *logion*; the beginning of the verse speaks of a προφητικὸς λόγος, and the second part (ἕως οὗ ἡμέρα διαυγάσῃ, καὶ φωσφόρος ἀνατείλῃ) could be understood as giving the content of this. The promise in *Rev.* 2:28 (δώσω αὐτῷ τὸν ἀστέρα τὸν πρωϊνόν) may also be a variant of the same theme.

knowledge imparted by him let us celebrate the divine festival; for the Word that throws light on things hidden, and by whom each created thing came to light and birth, is called Day (*Strom.* VI, 145: 4–6).

This passage yields two important pieces of information. The first is the quotation of *Ps.* 117: 24: 'This is the Day which the Lord has made.' The group of verses to which this belongs forms a part of the earliest *testimonia*,[84] and was an important source of material for Christology; hence it is understandable that the verse about the 'day' would be applied to Christ. It may be noted that in the passage quoted earlier from the *Eclogae propheticae*, Clement points out another verse where ἡμέρα stands for Christ, namely *Ps.* 18:3 (EVV 19:2): 'Day unto day uttered speech' (*Ec. proph.* III, 1).

Though, however, these exegeses are not decisive, the reference to *Gn.* 2:4 certainly is. Clement's exposition of this passage is very interesting. First, there is the parallel which he draws between *Gn.* 1:1 and *Gn.* 2:4; in the former verse the ἐν ἀρχῇ meant for Clement the Logos, and in the other, since ἡμέρα occupied a corresponding position, it was natural that it should be interpreted in the same way. Secondly, Clement refers explicitly to the Prologue of *John*; the 'Day' is the Logos, by whom all things were made, and without whom nothing was made. At the end of the passage he says that this is the principle of all creation (γένεσις) and of all knowledge (γνῶσις).

This interpretation was certainly not Clement's own invention. Philo before him had already applied the same passage of *Genesis* to the Logos, for we find in the *Allegorical Laws*:

This is the book of the Genesis of heaven and earth (*Gn.* 2:4) . . . he called the Word of God the 'book' (βιβλίον) upon which are inscribed and engraved the constitution of other beings. . . . On this day he made heaven and earth (*Gn.* 2:4). This is the 'day' (ἡμέρα) that he called the 'book' a little earlier since in either case he means the genesis of heaven and earth. For it is by his shining and splendid Word that God has made both (*Leg. All.* I, 9, 19–21).

Thus Philo gives an exegesis of *Gn.* 2:4 in which ἡμέρα already stands for the Word by which God created heaven and earth. There seems to be

84. Cf. p. 92 above. It will be remembered that in *Barnabas* this verse had been fused with *Mal.* 3:23, which has just been noted as one of the 'Day' *testimonia* in Justin (cf. n. 83 above).

no doubt that Clement was indebted to Philo in this matter. The curious exegesis will be noted in which βιβλίον also becomes a name of the Word; traces of this too are found in Jewish Christian theology, as may be seen in *Odes of Solomon* XXIII, 19, and above all in the *Gospel of Truth* 19:35–20:14, which speaks of the 'Book of the living, which is written in the Thought and Mind of the Father'.[85]

It is now possible to see the main context in which the term was applied to Christ. Ultimately, the reference is to the beginning of *Genesis*, but the immediate background is one of Jewish speculations on that chapter, of which Philo gives us an example, and which were continued in Jewish Christian theology, which made use of them not only in its christological, but also in its trinitarian thinking.[86] The reference to *John* in the logion: 'I am the Day' ultimately derives from the same early part of *Genesis*, and probably from 1:5.

This conclusion is confirmed by parallel speculations on the 'Day' as an appellation of Christ, which belong to the same context. Thus there are elaborations on the theme of the seven days of creation. Clement provides evidence for such speculations among Christian writers: 'The seventh Day is the Rest, which prepares by the cessation of sin the primordial (ἀρχέγονον) day, which is truly our repose, which is also the creation of the true light and the gnosis that shines upon us' (*Strom.* VI, 138:1). A comparison of this with the texts already studied leaves no doubt that this 'primordial day' is the Logos. A Christian feature appears in the detail that it is not the seventh day which is the image of the Logos, but the eighth, the Lord's day, which is also the first[87]; but of the Jewish background of such exegeses there can be no real doubt.

85. Cf. pp. 202 ff. below.   86. Cf. pp. 111 ff. above.
87. Cf. on this point, *Bible et Liturgie*, pp. 329–387.

Chapter Six

JEWISH CHRISTIAN APOCALYPTIC

A N examination of the world-view underlying Jewish Christian theology is indispensable to the present study, if only because this provided the characters and scenes in terms of which the Christian drama was unfolded. It was not cosmology as such which interested the Jewish Christian writers,[1] for they borrowed the greater part of their ingredients directly from Jewish apocalyptic.[2] Their concern was Christological; and they made use of cosmological data simply as a medium of expression. Nevertheless, Jewish Christian cosmology does present a number of original features; and it has, in addition, been the means by which certain elements, especially in the realms of angelology and demonology, have passed into Christian tradition.

THE COSMIC LADDER

The first topic of importance is that of the various spheres of the cosmos, the mythological geography of Jewish apocalyptic. The very word apocalyptic denotes the unveiling by which for the seer the veil that covers the supernal or infernal realities is drawn aside, and he is enabled to contemplate the secrets of the cosmos and of history. This feature appears again and again in Jewish Christian apocalyptic, which is likewise composed of ascensions or heavenly visions. Thus Isaiah passes through the successive spheres in the *Ascension of Isaiah*; Hermas writes: 'A spirit took me and bore me away through a pathless tract, through which no man could pass . . . the heaven was opened' (*Vis.* I, 1:3–4). Similarly Paul speaks of his being taken up into the Third Heaven (*II Cor.* 12:2–3), and John relates that he was 'in the Spirit . . . and saw a door opened in heaven' (*Rev.* 4:1 f.).

1. As BIETENHARD rightly stresses: *Die himmlische Welt im Urchristentum und Spät-judentum*, Tübingen, 1951.
2. Cf. H. H. ROWLEY, *The Relevance of Apocalyptic*, 2nd ed., London, 1947, pp. 91–150.

This hidden world includes first of all the heavens. Of these, traditional Judaism knew only three: the heaven of meteors, the heaven of stars and the heaven of God, and this is the scheme employed in the older Jewish apocalyptic. It is this system to which Paul alludes, and there is no ground for supposing that he implied seven heavens. Some Jewish Christian texts—as, for example, the *Testament of Levi* in the α recension (cf. III, 1–4)—retained the three heaven doctrine; indeed, the *Pseudo-Clementines*, which represent a traditionalist and anti-syncretist tendency, reduce them to two (*Rec.* IX, 3). In our period, however, this theory had to compete with the rival doctrine of the seven heavens. The latter system is not found in contemporary Jewish writings, such as *II*(4) *Esdras* or the *Apocalypse of Baruch*,[3] but only in Jewish Christian texts. It certainly derives from oriental, Irano-Babylonian influences, and appears as a characteristic feature of Syriac Jewish Christianity. It is remarkable that, having emerged with Jewish Christianity, it was to disappear with it also; Irenaeus and Clement kept it out of respect for tradition, but Origen rejected it explicitly.[4]

There is ample evidence on this point. To take first those texts in which the doctrine is directly stated, three typically Jewish Christian works are especially important.[5] The *Ascension of Isaiah* expounds the scheme three times: in connection with the ascension of Isaiah, and with the Incarnation and Ascension of Christ. The author distinguishes seven heavens, that of God being the highest, all inhabited by angels. Beneath the lowest heaven is the firmament, which is the prison of the apostate angels until such times as they are thrown into Gehenna at the last judgment. Lowest of all is the air, which is the domain of the demons. On this last point the author gives expression to a general opinion, which is independent of speculation on the seven heavens, and is found in St. Paul (*Eph.* 2:2; 6:12).[6]

In *II Enoch* (III–XX) there is a more precise and detailed account of the contents of the seven heavens. The first and lowest of them contains the higher waters, the reservoirs of snow and rain with the angels in charge of them, the stars and the angels who control their courses. The second is the prison of the apostate angels who fell from the fifth heaven. The third contains Paradise, where the souls of the just await the resurrection, and

3. Cf. L. GRY, 'Séjours et habitats divins d'après les apocryphes de l'Ancien Testament', *RSPT*, IV, 1910, p. 708.
4. *Contra Celsum* VI, 21.   5. Cf. BIETENHARD, *op. cit.*, pp. 3–8.
6. Cf. SCHLIER, *Christus und die Kirche im Epheserbrief*, pp. 9–13; J. DANIÉLOU, 'Les démons de l'air dans la Vie d'Antoine', in *Antonius Magnus Eremita* (*Stud. Anselm.*, XXXVIII), Rome, 1956, pp. 136–147.

Sheol, where the souls of the impious await punishment. The fourth is that of the sun and the moon and the angels that preside over them. The fifth is the heaven of the Watchers. The sixth contains the higher angels: seven archangels, seven cherubim, seven seraphim and seven phoenixes. The seventh is the heaven of God. It will be observed that nothing is said of what is below the firmament, nor are the apostate angels imprisoned there, but in the second heaven. Moreover the author sees the heavens rather in their relation to the mysteries of the dwelling places of souls and of the secrets of the cosmos than to those of the angels; and in this he seems to be more involved in the thought of traditional Jewish apocalyptic. The β version of the *Testament of Levi* also recognises seven heavens, which seems to be a strong indication of its Christian origin. The arrangement of the heavens is similar to that in the *Ascension of Isaiah*. The first heaven is sad, because it sees the faults of men. The second and third contain angels appointed to chastise the guilty among both angels and men; the fourth and the fifth contain the angels who intercede for men; the sixth is the heaven of the Thrones and the Powers; in the seventh resides the glory of God. Again nothing is said of what is below the firmament. It will be observed that, as in the *Ascension of Isaiah*, the heavens are exclusively the dwelling place of angels, and neither demons nor souls of the dead are found there. The author's main object[7] is to describe the liturgy in the seventh heaven, in order to show the spiritual character of the heavenly cult, which earthly worship should imitate—an emphasis which connects the passage with Christian Essenism.

These are the Jewish Christian texts which present the doctrine of the seven heavens in its pure form[8]; but the influence of this teaching is certainly visible, mixed with other elements, in later texts which serve as indirect evidence. Thus Irenaeus, describing the structure of the world at the beginning of his *Demonstratio* writes: 'The earth is encompassed by seven heavens in which dwell Powers and Angels and Archangels giving homage to the almighty God, who created all things' (9: *PO* XII, 761). He then compares the seven heavens to the seven-branched candlestick, a detail which may come from Philo; but the hierarchy of the Angels arranged according to the seven heavens comes directly from Jewish Christian

---

7. Cf. DE JONGE, *The Testaments of the Twelve Patriarchs*, pp. 46–49.
8. To these may be added the testimony of Aristo of Pella in the *Dialogue of Jason and Papiscus*, who speaks of seven heavens (ἑπτὰ οὐρανούς); cf. MAXIMUS, *Schol. Myst. Theol.* I, 17.

tradition on which he depended a great deal. On the other hand it will be observed that Irenaeus sees the seventh heaven as the dwelling place not of God, but of angels; and this suggests that beside the seven heavens he admits the existence not only of the lower heaven of air, but also of a higher domain which is the proper dwelling-place of God.[9]

This conception is found in another Jewish Christian author, who is in point of fact connected with the Asiatic tradition. The *Epistle of the Apostles* speak of the heavens on two occasions. In the first instance chapter 6 says that in the course of his Ascension Christ puts on the form of the angels until he reaches the fifth heaven. Now the *Ascension of Isaiah* (XI, 29) states that from the sixth heaven onwards Christ no longer puts on the form of angels. Both texts are manifestly dealing with the same conception; and the probable conclusion is that the *Epistle of the Apostles* knows of the doctrine of the seven heavens and is dependent on the *Ascension*. In a second passage, however, Christ declares: 'I have been in the Ogdoad which is the Κυριακή' (17).[10] In this conception the seven heavens represent the abodes of the angels, while the eighth is the abode of the Lord (κυριακή). It is a view influenced by the Hellenistic conception of the seven planetary spheres as opposed to the sphere of the fixed stars; and there is also an allusion to the Christian designation of the eighth day by the word κυριακή, which is here transferred to the eighth sphere.

This last feature reappears in Clement of Alexandria. He writes:

By the meadow (PLATO, *Rep.* IX, 616b) is to be understood the fixed sphere as being a peaceful and congenial spot, and the place of the saints; and by the seven days the motions of the seven (planets) and every art and operation which strives to attain its (true) end in rest (ἀνάπαυσις). But after the wandering orbs the journey leads to heaven, that is to the eighth motion and day (*Strom.* V, 106:3-4).

Here the temporal scheme of the seven days and the octave is transferred and adapted to the spatial conception of the seven planetary spheres and the sphere of the fixed stars. Clement explains this elsewhere:

Whether, then, it be a question of time which, (after passing) through the seven periods enumerated, is settled in the final rest, or of the

9. It will be seen that this fits in with the doctrine of the three principal heavens, the seven heavens being subdivisions of the second principal heaven.
10. As Karl Schmidt has pointed out (*Gespräche Jesu mit seinen Jüngern*, pp. 275-281) there is no question here of a Gnostic doctrine; the concepts belong to the main Christian tradition.

seven heavens, which some reckon in ascending order; and of the fixed sphere, which borders on the intellectual world, which is called the Ogdoad, it means that the Gnostic ought to rise out of the sphere of becoming and of sin (IV, 159:2).

It will be noticed that though Clement is aware of the distinction between the seven heavens and the ogdoad, he does not relate the seven heavens to the angelic hierarchies. He does indeed know a theory of the hierarchies, but it does not correspond with the seven heavens. It is in this vein that he writes in the *Stromateis*: 'From one original first Principle, which acts according to the (Father's) will, the first and the second and the third depend. Then at the highest extremity of the visible world is the blessed band of angels' (VII, 9:3). There is here therefore a hierarchy of only four degrees, and Clement envisages the seven heavens as a whole, which corresponds to the world of change, in opposition to the ogdoad of repose. This is not the view of Jewish Christian writers, who regard the seven heavens as constituting the heavenly kingdom. This would seem therefore to point to a different conception derived directly from a Hellenistic source, and influenced especially by Philo. The seven heavens are not the mystery of the heavenly world revealed to seers, but simply the planetary spheres of the cosmos.

The conception of the seven heavens is also found at this period in Gnostic literature, in which it constitutes one of the essential elements of the system. Thus Irenaeus writes in his notice on Ptolemy: 'They affirm ... (that there are) seven heavens, above which they say that he, the Demiurge, exists. And on this account they term him Hebdomas, and his mother Achamoth, Ogdoas. They affirm ... that these seven heavens are ... angels while they refer to the Demiurge himself as an angel' (*Adv. haer.* I, 5:2). There is here the same opposition of seven heavens and the ogdoad as in Clement, and indeed presented in exactly the same terms as those used in the *Epistle of the Apostles*: 'The repose of the spiritual ones (is) on the Lord's Day (κυριακή), that is, in the Ogdoad, which is called the Lord's Day. . . . The other faithful souls are with the Demiurge (i.e. in the Hebdomad).'[11] The structure has here been borrowed from Jewish Christianity, and allows for a hierarchy of angels, which was lacking in Clement. It has, however, been interpreted from a Gnostic standpoint; the seven heavens are the planetary spheres of the evil

11. CLEMENT ALEX., *Exc. Theod.* LXIII, 1.

cosmocrators,[12] to which are opposed not the abodes of the angels, but the Ogdoad itself.

On the other hand, this is not the complete picture of the Valentinian heavens, which is given in another passage: 'They next enumerate ten Powers: seven spherical bodies, which they call heavens; then a circle which contains these, and which they name the eighth heaven; and, last of all, the sun and the moon. These, being ten in number, they declare to be the image of the invisible Decad' (*Adv. haer.* I, 17:1). This text raises a difficulty, in that the sun and the moon are counted twice.[13] It may be that the general scheme of ten heavens ought to be retained, though interpreted differently; in which case, a probable suggestion[14] is that the system is an echo of the Stoic conception, which distinguished the heaven of air, the seven planetary heavens, the heaven of fixed stars, and the heaven of aether. The Gnostics would then have adapted this to form a scheme comprising the lower air, the hebdomad, the Ogdoad and the Pleroma.

Thus the Gnostic conception includes data borrowed from various systems, but it is easy to discern in it an original Jewish Christian basis. The conception of the wicked angels of the seven planets, for example, certainly looks like a corruption of the Jewish Christian conception of the angels of the seven heavens. Now Irenaeus remarked that with the Valentinians the heavens were likened to angels, and this is confirmed by Tertullian.[15] In view of the fact that Clement of Alexandria derived the same comparison from a Jewish Christian tradition,[16] the most probable conclusion is that the Gnostics incorporated this persistent conception of the seven heavens and their angels into a different scheme. Again, Irenaeus states elsewhere: 'They (the Valentinians) declare that Paradise, which is a power situated above the Third heaven, is a fourth archangel, from whom Adam received a certain (gift) when he had dealings with him' (*Adv. haer.* I, 5:2). This is clearly an echo of the Jewish Christian tradition of Paradise situated in one of the heavens. The Gnostics place it in the fourth, probably because this was the central one, that of the sun according to the arrangement of the Chaldean astronomers.[17]

12. Cf. p. 192 below, and Glossary s.v.
13. A similar duplication occurs in a fresco of the synagogue at Dura-Europos; cf C. H. KRAELING, *The Excavations of Dura-Europos, Final Report* VIII, 1, New Haven, 1956, p. 235.
14. Cf. ORBE, *op. cit.*, pp. 110–114.
15. *Adv. Valent.*, 20.
16. *Ecl. proph.* LII, 1.   17. Cf. ORBE, *op. cit.*, pp. 105–106.

It is possible therefore to distinguish several schemes for the structure of the heavenly cosmos: one, that of the Palestinian Jewish Christians, includes the air and the seven heavens; another, the Asiatic Jewish Christian, includes the air, the seven heavens and the Ogdoad; while the Gnostics present a third, influenced by Stoicism, which adds a heaven of fire. Moreover, there are variations in the contents of the heavens; sometimes they are regarded as the abodes of angels, at others as stages in the transformation of the soul. It is clear enough that several of these data are not Jewish Christian but come from Hellenism or from Gnosticism. Nevertheless they all seem to be grafted on to a Jewish Christian stock; the conception of the seven heavens as abodes of the angelic hierarchies, for example, first appears in Jewish Christianity.

It has been necessary to dwell on this question of the structure of the celestial world, because it was to play an important part in Jewish Christian dogmatic teaching. Indeed the principal dogmas were formulated in terms of cosmology. The Incarnation was presented as a descent of the Word through the angelic spheres; the Passion as Christ's combat with the angels of the air, followed by the descent into Hell; the Resurrection as an exaltation of Christ's humanity above all the angelic spheres; and after death the soul would pass through the various spheres, on its way encountering their guardians, to whom it would have to render an account. All these conceptions are based on a vision of the heavenly spheres which is part of the framework of Jewish Christianity.

The descent into Hell is relevant here, because in addition to the heavenly abodes, the cosmos also contains infernal dwellings. Here the most precise text is the *Ascension of Isaiah*. First it mentions Sheol, in which are the souls of the dead, guarded by the angel of death, who is, however, not an evil angel (X, 8–10). *II Enoch* places Sheol in the First Heaven, but the view given in the *Ascension* is the more common one. Sheol contains happy abodes for the souls of the just, and places of misery for those of sinners; but both kinds are only temporary dwelling-places where souls await the resurrection.[18]

After the resurrection the final dwelling-places are allotted. Beneath Sheol is the great Abyss, Gehenna, the place of perdition into which the evil angels and the damned of mankind are to be cast after the Judgment;

18. In the same way the firmament, or alternatively the second heaven, is conceived as the temporary prison of the fallen Watchers: cf. pp. 187 f. below.

this is the equivalent of our Hell,[19] and to this realm Christ does not descend (*Asc. Is.* X, 8). The righteous on the other hand will be brought into the final place of beatitude, called sometimes Heaven,[20] sometimes Paradise, sometimes the City. Irenaeus has preserved a Jewish Christian tradition which makes a distinction between these various abodes: 'The Elders say that those who are deemed worthy of an abode in heaven shall go there, others shall enjoy the delights of Paradise, and others shall possess the splendour of the City' (*Adv. haer.* V, 36:1).

There is, however, an exception to this waiting of the just before they enter into blessedness: in some cases their entrance is put forward. This seems to be a strictly Jewish Christian teaching. In the *Ascension of Isaiah* the visionary sees 'holy Abel and Enoch' already in the seventh heaven (IX, 8–9),[21] and with their raiment of glory (IX, 9), that is to say, they have been brought to life again. Resurrection is in fact a necessary condition for entry into this place. *II Enoch* shows the ascension of Enoch as a final entry into the highest heaven, which is the place of ultimate blessedness (LXVII, 2), whereas *I Enoch* only knows of a temporary ascension. Irenaeus ascribes the former doctrine to the Elders: 'Enoch of old, having pleased God, was translated in the body, foreshowing the translation of the righteous . . . . The Elders . . . say that those who have been translated are taken to Paradise, and remain there until the consummation of all things, being the first to enter upon incorruption' (*Adv. Haer.* V, 5:1).[22]

This condition only applies to certain saints of the Old Testament. Another Jewish Christian text, the *Clementine Recognitions*, explains this point:

> Others who, following the example of Enoch, pleased God have been translated to Paradise to await the Kingdom. But as for those who have not been able completely to fulfil the rule of righteousness their bodies are dissolved, but their souls are kept in the blessed regions, in order that at the resurrection of the dead they may obtain their reward, purified by the dissolution of their bodies (I, 52).

19. *Asc. Is.* X, 8; *II Enoch* X, 1–6. The distinction between Sheol and the Abyss is also found in the later Syriac tradition as represented by Ephraem and Isaac of Antioch: cf. P. KRÜGER, 'Gehenna und Scheol in dem Schrifttum unter dem Namen des Isaak von Antiochien', *OS*, II (1953), pp. 270–279.
20. In *Asc. Is.* IX, 6, it is the seventh heaven.
21. Cf. also IX, 28, where the author adds the name of Adam.
22. Cf. J. DANIÉLOU, *Les saints païens de l'A.T.*, Paris, 1956, pp. 69–71.

There is here a clear distinction between the exceptional state of those who are already restored to life, and the common condition of the souls of the righteous, who wait in Sheol for the resurrection, but in a happy region of that place.

THE ANGELS

As well as initiating men into a knowledge of the structure and extent of the whole cosmos Jewish Christian theology also aimed at describing all those who inhabited it. This knowledge bore especially on the world of the angels, angelology enjoying, as we have already seen in several connections, great importance in Jewish Christian thinking. The source of this importance was the influence of Jewish apocalyptic; the large part which the angels play in *I Enoch* is well known, and Josephus records that knowledge of the names of the angels was a feature of Essene gnosis. It certainly retained this prominence in Jewish Christian gnosis, establishing a tradition from which numerous doctrines were to pass into classical Christian teaching.[23] There is no need to emphasise every aspect of this tradition at this point; some of them will in any case be treated separately later. For the moment it will be sufficient to give a general impression of the angelic creation as it was conceived by Jewish Christians, stressing only those features which were peculiar to their presentation.

When he had organised the cosmos, and in particular the heavens, before making the other creatures God created the angels first: 'From the rocks I made a great fire break out, and from the fire I made all the incorporeal host and all the host of the stars, and the Cherubim and Seraphim and the Ophanim' (*II Enoch* XXIX, 3). It will be observed that the angels are not immaterial, their substance is fire.[24] They are, in the words of *Hermas*, the πρῶτοι κτισθέντες, the 'first created' (*Vis.* III, 4:1; *Sim.* V, 5:3), a conception found also in Clement of Alexandria (*Ecl. Pr.* LI; LVI, 7). One of the objects of the speculations on *Genesis* was to discover hidden allusions to their creation. In the expression, 'God created the heaven and the earth', heaven was understood by some as referring to the angels, while others identified them with the 'waters above the firmament'.[25] They are, in any case, created before other living things.

23. Paul, in the Captivity Epistles, and John, in the *Revelation*, had already incorporated a good deal of Jewish angelology into the New Testament.
24. Cf. H. B. KUHN, 'The Angelology of the Non-canonical Jewish Apocalypses', *JBL*, LXVII, 1948, pp. 211–219.
25. CLEMENT OF ALEXANDRIA, *Eclog. proph.* I, 2; III, 1.

As far as their appearance is concerned, another characteristic of Jewish Christian angelology is the gigantic stature of the angels. This feature, which is not found in the older apocalyptic, occurs in several texts. *II Enoch* speaks of 'Two men, very tall, such as I have never seen on earth' (I, 4). In the *Gospel of Peter*, the heads of the two angels who carry the Risen Christ 'touch the sky' (41). In the *Testament of Reuben* the angels are as high as heaven (V, 7). The Watchers of *II Enoch* are tall, 'more than great giants' (XVIII, 1). In the *Acts of John* the heads of the angels touch the sky (90), and the Elkesaites speak of two angels '96 miles high' (HIP-POLYTUS, *Elench.* IX, 13). The same feature appears in the Hermetic writings (cf. *Poimandres* I, 1).[26]

There were many ranks of angels, the highest orders forming the heavenly court, while the lower spirits administered the affairs of this world. It was characteristic of Jewish Christian apocalyptic in sketching out a hierarchy to relate it to the doctrine of the seven heavens. Highest of all, in the seventh heaven according to the *Ascension of Isaiah*, the sixth according to *II Enoch*, which reserves the seventh for the Great Glory, are of course the seven archangels. *II Enoch* mentions seven cherubim, seven seraphim and seven phoenixes. With regard to the other orders there are various arrangements. *II Enoch* places the Watchers in the fifth heaven, immediately preceding the heaven of the archangels; but in the *Testament of Levi* the fifth heaven is the abode of the 'angels of the presence', the sixth of the 'Thrones and Principalities'. In all cases there is a boundary drawn between the higher heavens, usually the seventh and the sixth, though sometimes including the fifth, which are the heavens of the angels who surround the sanctuary of God, and the lower heavens which are reserved to the angels who carry out their functions on earth.[27]

The higher heavens then are the sanctuary where the angels carry out the celestial liturgy.[28] Thus *II Enoch* shows us in the seventh heaven 'the hosts, drawn up according to their rank, advancing and bowing before the Lord, then retiring and going to their place in joy and gladness' (XX, 3-4). In the same way 'the Glorious serve him, neither retiring from him at night, nor leaving him during the day, standing before the face of the

26. FESTUGIÈRE thinks this may have had a Greek origin (*Révélation d'Hermès Trismégiste*, I, Paris, 1944, p. 8), but it is already to be found in the Qumran documents (*CDC*, II, 19) and was to endure in popular literature and iconography.
27. This is particularly clear in the *Ascension of Isaiah* and the *Epistle of the Apostles*, in which Christ only changes his form when he leaves the fifth heaven; cf. pp. 208 ff. below.
28. Cf. BIETENHARD, *op. cit.*, pp. 123-137.

Lord' (XXI, 1); and finally: 'All the host of Cherubim around his throne, singing before the face of the Lord' (XXI, 1). This does no more than continue the tradition of Jewish apocalyptic, but a Christian feature appears in the *Ascension of Isaiah* with the adoration of the Three Persons: 'In the sixth heaven . . . all had one appearance and their praise was equal. . . . And there they all named the primal Father and his Beloved and the Holy Spirit, all with one voice' (VIII, 16–18).

There is, however, more to be said on the subject of the angelic worship than this. The *Revelation* of John makes the immolation of the Lamb the centre of the heavenly liturgy. In a text of the *Testament of Levi* there is an analogous idea, but one expressed in a totally different key, which indicates an independent development[29]: 'In the (fifth) heaven are the angels of the presence of the Lord who minister ($\lambda\epsilon\iota\tau\sigma\nu\rho\gamma\sigma\hat{\nu}\nu\tau\epsilon\varsigma$) and intercede before the Lord for all the sins of ignorance of the righteous. And they offer ($\pi\rho\sigma\sigma\phi\epsilon\rho\dot{\sigma}\mu\epsilon\nu\sigma\iota$) to the Lord a sweet smelling savour ($\dot{\sigma}\sigma\mu\dot{\eta}\nu$ $\epsilon\dot{\nu}\omega\delta\dot{\iota}\alpha\varsigma$), a reasonable ($\lambda\sigma\gamma\iota\kappa\dot{\eta}\nu$) and bloodless ($\dot{\alpha}\nu\alpha\dot{\iota}\mu\alpha\tau\sigma\nu$) offering ($\pi\rho\sigma\sigma\phi\sigma\rho\dot{\alpha}\nu$)' (III, 5–6). At first sight this might seem to be concerned with spiritual worship as opposed to the offering of animal victims—a favourite theme of the Essenes especially, with their stress on the 'praise of the lips'. The same polemic against sacrifices appears also in *II Enoch* (XLV, 1–3), and it is indeed possible that the present passage is also inspired by the Essene spiritualisation of worship.

On the other hand, there can be no doubt that it is also strongly Jewish Christian in character. In a polemic against bloody sacrifices, the *Epistle of Barnabas*, after quoting *Ps.* 50:19 (EVV 51:17) adds another quotation: 'The smell of a sweet savour ($\dot{\sigma}\sigma\mu\dot{\eta}$ $\epsilon\dot{\nu}\omega\delta\dot{\iota}\alpha\varsigma$) unto the Lord is a heart that glorifies its maker' (II, 10). This is not a Biblical quotation; it may come from an apocryphal work, or it may be one of those *targumim* frequently to be found in Jewish Christianity. However that may be, *Eph.* 5:2 affords evidence of the existence of the expression $\dot{\sigma}\sigma\mu\dot{\eta}$ $\epsilon\dot{\nu}\omega\delta\dot{\iota}\alpha\varsigma$ to denote the sacrifice of the New Covenant in opposition to Jewish sacrifices; and similarly the expression $\lambda\sigma\gamma\iota\kappa\dot{\eta}$ $\pi\rho\sigma\sigma\phi\sigma\rho\dot{\alpha}$ clearly recalls the $\lambda\sigma\gamma\iota\kappa\dot{\eta}$ $\theta\nu\sigma\dot{\iota}\alpha$ of *Rom.* 12:1, though the word $\pi\rho\sigma\sigma\phi\sigma\rho\dot{\alpha}$ has a more liturgical ring.[30] Finally the term $\dot{\alpha}\nu\alpha\dot{\iota}\mu\alpha\tau\sigma\varsigma$, designating sacrifice, belongs to the technical language of Christianity.[31] This may well spring ultimately from

---

29. Cf. DE JONGE, *ad loc*.
30. In *Eph.* 5:2 it is associated with $\dot{\sigma}\sigma\mu\dot{\eta}$ $\epsilon\dot{\nu}\omega\delta\dot{\iota}\alpha\varsigma$; it appears also in *Barn.* II, 6.
31. Cf. DE JONGE, *The Testaments of the Twelve Patriarchs*, pp. 48–49.

Essenism, but the Christian author of the *Testaments* wishes to show that the true spiritual sacrifice which replaces the bloody sacrifices is the προσφορά, the liturgical offering of the sacrifice of Christ. It certainly looks as if this is the Syriac Jewish Christian equivalent of the Asiatic theme of the slain Lamb.

If the higher angels are devoted to the celestial liturgy, the lower ones are charged with administering the affairs of the cosmos and mankind. Here once more Jewish Christian angelology is greatly indebted to that of Judaism. Thus the angels are set over the various elements and over the life of nature; they preside over the movements of the stars (*Asc. Is.* IV, 18; *II Enoch* IV, XIX); they keep the stores of rain, snow and hail (*Test. Levi* III, 2; *II Enoch* V, 1–2); they watch over the rivers and the seas; they protect the harvests and the fruits (*Or. Sib.* VII, 34; *II Enoch* VI, XIX).[32] These are not specifically Christian features, but it is interesting to note that when Celsus later accused the Christians of a lack of piety toward the δαίμονες, who preside over the life of nature and distribute its benefits to men, Origen was happy to be able to retort that Christians also believe in these mysterious protectors, but do not venerate them as gods. In this he was the heir of the Jewish Christians.

The angels, however, preside not only over natural phenomena, but also over human communities. Jewish Christianity inherited from Jewish apocalyptic the doctrine of the angels of the nations (*I Enoch* XC, 22; *Or. Sib.* VII, 35),[33] and it must surely be through the medium of Jewish Christian tradition that the statement: 'The governments of the angels have been distributed over nations and cities' comes to appear both in Irenaeus (*Adv. haer.* III, 12:9) and in Clement of Alexandria (*Strom.* VI, 157:5). This teaching is particularly well developed in the *Clementines.* Thus *Rec.* II, 42, for instance, speaks of the sharing out of the seventy (or seventy-two) peoples among the angels; and *Hom.* XVIII, 4 states: 'In accordance with the number of the children of Israel, who were seventy souls when they entered into Egypt (*Gn.* 46:27), the Father marked out by seventy languages the boundaries of the nations.' There is in this passage quite plainly an attempt to harmonise the LXX translation of *Deut.* 32:8: 'When the Most High divided the nations, when he separated the sons of Adam, he set the bounds of the nations according to the number of the

32. In *Hermas* the angel Thegri is set in charge of the animals (*Vis.* IV, 2:4).
33. Cf. BIETENHARD, *op. cit.*, pp. 108–116.

angels of God', with Symmachus' version of the Hebrew text, which speaks not of the angels of God but of the children of Israel.[34]

Granted then that this is an inheritance from Jewish *haggada*, are there any signs of its having been christianised? It is interesting that the passage from the Clementine *Homilies*, the beginning of which has already been quoted, continues: 'To his own Son, who is also called Lord, God gave the Hebrews as his portion, declaring that he should be God of gods, that is, of the gods who received the other nations as their portions. These gods, then, gave laws each to their own portion; but from the Son himself came the Law which is established among the Hebrews' (XVIII, 4). In the Jewish texts God is the portion of Israel, but it is Michael who is given to the Hebrews as their protector, and it was he who taught them their language and gave them the Law on Sinai.[35] Moreover, if there are seventy peoples and seventy angels, each angel corresponding to a people, then Israel also ought to have its angel; and for this reason it certainly looks as if the *Clementines* identify Michael with the Son of God.[36] He is head over the sixty-nine angels, just as for Hermas he is the leader of the six archangels.[37] In the Clementines, however, the doctrine does not have an orthodox sense, since Christ is not truly the Son of God.[38]

Besides angels set over groups there are angels who are put in charge of individuals. This doctrine, of course, has antecedents in the Bible (*Tob.* 3:25) and in Judaism (*Jub.* XXXV, 17); it also occurs in the New Testament (*Matt.* 18:10) and even in paganism, in particular in the Middle Platonism of Plutarch.[39] Jewish Christianity, however, gave it a special

---

34. Origen must have received this doctrine, or at least some developments of it from these writings: cf. J. DANIÉLOU, 'Les sources juives de la doctrine des anges des nations chez Origène', *RSR*, XXXVIII, 1951, pp. 132–137; and R. CADIOU, 'Origène et les écrits pseudo-clémentines', *RSR*, XX, 1930, pp. 506–515. Origen's own explanation is as follows: 'The descent of the seventy souls (of Israel) into Egypt denotes the descent of the holy fathers (i.e., the angels) into the world, permitted by Providence for the instruction of the human race' (*Princ.* IV, 3:11–12). The question could in any case only arise for Hellenised Jews, and therefore the source here cannot be Palestinian Jewish apocalyptic.

35. JOSEPHUS, *Ant. Jud.* XV, 136; cf. *Gal.* 3:19.

36. Basilides taught that the prince of the angels (Michael) was set over the Jewish people, and that it was he whom the Jews took to be God (Irenaeus, *Adv. haer.* I, 24:4).

37. This is therefore another piece of evidence for the use of angelomorphic expressions in Trinitarian theology; cf. pp. 122 f. above.

38. On the Hellenistic parallels cf. ANDRESEN, *Logos und Nomos*, pp. 195–197.

39. Cf. G. SOURY, *La démonologie de Plutarque*, Paris, 1942, p. 131.

importance. Instances are to be found in the *Testaments* (*Test. Jos.* VI, 6–7), and also in *Hermas*, where the angel who appears to him says: 'I am the Shepherd unto whom thou wast delivered' (*Vis.* V, 3). In the *Epistle of Barnabas* (XVIII, 1) and in *Hermas* (*Mand.* VI, 2:2–5) the doctrine of the guardian angel has a counterpart in that of a personal demon, a development which seems to derive from the Essene doctrine of the Two Spirits.

It is a remarkable fact that later theology can be proved to have borrowed the doctrine of the guardian angel from Jewish Christianity. There are two valuable witnesses to this. The first is Origen, who cites the *Shepherd* and *Barnabas* as his authority for the doctrine of the two angels (*Princ.* III, 2:4). The second is Clement of Alexandria, whose evidence is fuller. He writes in the *Eclogae Propheticae*: 'Scripture says that little children who are exposed are entrusted to a guardian angel, who brings them up and makes them grow; and they shall be, he says, like the faithful here who are an hundred years old' (XLI, 1).[40] Later on Clement quotes a similar doctrine, which derives from the same background, and which he attributes explicitly to the *Apocalypse of Peter*: 'Divine Providence extends not only to those who are in the flesh. Peter, for example, says in his Apocalypse, "Aborted infants are entrusted to a guardian angel, so that having obtained a share in the gnosis they may arrive at a better destiny" ' (XLVIII, 1).

Among the various functions of the angel of the soul there are two that Christian theology has inherited from Jewish Christianity. First, Hermas speaks often of the Angel of Repentance. This angel is sent to Hermas both to beg him to mend his ways and to deliver to him tidings of pardon (*Vis.* V, 7; *Mand.* XII, 4:7; *Sim.* IX, 14:3). Origen was to take up this doctrine, referring explicitly to the *Shepherd* (*In Ps. hom.* 37). The Angel of Repentance had appeared in *I Enoch* (XL, 7–9) but it was Hermas who gave it prominence, and it was from him that Origen inherited the doctrine. Clement of Alexandria probably received it from the same source also: 'He who here on earth admits the angel of repentance will not then repent when he leaves the body' (*Quis div. salv.* XLII, 18).

Secondly, it is in Jewish Christian theology that the angel of peace occurs, who is charged with the task of receiving the soul as it leaves the body and

40. 'Scripture' here must refer to some Jewish Christian work, possibly the *Apocalypse of Peter* which Clement quotes immediately afterwards; if so, this would be a striking demonstration of how great was the authority which Jewish Christian works enjoyed in Clement's estimation by virtue of their antiquity. The concluding phrase is, of course, an echo of *Is.* 65:20.

leading it to Paradise. Thus *Test. Asher* states: 'If the man dies in peace, he goes to meet the angel of peace, who leadeth him to eternal life' (VI, 6; cf. also *Test. Benj.* VI, 1; *Test. Dan* VI, 5).[41] The doctrine does not appear in earlier apocalyptic, in which the angels have the task of watching over the bodies of the saints (*Life of Adam*, 46–47; and, in the New Testament, *Jude* 9, following the *Assumption of Moses*), and indeed is more reminiscent of the Hellenistic doctrine of the angel-escorts of the soul,[42] though it does not in fact derive from it. Later it was to have an important place in Christian liturgy ('In Paradisum deducant te Angeli'),[43] which seems to be one of the ancient inheritances from Jewish Christianity.

Other aspects of the activity of the angels are frequently to be found in our texts. They are intercessors of prayer,[44] messengers bringing divine revelations, instruments of God's punishment.[45] All these, however, derive from ordinary apocalyptic sources, though they passed into Christian theology by way of Jewish Christianity. It may justly be said that in this domain Jewish Christianity left a heritage of major importance to later theology, liturgy and spirituality. Indeed, such angelology may have oc-cupied an excessively important place in the early period, in view of the polemic which Paul, for instance, had to conduct against the angel cult among the Jewish Christians of Asia Minor, in Galatia (*Gal.* 1:8) and at Colossae (*Col.* 2:18).

THE DEMONS AND THE PROBLEM OF EVIL

Like angelology, demonology plays a big part in Jewish Christian theology, and it too is dependent on Jewish apocalyptic. The demons are usually regarded as fallen angels, and the normal explanation of their origin is the one given in *I Enoch*: angels of one of the higher orders, the Watchers, smitten with desire for the daughters of men, came down into the world under the direction of their leader; as a punishment they have been shut up in a prison, until the day when they are to be thrown into the great abyss after the Judgment. The *Testament of Reuben* alludes to this tradition (V, 5–7; cf. also *Test. Naphtali* III, 5), while the *Ascension of Isaiah* locates

41. The *Apocalypse of Paul*, 13–14, was later to elaborate this doctrine considerably.
42. Cf. F. CUMONT, 'Les vents et les anges psychopompes', *Pisciculi*, pp. 70–75.
43. Cf. J. DANIÉLOU, *Les anges et leur mission*, pp. 129–143.
44. *Test. Levi.* III, 5–7.
45. HERMAS, *Sim.* VI, 2:5; *Apocalypse of Peter*, passim.

the prison of Sammael in the firmament, between the heaven of meteors and the sphere of the moon. *II Enoch* places the fallen Watchers in the second heaven.

It is interesting however to note another tradition which was particularly well developed in Jewish Christianity, and which was to be taken over from it by the Fathers.[46] The doctrine of an angel set over the earth is attested by various writers in Jewish Christianity. According to Andrew of Caesarea Papias taught that 'God had given to certain angels the task of presiding over the government of the earth',[47] and *II Enoch* writes that 'God appointed two angels, Arioch and Marioch, to keep the earth and to govern temporal things' (XXXIII, 11). This is part of the general stock of apocalyptic teaching.[48] It will also be useful to note at this point the presence in Jewish apocalyptic at the close of the first century of the notion that Satan was jealous of Adam, because God had required that he should worship him (*Life of Adam*, 12, 17; *II Bar*. LVI, 10).

The doctrine referred to above, which was to play so large a part in patristic thought, arose from a fusion of the two conceptions mentioned so far, namely that of the fallen angels, and that of the angels set over the earth by God. Papias, after recalling that the earth had been entrusted to angels, goes on to say that 'this angelic order came to a bad end', and that 'he who had led astray the whole universe was cast down to earth with his angels'.[49] The passage in Andrew of Caesarea identifies this fallen angel with Satan, the great dragon, the old serpent (cf. *Rev.* 12:9). It seems to have been from Papias that Irenaeus acquired the doctrine which he develops at length in the *Demonstratio*.[50] According to this, God set a chiliarch 'over the angels charged with the earth'; this governor was an archangel who, however, became jealous of Man because of the many favours which the latter had received from God. Hence 'he brought about the ruin of Man by making him a sinner. For this he was punished; and on account of his rebellion he was called in Hebrew Satan, in Greek διάβολος' (11–16: *PO* XII, 762–764).

Among second century writers this conception is also found in Athen-

---

46. Cf. J. DANIÉLOU, *Les anges et leur mission*, pp. 61–66.
47. Cf. PREUSCHEN, *op. cit.*, p. 96.
48. Cf. also, in *III Baruch*, the concept of the Phoenix as guardian of the earth (VI, 4–7).
49. Cf. PREUSCHEN, *ibid.*
50. Justin appears to have held much the same doctrine; he describes Satan as one of the rulers (ἄρχοντες) who fell because he led Eve astray (*Dial.* CXXIV, 3).

agoras (*Suppl.* 24), who received it from the Jewish Christians; from him it was to pass to Methodius of Olympus (*De resurr.* I, 37), and from Methodius to Gregory of Nyssa (*Catech.* VI, 5), thus establishing beyond doubt the transmission of a doctrine from Jewish Christianity to the classical period. One may also wonder whether the frequent use of such phrases as 'prince of this world' (*Jn.* 12:31; *Asc. Is.* I, 3; IGNATIUS, *Eph.* XVII, 1; XIX, 1), 'king of this world' (*Asc. Is.* IV, 2) and 'god of this world' (*II Cor.* 4:4; *Asc. Is.* IX, 14) by New Testament and Jewish Christian writers may not be related to this conception of the archangel who had been set to preside over the world and had fallen.[51] However that may be, and whether the firmament is his natural domain,[52] or whether he came to be there as the result of his Fall (*Ascension of Isaiah, II Enoch*), it is none the less true that the terrestrial world is in fact the domain and sphere of action of the demon.

As an alternative to the various conceptions which associate the existence of evil angels with a Fall, the *Clementines* present a different point of view, which derives from Essenism. According to the *Rule of the Community* the Spirit of Truth and the Spirit of Perversity were established from the beginning by God himself: 'For he created the spirits of light and of darkness and upon them he founded every work' (*DSD III*, 25). Thus Mastema, the Satan of Qumran, also called Beliar, is not a good angel become wicked. This doctrine seems to be in the tradition of the figure of Satan in *Job*, who likewise is not a fallen angel but a God-appointed Tempter.

On this view the spirit of evil appears as an element in creation itself, and is mixed with the spirit of good throughout the present aeon, to be separated only in the day of visitation (*DSD IV*, 15–25).

The *Clementine Homilies* present a theory of the origin of the demon which seems to be related to the Essene doctrine, but is a more fully developed elaboration of it.[53] God did not create evil directly, but he created the various elements. The Evil One is born of the mixture of the elements (*Hom.* XIX, 12). His governing principle is not revolt against God, but an evil tendency which drives him to tempt men and to punish the wicked, and in this he is an instrument of God's plans. In any case it is impossible that anything should arise in the world against the will of God (VIII, 12).

51. BIETENHARD, *op. cit.*, p. 113, sees in such expressions no more than a reference to earthly tyrants.
52. So ATHENAGORAS, *Suppl.* 24.
53. Cf. H. J. SCHOEPS, *Aus frühchristlicher Zeit*, pp. 38–82.

The Evil One dwells in the lower places not in consequence of some punishment, but because of his innate taste for the darkness (IX, 9), and for this reason he also will have the chance of salvation in the end (IX, 9). He appears as the equivalent in personal terms of the tendency towards evil on the psychological plane, the *yeṣer hā-rā'*, which is also a tendency innate in man.[54] This doctrine does not seem to appear in orthodox Jewish Christian writings, but it may have influenced Origen's view, for it is known that he was acquainted with the *Clementines*.

Whatever the case may be with these various opinions as to the origin of demons, Jewish Christian writers agree in dividing them into two categories. In this they follow Jewish apocalyptic. On the one hand there are the higher demons—in the system of *I Enoch* the fallen Watchers—who are called Powers (*Eph.* 6:12; *Asc. Is.* I, 3; X, 15), Dominations (*Eph.* 6:12; *Asc. Is.* I, 3), Archons (*Eph.* 6:12; *Asc. Is.* X, 12; *Epist. Ap.* 28). Their chief is named Beliar (*II Cor.* 6:15; *Jub.* I, 20; *Asc. Is.* IV, 14), Satan, Sammael, Prince of darkness, Prince of this world, ὁ διάβολος, ὁ πόνηρος. He is often regarded as a parallel figure to the chief of the good angels, the Essene Prince of Light, or the archangel Michael (*Rev.* 12:7). In Jewish Christianity, however, there is a tendency to substitute for this Jewish opposition one between Christ or the Holy Ghost and the bad angel; and this ought perhaps to be regarded as one of the starting-points for the use of angelological terms in Christology.

Satan and the other fallen angels, then, are regarded as being shut up in a prison, which according to the *Ascension of Isaiah* is in the firmament, and according to *II Enoch* in the second heaven. The view that the present abode of Satan is in the lower heaven was already normal in the New Testament. Hence Christ 'beheld Satan fall like lightning from heaven' (*Lk.* 10:18); Paul places the malignant spirits ἐν τοῖς ἐπουρανίοις (*Eph.* 6:12); Michael casts Satan down to earth (*Rev.* 12:8–9). Jesus by his work of salvation dispossesses Satan of the power which he had retained, and drives him out of heaven[55]; but this action is eschatological, for Satan will be thrown into Abaddon, the Great Abyss, only at the Parousia, and for this reason he is always shown in Jewish Christian texts as still in the lower heavens.

Beside Satan and his angels there are the lower demons, the πνεύματα. *I Enoch* saw them as the souls of the giants who had been born of the union

54. Cf. SCHOEPS, *op. cit.*, p. 49.
55. Rightly emphasised by BIETENHARD, *op. cit.*, p. 214.

of the Watchers and the daughters of men, and Justin accepted this ex-planation (*II Apol.* V, 2–6) as did Athenagoras (*Suppl.* 24). It occurs again in the *Clementine Homilies* (VIII, 18). Whatever the origin ascribed to them, however, these demons live in the atmosphere surrounding the earth. Thus in the *Ascension of Isaiah* (X, 30) the angels of the air are explicitly distinguished from Sammael and his angels. The same work goes on to say, 'One was plundering and doing violence to another' (X, 31), a con-ception found also in Athenagoras who, speaking of the 'angels who have fallen from heaven and haunt the air and the earth', says that 'they stir up disorderly attacks, both against each other and against those without' (*Suppl.* 25). This idea is connected with the perpetual state of agitation found in the atmosphere in contrast to the serenity of the world of the stars. The doctrine of the demons of the air occurs in the Hellenistic world also, but it is the special characteristic of the Jewish Christian view to regard them as maleficent forces.

Jewish Christianity was especially insistent on the part played by these lower demons in the matter of temptation.[56] Several important doctrines emerge in this connection. First, a special demon was associated with each particular vice. This feature appears in the *Testament of Reuben* (III, 3–6), and was to be developed by Hermas, who, for example, declares, 'Slander is a restless spirit' (*Mand.* II, 3), 'angry temper is the most evil of spirits (πνεῦμα)' (*Mand.* V, 2:8), 'a mighty demon (δαιμόνιον) is stubbornness' (*Sim.* IX, 22:3). It was from the *Testaments* and *Hermas* that Origen took this doctrine and incorporated it in the Christian tradition.[57] Secondly, demons are shown as entering into bodies, which then become the objects of genuine possession. This doctrine is, of course, assumed by the Gospels; the seven demons that were driven out of the sinful woman (*Lk.* 8:2) seem indeed to be the seven demons of the vices in the *Testament of Reuben*. The *Epistle of Barnabas* (XVI, 7), the *Clementine Homilies* (IX, 10) and Valen-tinus (cf. CLEM. ALEX., *Strom.* II, 114:3) were all to develop this teaching; and it will be necessary to return to it when the time comes to examine Jewish Christian spirituality.

One final observation remains to be made. Whether it is a question of Satan and the fallen Watchers, or of the demons of the air, the common dwelling place of the evil angels is in the lower zones of heaven, those which are in direct contact with the earth. This has the important

56. Cf. J. DANIÉLOU, art. 'Démons', *Dict. Spir.*, IV, cols. 152–174.
57. Cf. E. BETTENCOURT, *Doctrina ascetica Origenis*, Rome, 1945, pp. 133–143.

consequence for the Jewish Christian world-view that souls must in their ascent to heaven after death pass through the spheres of the demons.[58] This implies first of all that in Jewish Christian teaching Christ meets the demons and triumphs over them in the course of his Ascension, and not in his descent to Sheol, which is concerned only with the deliverance of souls.[59]

According to *Col.* 2:14-15 Christ was already at grips with the powers of the air when he was raised up on the Cross—a view which was often repeated afterwards. It was, however, a strictly Jewish Christian conception, which was to become difficult to understand when people became accustomed to making Hell the abode of Satan.

The same implications were, moreover, equally important with regard to the ascension of each individual soul, which would have to escape the grasp of the demons who tried to restrain it. This it would be able to do only if there were nothing in itself to give them a hold. This doctrine must be distinguished from another, at first sight very similar, according to which each sphere was guarded by an angel who would require the appropriate password from the soul before allowing it to go through. This latter doctrine appears in the *Ascension of Isaiah*, and was applied by the Gnostics to the planetary cosmocrators in their own system. The two conceptions were in fact sometimes held in conjunction,[60] and were ultimately to be synthetised in the scheme by which both evil and good angels had their parts to play in the judgment of the soul. It will be clear, however, that these later elaborations would have been impossible, had it not been that the conception of the lower heavens as the dwelling-place of the demons constituted such an important element in the world-view of Jewish Christianity.

THE HEAVENLY BOOKS

Among the secrets of the cosmos shown to the visionary in the course of his journeyings the most important by far are those of the heavenly books in which the secrets of history are contained. The idea of the 'heavenly tablets', or 'book of destiny' in which the destinies of mankind were written down in advance in heaven is a very old one, as the Babylonian religion in particular testifies; and it is commonly connected with the

58. Cf. ORBE, *Los primeros herejes*, pp. 117-118.
59. As SCHLIER has rightly observed (*Christus und die Kirche im Epheserbrief*, pp. 17-18).
60. Cf. A. ORBE, *op. cit.*, p. 117.

idea of revelation to a prophet, or elect man of God, to whom the tablets are shown in the course of a heavenly ascension in order to enable him to proclaim God's plans to men. This conception was foreign to ancient Israel, and only made its appearance with *Ezekiel* (2:9); but in Jewish apocalyptic it underwent a remarkable development, thanks to its outstanding suitability as a vehicle for the central theme of these writers, namely that history is entirely determined in advance, and that men have only to wait for it to unfold.[61]

This conception, like that of the seven heavens, was clearly susceptible of varying interpretations. It might be regarded as implying a rigid theory of predestination, as it seems to have done in certain Jewish apocalypses, on the evidence of Josephus, in Gnosticism and in the Koran. On the other hand, it might refer simply to the general fulfilment of God's design, without detailed implications. The same variety of interpretation is evident in connection with a cognate conception, that of the 'book of life', which may denote either the list of those inscribed for ever on the heavenly records, or that of those who will be so inscribed if they make themselves worthy of it. What is of immediate concern, however, is not the mythical structure itself, which is simply an inheritance from Jewish apocalyptic, but the ideas which Jewish Christianity used it to express.

To be distinguished from the 'book of destiny' and the 'book of life' is a third conception, which was also taken up by Jewish Christianity, but which in fact falls into quite a different category, namely the 'Book of Works'. Here men's actions are thought of as recorded in heavenly books, which will be produced at the Day of Judgment, and the emphasis is on the importance of human acts and decisions. This conception also has its antecedents in Babylonian religion, and was to pass by way of Judaism and Jewish Christianity into the main Christian tradition; but it will not be necessary to consider it in this chapter.

Jewish Christian literature first of all takes up the conception, proper to Jewish apocalyptic, of the hidden plan of God, inscribed on heavenly tablets and revealed to a prophet during an ascension. In Judaism this was associated particularly with *I Enoch* LXXXI, 1–3; CIII, 1–3; CVI, 19;

---

61. Cf. G. WIDENGREN, *The Ascension of the Apostle and the Heavenly Book*, Uppsala, 1950; L. KOEP, *Das himmlische Buch in Antike und Christentum*, Bonn, 1952; H. BIETENHARD, *Die himmlische Welt im Urchristentum und Spätjudentum*, pp. 231–255; R. EPPELT, 'Les tables de la Loi et les tables célestes', *RT*, 1937, pp. 1–12; J. DANIÉLOU, 'Bulletin d'histoire des origines chrétiennes', *RSR*, XLII, 1954, pp. 610–614.

in Jewish Christianity it appears in *II Enoch*: 'The Lord called Vretil, one of the angels, a skilful being who wrote down all the works of the Lord. And the Lord said to Vretil: Take books from the store-house, and deliver to Enoch a reed-pen and dictate to him the works of heaven and of earth and of the sea' (XXII, 12). In an earlier chapter the work speaks of the angels who 'rule the whole of life and write it down before the face of the Lord' (XIX, 3-5).

The text goes on to show that the books contain the whole of God's design in nature and history. This is a picture of 'revelation' in the true sense of the word. Everything is inscribed beforehand in the heavenly books, and these books are shown or communicated or, as here, dictated. Thus the apocalypses are a copy of the heavenly books, and an angel is the minister of this revelation. It will be noted also that it is the angels who write the heavenly books. These various conceptions have antecedents in Jewish apocalyptic.

The same ideas are expressed in the *Ascension of Isaiah*. When Isaiah is taken into the seventh heaven,

> One of the angels who stood nigh . . . showed me some books . . . and he opened them, and the books were written, but not as the books of this world. And he gave them to me and I read them, and lo! the deeds of the children of Israel were written therein, and the deeds of those whom I know not. . . . And I said, In truth there is nothing done in this world, which is hidden in the seventh heaven (IX, 21-23).

The *Testaments of the Twelve Patriarchs* give a similar picture, as may be seen in the *Testament of Asher*: 'For I have read in the heavenly tablets that ye shall assuredly be disobedient and act ungodly' (VII, 5), and in the *Testament of Levi*: 'I destroyed at that time the sons of Hamor, as it is written in the heavenly tablets' (V, 4).[62] Thus the καιροί, the 'times', are determined in advance in the heavenly tablets. The ideas of revelation and determinism are the two components of the total conception.

The communication of a book signifies not only knowledge of future events, but also the revelation of a hidden teaching. This aspect may be seen in the *Shepherd*. In *Vision I* Hermas sees 'an aged lady in glistening raiment, having a book in her hand' (I, 2:2). She suggests to Hermas that she read him the book (I, 3:3), which ends with an account of the creation

62. Cf. also the *Prayer of Joseph*: 'I have read in the heavenly tablets everything that will come to pass upon you and your sons' (ORIGEN, *Com. Gen.* (*PG*, XII, 73B)).

of the world and of the Church (I, 3:4). This recalls the subject matter of the books which Vretil read to Enoch.

In *Vision II* Hermas again sees the aged woman 'walking and reading a little book' (II, 1:3). The following conversation takes place:

'Canst thou report these things to the elect of God? Lady, I say unto her, I cannot recollect so much; but give me the little book, that I may copy it. Take it, saith she, and be sure to return it to me. I took it, and retiring to a certain spot in the country I copied it letter for letter, for I could not make out the syllables. When then I had finished the letters of the book, suddenly the book was snatched out of my hand, but by whom I did not see' (II, 1:3-4).

Finally, after he has fasted for fifteen days, the contents of the books are revealed to Hermas (II, 2:1). It contains a message of repentance.

Similar imagery is employed by the heterodox Jewish Christian sect of the Elkesaites. Eusebius says that they received their revelation from a book fallen from heaven (*HE* VI, 38); Hippolytus states rather more explicitly that Elkesai possessed 'a book . . . revealed by an angel'. This angel, who was of enormous size, was accompanied by a female being equally gigantic. 'The male is Son of God, but the female is called Holy Spirit' (*Elench.* IX, 13). The communication of the book by the angel who is the Son of God recalls the *Ascension of Isaiah*, in which the heavenly books containing the revelations are communicated by Michael, a title which, as we have seen, is used to designate the Son of God. The imagery is still that of Jewish apocalyptic, but it is used to convey new teaching.

It will be observed that in a passage in the *Revelation* of John, 'book' is used in the same way as in the texts just examined:

And I saw another strong angel coming down out of heaven. . . . And he had in his hand a little book open. . . . And he cried with a great voice, as a lion roareth; and when he cried, the seven thunders uttered their voices. And when the seven thunders uttered their voices, I was about to write; and I heard a voice from heaven saying, Seal up the things which the seven thunders uttered, and write them not (10:1-4; cf. also 1:11).

The episode is strongly reminiscent of the *Shepherd*, even to the mention in each case of a little book ($\beta\iota\beta\lambda\iota\delta\acute{a}\rho\iota o\nu$).

It is important to note that the 'book of revelations' is also found in early pictorial representations. Sometimes there is an open book or a scroll unrolled, which Christ holds in his hand and shows to his Apostles[63]; sometimes a tablet is shown, proffered by a hand reaching down from heaven—an allusion to the giving of the law of Moses[64]; sometimes a scroll is shown coming down from heaven upon the Apostles.[65] In all these symbolic representations it is a question of a revelation made by Christ, a point on which more will have to be said later.[66] Since the *volumen*, generally rolled up, is a frequent adjunct of apostles and prophets, it is clear that the symbolism is in no way unusual.[67]

Together with the 'book of destiny' should be mentioned the 'book of life'. The expression is of biblical origin, and seems at first to have referred to earthly life: to be blotted out of the book of life means to die (*Ex.* 32:32; *Ps.* 69:28). But in the Jewish Christian period the term refers to eternal life: to be inscribed in the book of life is to be counted among the elect.[68] In a Graeco-Roman setting the idea was modified by that of the book in which citizens were enrolled, so associating it with the concept of the heavenly city[69]; but in Jewish Christian circles the book of life tended to become assimilated to the book of destiny. By insisting that God's chosen have been enrolled in the book of life since before the creation of the world, the theme of election is thrown into relief.

This motif is to be found in the New Testament. In *Luke* Christ tells the Seventy: 'Rejoice that your names are written in heaven' (10:20). The same idea, with explicit mention of the book of life, appears in St. Paul, who says of Clement and his colleagues that their 'names are written in the

---

63. This is an adaptation of a pagan motif; cf. J. VILLETTE, *La résurrection du Christ dans l'art chrétien du Ier au Vie siècle*, Paris, 1957, pp. 22–24.

64. Cf. G. WILPERT, *I sarcofagi cristiani antichi*, II, Rome, 1932, pl. 81.

65. Cf. BOTTARI, *Roma Sotterranea*, III, pl. 198.

66. Cf. pp. 199 ff. below.

67. One well-known example, which is closely connected with those mentioned above, and with the same background, will suffice. The sanctuary in the Viale Manzoni in Rome is a Gnostic building of the third century (*ibid.*, p. 109), of which one feature is relevant here. The southern room of the upper storey shows a man seated, with an unrolled *volumen* on his knees in which he is writing with a calamus; and the same scene is reproduced on another wall. CARCOPINO (*De Pythagore aux Apôtres*, Paris, 1956, p. 109; for a discussion of the whole building, cf. pp. 85–225) believes that it portrays an initiate communicating the gnosis to a disciple. The scroll which the master holds is the one containing the revelation. This picture illustrates admirably the scenes quoted from *Hermas* and the Elkesaites.

68. This may already be seen in Jewish apocalyptic; cf. *Dan.* 12:1.

69. Cf. KOEP, *Das himmlische Buch im Antike und Christentum*, pp. 68–124.

book of life' (*Phil.* 4:3). Three passages from the *Revelation* of John also indicate familiarity with this conception: those who worship the Beast are those 'whose name hath not been written in the book of life of the Lamb that hath been slain from the foundation of the world' (13:8); a variant of the same general form of words—'they whose name hath not been written in the book of life from the foundation of the world' (17:8)—is of interest for the emphasis on divine election even before the Creation; and finally, only those are to enter the heavenly city who 'are written in the Lamb's book of life' (21:27). The mention of the Lamb is, of course, a mark of the Christianisation of the Jewish phraseology.

Jewish Christian texts also exhibit this imagery. Thus the *Clementine Homilies* take up the Lucan passage quoted above: 'Rejoice . . . that through the good pleasure of God your names, as of the ever-living, are written in heaven' (*Hom.* IX, 22). Here the expression εὐαρεστία emphasises the gratuitous nature of the election. The *Apocalypse of Peter* uses the expression 'book of life' in this context: 'We prayed and went down from the mountain, glorifying God, which ha h written the names of the righteous in heaven in the book of life.'[70] The term was adopted throughout the patristic period, and in Saint Augustine's time was to give rise to discussions on predestination.[71]

However 'the book of life' can have a different meaning; it may stand for the book in which the just will be enrolled when they have made themselves worthy of it. This idea is already present in Jewish apocalyptic: 'If they transgress (the covenant)', says the *Book of Jubilees*, the Jews 'will be recorded on the heavenly tablets as enemies, and they will be blotted out of the book of life, and inscribed in the book of the guilty' (XXX, 22; cf. XXXVI, 10). It appears also in a passage in *Revelation* where, speaking of the Judgment, John says: 'And books were opened. And another book was opened, which is the book of life: and the dead were judged out of the things which were written in the books, according to their works' (20:12); the passage contin es: 'And if any was not found written in the bo_ok of life, he was cast int the lake of fire' (20:15). A variety of meanings attaches to 'the book of life' in this work; it may mean 'the book of revelation', 'the book of predestination' or, as here, 'the book of works' and the 'book of the saved'. The point of interest, however, is that this type of expression occurs in the majority of Jewish Christian works, or works belonging to

70. JAMES, *Apocryphal New Testament*, p. 519.
71. Cf. KOEP, *op. cit.*, pp. 83–85.

the Jewish Christian period. Thus, for example, Hermas writes: 'If they (thy children) shall repent with all their heart, they shall be written in the books of life with the saints' (*Vis.* I, 3:5). The actual words used, may, of course, vary somewhat; *Mand.* VIII, 6 has 'refrain from all these things (vices) that thou mayest . . . be enrolled among those who are free from them',[72] and elsewhere there is mention of 'the books of the living', upon which 'the righteous shall see his name enrolled' (*Sim.* II, 9).

The same conception is to be found in the *Odes of Solomon*: 'All those who overcome shall be written in the Book; for their book is the victory which is yours' (IX, 12–13). Here again there is a reminder of an expression in the *Revelation*: 'He that overcometh . . . I will in no wise blot his name out of the book of life' (*Rev.* 3:5). It is remarkable that in all these passages enrolment in the book of life should be regarded as resulting from man's fidelity. The predestinationist view, which was typical of the conception of the book of life in Jewish apocalyptic, and which endures in certain passages of Saint Paul (*Eph.* 1:18) and John (*Rev.* 13:8) seems here to be entirely set aside. It was to reappear i Gnosticism.

The book of life in this sense is known also by other names. Thus the expression 'the book of the memorial', appears in *I Clement*: 'But they that endured patiently in confidence inherited glory and honour; they were exalted and had their names recorded by God in their memorial ($\mu\nu\eta$-$\mu o\sigma\acute{v}\nu\omega$) for ever and ever' (XLV, 8). This alludes to a biblical expression in Malachi: 'The Lord hearkened and heard, and a book of remembrance ($\mu\nu\eta\mu o\sigma\acute{v}\nu o\nu$) was written before him for them that feared the Lord, and that thought upon his name. And they shall be mine, saith the Lord of Hosts, in the day that I do make, even a peculiar treasure' (3:16–17). It may be noted that this passage from Malachi is quoted in the *Damascus Document* (XX, 19) and was therefore in use in Essene circles. Similar wording appears in the Jewish *Testament of Levi* 'Thy seed shall be enrolled in the book of the memorial ($\mu\nu\eta\mu o\sigma\acute{v}\nu o\nu$) of life unto all ages'.[73]

These various examples have shown that the conception of the book of life was a familiar one in Jewish Christianity. They do not display any feature that can be regarded as original in comparison with the tradition of Jewish Apocalypses. Once again, however, it is not the symbolism itself which is of immediate concern but the Christian data expressed through it; this can be seen especially clearly in regard to the imagery at present under

72. Cf. also *Sim.* V, 3:2.
73. Cf. CHARLES, II, p. 366. N.b., *CDC* XX, 19 = *CDC* Ms. B, p. 2, sec. 19.

discussion. Henceforward 'Jesus himself is the Revelation; and there is no further use for visions, ecstasies and dreams'. There is now no need of a heavenly ascension in order to be initiated into the books of destiny: 'the revelation which Jesus brings comes down from heaven to earth.' Hence 'his word, his actions, his sufferings, his person now constitute the revelation authorised by God; God the Father reveals himself in his Son Jesus Christ'.[74] Such was the radical change brought about by the coming of Christ. The question now arises, did this have any repercussions on the concept of the heavenly book? Was this particular image used by Jewish Christianity to express the special character of the Christian revelation?

The judgments just quoted are borne out completely in a group of texts which constitute the specifically Jewish Christian expression of the heavenly book. The first of these is in the *Revelation* of John:

> And I saw in the right hand of him that sat on the throne a book written within and on the back, close sealed with seven seals. And I saw a strong angel proclaiming with a great voice: Who is worthy to open the book and to loose the seals thereof? And no one in the heaven or on the earth or under the earth was able to open the book or to look thereon (5:1–3).

Here the sealed book is clearly the one containing the secret of human destinies.[75] It is sealed because the knowledge of it is hidden from the regard of every creature. It is in the right hand of God and represents his decrees. Here again the task of manifesting it is committed to an angel, but the angel attests that neither he nor any creature is able to do this. This emphasises the absolute transcendence of the 'mystery' hidden in God, and recalls *Eph.* 3:9–11. The seven seals may perhaps denote the seven ages of the world.

It is now that one of the Elders declares: 'Weep not: behold, the Lion that is of the tribe of Judah, the Root of David, hath overcome, to open the book and the seven seals thereof' (5:5). Then the 'slain lamb' appears. 'He came, and he taketh it out of the right hand of him that sat on the throne' (5:6–7). This recalls the scenes in the apocalypses where the book is committed to the seer by an angel, but here it is God himself who gives the book, and therefore a higher revelation is implied. Thus, 'when he had taken the book, the four living creatures and the four and twenty

74. Cf. BIETENHARD, *op. cit.*, pp. 250 f.
75. Cf. SCHRENK, art. $B\iota\beta\lambda\iota o\nu$, *TWNT*, I, pp. 615–619

Elders fell down before the Lamb' (5:8). A comparison with the apocalypses indicates the completely unprecedented character of this new revelation, whose message was hidden even from the angels—a detail which recalls *I Pet.* 1:12; *Heb.* 1:1–14; *Gal.* 3:20.[76]

There is, however, by contrast with the apocalypses, another new feature, namely, that not only does the Lamb reveal the final destinies of the world, he also fulfils them. He is the very content of the revelation. He opens the book because He is the subject of the book. This application to the person of Christ of the apocalyptic doctrine of God's hidden plan may be seen already in St. Paul (*Eph.* 1:2–12), but without any explicit reference to the heavenly books. There is, however, a reference to the Father 'who hath blessed us with every spiritual blessing in the heavenly places in Christ: even as he chose us in him before the foundation of the world' (*Eph.* 1:3–4). Similarly, *I Peter* speaks of 'the Lamb . . . foreknown before the foundation of the world' (1:20); but only the *Revelation* alludes to the 'heavenly book'.

It will be observed that in the *Epistle to the Ephesians* the divine election embraces both Christ and those whom He has chosen eternally. This idea also appears in the *Revelation*, where it is the reason for the introduction of the 'book of life' which comes to be identified with 'the book of the Lamb'. Thus the notion of the 'book of life' is in its turn transformed, and embodied in the new conception of the Lamb, and those whom God has chosen in Him, as forming the content of God's plan. Thus we read: 'All that dwell on the earth shall worship him (sc. the Beast), every one whose name hath not been written in the book of life of the Lamb that hath been slain from the foundation of the world' (13:8). The meaning of the phrase is confirmed in another passage: 'And they that dwell on the earth shall wonder—they whose name hath not been written in the book of life from the foundation of the world—when they behold the beast' (17:8).

In the *Revelation* then, the slain Christ appears as the one who reveals and accomplishes the design of God contained in 'the sealed book'. This left one more stage to complete, namely that by which He would be identified with the book itself, in that his coming into the world constitutes revelation. This seems to be expressed in two texts based on Jewish Christian speculations on 'the heavenly book'.[77] The first is in the twenty-

76. Cf. J. DANIÉLOU, *Les anges et leur mission*, 2nd ed., pp. 11–35.
77. Cf. BIETENHARD, *op. cit.* It may be remembered that in a passage in Philo 'book' is a name of the Logos: 'The text calls the Logos of God "Book" (βιβλίον) in which are

third *Ode of Solomon*, perhaps the most difficult in the collection.[78] The relevant passage is as follows:

> His thought (i.e. of the Most High) was like a Letter; His will descended from on high (or from the Most High); and it was sent like an arrow which is violently shot from the bow. And many hands rushed to the Letter to seize it and to take and read it: and it escaped their fingers and they were affrighted at it and at the seal that was upon it, because it was not permitted to them to loose its seal: for the power that was over the seal was greater than they. But those who saw it ran after the Letter that they might know where it would alight, and who should read it and who should hear it (XXIII, 5-9).

'The description is something like that of the little sealed book in the Apocalypse which no one can open except the triumphant Lamb.'[79] It is a book, or letter,[80] which contains the 'will' of the Most High and was in his hand. Men and angels try to read it, but do not succeed, for it is sealed. No one dare even look at it, yet all try to master its contents and wait to know how it will be deciphered. The analogy is practically certain, the only difference being that in the *Odes* the book is sent and becomes a letter.

The last point is explained, however, precisely by the fact that the revelation, according to the *Ode*, is now made in the world and not during a heavenly ascension. Moreover, this revelation is the Word himself, who is, however, not at first recognised. This is why the letter is sealed.[81] With regard to the imagery of the letter, it is to be found in the *Song of the Pearl*, another text of Syrian origin,[82] which adds that the Father says to the Word: 'Thy name is named in the book of life' (47). Thus 'book' and 'letter' are clearly closely related terms.

This is strongly supported by the last verses, which give the key to the whole *Ode*: 'And the Letter was a great Tablet, which was wholly written by the Finger of God: and the name of the Father was on it and of the Son

78. Cf. RENDEL HARRIS, *The Odes and Psalms of Solomon*, Cambridge, 1909, p. 120.
79. So RENDEL HARRIS, p. 121, with remarkable insight.
80. O. ROLLER shows that in *Rev.* 1:11, βιβλίον denotes a letter ('Das Buch mit sieben Siegeln', *ZNW*, XXXVIII, 1937, p. 99), and LOHMEYER (*Komment Apok.*, p. 49) believes that the same applies to 5:1, and gives a reference to our *Ode*.
81. BATIFFOL recalls the Naassenian Hymn: 'Bearing the seals, I shall descend' (HIPPOLYTUS, *Elench.* V, 10).
82. Cf. JAMES, *op. cit.*, pp. 411-415.

---

enrolled and engraved the constitution of beings' (*Leg. All.* I, 8:19). Philo transposes the eschatological conception of the Bible into an exemplarist view.

and of the Holy Spirit, to rule for ever and ever' (19–20). Here is a final precious detail; the tablet written by the finger of God plainly refers to the tablets given to Moses on Sinai, and thus identifies the latter with the heavenly tablets of Jewish apocalyptic speculation. The tablet here is therefore the new revelation of the New Testament, contrasted with that of Sinai. Moreover, this revelation is that of the Father,[83] which completes the justification of the opinion quoted earlier: 'It is the words, the actions, the sufferings and the person of Jesus which constitute the revelation authorised by God; God the Father reveals himself in his Son Jesus Christ.'[84]

Thus the enigma of *Ode XXIII* seems best resolved by seeing it in the light of Jewish Christian speculations which identify the 'heavenly book' with Christ the Revealer, and see its contents as his act of redemption. Hitherto, however, there seemed to be no parallel to such an interpretation, and this led scholars to maintain a certain reserve with regard to this reading of the *Ode*. These reservations have now been dispelled by the discovery of a very similar exegesis in the *Gospel of Truth*.[85]

The allusions begin with the revelation of the gnosis to the disciples[86]:

In their hearts has been manifested the living Book of the Living[87] which was written in the Thought and (in) the Mind of the Father and which, from before the foundation of All-thing, abode in that part of him which is incomprehensible; that (Book) which it was impossible for anyone to take, since this was reserved for Him who was to take It and to be sacrificed. No one among those who believed in salvation was able to become manifest so long as that Book had not made its appearance. For this reason, Jesus the merciful and the faithful patiently accepted the endurance of suffering, until such time as He should have taken possession of that Book, since He knew that His death meant life for many (19:35–20:14).

83. BATIFFOL is surely right (*Les Odes de Salomon*, p. 85) in thinking that the mention of the Son and the Holy Ghost is a later doxology.
84. BIETENHARD, *op. cit.*, p. 250.
85. The points of contact between this work and the *Odes of Solomon* have been established by H. M. SCHENKE, *Die Herkunft des sogenannten Evangelium Veritatis*, 1959, pp. 26–29.
86. The translation followed is, with a few variations, that of H. C. PUECH, and the references are to his edition.
87. Cf. the expression 'book of the living' in Hermas (*Sim.* V, 2:9).

It is impossible to read this passage without being struck by the parallels to the *Revelation* and the *Ode*, as well as by its specifically Gnostic features. The book of life is the decree hidden in God which contains the names of the living. These names are enrolled in the Book from before the creation of the world, as in the *Revelation*. The Book is present in the world, like the Letter in the *Ode*, but no one dare take hold of it. In the Gnostic view, this signifies the rigorous predestination of the living, the spiritual ones, and at the same time the fact that they are unknown save in so far as they have been made known by the communication of the gnosis. This communication is the manifestion of the book, which Jesus takes upon Himself; but he cannot do this until he has been sacrificed and has taken suffering upon himself. This is clearly an allusion to the invisible Lamb of the *Revelation* who opens the sealed Book.[88]

The continuation of the passage is no less remarkable:

Just as, so long as a Testament has not been opened, the fortune of the deceased master of the house remains hidden,[89] so too the All remained hidden, so long as the Father of All was invisible, unique being existing through himself, from whom came forth all Spaces. This is why Jesus appeared and took that Book. He was nailed to a Tree; He fastened to the Cross the ordinance of the Father. Oh! great, sublime teaching (20:15-25).

This constitutes a most important exegesis of *Col.* 2:14. The χειρόγραφον is the ordinance of the Father, that is the Book itself, and this ordinance is promulgated on the Cross, for it is then that Christ wins the right to unfold it. Its content is the revelation of the Father, which until then had remained hidden.

Here once again is the theme from *Revelation*; the Lamb wins on the Cross the right to open the book. But the themes of the *Ode* are also present, for in the latter the scroll, letter or book is brought to the Cross, symbolised by a wheel (XXIII, 10), and is there opened up. Once more, it contains the revelation of the Father. There are, therefore, elements common to the *Ode* and the *Gospel* which do not appear in the *Revelation*, the link between

88. W. C. van UNNIK has already drawn attention to these similarities: *The Jung Codex*, 1955, pp. 79-130. He also emphasises other parallels, especially with the *Epistle to the Hebrews*; *Hebr.* 2:17 speaks of Jesus as 'merciful and faithful', a Jewish Christian expression connoting *hesed and 'emet*.
89. The influence of *Hebrews* is again apparent: cf. 9:15-17.

the letter and the Cross, and the revelation of the Father; and this confirms the presence of specifically Jewish Christian theological speculation. Moreover, the association of the *Ode* with *Col.* 2:14, which was not justified if the χειρόγραφον was in fact a decree of condemnation, now becomes certain and attests an unexpected Jewish Christian exegesis of the *Colossians* passage.

Some other references to the 'Book of the Living' in the *Gospel of Truth* remain to be mentioned. First of all there is the enrolment in the book of life: 'Those who have received the Teaching, namely the Living who are inscribed in the Book of the Living, receive it for themselves alone' (21: 4–6)—an allusion to *Rev.* 13:8–9. A later passage reads: 'Such is the Gnosis of this living Book, which has been revealed to the Aeons in the end' (22:38–39). These passages emphasise the character of the Book as revelation. At the same time Gnostic transformation of the theme, which becomes more marked in what follows, where the text speaks of the vowels and consonants of the Book which cannot be uttered by those who do not know them (23:1–5),[90] leaves a clear field for those speculations on letters which occur in Mark the Magician.

We have now traced some of the characteristics of the world-view of Jewish Christian theology. It is a conception which stems largely from Jewish apocalyptic, but it contains also a number of important ideas, the seven heavens, the two angels, the demons of the air and the angels of the nations, which have their parallels in the Hellenistic world. It seems to be the product of a period in which Jewish apocalyptic felt the influence of the Greek society that surrounded it, and one also in which the Jewish Christians of Syria or Asia Minor were in contact with Oriental religions. But even with this particular colouring which gives it a character of its own, distinct from that of the old apocalyptic, it remains a fundamentally Jewish Christian construction, and the traces of it which appear later can definitely be assigned to this source. Its chief interest, however, lies not in itself but in the fact that it provided the symbolism for the expression of the theology of the Incarnation and the Redemption.

90. This is reminiscent of Hermas: cf. *Vis.* II, 1–2.

CHAPTER SEVEN

THE LION AND THE STAR:
THE THEOLOGY OF THE INCARNATION

IN the last chapter some account was given of the structure of the cosmos according to Jewish Christian teaching; and it was then remarked that the Jewish Christians were interested in this structure not for its own sake, but for the imagery it supplied with which to express theological truth. By means of this imagery they sought to sketch out an overall picture of the divine economy of salvation, a picture which was in fact the earliest theological elaboration of the New Testament data in Christian history, and one which issued in a Christology of a very distinctive kind. The symbolism in which this Christology was expressed was not that of the historical vision of the Old Testament, which Irenaeus was to adopt, nor that of Hellenistic metaphysics, such as appealed to Origen and the Greek theologians who came after him; instead it was borrowed from the apocalyptic of Later Judaism.

The structure so employed might be called both 'mythical' and 'gnostic', but it is important to be precise in the meaning to be attached to each of these terms. It is 'mythical' if the word 'myth' is used to mean a system of symbolism, but not if it is taken to connote a 'mythological' or 'legendary' vision of the world,[1] the vital difference being that in the former sense the 'myth' does not falsify the original content of revelation, it is merely a mode of expressing it, and this mode of expression is just as valid as a metaphysical or existential one.[2]

1. 'The word "myth", as a technical term in the phenomenology of religion, no longer has the sense of "fable". It means "an imaginative (not imaginary) representation used to convey statements of value" ' (H. DUMÉRY, *Philosophie de la religion*, Paris, 1957, I, p. vi).
2. BULTMANN falls into the error of imagining that the myth alters the content of the message, and that he is successful in distinguishing that message, whereas all he achieves is to transfer it from one mode of expression to another. Obviously some mode of

This general picture may also be called 'gnostic', but here again it is important to be precise as to the meaning of the word. Gnosis is to be understood not in the general sense of a higher knowledge, nor in the restricted one of the dualism of Valentinus, but as something in between, namely the particular form taken by religious knowledge in the second century after Christ. This gnosis is of Jewish origin, with elements borrowed from Iran and Greece, and it constitutes a stock of symbolism common to Jewish apocalyptic, Jewish Christian theology, Egyptian Gnosticism and Hellenistic Hermeticism. Each one of these groups, however, treats it in its particular way, adapting it to express its own doctrine. Thus, the fact that a particular work mentions the seven heavens and the ogdoad does not mean that the work in question must have been influenced by Valentinian Gnosticism, but that on the contrary Valentinian Gnosticism belongs to a cultural background in which these symbols were common property.

It may be noted that apocalyptic categories are already to be found in St. John and in St. Paul. The captivity Epistles are full of Gnostic symbolism, in particular that of the descent of Christ (*Eph.* 4:9), of Christ's struggle on the Cross against the principalities and powers (*Col.* 2:15), of the exaltation of Christ above all the heavens (*Eph.* 1:21; 4:10; *Phil.* 2:10). There is a definite kinship between Paul's view of the world and that of the *Epistles* of Ignatius, *II Clement* and the *Shepherd of Hermas.*[3] This symbolism does not appear in purely Jewish or purely Greek texts, but may be called Oriental-Hellenistic. The Pauline Epistles do not, of course, fall within the scope of the present study, but it is interesting to see that the Jewish Christian theologians have the same intellectual background as that of the Epistles of the Captivity.

THE HIDDEN DESCENT

One of the first characteristics of Jewish Christian Christology is that the mystery of the descent of the Son was hidden from the angels. The most

3. Cf. SCHLIER, *Christus und die Kirche im Epheserbrief*, p. 75.

---

expression is always necessary, and it will normally be the mode current in the society, whatever its state of civilisation, in which the message is expressed. Jewish Christian theology therefore represents one particular mode of expressing Christianity which is neither more, nor less valid than another.

primitive form of this idea is probably preserved in the *Physiologos*.[4] The text runs as follows:

So our Saviour, the spiritual lion sent by the Eternal Father, hid the signs of His spiritual being, that is His divinity. With the Angels He became an Angel, with the Thrones a Throne, with the Powers a Power, with men a man during his descent (κατάβασις). For he descended into the womb of Mary, to save the race of human souls that had strayed. Consequently, they did not recognise Him in his descent from on high, and they said: 'Who is this King of Glory?' Then the Holy Spirit answered: 'The Lord of Hosts, He is the King of Glory.'[5]

This text is interesting because it gathers together all the themes to be found in any of the various texts where this conception appears. Attention should be drawn first of all to the idea that the Word, descending to earth to take flesh, passes successively through all the orders of angels, a feature which is also present in the *Ascension of Isaiah*. The theological point is that the Incarnation remained hidden from the Angels, and this seems to have been a characteristic emphasis of Jewish Christian thinking. It is already to be found in St. Paul (*I Cor.* 2:8; *Eph.* 3:10–12), and occurs again in a famous passage of Ignatius of Antioch: 'And hidden from the prince of this world were the virginity of Mary and her child-bearing and likewise also the death of the Lord—three mysteries to be cried aloud—the which were wrought in the silence of God' (*Eph.* XIX, 1).[6] Irenaeus was to say the same, with an allusion to the angels: 'But because the Word came down invisible to creatures, He was not known to them in His descent' (*Dem.* 84).

The direct source of both these passages seems to be the *Ascension of Isaiah* (XI, 16): 'This hath been hidden from all the heavens and all the princes and all the gods of this world.'[7]

It is this theme and the preceding one taken together, however, which produce the most curious feature of the passage from the *Physiologos*,

4. This work in its final form seems to belong to the end of the fourth century, but it has made use of elements borrowed from early Jewish and Jewish Christian literature; cf. ERIK PETERSON, 'Die Spiritualität des griechischen Physiologos', *BZ*, XLVII, 1954, pp. 70 f.
5. Cf. PITRA, *Spic. Solesm.* III, p. 339.
6. Cf. SCHLIER, *Untersuchungen*, pp. 5–32.
7. The theme was to pass into the main Christian tradition: cf. ORIGEN, *Hom. Luc.* 6; AMBROSE, *Exp. Luc.* II, 2; ZENO, *Tract.* II, 29.

namely that in the course of his descent the Word is assimilated successively to the different orders of angels through which he passes. It is important to be precise about this assimilation. In Origen the conception occurs of the Word becoming incarnate in all orders of creatures, that he might save them all; hence he also becomes an angel with the angels. This is not the idea in the *Physiologos*, nor is it Jewish Christian, but a part of Origen's own system. In the present instance the only reason that leads the Word to put on the form of the angelic worlds through which he passes is that he should not be known. This is quite apparent in the *Physiologos* passage, and also in the other Jewish Christian texts which treat of the same theme.

The most important of these is the *Ascension of Isaiah*, and the other works probably depend on this one.[8] The relevant passages begin as follows: 'I heard the voice of the Most High, the Father of my Lord, saying to my Lord Christ, who is to be called Jesus: Go forth and descend through all the heavens; then Thou shalt descend to the firmament and to the (terrestrial) world. . . . And Thou shalt transform thyself into the likeness of all who are in the five heavens, and Thou shalt be careful to change into the form of the angels of the firmament. And let none of the angels of the world know that Thou art Lord with Me of the seven heavens and of their angels . . . in order that thou mayest judge and destroy the princes and angels and gods of the world' (X, 7–12).

The work then describes the actual descent of the Word. He goes down first into the sixth heaven where he keeps his form and the angels adore him. 'And I saw when He descended into the fifth heaven that in the fifth heaven He made Himself like unto the form of the angels there, and they did not glorify Him; for His form was like unto theirs' (X, 20). It is the same with the other heavens. As regards the third heaven there is the added detail that: 'Those who kept the gate of the heaven demanded the password and the Lord gave it to them in order that he should not be recognised' (X, 24). He arrived then at the firmament 'where dwelleth the ruler of this world, and He gave the password to those on the left, and His form was like theirs, and they did not praise Him there, but from envy they were at strife one with another' (X, 29).

These passages are of the first importance. It will be observed that the Word takes not only the form of the good angels, but also of the fallen

8. The reason for beginning with the *Physiologos* rather than the *Ascension* was that, as Peterson has suggested, the former work probably depends on an older version of the *Ascension* than the one extant; cf. pp. 209 f. below.

angels of the firmament. This is clear evidence that it is essentially a question of appearances, and that the emphasis is placed on the fact that the Word must stay invisible so as not to be recognised. This characteristic appears also in the allusion to the password, which is connected with the idea of the angels who guard the gates, the doorkeepers or customs-men (τελῶναι), who play an important role in the doctrine of the ascent of souls to Paradise.

Another, slightly later Jewish Christian text takes up the same themes. It is the *Epistle of the Apostles*, in which the following passage occurs:

> When I come from the Father, and pass through the heavens, and am clothed with the Wisdom of the Father and with his Power, then am I like to the heavenly beings, the angels and archangels. When I pass through the heavens in their form, then am I as one of them. Next I find the Orders, the Powers, the Dominations; the archangels Michael, Gabriel, Uriel and Raphael followed me as far as the fifth firmament, since I resembled one of them, for power to do so had been given me by the Father. But then I terrified the archangels by my word, telling them to return to the altar of the Father and to serve the Father according to their wont, until I should return to Him (13).

It should be noted that, as in the *Ascension*, the archangels do not go beyond the sixth heaven, and that the Word sends them back to the Father when he continues his descent.[9]

There is a final detail of the *Physiologos* still to be considered, which seems to be markedly archaic and yet is not in the extant text of the *Ascension of Isaiah*. It will be remembered that the passage ended as follows: 'The angels did not recognise the Word in his descent, and they said: "Who is this King of Glory?" And the Holy Spirit answers: "The Lord of Hosts, he is the King of Glory." '[10] There are two noteworthy

9. An almost identical group of four archangels is found at Qumran (*DSW* IX, 15).

10. The reason for thinking that we are dealing with a tradition of the *Ascension of Isaiah* different from the extant text is that this feature reappears in the fourth century in a remarkable passage of Gregory of Nyssa, in which, however, the Holy Spirit is replaced by the angels who accompany Christ: 'When the hypercosmic powers accompany the Lord in his descent, they order the angels who surround the earth, to whom is confided the care of human life, to lift up their gates, saying: Be lifted up, you eternal gates, and the king of glory shall enter. But as he who contains all within himself proportions himself wherever he goes to those who receive him, he not only becomes man with men, but coming amongst angels he likens himself to their nature. Hence the doorkeepers enquire of those who speak, saying: Who is this king of glory?' (*Serm.*

points here. First of all there is the use of *Ps.* 23:10 (EVV 24), which seems to have become associated at an early date with the theme of the passage of the Word through the angelic spheres, except that in all other cases it refers to the ascent and not to the descent of the Word.[11] On the other hand, the fact that it is the Holy Spirit who replies is quite in conformity with the usage of the *Ascension of Isaiah*, and is a mark of primitiveness.[12]

All the texts so far quoted belong to the main Christian tradition, but the theme was also taken up by the Gnostics, and here again it appears as extremely archaic, since it is found in the gnosis of Simon Magus. Irenaeus' account states: 'Since the angels ruled the world ill, because each one of them coveted the principal power for himself, he came to amend matters, and descended, changing his appearance and making himself like to the Powers and Principalities and Angels.'[13] Similarly Epiphanius has: 'I change my form in each heaven, according to the likeness of those that are there, so as not to be recognised by my powers' (*Pan.* XXI, 2:4). Tertullian says that Simon claimed 'to have come down to deliver men from the angelic powers, to which he assimilated himself so as to deceive them and that in this way he also falsely caused himself to pass as a man amongst men'.[14]

But it is obvious that the context of the thought is here quite different. The powers are now the planetary powers, the cosmocrators who dominate the lower world, the work of the Demiurge. An analogous conception, one more developed and very close in its form to the *Epistle of the Apostles*, but

11. Except in the case of the *Gospel of Nicodemus*, where it is applied to the Descent into Hell (V, 1–3). We should possess another example of great importance if the Κύριος τῆς δοξῆς of *I Cor.* 2:8 could be derived from this psalm. Cf. A. CABANISS, 'The Harrowing of Hell, Psalm 24 and Pliny the Younger', *VC*, VII, 1953, pp. 64–75.

12. So PETERSON, *op. cit.*, pp. 73 f.

13. *Adv. haer.* I, 23:3. Cf. the texts collected by BARBEL, *op. cit.*, pp. 299–300; also SCHENKE, 'Das Evangelium nach Philippus' (26), *TL*, LXXXIV, 1959, p. 10.

14. *De Anima* XXXIV, 4; cf. WASZINK, *Tertullianus de anima*, Amsterdam, 1947, pp. 401–410.

Asc., *PG* XLVI, 693A). The text is coloured by Origenist influences, especially in the theme of the multiple ἐπίνοιαι of the Word, and his aptitude for proportioning himself to the capacity of those who receive him. But the Jewish Christian basis shows through: the angels do not recognise the Word because he has taken the form of an angel. The doorkeepers are those of the *Ascension of Isaiah*, and the use of *Ps.* 23:9 is an indication, not of the influence of the *Physiologos*, but of the use of some common source, which would probably be a lost Greek version of the *Ascension of Isaiah* which is known to have existed from a fragment quoted by Epiphanius (*Pan.* LXVII, 3:4).

related to Gnostic dualism, occurs in *Pistis Sophia*. In this work the Saviour takes the form of the Angel Gabriel, so as not to be recognised by the Archons (VII, 12). This is an instance of the theme of Christ appearing under the guise of Gabriel, which is to be found in various texts,[15] and is connected with the biblical theme of the Word manifesting himself in the form of an angel,[16] not with a use of the angel symbolism to denote the Word. In the *Pistis Sophia*, however, this theme is combined with that of the Word's dissimulating his identity. In the Simonian teaching, as reported above by Tertullian, the Word also takes on the appearance of a man when he comes amongst men in order not to be recognised by them. This theme too occurs both in the *Physiologos*, and in the *Ascension of Isaiah*. The relevant passage from the latter may be quoted: 'This hath been hidden from all the heavens and all the princes . . . And I saw: In Nazareth He sucked the breast as a babe, and kept in all things the common law of life in order that He might not be recognised' (XI, 17). There is thus a common train of thought in which the Word becomes a man among men, as he was an angel amongst angels, in order not to be known. In Gnosticism this corresponds to a Docetist tendency and a denial of the Incarnation. In the *Ascension of Isaiah*, however, it is accompanied by an affirmation of the Incarnation, and simply underlines the fact that this Incarnation is hidden from men as it is from angels.[17]

Among the Gnostics these conceptions were especially well-developed by the Ophites. A text of this sect came into Origen's hands: it describes the descent through the seven planetary spheres, each one of which the sect identified with a Jewish archangel, who thus became assimilated to an Archon. In order to pass through the sphere it was necessary to give the password to the one who guarded the gate.[18] Irenaeus also mentions that the Ophites speak of 'the descent of Christ, which throws the Archons into stupor and amazement by its novelty' (*Adv. haer.* I, 30:11), adding that for them 'Christ descended through the seven heavens, assuming the likeness (*assimilatum*) of their sons' (30:12) and that 'many of the disciples of Jesus were not aware of the descent of Christ upon him' (30:13).

Once again it is easy to recognise the Jewish Christian theme of the

---

15. BARBEL., *op. cit.*, pp. 235–262.   16. Cf. pp. 131 f. above.
17. Cf. also *Orac. Sib.* XII, 32–33: 'Then will be the hidden (κρύφιος) coming of the Word of the Most High, having flesh like mortals.'
18. *Contra Celsum* VI, 30–31, also VI, 34; cf. H. CHADWICK, *Origen Contra Celsum*, Cambridge, 1954, pp. 345–348.

assimilation of the Word to the angels in the course of his descent. As in Ignatius, the angels are the astral powers. This whole conception, which originates in archaic Christian theology, is, in a Gnostic system, transferred together with the assimilation to the Jewish archangels to evil powers. The symbolic framework is the same for both the Jewish Christians and the Gnostics; but the symbolism, common to both, is used to express a radically different system of theology in each case.

A third witness to the presence of this theme among the Ophites is the *Naassenian Hymn* preserved by Hippolytus. In it Christ declares:

> Bearing the seals I shall descend
> I shall pass through all the aeons

(*Elench.* V, 10). The most interesting feature here is that of the seals (σφραγίδες). This introduces a new conception, the point of which is not that the Word is invisible, but that he is invulnerable. The σφραγίδες are in fact his protection; and this throws into stronger relief the maleficent character of the Archons through whom he has to pass in his descent. The conception is quite certainly already present in the *Odes of Solomon*:

> His thought (i.e., the Word) was like a letter, his will descended from on high. Many hands (i.e., the angels) hurled themselves upon him to seize it, to take and read it; but it escaped from their fingers, and they were afraid of it and of the seal that was on it, because they had not the power to break the seal, for the power that was on the seal was more mighty than they (XXIII, 5–9).

An echo of this hidden descent appears also in the gnosis of Basilides. Christ 'transfigured himself as he pleased' (*Adv. haer.* I, 24:4). Thus before his Passion he puts on the shape of Simon of Cyrene, and the latter is crucified in his place, while he himself 'ascended to him who had sent him, deriding them, inasmuch as he could not be laid hold of, and was invisible to all' (24:4). This is the Christ who is invisible to men. But a later passage speaks of the angelic spheres which, according to Basilides number three hundred and sixty-five. Christ 'ascended and descended' through them (24:5). 'He who . . . has known all the angels . . . is rendered invisible and incomprehensible to the angels and all the powers. . . . And as the Son was unknown to all (the angels and the powers) so must he also (the Gnostic) be known by no one. But while he knows them all, and passes through them all, he himself remains invisible and unknown to all' (24:6).[19]

There is a plain parallel drawn here between Christ and the Gnostic, so that what is true of the one holds for the other. Hence it is possible to discern once again the conception of Christ as able to take on what form he wishes and therefore also the form of an angel, in order to disguise himself to all in his descent and ascent. Conversely, this gives the Gnostic the right to dissimulate 'by making himself like to all' (24:6), that is, by denying what he is in order to avoid persecution. Once more the Jewish Christian doctrine of the concealment of the Word from the angels undergoes in Gnosticism a transformation which alters its whole inner meaning.[20]

One other feature of the archaic doctrine of the descent of the Word must be considered, and that is the frequent inclusion of the figure of the Holy Ghost. In the *Physiologos* it was he who revealed the true nature of Christ to the angels who failed to recognise him in his descent; and in the *Epistle of the Apostles* the Word is said to descend clothed in the Wisdom of the Father. This Wisdom, as in the writings of Theophilus of Antioch, is the Third Person of the Trinity.[21] There seems also to be a vestige of this conception in the teaching of the Ophites. According to them, 'Christ, united with Wisdom (*perplexum Sophiae*), descended into him, and thus Jesus Christ was produced' (*Adv. haer.* I, 30:12). In the Ophite doctrine this descent of Christ, which as in the *Epistle* passes through all seven heavens, takes place at the Baptism.

It is interesting to compare these texts with a passage in Irenaeus:

But the earth is encompassed by seven heavens, in which dwell Powers and Angels and Archangels, giving homage to the almighty God who created all things . . . That is why the Spirit of God in His indwelling is manifold, and is said by Isaiah the prophet to rest in seven forms on the Son of God, that is, on the Word in His Incarnation (*Is.* 11:2) . . . Now the first of these forms and that which includes all the others is Wisdom. . . . And Moses revealed the pattern of this in the seven-branched candlestick (*Dem.* 9).

19. Cf. also APELLES, according to Hippolytus: 'He lived in a body, unknown to the cosmic powers during all the time he spent in this world' (*Elench.* VII, 38; cf. also VIII, 10; also the *Apocryphon of John* LI, 10–15: TILL, p. 143).
20. Cf. A. ORBE, *Los primeros herejes ante la persecución*, pp. 26–33.
21. Cf. KRETSCHMAR, *op. cit.*, p. 50.

This passage must have come to Irenaeus from an earlier source, almost certainly Theophilus of Antioch.[22] In it once again is the association of the Spirit or of Wisdom with the Word at the Incarnation, but this time with the addition of an explicit connection between the seven heavens and the seven gifts of the Holy Ghost.[23]

It would seem that there is here a fusion of two themes. The association of the seven heavens and the seven gifts of the Spirit with the seven-branched candlestick, interpreted as an image of cosmic worship, is in the direct tradition of Asiatic theology, and echoes the imagery of the 'seven lamps of fire burning before the throne, which are the seven Spirits of God' (*Rev.* 4:5). The same tradition (*Rev.* 5:6) also presents the seven Spirits as belonging to the slain Lamb. There is no need, therefore to derive this particular exegesis from Theophilus of Antioch. On the other hand, the association of the doctrine of the descent through the seven heavens with that of the communication of the seven gifts of the Spirit to the Word in the course of his descent, so that he is 'anointed with the fulness of the Spirit',[24] is an element which does seem to be more specifically Syriac.

THE STAR OF JACOB

If the first characteristic of the Jewish Christian theology of the Incarnation is the emphasis placed on the hiddenness of the event, the second is the stress on its supernatural character. The latter is achieved primarily by developing the Gospel traditions in the direction of the marvellous, a feature typical, for example, of the Apocryphal Gospels. The interest of this process lies in the theological meaning which is given to the events of the life of Christ by presenting them as 'mysteries'. Thus Ignatius of Antioch calls the virginity ($\pi\alpha\rho\theta\epsilon\nu\iota\alpha$) of Mary and her child-bearing 'mysteries to be cried aloud' (*Eph.* XIX, 1), and Justin terms the birth of Christ a 'mystery' (*Dial.* XLIII, 3). Three of these mysteries will be examined here, the Nativity, the Adoration of the Magi and the Baptism.

To begin then with the Nativity, it should be noted that Mary's child-bearing is presented as just as much a mystery in its own right as her virginal conception. Indeed, as regards the latter, Jewish Christian theology

22. Cf. KRETSCHMAR, *op. cit.*, pp. 48–49.
23. KRETSCHMAR (*op. cit.*, p. 48) stresses the purely apocalyptic character of this symbolism; cf. also VICTORINUS OF PETTAU, *De fabrica Mundi*, 7–8.
24. KRETSCHMAR, *op. cit.*, p. 48.

shows no sign of any development beyond *Luke* and *Matthew*. The statement that Mary conceived by the Holy Ghost is quite explicit in the New
Testament, and the Jewish Christian writers do no more than repeat this
affirmation. The only new elements are some additional *testimonia* to
supplement *Is.* 7:10-16, notably that of the stone cut from the mountain
(*Dan.* 2:34), which is found in the *Acts of Peter* (24) and in Irenaeus (*Adv.
haer.* III, 21:7), and which goes back to a very ancient collection on the
subject of Christ as the Stone.[25]

By contrast the supernatural character of Christ's birth is not emphasised
in the New Testament, though it is a theme that plays an important part in
Jewish Christian theology.[26] Attention may be drawn first of all to the
Apocryphon of Ezekiel, 'She has brought forth (τέτοκε) and has not
brought forth', which is widely quoted.[27] Similarly, *Is.* 7:13, 'Is it then a
small thing for you to strive with men? And how will you strive with the
Lord?' is used in several texts[28] to emphasise the miraculous quality of the
event, of which the succeeding verse is of course the classic prediction.

Above all, however, the birth of Jesus is presented as having occurred in
a miraculous manner. Thus the *Ascension of Isaiah* states:

> It came to pass, when (Joseph and Mary) were alone, that Mary
> straightway looked with her eyes and saw a small babe and was
> astonished. And after her astonishment her womb was found as for-
> merly before she had conceived. And when her husband Joseph said
> unto her, 'What has astonished thee?' his eyes were opened, and he
> saw the infant and praised God . . . And many said: 'She has not
> borne a child, nor has a midwife gone up, nor have we heard cries of
> pain' (XI, 8-14).

The last phrase is quoted in the *Acts of Peter* as the testimony of 'a prophet'
on the virginal motherhood (24).

Evidence of the antiquity of the account given in the *Ascension of Isaiah*
is afforded by the fact that it is imitated in *II Enoch*. Here, however, the

---

25. Cf. VINCENT TAYLOR, *The Names of Jesus*, pp. 93-100.
26. Cf. H. J. PLUMPE, 'Some little-known early witnesses to Mary's virginitas in partu',
TS, IX, 1948, pp. 567-577.
27. Cf. *Acts of Peter* 24; CLEM. ALEX., *Strom.* VII, 94:2; TERTULLIAN, *De Carne
Christi* XXIII, 1-3: cf. also EPIPHANIUS, *Pan.* XXX, 30, who presents the text in the
form of dialogue, and seems to ascribe it to the *Ascension of Isaiah*; and RESCH, *Agrapha*,
pp. 305 f.
28. Cf. *Protev. Jac.* XX, 1; *Acts of Peter* 24; JUSTIN, *Dial.* XLIII, 5; LXVI, 2.

subject is not the birth of Jesus, but that of Melchizedek.[29] The text relates first of all how Sophonim, wife of Nir, conceived without having slept with her husband; she then gives birth to Melchizedek in marvellous circumstances. 'And Noah and Nir went in, and saw the child sitting up; and his body was perfectly formed, and he was speaking and blessing the Lord. And Noah and Nir examined him, saying, "This is of the Lord" ' CHARLES: III, 1–20).[30]

Another witness, the *Odes of Solomon*, also combines the two elements of virginal conception and virginal motherhood. Thus *Ode* XIX states: 'The Holy Spirit spread his wings over the womb of the Virgin, and she conceived, and bore a child, and became a Virgin Mother with much mercy. She grew great with child and brought forth a son without pain. And that nothing might be done needlessly, she did not ask for a midwife to help her.' It will be remembered that the two details of freedom from pain and of the absence of the midwife were also present in the *Ascension of Isaiah*, and were quoted by the *Acts of Peter*. These works, therefore, share a common tradition.

This tradition is recorded and developed in the *Protevangelium of James*. The text first describes the amazement that overcame all nature at the moment the Nativity took place. Joseph sees 'the air in amazement . . . the pole of heaven . . . standing still, and the fowls of heaven without motion' (XVIII, 2). Joseph and the midwife whom he went to fetch 'stood in the place of the cave: and behold a bright cloud overshadowing the cave . . . the cloud withdrew itself out of the cave and a great light appeared in the cave so that our eyes could not endure it, and by little and little that light withdrew itself until the young child appeared' (XIX, 2). Other apocrypha were to take up this account and develop it still further. They belong to the literary genre of *haggada*, which sought by marvellous details to emphasise the theological significance of historical episodes.[31]

The second theme to receive theological elaboration in Jewish Christ-

29. A. VAILLANT (*Le livre des secrets d'Hénoch*, p. 75, n. 17) remarks that this 'springs from a desire to suggest a parallel between the miraculous birth of Melchizedek and that of Christ', and adduces it as one of his principal arguments for the Christian origin of the work. The story is printed as a detached appendix in CHARLES.

30. H. SAHLIN (*Der Messias und das Gottesvolk*, Uppsala, 1945, pp. 370–372) regards this passage as quite clearly dependent upon *Luke*.

31. This theology of the Nativity has sometimes been regarded as a sign of Docetism, but to do so is to risk casting doubt on the miraculous birth itself as an event. This was the error of TERTULLIAN (*Adv. Marc.* IV, 21) who through this fear of Docetism strayed from orthodoxy.

ianity was that of the Magi and the Star. The most ancient evidence of this development, and among the most characteristic, is that of Ignatius of Antioch. The fact that it comes in the same context as the passage on the 'hidden mysteries' bears witness to its Jewish Christian origin. He writes:

> How then were they (these mysteries) made manifest to the aeons (αἰῶσιν)? A star (ἀστήρ) shone forth in the heaven above all the stars; and its light was unutterable, and its strangeness caused amazement; and all the rest of the constellations with the sun and moon formed themselves into a chorus about the star; but the star itself far outshone them all; and there was a perplexity to know whence came this strange appearance which was so unlike them. From that time forward every sorcery (μαγεία) and every spell was dissolved, the ignorance of wickedness vanished away, the ancient kingdom was pulled down, when God appeared in the likeness of man unto newness of everlasting life' (*Eph*. XIX, 2–3).

There are several important elements in this passage. The first of these is the appearance, at the moment of Christ's birth, of a star of superior brightness to all the others. The significant development of *Matthew's* account of the star of the Magi,[32] is the emphasis on the size and brightness of the star. This appears again in the *Protevangelium of James*, with an explicit reference to *Matthew*: 'The wise men said: We saw a very great star shining among the stars (λάμψαντα ἐν τοῖς ἄστροις) and dimming them, so that the stars appeared not' (XXI, 2). Similarly in the *Sibylline Oracles*: 'When a star shall appear coming from heaven in the midst of our days, equal to the sun in splendour (λαμπρός), then shall be the hidden coming of the Word of the Most High, having flesh like mortals' (XII, 30–34). There is a remarkable similarity to Ignatius here, particularly in the reference to the hidden coming.

Thus the accent is placed on the exceptional nature of the star that appears, a quality due not simply to its size, but also to its meaning. This seems to be firstly to symbolise the messianic light that dissipates the darkness, an aspect found in the *Testament of Levi*. In a passage dealing with the coming of the new (καινός) priest, the author continues: 'His star (ἄστρον) shall arise (ἀνατελεῖ) in heaven like that of a king, beaming with

32. Cf. P. CAMELOT, *Saint Ignace d'Antioche, Lettres*, p. 88, n. 2. H. KÖSTER (*op. cit.*, pp. 31–32), however, disputes this connection, and sees in Ignatius' text a symbol of the Ascension.

the light of knowledge (φῶς γνώσεως), as the sun beams forth the day . . . He shall shine (ἀναλάμψει) like the sun on the earth, and shall remove (ἐξαιρεῖ) all darkness from under heaven' (XVIII, 2–4). The point to observe here is that the star becomes a symbol of the Messiah himself, as a sign of the light he is to shed upon the world.[33]

This indicates the link between the theme of the star of the Magi and that of the star as a symbol of the Messiah. The passage just quoted must certainly refer to *Mt.* 2:2,[34] but there is also an allusion to *Num.* 24:17: 'A star shall arise (ἀνατελεῖ ἄστρον) out of Jacob.'[35] There is an explicit linking of these texts in Justin, who adds a reference to *Zech.* 6:12[36] in the LXX version:

And that He was to spring up as a star by means of the race of Abraham, Moses gave us to understand when he said thus: A star shall spring up out of Jacob, and a leader out of Israel. And another Scripture saith: Behold, the man—His name is Dayspring (ἀνατολή). When therefore a star sprang up also in heaven at the very time of his birth, as is written in the memoirs of his Apostles, the Wise Men from Arabia recognised Him from this, and came and worshipped Him (*Dial.* CVI, 4).

The introduction of *Num,* 24.17 is especially interesting, for this text was among the earliest to be quoted in collections of Messianic *testimonia*, and already figured in such collections at Qumran.[37] It is applied to 'the Interpreter of the Law in the land of Damascus' in the *Damascus Document* (VII, 19)[38]; is used as a promise of victory in the *War of the Sons of Light and*

33. Cf. also *Test. Jud.* XXIV, 1: 'After these things shall a star (ἄστρον) arise to you . . . in peace, and a man shall arise from my seed.'
34. As DE JONGE maintains, *The Testaments of the Twelve Patriarchs*, p. 154, n. 255.
35. There is already an allusion to *Num.* 24:17 in *Mt.* 2:2, as the word ἀνατολή indicates. Cf. K. STENDAHL, *The School of St. Matthew*, p. 136; E. BURROWS, *The Oracles of Jacob and Balaam*, London, 1938, p. 98.
36. In *Zech.* 6:12 and *Jer.* 23:5 ἀνατολή means the 'shoot' on a plant, but as early as the time of Philo the word was interpreted differently; cf. SCHLIER, art. 'Ανατολή, in *TWNT*, I, p. 355.
37. It occurs, in fact, in a collection of *testimonia* discovered in Cave IV, and customarily referred to as 4Q *Testimonia*, published by J. M. ALLEGRO in *JBL*, LXXV, 1956, pp. 182–187; cf. D. BARTHÉLEMY and J. T. MILIK, *Qumran Cave I*, Oxford, 1955, p. 121.
38. LURIA (*Eretz Israel*, IV, 1956, as quoted by R. North in *Verbum Domini*, XXXV, 1957, pp. 48 f., who, however, by mistake writes *Deut.* for *Num.*) thinks there may be some connection with Kokhba, the home of Dositheus in the neighbourhood of Damascus. Dositheus is certainly related to the Essenes; cf. R. McL. WILSON, 'Simon, Dositheus and the DSS', *ZRGG*, XIX, 1957, pp. 21–40.

the Sons of Darkness (XI, 6); and is included in the *4Q Testimonia* (12).[39]
Lastly it was to be the inspiration for the surname of the last chief of the
Zealot movement, Bar Kokhba, the 'son of the Star'.[40]

From the Essene collections this text passed into the Christian *testimonia*.
In addition to the passages already quoted,[41] Justin refers to it when he
makes ἄστρον one of the titles of Christ: 'He is called Star by the mouth
of Moses, Dayspring by that of Zechariah' (*Dial.* CXXVI, 1). The same
two texts are associated here as in the earlier passage mentioned (*Dial.*
CVI, 4). Justin again mentions *Num.* 24:17 in *I Apol.*: 'Isaiah, another
prophet, foretelling the same things in other words, spoke thus: "A star
shall arise out of Jacob and a flower shall spring from the root (ῥίζης) of
Jesse, and in His arm shall the nations trust." And this star of light which
has arisen, and this flower which did spring from the root of Jesse is the
Christ' (XXXII, 12–13).[42] *Mt.* 2:2 and *Num.* 24:17 are again linked in
Irenaeus: 'Emmanuel, whose star Balaam thus prophesied: There shall
come a star out of Jacob, and a leader shall rise in Israel. Now Matthew
says that the Magi coming from the East exclaimed thus: We have seen his
star in the East and are come to worship him' (*Adv. haer.* III, 9:2). The
Demonstratio (58) adds other details. First, the fact that the star appears in
heaven signifies that he who is born of Jacob comes from heaven; this
recalls Ignatius of Antioch. Secondly, the star rests on the head of Jesus, a
detail echoed in the *Protevangelium of James*. Lastly, the paragraph immediately following cites *Is.* 11:1, which suggests that Irenaeus too was
using the traditional *testimonia*.

Origen was to inherit from this tradition. 'The Star which appeared at
the birth of Jesus was prophesied by Balaam', he writes (*Contr. Cels.* I, 59),
and in *Hom. Num.* (XVIII, 4) he adds a noteworthy development of his

---

39. PETERSON ('Die geschichtliche Bedeutung der jüdischen Gebetsrichtung', *TZ*, III,
1947, p. 5) thinks that it may be associated with the Essene custom of turning to the
East when praying.
40. On the role of the star in archaic Jewish art, cf. E. GOODENOUGH, *Jewish Symbols*, I,
pp. 61, 187; II, pp. 29, 216.
41. I.e., *Test. Levi.* XVIII, 2–4; *Test. Jud.* XXIV, 1, and in the New Testament *Mt.*
2:2, to which may be added *Lk.* 1:78; *Rev.* 2:28, 22:16.
42. It will be observed that Justin brings together *Num.* 24:17 and *Is.* 11:1 and welds
them into a single quotation which he attributes to Isaiah in a way which presupposes
his use of one of the early collections of *testimonia* rather than the Biblical text itself.
That this particular combination of texts is early is attested by *Rev.* 22:16: 'I am the
Root (ῥίζα) and offspring of David, the bright, the Morning Star (ἀστήρ)', and by
Test. Jud. XXIV, 1–6.

own. He remarks that the star, after coming to a halt above Jesus, 'halted so as never to leave him', like the Spirit at the Baptism, and he concludes from this that it is 'a symbol of divinity'. In another passage (XIII, 7) he witnesses to the tradition which sees the Magi as Balaam's heirs and aware of his prophecy: 'Hence when Jesus was born they recognised the star.'[43]

Beside the allusion to the dazzling star that manifests the birth of Christ to the celestial aeons (αἰῶσιν), the text of Ignatius of Antioch adds that 'all the rest of the constellations with the sun and the moon formed themselves into a chorus about the star; but the star itself far outshone them all' (Eph. XIX, 2). Some have suggested interpreting this text in terms of Hellenistic astrological ideas,[44] but the passage as a whole seems to be Jewish Christian having as its background a collection of testimonia,[45] and it may be asked whether this final detail cannot also be explained in this way.

There is a text in the Old Testament which also describes the sun, the moon and the stars paying homage to a brighter star. This is Joseph's dream: 'Behold, I have dreamed yet a dream; and behold, the sun, and the moon and eleven stars made obeisance to me' (Gn. 37:9). Now this text has in fact been interpreted as applying to Christ. In the Blessings of Isaac and Jacob Hippolytus comments on Joseph's vision. Joseph, he says 'saw the Word in advance' (PO XXVII, 3), and commenting on the text in question he adds:

> Why be indignant if the sun and the moon and the eleven stars adore him? They are there in ancient times as prefiguring what was to come. Where then has that which was said been fulfilled, namely: Must we come, I and thy mother and thy brethren and adore thee falling to the ground? if it was not when the blessed Apostles, together with Mary and Joseph, being come to the Mount of Olives adored Christ? (ibid. 5–7).[46]

Once again it is the Testaments of the Twelve Patriarchs which testify to the use of the text in the primitive Jewish Christian community; and they

43. Cf. BIDEZ-CUMONT, Les Mages hellénisés, I, Paris, 1938, pp. 48–49.
44. So SCHLIER, Untersuchungen, pp. 14–15.
45. A. CABANISS sees here in particular the influence of Sap. Sol. 18:14–16 ('Wisdom 18:14, an Early Christmas Text', VC, x, 1956, pp. 100–101).
46. It will be noticed that Joseph is shown as still living at the time of the Ascension, which took place on the Mount of Olives. The eleven stars are explained by the absence of Judas. Ignatius' interpretation differs, but may well be a parallel interpretation of the same text.

include a detail which suggests that, as on a number of occasions, it was this usage which inspired Hippolytus. The *Testament of Naphtali* contains the following passage:

> I saw a vision on the Mount of Olives, on the East of Jerusalem; the sun and the moon were standing still. And behold Isaac, the father of my father, said to us: Run and lay hold of them, each one according to his strength; and to him that seizeth them will the sun and moon belong. And we all of us ran together and Levi laid hold of the sun and Judah . . . seized the moon, and they were both of them lifted up with them. And when Levi became as a sun, lo, a certain young man gave to him twelve branches of palm; and Judah became bright as the moon, and under his feet were twelve rays (V, 1–4).[47]

There are obvious differences here from the texts of Hippolytus and Ignatius, especially in the matter of the two Messiahs,[48] who are identified the one with the sun and the other with the moon. Nevertheless it is worth noting that they retain the pre-eminence of the sun and moon above the twelve other stars, and this small detail makes it very probable that there is here a reminiscence of *Gn.* 37:9.[49] The allusion to the Mount of Olives is also so precise that Hippolytus must have taken it from the *Testaments*. The detail about the East ($\dot{\alpha}\nu\alpha\tau o\lambda\dot{\eta}$) of Jerusalem is equally interesting, and recalls *Zech.* 6:12; *Mt.* 2:2 and *Lk.* 1:78.

With all this, however, the theology of the text in Ignatius is not yet exhausted. The appearance of the new star throws the astral powers into consternation. It heralds the destruction of all sorcery ($\mu\alpha\gamma\epsilon i\alpha$), the abolition of all wickedness, the ruin of the Ancient Kingdom (*Eph.* XIX, 3). There seems to be in this passage an allusion to the domination exercised by the stars over the world, and to the magical and astrological practices that were an expression of it. Nevertheless, the allusion to magic may also in this context refer to the Magi. If so, then it is both the astral powers and the Magi, their ministers, who are stupefied by the appearance of the new star which marks the end of their reign.

47. It is not impossible that *Rev.* 12:1 was inspired by this text: 'And a great sign was seen in heaven; a woman arrayed with the sun, and the moon under her feet, and upon her head a crown of twelve stars.'
48. This feature is evidence of the Essene origin of the text.
49. Cf. M. D. GOULDER and M. N. SANDERSON, 'St. Luke's Genesis', *JTS* (*NS*), VIII, 1957, p. 26.

This interpretation is in fact confirmed by other evidence, and firstly that of Justin, who writes:

For that saying also of Isaiah: He shall take the power of Damascus and the spoils of Samaria (*Is.* 8:4), meant that the power of the evil demon who dwelt at Damascus should be overcome by Christ at his very birth. And this is manifestly what took place. For the Wise Men had been carried off as spoil (ἐσκυλευμένοι) for all kinds of evil actions to which they were driven by that evil demon; but by coming and worshipping Christ they were shown to have escaped from that power which had taken them as spoil (*Dial.* LXXVIII, 9).[50]

This calls for several observations. First of all it should be noted that *Is.* 8:4 is quoted twice more in Justin, inserted into *Is.* 7 between verses 16 and 16b (*Dial.* XLIII, 6; LXVI, 3). This is clearly another of the conflations characteristic of the passages grouped together in primitive collections of *testimonia*, and this shows that *Is.* 8:4 was at a very early date linked with the prophecies of the childhood of Christ. Secondly, the episode of the Magi, when associated with this text, takes on a theological significance. The Magi were from Damascus,[51] that is, they were dependents of the Prince of Darkness, localised at Damascus, no doubt in opposition to Jerusalem.[52] Christ's coming brings about their conversion by snatching them from the evil powers which they had served by their magic and astrology.

Two points stand out. First, the Gospel Magi are here assimilated to the priests of the idols, and in particular to the magi of Syria. In this connection the story of Simon Magus should be borne in mind,[53] as also the fact that Syria was much cultivated by the Magians, Iranian missionaries. Secondly, there is the fact that Balaam, sometimes identified with Zoroaster,[54] was regarded as the ancestor of the Gospel Magi. All these

---

50. Cf. also LXXVII, 2–4; LXXXVIII, 1. The theme is taken up also by Tertullian, *Adv. Marc.* II, 13.

51. It will be remembered that *CDC* VII, 17–19 establishes a link between *Num.* 24:17 and the sojourn of the Zadokite Community at Damascus.

52. The *Epistle of the Apostles* (44) adduces the same passage from *Isaiah* to prove that the preaching of Paul at Damascus with the entry of the Gentiles into the Church constitutes the beginning of the New Jerusalem; cf. T. Schneider, 'Das prophetische Agraphon der Epistola Apostolorum', *ZNW*, xxiv, 1925, pp. 151–154.

53. Schoeps (*Aus frühchristlicher Zeit*, pp. 249–254) has shown that Balaam in *Rev.* 2:14 may represent Simon.

54. Cf. Bidez-Cumont, *op. cit.*, pp. 47–48.

details suggest some contact between Jewish and Jewish Christian circles on the one hand and the magi from Syria on the other,[55] though it should be noted that the relevant passage from Justin does not support Ignatius in the allusion to astral powers.

What is, however, theologically the most important feature is Christ's victory over the Devil 'at his very birth', which becomes apparent with the conversion of the Magi. This sees in the Nativity and the Adoration of the Magi an anticipation of Christ's combat with the powers of evil, a point also made explicit in Ignatius' text with reference to the Magi episode. Origen was to develop this point in the *Contra Celsum* (I, 60). He declares that 'Magi are in communion with demons', and adds that they succeed in these practices only so long as no influence more divine or potent appears. But at the birth of Jesus the demons lost their strength: 'They were not only overthrown by the angels who visited the earthly regions at the time of the birth of Jesus, but also by the soul of Jesus and the divine power which was in it. Beholding a sign of God in heaven they wished to see what was indicated by it. Without doubt they possessed the prophecies of Balaam; and when they had found him who was superior to all demons, they worshipped him.' This is very close to Ignatius's view of Christ destroying the power of sorcery at his coming, but there is no mention of the astral powers. The latter are mentioned, however, with reference to the star of the Magi, by the Gnostic Theodotus (CLEMENT, *Excerpta* 69–75). The text first describes the nature of Destiny, which results from the action of the Powers, who work through the stars (69). Men are subject to its domination, but the Lord snatches us from it: 'That is why a strange and new star (ξένος ἀστὴρ καὶ καινός) arose (ἀνέτειλεν), doing away with the old ordinance of the stars, shining with a new light which was not of this world, as did the Lord himself' (74). There is a striking resemblance to Ignatius in these expressions. Nevertheless, the line of thought pursued by Theodotus gives further emphasis to the power of the cosmocrators, and thus betrays its Gnostic outlook. Furthermore he sees the Magi as astrologers who by their science know of the birth of Christ, as is shown clearly by the next paragraph in the *Excerpta*: 'The Magi not only saw the Lord's star, but they recognised the truth that a king was born' (75).

These texts taken together reveal a tradition linking the Magi episode with the theme of Christ's coming as putting an end to those magical and

55. Dositheus, Simon's teacher, had had contacts with the refugee Zadokites in the region of Damascus; cf. R. NORTH, *op. cit.*, p. 49.

astrological practices which were looked upon as a cult of the devil. Now the theory which connects these practices with evil powers is specifically a Jewish Christian one, and derives from the Jewish apocalypses. The crucial text is *I Enoch* VIII, 3, which describes the evil angels revealing the magic arts to men, and is often made use of in the *Clementine Homilies* (VIII, 12–14; IX, 13–19, etc.). The interpretation of the story of the Magi as reported by Justin and Origen is therefore seen to derive from a Jewish Christian background, influenced by apocalyptic.[56]

The reference to astrology implied by the text in Ignatius, which supposes man to be dominated by astral powers, seems to be more specifically related to a Syrian setting, for the same belief in astrology is found in other Syrian authors such as Tatian and Bardaisan. In this environment the appearance of the star of the Magi comes as a sign of the breaking of the domination exercised by the evil powers through the medium of the stars and their influence.[57]

THE BAPTISM OF JESUS

Another significant feature of Jewish Christian theology is the prominent place which it accords to the Baptism of Christ. In some respects it seems to enjoy more importance than the Nativity[58]; but that this should be so in a Jewish Christian environment is hardly surprising.

The Baptism of Christ was bound to bulk large if only from the fact of

56. Cf. J. DANIÉLOU, art. 'Démons', *Dict. Spir.*, IV, cols. 155–159.

57. The theology of the star would thus seem to be connected originally with the Jewish Christians of Damascus, possibly through Damascus Zadokites converted to Christianity. It is to these circles that the New Testament *Gospel of Matthew*, the *Testaments of the Twelve Patriarchs* and the *Epistles* of Ignatius are to be assigned. Cf. L. GOPPELT, *op. cit.*, pp. 178–199; J. DANIÉLOU, *Les manuscrits de Qumran et les origines du christianisme*, Paris, 1957, pp. 91 ff.; 'L'étoile de Jacob et la mission chrétienne de Damas', *VC*, XI, 1957, pp. 121–138.

58. Thus the Gospel of *Mark* begins with the Baptism, and this may derive from a primitive form springing from the lectionary readings for a twelve month period, beginning one September with the account of the Baptism, and ending the next with the Entry on Palm Sunday (cf. J. DANIÉLOU, 'Les quatre-temps de septembre et la fête des Tabernacles', *Maison-Dieu*, XLVI, 1956, pp. 114–137). Heterodox literature, both Ebionite and Gnostic, seems to presuppose some usage of this kind, though interpreting it in a non-orthodox manner, when it sees in the Baptism the descent of the Godhead on the man Jesus; at any rate this certainly points to the prominence of the Baptism in the tradition. For the teachings of Cerinthus cf. IRENAEUS, *Adv. haer.* I, 26:1; for the Ebionites, EPIPHANIUS, *Pan.* XXX, 16; and on the subject as a whole, E. FABBRI, 'El bautismo de Jesus y la unción del Espiritu', *Ciencià y Fé*, XII, 1956, pp. 8–9.

the contacts between the Essenes and John the Baptist, whose practice of immersion in living water falls into the framework of the Essene baptist movement. Similarly the outpouring of the Holy Spirit is seen as the fulfilment of the promise of an eschatological outpouring such as occupies an important place in the Qumran documents. All these details will have to be discussed later in considering the sacrament of baptism in Jewish Christian theology.[59] For the present, however, they need not concern us; nor will it be necessary to examine the accounts of the Baptism of Christ in the Synoptics and Saint John, or the special variations in treatment exhibited by the apocryphal writings.[60] The present section will be confined to a survey of the theological data presented by Jewish Christianity.

The first element of the Baptism narrative to be considered is Christ's descent into the Jordan, which has been given several interpretations in Jewish Christian texts. First, it is regarded as a descent into the waters of death where the dragon lives. Thus the *Testament of Asher* comments: 'When the Most High shall visit ($\epsilon\pi\iota\sigma\kappa\epsilon\psi\eta\tau\alpha\iota$) the earth, coming Himself as a man among men, eating and drinking and in peace ($\dot{\eta}\sigma\upsilon\chi\iota\alpha$) breaking the head of the dragon by means of water ($\delta\iota\ \ddot{\upsilon}\delta\alpha\tau\sigma\varsigma$), He shall save Israel and all the Gentiles, God bearing the likeness ($\dot{\upsilon}\pi\sigma\kappa\rho\iota\nu\dot{\sigma}\mu\epsilon\nu\sigma\varsigma$) of man' (VII, 3). This passage is clearly Christian[61]; there is an allusion to *Ps.* 74:13 and the expression $\delta\iota\ \ddot{\upsilon}\delta\alpha\tau\sigma\varsigma$ is certainly a reference to Baptism.

The same quotation from *Ps.* 74:13 was to be applied explicitly to baptism in a later text. Cyril of Jerusalem wrote in the *Catechetical Lectures*: 'Since, therefore, it was necessary to break the heads of the dragon in pieces, He went down and bound the strong one in the waters' (III, 11). The theme of the dragon hidden in the waters of death, and of Christ's baptism as a descent into the dragon's domain was to endure in tradition.[62]

The important point here is the link established between Christ's Baptism and his Passion. Paul had drawn a connection between the death and

59. Cf. chap. 11, pp. 316, 323 f., 325 f. below.
60. On all these points the reader is referred to the excellent account in the relevant chapter of W. BAUER, *Das Leben Jesu*, pp. 110–141.
61. Cf. DE JONGE, *op. cit.*, p. 152, n. 222.
62. PER LUNDBERG has demonstrated its origins, and adduced examples of it in the liturgy (*La typologie baptismale dans l'Ancienne Église*, pp. 64–166); OLIVIER ROUSSEAU has shown that it was a symbolical anticipation of Christ's descent into hell, and of his victory over Satan ('La déscente aux enfers figure du baptême chrétien', *Mél. Lebreton*, II, p. 286); and ANTON BAUMSTARK has pointed out how it persisted in the Greek prayer for the consecration of baptismal water (*Liturgie comparée*, 1st ed., Chevetogne, 1939, p. 147).

resurrection of Christ and Christian baptism, but here there is a definite symbolic system. Christ's Baptism prefigures his Passion. In this sense, the episode should be compared with the Marriage Feast of Cana in St. John's Gospel where the allusion to the Passion seems to be certain.[63] The Baptism of Christ would thus prefigure Christian baptism not only in consecrating the water-ritual, but also[64] in associating the descent into the water with the mystery of death and resurrection.[65]

This association of Christ's Baptism and his Passion seems to be present in several Jewish Christian texts. In an interesting passage the *Odes of Solomon* brings together the descent into Hell and the descent of the Spirit on Christ at the Baptism, a combination which can hardly be interpreted otherwise than as an allusion to the Baptism as a descent into the world of death.[66] The text reads: 'The dove fluttered over the Messiah . . . and sang over him, and her voice was heard. . . . The abysses opened, which had been hidden' (XXIV, 1–3).

There seems to be a similar association of ideas in a passage of Ignatius of Antioch which immediately precedes the one on the hidden character of the Incarnation. Ignatius writes: 'Our God, Jesus the Christ . . . was born and was baptised that by his Passion he might cleanse water' (*Eph.* XVIII, 2). The most natural explanation of these expressions is that Christ, by descending into the water destroyed the demonic forces that dwelt in it, thus purifying them by his Passion, that is to say, by his death, which is a descent into the world of death.[67]

63. Cf. CULLMANN, *Early Christian Worship*, pp. 66–71.
64. Cf. H. RIESENFELD, 'La signification sacramentaire du baptême johannique', *Dieu vivant*, XIII, 1949, pp. 29–37.
65. This would tell against the view of A. BENOIT (*Le baptême au Second Siècle*, p. 228) who refuses to admit any trace of Pauline theology in Jewish Christian circles.
66. 'There is a possible suggestion that the Psalm may refer to the Descent into Hades and to the Baptism as events happening in close connexion . . . In the earliest times the Baptism of Christ was the occasion of his triumph over Hades' (RENDEL HARRIS, *The Odes and Psalms of Solomon*, p. 123). Cf. also *Ode* XXII, 5, which speaks of 'him who overthrew the dragon with seven heads', and which also seems to have some connection with the Baptism of Christ (cf. C. M. EDSMAN, *Le baptême de feu*, Uppsala, 1940, p. 47; J. H. BERNARD, *The Odes of Solomon*, London, 1912, pp. 32–39).
67. P. CAMELOT rightly observes that 'by the baptism of Jesus, an image and prophecy of his death and resurrection, the water shares in the virtue of his passion' (*Ignace d'Antioche, Lettres*, p. 87, n. 2; cf. LUNDBERG, *op. cit.*, p. 226; SCHLIER, *Untersuchungen*, pp. 44–45). A. BENOIT comments: 'We find in Ignatius the first formulation of an idea which was to remain current in later times, and the roots of which go back to Jewish cosmology: the baptism of Christ purifies the waters infested with demons' (*Le Baptême chrétien au Second Siècle*, p. 69).

There is a conception closely related to that of Ignatius in the *Eclogae Propheticae* of Clement of Alexandria. Clement writes:

The Lord had himself baptised, not that he had need of it for himself, but so that he might sanctify all water for those that are regenerated in it. In this way not only are our bodies cleansed but our souls also, and the sanctification of the invisible parts of our being is signified by the fact that even the impure spirits which cleave to our soul, are rooted out from the time of the new spiritual birth' (7).

Here again the object of Christ's descent into the water is to purify it from the presence of demonic beings, and so to make it able to purify from the same powers those who are baptised.

There is another line of development which is related to the eschatological significance of Christ's Baptism: this is the imagery which links the baptism of water with a baptism of fire.[68] This theme goes back to the pericope of *Mt.* 3:11: 'I baptize you with water . . . He shall baptize you with the Holy Ghost and with fire', which, of course, is strongly eschatological in character.[69] There seems to be an allusion here to the last judgment by fire, and to the quality of judgment inherent in the coming of the Messiah. Nevertheless, by the time of *Mark* 1:8 this archaic feature has already disappeared from the New Testament, and only a reference to Baptism with the Holy Spirit remains.

In Jewish Christian tradition, however, it persisted, and was developed into an imagery of fire in or over the water of the Jordan, which symbolised the fulfilment of John's prophecy in the actual Baptism of Christ. Thus several archaic texts, the *Gospel of the Ebionites*,[70] the *Diatessaron* and certain Latin MSS of the New Testament mention the presence of a fire or of a light over the Jordan.[71] Normally, however, sufficient care is not taken to distinguish the two forms of this tradition. The only one which is relevant here is that in which the fire appears at the moment of Christ's descent into the water, and of which a clear instance is found in Justin: 'While Jesus was going down into the water, a fire was kindled in Jordan; and while he was coming up out of the water again, the Holy Spirit, like a dove, fluttered over him' (*Dial.* LXXXVIII, 3).[72]

68. Cf. C. M. EDSMAN, *op. cit.*, pp. 182–190.
69. Cf. VAN IMSCHOOT, 'Baptême de feu et baptême d'eau', *ETL*, XIII, 1936, pp. 653 ff.
70. Cf. EPIPHANIUS, *Pan.* XXX, 13.   71. Cf. W. BAUER, *Das Leben Jesu*, pp. 134–136.
72. A. ORBE believes that Clement of Alexandria knew of this tradition: 'Teologia bautismal de Clemente Alexandrino', *Gregorianum*, XXXVI, 1955, pp. 434–439.

In this tradition the fire appears to be an allusion to the destructive fire of Judgment, and a number of texts mention it. The following instance occurs in the *Sibylline Oracles*: 'After he (the Son of God) has received a second birth according to the flesh, being washed in the blue, sluggish stream of Jordan, when he has escaped the fire, he will be the first to see a God coming with good favour by means of the Spirit on the wings of a white dove' (VI, 3–7). The text certainly seems to suggest that Christ was delivered from the fire by baptism, and that it was then that the Spirit descended, a view quite in line with the text of Justin in which the fire appears over the water at the moment when Christ goes down into the Jordan.[73] The idea of Christ's having been delivered at his Baptism from the fire appears elsewhere in the *Oracles*, in a passage which speaks of: 'the Father who has spread abroad Thy Baptism in pure water, at which Thou (the Word) didst appear, coming out of the fire' (VII, 83–84).[74]

The same conception occurs in the *Excerpta ex Theodoto*. Clement, giving an account of the teaching of this disciple of Valentinus, writes: 'Just as the birth of the Saviour delivered us from the (flux of) becoming and from Fate, so also his Baptism rescued us from the fire and his Passion rescued us from passion' (76, 1). The chief interest of this passage is the parallel set up between the three mysteries of deliverance: that of the Magi, which delivers from *fatum*, that of baptism which delivers from fire, and that of the Passion which delivers from passion. Here, behind the Gnostic interpretation, there is a theology of the stages of redemption in the life of Christ.

This is proved by the parallel between this text and the one in which Justin also speaks of fire at the Baptism. Justin wishes to show that the power ($\delta \acute{\upsilon} \nu \alpha \mu \iota \varsigma$) of Christ is first manifested at his birth in the Magi episode (LXXXVIII, 2), and then a second time at his Baptism, when 'fire was kindled in the Jordan'; and, he adds, 'if Christ went down into the river, it was not through any need of being *baptized*, just as he had no need to be *begotten* or *crucified*. He underwent these things for the race of men, which had fallen into the power of death' (LXXXVIII, 4). Thus, as with Theodotus, the three mysteries are related to the theology of the redemption as three stages in the struggle of the incarnate Son of God against the Powers. In this sense the themes of the descent into the Jordan as a struggle against the dragon of the sea, or as a passing through the fire of judgment have a parallel theological significance.

73. Cf. DANIÉLOU, *Sacramentum futuri*, pp. 63, 77 f.
74. For the meaning of $\dot{\epsilon} \xi \epsilon \phi \alpha \acute{\alpha} \nu \theta \eta \varsigma$, cf. *Odyssey* XII, 441.

The Jewish Christian origin of this contrast between judgment by water and judgment by fire is shown by two facts. Firstly, this opposition on the eschatological level strictly speaking only appears in Jewish and Christian circles in the second half of the first century. The doctrine of a judgment by fire was certainly not unknown to the Old Testament, but it was greatly developed in the Qumran manuscripts, especially in the *Psalms of Thanksgiving* (III, 28–36), where fire is described as consuming the water. It appears also in the *Sibylline Oracles* (IV, 152–161). But the actual opposition of the two judgments, by fire and by water, emerges only in the second half of the first century, in such works as the *Life of Adam and Eve* (L, 1–2), the New Testament *II Peter* (3:5–7), and Flavius Josephus (*Ant.* I, 70).[75]

But there are more precise data than this. In a text which has yet to be considered, connected with the heterodox Jewish Christianity of the Ebionites, the opposition of fire and water is presented in connection with the Baptism of Christ. This is a passage from the oldest stratum of the *Clementine Recognitions*, that of the *Preaching of Peter*, which reads: 'After Aaron, who was High Priest, another was taken, drawn out of the waters. I do not speak of Moses, but of Him who, in the waters of baptism, was named Son of God. You have understood that I am speaking of Jesus, who has put out by the grace of baptism, that fire which the High Priest kindled for sins' (*Rec.* I, 48).

The text is an expression of the Ebionite polemic against animal sacrifices offered by fire,[76] and therefore represents a different theological interpretation from that of the passages mentioned hitherto. But it obviously rests on the same original conception of the conflict of water and fire at the Baptism of Christ, and the affirmation of the triumph by water over the destructive force of fire.[77] This is connected with a pessimistic conception of fire which corresponds to an exaltation of water which is a mark of Ebionism, but which may also originally have belonged to Jewish Christianity in general, and represented an anti-Iranian tendency.[78]

75. Cf. G. VERMÈS, 'La secte juive de la Nouvelle Alliance', *Cah. Sion*, Sept. 1950, pp. 18–21.

76. Cf. H. J. SCHOEPS, *Theologie und Geschichte des Judenchristentums*, p. 210.

77. Cf. H. J. SCHOEPS, *op. cit.*, pp. 206–207, who cites another passage in the same vein: 'Flee to the water which alone can extinguish the power of fire' (*Hom.* XI, 26). For the same feature in Elkesaism, cf. EPIPHANIUS, *Pan.* XIX, 3. It may derive ultimately from Essenism; cf. SCHOEPS, *Urgemeinde, Judenchristentum, Gnosis*, p. 81.

78. Cf. SCHOEPS, *Theologie*, p. 207; also SCHLIER, *Untersuchungen*, pp. 146–147; E. MOLLAND, 'La circoncision, le baptême et l'autorité du décret apostolique dans les milieux judéo-chrétiens', *ST*, IX, 1955, pp. 16–21.

This is not, however, the most usual treatment of the Baptism.[79] First of all, the early evidence as a whole does not connect the manifestation of fire precisely with the descent of Jesus into the Jordan, but only with the Baptism in general.[80] In the *Gospel of the Ebionites*, indeed, it actually occurs after the Baptism: 'When Jesus came up from the water, the heavens were opened and He saw the Holy Ghost descending upon him and entering into him: and a voice came from heaven saying: Thou art my beloved Son, in whom I am well pleased: and again: This day have I begotten thee. And straightway there shone about ($\pi\epsilon\rho\iota\acute{\epsilon}\lambda\alpha\mu\psi\epsilon$) the place a great light.'[81]

Secondly, the greater number of texts do not speak of a fire ($\pi\hat{\upsilon}\rho$) but of a light ($\varphi\hat{\omega}s$). This was the case with the *Gospel of the Ebionites* just quoted; the Latin *codices* render by *lumen magnum* or *lumen ingens*; and the same sense is given in the *Diatessaron*. This points in quite a different direction, being clearly concerned with a light of glory which accompanies the manifestation, or divine epiphany of Jesus, and which is to be associated not with the Baptism, but with the voice from heaven and the descent of the Holy Spirit. There is here a striking parallel with the Transfiguration; in both cases the voice of the Father witnesses to the sonship of Jesus, and the ray of light which appears at the Baptism seems to be equivalent to the blaze of glory which emanates from Jesus transfigured.

Can anything more precise be said on this point? The *Gospel of the Ebionites* says that 'there shone about ($\pi\epsilon\rho\iota\acute{\epsilon}\lambda\alpha\mu\psi\epsilon$) the place a great light'. Now in *Lk.* 2:9 the Nativity story reads: 'The glory of the Lord shone round about ($\pi\epsilon\rho\iota\acute{\epsilon}\lambda\alpha\mu\psi\epsilon$) them, and they were sore afraid.' The theme of fear does not appear in the *Gospel of the Ebionites*, but it does in the Latin *codices* which keep strictly in line with *Luke*. Thus the texts of the *Codex Vercellensis* runs: 'A great light shone over (*circumfulsit* = $\pi\epsilon\rho\iota\acute{\epsilon}\lambda\alpha\mu\psi\epsilon$) the water, such that all those present were seized with fear.' In *Luke*, as in the present texts, the appearance of the light is linked with the opening of the heavens: it is the heavenly light which shines upon earth, and thus underlines the divine character of the action which is taking place.

There is no reason to believe that this theme has been transposed from the Nativity to the Baptism; on the contrary the reverse process seems more probable. The Baptism episode clearly occupied a position of excep-

79. As BAUER (*op. cit.*, p. 136) has remarked in opposition to Zahn.
80. As, for instance, in the *Predicatio Pauli*, quoted by the pseudo-Cyprian, or in the variant readings of the Latin New Testament codices: cf. BAUER, *op. cit.*, p. 137.
81. PREUSCHEN, p. 11.

tional importance in the early days of Jewish Christianity. But the whole body of heterodox authors, Ebionites as well as Gnostics, Cerinthus as well as Carpocrates, drew from it heterodox conclusions, namely that this was the moment of the descent of the Holy Spirit into the man Jesus. This appears very clearly in the passage from the *Gospel of the Ebionites* already quoted, in which the Holy Spirit is said to enter into (εἰς) Jesus.[82] It is easy to see why from then onwards the tradition of the Great Church tended to play down the Baptism in favour of the Gospel of the Infancy, and to bring out the divine aspect of the latter. This point has already been established in regard to the Magi episode, and it appears equally clearly in that of the Shepherds.

It seems reasonable to conclude then that the presence of the light of glory at the Baptism is a primitive datum. But what is its real context? Attention may be drawn to the use at an early date of the terms φώτισμα (CLEM. ALEX., *Paed.* I, 6:26) or φωτισμός (JUSTIN, *I Apol.* 1:61) as names for Christian baptism. This usage is very ancient, since baptised persons are already called φωτισθέντες in *Heb.* 6:4 and 10:32, but the explanations given for the terminology are mostly obscure.[83] The one given by Justin, that baptism is an illumination of the intelligence (*Dial.* CXXII, 4–5), appears to be secondary and betrays Hellenistic influences. A more profitable line of investigation, as will be seen in a later chapter,[84] is to examine the relation of the Baptism of Christ as presented in these texts to the liturgy and calendar of Jewish Christianity.

A comparison, therefore, of the characteristic details of Jewish Christian theology in the various episodes just studied, reveals first of all the care that is taken to give the events of Christ's life their cosmic dimension: Christ passes through the angelic worlds at his Incarnation, he dispossesses the demonic powers by his Nativity, at Baptism he confronts the prince of the abyss. At a deeper level, these episodes thus become mysteries, divine actions, witnessed to by the star of the Magi, the light at the Baptism; and in them God's glory manifests itself. These features will be found developed to a high degree in the Jewish Christian understanding of the mystery of the Cross.

82. Cf. E. FABRI, 'El bautismo de Jesus en el evangelio de los Hebreos', *Riv. de Theol.*, VI, 1956, pp. 49 f.
83. Cf. A. BENOIT, *Le baptême chrétien au Second Siècle*, p. 168; BAUER has drawn attention to the fact, but without pursuing the matter.
84. Cf. pp. 339 ff. below.

CHAPTER EIGHT

THE THEOLOGY OF REDEMPTION (I)

THE DESCENT INTO HELL

THE descent into hell was a subject of central importance for Jewish Christianity. Before discussing it, however, it is essential to define precisely the reference of the term. The most frequent view in the ancient world placed the habitations of the dead (in Hebrew, *Sheol*, in Greek, *Hades*) in the regions under the earth, the *inferi* strictly so-called. It is to these regions that the term 'Hell' in the phrase 'Descent into Hell' refers, and the purpose of the Descent, in Jewish Christian thinking, was to enable Christ after his death to preach deliverance to the righteous who were imprisoned there. This doctrine appears to be unknown to the New Testament,[1] and to be purely Jewish Christian; it in fact constitutes a dogmatic development which was to be accepted by the common tradition, and finally included in the Creed.[2]

This doctrine was, however, also intruded into other themes. First, it was integrated with the general theme of Christ's descent, the *katabasis*, which was considered in an earlier chapter. In the New Testament the Word of God descends from heaven to the earth, and this certainly appears to be the sense in which the texts which speak of his descent should be interpreted, especially *Eph.* 4:9, and *I Pet.* 3:18–22.[3] The Word passes through the angelic worlds and comes down to men, and the limit of his descent is the Incarnation,[4] as is clear in *Phil.* 2:7 where *kenosis* consists for the Word in his making himself 'like unto men'.

Thus, in Jewish Christian theology, two themes were present: the descent of the Word from heaven to earth, and Christ's descent from earth

1. So W. BIEDER, *Die Vorstellung von der Höllenfahrt Jesu Christi*, p. 128; H. SCHLIER, *Christus und die Kirche im Epheserbrief*, pp. 3–18; B. REICKE, *The Disobedient Spirits and Christian Baptism*, Copenhagen, 1945, pp. 115–118.
2. Cf. J. N. D. KELLY, *Early Christian Creeds*, London, 1950, pp. 378–383.
3. BIEDER and SCHLIER have shown that these passages did not refer to the infernal regions.
4. This pattern is especially clear in the *Physiologos*.

to hell. But the fact that a comprehensive cosmology, such as that of *Phil.* 2:10, includes 'things in heaven and things on earth and things under the earth', would tempt writers to amalgamate the two themes in one vision; and this is precisely what happens in the *Ascension of Isaiah*, in which the Word, after passing 'through all the heavens . . . the firmament and this world', descends as far as 'the angel who is in Sheol and transforms himself into the likeness of the angels who are in Sheol' (X, 8–10), but does not go as far as Haguel, the great abyss where the wicked angels will be imprisoned after the Last Judgment.

Secondly, however, the doctrine has been intruded into Christ's combat with the evil angels in his Passion. This conflict is mentioned in *Colossians*: 'Having put off from himself the principalities and the powers, he made a show of them openly, triumphing over them in it (sc. the Cross)' (2:15). According to Jewish Christian ideas the habitat of the fallen angels, their prison, is the air, and it is there that their struggle with Christ must take place[5]; but the descent into Hell attracted this theme to itself, and by the end of the second century had substituted for it that of a struggle between Christ and the evil angels in Hell after the Passion, a theme that was destined to endure.

The first passage to be considered comes in the *Gospel of Peter*, after the account of the Resurrection: 'And they heard a voice which came from heaven saying: Hast thou preached to them that sleep? And the Cross answered: Yes' (41–42).[6] The expression 'them that sleep' appears in a similar context in *Mt.* 27:52, with reference to the righteous of the Old Testament who came out of their tombs at the moment of the Passion.[7] The present text may also, therefore, be presumed to refer to the righteous of the Old Testament who were shut up in Sheol.

This comparison between the *Gospel of Peter* and *Matthew* makes it possible also to determine what is meant by Christ's preaching ($\kappa\eta\rho\acute{\upsilon}\sigma\sigma\epsilon\iota\nu$), namely his proclamation of deliverance to the saints of the Old Testament. This is the primitive theme, which was to remain the essential one of the descent into Hell, and which seeks to answer the theological problem of the fate of the righteous who died before Christ. It is understandable that this problem must have preoccupied Jewish Christians. The question with

---

5. As SCHLIER has shown (*Christus und die Kirche im Epheserbrief*, pp. 3–18), this feature is still very apparent in the *Homily* of the Pseudo-Hippolytus (51–52).
6. On the details of this passage cf. BIEDER, *op. cit.*, pp. 129–135.
7. The same sense is to be found in the *Apocryphon of Jeremiah*.

which it is concerned is in no way similar to that of the preaching (κηρύσσειν) of Christ to the 'spirits in prison', which is mentioned in *I Peter* (3:18-20). In the latter case Christ is proclaiming to the demons in their prison, which is the air, his victory over them—an idea which recalls *Col.* 2:15.[8] Such passages are directed at the Christian, to whom Christ is proposed as an example. He must renounce Satan and profess his faith; the setting of the thought is sacramental. In the *Gospel of Peter*, however, the concern is purely theological; this is a first attempt at reflection, in purely mythic terms, on the problem of the scope of the salvation wrought by Christ.

A parallel witness, who should be compared with the *Gospel of Peter*, since he also represents a very old doctrinal standpoint, is the Elder quoted by Irenaeus. This Elder taught that 'the Lord descended into the regions beneath the earth, preaching (*evangelizantem*) His Advent there also and the remission of sins received by those who believe in Him' (*Adv. haer.* IV, 27:2). Here once more is a proclamation of salvation to the dead. The allusion to those who believe might suggest the possibility of conversion, but the context makes it clear that 'those who believe' are only those 'who had hoped in him', that is, the Old Testament saints.

The descent into Hell appears in another very ancient Jewish Christian text, the fragment called the *Apocryphon of Jeremiah* which is quoted by Justin (*Dial.* LXXII, 4) and by Irenaeus (*Adv. haer.* III, 20:4; IV, 22:1; 33:1; 33:12; V, 31:1; *Dem.* 78). The text runs thus: 'The Lord God remembered His dead, the saints of Israel that have fallen asleep (κεκοι-μημένων) in the dust of the tomb, and He went down (κατέβη) unto them, to proclaim the good news (εὐαγγελίσασθαι) of the salvation which he was bringing to them.'[9]

This text serves to confirm the previous one, with which moreover it has, from a literary point of view, certain things in common, in particular the word (κεκοιμημένων). Furthermore, it speaks expressly of the 'dead of Israel', which makes it quite clear that the work belongs to Jewish Christianity, and is concerned with the question which was bound to exercise Jewish Christians, namely that of the fate of the saints of Israel, the

8. This is the conclusion reached by H. SCHLIER and B. REICKE, and to which R. BULT-MANN now adheres ('Bekenntnis und Liedfragmente im I Pt.', *Conj.Nest.*, II, p. 5).
9. The Christian origin of the text is certain. BIEDER is inclined to regard it as a Christian interpolation introduced into the canonical *Jeremiah* (*op. cit.*, p. 140), but it is hard to see where it could have been inserted. It seems more probable that it is an example of a Christian *midrash* on the prophet, of the type discussed in chap. III above, pp. 97 ff.

patriarchs and prophets. Moreover, the abode of the dead is explicitly fixed in a place situated in the depths of the earth. The expression χῶμα, tomb, recalls the μνημεῖον of Mt. 27:53 which is also concerned with 'them that sleep'. The three texts, Mt. 27:53, the *Gospel of Peter* and the *Apocryphon of Jeremiah* are therefore developments of the same idea.

The interesting point about the *Apocryphon* is in the first place that the idea of the descent (κατέβη) is explicitly stated. It is the descent into hell in the strict sense of the word, and it has a very definite object. On the one hand, it is a proclamation (εὐαγγελίσασθαι), a feature which links up with the *Gospel of Peter* (ἐκήρυξε) and also recalls *I Pet.* 4:6. This proclamation is of the salvation which has been wrought. However the Latin translation of Irenaeus gives a different version: 'He came down to them that He might deliver them and save them' (IV, 33, 1). The other translations of the passage combine the motifs of proclamation and deliverance. It is possible that the second of these ideas represents another version of the *Apocryphon*, in which case it would be a question not simply of a salvation won by Christ which would be completed at the resurrection of the dead, but of a liberation, a resurrection already accomplished. This is the conception found in *Mt.* 27:52 f. The present text would, therefore, combine the ideas of the descent into Hell and of the already accomplished resurrection of the saints of the Old Testament.

In view of this combination the text takes on a considerable dogmatic importance. To begin with it is the first text in which Christ's descent into Hell is seen as having its object in the actual deliverance of the righteous and not merely in the proclamation of their deliverance in the future. In this form the doctrine was to endure in tradition. Moreover, it is also very plain that the text speaks of a resurrection of bodies, and not merely of a liberation of souls, and this testifies to the existence in Jewish Christian tradition of the doctrine of a resurrection of the body already accomplished in the case of the saints at the time of Christ's Resurrection, and anticipating the eschatological resurrection.[10]

The presence of this doctrine in the works of Ignatius of Antioch is another witness to the fact that it belongs to early Jewish Christian tradition,[11] especially since it occurs in only one passage (*Magn.* IX, 2), and

10. Cf. H. ZELLER, 'Corpora sanctorum', *ZKT*, LXXI, 1949, pp. 385-465. The point is of considerable importance for the doctrine of the Assumption of the Virgin, which thus appears to fit into the context of primitive tradition.

11. So BIEDER, *op. cit.*, pp. 142-143.

therefore, like the doctrine of the concealment of the *katabasis* from the angels, is more probably to be classed as an extraneous teaching which he has incorporated than as a theological statement of his own. The text is as follows: 'How shall we be able to live apart from Him? seeing that even the prophets, being His disciples, were expecting Him as their teacher through the Spirit. And for this cause He whom they rightly awaited, when He came (παρών) raised them (ἤγειρεν) from the dead.'

Here the evolution begun with the *Apocryphon of Jeremiah* is completed. There is no longer any question of a proclamation; only two elements survive: first, the descent into Hell (παρών), which is genuinely Jewish Christian and may come from the *Gospel of Peter*, and secondly the resurrection of the dead which seems to have an undeniable connection with *Mt.* 27:52[12]; and these themes have been combined. The object of the descent into Hell is the resurrection of the saints of the Old Testament. The date of the letters of Ignatius gives us a valuable *terminus ad quem* for this view, for to have been incorporated by him in his works it must have been common in Jewish Christianity at the end of the first century.

At this stage the *Shepherd of Hermas* once more contributes some valuable information, and reveals new developments of the same doctrine. The *Ninth Similitude* speaks of stones which 'did . . . come up from the deep though they had already received the seal (σφραγίς)'. Hermas explains their meaning thus:

> These, the apostles and the teachers who preached the name of the Son of God, after they had fallen asleep in the power and faith of the Son of God, preached also . . . to them that had fallen asleep before them (προκεκοιμημένοις), and themselves gave unto them the seal (σφραγίς) of the preaching. Therefore they went down with them into the water, and came up again. . . . So by their means they were quickened into life, and came to the full knowledge of the name of the Son of God (IX, 16:5–7).

The symbolism of this passage is beyond doubt. The water represents the infernal regions, the lower waters, in which the dead abide. From what has already been said, it is clear that those who 'had fallen asleep before' must be the men of the various generations of the Old Testament, who died before the coming of Christ. The most curious point, however, is the last:

---

12. Cf. E. MASSAUX, *Influence de l'Évangile de Matthieu sur la littérature chrétienne avant Irénée*, pp. 101–103. This view is contested by KÖSTER, *op. cit.*, pp. 28–31.

it is not Christ who goes down to them but 'the Apostles and the teachers'. They, after their death go down to the infernal regions, and this descent has a twofold purpose; they proclaim ($\dot{\epsilon}\kappa\acute{\eta}\rho\upsilon\xi\alpha\nu$) salvation, but above all they procure the salvation which they proclaim by giving the seal ($\sigma\varphi\rho\alpha\gamma\acute{\iota}s$), that is, by baptism; after this both parties rise from the waters, that is, they are restored to life.

Once again this is a reflection on the salvation of the saints of the Old Testament. The context is still strictly Jewish Christian, but a new problem is raised. Baptism is absolutely necessary for salvation, but the saints of the Old Testament were not baptised; hence they have to receive baptism. This is clearly stated in the previous passage:

> It was necessary for them to rise up through the water, that they might be made alive; for otherwise they could not enter into the Kingdom of God, except they had put aside the deadness of their former life. So these likewise that had fallen asleep received the seal ($\sigma\varphi\rho\alpha\gamma\acute{\iota}s$) of the Son of God and entered into the Kingdom of God. For before a man, saith he, has borne the name of (the Son of) God, he is dead; but when he has received the seal ($\sigma\varphi\rho\alpha\gamma\acute{\iota}s$), he layeth aside his deadness, and resumeth life (IX, 16:2–3).

At this stage the descent of the Apostles to Hell intervenes. It was to the Apostles that the mission of giving baptism had been entrusted, and if baptism was necessary to every soul, then their mission must take them to every soul. Now the souls of the saints of the Old Testament were in Hell; and so to Hell the Apostles must go. This strange conception, the naive solution of a problem which is a living issue in every generation, reappears in Clement of Alexandria, who refers to this passage from the *Shepherd*, but enlarges the conception by extending baptism to the Gentile righteous who have been pleasing to God, whether after the Law or before it, and among whom he mentions Abel and Noah (*Strom.* II, 43:5; cf. also *Strom.* VI, 45:4).

It will be observed that here the interest is shifted from the eschatological problem to the soteriological one. The question of the return from Hell is secondary, and it is not said whether this refers to a resurrection or to a liberation of souls from the subterranean prison. The latter interpretation is surely the better one, since the fate of the righteous of the Old Testament is the same as that of the Apostles, who are certainly not raised from the dead. It is, therefore, no longer a question of resurrection but of the entry of souls into the Kingdom, a view which assumes two different abodes for souls. But what is especially noteworthy in this view is the link between the descent into Hell and baptism. The water is both baptismal water and the water of death, and the descent and the rising are allusions to the baptismal rite. This comes very close to the theme of baptism as an imitation of Christ's descent into Hell, which was to become so important later.[13]

The descent of the Apostles to Hell in order to baptise the saints of the Old Testament is one of the most curious features in the *Shepherd*; but this baptism in Hell is found elsewhere attributed to Christ himself. This is so, for example, in the *Epistle of the Apostles*:

> I willed to give their reward to those whom I had caused to set their hope upon it. Therefore I descended, and spake with Abraham, Isaac and Jacob, and with your fathers the Prophets, and proclaimed to them in Hell that rest in Heaven to which they are to come. With my right hand I gave them the baptism of life, pardon and remission of all evil, as I did for you (26–27).

It will be observed that this passage has certain points in common with the teaching of the Elder in Irenaeus. The object of the descent into Hell is that Christ may visit 'those who had hoped', that is to say, none but the righteous of the Old Testament. In the course of this visitation Christ speaks with them, and proclaims to them the good news of salvation, that they are to enter into rest. There is, however, no trace of an immediate resurrection with Christ, though there is mention of the remission of sins. In the case of the Elder this remission was only announced, whereas here it is actually effected by baptism, a variation which provides a link with *Hermas*. Since, however, there can be no question of a direct relationship between the *Shepherd* and the *Epistle*, it follows that the baptism given to the patriarchs in Hell must have been part of the common stock of Jewish Christian teaching.

With the *Testaments of the Twelve Patriarchs* a new aspect of the descent to Hell appears, namely the conflict with the Devil who there keeps souls in his power. Christ goes down to Hell to triumph over him and to snatch the souls from him. This represents an important development. In Saint

13. Cf. P. LUNDBERG, *La typologie baptismale dans l'ancienne Église*, pp. 64–74; O. ROUSSEAU, *La déscente aux enfers fondement sotériologique du baptême chrétien* (*Mélanges Lebreton*, II, pp. 277–297).

Paul, Christ's struggle with the demon takes place on the Cross, the place where he casts off the principalities and powers (*Col.* 2:15), and this view was bound up with the old Jewish Christian conception of the air as the dwelling place of the demons. The latter is not absent altogether from the *Testaments*, but it is combined with the different conception of the presence of the demons in the infernal regions; and the struggle with Satan is no longer associated with the Cross, but with the descent into Hell.

The *Testament of Levi* describes the circumstances of Christ's death thus: 'The rocks are rent, and the sun quenched, and the waters dried up, ... the invisible spirits mourn, and Hell ($ᾅδης$) is despoiled ($σκυλευομένου$) through the Passion of the Most High' (IV, 1). The text is clearly Christian,[14] and belongs to the context of *Mt.* 27:51-52 with its cosmic signs accompanying Christ's Passion, which is the fulfilment of the eschatological judgment. At the beginning the text speaks of 'judgment' ($κρίσις$) upon the sons of men (IV, 1a).

In these conditions the expression 'Hell is despoiled' clearly relates to the resurrection of the saints of *Mt.* 27:52. But the accent is no longer placed on the saints who are set free, but on Death which is overcome and from whom the saints are snatched. There is a deliverance, not a resurrection, and the defeat of the Devil receives more attention than the salvation of the saints. From now on the primary concern is no longer with the theological problem of the salvation of the saints of the Old Testament; what matters for the author is to show that Christ's Passion fulfils the eschatological judgment. This is still more in line with the view of the New Testament: 'Now shall the prince of this world be cast out' (*Jn.* 12:31). The same approach is found in *Mt.* 27:52, where the resurrection of the dead is mentioned as an eschatological sign. The interesting point about the Testaments, however, is that they take up a New Testament theme, the victory of Christ over the Powers by his Passion, and associate it with the specifically Jewish Christian theme of the descent into Hell.

The *Testament of Dan* defines even more clearly the conception of the combat with the Devil: 'And there shall arise unto you from the tribe of Judah and of Levi the salvation of the Lord; and He shall make war against Beliar and shall obtain the victory for your fathers. And the captivity shall he take from Beliar, the souls of the saints, and turn disobedient hearts unto the Lord, and give to them that call upon him eternal peace' (V, 10-11).

14. De Jonge has remarked on the archaic Christology indicated by the word $ὕψιστος$ applied to Christ (*The Testaments of the Twelve Patriarchs*, p. 126).

The descent into Hell is not expressly mentioned,[15] but a comparison with other passages in the *Testaments* shows without doubt that the combat in Hades was intended.[16] The victory over Beliar is indeed associated with the deliverance of the holy patriarchs (πατράσιν), but the dominant idea is the universality of Christ's victory, which extends both to the living and the dead.

Attention should be drawn to the allusion to captivity (αἰχμαλωσίαν) followed by that to the gift (δώσει) of eternal life and the conversion of the disobedient (ἀπειθεῖς). These three ideas are linked together in *Ps.* 67:19 (EVV 68:18): 'Thou art gone up on high, thou hast led captivity (αἰχμα-λωσίαν) captive, thou hast received gifts (δόματα) among men, yea, for they were disobedient (ἀπειθοῦντες) to thy abiding.'[17] Now Saint Paul had already used this psalm to describe the victory of Christ over the Devil. 'When he ascended on high he led captivity captive, and gave gifts unto men. Now this, He ascended, what is it, but that he also descended into the lower parts of the earth?' (*Eph.* 4:8-9).

Comparison of the three texts reveals the following resemblance between the *Testaments* and *Ephesians*, namely the alteration of 'receive gifts' into 'give gifts'. On the other hand, the allusion to 'disobedience' does not occur in Saint Paul. Furthermore, the text in the *Testaments* has a different meaning from that in Paul. The latter places the emphasis on the out-pouring of gifts in the Church, and does not appear to allude to the descent into Hell; the lower regions are the earth itself.[18] The *Testament of Dan*, on the other hand, insists on the deliverance of the souls of the dead, and consequently suggests the descent into Hell. The *Testaments* do not appear therefore to be dependent on Saint Paul; rather, the text from *Ps.* 67, which belonged to the collection of *testimonia*, and in which it is frequently quoted,[19] had been modified in a Christological sense in the primitive community,[20] and Paul and the *Testaments* made a parallel use of it.

It is interesting to note that Origen was later to synthesise the two interpretations, that of Christ's combat with the powers on the Cross, and that of the descent into Hell in order to liberate the captives. He writes: 'He began by binding the Devil on the Cross, and, entering into his house,

---

15. Cf. DE JONGE, *op. cit.*, p. 91.   16. Cf. BIEDER, *op. cit.*, p. 164.
17. Cf. also *Test. Zeb.* IX, 8, which alludes to this psalm.
18. Cf. BIEDER, *op. cit.*, p. 87, SCHLIER, *op. cit.*, p. 13.
19. Cf. DANIÉLOU, *Bible et Liturgie*, pp. 420-424; also p. 90 above.
20. Cf. B. FISHER, 'Le Christ dans les Psaumes', *Maison-Dieu*, XXVII, 1951, p. 100.

that is, into Hell, and ascending thence on high, he took with him the captives, those who have risen again with him and have entered the heavenly Jerusalem' (*Com. Rom.* V, 10). This text confirms the existence in tradition of a link between the Psalm and the descent into Hell; and the *Testament of Dan* is the first text in which this link appears.

That the *Testaments* present the doctrine of Christ's descent into Hell as the scene of his victory over Satan is confirmed, and this time quite explicitly, in another text, the *Testament of Benjamin*. This text,[21] which describes the signs that accompany the death of Christ, belongs to the same context as the *Testament of Levi* and continues the theme of *Mt.* 27:51. The author first describes the rending of the veil of the Temple, and then continues: 'And He shall ascend (ἀνελθών) from Hades and shall pass (μεταβαίνων) (*var.* he shall rise, ἀναβαίνων) from earth to heaven' (IX, 5).

The expression ἀνελθών indicates quite positively that Christ first went down to Hades. The descent into Hell is here therefore quite explicit, more so than in the previous texts; but since Hades was mentioned in the *Testament of Levi*, it is likely that that passage also implied an infernal Hades. It is, moreover, important to note that the theme of the descent into Hell is explicitly distinguished from that of the descent of the Word upon earth. Christ's Ascension is from earth to heaven and therefore presupposes that his descent was from heaven to earth. This is the Pauline theme of the *katabasis* and *anabasis*. The theme of the descent into Hell is different. It is not Pauline, nor does it belong to the primitive *katabasis-anabasis* scheme, but rather to a liturgical context as already stated.[22] The two themes may, however, have interfered with one another, as in the case of the *Ascension of Isaiah*.

One of the first texts in the last-named work mentions 'the descent of the Well-Beloved into Sheol' (IV, 21) only in order to connect the death of Christ with *Is.* 52–53. This derives from an interpretation, found also in the *Sybilline Oracles*, in which the descent into Hell means no more than the reality of Christ's death.[23] A second passage, on the other hand, presents the theme of Christ's conflict with the angel of death in Sheol. After describing the crucifixion, which 'the God of this world' has accomplished, 'without knowing who He is', the author continues: 'And when He hath plundered the angel of death, He will ascend on the third day, . . . And

---

21. Already quoted in a previous connection; cf. p. 145 above.
22. Cf. pp. 233, 238 f. above.   23. Cf. also XI, 19.

then many of the righteous will ascend with Him and He will send his preachers all over the earthly globe and will ascend into heaven' (IX, 16–17).

The doctrine of this passage covers exactly the same ground as that of the *Testaments of Levi* and *Benjamin*. As in the former, there is the idea of the despoiling of the angel of death, that is to say, a combat with him who holds the dead in captivity in Hell. That this despoiling does take place in Hell is proved by the mention of rising again. Moreover, as in the *Testament of Benjamin*, this rising again from Hell is carefully distinguished from the Ascension proper, which is an ascent from earth to heaven. The resurrection is still that of the saints of the Old Testament, and it is definitely stated that it took place on Easter Day, a different interpretation from that of *Mt.* 27:52 which associates it with the Passion in the strict sense of the word. The angel of death does not seem to represent the Devil, since the abode of the demons is the firmament.

The Ethiopic version of the *Ascension* gives a slightly different text: 'He will ascend on the third day, and He will remain in that world 545 days. And then many of the righteous will ascend with Him, whose spirits do not receive their garments until the Lord Christ ascend and they ascend with Him' (IX, 16–17). This is a later elaboration in which the resurrection of the saints, symbolised by the garments, is delayed until Christ's Ascension which, according to a speculation which appears again in the Gnostics,[24] only takes place 545 days after the Resurrection.

The passages from the *Ascension* mentioned so far are homogeneous with those of the *Testaments*, but they have a more archaic character than the latter. There is, however, one more text which introduces a new element by amalgamating the doctrine of the descent into Hell with the doctrine already discussed of Christ's descent through the various worlds, and his clothing himself in their forms in order to remain hidden from them. In this version it is even clearer than in the previous passages that the angel of death is not the Devil, for Christ in fact passes through the sphere of the evil angels in the firmament and in the air. Sheol thus appears as simply the abode of the dead, where they are guarded by an angel who is perhaps dangerous, but not wicked.

The Father says to the Beloved:

Go forth and descend through all the heavens; and after that thou shalt descend to the firmament and the terrestrial world, even as far as

24. IRENAEUS, *Adv. haer.* I, 3:2; cf. pp. 251, 253 below.

to the angel in Sheol; nevertheless to Haguel thou shalt not go. And thou shalt become like unto the likeness of all who are in the five heavens, and to the form of the angels of the firmament, and also of the angels who are in Sheol. . . . Afterwards from the realms of death thou shalt ascend to Thy place, and thou shalt not be transformed in each heaven' (X, 8–14).

The descent to Hell is not envisaged here as signifying the death of Christ, nor as a solution to the problem of the salvation of the patriarchs, nor, above all, as a victory over Satan, for this is formally excluded. It is simply related to the hidden character of Christ's coming. The *katabasis* theme here includes the descent to Hell as its final stage. But the author excludes Haguel, the great abyss spoken of in *I Enoch*, into which the evil angels will be thrown at the end of time.

The Jewish Christian *Sybilline Oracles* introduce a new development. A passage in *Book* VIII reads: 'He shall go into Hades to proclaim hope to all the saints, the end of the ages and eternal day; and he will fulfil the law ($\mu o\hat{\imath}\rho\alpha\nu$) of death by sleeping for three days' (VIII, 310–312). The first two verses recall the *Gospel of Peter*, and reduce the descent into Hell to a proclaiming of salvation. The most interesting is the last verse, in which appears the conception of the descent into Hell as 'fulfilling the common law of humanity'.[25] This reappears in Tertullian (*De anima* LV, 2), but it is a purely Greek theme which is not relevant to the present study.

The *Odes of Solomon* introduce the final stage of this particular topic: the linking of the theme of Christ's victory over death in Hell with the liturgical theme of Baptism. The latter thus becomes the victory of the baptised over the demon in the baptismal font. This is the first appearance of a theme which was destined to play a great part in Oriental liturgy, especially that of Syria. The particular style of the *Odes*, with their constant transition from the Christian to Christ, is especially suited to this identification of the two ideas. It may perhaps be added that the Qumran *Psalms*, in which there is the same personal emphasis, and the same transition from the Teacher of Righteousness to the Community, confirms the Jewish Christian, and perhaps the Essene Christian, origin of the *Odes*.

In *Ode* XVII the baptised first celebrates his deliverance from vanity, and the new birth which has followed. Then Christ begins to speak: 'I opened doors that were closed and I brake in pieces the bars of iron; and

25. BIEDER, *op. cit.*, p. 159.

the iron became red-hot and melted before me; nothing any more appeared closed to me, because I was the Door of everything. Then I went forth to all my prisoners to loose them' (XVII, 8–11). The allusion here is either to *Is.* 45:2 or to *Ps.* 106:16 (EVV 107), a verse which belonged to the oldest collections of *testimonia*, and which reappears constantly in connection with the descent into Hell. Now it is precisely on the subject of baptism that this quotation is given in a list of *testimonia* in *Barnabas*: 'I will go before thee . . . and crush gates of brass, and break in pieces bolts of iron' (XI, 4).[26] Baptism here is the baptism of the ordinary Christian, whereas in the *Odes* the reference oscillates between this and the Baptism of Christ; but as has already become clear, the theological themes of the two are closely connected.

This introduces a new element; Christ has been a prisoner of Death, but he has broken its power, and thus liberated all the dead. The two themes of the descent into Hell, the first regarding it as the death of Christ, and the second as the deliverance of the dead, are now associated as two temporally successive actions, whereas hitherto the former has been practically absent. Christ's combat with Satan now has for its primary object his own deliverance in the Resurrection, and the theme of the fight between Christ and Satan in Hell has become more precise; it is already *mors et vita duello conflixere mirando*. Finally, those set free are no longer the saints of the Old Testament. The interest is no longer in the past, but is centred on the liberation from Hell achieved in the present by Christ for all those who are baptised. Christ's actual coming out of Hell is continued sacramentally by baptism, which liberates the Christian from Hell by giving him a share in Christ's deliverance. The descent into and ascent from the water are a sacramental imitation of the descent and ascent of Christ which bring about the real effect of the sacrament. Here the theological and liturgical themes coincide completely.

In *Ode* XVII the theme of the descent was no more than suggested, by the imagery of the prison. In *Ode* XXII, on the other hand, it is explicit, for there Christ's descent into hell and his victory over the powers, the descent of the baptised into the font and his deliverance, and finally the resurrection of the dead are all closely associated:

It is He who brought me down, and who has also brought me up from the regions below; and it is He who gathers together the things that are between. It is He who has scattered my enemies and my adversaries,

26. Cf. P. LUNDBERG, *op. cit.*, p. 179.

and has given me power over bonds that I might loose them, He that has bruised by my hands the dragon with seven heads, and caused me to tread his roots under my feet, that I might destroy his seed. Thou wast at my side, and didst protect me, and in every place Thy name encircled me like a rampart. Thy right hand has dissolved the poison of the Accuser, and Thy hand has levelled the way for those who believe in thee (XXII, 1–7).

Here once again the text begins with an allusion on the part of the baptised to the baptismal rites. It is not a question of the crowns, as in *Ode* XVII, but of the descent into and the rising from the font. The text then describes Christ's struggle with Satan, and here an interesting point emerges. The triple allusion to what is on high, what is between and what is below seems to be echoed in the description of Christ's combat, in which he scatters the enemies, bruises the dragon with his hands, and tramples its roots under his feet. It would seem that this struggle takes place in the air, on earth and in Hell at one and the same time, and there is thus a synthesis of the conception of the combat against the Powers on the Cross and the combat against Death in Hell. The Pauline and the Jewish Christian themes are at last synthesised.

The expression: 'Thou wast at my side and didst protect me' seems to be an allusion to baptismal immersion conceived as a descent into Hell and a confrontation of the demon. Here is the origin of the pre-baptismal anointing, which was intended to strengthen the baptised for his fight against the dragon of the waters.[27] There seems to be moreover a probable echo of *Ps.* 22:4 (EVV 23). 'Even if I walk in the midst of the shadow of death I will not be afraid of evils, for thou art with me'; if so, this would be the first indication of the baptismal use of this psalm which was to have such an important place in the liturgy of Christian initiation.[28] The final point of interest is the archaic, Jewish Christian use of the term 'the Name' to denote the divine activity in baptism; this is an allusion to the σφραγίς and its protective power.[29]

The rest of the *Ode* is concerned with the resurrection:

Thou hast chosen them from the graves, and separated them from the dead; thou hast taken dead bones and covered them with bodies; they

27. Cf. DANIÉLOU, *Bible et Liturgie*, pp. 58–60.
28. *Ibid.*, p. 246, on the baptismal interpretation of this verse.
29. *Ibid.*, pp. 76–89; also E. DINKLER, 'Jesus Wort vom Kreuztragen', *Neut. Stud. R. Bultmann*, 1954, pp. 117–119.

became solid, and thou didst give them the energy of life. Thy way was without corruption; yet thou didst bring thy face into the world which belonged to thee to subject it to corruption, that all things might be dissolved and then renewed (XXII, 8–11).

Here the resurrection seems to be the eschatological resurrection promised to the baptised, and already virtually accomplished in the emergence from the baptismal font. The end of the passage returns to the idea of Christ's descent to Hell. This proves beyond question the synthesis of the Pauline theme of descent to earth and the Jewish Christian theme of the descent to Hell. The sojourn on earth is no longer even mentioned.

Ode XLII, the last of the collection, offers a notable contribution to the evidence on this subject:

Sheol saw me and was overcome; Death suffered me to return and many with me. I was gall and bitterness to him, and I went down with him to the utmost of his depths. I held an assembly of living men among the dead, and I spake to them with holy lips; and those who had died ran towards me, they cried and said: Son of God have pity on us, and deal with us according to thy loving kindness; bring us out from the bonds of darkness, and open to us the door, that we may come forth to thee. For we see that our death has not come nigh thee. As for me, I heard their voice, and I traced my name upon their heads; therefore they are free men and they are mine (XLII, 15–26).

This remarkable text first takes up and summarises the general theme: descent into Sheol, victory over death, departure from Sheol and the deliverance of many. But after this the various actions of Christ in Sheol are noted in detail for the first time. In the first place, Christ not only goes down to Sheol but also into its deepest part, where Death abides[30]—the first instance of this conception. This proves first that Death is here identified with Satan himself, who is moreover no longer in the firmament, but in the bowels of the earth; and secondly, that Christ goes down to the deepest place of Hell, a belief denied by the *Ascension of Isaiah*. The placing of Satan at the centre of the earth was to become the standard symbolism.

The passage goes on to record Christ's acts in Sheol proper in detail. First of all there is a repetition of His preaching to the dead, a feature which occurred in the very first texts quoted. Until now, however, it had never

30. Cf. BIEDER, *op. cit.*, p. 179.

been associated with the theme of the conflict with Death. For the first time also the dead appeal to Christ, an idea that was to be taken up in the *Gospel of Nicodemus* and was to become a common theme. Next there is the baptism of the dead, given by the imposition of the Name, which recalls the evidence of the *Shepherd*. Thus Christ, during his sojourn in Hell, brings together an assembly, an *ecclesia* of those who already belong to him and to the number of living, and who will rise with him on the third day.

It is a point of special interest that even in Sheol Christ's condition is not the same as that of the dead; their death has not come near him, which is why the dead ask that they may come forth to him. And Christ responds to their desire and brings them life, thus instituting a first deliverance within Sheol itself. There is a remarkable parallel to this in the *Shepherd*, which says of the Apostles that 'these went down alive' into Sheol, whereas the others 'went down dead' (*Sim.* IX, 16:6). A little before this the text reads: 'Before a man has borne the name of God he is dead; but when he has received the seal he layeth aside his deadness' (IX, 16:3). The situation is exactly the same, save that in the one case the deliverer is Christ, and in the other the Apostles. The allusion to the Name, meaning baptism, which brings a person to life even if he is still in Sheol, is common to both texts.

THE ASCENSION

Just as Christ's Incarnation was expressed within the framework of Jewish Christian sacred cosmology as a descent (κατάβασις) of the Beloved through the angelic spheres, so his Glorification is presented as an ascension (ἀνάβασις). The contrast of these two movements, that which begins and that which completes the earthly life of Christ, is already present in the New Testament. It is emphasised in *Ephesians* especially: 'Now this, He ascended, what is it but that he also descended into the lower parts of the earth?' (4:9, cf. also *Phil.* 2:5–10). Similarly in *John*: 'I came out from the Father, and am come into the world; again, I leave the world, and go unto the Father' (16:28). It is the second of these movements which must now be considered.

It is the Ascension as a theological symbol, the exaltation above every creature of that humanity which the Word of God united to himself, which is of central importance, and which interested the primitive tradition more than any other: 'It is clear that the invisible, transcendent accession of the risen Christ to the divine world is the essential part of the mystery. His visible departure from this world is only a secondary aspect of it. This explains why primitive Christian tradition insists so much on the essential affirmation of the heavenly triumph of Christ.'[31] This is true also of the Jewish Christians. Nevertheless this exaltation of Christ exhibits various elements and aspects,[32] and these must be studied first, before turning to the strictly Jewish Christian developments of the theme of the ἀνάβασις.

Among the Jewish Christian texts which deal with the glorious exaltation of Christ, one group associates it directly with the Resurrection, of which it was regarded as expressing the theological import. This does not mean, however, that the authors in question did not believe that the risen Christ remained for a while on earth, and then departed at the end of that period. It does mean that the exaltation of Christ does not depend on the latter event, but was already effective from the time of his Resurrection. Contrary to the practice of later theology Jewish Christianity expresses the glorification of Christ from the point of view of the Ascension rather than that of the Resurrection, an approach which fits better into the structure of Jewish Christian theology with its more cosmological than anthropomorphic world-view.

This approach appears first in texts where the Resurrection as such is not mentioned, but where its content is given expression in the conception of the heavenly exaltation. This is the case with the *Testament of Benjamin*: 'And He shall ascend from Hades and shall pass (μεταβαίνων)[33] from earth to heaven. I know how lowly (ταπεινός) He shall be upon earth, and how glorious (ἔνδοξος) in heaven' (IX, 5). The ideas are formulated here in a manner very close to that of the Pauline Captivity Epistles. A contrast is drawn between the abasement of the Incarnation and the exaltation of the Resurrection, but with the latter presented as an entry into heaven. The descent into Hell is mentioned as immediately preceding the exaltation, with no intervening incident.

The *Gospel of Peter* has the same conception. The account of the Resurrection describes how 'the heavens opened and two men descended thence shining with a great light'; then 'three men come out of the sepulchre, and the two young men were bearing up the other. The head of him whom they were escorting out-topped the heavens' (36–40). The details of this scene will call for further consideration later; but the opening of the heavens,

31. P. BENOIT, 'L'Ascension', *RB*, LVI, 1949, p. 195.
32. Cf. V. LARRANAGA, *L'Ascension de N.-S.*, Rome, 1938, pp. 492–566.
33. A variant reading is ἀναβαίνων.

the elevation of the risen Christ on the angelic throne (the Jewish *mer-kaba*[34]), the fact that his head reaches above the skies, all describe the Resurrection in terms of a heavenly ascension. Moreover, the continuation of the *Gospel* confirms that the Resurrection is identified with Christ's entry into heaven, for the angels answer the women who seek Christ's body in the tomb: 'He is not there for he is risen and has departed to the place from which he had been sent' (56). Again the Ascension follows directly upon the descent into Hell (41).

Side by side with this line of thought, which is close to Pauline theology, there is another which may be called Johannine. This distinguishes the Resurrection from the Ascension, but places the latter nevertheless on Easter Day: 'The Fourth Gospel certainly speaks of a heavenly exaltation of the Lord on Easter Day itself. The words: I have not yet ascended to my Father, can have no other meaning.'[35] In this case Christ manifests himself after his Resurrection but before his Exaltation. This view is precisely that of the *Epistle of Barnabas*: 'We keep the eighth day for rejoicing, in the which also Jesus rose from the dead and having been manifested ascended into heaven' (XV, 9). A passage in the *Apology* of Aristides probably belongs to the same line of thought: 'After three days He came to life again and ascended into heaven' (15).

The most important school of thought in Jewish Christianity, however, associates the exaltation of Christ with his final departure, and what is more, it attributes great importance and considerable length to Christ's stay on earth between the Resurrection and the Ascension. This view is expressed in the *Ascension of Isaiah* where the exaltation is one of the main themes, recurring several times. In one of the first passages the Resurrection and the Ascension are spoken of as successive events:

> And I saw the angel of the Holy Spirit, and Michael, the chief of the holy angels, on the third day open the sepulchre; and the Beloved sitting on their shoulders will come forth and send out His twelve Apostles; and they will teach all nations and tongues concerning the Resurrection of the Beloved; and those who believe in His cross, and in His ascension to the seventh heaven whence He came, will be saved (III, 16–20).

This text is of great interest, since it distinguishes two exaltations of the Lord. It first describes the Resurrection, in terms which recall the *Gospel*

34. Cf. Glossary s.v.   35. BENOIT, *op. cit.*, pp. 169–170.

of Peter, as an ascent of the risen Christ on the shoulders of angels. But the author distinguishes from this first exaltation the ascent through the seven heavens which is separated from the first by the sending of the Apostles. There is also a definite allusion to *Mt.* 28. Thus the exaltation themes are shared out between the Resurrection and the Ascension, though the main emphasis is reserved to the latter. Furthermore, it may be said that in general the attaching of exaltation themes to the Resurrection in the *Ascension of Isaiah* does not imply a denial of the actual historic departure of Jesus. The two questions are quite separate. The fact of Christ's sojourn on earth after the Resurrection, and of his departure at the end of that period, is affirmed by the whole tradition.

The peculiarity of Jewish Christian theology is that it prolongs this sojourn. This may be seen in a second passage from the *Ascension of Isaiah*:

> When He hath plundered the angel of death, He will ascend on the third day, and He will remain in this world 545 days. And then many of the righteous will ascend with Him, whose spirits do not receive their garments till the Lord Christ ascend and they ascend with him. Then indeed they will receive their garments and thrones and crowns, when He has ascended into the seventh heaven' (IX, 16–19).

Here there is the sequence of descent into Hell and ascent, but the latter plainly refers to the Resurrection. This ascent is in fact separated by 545 days from the ascension to the seventh heaven.[36]

A final passage from the work reveals a similar view:

> I saw Him . . . likewise after the third day rise again and remain some days. And the angel who conducted me said: Understand, O Isaiah. And I saw when He sent out the twelve Apostles and ascended. . . . And I saw how He ascended into the seventh heaven and all the righteous and all the angels praised Him, and then I saw Him sit down on the right hand of that Great Glory, whose glory I told you that I was not able to look upon (XI, 21–32).

Here the exaltation of Christ, with some of its chief features, the session

36. The same lengthy period is to be found in later texts (cf. p. 253 below), betraying their dependence on the *Ascension*. Cf. particularly the *Apocryphon Jacobi*, discovered at Nag Hammadi; for the points of contact between this work and the *Ascension*, cf. W. C. van Unnik, 'The Origin of the Recently Discovered Apocryphon Jacobi', *VC*, x, 1956, p. 155.

at the right hand, the elevation above the seven heavens, the praise of the angels, is again explicitly related to the final departure of the risen Christ.

A similar conception is to be found in the *Epistle of the Apostles*. The entire work consists of revelations made by Jesus between the Resurrection and the Ascension. The following passage distinguishes clearly between the two events: 'after he was crucified, and dead and risen again, when the work had been fulfilled which was accomplished in his flesh while he was crucified, and when his ascension came to pass at the end of a few days, then he said to us: Now that I am going to my Father which is in heaven, I give you a new commandment, that you should love one another' (18; *PO* IX, cols. 200–201). The length of Christ's sojourn is not stated precisely, but it involves only 'a few days'. The most important feature is that Christ's teaching on fraternal charity is placed before the Ascension and not before the Passion, as in *John*. This would seem to suggest that there was a tradition by which the discourses which John for unknown reasons placed after the Supper actually took place after the Resurrection.

Elsewhere the *Epistle of the Apostles* gives us an account of Christ's Ascension at the end of his stay on earth:

> When he had said this, and had finished his discourse with us, he said unto us again: Behold, on the third day and at the third hour he shall come which hath sent me, that I may depart with him. And as he so spake there was thunder and lightning and an earthquake, and the heavens parted asunder and there appeared a bright cloud which bore him up. And there came voices of many angels, rejoicing and singing praises and saying: 'Gather us, O priest, into the light of thy majesty.' And when he drew nigh to the firmament of heaven, we heard his voice saying unto us: 'Depart hence in peace' (51; *PO* IX, col. 239).

The detail of the third day seems to be a literary reminiscence of texts in which the Ascension was placed on Easter Day.[37] Further consideration will have to be given to the ascension themes which appear here, the luminous cloud and the dialogue with the angels.

The texts so far examined belong to the Great Church, but Gnosticism also exhibits certain Jewish Christian elements relating to this theme, which supplement those already quoted. The theme of a teaching by the risen Christ, which ended only with his Ascension, is a common one among the Gnostics. The disciples of Ptolemy (*Adv. haer.* I, 3:2) and the Ophites

37. Cf. C. Schmidt, *Gespräche Jesu mit seinen Jüngern*, p. 301.

(*Adv. haer.* I, 30:14) make this delay last eighteen months, which fits in with the 545 days of the *Ascension of Isaiah*. This certainly seems to be a case of a Jewish Christian tradition which was simply copied by the Gnostics.[38] *Pistis Sophia* in the third century was to assign eleven years to this teaching of Christ (I, 1), concluding it with an account of the Ascension. This long delay is explained by saying that Christ gave the true gnosis to his disciples during the time between the Resurrection and the Ascension, and that this necessitated the prolongation of his stay on earth. This theme may, however, derive from Jewish Christianity if, as already suggested, Jewish Christian speculations are represented as constituting a higher teaching belonging to Apostolic times, and thus fictitiously attributed to Christ.

It is now clear that the exaltation of Christ might be connected with various stages of the glorification which constitutes his Ascension in the theological sense of the word. For ascension, that is to say, the raising up of a person above the heavens, is a stock piece of Jewish and Jewish Christian apocalyptic symbolism, and is susceptible of various interpretations,[39] the most ancient being that which was used to describe the elevation of a visionary—'whether in the body or apart from the body, I know not' (*II Cor.* 12:2)—so that he is able to contemplate the heavenly world normally hidden from his eyes. *I Enoch* presents an ascension of Enoch in these terms; the *Ascension of Isaiah* shows us Isaiah passing through the seven heavens in the course of his vision; in the *Apocalypse of Peter* there is an ascension of Christ at the moment of his Transfiguration; Paul describes how he was taken up to the Third Heaven; and in the *Shepherd* a spirit seizes Hermas and carries him away to an inaccessible region (*Vis.* I, 1:3–4).

Moreover, there is also the theme of a just man taken up after his death into the highest heaven, though only, it seems, in the case of Enoch as related by *II Enoch*. However, in the *Ascension of Isaiah* Isaiah sees both Adam, Abel and Enoch in the seventh heaven. These ascensions are of the same type as the previous ones, although their meaning may be quite

---

38. The Ophites distinguish two ascensions: a return of the heavenly Christ to the Father (ἄνοδος) before the Passion and a taking up (ἀναληφθείς) of the psychic Jesus after eighteen months (*Adv. haer.* I, 30:13 f.). Cf. A. HOUSSIAU, *La christologie de St. Irénée*, p. 155.

39. Cf. G. BERTRAM, 'Der religionsgeschichtliche Hintergrund der Erhöhung', *ZNW*, LXVIII, 1956, pp. 63–68; G. KRETSCHMAR, 'Himmelfahrt und Pfingsten', *ZKG*, LXV, 1956, pp. 220–224.

different, representing glorification after death. In Jewish Christian texts this glorification was to be extended to a certain number of saints of the Old Testament, but only after the Resurrection of Christ whom they accompany in his Ascension.[40]

It is an ascension in this sense which is attributed to Christ in the texts considered in this chapter, and which serves to denote his glorification. Formally it does not in fact differ from the other ascensions mentioned, as is especially obvious in the *Ascension of Isaiah*, in which the passage through the seven heavens is described in the same way, whether in the case of the vision of Isaiah or of the Ascension of the Beloved. Similarly in the *Apocalypse of Peter* the account of the vision of Christ at the Transfiguration is so like the account of the Ascension in the *Epistle of the Apostles* that the two could be interchangeable. The important point, therefore, in the accounts of Christ's Ascension is the essential meaning, not the cosmological expression. Nevertheless, since this cosmological symbolism serves as a means of presenting doctrine, it calls for careful examination, and the next step must therefore be to study the structure of the various accounts of the Ascension.

One of the oldest forms is that which occurs in the *Gospel of Peter* and in the *Ascension of Isaiah*, in which Christ is borne up on a throne formed of angels. The two relevant passages are as follows: 'The two young men (i.e., the angels) bore up the other (i.e., the Risen Christ) . . . and a Cross followed them' (*Gospel of Peter* 39), and: 'The Beloved sitting on their shoulders will come forth, and send out His Twelve Apostles' (*Asc. Is.* III, 17). In spite of objections which have been raised with regard to the first of these texts, it is clear that they are both representations of an ascension, and may legitimately be compared with a passage in the *Shepherd* where, when the Woman, who symbolises the Church, has finished teaching Hermas, 'two men (i.e., two angels) appeared, and took her by the arms, and they departed toward the East' (*Vis.* I, 4:4).[41]

The imagery here is in fact that of the *merkaba*,[42] the heavenly chariot

40. Cf. pp. 239–243 above.

41. Cf. ERIK PETERSON, 'Beiträge zur Interpretation der Visionen in Pastor Hermae', *OCP*, XIII, 1947, p. 631. Even though it is a vision that is being described, and not an ascension, the cases are strictly comparable since the same symbolic scheme served for both.

42. The link between the Ascension and the *merkaba* has recently been emphasised by LOUIS BOUYER (*La Bible et l'Évangile*, pp. 153–157) in a modern rediscovery of the ancient symbolism of Jewish Christian theology.

formed of angels. The importance of this theme in *Ezekiel*[43] is well known, but the fact that it is not applied to Christ in the New Testament makes it all the more interesting to find it in these texts. It is patently Jewish in character, and derives from the oldest stratum of Jewish Christianity, that of Palestine; hence it is not surprising that its first appearance should be in texts of a markedly archaic type. The exaltation of Christ upon the two angels[44] appears therefore as a manifestation of his extraordinary glory, and as a hidden mystery, the knowledge of which is carefully restricted. It is a point that cannot but strike the modern reader that these authors should presume to supplement the reticence of the New Testament in this way by giving a 'higher' teaching.

A second theme is that of the passage through the heavens and the angelic hierarchies. In the *Ascension of Isaiah* Christ ascends through the seven heavens, and the *anabasis* is, moreover, made to balance the *katabasis*. In the latter the angels had not recognised the Word of God, who hid his glory by taking their likeness; now his glory is revealed and the angels adore him. The Ascension appears here in its full meaning of a glorious exaltation, and this text was to have a great influence.

Christ first passes through the firmament, the abode of the fallen Watchers, and the angels are filled with a great sadness at not having recognised the glory of the Lord at his descent (XI, 23–24). This idea recurs throughout the *Ascension*: '(Christ) ascended into the second heaven, and He did not transform Himself, but all the angels who were on the right and the left of the throne which is in the midst of them both worshipped Him and praised Him and said: How was Our Lord hidden from us whilst descending and we perceived not?' (XI, 25–26). It is the same until the sixth heaven, 'but in all the heavens the praise increased' (XI, 31). Finally the risen Christ reaches the seventh heaven: 'And then I saw Him sit down on the right hand of the Great Glory' (XI, 32).

The characteristic theme of the Angels' regret for not having recognised Christ at his descent is repeated exactly in *Pistis Sophia*, which clearly depends on the *Ascension*, but with this difference, that the successive

43. It should not be forgotten that the opening chapter of *Ezekiel*, like the beginning of *Genesis*, was included by the Jews among those books which were given an esoteric interpretation.
44. The peculiar form taken by the Ascension in the *Apocryphon Jacobi* should be noted. Christ rises upon a chariot of cloud; two *disciples* (not angels) accompany him through the first two heavens, but stop at the threshold of the third: cf. VAN UNNIK, *op. cit.*, p. 152.

spheres through which the Saviour passes in his ascension are now the seven planetary spheres with their Archons, which constitute the world of the Demiurge:

> When I saw the vesture (of light) which (the Power) had sent me, then I clothed myself therewith, and I shone most exceedingly and I soared into the height. I came before the gate of the firmament . . . and the gates of the firmament were shaken and opened at once. . . . And I left that region behind me and ascended to the first sphere, shining most exceedingly, forty-nine times more brightly than I had shone in the firmament. And when I reached the gates of the first sphere, all the gates were shaken and opened of themselves at once. I entered into the houses of the sphere . . . and all the rulers were amazed and shook when they saw the great light that was about me. And beholding my vesture they saw upon it the mystery of my Name, and they fell into still greater agitation, and were in great fear, saying: 'How hath the Lord of the universe passed through us without our knowing?' (11–12).

The Ascension then continues through the other spheres.

In the *Epistle of the Apostles* there is a slightly different presentation of the story. Here a procession of angels accompanies the Word. At his descent it was the higher powers who accompanied him down to the fifth heaven: 'The (archangels) Michael, Gabriel, Uriel and Raphael followed me unto the fifth firmament' (13), but when they arrive at this heaven the Beloved sends them back: 'On that day I terrified the archangels by my word, bidding them go to the altar of the Father and serve the Father after their wont until I should return unto Him' (*ibid.*). Now, at the Ascension the action is in reverse; the lower angels form a procession for the risen Christ in his ascent, until he sends them back: 'Then came the voices of many angels rejoicing and singing praises and saying: Gather us, O Priest, unto the light of thy majesty. And when they drew nigh unto the firmament of heaven we heard his voice saying, Depart hence in peace' (51).

So far consideration has been limited to some Jewish Christian cosmological forms which were used for expressing the glorification of Christ. But the Jewish Christian theology of the Ascension has another source as well: the *testimonia*, which will later be seen also to play an important part in the theology of the Cross. In themselves the *testimonia* belong to the primitive tradition and to biblical theology, but Jewish Christianity has on the other hand added to them, by combing the ancient Scriptures, and on the other hand, has used them as a starting-point for developing various theological speculations. This process is especially noticeable in the case of the present theme. The relevant *testimonia* come originally from the *Psalms*, and express the establishment of the Messiah in his royal state: from this point of view, the application of them to the Ascension is a clear illustration of its theological meaning.[45]

The first psalm to play a role in the theology of the Ascension is *Psalm* 109 (EVV 110). The use of it dates back to the earliest stratum of the *testimonia*, since the New Testament quotes it several times to designate the glory of Christ. It forms part of the earliest Christian profession of faith, that of Peter on the day of Pentecost:

> (David) being therefore a prophet, and knowing that God had sworn with an oath to him, that of the fruit of his loins he would set one upon his throne; he foreseeing this spake of the resurrection of the Christ. . . . This Jesus did God raise up, whereof we all are witnesses. Being therefore by the right hand of God exalted, and having received of the Father the promise of the Holy Ghost, he hath poured forth this, which ye see and hear. For David ascended not into the heavens: but he saith himself: The Lord said unto my Lord, Sit thou on my right hand, till I make thine enemies the footstool of thy feet (*Acts* 2:30–35).

The same psalm is quoted in the principal passages on the Ascension in the New Testament. Thus in *Ephesians*: 'According to that working of the strength of his might which he wrought in Christ, when he raised him from the dead, and made him to sit at his right hand in the heavenly places, far above all rule, and authority, and power, and dominion, and every name that is named, . . . and he put all things in subjection under his feet' (1:19–22). Here there are two allusions to the psalm—the session at the right hand, and the footstool. The latter reappears in *I Cor.* 15:25–27: '(Christ) must reign until (the Father) hath put all his enemies under his feet. The last enemy that shall be abolished is death. For, He put all things in subjection under his feet.' Here the 'footstool' symbolises the eschatological completion of that which was begun by the heavenly session. The two expressions are again associated in *Hebrews*: '(Christ), when he had offered one sacrifice for sins for ever, sat down on the right hand of God; from henceforth expecting till his enemies be made the footstool of his feet' (10:12–13).

45. Cf. DANIÉLOU, *Bible et Liturgie*, pp. 409–429.

Thus *Psalm* 109 affords an outstanding example of the use of *testimonia* for the formulation of theology in primitive Christianity. Its formulas have even passed into the Creeds in those clauses which speak of Christ's 'sitting at the right hand' of the Father, and this particular imagery, which must go back to the very first apostolic generation, was to be used by Jewish Christianity in its turn, in conjunction with that of the exaltation above the angels to designate the glorification of Christ. This is true, for instance, of the *Ascension of Isaiah*: 'I saw him sit down on the right hand of that Great Glory' (XI, 32); and Justin is simply an heir to this tradition, when he writes: 'And that God the Father of all would bring Christ up to heaven after He had raised Him from the dead, and would keep Him there until He has subdued His enemies the demons, . . . hear what was said by the Prophet David: The Lord said unto my Lord, sit thou at my right hand, until I make Thine enemies Thy footstool' (*I Apol.* XLV, 1–2).[46]

The second psalm to be applied to the Ascension by the *testimonia* is *Psalm* 67 (EVV 68). Here again the use of it in this connection is very ancient, since it occurs in Saint Paul: 'But unto each one of us was the grace given according to the measure of the gift of Christ. Wherefore he saith, When he ascended on high, he led captivity captive, and gave gifts unto men. Now this, He ascended, what is it but that he also descended into the lower parts of the earth?' (*Eph.* 4:7–9). It has already been pointed out that this text was one of the *testimonia* relating to the Descent into Hell. In *Ephesians*, however, and in the passages about to be quoted, the deliverance of the captives is not applied in this sense, but as representing the conversion of the pagans.

This is the interpretation in a whole series of writers who take their exegesis from the Jewish Christian tradition. One example comes from the *Odes of Solomon*: '(The Lord granted me) to convert the souls of those who wish to come to Him, and to lead captive a blessed captivity for freedom'[47] (X, 3). Similarly Justin writes: 'It was prophesied that after the ascent of Christ into heaven He would take us captive from error ($\pi\lambda\acute{\alpha}\nu\eta s$) and would give us gifts' (*Dial.* XXXIX, 4), and he quotes in support *Ps.* 67:19 (EVV 68:18). The liberation therefore takes place after the Ascension, the pattern being the same as in the interpretation of *Psalm* 109. In both cases the mission follows immediately after the Ascension. Thus Justin quotes

46. Cf. also IRENAEUS, *Adv. haer.* IV, 33:13.
47. N.b. the interpretation of $\alpha\acute{\iota}\chi\mu\alpha\lambda\omega\sigma\acute{\iota}\alpha\nu$ as the accusative of the direct object. The conversion of the Gentiles is mentioned in v. 6.

this same verse again later, this time applying it to Pentecost: 'It was prophesied that this (the outpouring of the gifts of the Spirit) would be effected by Him after His ascent into heaven' (LXXXVII, 6).

Of special importance is Irenaeus, not only because he is a privileged witness to Jewish Christian traditions, but also because he has a more developed exegesis of this particular Psalm. He writes:

And when raised from the dead Christ was to ascend into heaven, as David says: The chariot of God is thousands and thousands of angels; the Lord is among them in Sinai, in the holy place. He ascends on high, leading the throng of captives; he hath given gifts to men. By 'captivity' the prophet means the destruction of the power of the rebel angels (*Dem.* 83).

Later in the passage Irenaeus explains that 'after His resurrection from the dead Christ assembled His disciples, and it was in their sight that He ascended, and the heavens opened to receive Him' (*ibid.*).

Nevertheless, in the two cases just examined the use of the Psalms in Jewish Christianity is strictly dependent on the New Testament, and does not introduce any new theological developments. The case is rather different with another Psalm, which was first applied to the Ascension only with the advent of Jewish Christian theology, and was to lend itself to important theological elaboration. This is *Ps.* 23 (EVV 24). The oldest indication of its use in this connection appears in the *Apocalypse of Peter*[48]: 'A great fear and terror seized the angels in this heaven, and they pressed one upon another that the word of the Scripture might be fulfilled which saith: Open your gates, ye Princes. Thereafter was the heaven shut, that had been open.' The context of this scene is obvious. Christ arrives at the gates of heaven; the sight of him throws the angels into amazement; they hasten to open the gates for him, and then shut them again after he has passed through.

The theme is the same as that already encountered in the *Ascension of Isaiah* and the *Pistis Sophia*, especially as regards the terror of the angels in the face of the glorified Christ, a feature common to all these texts. The guarding of the gates of heaven by angels also occurs in the *Ascension of Isaiah* (X, 24–25). The only new element is the application of *Psalm* 23:7 to the Ascension, to which it was admirably suited with its reference to the ἄρχοντες and the gates; and the transposition from the installation of the

48. Text ed. by GRÉBAUT, *ROC*, v, 1910, p. 317.

Messiah in the Temple of Jerusalem to the enthronement of the glorified Christ in the heavenly Temple was certainly a natural one.

This Psalm must have belonged to the *testimonia* of the Ascension at an early date, as is indicated by the frequent use of it in later texts. It is often associated with *Psalm* 110, as in the following quotation from Justin: '(The princes) were bidden to open their gates that this very one who is King of glory might enter in, and ascend to sit on the right hand of His Father, until he had made His enemies the footstool of His feet' (*Dial.* XXXVI, 5). This must have been a common grouping of texts, for it occurs again in the Gnostic Justin, who applies it to the ascension of Elohim the Demiurge into the presence of the Good: 'Elohim . . . wished to ascend up to the heights of heaven. Coming to the highest part of all, he cried out, Open me the gates, that I may enter in and give glory to the Lord. And immediately the gate was opened, and the Good One said to him: Sit thou on my right hand' (HIPPOLYTUS, *Elench.* V, 26).

One of the first developments of this theme occurs in Irenaeus, who here follows the *Apocalypse of Peter*:

Again David says this very thing: Open your gates, O ye Princes, and be lifted up, O eternal gates; and the king of glory shall enter in. The 'eternal gates' are the heavens. Because He was by nature invisible, the Word could not be perceived by creatures when He came down to earth. But once He had been made visible by His Incarnation, He was seen as He ascended into heaven; and when the Powers saw Him, the angels below cried to those that were above: Open your gates; be lifted up, O eternal gates, and the king of glory shall enter in. And when the angels in the highest were astonished and said: Who is this? those who had already seen Him hailed Him a second time, crying: It is the Lord strong and mighty, it is He the king of glory (*Dem.* 84).

It will be observed that in this passage, in contrast to the texts studied earlier, the hidden character of Christ's descent is due to his divine nature. By contrast he is made visible at his Ascension by his body, and the sight of this glorified body throws the angels into amazement.

This is expressed still more explicitly in the *Paschal Homily* attributed to Hippolytus:

At the sight of this great mystery of a man ascending now with God, the Powers shouted with joy this order to the hosts on high: Lift up your gates, you princes. Be lifted up, eternal gates. And the king of glory will enter. They, seeing this unheard-of marvel of a man mingled with God, cry in answer: Who is this king of glory? And those from whom they thus enquired answer again: The Lord of Hosts, he is the king of glory (61).

It is the unheard-of marvel of the Man-God which here astonishes the Powers; another interesting detail is the dialogue of the latter with the lower angels.

The application of this Psalm to the Ascension was, however, to lead to a new and curious development. The Psalm, as has just been remarked, involves a dialogue between the angels who accompany Christ and those who guard 'the eternal gates'. These interrogate the former and ask them who it is that they accompany, which seems to indicate that they do not recognise him. This theme had, of course, been applied to Christ's descent, when he put on the form of the angels in order not to be recognised by them; indeed, it is in this context that in the *Physiologos* the angels ask: 'Who is this king of Glory?', and receive from the Holy Ghost the reply: 'The Lord of Hosts, he is the king of glory' (IV, 5).

But when the Psalm was associated with the *anabasis* a difficulty was discovered. If the glory of Christ was manifest, it was not clear to what the angels' question referred; and it therefore became necessary to disguise the Word in his ascent in the same way as in the descent. This gave rise to a whole new tradition, which seems to be a development of the Jewish Christian theme. What now hides the Word from the angels is no longer his putting on their form when he passes through their regions, but the fact that he is henceforth united to human nature; the Incarnate Word is an absolutely new reality which overcomes them with amazement. This emphasis on the novelty of the Incarnation, as a mystery which has been hidden from the angels and which throws them into astonishment, is a revival of a Pauline theme (cf. *Eph.* 3:9–10).

The first text to present this theme occurs in Justin:

When Christ rose from the dead and ascended into heaven, then they who were appointed by God rulers in the heavens were commanded to open the gates of the heavens that this very One who is King of glory might enter in, and ascend and sit on the right hand of the Father, until He has made His enemies the footstool of His feet, as is made plain by another Psalm.[49] When, therefore, the rulers in heaven saw Him

49. Note again the use of *Ps.* 109 (EVV 110) in this context.

wearing a form without form and without honour or glory, they did not recognise Him, and were enquiring: Who is this king of glory? And the Holy Spirit answers them, either in the person of the Father or in His own person: The Lord of Hosts, He is the King of glory (*Dial.* XXXVI, 5–6).

There is a close relationship between this treatment and that in the *Physiologos*.[50] Each makes the same use of *Psalm* 23, and in each case it is the Holy Ghost who replies to the princes. This is an archaic feature, which was later to disappear entirely, and is thus an argument in favour of the antiquity of the tradition recorded by the *Physiologos*. The chief difference from the *Physiologos* is that Justin places the episode in the context of the Ascension and not in that of the descent prior to the Incarnation.

Justin's theme reappears in a passage of Origen:

When He comes, conquering and triumphant, with His body which has risen from the dead, then certain of the Powers say: Who is this that cometh from Edom, with reddened garments from Bozrah in such splendour? Then those who escort Him say to those who are set in charge of the heavenly gates, Open your gates, ye rulers, open your everlasting doors, and the king of glory shall come in. But they enquire yet again, if one may so describe it, seeing His right hand red with blood, and His whole body covered with the marks of his valour (*Com. Joh.* VI, 56).

It will be observed that to *Psalm* 23 is added *Is.* 63:1, introducing the idea of the wounds of the Passion, which the risen Christ continues to bear; but apart from this new feature the train of thought is still the same as in the text from Justin.[51]

In the form which Origen gave to it the theme was to pass into the common tradition of the fourth century. Thus Gregory Nazianzen writes:

Join yourself to those angels who escort Him or those who receive Him. Bid the gates raise their lintels to receive Him whose stature is now exalted by virtue of His Passion. To those who are in doubt because He bears in His Ascension a body and tokens of His Passion, which

50. As PETERSON has rightly emphasised: 'Die Spiritualität des griechischen Physiologos', *BZ*, XLVII, 1954, pp. 70–71.
51. The theme is also found among the Naassenians, though to the question 'Who is this King of glory?' their answer is: 'A worm and no man' (*Ps.* 21:7 (EVV 22:6); cf. HIPPOLYTUS, *Elench.* V, 8).

He had not when He came down, and who therefore enquire, Who is this King of Glory?, reply that it is the Lord strong and mighty.[52]

A very similar passage is found in Saint Ambrose: 'The angels also doubted when Christ arose, seeing his flesh ascending from earth to heaven. So they said: Who is the King of glory? And when some said: Lift up your gates, ye princes, and the King of glory shall come in; then others doubted and replied: Who is this that cometh up from Edom?'[53]

The most interesting case, however, is that of Gregory of Nyssa, who, it will be remembered, also reproduced the theme from the *Ascension of Isaiah* of the Word's being concealed during his descent by putting on the angelic forms.[54] In the same passage he describes the Word as still hidden from the angels on his return, but this time because he has a human body. Here, for the first time the hidden descent and the hidden ascent come together. When Christ ascends 'our guardians form a procession for Him, and command the hypercosmic powers to open the heavens that He may be adored there once more. But they do not recognise Him because He has put on the poor coat of human nature, and His garments are red from the wine-press of our ills. And this time it is they who cry: "Who is this king of glory?"'[55]

52. *Or.* XLV 25.   53. *De. myst.* 36.   54. Cf. p. 209, n. 10 above.
55. *Or. Asc.*

CHAPTER NINE

THE THEOLOGY OF REDEMPTION (II):
MYSTERIUM CRUCIS

JEWISH Christian theology is a *theologia gloriae*, in which the accent is placed on the victory of Christ and its cosmic efficacy. This is especially apparent in the part played in this theology by the Cross. In primitive Christianity there were two main lines of thought with regard to the Cross. On the one hand, the fact that Christ had been crucified meant that the Cross was one of the historic data of his earthly life; on the other, it was from the very first, either in the form + or ×, a Christian cultic symbol[1] which, though an inheritance from pre-Christian Judaism,[2] had acquired a new and decisive significance from its association with the historic Cross of Christ.[3]

This chapter will, however, be concerned with the use of the Cross as a theological symbol. Here is yet another example of a mythic scheme of concepts, of imagery used to represent religious truth, such as will by now be familiar enough as a feature of Jewish Christianity. In this particular pattern the Cross appears under various aspects: as the power of Christ in his resurrection, as a sign of the cosmic scope of the redemption, and as an object of eschatological expectation.[4] To throw these various aspects into relief, reference will be made to Jewish Christian texts, and also to the Gnostic treatises which took up the theme and developed it according to their own point of view.

1. The σφραγίς as a *signatio* of the Christian with the cruciform sign formed part of the primitive rites of initiation.
2. Cf. pp. 154 f. above.
3. Cf. E. DINKLER, *Jesus Wort vom Kreuztragen*, in *Neutest. Stud. für R. Bultmann*, 1954, pp. 117–123; 'Zur Geschichte des Kreuzsymbols', *ZKT*, XLVIII, 1956, pp. 148–172; W. MICHAELIS, 'Zeichen, Siegel, Kreuz', *TZ*, XII, 1946, pp. 505–526; A. GRILLMEIR, *Der Logos am Kreuz*, pp. 67–80; H. RAHNER, 'Das mystische Tau', *ZKT*, LXXV, 1953, pp. 385–410; J. L. TEICHER, 'The Christian Interpretation of the Sign × in the Isaiah Scroll', *VT*, V, 1955, pp. 189–198.
4. In this context little or no attention is paid to the Cross either as a cultic symbol or as an instrument of execution.

THE GLORIOUS CROSS

The first text in which the Cross appears with a theological significance is the *Gospel of Peter*. At the moment of the Resurrection the guards 'saw three men come out of the sepulchre; two of them bore up the third, and a Cross followed after them. And the heads of the first two reached up to heaven, but the head of him whom they were escorting out-topped the heavens. And they heard a voice out of the heavens saying: Hast thou preached unto them that sleep? And an answer was heard from the Cross, saying: Yea'. This text has already proved of great importance in connection with the Resurrection and the Descent into Hell; now it yields a third datum of interest, the conception of the Cross as having gone down to Hell with Christ and come back with him. Moreover, it is the Cross which answers the voice from heaven, which is clearly that of the Father.

This one passage already contains a whole range of concepts. In the first place the Cross is associated with Christ's glory. No longer merely the gibbet on which Christ had hung, it comes out of the tomb with him,[5] and is associated with his victory and his ascent from Hell to glory. Secondly, it is living and answers the question put by the Father. 'The Cross is often made to play an active part like a living being.'[6] It is therefore something more than a mere sign; it is a reality in its own right, the nature of which it is important to define with some precision.

Analogous and still more ancient data appear in a quotation given by the *Epistle of Barnabas*, which probably comes from a Jewish Christian *midrash* of *Jeremiah*[7]: 'And when shall these things be accomplished? saith the Lord: Whensoever a tree shall be bended and stand upright (ἀναστῇ)' (XII, 1). There is a parallel here with the Gospel of Peter[8]: the Cross is laid in the tomb and rises to life again out of the tomb. It is possible, therefore, that this very ancient *midrash* is the source of the *Gospel of Peter*, a conjecture which seems to be all the more probable in view of the fact that the *Gospel* is apparently dependent on another fragment of the same *midrash* in the matter of the descent into Hell.

---

5. This feature is also found in an apocryphon preserved in Sahidic (*Frag.* 5; FORBES ROBINSON, *Coptic Apocryphal Gospels*, p. 185). It may also be present in the *Odes of Solomon* (XXIII, 14).
6. VAGANAY, *Évangile de Pierre*, p. 303.
7. The same quotation appears in the *Testimonia adversus Judaeos* of Gregory of Nyssa, who explicitly attributes it to Jeremiah (*PO*, XLVI, 213D).
8. Emphasised by RESCH, *Agrapha*, p. 320.

The various elements to be found in the *Gospel of Peter* reappear in later works. The first of these is the ascension of the Cross as an accompaniment of Christ's Ascension. This occurs in the Jewish Christian *Sibylline Oracles*. The sixth canticle ends with a hymn to the Cross of a kind to be met with several times in Jewish Christian literature: 'O happy wood on which Christ was stretched, earth shall not keep thee, for thou shalt see the heavenly dwelling, when thou, O God, wilt cause thy burning eye to scatter fire' (VI, 26–28). This theme was to endure in the homiletic and liturgical tradition, and may be observed in the *Acts of Pionius* (13), in the Pseudo-Chrysostom (*De cruce et latrone* II, 4) and in the Pseudo-Methodius (*Fragment* 14).

The theme of the living Cross of light was borrowed by the Gnostics. In particular it occurs in a group of apocryphal Acts, many of which have hymns to the Cross in which this aspect is especially prominent. Thus in the *Acts of John*:

Christ showed me a Cross of light. And I saw the Lord Himself on the Cross,[9] not having any shape but only a voice: And a voice not such as was familiar to us, but one sweet and gentle and truly divine, saying unto me: This Cross of light is called by Me sometimes Word, sometimes Mind, sometimes Jesus, sometimes Christ, sometimes Door, sometimes Way, sometimes Bread, sometimes Seed, sometimes Resurrection, sometimes Father, sometimes Son, sometimes Spirit, sometimes Life, sometimes Truth, sometimes Faith, sometimes Grace (98).

Quite clearly this is no longer simply a matter of the wooden gibbet. The latter had been but a sign of a mysterious reality; here Christ himself is present in his hidden essence, and therefore all the names of Christ in Scripture are attributed to it. Especially interesting is the divine voice which comes from the Cross, a detail which appeared in the *Gospel of Peter*.[10] In the *Acts of John* this conception of the Cross has a Gnostic character; Christ is the Cross of light, and the man who was on the wooden Cross was not he[11]: 'This Cross (of light) is not the wooden cross which you will see when you go down from here. Nor is it I who is on that cross, I whom now you do not see, though you hear my voice. Men have taken me for that which I am not, for indeed I am not that which I was among

9. Or 'above the Cross' (JAMES, *Apocryphal New Testament*, p. 254).
10. Cf. pp. 234 f. above
11. Cf. also *Acts of Peter* 38, and the comments of A. ORBE, *op. cit.*, pp. 176–212.

the multitude' (99).[12] Here again is the Gnostic theme of the distinction between the Christ who is on high and the earthly Jesus, as well as their perversion of the theme of the non-recognition of the Word into the pretence by which a substitute replaces the heavenly Christ in the Crucifixion.

Just as the Cross accompanied Christ in his ascent to heaven, so it will precede him at his coming again. This eschatological significance of the Cross is particularly important. The key text for Jewish Christian writers was *Mt.* 24:30: 'Then shall appear the sign ($\sigma\eta\mu\epsilon\hat{\iota}ον$) of the Son of Man in heaven.' This is the phenomenon which the *Didache* designates by the term $\sigma\eta\mu\epsilon\hat{\iota}ον\ \dot{\epsilon}\kappa\pi\epsilon\tau\acute{a}\sigma\epsilon\omega s$ as the first sign of the Parousia.[13] Similarly the *Apocalypse of Peter* says of the Second Advent: 'As the lightning that shineth from the east unto the west, so will I come upon the clouds of heaven in my glory while my Cross shall go before my face' (*ROC*, V, 1910, p. 209). It will be observed that, as in the *Gospel of Peter*, the Cross is presented as a living being; but here it precedes Christ, whereas there it followed him. Similarly the *Epistle of the Apostles* has: 'I shall come in brightness seven times the brightness of the sun, borne on the wings of the clouds in my glory, while my Cross shall go before me' (16).[14]

These texts have a special interest from the liturgical point of view. It will be noted that Christ's coming, preceded by his glorious Cross, is expected 'in the East'. The practice of praying 'ad orientem' must have been originally connected with this view that Christ would return at the End 'in the East'. There is a passage in the *Acts of Hipparchus and Philotheus* which runs as follows: 'There was in the house of this same Hipparchus a well-ordered room, on the Eastern wall of which he had painted a Cross. There, before the image of the Cross, with his face turned towards the East, he prayed seven times a day.'[15] This seems to suggest a connection between the practice of painting a Cross on the wall of a house and that of praying 'towards the East'.[16] The purpose of the cross is to indicate the eastern wall,[17] for the emphasis is first and foremost on praying towards

12. On this text of A. Orbe, *op. cit.*, pp. 205–209.
13. Cf. E. Stommel, $\Sigma\eta\mu\epsilon\hat{\iota}ον\ \dot{\epsilon}\kappa\pi\epsilon\tau\acute{a}\sigma\epsilon\omega s$, in *RQ*, XLVIII, 1953, pp. 21–42.
14. The *Sibylline Oracles* present the Cross as appearing at the time of the Judgment 'as a sign ($\sigma\hat{\eta}\mu\alpha$) for all men' (VIII, 244). Cf. also 'Apoc. Elijah', *TU* (*NF*) XI, 1899, 3rd edn., p. 87; also F. Dölger, *Sol salutis*, 2nd edn., Münster, 1925, pp. 215–217.
15. Assemani, *Act. Mart.*, 1748, II, p. 125.
16. Cf. Peterson, 'La croce e la preghiera verso l'Oriente', *EL*, LIX, 1945, pp. 52 ff.; 'Die geschichtliche Bedeutung der jüdischen Gebetsrichtung', *TZ*, III, 1947, pp. 1–15. It is Peterson who has drawn attention to this interesting text.
17. Cf. also *Acts of Xanthippe and Polyxena*, 15; James, *Apocrypha anecdota*, pp. 68–69.

the East, not on prayer facing the cross. Hence the origin of the crucifix in houses is connected with praying toward the East, and with the eschatological expectation.

This is, however, obviously not the Cross as an image of Christ suffering, but the glorious Cross which will precede him at the Parousia. The modification of its significance in the former sense was brought about by later Christian asceticism, which saw in it not a prophecy of the Parousia, but a memorial of the Passion. Moreover, the connection with the Eastern wall was forgotten, and the crucifix was placed on any wall. Nevertheless, it is still true that the use of the crucifix in houses is a survival from the Jewish Christian theology of the eschatological Cross, and can be shown from the present texts to go back, at least in its roots, to the primitive community, of whose spirituality it is an expression.

Another feature not unconnected with this Jewish Christian theology of the eschatological manifestation of the Cross is the reference in writings of the fourth century to appearances of the Cross in the sky. It will be better to pass over the still obscure question of the vision at the Milvian Bridge[18] and to examine instead one reported by Cyril of Jerusalem, who in his *Catechetical Lectures* also propounds the doctrine of the eschatological Cross: 'The saving trophy of Jesus shall one day appear again, coming from heaven. The King's trophy shall go before him, so that seeing Him whom they pierced, and recognising by the Cross Him who was dishonoured, the Jews may repent and mourn, but we may glory, exalting the Cross' (XIII, 41). Cyril describes this eschatological Cross in still more precise detail in another place: 'What shall be the sign (σημεῖον) of His coming, such that no power may be able to halt it? "And then", He has said, "shall be seen the sign of the Son of Man in heaven." Now Christ's own true sign is the Cross; a sign of a luminous (φωτοειδής) Cross shall go before the King' (XV, 22).

Now in his *Letter to Constantius* Cyril describes the appearance of just such a Cross at Jerusalem:

> For in these very days of the holy feast of Pentecost, on the Nones of May, about the third hour, a gigantic cross formed of light (φῶς), appeared in the sky above holy Golgotha stretching out as far as the holy Mount of Olives. It was not seen by just one or two but was most

18. Rufinus thus describes Constantine's dream before the vision: 'In his sleep he saw in the eastern sky the sign of the cross shining as if on fire' (*HE* IX, 8:15).

clearly displayed before the whole population of the city. Nor did it as one might have supposed, pass away quickly like something imagined, but was visible to sight above the earth for some hours, while it sparkled with a light brighter than the sun's rays (4).[19]

Significant here is the mention of the Mount of Olives, which is east of Jerusalem.

Cyril expressly relates this phenomenon to the eschatological Cross of which it is an anticipation:

> This portent, God-beloved emperor, has now been accomplished in accordance with the testimonies of the prophets and with the sacred words of Christ contained in the Gospels, but in days to come it will be accomplished more fully. For in the *Gospel according to Matthew* the Saviour, giving to his disciples a knowledge of things to come, tells them in a prediction itself full of light, And then shall be seen the sign of the Son of Man in heaven (6).

Here the Jewish Christian eschatological Cross is being developed by the tradition no longer along cultic, but along mystical lines. It is interesting that Cyril refers to a collection of testimonies ($\mu\alpha\rho\tau\nu\rho\acute{\iota}\alpha\iota$) of the Old and the New Testaments relating to the appearance of the glorious Cross in the East.

THE TYPOLOGY OF THE CROSS

For the Jewish Christian then, the Cross is something more than the wood on which Jesus was crucified. It is a spiritual, mysterious, living reality which accompanies the risen Christ. The attempt to determine more exactly what it represented has so far indicated that in some cases it was identified with Christ himself, as in the *Acts of John* or the *Gospel of Peter*; and this was, indeed, one of the ways in which Jewish Christian teaching sought to detach the wood of the Cross from its mere historical factuality and to give it a theological significance. It was, however, far from being the only, or even the normal way. In its more usual significance the Cross, though it may at first indeed have been a gibbet, comes principally to express the saving power, the $\delta\acute{\nu}\nu\alpha\mu\iota\varsigma$, of Christ's Passion. As Justin puts it: 'It is the great sign ($\sigma\acute{\nu}\mu\beta o\lambda o\nu$) of Christ's strength and power' (*I Apol.*

19. On the cross of light in the vault of heaven cf. L. HAUTECOEUR, *Mystique et architecture. Symbolisme du cercle et de la coupole*, Paris, 1954, p. 209.

LV, 2).[20] This soteriological significance is expressed in the documents through the visible attributes of the Cross, its material, its form, its position, thus giving rise to an extremely rich and varied series of speculations on the different symbolic meanings of the Cross, its hidden content, its mysterious efficacy. The symbols themselves were borrowed either from figures of the Old Testament, or from natural objects, and between them they make up the second major part of the Jewish Christian theology of redemption.

The use of the Old Testament is especially interesting here from the methodological point of view. The *testimonia* as such do not belong to Jewish Christianity; they simply represent the prophetic argument for the continuity of the two Testaments. Jewish Christian theology, however, detaches the *testimonia* from their historical reference, using their images, but transforming them into mythic categories through which it expresses its conceptions. Philo had already subjected Scripture to a similar transformation in order to express his own theology through the images of Scripture. This turning of the Old Testament into a mythology for theological purposes was one of the characteristics of Jewish Christianity, and one which is particularly in evidence in the case of the Cross.

One group of *testimonia* relates to types of the Cross in the Old Testament, and the antiquity of these particular interpretations is indicated by the fact that they are already to be found in the New. Thus the brazen serpent occurs in *Jn.* 3:14, before reappearing in the *testimonia* of the Cross in *Barnabas*: 'Another time when Israel was falling Moses maketh a type of Jesus, to show how He was to suffer and to give life, He whom they thought to have perished on the Cross' (XII, 5). This type is found in all the collections; it comes in the *Dialogue* of Justin (XCIV, 3; CXXXI, 4),[21] and in Tertullian's *Adversus Marcionem* (III, 18; cf. *De. idol.* V, 3).

This type is continually associated with another, that of Moses praying with his arms in the form of a Cross and so ensuring the victory of the Jews. Being so closely parallel to the first, it is likely that it too formed part of the Apostolic *testimonia*,[22] and it may, therefore, have been only by chance that one was recorded in the Gospel and the other not. This type

20. A heterodox variant of this basic conception plays a large part in the Valentinian gnosis: cf. SAGNARD, *La gnose valentinienne*, p. 251; ORBE, *op. cit.*, pp. 150–176.
21. Cf. also II, 1; XCI, 4; CXII, 1.
22. Cf. T. W. MANSON, 'The Argument from Prophecy', *JTS*, XLVI, 1945, p. 135.

occurs in *Barnabas*: 'The Spirit speaketh to the heart of Moses, inspiring him to perform a type of the Cross and of him that was to suffer upon it' (XII, 2). It comes also in the *Sibylline Oracles*, significantly in a passage which enumerates the virtues of the cross: 'It was thou whom Moses figured (ἐτύπωσε) when he stretched out his holy hands, triumphing over Amalek by faith, that the people might know that the staff (ῥάβδος) of David had been chosen by God the Father and honoured' (VIII, 250–253). Justin mentions the theme several times: 'Not because Moses prayed thus did the people gain the victory, but because . . . he himself formed the sign of the Cross' (*Dial.* XC, 5; cf. also XC, 4; CXI, 1; CXII, 2; CXXXI, 4).[23] Cyprian quotes the text in his *Testimonia* and adds: 'By this sign of the cross, Amalek was overcome by Josue (= Jesus), thanks to Moses' (II, 21).[24]

Beside these major *testimonia* relating to the shape of the cross, the Old Testament collection contains others. Barnabas quotes *Is.* 65:2: 'All the day long have I stretched out My hands to a disobedient people' (XII, 4). The same quotation is found in Irenaeus (*Dem.* 79), Cyprian (*Test.* II, 20), and Justin (*Dial.* XXIV, 4; CXIV, 2).[25] Moreover, in the *Excerpta ex Theodoto* appears the statement: 'The Cross is the sign of the Limit in the Pleroma. . . . Therefore Jesus, by that sign (σημεῖον), carries the seeds on his shoulders and leads them into the Pleroma. For Jesus is called the shoulders of the seed, and Christ is the head . . . but they (the psychics[26]) did not know the power (δύναμις) of the sign' (42–43). Irenaeus gives us the origin of this theme in a commentary on *Is.* 9:5: 'The government is set upon His shoulders.' He writes: 'This means allegorically the Cross, on which His arms were nailed: for this Cross is the mark of His power, that is, the sign of His empire' (*Dem.* 56: cf. TERTULLIAN, *Adv. Marc.* III, 19).[27]

Also to be included among the primitive types of the Cross is that of the door-posts and lintels of the Jewish houses which were smeared with the blood of the lamb to keep away the destroying angel at the time of the

23. Similarly also IRENAEUS (*Dem.* 46) and TERTULLIAN (*Adv. Marc.* III, 18).
24. Cf. DANIÉLOU, *Sacramentum futuri*, pp. 144–147.
25. Cf. also HIPPOLYTUS, *Ben. Mos.*, PO, XXVII, 131, which adds *Deut.* 33:3: 'All his sanctified ones are under thy hands'; cf. also 142. Similarly *Ben. Isaac*, 16 adds *Gn.* 49:8: 'Thy hands shall be on the neck of thine enemies', referring it to Christ's victory over the Powers on the Cross.
26. Cf. Glossary s.v.
27. Cf. also *Ben. Mos.*, PO, XXVII, 165, which adds *Deut.* 33:12: 'and he rested between his shoulders.' The theme is already to be found in JUSTIN, *I Apol.* XXXV, 2.

Exodus.[28] This is the starting point for a whole liturgical symbolism which regards the Jewish houses marked with the sign of the cross in the blood of the lamb as a type of the soul of Christians marked with the sign of the Cross at baptism.[29]

Another theme relating to the Cross is that of the horns. The word denoted both the horns of an animal and the transverse arms of the Cross.[30] Thus Justin sees in *Deut.* 33:13–17 a type of the Cross:

These words, *the horns of that which hath but one horn*, cannot be interpreted of any other thing or shape than of that which the cross presents to us. The single horn is the vertical wooden beam, of which the very top sticks up like a horn when the other wooden beam is fastened to it; and the ends of this second beam appear on each side like horns joined to a single horn. That which is fixed in the middle (of the upright) is also a projection, like a horn, on which the crucified are supported; it even looks like a horn, fashioned and fixed like the others (*Dial.* XCI, 2).[31]

In this text, in addition to the three main arms of the Cross there is an allusion to a horn represented by the projection at the front of the Cross upon which the condemned man was seated. Tertullian mentions the same detail (*Ad. Nat.* I, 12), and Irenaeus speaks of the middle horn *in quo requiescit qui clavis affigitur* (*Adv. haer.* II, 24:4).[32] But the point of immediate concern, however, is that the text of Deuteronomy alludes to the *strength* of the buffalo or of the rhinoceros, and it is in this sense that Justin understands it. The Cross is also a manifestation of an irresistible power. Justin prefaces the quotation by the words: 'God pointed out in another way the strength (ἰσχύς) of the mystery of the Cross' (XCI, 1). The theme is found also in Tertullian (*Adv. Marc.* III, 19).[33]

28. This comes in JUSTIN (*Dial.* CXI, 4); cf. also HIPPOLYTUS, *Ben. Mos.* 191. The form inscribed is the Π, but Sulzberger has pointed out that some crosses were formed of a horizontal bar resting on two uprights ('Le symbole de la croix', *Byzantion*, II, 1925, pp. 364–365).

29. Cf. DANIÉLOU, *Bible et Liturgie*, pp. 219–227. This may be compared with the lamb roasted on two spits, forming a cross (JUSTIN, *Dial.* XL, 3).

30. H. RAHNER, *Griechische Myten in christlicher Deutung*, Zürich, 1945, p. 415.

31. Cf. also CV, 2. The *Sibylline Oracles* (VIII, 245) call the cross 'desired horn (κέρας)'. HIPPOLYTUS, *Ben. Mos.* 173–174, takes up Justin's elaboration, as does Apollinarius of Hierapolis (cf. ROUTH, *Rel. Sacr.*, I, p. 161).

32. This recalls the form of cross (+) which is to be seen in the catacomb of St. Callistus: cf. SULZBERGER, *op. cit.*, p. 383.

33. Cf. an allusion to *Deut.* 23:17 in Hippolytus' account of the Naassenians, *Elench.* IX, 100.

10—T.J.C.

To these types borrowed from the Old Testament, and dating back to Jewish Christianity, were added symbols borrowed from Nature and from Man. Justin gives an interesting list of these:

(The cross) . . . is the greatest symbol of His (Christ's) power and rule. Pagans could have no idea of this, and everything they have said on this subject is put symbolically, as is also proved by the things which fall under our observation. For consider all the things in the world, whether without this form they could continue to exist. . . . For can the sea be traversed, except this trophy (τρόπαιον) which is called the mastage (ἱστίον) stand intact in the ship? Can the earth be ploughed without it? Can labourers and mechanics do their work except with tools which have this shape? And Man himself differs in appearance from the other animals only because he stands erect, and can stretch out his hands, and because his nose, the organ of vital respiration, projects and so traces a cross in the middle of his face. And therefore it was said by the prophet, The breath of our nostrils is the Lord Christ (*Lam.* 4:20). You also have signs (σύμβολα) which tell the power of the Cross, I mean the banners and trophies which go before your armies. Thus you show that the Cross is also the sign of your own power and strength, even though you do so unwittingly (*I Apol.* LV, 1–6).

Here assembled at an early date are themes that were to enjoy a great history. The symbol of the mast[34] was to be developed in particular by Hippolytus,[35] while that of the plough was to prove an outstandingly fruitful symbol, as recent research has shown.[36] An excellent example is to be found in Irenaeus (*Adv. haer.* IV, 34:4). The theme of the erect statue with arms outstretched recalls the typology of Moses, and that of the facial cross the biblical image of the unicorn.[37] Finally, the image of the military

34. H. RAHNER, 'Das Kreuz als Mastbaum und Antenne', *ZKT*, LXXV, 1953, pp. 129–173.
35. *De Antichristo*, 4.
36. Cf. J. DANIÉLOU, 'La charrue figure de la croix', *RSR*, XLII, 1954, pp. 193–204; DOIGNON, 'Le salut par le fer et le bois chez Irénée', *RSR*, XLII, 1955, pp. 535–545. HIPPOLYTUS, *Ben. Isaac, PO*, XXVII, pp. 90–91, should be added to the texts quoted in the first-named article. It is possible that the symbol of the axe (ἀξίνη), the importance of which in archaeology has been demonstrated by CARCOPINO (*Le mystère d'un symbole chrétien*, Paris, 1955, pp. 69–76), should be associated with this group.
37. These two themes are combined in a graffito on a tomb in the Viale Manzoni: cf. CARCOPINO, *De Pythagore aux Apôtres*, p. 94.

ensign was to take on a new lease of life in the fourth century, when it was identified with the *labarum* of Constantine.[38] It should be noted that the image recalled by these various symbols is not the *tau* nor the Greek cross but the Latin cross.[39]

These various symbols are in no way specifically Christian, and it is significant that Justin puts them forward in the Apology where he is addressing pagans. He wishes to show that even for them the Cross is not without precedent. But does this exclude the possibility of their being Jewish Christian in origin? Study of the various themes seems to suggest that having first existed in Jewish Christianity they were transferred to a Hellenistic setting, just as, in the case of the man with arms outstretched, there was a profane transposition of the theme of the prayer of Moses. Moreover, the Jewish Christian origin of this particular theme is confirmed by the *Odes of Solomon*, as in *Ode* XXVII: 'I stretched out my hands and sanctified my Lord, for the stretching forth of my hands is His sign, and the upward reach (of my body) is the upright tree' (1–2). The same expressions recur in *Ode* XLII: 'I stretched out my hands and consecrated myself to the Lord. The stretching forth of my hands is the sign thereof, as the tree was stretched forth on which was hung by the wayside the Righteous One' (1–3).

The same seems to be true of the plough. Irenaeus connects this symbolism with *Is.* 2:3–4, an important text in the *testimonia*. Justin also mentions it several times. It is, therefore, very likely that he had this in mind when he saw the plough as a figure of the Cross. The *Odes of Solomon* likewise seem to contain an allusion to the theme in the strange passage in which the Cross is compared to a wheel which 'mows, cuts, uproots' (XXIII, 12), just as Irenaeus, describing the function of the Cross as a plough, says that it has 'hoed the uncultivated land' (*Adv. haer.* IV, 34:4).

The axe ($\dot{\alpha}\xi\acute{\iota}\nu\eta$) also has biblical antecedents. The axe which Elisha caused to rise to the surface after it had sunk in the water is an ancient type of the Cross, which is found in Justin (*Dial.* LXXXVI, 6), and was taken up and developed by Irenaeus (*Adv. haer.* V, 17:4). The latter moreover comments on *Mt.* 3:10, the axe which is laid to the root of the tree, by observing that the Word of God resembles the axe (*ibid.*). Now Josephus

---

38. *Physiologos* 42 (PITRA, *Spic. Solesm*, III, 364) adds the sun's rays, the horns of the moon, the outspread wings of a bird; the last appears also in TERTULLIAN, *De Orat.*, XXIX, 4 and HIPPOLYTUS, *De Antichristo* 61.
39. Cf. SULZBERGER, *op. cit.*, p. 356.

records that at the moment of their admission into the community 'the Essenes received a white robe and an axe' (ἀξινάριον),[40] an interesting detail in view of the connection of the text just quoted with John the Baptist, who has links with the Essenes. It also suggests that in Essene circles the axe already had a symbolic value.[41]

The symbols of the Cross so far considered all had some reference to its shape. There is another group which refers to the material, in which the symbolism is that of wood, and the truth expressed is still the power and virtue of the Cross. In this group wood is generally associated with water, so that the context appears to be a sacramental one, water constituting the matter of the sacrament, wood symbolising the divine power communicated to it.[42] Since, therefore, it is the power of the Cross which acts through the water and communicates to it the power of effecting the divine operations, writers single out those cases where wood appears to be endowed with a special efficacy.

Here once again the Old Testament provides the first series of *testimonia*. Thus the author of *Barnabas* writes: 'Let us enquire whether the Lord took care to signify beforehand concerning the water and the Cross' (XI, 1), and gives as an example *Ps.* 1:3: 'the tree that is planted by the streams of waters.' He continues: 'Ye perceive how He pointed out the water and the Cross at the same time. . . . Blessed are they that have set their hope on the Cross, and go down into the water' (XI, 8). The same quotation is given by Justin (*Dial.* LXXXVI, 4) in a group of *testimonia*. Here there is only the association of water and the Cross, not the power of the wood to give life to the water; but this additional element appears in other passages.

Justin gives a collection of *testimonia* relating to wood: the Tree of Life in Paradise; the staff of Moses which divides the waters of the Red Sea,[43] makes water spring from the rock, and sweetens the bitter waters of Mara; the staves thrown by Jacob into the water ducts; Jacob's ladder[44]; the blossoming rod of Aaron; the stem of Jesse; the oak of Mamre; the seventy

40. *Bell. Jud.* II, 8:7.
41. There is therefore no reason for seeing in it a Pythagorean influence as CARCOPINO does: *op. cit.*, p. 55.
42. Cf. LUNDBERG, *Typologie baptismale*, pp. 167–228.
43. Cf. also *Dial.* CXXXVIII, 2.
44. 'The ladder is an image of the cross; by it those who believe in Him mount to heaven' (IRENAEUS, *Dem.* 45). Cf. also Ps.-HIPPOLYTUS, *Hom. Pasc.* LI, 8. On the later history of the theme cf. EDSMAN, *Baptême de feu*, pp. 51–57; LUNDBERG, *op. cit.*, pp. 192–197.

willow trees that the people find near the twelve springs after crossing the Jordan; the rod and staff which 'comfort David' in *Ps.* 22:4 (EVV 23); the staff which designates Judah; the wood of the axe thrown into the Jordan.[45] Justin follows up the last example with an allusion to Christ's 'being crucified on the tree and sanctifying us by water' (*Dial.* LXXXVI, 1-6). Finally, in a later passage he adds the combination of the wood of the Ark and the Deluge: 'Christians have been begotten anew (of Christ) by water and faith and wood, which contained the mystery of the Cross, even as Noah also was saved by the wood of the Ark when he was borne upon the waters' (*Dial.* CXXXVIII, 2).

This list calls for several remarks. In the first place it is clear that it only reproduces a more ancient collection, such as those which existed for other themes, that of the 'Rock' for example.[46] Secondly, many of these themes were later to have a different significance: the Tree of Life was to be a figure of Christ himself, as was the stem of Jesse[47]; the staff of comfort became a type of the Holy Spirit, Noah's Ark of the Church.[48] What is characteristic here is that these symbols should by preference be associated with the Cross, a fact which points to a privileged position of the Cross, and so suggests an archaic stage of theology.

Furthermore, in the case of several at least of these evidences it can be seen that they emphasise the power of wood in relation to water, and that this is also the feature stressed by Justin. This is true in the case of the rod of Moses dividing the waters, sweetening the bitter lake of Mara, or making water spring from the rock; but it is also true of the Ark and the Deluge; of the wood of the axe in the Jordan, of the willow trees and the springs, of the staves and the water ducts. This suggests that there had been a search for passages which might pre-figure the present operation of the Cross as the active $\delta \acute{\upsilon} \nu \alpha \mu \iota \varsigma$ in baptism. The important point here is not the types in themselves, which are highly disputable, but the desire to make them express the vivifying action of the Cross; for it is this that seems to be Jewish Christian.

45. Jacob's ladder and the rod and staff of *Ps.* 22:4 are linked together in ZENO OF VERONA, *Tract.* II, 13:3; cf. also II, 14:3.
46. The same list occurs also in TERTULLIAN, *Adv. Jud.* XIII, 11-19. The comparison with the Tree of Life occurs in IGNATIUS OF ANTIOCH, *Trall.* XI, 2. These associations were already being made in Judaism; cf. Ps-PHILO, *Lib. Antiq. Jud.*, XVIII, 1-3.
47. There must have been a collection in which $\dot{\rho} \acute{\alpha} \beta \delta o \varsigma$ stood for Christ, not for the Cross. JUSTIN makes it a title of Christ (*Dial.* CXXVI, 1); and IRENAEUS links Moses' rod, the royal sceptre and the stem of Jesse as figures of the Incarnation (*Dem.* 59).
48. Cf. DANIÉLOU, *Sacramentum futuri*, pp. 80-85.

Examples of this aspect of the Cross may be quoted. Thus the Jewish Christian *Sibylline Oracles* include in a eulogy of the Cross this remarkable passage, in which Justin's themes appear yet again: 'Sign (σῆμα) then for all men, pre-eminent (ἐπίσημος)[49] sphragis shall the wood be for all believers, the desired horn, life of the devout, scandal to the world, enlightening (φώτιζον) the elect in the waters by means of the twelve springs, rod of iron which shall give pasture and rule' (VIII, 244–247). Later there is mention of the staff (ῥάβδος) of David (VIII, 254). The powers of the Cross should be noted: it vivifies and enlightens, and it acts especially in baptism (φώτιζον) by means of the springs which are the twelve Apostles. A new theme will also be observed, that of the iron sceptre, which comes from the *Revelation* (2:27; 12:5).

Gnostic writings provide other types of the Cross which were almost certainly borrowed from Jewish Christian *testimonia*. The first of these is the winnowing fan (cf. *Lk.* 3:17). Irenaeus, summarising the Valentinian gnosis, writes that it held 'the fan to be the cross, which consumes . . . all material elements, as fire does chaff; but it purifies all them that are saved, as the fan does the wheat' (*Adv. haer.* I, 3:5). Another is the whip which chases the traffickers from the Temple, in which Heracleon distinguishes the cords 'which are the *dynamis* of the Spirit' and the wood 'which is the figure of the Cross; by this wood are consumed and destroyed merchants and universal malice' (*Frag.* 13). Here again the connection between the Cross and spiritual power is characteristic.

There is a similar theme in a curious passage of Ignatius of Antioch: 'Ye are stones of a temple which were prepared beforehand for a building of God the Father, being hoisted up to the heights by the engine of Jesus Christ, which is the Cross, and using for a rope the Holy Spirit' (*Eph.* IX, 1). Here the Cross is again associated with the power of the Spirit: the machine and the cable are the two divine δυνάμεις which carry out the exaltation of believers. In Ignatius this seems to be an original contribution designed for a pagan environment; but its starting point is the Jewish Christian symbolism of the Cross as an efficacious power.[50]

49. It should be noted that ἐπίσημος also stands for the number 6 in the Greek alphabet, which was represented by the sign *waw*, a symbol of Christ (cf. DUPONT-SOMMER, *La doctrine gnostique de la lettre Waw*, pp. 51–68). JEROME saw in it a type of the Cross (cf. G. MORIN, 'Hieronymus de Monogrammate', *RBen.*, XX, 1903, pp. 225–236).

50. Cf. SCHLIER, *Untersuchungen*, pp. 112 f. LEBRETON is mistaken when he writes: 'Without the Spirit the Cross is an inert machine, erect before our eyes, but without any hold on our souls' (*Histoire du dogme de la Trinité*, II, p. 327). The theme is taken up by HIPPOLYTUS, *De Antichristo* 59.

THE COSMIC CROSS

The texts so far considered have shown the Cross, both in its shape and in its substance, as a sign of the power of the risen Christ working in the Church with the Spirit to achieve the divine purposes. Towards the middle of the second century these symbolisms may be seen developing in a speculation on the Cross, found among both the orthodox and the Gnostics, in which the dimensions of the Cross are used in a great variety of ways to express the cosmic universality of the action of the risen Christ.

To begin with Irenaeus broaches this theme in a passage on the symbolism of the Cross. Having shown that the wood is a figure of the Incarnation of the Word he continues:

For as we lost him by means of a tree, by means of a tree again has he been manifest to all, showing the height, the length, the breadth, the depth in himself; and, as one of our predecessors has said, reuniting the two peoples in one only God by the stretching forth of his hands. For there were two hands, because there were two peoples scattered to the ends of the earth; and there was but one head as there is but one God (*Adv. haer.* V, 17:4).

This text is of great interest because it reveals the origin of speculation on the Cross as a sign of the life-giving power of Christ. On the one hand it links this theme with the New Testament, to which there are two allusions. The first is to *Eph.* 3:18 which speaks of 'the breadth and length and height and depth' of the love of Christ. Whatever may be the literal sense of the text, it was sure to be interpreted by tradition as a symbol of the Cross.[51] The second is to *Eph.* 2:14–16: '(He) has broken down the middle wall of partition (φραγμός), having abolished in his flesh the enmity . . . that in himself he might make of the two one new man, so making peace; and that he might reconcile both unto God in one body through the cross, having slain the enmity thereby.' This second text is most important, since it already contains a speculation on the Cross which later authors had only to develop.

This text presupposes a conception of the φραγμός, the wall of separation, which calls for the image of the Cross as its counterpart. Paul's text

51. Cf. HIPPOLYTUS, *Elench.* VI, 34 which sums up the teaching of the Valentinians. FEUILLET seems to have proved decisively that the literal meaning of the text refers to the four domains of the universe in the Wisdom Literature ('L'Église plérôme du Christ', *NRT*, LXXXVIII, 1956, pp. 595 ff.).

in fact assumes a double φραγμός.[52] In the first place there is the one that separates the two peoples; and in this sense the expression, like the idea, seems to be truly Pauline; but there is also the φραγμός separating the world below from the world above. This was a stock conception. It appears in a letter of Ignatius, where it is said that Christ 'has made a breach in the wall of separation' (Trall. IX, 4: long recension), and also among the Mandaeans, for whom it represents the heavenly wall separating the world below from the Pleroma.[53] The Apocryphal Acts also have it, in this case conceived as a wall of fire.[54]

In this view Christ restores unity in a two-fold sense. He destroys both the vertical wall which separates the two peoples, and the horizontal one which separates man from God; and he does this by the Cross, which now seems to represent the double operation of Christ extending both vertically and horizontally to form a cross. There are also in a sense two crosses: the cross of separation which existed before the coming of Christ, and the cross of unification which is the coming of Christ. This distinction will be found useful when considering the various modifications of the theme that are to be found among the Gnostics.

The text of Irenaeus exhibits a first elaboration of this theme, which he ascribes to 'one of our predecessors', and therefore reaches a fairly long way back into the history of theology. By re-stating the Pauline image in more detail, he explicitly connects Christ's stretching out his hands on the Cross with the drawing together of the two peoples, while the head symbolises the achievement of their union.[55] However, this image of the head and the outstretched arms was, as will have been noted earlier, equivalent to the Cross. It seems therefore that Irenaeus received from Jewish Christianity this symbolism by which the Cross represented the gathering of the two peoples into one.[56] On the other hand, he has associated this symbolism with the passage in Ephesians on the dimensions of the love of Christ. The passage therefore comprises all the necessary elements for a Cross-symbolism indicating explicitly the gathering together of all things both among themselves and in God.

52. Cf. SCHLIER, Christus und die Kirche im Epheserbrief, pp. 23–24.
53. Cf. SCHLIER, op. cit., pp. 20–21.   54. Cf. SCHLIER, op. cit., p. 22.
55. The stretching out of the hands is found in an Apocryphon of Ezra (HIPPOLYTUS, Ben. Mos., PO, XXVII, 131).
56. It occurs in the Jewish Christian Sibylline Oracles: 'He will stretch out his hands and measure the whole world' (I, 372; VIII, 302). Cf. also HIPPOLYTUS, De Antichristo 61.

Whether Irenaeus received this elaborated symbolism from tradition, as is generally the case, or whether he is himself responsible for it, it is certainly present in the *Demonstratio*:

By the obedience which He practised unto death hanging on the tree, He undid the old disobedience occasioned by the tree. And because He is himself the Word of God Almighty, whose invisible presence is spread abroad in us and fills the whole world, He extends His influence in the world through its (whole) length, breadth, height and depth. For, by the Word of God, all things are subject to the influence of the economy of redemption, and the Son of God has been crucified for all, having traced the sign of the Cross on all things. For it was right and necessary that He who made Himself visible, should lead all visible things to participate in His Cross; and it is in this way that, in a form that can be perceived, His own special influence has had its sensible effect on visible things: for it is He that illumines the heights, that is the heavens; it is He that penetrates that which is beneath; He that traverses the whole vast extent from East to West, and He that covers the immense distance from North to South, summoning to the knowledge of His Father those scattered in every place (34).

This text is based on *Eph.* 3:18, and there is also a reference to *Eph.* 2: 15–16. On the other hand, the influence of another Pauline text is discernible, namely *Col.* 1:15–20. This influence appears firstly in the parallel with the universal action of Christ the Redeemer. Secondly, the height here does not mean God but the angels, as in *Col.* 1:20: 'It pleased the Father . . . through him to reconcile all things to himself; through him, I say, whether things upon the earth, or things in heaven, having made peace through the blood of his cross.' There is, therefore, an association here of *Eph.* 2:15 and *Col.* 1:20 to present Christ as at the same time gathering together both those who are separated by the vertical wall, the peoples of the world, and those separated by the horizontal wall, men and angels.

Furthermore, the passage brings in a special element, for on the one hand there is a vertical cross, since Christ gathers together those here below and those on high, those to the East and those to the West, and there is also a horizontal cross related to the four cardinal points. This introduces a new image, 'the cross of the winds'. It is no longer a question simply of the reconciliation of Jew and Gentile, but of universal evangelisation. This may possibly be an Asiatic Cross-symbolism, continuing the tradition of *Jn.* 12:32.[57]

This symbolism of the Cross in Irenaeus seems to come from a Jewish Christian tradition, and in fact may be present in the *Odes of Solomon*. Thus *Ode* XXII reads: 'It is He who makes me descend from on high and brings me up from the regions below; it is He also who gathers together the things that are between' (1–2). This is extraordinarily reminiscent of the *Demonstratio*. There is, however, a different idea present; the vertical dimension of the Cross seems to represent the *katabasis* and *anabasis* of the Word. The cosmic symbolism of the Cross is the same, but the application of it is different.

This point supplies the probable explanation of the next *Ode*, in which the Word is compared to a letter[58]:

Now a Wheel received it, and it came upon it. And with (the wheel) was a sign of Kingship and of Government; and everything that shook the Wheel it scythed and cut down. The head went down to the feet, because down to the feet the Wheel ran and that which was marked upon it. The Letter was one of command. Thus every region was reunited in one single place; and at its highest point was manifest the head now unveiled, even the True Son, who came forth from the Most High; and He inherited the universe (XXIII, 10–17).

A comparison with the previous *Ode* leaves scarcely any doubt that the Letter is the Word, who is also called the Head. The Wheel which receives it seems to represent His redemptive action, and the latter implies a hidden descent: the head goes down to the feet; a glorious ascension: the head is unveiled at the summit; and a gathering together of what is in between: the letter gathers together all regions. Here, therefore, the wheel seems to be a symbol of the Cross as expressing the universality of the redemptive action.[59]

Moreover, there seems to be confirmation of this in a text which is explicitly a symbolical commentary of the mystery of the cross, namely the *Acts of Peter* (38), where the head is again spoken of as going down to the feet. Here the Cross signifies in the first place the fall of the first man,

---

57. Cf. ORBE, *Los primeros herejes*, p. 227.   58. Cf. p. 201 above.
59. It will be remembered that the letter and the Cross are linked in the *Gospel of Truth*. It is also possible that the word *rotas* in the magic square, the whole symbolism of which refers to the Cross, ought to be interpreted in the sense of this *Ode*.

which involves a reversal of values and puts on the right what was on the left. This has to be corrected by a movement in the opposite direction (ἐπαναδραμεῖν), constituting a conversion (μετανοία). This was the operation which was carried out by Christ, and which is symbolised by the Cross, whose vertical dimension represents the upward movement, while the horizontal dimension stands for universal extension (τεταμένος λόγος).[60]

There is one more text from Irenaeus relating to this subject, although it is not so explicit:

> For the Creator of the world is truly the Word of God; and this is our Lord who in the last times was made Man, existing in this world, and who in His invisible nature contains all created things, being implanted (*infixus*) in the whole Creation, since the Word of God governs and arranges all things; and that is why He came to His own in a visible manner, and was made flesh, and hung upon the tree, that He might sum up all things in Himself, in such a way that His own creation bore Him, which itself is borne by Him (*Adv. haer.* V, 18:3–19:1).

There is certainly an allusion to the Cross here, which is confirmed by a parallel text in Melito: 'He who bears the Universe is borne by the tree.'[61] In the text of Irenaeus the Cross symbolises the summing up of all things by the Word, but this summing up is only possible because the Word contains all things. The train of thought is the same as that of *Col.* 1:20.

Significant is the expression: 'He who is borne by the Cross is he who bears all things.' The Cross here takes on another meaning. It emphasises not so much the fact that the Word as Creator contains and unifies all things, as the fact that he sustains and carries them. Once again it is a symbol of the Logos himself in his action in the cosmos, but this time recalls analogous expressions, such as were cited earlier, relating to the Name. Thus Hermas writes, for instance: 'The Name of the Son of God is great and incomprehensible and sustaineth (βαστάζει) the whole world. . . . Seest thou then what manner of men He sustaineth? even those that bear His name' (*Sim.* IX, 14:5). Here the ideas of bearing and being borne are juxtaposed in the same way as in Irenaeus, the only difference being that

60. ORBE, who has subjected this passage to a long analysis (*op. cit.*, pp. 176–204), sees in it a Gnostic symbolism, but this does not seem to the present writer to be at all certain.
61. *Hom. Pasch.* XVI, 12–15.

the Name stands in place of the Cross, an equivalence which suggests that the Cross too in such phraseology represents the Word himself in his unifying and consolidating activity. This idea reappears in the Gnostics. In the *Acts of Peter* the Cross is the Logos himself in his cosmic extension (τεταμένος λόγος) (38)[62]; but in this Gnostic conception the Christian theme is adapted and deformed.

Parallel with the elaborations of Irenaeus is a Gnostic speculation on the Cross which, despite the modifications it has undergone, preserves the elements of what has been called 'a Christian sermon on the Cross in the second century'.[63] The essentials of this are to be found first of all in the account in Irenaeus (*Adv. haer.* I, 2), where it is said that when Sophia, the last of the aeons of the Pleroma was in danger of dissolving through her passion for the Father, the Father gave forth a new aeon, Horos (limit), namely a power which consolidates (ἐστηρίχθαι) all the aeons and preserves them outside the inexpressible greatness of the Father (I, 2:2). Now this power is also called 'Cross (σταυρός), Redeemer (λυτρωτής), Reaper (καρπιστής),[64] Guide of the Return (μεταγωγεύς)' (I, 2:4).[65]

A little later Irenaeus explains how the Gnostics show in regard to this Power that it has two functions, the consolidatory (ἑδραστική) and the divisive (μεριστική):

> In so far as he consolidates and sustains, he is called Stauros, while in so far as he divides and separates, he is Horos. They then represent the Saviour as having indicated this twofold faculty; first the sustaining power when He said: 'Whosoever doth not bear his Cross, and follow after me, cannot be my disciple' (*Lk.* 14:27); . . . but the separating power when He said: 'I came not to send peace, but a sword' . . . also . . . 'The fan is in His hand'. . . . Moreover, they affirm that the Apostle Paul made mention of this Cross in the following words: 'The doctrine of the Cross is to them that perish foolishness, but to us who are saved it is the power (δύναμις) of God' and again, 'the Cross of Christ, by whom the world is crucified to me, and I unto the world (*Gal.* 6:14)' (I, 3:5).

There is no need to enlarge upon the significance of this Gnostic doctrine

62. Cf. ORBE, *op. cit.*, pp. 196–199; GRILLMEIER, *op. cit.*, pp. 79–80.
63. F. M. SAGNARD, *op. cit.*, p. 253.
64. On this word cf. C. BARTH, *op. cit.*, pp. 86–87.
65. On this collection of names cf. SCHLIER, *Untersuchungen*, pp. 102–105; ORBE, *op. cit.*, p. 167.

here.[66] It may be noted that similar teaching appears in the *Excerpta ex Theodoto*: 'Those who possess the Name are not halted by the Limit and the Cross and hindered from entering the Pleroma' (22); and later: 'The Cross is the sign ($\sigma\eta\mu\epsilon\hat{\iota}o\nu$) of the Limit in the Pleroma; for it divides the unfaithful from the faithful, as the Limit divides the world from the Pleroma' (42).[67] Thus the Cross-Limit is conceived as both the division of the Pleroma from the Kenoma and the separation of the faithful from the infidel.[68]

The *Acts of John* include a passage on the Cross, which is of a piece with the Valentinian texts. It speaks of a Cross of light planted on earth, a conception that recalls the glorious Cross. This Cross has various names, which manifest the various powers of Christ. It is 'the marking-off ($\delta\iota o\rho\iota\sigma\mu\delta s$) of all things' (98), a notion which is pure Gnosticism; 'it has fixed ($\delta\iota\alpha\pi\eta\xi\dot{\alpha}\mu\epsilon\nu o s$) all things . . . by the Word' (99), a statement which recalls the Gnostic idea of consolidation. Moreover, the doctrine expounded is the same as that in the so-called Great Notice of Irenaeus (*Adv. haer.* I, 2) cited above.[69] The corrupt state of the text, however, makes it impossible to draw any further conclusions. The only new element is the linking of the glorious Cross with the $\delta\dot{\nu}\nu\alpha\mu\iota s$ of the Cross, which serves to emphasise that the Cross of the crucifixion is only a symbol of the real Cross (99), and clearly confirms that the latter is a divine power.

Is it possible to determine more precisely the origin of this theme of the Cross-Limit? There do not seem to be any grounds for suggesting the image of an erect pike or of a palisade,[70] and such a symbolism would in any case be misleading. The best suggestion is that the Platonic X of the *Timaeus* underlies the Gnostic Stauros, and that this was thought of as a great cross of light traced in the sky.[71] For Plato the cosmic X was constituted by the intersection of the sphere of the planets and the sphere of the fixed stars at the ecliptic, and thus formed a cross marking the boundary

66. This has been well done by F. M. SAGNARD, *op. cit.*, pp. 244–255; and A. ORBE, *op. cit.*, pp. 160–213.

67. Cf. also HIPPOLYTUS, *Elench.* VII, 31, 5.

68. CARCOPINO (*De Pythagore aux Apôtres*, 1956, pp. 95, 118) has suggested that a tomb-painting in the Viale Manzoni contains a representation of this Gnostic Cross separating the Pleroma from the Kenoma. For the meaning of the latter term, cf. Glossary s.v.

69. Cf. p. 284 above.

70. As do HARVEY and SCHLIER.

71. So SAGNARD, *op. cit.*, pp. 245–246, 252, following BOUSSET, 'Platos Weltseele und das Kreuz Christi', *ZNW*, XIV, 1913, pp. 273–285.

between the planetary world and the heaven of the stars.[72] Now the Gnostics regarded the planetary world or hebdomad as the sphere of the Demiurge, who was a stranger to the Pleroma, and it is, therefore, easy to see how on this view the Cross could come to be regarded as separating the lower world from the world above. The reference to the *Timaeus* appears, therefore, to be by far the best explanation of the definition of the Cross as the Limit.

But are there sufficient grounds for linking these ideas in this way? Gnostic texts make no allusion to the Platonic X, but on the other hand, this was identified with the Cross of Christ by second century writers of the Great Church. Thus the *Demonstratio* of Irenaeus states: 'He has imprinted the sign of the Cross on the universe,' which is in fact a scarcely altered quotation from the *Timaeus* of Plato (26 B–C), which Justin had seen as a prefiguration of the Cross in his *First Apology*: 'Plato, in the *Timaeus*, seeks to discover, in accordance with the laws of Nature, what the Son of God is, and puts it in these words: "He has marked Him in the form of a X on all things"' (LX, 1). Justin then explains that Plato borrowed this symbolism from the episode of the brazen serpent, and continues: 'which Plato reading, and not accurately understanding it, and not apprehending that it was a figure of the Cross, but taking it to be a X, he said that next to God the first principle, the second power, was traced in the form of a X upon the universe' (LX, 5–6).

There is another detail in the text of the *Timaeus* which permits a still more definite conclusion. Plato explains that the function of the sphere of the fixed stars is to restrain ($\pi\epsilon\delta\hat{\alpha}\nu$) the movement of the planets. Now in the *Acts of Andrew* a eulogy of the Cross includes the following words: 'O Cross that hast restrained ($\pi\epsilon\delta\eta\sigma\alpha\varsigma$) the moving sphere of the world' (JAMES, p. 360). It is impossible to avoid seeing in this an allusion to the *Timaeus*; moreover, the fact can be quite definitely established, thanks to a passage in Hippolytus on the disciples of Mark: '(The eighth heaven) has been added to the planetary sphere to restrain its rapid movement. . . . Hence it is an image of Horos' (*Elench.* VI, 41; cf. also Irenaeus, *Adv. haer.* I, 17:1). Here the Gnostic Stauros-Horos is explicitly identified with the Platonic X.

It is now possible to draw a conclusion regarding the conception of the Cross as the Limit. It appears to be a Gnostic development of a theme

72. *Timaeus* 26B.

which existed in the Great Church, namely the Platonic X as a symbol of the Cross. But the Christians saw it as expressing the unification of all things by the Cross, which constituted the form of the whole creation, and thus indicated the presence of the Word in all things. The Gnostics perverted this image to suit their radical dualism, affording yet another example of a Gnostic adaptation of an older theme. This was not, however, a Jewish Christian conception, but was derived by Justin from a presentation of the Gospel in a Hellenistic form of symbolism.[73]

The situation is the same with regard to the other function of the Cross, namely consolidation. Here a new symbolism appears in which the Cross is seen as a pillar supporting the world above, and this image is found in orthodox writers of the second century. Thus in the *Paschal Homily* of Melito of Sardis there is a contrast between the cosmic role of the Word and the crucified Christ: 'He who hung the earth in its place is hanged on the wood; he who made all things fast ($\sigma\tau\eta\rho\acute{\iota}\xi\alpha\varsigma$) is made fast upon the tree' (XVI, 12–15). The same verb ($\sigma\tau\eta\rho\acute{\iota}\zeta\omega$) that was used by the Valentinians appears here.

This is even plainer in the *Paschal Homily* inspired by Hippolytus:

The Cross is Jacob's ladder, and the path of the angels, on the top of which the Lord Himself is supported. This tree of heavenly dimensions has raised itself from earth to heaven, fixing itself ($\sigma\tau\eta\rho\acute{\iota}\xi\alpha\varsigma$), an eternal plant, between heaven and earth, to uphold the universe, support ($\check{\epsilon}\delta\rho\alpha\sigma\mu\alpha$) of all things, mainstay ($\sigma\tau\acute{\eta}\rho\iota\gamma\mu\alpha$) of the world, prop ($\check{\epsilon}\rho\epsilon\iota\sigma\mu\alpha$) of the whole inhabited earth, joint of the terrestrial globe, holding together the variety of human nature, and nailed by the invisible bolts of the spirit, that being fixed to the divine, it may never more be sundered from it. Touching with its crown the summit of heaven, making firm ($\sigma\tau\eta\rho\acute{\iota}\zeta\omega\nu$) the earth with its feet, and embracing on every side in its mighty arms the many spirits of the air between heaven and earth, it was wholly in all things and in every place (51).

The *Acts of Andrew*, an orthodox work, develops the theme of the cosmic Cross in the same tradition as Irenaeus and Hippolytus, namely by emphasising the symbolism of the four dimensions and of the cosmic pillar,

73. Cf. the words of CLEMENT OF ALEXANDRIA in a catechetical exposition of this subject: 'We have as a limit ($\acute{o}\rho o\varsigma$) the cross ($\sigma\tau\alpha\upsilon\rho\acute{o}\varsigma$) of the Lord' (*Paed.* III, 12).

unification and consolidation. The following passage occurs in the *Martyrdom of Andrew*:

> I know thy mystery, (O Cross), for the which thou art set up; for thou art planted in the world to establish (στηρίξῃς) the things that are unstable. And the one part of thee stretcheth up toward heaven that thou mayest signify the heavenly Word; and another part of thee is spread out to the right hand and the left that it may put to flight the envious and adverse power of the Evil One, and gather the world into unity; and another part of thee is planted in the earth, . . . that thou mayest join the things that are in the earth and those that are under the earth unto the heavenly things (JAMES, p. 359).

It will be observed how closely this text is related to the one in Hippolytus; but this is still more apparent in the comparison of the Cross to a tree:

> O Cross, engine of the salvation of the Most High! O Cross, trophy of the victory of Christ over his enemies! O Cross, planted upon the earth and having thy fruit in the heavens! O name of the Cross, filled with all things! O Cross, that hast restrained (πεδήσας) the moving sphere of the world! Hail! O form of that Mind which gave form to the formless earth! Hail! thou that wast the vesture of the Lord, and didst bear the thief as a fruit (*ibid.*, pp. 359–360).

Here are to be found in one single text the theme of the μηχάνημα of Ignatius of Antioch, Justin's τρόπαιον, the axe of Hippolytus, and finally the theme of the brake.

It remains to enquire how the equation of Stauros and Sterigma is to be explained. In the first place the connection was probably assisted by a false etymology which derived both words from the same root. Is it possible, however, to assign the verb στηρίζειν definitely to its proper context? It is interesting to observe that it comes in *I Clement*: '(The Creator) by His exceeding great might established (ἐστήρισεν) the heavens, and in His incomprehensible wisdom He set them in order (διεκόσμησε). And the earth He separated (διεχώρισε) from the water that surroundeth it' (XXXIII, 3). There are two things that should be noted in this text. Firstly, the verb στηρίζειν is related to God's creative action; but it has been remarked several times that the action of the Cross was represented as the re-enactment by the Word of his work in the Creation.[74]

The second point to notice is that the text associates in the creative action both the themes of consolidation and of separation (διεχώρισεν). In the New Testament one of the characteristic features of the Logos is that he is the one who divides, a theme which occurs in particular in *Heb.* 4:12 and *Rev.* 19:15. In view of the fact that in the texts quoted the Logos is identified with the Cross, it may be asked whether there may not have been a symbolism of the Cross dividing and distinguishing, which might have belonged to the common Jewish Christian tradition. If that were so then this aspect of the Cross also would belong to Jewish Christianity, Justin identifying it with the Platonic X, and the Gnostics interpreting the concept of separation in accordance with their dualism. The various functions attributed to the Cross by the Gnostics would then ultimately be based on Jewish Christian symbolism, belonging to the main Christian tradition.

This Cross-symbolism produced by Jewish Christianity was to continue. The *Catechetical Lectures* of Cyril of Jerusalem give the Cross an important place, possibly as a result of the discovery of it by the Empress Helena. They include elements of speculation in the tradition of Irenaeus: 'He stretched out His hands on the Cross that He might embrace the ends of the world; for this Golgotha is the very centre of the earth. . . . He stretched forth human hands, who by His spiritual hands had established the heaven' (XIII, 28). There are two Irenaean features here: in the first place, the stretching out of the hands indicates the ends of the earth, not the powers of the air; secondly, there is the parallel between the cosmic action of the Word as Creator and the stretching out of Christ on the Cross, one of the standard themes of sermons on the Cross, as was shown by the passage from Melito quoted above.[75]

Athanasius, on the other hand, in his Cross-symbolism combines the theme of the union of the two peoples with that of the combat against the powers of the air:

If the Lord's death is the ransom of all, and by His death the middle wall of partition (φραγμός) is broken down . . . how would He have

74. IGNATIUS OF ANTIOCH uses the word to describe strengthening by the Holy Spirit (*Philad., Inscr.; Eph.* XII, 1). Cf. SCHLIER, *Untersuchungen*, p. 87. This recalls the importance of speculation on *Genesis* at this period.
75. Cf. p. 283 above.

called us to Him if He had not been crucified? For it is only on the cross that a man dies with his hands spread out. Whence it was fitting for the Lord to bear this also and to spread out His hands: that with the one He might draw the ancient people, and with the other the Gentiles and unite both in Himself. For this is what He Himself has said, signifying by what manner of death He was to ransom all: 'I, when I am lifted up,' He saith, 'shall draw all men unto Me' (*Jn.* 12:32). Again, if the devil, the enemy of the human race, . . . wanders about our lower atmosphere . . . and the Lord came to cast down the devil . . . by what other kind of death could this have come to pass than by one which took place in the air, I mean the cross? (*De Inc.* XXV, 3–5).[76]

The most remarkable treatment, however, is certainly that of Gregory of Nyssa, who gathers together several of the themes so far considered. Gregory declares first of all that 'it is impossible to expound all the meaning contained in the Cross' (*Or. Res.* I). Then, following Athanasius, he states that there was a hidden reason for the death on the cross, and finds this reason in *Eph.* 3:18, 'Paul knows indeed that the Cross, divided into four branches from the central joint, signifies the power ($\delta\acute{v}\nu\alpha\mu\iota s$) and the Providence which come from Him who is seen upon it, and which penetrate everything, and for this reason he gives each branch a special name.' Here as in Irenaeus the ideas of power and of universality are closely linked.

Gregory then describes the four dimensions. 'He calls "depth" the long branch going down from the centre, "height" the one rising from it, "length and breadth" those which extend transversally from either side of the joint, in such a way that the one on one side of the centre is called "length" and the one on the other side is called "breadth".' This involved explanation shows that the text from Paul is being made to fit into the classic conception of the Cross. Now 'this signifies that there is nothing which is not under the empire of the divine power, neither that which is above heaven, nor that which is under the earth, nor that which extends transversally to the limits of being'. This is the Irenaean conception.

Here the symbolism of the Cross appears to represent above all the universal Providence of the Logos. This is seen still more clearly in the next section, where Gregory expresses himself in Stoic language: the Cross

76. Cf. DANIÉLOU, 'Les démons de l'air dans la Vie d'Antoine', *Stud. Ans.*, XXXVIII, pp. 136–138.

is 'in a manner the bond (σύνδεσμος) of the universe'; 'it penetrates (ἥκων) all things.' Referring to *Phil.* 2:10, Gregory sees in the upper part of the Cross 'the super-celestial part', in the middle part the earth, and in the lower part the regions under the earth. Thus the form of the cross represents 'him in whom all things consist' (*Col.* 1:17), 'him who exists before everything which is under his control', 'him whose power conserves (συντηρητική) all beings.' Thus 'for those whose vision can penetrate, the Cross becomes a theologian (θεόλογος), proclaiming by its form the sovereign power of him who appears upon it, and who is all in all'. The Cross is thus the sign of the divinity of the Word.

The Jewish Christian theology of the Cross can now be seen in all its rich diversity. It is regarded as the sign of the victory of Christ; it is a Cross of glory. It is like a living being, Christ's companion in his works of power, in Hell and at the Parousia. Some texts identify it with Christ himself. The *testimonia* of the Old Testament show the Cross prefigured in the many symbols, which illustrate in detail the various forms of its efficacy. It is the instrument by which the incarnate Word accomplishes his work of salvation. Finally its shape suggests a cosmic symbolism in which it expresses the universality of the redemptive action, unifying all things, consolidating the new creation, distinguishing what belongs to Christ from what is foreign to him.

This theology of the Cross is also seen to derive from all the various sources of Jewish Christianity. As a Cross of light it is in the tradition of Apocalyptic, and recalls the star of the Magi and the fire over the Jordan with which it is sometimes identified.[77] As the δύναμις of Christ it is connected with the *testimonia*, of which it forms the subject of one of the major collections, and it is speculations on these texts which constitute its theology. Finally as a cosmic Cross it has the attributes of God the Creator, the powers of consolidation, of distinction, of unification, and attaches to itself the functions of the Logos in Philo's theology.[78] In this respect it stands in the tradition of those esoteric speculations on *Genesis*, the importance of which in Jewish Christian theology has been noticed several times.

The Cross has thus been promoted to represent the whole plan of redemption. It reaches out to the whole of Creation; it symbolises the action

77. Cf. EDSMAN, *op. cit.*, pp. 166 ff.
78. Cf. *Heres* 235 (distinction); *Plant.* 8 (ἔρεισμα τῶν ὅλων); *Fug.* 112 (δεσμός); *Somn.* I, 158 (στήριγμα καὶ ἔρεισμα).

of the Word as well in the farthest heaven as in the abysses of hell, and represents the spread of this action over the breadth of space and the length of time. The next step must be to consider the results of this redemptive work of Christ, beginning with the theology of the Church.

Chapter Ten

THE CHURCH

ONE of the most striking points about Jewish Christian theology is the importance attached to the theology of the Church. One might have believed that at a time when the Church was still in process of formation, there would be little developed thought on that subject; but the facts prove just the contrary. The Church can be seen at a very early date to have been conscious of its existence as a theological entity; indeed this topic seems to have occupied a much more important position at this time than it was to do later in patristic and mediaeval theology, the second of which concentrated on Mariology the attention which had at first been devoted to ecclesiology. It is only at the present day that the desire has revived to go back to the plan of ancient theology, and to try to develop its themes.

This aspect of Jewish Christian theology is, however, less surprising if it is remembered how vitally important a theological reality in biblical thought was the position of the people of God. The prophets in particular had built up an entire theology of Israel as the spouse of Yahweh, as the vine of the Lord, as the city of the Most High; and Apocalyptic had enriched these symbols. In *II* (4) *Esdras* Israel is a 'dove', a 'lily', a 'sheep' (5: 23–26). Again, the Qumran manuscripts have shown how aware was the Essene community of its own eschatological significance. It is 'an eternal plant' (*DSD*, VIII, 5); 'a sanctuary for Israel' (VIII, 5; IX, 6). These expressions reappear applied to the Church in Jewish Christianity. The Church is the 'plantation planted by the Apostles of the Beloved' (*Asc. Is.* IV, 3), and the *Epistle to the Ephesians* describes her as the sanctuary 'built upon the foundation of the Apostles and the Prophets' (2:20).

All this provided the ingredients for a biblical theology of the Church, which was in existence from the beginning, and which has endured in all Christian tradition. The Church was to be 'the new Jerusalem', 'the true vine', 'the perfect dove', 'the only house'. This theology, however, is not specifically characteristic of Jewish Christian thought, and the concern of this chapter will be with another more distinctive feature. Several ancient texts speak of the Church as a pre-existent reality.[1] Hermas says of her, 'She was created before all things; . . . and for her sake the world was framed' (*Vis.* II, 4). *II Clement* speaks in its turn of 'the first Church, which is spiritual, which was created before the sun and the moon' (XIV, 1). These texts have been associated by some scholars with Gnostic speculations.[2] If by this is meant Hellenistic or dualist influences, it is not true; but it is true if it refers to the speculative thought of Jewish gnosis, that is to say, to the imagery of apocalyptic and the conceptions that went with it.[3]

THE AGED WOMAN

A good starting point may be found in Hermas, who pursues a line of thought on this subject which is linked directly with Palestinian Jewish Apocalyptic. According to Hermas God created all things 'for His holy Church's sake' (*Vis.* I, 1:6), a statement which already implies the pre-existence of the Church in the divine thought. In a very similar way Jewish apocalyptic had held in high esteem the idea that everything was created with Israel in view. Thus in *II (4) Esdras* God says: 'I created the world for the sake of Israel' (7:11). This conception of the Church as the goal of Creation, already present to the mind of God before the foundation of the world, and the purpose to which all else must be subordinated, also appears in Paul, for whom 'the mystery which from the beginning of the world hath been hid in God, who created all things' is manifested in the Church (*Eph.* 3:9–10). Ignatius of Antioch speaks of the Church 'fore-ordained before the ages (αἰώνων) to be for ever' (*Eph. Inscr.*).[4]

The fact that the Church is the first of all created things is indicated by the various guises in which she appears to Hermas. First, there is the Aged Woman. She appears first without her identity being revealed (*Vis.* I, 2:2), but later it is disclosed to him by an angel:

Whom thinkest thou the aged woman . . . to be? I say, The Sybil. Thou art wrong, saith he, she is not. Who then is she? I say. The

---

1. Cf. J. Beumer, 'Die altchristliche Idee einer präexistierenden Kirche und ihre theologische Auswertung', *WW*, IX, 1942, pp. 13–22.
2. Cf. H. Schlier, *Christus und die Kirche im Epheserbrief*, pp. 66–68.
3. This already applies in the case of Paul; cf. L. Cerfaux, *La théologie de l'Église suivant Saint Paul*, Paris, 1942, pp. 276–282.
4. Cf. Schlier, *Untersuchungen*, pp. 82–88.

Church, saith he. I said unto him, Wherefore then is she aged? Because, saith he, she was created before all things; therefore is she aged; and for her sake the world was framed (*Vis.* II, 4:1).

The last phrase emphasises the connection between this passage and those just studied.

To the image of the Aged Woman is added a second, that of the building. The woman shows Hermas a great tower being built, and when he asks her the meaning of it, she replies:

The tower which thou seest building, is myself, the Church, which was seen of thee both now and aforetime. . . . The tower is builded upon waters . . . because your life is saved and shall be saved by water. But the tower has been founded (τεθεμελίωται) by the word (ῥῆμα) of the Almighty and Glorious Name, and is sustained by the unseen power (δύναμις ἀόρατος) of the Master. . . . The six young men that build . . . are the holy angels of God, that were created first of all, and unto whom the Lord delivered all His creation (*Vis.* III, 3:3–4:1).

The context of the thought is still the Creation, which accounts for the present of the six angels charged with the administration of created things; but there is another element more important than this. The Tower is founded on the Word and built upon the water, and when Hermas asks the reason for this, the woman answers that the reason had been given him before. This is a reference to *Vision* I, where it was said: 'The God of Hosts, Who by His invisible . . . power (δύναμις ἀόρατος) created the world . . . by his strong word (ῥῆμα) fixed the heaven and founded (θεμελιώσας) the earth upon the waters, and by His own wisdom and providence formed His holy Church, which also He blessed' (3:4).

It is quite clear that any explanation of the two mysterious details of the Church founded upon the Word and built upon the water must begin with the account of the Creation. The text is based on an analogy on the one hand between the primordial waters and those of baptism and on the other between the creative utterance of God and the incarnate Word. This is, therefore, the first example of that explicit association of the waters of creation with those of regeneration which was ultimately to enjoy such an important position in baptismal typology, especially from Tertullian onwards (*De bapt.* III, 1). It is possible, indeed, that this analogy already formed the background to *Jn.* 3:5.

The context of thought, therefore, is still the same as that considered hitherto. The only new feature is the image of the Tower in place of that of the Aged Woman. It should be noted that it is not a city or a temple that is being built, but a tower; and it is not impossible that the image itself derives from some creation context, the earth being considered as an edifice in pyramid form built over the lower waters. The image of the cosmic tower or mountain is familiar to the Semitic mind, as is shown by the Babylonian *zikkurat*; and at a later date the *Hymns* of Ephraem also refer to the earth as a paradise mountain.

The elements of this vision of the Church resolve themselves into three: the comparison of the Church to a woman and a tower; the existence of the Church prior to the rest of creation; the relationship of this symbolism to the account of Creation in *Genesis*. Is it possible to determine the original context of these elements?

The first clearly recalls two important passages in apocalyptic literature, which are very close to *Hermas*, and which also associate the image of a woman and that of a building. The first is a vision in *II* (4) *Esdras*. In a setting very similar to that of the *Shepherd*, Ezra 'lifted up (his) eyes and saw a woman upon the right hand' (9:38). This woman is aged (9:45–10:1), and she represents Sion (10:44); but a little later we are told: 'the woman was no longer visible to me but there was a city builded on large foundations' (10:27). The second text is in the *Revelation* of John. Here are to be found both the woman and the city and the creation context: 'And I saw the holy city, the new Jerusalem coming down out of heaven from God prepared as a bride adorned for her husband' (21:1–2). It is true that this is not an aged woman, but the essential feature of the image is the use of a woman as such. Moreover, Hermas does in any case show us the Church elsewhere in a symbolism which comes closer to that of the *Revelation*. At her earliest manifestation the woman does indeed appear 'very aged'; but later she is seen to be 'youthful', and finally 'altogether youthful' (*Vis.* III, 10:3–5). Above all, another passage presents her as a bride: 'There meeteth me a virgin arrayed as if she were going forth from a bride-chamber, all in white . . . veiled up to her forehead, and her head-covering consisted of a turban, and her hair was white. I knew from the former visions that it was the Church' (*Vis.* IV, 2:1–2). In this vision Hermas combines the antiquity of the Church, indicated by the white hair, with her character of a young spouse which recalls the *Revelation* of John.

The second characteristic of this ecclesiology is the assertion of the pre-existence of the Church: she is the first of all creatures. This is the most important affirmation of all, and constitutes the characteristic mark of Jewish Christian theology in this regard. It occurs both in *Hermas* and in *II Clement*, and has an important place in Gnosticism, in which Ecclesia is one of the aeons of the Pleroma. The *Treatise of the Three Natures*, discovered at Nag Hammadi, speaks of the Church 'which exists before the aeons',[5] and Theodotus refers to 'the Church . . . chosen before the foundation of the world'.[6] Further reference will have to be made to these Gnostic texts, but for the moment all that is necessary is to decide to which context of ideas this conception belongs. It is often regarded as a Gnostic doctrine adopted by the first Christian theologians, Paul especially,[7] and implying the existence of a spiritual world of which ours is but a later and degraded form. There are, however, no other grounds for supposing Gnostic influences in *Hermas*, whose thought context is uniformly that of Palestinian Judaism. Does the latter then afford any analogies to the idea of a pre-existent Church?

The conception is indeed very close to one of the essential concepts of Apocalyptic, namely that of the hidden pre-existence of eschatological realities in God. One of the most important examples is that of the 'Son of Man' in *Daniel* and *I Enoch*, who is an eschatological figure. *I Enoch* says of him: 'Before the sun or the signs (of the Zodiac) were created, . . . his Name was named before the Lord of Spirits' (XLVIII, 3). Similarly in the case of the Church, the *Revelation* of John describes the new Jerusalem 'coming down out of heaven from God'. The same symbolism certainly seems to be implied in the passage from *I Enoch* where the Lord of the sheep, after having folded up the old house, the first Jerusalem, 'brought a new house greater and fairer than the first' (XC, 29). *II Baruch* speaks still more explicitly of the building as 'that which was prepared here beforehand from the time when I (God) took counsel to make Paradise, and showed it to Adam before he sinned, but when he transgressed the commandment it was removed from him, as also was Paradise. . . . And now, behold, it is preserved with Me, as also is Paradise' (IV, 3–6).

Thus the holy city, like Paradise, belongs to those realities which were the first to be created, and which God holds in safe keeping in his presence. This is exactly the case with Paradise in *I Enoch*. The Tree of Life which is

---

5. Cf. Puech and Quispel, *Le quatrième écrit du Codex Jung, VC*, ix, 1955, p. 96.
6. *Excerpta* 41, 2; cf. also *Sophia J. C.* 110:5–10 (Till 261).
7. Cf. H. Schlier, *op. cit.*, pp. 60–75.

near the Mount of Paradise 'no mortal is permitted to touch till the great judgment. . . . It shall then be given to the righteous and holy. Then blessed I the God of Glory because He had prepared such rewards for the righteous, and had created such things' (XXV, 4-7). Thus the Son of Man, Paradise and the Holy City all belong to a group of realities created in the very beginning, the memory of which was to be preserved in Jewish tradition: 'Seven things were created before the creation of the world: the Law, Repentance, Paradise, Hell, the Throne of Glory, the Sanctuary and the Name of the Messiah' (*B. Pesakhim*, 53a). The pre-existence of the Sanctuary is manifestly a Jewish apocalyptic theme which Christian apocalyptic later applied to the Church.

However, Christian apocalyptic itself can offer other examples earlier than Hermas. The *Revelation* of John has already been quoted; but side by side with that should be mentioned the *Epistle to the Hebrews*, which speaks of 'the heavenly Jerusalem', and of the 'assembly of the firstborn, which are written in heaven' (12:22-23), phrases which can only refer to the elect, inscribed on heavenly tablets, that is to say, predestined in God's plan.[8] In the writings of Jewish Christianity in the strict sense of the word there is also the very archaic text of the *Ascension of Isaiah* which speaks of 'the descent of the Angel of the Christian Church, which is in the heavens' (III, 15), a descent which takes place between the Passion and the Resurrection. By the Angel of the Church the author means the Church itself in its pre-existent reality, and the image is therefore parallel to that of the aged woman in *Hermas*.[9]

How is this theme, received by Christian apocalyptic from the Jewish, to be interpreted? Is it the Gnostic conception of a supernal world of which this world is a debased form? Such a notion seems to be entirely foreign to Jewish apocalyptic, which was concerned with the pre-existence of eschatological realities hidden in God before time was, and only to be revealed at the End. This is Paul's concept in *Eph.* 3:9 f. The expressions 'kept', 'preserved', which are regularly applied to these realities, show that they are still not yet accomplished, and as yet exist only in the counsels of God, but Semitic realism calls this mode of existence a first creation. Proof of this is afforded by the fact that in *I Enoch* the names of the just are also included in the pre-existent realities, a conception which clearly

8. The idea of the pre-existence of the eschatological community is also found in *I Enoch*.
9. Cf. also *Odes of Sol.* IV, 3; CLEM. ALEX., *Stromateis* VII, 107:3-6.

does not imply a pre-existence of souls in the Platonic sense, but rather predestination in the Pauline.[10]

The theology of the pre-existent Church in the *Shepherd* appears then to belong to a line of speculative thought common to both Jewish and Jewish Christian apocalyptic. Ultimately, however, these speculations were taken over and altered to fit outlooks which were foreign to them, so that in Gnosticism the notion of the pre-existent eschatological Church became that of the aeon Ecclesia, one of the most important in the Pleroma.[11]

There still remains one point connected with the teaching of *Hermas* on the pre-existent Church which calls for attention: the relationship between these doctrines and the account of Creation in *Genesis*. The references to apocalyptic have not entirely clarified the background of Hermas' thought. The allusions to *Genesis* seem to imply a further element, that of an exegesis of the Hexaemeron in which the various parts of the account of Creation are not interpreted in their literal sense but in a hidden one, and are made to stand for realities which in a mysterious way existed before the material world.[12]

Exegeses of this kind did in fact enter the Jewish Christian world from Judaism, and they were particularly concerned with the doctrine of the Church. Anastasius Sinaites, when he comes to interpret the Hexaemeron as a prophecy of the future Church, wishes to show that he is supported by precedents, and writes: 'Let us begin from Papias, the famous bishop of Hierapolis, who was a follower of the Beloved Disciple, from Clement, and Pantaenus, the priest of the Church of Alexandria, from the very learned Ammonius, and the ancient exegetes before the first councils, who interpreted the entire Hexaemeron as applying to Christ and the Church.'[13] This could hardly be more explicit. Unless the evidence of Anastasius is to be rejected out of hand, it must be admitted that the Asiatic Elders knew an exegesis of the Creation which interpreted it as applying to the Church. This is curiously reminiscent of the beginning of the *Shepherd*. As far as

10. Cf. N. A. DAHL, 'Christ, Creation and the Church', *The Background of the NT*, pp. 428 f., who distinguishes pre-existence, prefiguration and predestination.

11. This raises the question of the elements which go to make up the Origenist conception of the pre-existence of souls. These conceptions in themselves are not immediately relevant, but they will be referred to later in so far as they have preserved data taken from Jewish Christian apocalyptic.

12. Speculations of this type form the background to Philo's *Questions on Genesis*, which quotes earlier interpretations. It will also be remembered that the beginning of *Genesis*, together with the first chapter of *Ezekiel* and the *Song of Songs* were among those biblical texts that were held to contain secret doctrines, and might not be divulged.

13. PREUSCHEN, *Antilegomena*, p. 96.

Papias is concerned, there are, however, no extant texts to confirm this exegesis; but Anastasius also refers to Pantaenus, Clement of Alexandria and Ammonius Sakkas. Does the Alexandrian tradition bear out his statement?

There is noteworthy support for it in the *Eclogae Propheticae* of Clement of Alexandria. In this work Clement was passing on traditions going back to the Elders, that is to say, to the primitive Palestinian community (cf. *Strom.* I, 1:11), as Eusebius confirms:

> In the first book of the *Stromateis*, he (Clement) shows . . . that he is himself very close to the tradition of the Apostles; and he promises in them also to write a commentary on *Genesis*. And in his treatise *On the Pasch* he professes that he was compelled by his companion to commit to writing traditions that he had heard from the elders of olden time (*HE*, VI, 13: 8–9).

The mention of commentaries on *Genesis* in this context puts them in a direct relation with the traditions of the Elders, that is the Apostolic circle, the Jewish Christian community.

Moreover, the *Eclogae* do in fact consist largely of commentaries on *Genesis*. The heavens and the waters mentioned in the account of Creation represent the pure powers (1:2); the heaven and the earth of *Gn.* 1:1 signify heavenly and earthly things respectively, that is, spiritual and carnal realities (3:1–3); the Beginning (ἀρχή) is the Son (4:1). In regard to *Gn.* 1:2 it is said that 'regeneration (ἀναγέννησις) is produced by water and the spirit, as indeed is all creation (γένεσις)' (7:1), while the heavenly waters represent the Holy Spirit (8:2). Moreover, the protoctist angels are named several times (51: 2; 56: 7; 57:1).

There are two noteworthy points of contact between this work and the *Shepherd*. First, there is the baptismal typology of the primordial waters, with an allusion to *Jn.* 3:5; and secondly, this is the only other work besides the *Shepherd* which names the protoctist angels.[14]

It is clear, however, that Clement does not depend here on Hermas. His interpretation, though it may share the same material elements, has

14. It is not without significance that this should be in a commentary on the Hexaemeron. It may be remembered that in the Pseudo-Cyprianist treatise *De centesima sexagesima tricesima*, in which Jewish Christian material was identified, the creation of the six days signified that of the six archangels. Now Hermas speaks of six protoctists, since for him as for the anonymous author the seventh is the Word; and Clement, in the same context in which he speaks of the protoctists, says that 'the angels are called days' (*Ecl. Proph.* LVI, 6). Thus the doctrine of the protoctists appears also to be connected with an anagogical interpretation of *Genesis*.

quite a different inspiration, more Platonist and less eschatological. Nor is there any reason for supposing that Hermas depends on Papias. The only possible explanation is, therefore, the existence of an exegesis of *Genesis* in the primitive community, among the Elders, which must have been the common source for all these authors. This exegesis would be characterised by the fact that the episodes of the Hexaemeron were not interpreted as referring to the creation of the material world, but to pre-existent spiritual realities. Hermas saw these realities in an eschatological perspective as the Church pre-existing in the divine thought, whereas Clement saw them in a Platonic, realist sense as the spiritual, angelic creation, preceding that of men.

The Bride of Christ

The second form of the theme of the pre-existent Church is to be found in *II Clement*:

Wherefore, brethren, if we do the will of God our Father we shall be of the first Church (ἡ Ἐκκλησία ἡ πρώτη), which is spiritual, which was created before the sun and the moon; . . . the Church of life. . . . And I do not suppose ye are ignorant, that the living Church (ζῶσα) is the body of Christ, for Scripture saith: God made man, male and female. The male is Christ and the female is the Church. And the Books and the Apostles plainly declare that the Church existeth not now for the first time, but cometh from on high (ἄνωθεν); for she was spiritual, as our Jesus also was spiritual, but was manifested (ἐφανερώθη) in the last days that He might save us (XIV, 1–2).

There are obvious contacts between this text and those studied earlier, even to the actual expression used by Hermas in speaking of the Church 'which was the first created' (πρώτη ἐκτίσθη). This reference to the 'protoctist' Church is one indication which points toward a common context of Jewish Christian apocalyptic. On the other hand, it is difficult to avoid recognising a Pauline influence, and more particularly that of the *Epistle to the Ephesians*, in the conception of the Church as the 'body of Christ', and in the typology of Adam and Eve as a figure of the union of Christ and the Church. Finally, the actual theme of the Church as the bride of Christ appears, as in the *Revelation* of John, and is linked with the nuptial imagery by which the Prophets had described the union of Yahweh and Israel. It is clearly an allusion to the Old Testament and to Paul which *II Clement* intends when it speaks of 'the Books and the Apostles'.

There is here nevertheless a new element, the pre-existent marriage of Christ and the Church, and this theme deserves special study for two reasons. First, although comparatively rare among the orthodox, it occupies an absolutely central position in Gnostic teaching. Is it then a Jewish Christian theme transferred to Gnosticism, or is it specifically Gnostic? This in turn raises the notorious question: Is there a Hellenistic myth at the source of this theme?[15] Or is it an elaboration of a Jewish Christian speculation of biblical origin?

The importance of Ecclesia among the aeons of the pre-existent Pleroma in the Valentinian gnosis is a remarkable and curious fact, which can only be explained on the assumption of previous speculations on the pre-existent Church. As Valentinianism uses Jewish Christian material, this development permits the use of Valentinian teaching as documentary evidence for Jewish Christian theology.[16] Nevertheless, the very varied forms of these speculations mean[17] that a careful examination of detail and some degree of reconstruction will be necessary before it is possible to arrive at the Jewish Christian teaching which underlies them.

The important notice which begins the *Adversus haereses* of Saint Irenaeus probably provides a résumé of the doctrine of the western Valentinian school, and in particular of that of Ptolemy[18] up to the end of the second century. In this teaching the syzygy[19] Anthropos-Ecclesia is the fourth of the primordial ($\dot{\alpha}\rho\chi\acute{\epsilon}\gamma o\nu o\nu$) ogdoad (*Adv. haer.* I, 1:1), and is immediately preceded by the pair Logos-Zoë. It is these two couples who engender the twenty-two aeons that complete the Pleroma. It certainly looks as if there is here a duplication of an original couple Christos-Ecclesia[20]; and this would seem to be confirmed by the notice itself, which goes on to say: 'They declare also that Paul has referred to the conjunctions within the Pleroma, showing them forth by means of one; for when writing of the conjugal union in this life, he expressed himself thus: This is a great mystery, but I speak concerning Christ and the Church' (I, 8:4).

15. So SCHLIER (*Christus und die Kirche im Epheserbrief*, pp. 60–75) following REITZEN-STEIN; cf. also L. CERFAUX, *Le théologie de l'Église suivant Saint Paul*, pp. 275-287; A. ORBE, 'Cristo y la Iglesia en su matrimonia anterior a los siglos', *EE*, XXIX, 1955, 299-344.
16. The accounts given by Irenaeus and Hippolytus had long witnessed to this fact, and it has now been confirmed decisively by the manuscripts of the *Jung Codex*.
17. Cf. PUECH and QUISPEL, 'Le quatrième écrit gnostique du Codex Jung', *VC*, IX, 1955, pp. 94-102.
18. Cf. SAGNARD, *La gnose valentinienne*, pp. 140-198; also Glossary s.v. PTOLEMAEUS.
19. Cf. Glossary s.v.   20. Cf. ORBE, *op. cit.*, p. 312.

Several valuable references will already have been noted here. The pair Christos-Ecclesia is related to the doctrine of the *Epistle to the Ephesians*, which appears indeed to be one of its sources. Secondly, through the *Epistle*, it is linked with the typology of Adam and Eve. All this is already indicative of a Jewish Christian context. Again, several expressions are reminiscent of *II Clement*. The term ἀρχέγονον certainly seems to be a modification of the 'protoctist' of the apocalypses. Above all the terms Ecclesia and Zoë, which occupy corresponding positions in their respective syzygies, are echoed in *II Clement* where the Church is called the living (ζῶσα) Church or the Church of life (τῆς ζωῆς).[21]

Irenaeus' note on Mark the Magician shows that the latter had the same conception as Ptolemy, making Anthropos-Ecclesia the fourth syzygy of the ogdoad (I, 14:5). Nevertheless, Mark offers two curious exegeses. In one of them he sees the Annunciation as a figure of this particular tetrad: Gabriel corresponds to Logos, the Holy Spirit to Zoë, the Power of the Most High to Anthropos, the Virgin to Ecclesia (I, 15:3). It seems likely that these identifications are based on Jewish Christian speculation, as is that of the Church and the Spirit, which will have to be considered in a moment.[22] Finally, the theme of the Church as a Virgin occurs frequently. It is already found in Paul (*II Cor.* 11:2), and the evidence of Hegesippus shows it to be Jewish Christian (EUSEBIUS, *HE* IV, 22:4). The curious feature of Mark's exegesis is that the Virgin is the Virgin Mary, and this is, therefore, the first instance of that identification of Mary with the Church which was to lead to such great developments.[23]

Of greater immediate interest, however, is Mark's other exegesis, since it again introduces the Hexaemeron. According to Irenaeus Mark's commentary on *Gn.* 1:2: 'Darkness was upon the face of the deep and the Spirit of God moved upon the face of the waters', sees in this the second tetrad. It is not stated whether Ecclesia is identified with the Spirit or with the primordial waters; either interpretation is possible and full of interest. The first would link up with the tradition which identified the Spirit and the Church; the second would be reminiscent of various features in Hermas and Clement of Alexandria. Thus yet another route proves to lead back to

21. It will also be observed that the expression 'the Church comes from on high' (ἄνωθεν) has its equivalent in Ptolemy, who speaks of 'the Church on high' (ἄνω) (I, 5:6). A group of disciples of Ptolemy makes Anthropos-Ecclesia the third syzygy and Logos-Zoë the fourth (I, 12:3).
22. Cf. pp. 305 f. above.
23. Cf. A. MULLER, *Ecclesia-Maria, Die Einheit Mariens und die Kirche*, 1951, p. 34.

the same ecclesiological exegesis of the *Genesis* cosmogony, and so to the Jewish Christian gnosis.

Another tradition of the Western Valentinian school is that of Heracleon. The Extracts from him which are preserved by Origen include no speculation on the pre-existent Church, but they do contain the expression the 'spiritual (πνευματική) Church' (*Com. John.* XIII, 51), which occurred in *II Clement* as a synonym for the Church as the first-created; and it would therefore not be unreasonable to conclude that the latter expression is implied here also.

This lacuna with regard to Heracleon's ecclesiology has now, however, been filled, if the *Treatise of the Three Natures*, discovered at Nag Hammadi, is accepted as his work[24]; and since the text is a Western Valentinian gnosis, and yet differs from that of Ptolemy, to attribute it to Heracleon is a fairly natural conclusion. The work presents a theology of the pre-existent Church closer to that of *II Clement* than anything so far considered, since the Church appears not as an aeon among other aeons, but associated in pre-existence with the only Son.

One passage which is relevant here reads as follows: 'Not only does the Son exist from the beginning, but the Church also exists from the beginning.'[25] A little farther on the author speaks of 'the Church that exists before the aeons' (p. 58, l. 30). The following comment could hardly be bettered:

> If we understand it rightly, the Church is born from all time, in a state of permanence without beginning or end, from the act by which the Son conceives himself as such, from the embrace that unites the Son to the Father. . . . In any case it certainly seems as if the generation of the Church, like that of the Son, is prior to the generation of the aeons and distinct from it. Most probably regarded as the Spouse of the Son, this 'Εκκλησία is, without doubt, the pre-existent Church, the first or primordial Church, which, at about the same period, the homily known as *II Clement* conceived in its turn as 'spiritual', 'originating from on high', 'created before the Sun and the Moon'.[26]

The *Treatise of the Three Natures*, then, presents a conception of the pre-existent Church very close to that of *II Clement*. At the same time,

24. This seems very probable in the light of the arguments adduced by PUECH and QUISPEL, *op. cit.*, pp. 100–102.
25. P. 57, l. 35. Cf. PUECH–QUISPEL *op. cit.*, p. 94.
26. PUECH–QUISPEL, *op. cit.*, p. 97.

however, it places it in a new scheme; by putting its generation on the same plane as that of the Son, it makes it the Third Person of the Trinity.

All this is done as if the author of the *Treatise* had deliberately re-modelled the existing scheme. By joining the Church with the Son, and thereby raising it to the second rank, immediately after the Father, he simplifies and modifies the Ogdoad of classical Valentinianism in the direction of a Triad, or Trinity; and furthermore, when he affirms that the Son and the Church exist 'from the beginning', that is from all eternity, it is possible that he came very close to conceiving this Triad as a kind of ontological Trinity.[27]

This opens up a new line of thought. Attention has already been drawn to the relationship between the Church and Pneuma, the Holy Spirit, on the one hand, and Wisdom, Sophia, on the other. In this latest concep-tion, however, the Church is described in terms of the Third Person of the Trinity. For Heracleon this is bound up with a Gnostic conception of aeons quite foreign to the Great Church; but once again he is simply borrowing his scheme from the latter, for there is in fact an orthodox line of Trinitarian thinking in which the Third Person is Wisdom, and more or less closely identified with the Church,[28] that, namely, of Theophilus of Antioch, which is definitely Jewish Christian in character. This, however, lies along another line of research regarding the Church and Wisdom, which will have to be reserved for the later part of this chapter.

Speculations on the pre-existent Church analogous to those so far met with in the Valentinian gnosis are to be found in other Gnostic sects. Irenaeus' note on the Ophites, for example, shows that for them the Father was identified with the First Man, who begets the Second Man and the Holy Spirit. These in their turn beget Christ and 'the true and holy Church', which is 'an incorruptible Aeon' (I, 30:2). Here once again is the Pauline group Christus-Ecclesia, and this genealogy, moreover, is in the context of an exegesis of the first verses of *Genesis* (I, 30:1).

Both in *II Clement*, therefore, and in the Valentinian speculations is to be found a doctrine of the pre-existent Church characterised by the representation of the Church as the Bride of Christ. Is it possible to determine the background from which this symbolism originated? It has

27. *Ibid.*, p. 96.
28. Cf. KRETSCHMAR, *Studien zur früchristlichen Trinitätstheologie*, 1956, pp. 27–62.

often been regarded as a Christian adaptation of the myth of the androgynous Anthropos,[29] but the few references attesting the existence of the
myth in Hellenistic thought at the time do not appear to be decisive. It is
certain, however, that this influence does appear in Gnostic texts, where
the masculine-feminine opposition forms a part of the very structure of the
Pleroma, and it must be connected with an essential element of paganism,
that of the pairs of gods and goddesses. This, however, seems on the face
of it to be utterly foreign to Jewish and Christian thought, and a more
probable explanation would appear to be that the Gnostics have once more
taken over a theme older than Jewish Christianity. If so, is it possible to
discover its original setting?

At this point it is necessary to go back to the text of *II Clement* and study
it further, for it not only emphasises the pair Christ-Ecclesia, but also that
of Church–'body of Christ'. 'I do not suppose ye are ignorant that the
living Church is the body of Christ, for the scripture saith: God made man,
male and female. The male is Christ and the female is the Church' (XIV,
2). Farther on the text continues with this difficult passage: 'Now the
Church, being spiritual, was manifested in the flesh of Christ . . . this flesh
is the counterpart and copy of the Spirit. . . . But if we say that the flesh is
the Church and the Spirit is Christ, then he that hath dealt wantonly with
the flesh hath dealt wantonly with the Church' (XIV, 3-4). Here there is
a double antithesis: that between the spiritual Christ and the spiritual
Church which is his body, and that between the Christ who is Spirit
and the carnal Church.[30] What was the origin of this double theme?

The immediate context of the first antithesis is clearly the Pauline
Epistles and in particular the *Epistle to the Ephesians*, which states: 'He
(God) gave him (Christ) to be the head over all things to the Church,
which is his body ($\sigma\tilde{\omega}\mu\alpha$)' (1:22–23). It will nevertheless be observed that
with Paul the antithesis is between the head and the body, a feature which
appears again in *Colossians*: '(Christ) is the head of the body, the Church'
(1:18). Now the passage in *II Clement* makes no allusion to Christ as the
head. The Church is the body, not as opposed to Christ as the head, but
as the feminine element in opposition to the masculine. Nevertheless, that
a transition from the head-body to the man-woman antithesis was easily
made is clear from Paul himself, as a later passage in *Ephesians* proves:

29. Cf. Glossary s.v. SCHLIER writes concerning *II Clement*: 'He shows clearly that the
myth of the androgynous Anthropos was not unknown to him' (*op. cit.*, p. 67).
30. As ORBE clearly sees: *op. cit.*, pp. 336–340.

Husbands, love your wives, even as Christ also loved the Church. . . . So ought men to love their wives as their own bodies. . . . For no man ever yet hated his own flesh; but nourisheth and cherisheth it, even as the Lord the Church; for we are members of his body, formed of his flesh and of his bones. For this cause shall a man leave his father and mother, and shall be joined to his wife, and they two shall be one flesh (*Gn.* 2:24). This is a great mystery: but I speak concerning Christ and the Church (5:25–32).

Another passage may be compared: 'Know ye not that your bodies are members of Christ? Shall I then take the members of Christ and make them the members of an harlot . . . for two, saith he, shall be one flesh' (*I Cor.* 6:15–16).

This belongs very definitely to the same context as *II Clement*. But this only places the problem a stage further back, since the question of sources is now posed at the level of the *Epistle to the Ephesians*. It has been suggested that the problem can be resolved by reference to the androgynous Anthropos, which is one single body, of which the man and the woman are two aspects.[31] Here the ἐν σῶμα is not the union of head and members but of the masculine and feminine elements. This is certainly a possible explanation,[32] but is there not possibly another—and better—one?[33]

Now there is one remarkable detail common to the two texts quoted from Paul and the one from *II Clement*, and that is the reference to the first and second chapters of *Genesis* relating to the creation of woman. *II Clement* quotes *Gn.* 1:27 on the distinction between man and woman; but when it recalls that the Church is the body of Christ, it alludes by implication to 2:24: 'They two shall be one flesh', and this is the verse quoted by Paul. There are other points in *II Clement* which also relate to these chapters, as, for example, the expressions 'Church of life', 'living Church', which, among other things, are allusions to *Gn.* 3:20 where Eve is called the

31. Cf. SCHLIER, *loc. cit.*, also D. DAUBE, *The NT and Rabbinic Judaism*, London, 1956, pp. 71–86.
32. ORBE accepts this explanation for *II Clement* but not for the *Epistle to the Ephesians*, which seems to be a quite arbitrary discrimination, since the thought context is obviously the same.
33. CERFAUX suggests that there is, when he speaks of the 'clearly exaggerated role that the Anthropos myth has been made to play in explaining the theology of the mystical body' (*La théologie de l'Église selon Saint Paul*, p. 285); but he leaves the matter there, and gives no indication of what might have been the starting point of the theme.

'mother of all living'.[34] All this constitutes a context in which the terminology of a bodily unity between Christ and the Church is sufficiently justified without recourse to the problematical intervention of the Anthropos myth, namely the context of the biblical account of the creation of woman. Once again, therefore, the opening chapters of *Genesis* are indicated as the starting point for the theology of the Church.

Furthermore, it should be noted that Jewish Christianity has another important piece of evidence to offer on the subject of the ἓν σῶμα, namely that of *Hermas*.[35] Hermas is clearly concerned here with the pre-existent Church. The passage reads: 'Thou seest the tower made a single stone with the rock. So also they that have believed in the Lord through His Son . . . shall become one spirit and one body (ἓν πνεῦμα, ἓν σῶμα)' (*Sim.* IX, 13:5). A little earlier the tower had been identified with the Aged Woman, who is the pre-existent Church, and the unity of the Rock and the Tower is, therefore, another version of the unity of the Man and the Woman, giving the passage the same meaning as that in *Ephesians*.[36]

The ecclesiological exegesis of *Gn.* 2:24 in Jewish Christianity, of which this is yet another example, involves on the one hand a typological line of thought which is not specifically Jewish Christian, and which may therefore be left aside[37]; but it also involves another of a different kind, in which the creation of Adam and Eve is regarded not as a figure of Christ and the Church to come, but as an expression of the pre-existence of Christ and the Church. This exegesis is analogous to that of the six days of Creation, and is attested by Papias, Hermas, the *Epistle to the Ephesians* and *II Clement*.

Has this exegesis any antecedents in Judaism? There is a strange statement of Anastasius Sinaites[38] which compares Papias with Philo of Alexandria on the grounds that the latter also was acquainted with speculation (θεωρία) of a spiritual type (πνευματικῶς), in which the things of Paradise were interpreted anagogically[39] (ἀναφέρειν). This observation contains a certain amount of truth. Philo does indeed give an exegesis of the creation of Adam and Eve in which they are shown not, of course, as the pre-existent Christ and the Church, but as the faculties of intellect and sensation which went to make up the archetypal Man, pre-existent in the

34. Cf. ORBE, *op. cit.*, p. 317.
35. As rightly pointed out by SCHLIER, *op. cit.*, pp. 53–56.
36. The expression 'one spirit and one body' is also found in *Eph.* 4:4.
37. Cf. DANIÉLOU, *Sacramentum futuri*, pp. 37–44.
38. Cf. PREUSCHEN, p. 96.   39. Cf. Glossary s.v. under Sense.

intelligible world prior to his creation in the sensible world[40]; and this obviously constitutes the closest analogy to the Christian conception in question.[41]

On the other hand, it is hardly likely that Philo influenced Paul or Hermas, especially as the theme is interpreted in a philosophical tradition to which Paul was a stranger. The question arises, therefore, whether there could have been a common source, namely speculation in later Judaism on the account of the creation of man and woman; and such speculations did in fact exist.[42]

First, there is the importance increasingly accorded to Adam: examples of this are to be found in the *Life of Adam and Eve*, in *II* (4) *Esdras*, in *II Baruch* and in the Jewish *Sibyllines* (III, 24–26), works between them cover a period from the middle of the first to the middle of the second century A.D., and are therefore contemporaneous with Jewish Christian literature. A number of speculations to be found in the *Talmud* can also probably be assigned to this period.

In these particular texts, it is true, there is no question of a pre-existent Adam, but simply of his greatness before his fall. There is, however, another trend in which are to be distinguished traces of a pre-existent celestial Adam distinct from the earthly one who sinned. This conception appears in *I Enoch* with the figure of the Son of Man who pre-exists with God, together with the other eschatological realities of which he is a part, and whose name is 'named before the sun' (XLVIII, 3). Similar features are present in the Greek *Wisdom of Solomon* in a remarkable passage[43]: 'She (Wisdom) guarded to the end the first formed father of the world ($\pi\alpha\tau\dot{\eta}\rho$ $\kappa\acute{o}\sigma\mu o\upsilon$) that was created alone, And preserved him from all personal sin, and gave him strength to get dominion over all things' (X, 1–2). This certainly seems to be an example of a speculation on *Genesis*, showing an archetypal Man, unique and a stranger to sin.

It should be observed that these speculative exegeses appear at the same time in a Hellenistic and in a Palestinian setting, which explains why they have a twofold course of development. With Philo they encounter Platonic thought, the realism of which results in a conception of the first Adam as

40. *Leg. All.* I, 23.
41. As ORBE recognises: *op. cit.*, p. 321.
42. As W. D. DAVIES has observed: *Paul and Rabbinic Judaism*, pp. 36–57; cf. also D. DAUBE, *The New Testament and Rabbinic Judaism*, pp. 172–185.
43. To which DUPONT-SOMMER has drawn attention: 'Adam père du monde', *RHR*, CXII, 1939, pp. 182–196.

the archetype of humanity, standing at once for the idea of man and the idea of woman, identified with νοῦς and αἴσθησις respectively.[44]

The conception was also developed, however, in a Palestinian tradition, one expression of which is to be found in the *Pseudo-Clementines*. The part played by Adam in these writings is significant[45]: he is the first incarnation of the true prophet; he is a stranger to sin; and he is to reappear in Christ. Secondly, the idea appears in those Gnostic speculations in which Anthropos becomes one of the pre-existent aeons of the Pleroma. Finally, there is a third tradition, the Pauline development, which keeps to the strict line of *I Enoch*: the pre-existent heavenly Adam belongs to the eschatological realities, whose existence is existence in the μυστήριον, in God's hidden plan, and not real existence. This stands in opposition both to Philo and to the *Clementines*.

This may be seen very plainly in the remarkable passage in *I Corinthians* where Paul comments on *Gn.* 2:7: 'The first man Adam was made a living soul; the last Adam became a quickening spirit (πνεῦμα). Howbeit that was not first which is spiritual (πνευματικόν), but that which is natural; and afterwards that which is spiritual. The first man is of the earth, earthy: the second man is the Lord from heaven' (15:45–47). Here is the theme of *I Enoch*, the eschatological coming of the Son of Man, pre-existent with God, but second in order of manifestation. What Paul adds is to place this conception in the setting of a polemical exegesis of *Genesis*, and so to relate it to current discussions regarding these texts, which presupposed speculations on the subject of the first spiritual and pre-existent Adam.

It will immediately be objected that this may apply well enough to Adam, but not to Eve. However, with Paul ἄνθρωπος stands for the whole man, male and female together; and this too is a conception which derives from Jewish thought. In the apocalyptic view the Chosen One, the Son of Man, is inseparable from the community of the saints, the ἐκκλησία; both are hidden in God, and both are manifested eschatologically.[46] Consequently Paul simply develops this eschatological view in an exegesis of

44. The Philonian development was, of course, not the only one in Hellenistic circles. E. PETERSON ('La libération d'Adam de l'Ananké', *RB*, LV, 1948, pp. 210–211) has drawn attention to Jewish Christian magical papyri in which Adam is called πατὴρ κόσμου exactly as in *Wisdom*, and in which there is no longer any question of a personal παράπτωμα. Similarly, there existed a pagan speculation on *Genesis* in the form of the *Poimandres*: cf. C. H. DODD, *The Bible and the Greeks*, pp. 145–170; E. HAENCHEN, 'Aufbau und Theologie des Poimandres', *ZTK*, LIII, 1956, pp. 170–175.
45. Cf. H. J. SCHOEPS, *Theologie und Geschichte des Judenchristentums*, pp. 100–106.
46. Cf. DAVIES, *op. cit.*, p. 56.

Genesis. Just as Adam appears as the pre-existent Son of Man, so Eve is seen as the eschatological community, the Church, which like Adam is created in the beginning, but manifested only in the last days.

It is now clear that the text of *II Clement* is simply a more ecclesiological development of this view. As in the case of Paul, it is an apocalyptic exegesis of *Genesis*; and what Paul said of Christ, that he is the spiritual Adam, pre-existent and manifested at the End, *II Clement* says of the Church. She is the spiritual ($\pi\nu\epsilon\upsilon\mu\alpha\tau\iota\kappa\acute{\eta}$) Eve, named before the Sun, and like the Son of Man in *I Enoch*, is among the 'good things prepared', and is manifested in the last ($\dot{\epsilon}\sigma\chi\acute{\alpha}\tau\omega\nu$) days (XIV, 2), like the Adam of *I Corinthians*. This manifestation is made in the flesh, like that of Christ, but unlike Christ, who by the Resurrection is Spirit, the Church is still flesh until the Parousia. Hence *II Clement* can say that 'the flesh is the Church and the Spirit is Christ' (XIV, 4).[47]

Thus the evidence of *II Clement* points to the same conclusion as that of *Hermas*. The context of its speculative doctrine of the pre-existent Church is Jewish Christian apocalyptic, and there is, therefore, no point in invoking Gnostic sources. There is indeed a gnosis involved, but it is one in the Pauline sense of the word. This apocalyptic speculation is characterised by the fact that, just as in the *Shepherd*, it rests on an anagogical exegesis of *Genesis*. Exegesis of this kind, which is quite distinct from typological interpretation, is the chief mark of the kind of thought studied in this chapter, and is typically Jewish Christian. The only difference between Hermas and the author of *II Clement* is that the former commented on the Hexaemeron, whereas the Pseudo-Clement drew his inspiration from the account of the creation of man and woman.

THE CHURCH AND WISDOM

In conclusion these speculations on the pre-existent Church raise once more a question already touched on, namely that of the relation between the Church and Sophia, the Wisdom of God. It has recently been suggested by more than one scholar that in primitive Christianity there was an identification of the Church with pre-existent Wisdom.[48]

47. Cf. ORBE's apt remarks on this last point: *op. cit.*, p. 329.
48. SCHLIER sees this as a Gnostic speculation which influenced Saint Paul (*op. cit.*, p. 62), while KRETSCHMAR rejects this opinion, and thinks that the identification goes back to Jewish Christian speculations on Wisdom influenced by Hellenistic Judaism (*op. cit.*, pp. 36–37); but both are of the opinion that there was such an identification in primitive Christianity.

The texts cited, however, are by no means decisive on this point. In *Eph.* 3:10, Paul writes that 'now unto the principalities and powers (is) made known by the Church the manifold (ποικίλος) wisdom of God'.[49] There is obviously some relationship here between Wisdom and the Church, but all that is said is that the Church manifests the Wisdom of God. There is no mention whatever of her pre-existence. It should be remembered moreover that it is to the Word that Paul applies those attributes which the *Wisdom of Solomon* applied to Wisdom. There are, therefore, no grounds for supposing that Paul held a doctrine of the Church-Wisdom.

Is there better evidence in the early Christian authors?[50] There is in Theophilus a doctrine of considerable interest in which Wisdom is identified with the Holy Spirit (*Ad. Aut.* I, 7). Furthermore, in an exegesis of *Gn.* 1 the first three days of creation are called 'figures' (τύποι) of the Trinity (II, 15); and at another point in the same exegesis the Churches are compared to the islands created on the third day with the sea (II, 14). But all this hardly provides sufficient grounds for positing a relationship, and indeed an identity between the Church and Wisdom.[51] Theophilus cannot, therefore, be held to provide a basis for such an identification.

Other authors adduced in support of a 'Sophia-ecclesiology' in non-Gnostic primitive Christianity are no more convincing. The examples from *Hermas* prove nothing. The fact that the aged Woman, who is the Church, changes form cannot really be held to justify equating her with the Wisdom which is ποικίλος, nor does the statement that the Church was created by Wisdom entail an identification of the two.[52] Nor is the designation of the Church as παρθένος in Hegesippus a more valid argument.[53]

This would seem, therefore, to confirm the view that the pre-existence of the Church in Jewish Christianity is not that of the hypostatic Wisdom,

49. This is the passage on which SCHLIER (*loc. cit.*) chiefly bases his case.
50. The views challenged in this paragraph and the next are those of KRETSCHMAR; references to the relevant passages of the *Studien zur früchristlichen Trinitätstheologie* are given at the appropriate places.
51. KRETSCHMAR himself has to admit: 'It is true that the actual word Wisdom is missing' (*op. cit.*, p. 36).
52. *Op. cit.*, p. 55.
53. With regard to the pre-existent Church in *II Clement* KRETSCHMAR himself writes: 'Explicit references to Wisdom are lacking' (p. 56); and again, in dealing with the *Epistle of the Apostles*: 'There is admittedly no reference here to a connection between Sophia and the Church' (p. 57). It is significant that the words 'missing' and 'lacking' should recur so often.

but a pre-existence of intention in God's plan. There certainly is an assimilation of the Church to Wisdom, but this is strictly a Gnostic doctrine, and in no sense a source of primitive Christian thought. Rather is it a corruption of the Jewish Christian doctrine, making the Church an aeon pre-existing in the Pleroma, and placing it on the same plane as Logos, Pneuma or Sophia.

This Gnostic doctrine is found in Theodotus as well as in Ptolemy. Of the former Clement records: 'The visible part of Jesus was Wisdom and the Church of the seeds . . ., as Theodotus says' (*Excerpt.* 26, 1). In this teaching the Church was regarded as the collection of spiritual 'seeds' which made up Sophia, while the Saviour was constituted by the whole body of angels.[54] Furthermore, the Great Notice in Irenaeus describes Ptolemy as identifying the Church and Wisdom in the same way. The Church on earth is therefore the pre-existent Church-Wisdom fallen from the Pleroma.

The *Treatise of the Three Natures*, as already noted, revealed an even more remarkable teaching, in which Ecclesia is identified with the Third Person of the primordial Triad. This is obviously based on Jewish Christian conceptions in which the Holy Ghost is identified with Sophia, and of which there is an echo in Theophilus and Irenaeus. This certainly made possible a radical identification of the Church and the Holy Spirit, but that conception is foreign to Jewish Christianity, and represents a wholly Gnostic speculation. The identification of the Church with Wisdom may therefore be regarded as a purely Gnostic doctrine, quite extraneous to Jewish Christianity.

Our examination of Jewish Christian ecclesiology may perhaps be summed up with the following remarks. This doctrine of the Church, for which *Hermas*, *II Clement* and Papias are the chief witnesses, derives one of its fundamental conceptions from Apocalyptic, in so far as the object of the latter is to show the pre-existence of eschatological realities in God's plan; and the traces of such an inspiration are already visible in the Pauline Captivity Epistles. The Jewish Christian theologians are, however, characterised by the introduction of this apocalyptic theology into an anagogical exegesis of the first chapters of *Genesis*, and it is this which seems to have been typical of Jewish gnosis in the first century after Christ.

54. Cf. ORBE, *op. cit.*, pp. 336–339.

CHAPTER ELEVEN

BAPTISM AND EUCHARIST

IT is probably in the organisation of worship that Jewish Christianity has made its deepest and most enduring mark on the Church. Half a century ago the Jewish origin of the general framework of Christian worship was usually contested. The sacraments were regarded as being influenced by the Hellenistic mysteries. Today the situation is quite different, especially in the light of the discoveries at Qumran. The *Sitz im Leben* of the first Christian liturgy must obviously be sought in the religious practices of Jewish communities of the Essene type,[1] for it is there that the closest parallels are to be found to the practices of baptismal initiation, the setting of the Institution of the Eucharist, the hours of prayer, and the ritual of festivals.

Many of these practices endured in the Hellenistic Church, though in some cases a different interpretation was put upon their symbolism. But the change from the Semitic to the Greek world involved profound modifications. Living water was no longer of obligation for Baptism, the Eucharist was separated from the common meal, the arrangement of the liturgical year was upset by the Greco-Roman calendar, the practice of spiritual marriage became suspect. It is possible, however, by means of the documents and some surviving practices, especially in the Syriac communities, to discover some of the lost details that gave Jewish Christian liturgy its distinctive character; and it is more especially on these features that attention will be concentrated, some indication also being given of the Jewish Christian origin of such practices as have endured.

One ought clearly to speak of Jewish Christian 'liturgies' rather than of one liturgy, for liturgical development moved from diversity to uniformity.[2] Thus there are practices that might have belonged to one Jewish Christian

1. Cf. DANIÉLOU, 'La communauté à Qumran et l'organisation de l'Église ancienne', *La Bible et l'Orient*, 1955, pp. 104–115.
2. As BAUMSTARK has shown: *Liturgie comparée*, pp. 12–20.

group and not to another. This is manifestly true, for example, in the matter of the opposing opinions on the question of the obligation, toleration or rejection of the Jewish customs of the sabbath or circumcision. It is wise, therefore, to be wary of generalising about Jewish Christianity as a whole simply on the evidence of certain texts. However, there is a certain overlapping of ideas in the various authors which permits of piecing together the primitive material of the Palestinian liturgy of Jerusalem by way of its later developments. The first topic for consideration must be the theology of the sacraments as it is to be seen in Jewish Christian texts.

CHRISTIAN INITIATION

There can be no doubt that Christian Baptism is related to Jewish customs. It is directly connected with the baptism of John the Baptist, and he in his turn depended on his Jewish environment. Having established thus much, however, there still remain several possible Jewish antecedents, which are not mutually exclusive since they could each have exerted an influence at different moments in history. It seems as though the baptism of John the Baptist is especially closely connected with the eschatological prophecies on the pouring out of living water[3]; but this does not prevent its showing signs of contact with the Essene initiation, which consisted of the first participation in the ritual bath of the community. There is, therefore, a connection between the origins of Christian Baptism and the baptist movement in first-century Palestine. Nor is it impossible that Christian Baptism may have borrowed certain practices from the baptism of proselytes, as, for example, in the case of the baptismal ritual of the *Didache*, which even if not initially inspired by it, seems to have imitated the Jewish ritual for proselyte baptism.[4] The question here, however, is not the Jewish origin of baptism, which nobody doubts, but what baptismal practices were the usage of Jewish Christianity, and whether they were later lost or preserved.

One of the basic features seems to have been a preparatory instruction. This may have been at first quite short. Thus in the *Acts* Philip contented himself with explaining a chapter of Isaiah to the Candace's eunuch before baptising him in the living water of the river (8:35–36). Moreover, Jewish usages do not seem to have exerted an influence on the most primitive

3. Cf. LAMPE, *The Seal of the Spirit*, pp. 25–27.
4. Cf. BENOIT, *Le baptême chrétien au Second Siècle*, p. 31.

practice, but to have appeared only when the need was felt of giving some kind of organisation to the sacraments instituted by Christ. This organisation is to be found in the *Didache*, where the relevant part of the work begins with a Treatise on the Two Ways, which is a catechism in preparation for baptism, and concludes with these words: 'But concerning baptism, thus shall ye baptise. Having first taught all these things' (VII, 1).

This preparatory catechesis was certainly necessary for its own sake, without its having to be derived from Judaism, but nevertheless, once it existed, it was natural that people should take their inspiration from the analogous institutions which Judaism had to offer. There are in this case two possible derivations. One is from the practice in the baptism of proselytes,[5] which included a preparatory instruction; but it must be admitted that there is not a great deal of information on this subject. The other is from the initiation ritual of the Zadokite order, as this is known from the *Rule of the Community*. Here the details are clear: he who wishes to enter the community must first be instructed for a year; if he is accepted he is admitted to the ritual bath (VI, 13-23cf. III, 9).

Perhaps the most remarkable and decisive piece of evidence in this connection is the actual content of the Jewish Christian pre-baptismal catechesis. There are quite a number of documents which make it possible to reconstruct its chief elements and establish its Jewish origin. The first is obviously the *Didache*. This begins by explaining the existence of the Two Ways: 'There are Two Ways, one of life and one of death' (I, 1); then comes the declaration of the way of life: 'First of all thou shalt love the God that made thee; secondly, thy neighbour as thyself.' And the second rule is: 'And that which thou wouldst not have befall thyself, neither do thou unto another' (I, 2). The second part of the *Epistle of Barnabas* expounds a treatise of the Two Ways on exactly the same lines, adding that 'on the one are stationed the light-giving angels of God, on the other the angels of Satan' (XVIII, 1). The first commandment is: 'Thou shalt Love Him that made thee' (XIX, 2). *I Clement* records a teaching attributed to the Lord: 'Have mercy that ye may receive mercy; . . . As ye do, so shall it be done to you; as ye give, so shall it be given unto you; with what measure ye mete, it shall be measured withal to you' (XIII, 2).

At the end of the *Paedagogus* Clement of Alexandria gives a different form of this instruction. His version, which he calls a résumé ($\kappa\epsilon\varphi\alpha\lambda\alpha\iota\dot{\omega}\delta\eta s$

5. Cf. A. BENOIT, *op. cit.*, pp. 13-14; cf. also DAVIES, *Paul and Rabbinic Judaism*, pp. 111-146.

ἐπιδρομή) of Christian morality begins with a quotation from *I Pet.*
1:17–19 and 4:3 (III, 12:85), followed by an allusion to Baptism (ἀνα-
γεννηθέντες). The instruction, intended for those who are still spiritually
children, begins with a statement of the Two Ways: 'I lead thee by the way
(ὁδός) of salvation. Depart from (ἀπόστα) the paths (ὁδοί) of deceit.'
There follows an exposition of the good Way, which is summed up
(κεφαλαιώδης) in one all-embracing word: 'As ye would that men should
do unto you, do ye likewise to them.' Again, 'We may sum up the commandments in these two sayings: "Thou shalt love the Lord thy God with
all thy heart, with all thy soul and all thy strength; and thy neighbour as
thyself." ' Clement then expounds the commandments in detail according
to the Law and the Gospel.[6]

The *Clementine Homilies* provide a final example. They speak of a baptismal catechesis given by Peter to the inhabitants of Tyre[7] which includes
first of all an exposition of the doctrine of the Two Spirits: 'From the
beginning was a law laid by God, the Creator of all things, on each of the
two princes, him of the right hand and him of the left . . .' (VII, 3). Until
now the Tyrians had followed the way of death; now they may recover
life. Peter then gives the conditions for this:

Pray to Him (God); abstain from the table of devils; do not taste dead
flesh; do not touch blood; purify yourselves by washings; and the rest
in one word—let each man be minded to do to his neighbour those
good things he wishes for himself. You would not like to be murdered;
do not murder another man; you would not like any of your things to
be stolen from you; steal nothing from another (VII, 4).

Then follows a second catechesis for the Sidonians, consisting of a treatise
of the Two Ways (VII, 7), followed by certain precepts (VII, 8).

The contents of the precepts in the first passage correspond almost
exactly with the Apostolic decree in *Acts* 15.[8] This decree was therefore
used, at least in some groups as a catechetical instruction. But very soon the

6. For IRENAEUS this double commandment constitutes the λόγος συντετμημένος
proclaimed by *Is.* 10:23 (*Dem.* 87).
7. According to STRECKER (*op. cit.*, pp. 69–70) this passage does not form part of the
Preaching of Peter, but of the *Grundschrift*, which comes from the third century. It does
not, however, for that reason, as MOLLAND has seen, contain any fewer archaic Jewish
Christian elements.
8. Cf. MOLLAND, 'La circoncision, le baptême et l'autorité du décret apostolique', *ST*,
IX, 1955, pp. 25–33, which should be supplemented by B. HEMMERDINGER, 'Trois
nouveaux fragments grecs du Livre III de Saint Irénée', *Scriptorium*, x, 1956, pp. 268 f.

ritual character of its prescriptions was no longer understood, and it was taken more in a moral sense. This development may be observed in other passages of the Clementines (*Rec.* IV, 36). It should be noted nevertheless that traces of the original ritual aspect have endured. Thus the *Didache* speaks of abstaining from things offered to idols (VI, 3), a relic of the archaic period. It has also been noted that 'to this little moral treatise the Golden Rule'[9] was very soon added. The latter is found elsewhere in the Clementines (*Hom.* II, 6; XII, 32; *Rec.* VIII, 56).

All these documents clearly belong to a standard type of instruction connected with Baptism, and their elements are all either Jewish Christian, like the Apostolic decree, or Jewish. The doctrine of the Two Ways bears distinctly the mark of the Qumran catechesis. The Golden Rule: 'That which thou wouldst not have befall thyself, do not thou to another', is the negative version of a formula already familiar to the New Testament; indeed, the very fact that it is the negative form, as distinct from the Dominical, is significant, for it was this negative version which, though not to be found in the Old Testament, was the one taught by Hillel, and represented the norm of all morality for Jewish catechetical instruction.[10]

Finally, the formula of the two commandments, even though it appears in *Mt.* 22:37–39, is a grouping together of *Deut.* 6:5 (the *Shema*) and *Lev.* 19:18 which had already been made in Judaism. It is an element of Jewish catechesis taken over by the New Testament.[11]

The rest of the instructions naturally contain specifically Christian elements, borrowed especially from the Sermon on the Mount, but they also include material of Jewish origin, such as the allusion to simplicity (ἁπλότης) so dear to the Essenes (*Barn.* XIX, 2); and the most important point of all is that the Gospel material is presented in Jewish forms. The text of Clement of Rome is typical in this regard.[12] It is also a striking

9. MOLLAND, *op. cit.*, p. 28.
10. Cf. D. DAUBE, *The NT and Rabbinic Judaism*, pp. 109, 124.
11. It appears frequently in the *Testaments* (*Iss.* V, 2; VII, 6; *Dan.* V, 3; *Benj.* III, 3). Cf. PAUL WINTER, 'Zadokite Fragments IV, 20–21', *ZNW*, LXVIII, 1956, p. 72. The *Testaments* represent the transition from the Jewish to the Christian catechesis. H. KÖSTER (*op. cit.*, p. 71) sees in the two-commandment formula a Christian feature; if this view is correct, it would be yet another argument for the Christian character of the *Testaments*.
12. Thus MASSAUX can write: 'For these reasons we believe that Clement drew on a source whose compilers were inspired by Matthew. This was probably a kind of catechism summing up the teaching of Christ' (*Influence de l'Évangile de Saint Matthieu sur la littérature chrétienne avant Irénée*, p. 13). Cf. also H. KÖSTER, *op. cit.*, pp. 159–173.

feature of the passages quoted from the *Clementine Homilies* that while the content is that of the Gospel, the formularisation follows the negative pattern of Hillel's rule. In the same way Clement of Alexandria begins by quoting *I Peter* which is a typically Christian catechesis,[13] but then in his summary he adopts the schema of the Two Ways.

Taken together all these observations suggest that there did exist in Apostolic times a purely Christian catechesis, the elements of which are given by the New Testament in *I Peter* and the Pauline *Epistles*. Later, however, in Jewish Christian circles, and certainly from the first in Palestine, there was a desire to organise this catechesis according to a common and simple norm; and for this the Jewish Christians borrowed the framework of the Jewish catechesis, the teaching of the Two Ways. This does not mean that the doctrine of the Two Ways had not already influenced the New Testament, but that the use of a pattern consisting of the Two Ways, the Golden Rule, and the two great commandments as a framework for catechetical instruction was non-apostolic and specifically Jewish Christian.[14]

The preparation for Baptism therefore included a preparatory instruction of plainly Jewish character; but it also had its ascetic aspect, a number of texts attesting the requirement of a fast. The *Didache* says explicitly: 'Before the baptism let him that baptiseth and him that is baptised fast, and any others also who are able; and thou shalt order him that is baptised to fast a day or two before' (VII, 4). The *First Apology* of Justin gives evidence of the same practice: 'As many as . . . believe that what we teach and say is true, and undertake to be able to live accordingly, are instructed to pray, and to entreat God with fasting for the remission of their sins that are past, we praying and fasting with them' (*I Apol.* LXI, 2).[15] In addition to the fast, Justin's text confirms the existence of the pre-baptismal catechesis. This catechesis appears to terminate in a personal commitment,

13. Cf. E. G. SELWYN, *The First Epistle of St. Peter*, London 1947, pp. 363–467; E. BOISMARD, 'Une liturgie baptismale dans la Prima Petri', *RB*, LXIII, 1956, pp. 182–208; F. L. CROSS, *I Peter, A Baptismal Liturgy*, 1954.

14. Side by side with the moral catechesis there was a dogmatic catechesis, parts of which are to be found in *Barnabas*, Justin's *Dialogue* and the *Demonstratio* of Irenaeus: cf. G. SCHILLE, 'Katechese und Taufliturgie', *ZNW*, LI, 1960, pp. 112–131; 'Zur urchristlichen Tauflehre', in *ZNW*, XLIX, 1958, pp. 31–52.

15. Cf. also the practice of the Valentinians: 'It is for this reason (to send demons away) that there are fastings, supplications, prayers, (impositions) of hands, kneelings' (CLEM. ALEX., *Exc. Theod.* 84, 1). Cf. also SAGNARD, *op. cit.*, p. 234, who shows that this text gives evidence of Christian practices in the middle of the second century.

and would seem, therefore, to be concerned with the general instruction and not the immediate preparation. For Justin the essential constituent of the immediate preparation would be the fasts and prayers.

The practice of fasting is obviously of Jewish origin, but the Jewish origin of the pre-baptismal fast is further confirmed by its presence in the *Pseudo-Clementines*. There is a passage in the *Recognitions* which is rather curious: the mother of the two young people asks to be baptised at once. Peter answers: 'She must fast at least one day first and so be baptised; and this because I have heard from her a certain declaration, by which her faith has been made manifest to me . . . otherwise she would have been instructed and taught many days before' (VII, 34). Thus the preparation would have to last normally for some weeks. Peter agrees to reduce it, but at least one day's fast is necessary. The *Didache* also demands the same as a minimum (VII, 4).[16]

What was the significance of this fast? Justin makes its object 'the remission of sins' (*I Apol.* LXI, 2). The fast is clearly linked with some kind of purification. Now in contemporary Judaism purification involved not only interior conversion, but also deliverance from demons, and this was especially important in the case of pagans. The author of *Barnabas* writes: 'Before we believed on God, the abode of our heart was . . . a house of demons' (XVI, 7). The best interpretation would, therefore, seem to be that 'Judaism attributed to fasting the power of casting out devils. This would bring us to the origins of the later baptismal exorcism'.[17] Justin associates fasting with prayer, and this recalls *Mt.* 17:21: 'This kind (of devil) is not cast out save by prayer and fasting.'

There is one more element in the preparation for Baptism that seems to be suggested by these texts.[18] It will be remembered that Clement of Alexandria writes regarding the Two Ways: 'I lead thee by the way of salvation; renounce (ἀπόστα) the paths of error.' Justin speaks of an undertaking to observe the precepts, which is made before the immediate preparation for Baptism, and also describes converts as renouncing

16. It may be noted that the time of probation at Qumran involved 'practising temperance' (JOSEPHUS, *Bell.* II, 8:7[138]).
17. A. BENOIT, *op. cit.*, p. 11. This seems to be confirmed by *Exc. Theod.* 84, where the pre-baptismal fast, combined with prayer, has the object of casting out devils. On the link between fasting and exorcism cf. H. MUSURILLO, 'The Problem of Ascetical Fasting in the Greek Patristic Writers', *Traditio*, XII, 1956, pp. 19-23.
18. The imposition of hands will also be observed (*Hom. Clem.* III, 73; *Exc. Theod.* 84, 1).

(ἀπετάξαντο) idols and adhering (ἀνέθηκαν) to Christ.[19] The *Shepherd* declares: 'It is good to follow (ἀκολουθεῖν) the angel of righteousness and to renounce (ἀποτάξασθαι) the angel of wickedness' (*Mand.* VI, 2:9). The expression used by Hermas and Justin was to become the technical term for the renunciation (ἀπόταξις) of Satan and his angels, as is already attested by Tertullian (*De spect.* 4) in the pre-baptismal rites which he describes.

This seems to be an allusion to a rite of renouncing Satan and adhering to Christ which was already spoken of as an ancient tradition at the end of the second century.[20] It is even possible that the holding out of the hand which, according to Cyril of Jerusalem,[21] used to accompany this rite in the Syriac Church is to be seen in the opening of one of the *Odes of Solomon*, 'My arms I lifted up on high, even to the grace of the Lord' (XXI, 1). The gesture is in fact not the same as that for praying with arms outstretched, which is mentioned elsewhere in the text. It may be noted also that Saint Basil mentions the renunciation of Satan as one of the παραδόσεις (*De Sp. Sanct.* 27). Now it seems likely that παράδοσις will have the same meaning in the Fathers, whether it is applied to beliefs or customs, and be used of material handed down from the Apostolic period, that is, of Jewish Christian origin.

This last point is the one of immediate concern. There are two elements which seem to indicate that the practice had some connection with the Qumran community. First of all, in the *Rule of the Community*, incorporation into the community was preceded by a double oath: 'He shall bind himself by an oath to submit to the law of Moses' (*DSD* V, 8) and: 'Let him bind himself by the covenant to separate himself from all men of evil ways' (V, 10).[22] This constitutes the closest known analogy to the Christian renunciation of Satan and adherence to Christ. That *Hermas* uses the technical term ἀποτάσσειν in relation to the Essene doctrine of the two angels has already been noted. It seems, therefore, as if the actual formula of the renunciation may come from the Essene ritual. Only the content of the undertaking is changed: its object is no longer the 'Law of Moses', but the 'precepts that have been taught'.

19. *I Apol.* XLIX, 5. Cf. also *II Clem.* VI, 4–5 with ἀποτάσσεσθαι.
20. Cf. BERNARD, *The Odes of Solomon*, p. 90. REICKE sees a mention of the practice as early as *I Pet.* 3:21 (*op. cit.*, p. 185); cf. also SELWYN, *The First Epistle of Peter*, pp. 205–206.
21. *Cat. Myst.* I, 2.
22. This evidence is confirmed by JOSEPHUS (*Bell.* II, 8:7[139]).

It may be concluded that the Jewish Christian texts reveal a complete preparation for Baptism, containing: a moral instruction arranged on the plan of the Two Ways; a period of fasting; a personal undertaking to observe the precepts that have been taught, and to break with the old life. Moreover, this whole pattern is found in basic outline, and even in certain precise details, in the *Rule of the Community* of Qumran, with the difference that there it is duplicated to cover the two degrees of initiation. It is legitimate, therefore, to conclude that the whole was used and adapted by the Jewish Christians in Palestine when they had to organise a course of preparation for Baptism; but this does not necessarily imply that Baptism itself was connected with the Qumran sect.

BAPTISMAL RITES

Next to be considered is the act of baptism itself, though not the origin of the sacrament, since that goes back to the direct institution of Christ. It has already been remarked that the Christian rite derived from the baptism of John, which probably had an eschatological meaning.[23] The concern of this section will be with the particular Jewish Christian forms of the rite.

A good starting point is the following text from the *Didache*:

> But concerning Baptism, thus shall ye baptise. . . . Baptise in the name of the Father and of the Son and of the Holy Spirit. . . . But if thou hast not living water, then baptise in other water; and if thou art not able in cold, then in warm. But if thou hast neither, then pour water on the head thrice in the name of the Father and of the Son and of the Holy Spirit (VII, 1–3).

The baptismal formula and the triple effusion are purely Christian and in no way Jewish. As regards the practice of Baptism by immersion, it is true that this was so with Jewish baptisms, both in the case of proselytes and in the Qumran purification; but it is in fact a general feature, and was to be the practice in a pagan environment also. What is more interesting is the reference to living water, which assumes that baptism is given in a river or some running water (cf. *Acts* 8:36). It is presented as the primitive and preferred usage,[24] although it is allowed that any water may suffice,

23. Cf. LAMPE, *The Seal of the Spirit*, p. 26.
24. Cf. T. KLAUSER, 'Taufet in lebendigem Wasser! Zum religions- und kulturgeschichtlichen Verständnis von Didache, VII, 1–3', *Pisciculi*, pp. 157–165.

and, if there be only a small quantity, that effusion may replace immersion. The same direction as to the use of living water appears in the Clementine *Recognitions* (VI, 15), which also refer to Baptism given in the sea (IV, 32; VII, 38: cf. also *Acts of Peter* 5). Apart from these direct references, there is probably an allusion to this feature in the fact that Baptism is denoted by the expression 'living waters' in a number of texts. Thus one of the *Odes of Solomon* which is in all probability an invitation to Baptism begins as follows: 'Fill ye waters for yourselves from the living fountain of the Lord' (XXX, 1).[25]

The rite of immersion in living water seems to have been accompanied in the Jewish Christian era by complementary ceremonies. First, there is the mention of a pre-baptismal anointing with oil in a passage of the *Testament of Levi* which purports to describe the installation of the High Priest, but which is in fact a symbolic description of the baptismal initiation.[26] The passage runs as follows: 'The first anointed me with holy oil; ... the second washed (ἔλουσε) me with pure water, and fed me with the consecrated (ἅγιον) bread and wine, and clad me with a holy and glorious robe' (VIII, 4–5).

Certain details here might possibly call to mind the Messianic banquet described in one of the Qumran fragments,[27] but it certainly looks as though the passage as a whole could apply only to Christian initiation. The point of immediate interest is the recurrence of the pre-baptismal anointing with holy oil. It is at first sight curious that this should precede the actual baptism, the more so as the reference is certainly to an anointing with consecrated oil; but whereas Western custom places this rite after the baptism, in the Syriac liturgy it occurs beforehand.[28] Here once again it would seem that the Syriac liturgy shows traces of archaic usages and preserves Jewish Christian features.[29]

These are the two most detailed witnesses on the subject of the anointing in the Jewish Christian ritual, but there are others to confirm the fact of its

25. Cf. BERNARD, *op. cit.*, p. 114.
26. Cf. T. W. MANSON, 'Miscellanea apocalyptica', III, *JTS*, XLVIII, 1947, pp. 59–61. DE JONGE has also adopted this hypothesis: *The Testaments of the Twelve Patriarchs*, p. 128.
27. Cf. BARTHÉLEMY–MILIK, *Qumran Cave I*, p. 117.
28. Cf. DE JONGE, *op. cit.*, p. 128.
29. This position before baptism might seem also to corroborate the thesis of Gregory DIX, who held that the Christian initiation reproduced the order of the initiation of proselytes, so that the anointing corresponded to circumcision; but there is nothing in the texts under consideration to justify such a parallelism: cf. LAMPE, *op. cit.*, p. 114.

existence. On the one hand, the Coptic text of the *Didache* includes after the Eucharist the text of a prayer of consecration of the oil ($\mu\acute{\nu}\rho o\nu$) (X, 7).[30] There is an indication of the same kind among the Gnostics: 'The bread and the oil are sanctified ($\mathring{\alpha}\gamma\iota\acute{\alpha}\zeta\epsilon\tau\alpha\iota$)' (*Exc. Theod.* 82), and such a consecration appears to be implied by the expression 'holy ($\mathring{\alpha}\gamma\iota o\nu$) oil' which came in the *Testament of Levi*. It seems therefore that while there is no question in Jewish Christianity of consecrating baptismal water—the first allusion to such a consecration is in Ignatius of Antioch (*Eph.* XVIII, 2), and the notion seems indeed quite incompatible with the idea of baptising in rivers or in the sea—in the case of the oil an epiclesis was pronounced, comparable to that over the bread and the wine. This is no doubt connected with the conception of anointing with holy oil in Judaism.

On the other hand, the existence of an anointing of some kind, even though its precise purpose is not clear, is presupposed by allusions in authors who were either Jewish Christians themselves or in some way dependent on Jewish Christianity.[31] Theophilus of Antioch writes: 'Are you unwilling to be anointed with the oil of God? Why, this is the very reason, as I think, that we are called Christians, because we are anointed with the oil of God' (I, 12). Anointings also play a large part in Gnostic rituals. Irenaeus mentions them several times: after baptism some 'anoint the initiated person with balsam, for they assert that this unguent is a type of sweet odour which is beyond all things' (*Adv. haer.* I, 21:3). Others replace baptism by an anointing 'on the head with oil mixed with water' (I, 21:4).[32]

It has been acutely observed that 'all these features are like tracings of rites used in the Church'.[33] Yet they raise an interesting question. It has been suggested that the anointing spoken of in Jewish Christian texts was a special rite associated with the outpouring of the Holy Spirit, whereas the object of Baptism was simply to remove sins. Now this is certainly not true of Jewish Christianity, in which the anointing plays a subsidiary role

30. Cf. PETERSON, 'Über einige Probleme der Didache-Überlieferung', *RivAC*, XXVII, 1952, pp. 46–54.
31. Cf. *Odes of Solomon* XXXVI, 5 (BERNARD, p. 121).
32. According to Hippolytus the Naassenians held that at baptism man 'is washed in living water and anointed with ineffable ointment' (*Elench.* V, 7: 19). Cf. also the inscription of Flavia Sophe: 'Anointed in the baths of Christ with the sacred unction.' On the Gnostic character of the inscription cf. QUISPEL, 'L'inscription de Flavia Sophè', *Mél. de Ghellinck.*, I, 1951, pp. 205–214.
33. BENOIT, *op. cit.*, p. 203, quoting DUCHESNE; cf. also QUISPEL, *op. cit.*, pp. 212–213.

whose meaning is not clear. It is Baptism which gives the Holy Ghost. It is true on the other hand that such a distinction is found among the Gnostics and is associated with a certain depreciation of Baptism, anointing then becoming the sacrament of the perfect (*Adv. haer.* I, 21:2–3). This conception was to influence third-century writers, especially Tertullian, but Clement of Alexandria condemned it as a Gnostic error,[34] as did Irenaeus.[35] This leaves two questions still unsolved: the significance of the baptismal anointing, and the existence of a sacrament of Confirmation distinct from Baptism.

The text of the *Testament of Levi* spoke of putting on a garment.[36] Baptism by immersion obviously involved stripping off the tunic and dressing again afterwards. It seems, however, that in the Jewish Christian period this simple action was given a ritual significance, in particular through the symbolism of re-clothing with a white tunic after Baptism. In addition to the evidence of the *Testament of Levi* this seems to be presupposed by several allusions in the *Odes of Solomon*: 'I stripped off (folly) and cast it from me; and the Lord renewed me with His raiment' (XI, 9–10).[37] 'I have put on incorruption through his name: and have put off corruption by his grace' (XV, 8)[38]; 'I put off darkness and clothed myself with light' (XXI, 2).[39]

These texts raise a question. They may only have a symbolical meaning: the putting off of sin and the putting on of grace. It is, nevertheless, remarkable that in the *Clementines* Baptism is called 'garment' ($\H\epsilon\nu\delta\nu\mu\alpha$) (*Hom.* VIII, 22; *Rec.* IV, 36), and that this feature was to recur (*Const. Apost.* VIII, 6), 'garment' becoming a regular name for the sacrament.[40]

34. Cf. Orbe, 'Teologia bautismal de Clement Alejandrino', *Gregorianum*, xxxvi, 1955, pp. 410–448.
35. Benoit is right in saying with regard to the anointing and the imposition of hands: 'Irenaeus, agreeing in this regard with the other Fathers of the second century, does not allow these rites any importance in his teaching on baptism' (*op. cit.*, p. 208). Later we will have the same remark to make with regard to the *sphragis*.
36. *II Enoch* may be inspired by a baptismal ritual when it writes concerning Enoch's entry into the seventh heaven: 'And Michael stripped me of my garments and anointed me with the good oil' (XXII, 9).
37. Cf. Bernard, p. 72.   38. Cf. Bernard, p. 78.
39. Cf. Bernard, p. 90. Cf. also XXV, 8: 'I was clothed with the covering of thy good Spirit, and thou didst remove from me my raiment of skins' (Bernard, p. 167). The theme of the stripping off in Baptism of the skin-tunics of *Gn.* 3:21 was to prove a popular one; cf. Daniélou, *Bible et Liturgie*, pp. 53–57.
40. Cf. Daniélou, 'Catéchèse pascale et retour au Paradis', *Maison-Dieu*, xlv, 1956, p. 115.

But does not this name express a real rite, the putting on of a white robe and the laying aside of the old garments?[41] This seems to be presupposed by the text of the *Testament of Levi*, where there is presumably yet another example of Essene influence, since Josephus records that those who were allowed to enter on the first probation were clothed in a white garment.[42] Hermas also mentions a white garment in a baptismal context (*Sim.* VIII, 2:3–4), and associates it with the σφραγίς (VIII, 2:4).

The rite of the white garment is probably then of Jewish Christian origin, but it survived longer than its source. It seems, however, to have been accompanied in the Jewish Christian liturgy by another rite, which could not be preserved in a pagan environment, the coronation. No explicit description of this rite is extant, but it seems to be indicated by the *Odes of Solomon*: 'The Lord is on my head like a crown and I shall not be without Him. A crown of truth has been woven for me' (I, 1–2).[43]

It will be observed that the garment and the crown appear to be related elsewhere in Jewish Christian circles. Thus in the *Ascension of Isaiah*, 'The garments and the crown' are laid out in the seventh heaven, that Isaiah may put them on when he arrives there; they symbolise the glory of the Elect (VII, 22; cf. also VIII, 26; IX, 25). The crown represents a higher beatitude than the garment (IX, 12),[44] a symbolism which must be a product of ritual practice. The *Testament of Levi* links the garment with the crown in a baptismal context (VIII, 5–9),[45] while a passage from *Hermas* describes the Angel of the Lord as giving palm crowns to some, and to others garments and a seal (σφραγίς) (*Sim.* VIII, 2:1–4), before he brings them into the Tower which is the Church.[46] This refers to the heavenly Church, but the mention of the σφραγίς, which denotes baptism

41. LAMPE, *op. cit.*, p. 112, accepts this.
42. *Bell.* II, 8:7 [137]. Cf. LAMPE, *op. cit.*, pp. 112–113; DANIÉLOU, *op. cit.*, pp. 113–119. Cf. also the allusion to the putting on of a white garment after the ritual purifications in the Temple, *Pap. Oxyr.* V, 840, l. 27; commentary by J. JEREMIAS, *Conj. neotest.*, XI, pp. 103–104, and in *Unbekannte Worte Jesu*, pp. 42–44.
43. BERNARD (*op. cit.*, p. 45) again refers to the Syrian rite, in which the neophyte was crowned with flowers. LAMPE accepts this hypothesis: 'The neophyte (for the author of the *Odes*) is apparently crowned with a garland symbolising the presence of Christ, like a crown on the head of the believer' (*op. cit.*, p. 112).
44. Cf. RENDEL HARRIS, *The Odes of Solomon*, p. 45; also *Psalms of Thomas* IX, 13–14.
45. Cf. also 'Apocalypse of Peter', *ROC*, V, 1910, pp. 317, 319.
46. ORIGEN speaks of a book in which 'all the believers receive a crown of willow' (*Hom. Ezek.* I, 5), though this seems to be some other book than the *Shepherd* of Hermas. The presence of the rite of of coronation in the Mandaean baptism ritual should also be noted; cf. E. SEGELBERG, *Masbūtā*, p. 61.

in *Hermas*, seems to indicate that the conception has been borrowed from the baptismal ritual.

The symbolism of 'the garment and the crown' as representing eschatological blessings recalls the Qumran manuscripts (*DSD* IV, 7–8); but it is the passage from *Hermas* which may well identify the origin of the rite. The context is that of the Feast of Tabernacles with its pouring out of water (*Sim.* VIII, 2:8), and the presentation of willow-branches to the Priests (*Sim.* VIII, 3:4). Now the use of palm-crowns is also connected with the customs of the Feast.[47] This would explain their appearance in the *Revelation* of John, which is inspired by the Feast of Tabernacles, and in which white robes, branches (of palms) and living water (7:9–17) also feature, as well as the eschatological character of the crown in the *Ascension of Isaiah*. Now the Feast of Tabernacles played an important role in the Qumran community, and it seems also, as will be noted later, that it was not without its importance in Jewish Christianity, where it was certainly a baptismal festival. The practice of crowning the neophytes therefore could be a Jewish Christian adaptation of one of the customs of the Jewish Feast of Tabernacles.[48]

Another interesting point about this ritual is that it seems to be a typical example of a practice which Christianity was obliged to abandon when it moved into pagan society. In such a society the wearing of the crown had idolatrous implications. It was worn by the pagan priests; and the award of a crown to a soldier was in the nature of a cultic act, which is the reason why Tertullian condemns the practice in the *De Corona Militum*. Under these conditions it is clear that the wearing of a crown would appear somewhat equivocal to the baptised persons, and might seem to put Baptism on the same plane as the worship of idols.[49] Hence it completely dis-

47. Cf. *Jub.* XVI, 30: 'It was laid down that they should celebrate the Feast (sc. of Tabernacles) dwelling in booths, wearing *crowns* on their heads, and holding leafy branches and boughs of willow', with which may be compared TACITUS, *Hist.* V, 10: 'The Jewish priests used to wear crowns of ivy.' In this connection E. GOODENOUGH cites the inscription of Berenice (*Jewish Symbols*, II, pp. 143 f.), and further (III, p. 471; IV, p. 157) observes that the crown is often associated with the *lulāb* (cf. Glossary s.v.) on Jewish monuments. On the use of crowns in Judaism cf. *Jdt.* 15:13 (LXX); *III Mac.* VII, 16: also I. ABRAHAMS, *Studies in Pharisaism and the Gospels*, Cambridge 1917, I, pp. 169–170; H. RIESENFELD, *Jésus Transfiguré*, 1947, pp. 48–51; C. H. KRAELING, *The Excavations of Doura-Europos: Final Report*, VIII, 1, pp. 114–115.

48. *Odes of Solomon* XX, 7–8: 'Come into Paradise, and make thee a garland from its tree and put it on thy head', suggests that the crown was a crown of leaves.

49. BÜCHLER ('La fête des Tabernacles chez Tacite et Plutarque', *REJ*, XXXVII, 1898, p. 196) sees a Greek influence in the origin of this practice, but it is difficult to reconcile this with the fact that the crowns are mentioned in *Jubilees*.

appeared. Similar problems arose in connection with other rites, and certain Jewish practices were also abandoned for the same reasons.[50]

There is a final question to be considered regarding the post-baptismal rite of the *sphragis*, a question that has been much debated in recent years. However, certain points seem to have been established. First, in archaic texts the word σφραγίς does not denote a special act distinct from baptism and connected with the outpouring of the Spirit; and in particular there is no ground for seeing a parallelism between a Jewish circumcision-baptism and a Christian *sphragis*-baptism. The term *sphragis* refers to baptism itself, and this is the outpouring of the Spirit.[51] The sum of the evidence in archaic texts is decisive in this regard. The word σφραγίς is found with this meaning in Saint Paul (*Eph.* 1:13; *II Cor.* 1:22) and in Jewish Christian authors such as *II Clement*,[52] or the *Shepherd* of Hermas,[53] which states: 'The seal then is the water' (*Sim.* IX, 16:4). The *Odes of Solomon* allude to it frequently (IV, 8; VIII, 16), and the *Epistle of the Apostles* also mentions it (41).[54]

Thus the *sphragis* is one of the names given to Baptism in the Jewish Christian community. The origin of this term ought probably to be looked for in Judaism. The word itself does indeed occur in a number of ancient texts to denote circumcision, as for example, *Rom.* 4:11, and *Barn.* IX, 6–8. Baptism is the *sphragis* in so far as, like circumcision, it is the sign which incorporates a person into the people of God.[55] Even in the Jewish Christian communities which retained the practice of circumcision, as they had done that of the Sabbath, it was Baptism which represented the true equivalent of circumcision.[56] This equation of Baptism with circumcision in Jewish Christian society justifies the opinion that the baptism of infants is a Jewish Christian custom, which would seem normal since the Jewish child was circumcised on the eighth day.[57] The practice was to disappear in pagan environments, and only reappeared at a later date.

50. Cf. GOODENOUGH, *Jewish Symbols*, IV, p. 157.
51. Cf. LAMPE, *op. cit.*, pp. 97–149.   52. Cf. BENOIT, *op. cit.*, pp. 97–112.
53. *Ibid.*, pp. 131–132.
54. Cf. also the phrase 'baptismo consignari' (= σφραγίζεσθαι) in *Clem. Rec.* VI, 8.
55. DIX was right in associating circumcision and *sphragis*, but he was mistaken in seeing the *sphragis* as something other than Baptism: 'The Seal in the Second Century', *Theology*, LI, 1948, p. 7.
56. E. MOLLAND, 'La circoncision, le baptême et l'autorité du décret apostolique', *ST* IX, 1955, pp. 8–14) has shown, against Schoeps, that this was the case with the Jewish Christians of the Clementines.
57. Cf. CULLMANN, *Baptism in the New Testament*, pp. 56–69, 76–79.

When all is said, however, it has still not been decided whether the word *sphragis* denoted a special rite within Baptism. The problem is parallel to that of the garment, which was a name given to Baptism as a whole, but by extension from a particular action. Is the case really the same with the *sphragis*? The term was later used to denote the sign of the Cross which was made on the foreheads of Christians, and this ceremony formed a part, and still forms a part, of the baptismal rites. It is necessary to decide, therefore, whether this custom goes back to Jewish Christianity.

Several texts seem at first to suggest that the *sphragis* really is a sign imprinted on the forehead, as, for example, *Odes of Solomon* VIII, 16: 'On their faces I set my seal.' It has been said of this text: 'There appears to be a reference to the use of the sign of the Cross in the baptismal ritual, and this sign set upon the newly baptised is related to the conception we have noted in the Apocalypse of the elect being visibly marked with the stamp of divine ownership on their forehead.'[58] This comparison is of the highest importance. It was noted in a previous chapter that for Ezekiel the sign with which the elect were marked was the *tau*, written + or ✕ ; and this is the sign of which the *Revelation* speaks. The question now arises, was this sign, which marked the members of the eschatological community with God's seal, the one used by the Jewish Christians? In all probability it was, since the relevant text from Ezekiel is mentioned in the *Damascus Document* (XIX, 12),[59] and the marking with the *tau* figured in Essene circles as the seal of the members of the eschatological community.

This practice must be considered in conjunction[60] with the expression 'bear the name', which refers in *Hermas* to Baptism (*Sim.* IX, 13:2–3). The Name in this expression is the Person of Christ, and therefore to 'bear the Name' could at that period mean to bear the sign of the deity, the *tau*. It is clear that in Greek circles this meaning of the *tau* was lost, and that it was for this reason interpreted either as referring to the Cross of Christ, to which the form + corresponded, or to the name $X\rho\iota\sigma\tau\delta s$ itself, the first letter of which resembled the form ✕. The expression 'bear the Cross' would then have been substituted for the more archaic and

58. Cf. LAMPE, *op. cit.*, p. 113.

59. Cf. TEICHER, 'The Christian Interpretation of the Sign X in the Isaiah Scroll', *VT*, v, 1955, p. 196.

60. For a detailed discussion of this topic, and the citation of the relevant evidence, cf. chap. 5 above, and in particular pp. 154 ff.

Jewish expression 'bear the name'.[61] In this case marking the forehead of the baptised, probably after baptism, would be a Jewish Christian practice related to the conception of Baptism as incorporation into the Messianic community—which is precisely the archaic conception, and in the Essene tradition. The sign used for the marking was the Hebrew *tau*, and the interpretation of this as the sign of the Cross originates in the mystique of the Cross as this existed in the Jewish Christian community. The first origins of the rite therefore derive from two stages in Jewish Christian history: the first, the eschatological community of Palestine, and the second, Syriac Jewish Christianity after A.D. 70.

These views are confirmed by the data left by the Valentinians. They took over and adapted Christian Baptism in a way which preserves many of its elements, and these of an archaic character. Close study of the doctrine of the $\sigma\phi\rho\alpha\gamma\ell\varsigma$ in the *Excerpta ex Theodoto*[62] shows that the seal is given in Baptism by the 'invocation of Father, Son and Holy Spirit' (80, 3); the baptised receives the seal as he goes down into the water. The seal, therefore, clearly refers to the baptism itself. In another passage it is stated that 'the faithful bear through Christ the Name of God as if it were an inscription. Even dumb animals show by the seal ($\sigma\phi\rho\alpha\gamma\ell\varsigma$) they bear whose property they are' (86, 2). Thus the Name of God is like the *sphragis*, the mark of ownership carried by animals. This seems to be a decisive indication that in Baptism the faithful were marked with the Name of God, and this sign could only have been the *tau*, which in Theodotus still kept its old meaning.

THE EUCHARIST

Jewish Christian texts describe the Christian initiation as concluding with the Eucharistic feast. Thus the *Testament of Levi* says: 'The second washed me with pure water and fed me ($\epsilon\psi\omega\mu\iota\sigma\epsilon\nu$) with consecrated ($\alpha\gamma\iota\rho\nu$) bread and wine' (VIII, 5). The text of the *Didache* inserts after the section dealing with Baptism a remark about the pre-baptismal fast, designed to distinguish it from ordinary fasts, and then proceeds to the instruction in the Our Father. The latter, however, resumes the account of the initiation procedure, for in the later Syriac catecheses this prayer

61. That is if the views of DINKLER ('Jesus Wort vom Kreuztragen', *Neut. Stud. Rud. Bultmann*, 1954, pp. 110–112) are to be accepted; cf. however, the reservations of E. GOODENOUGH, *Jewish Symbols*, I, pp. 131–132.
62. Cf. SAGNARD, *Extraits de Théodote*, pp. 234–239.

was only communicated after Baptism, and constituted the first prayer of the baptised. The *Didache* then goes on at once to deal with the Eucharist (IX, 1), which therefore falls naturally into place in the general framework of initiation.

The Jewish origins of the pattern of the Eucharistic prayer are well established,[63] but, as in the case of Baptism, it is not the basic structure of the Eucharist, whether as recorded in the original Jewish community, or as it has endured down to the present time, which is of immediate importance, but the special features which the Eucharist presented in the Jewish Christian environment, and which have since been lost or transformed. Now the clearest point here is the link between the Eucharist and the common meal, which is clearly to be seen in the ritual of the *Didache*. The latter includes first a eucharist over the wine (IX, 2), then another over the broken (κλάσας) bread (IX, 3). The sacramental character of this is emphasised: 'Let no one eat or drink of this Eucharist but they that have been baptised in the Name of the Lord; for concerning this also the Lord hath said: Give not that which is holy to the dogs' (IX, 5). Then comes a final thanksgiving preceded by the words: 'And after you are satisfied' (X, 1).

There are various opinions about this ritual. Is it the actual order of the Eucharist? Is it an adaptation of Eucharistic prayers for use at a meal? Whatever the case may be, the prayers certainly seem to be Eucharistic, a point to which it will be necessary to return. On the other hand, the structure equally certainly corresponds to that of a common meal: the blessing of a cup before the meal, followed by the eucharist over the wine, an order which seems to be the same as that of the Institution in *Luke*. In that case only the second and third thanksgivings would be sacramental. The link between the Eucharist and the meal is here very clearly marked, but this combination was quickly abandoned. Why this was so in Greek circles may be gathered from St. Paul's account of the abuses to which the practice gave rise at Corinth, while in Jewish Christian communities the feasts became hotbeds of Messianic enthusiasm.[64] Despite this, however, did any traces of these common meals survive into later times?

The most interesting data on this point come from the *Apostolic Tradition* of Hippolytus of Rome, who records that with the bread and the wine,

63. Cf. DANIÉLOU, 'La communauté de Qumran et l'organisation de l'Eglise ancienne', *La Bible et l'Orient*, p. 107.
64. Cf. REICKE, *Diakonie, Festfreude und Zelos*, p. 49. DIX is therefore right in supposing that the practice was abandoned by Jewish Christians after A.D. 70 (*Jew and Greek*, pp. 103–104).

sacraments of the body of Christ, the bishop blessed at Mass 'milk and honey mingled together' (23).[65] What is of importance here is not the symbolic meaning which Hippolytus gives to the rite—for this is secondary[66]—but that this symbolic meaning indicates a desire to give some interpretation of an action the natural meaning of which had been lost. Now the most natural meaning is that the action was a survival of a meal which had been associated with the Eucharist, or rather in the course of which the Eucharist had been consecrated. At the same time this text of Hippolytus justifies the interpretation of the various passages where Jewish Christian texts speak symbolically of milk and honey as allusions to this meal.

Such allusions are numerous. The *Epistle of Barnabas* (VI, 8-17) gives the same allegorical interpretation as the *Apostolic Tradition*, a fact which is enough by itself to make one suspect the existence of a real rite, since the *Epistle* tends to allegorise everything. If their baptismal character is admitted, however, the allusions in the *Odes of Solomon* are of greater value. Thus, for example, IV, 10 reads: 'Open thy rich fountains that pour forth to us milk and honey.'[67] In *Ode* XIX only milk is mentioned: 'A cup of milk was offered to me' (XIX, 1). It will be remembered that *I Pet.*, which is a baptismal catechesis, reads: 'As new-born babes, desire the sincere milk of the word' (2:2), and in the *Apostolic Tradition*, where the offering of milk is certainly present, the theme of 'little children' also appears (23) side by side with that of 'the land of promise'. Clement of Alexandria also combines the two themes (*Paed.* I, 6: 34-35).

Evidence may also be adduced here from authors who did not belong to the Great Church, since they, as has been said before, often preserve archaic practices. Tertullian states that the rite was practised by the Marcionites, which takes us back to the first half of the second century (*Adv. Marc.* I, 14). Moreover, Hippolytus records that the Naassenians make milk and honey the symbol of the food of the perfect. After quoting the passage from *Deut.* 31:20 about the 'land flowing with milk and honey' he adds: 'This . . . is the milk and honey by tasting which those that are perfect are liberated from all domination, and share in the Pleroma' (*Elench.*

---

65. Cf. N. A. DAHL, 'La terre où coulent le lait et le miel', *Aux Sources de la Tradition chrétienne, Mél. Goguel*, pp. 62-70.
66. Cf. also TERTULLIAN, *De Cor.* III, 3.
67. On this passage BERNARD (*op. cit.*, p. 53) comments: 'There are many traces in early Christian literature . . . of a rite of administering milk and honey to the newly baptised.'

V, 8: 30).[68] The fact that the Naassenians interpret the rite as referring to the food of the perfect would seem to imply knowledge of its existence. All these evidences, therefore, suggest that the Eucharist, which was originally connected with the common meal in the first community, continued throughout the whole Jewish Christian epoch to imply at least a participation in milk and honey.[69]

A second area of investigation is that of the actual composition of the Eucharistic prayers. The *Didache* has preserved two, one over the wine and the other over the bread, which have been shown to be Jewish Christian. 'They are fragments of an ancient christological hymn formerly used by the Jewish Christians of Palestine, and we find in them a very ancient form of Jewish Christian epiclesis.'[70] There are indeed numerous Jewish Christian features, a few of which must now be considered.

The text begins with these words: 'We give Thee thanks, O our Father, for the holy vine of Thy servant David, which Thou madest known unto us through Thy servant Jesus' (IX, 2). The conception of Israel as the vine of the Lord is eminently Biblical,[71] while the allusion to David also indicates the Jewish background.[72]

Equally, the term $\pi\alpha\hat{\iota}s$ to designate Jesus as a servant is Jewish Christian in provenance, being connected with the application to Christ of the Old Testament passage on the Servant of Yahweh—a text that had an important place in primitive liturgy. 'We can see the connection between *Is.* 52:13 and the beginnings of Christian liturgy through the history of the term $\pi\alpha\hat{\iota}s\ \theta\epsilon o\hat{v}$, which reappears in liturgical contexts.'[73] The first prayer concludes with a doxology in a very ancient form: 'For Thine is the power and the glory for ever and ever.' The form shows that it was a response made by the people.[74]

---

68. Cf. K. USENER, *Kleine Schriften*, IV, pp. 398 ff.

69. DE JONGE (*op. cit.*, p. 80) sees also some suggestion that fruits were eaten: *Test. Iss.* V, 3. It will be noted also that the ritual use of salt, which continued to form a part of the baptismal rites, has Essene counterparts. It is found among the Therapeutae (PHILO, *Cont.* 37) and the Ebionites (*Diamart.* 1).

70. E. PETERSON, 'Didache cap 9 e 10', *EL*, LVIII, 1944, pp. 3–13.

71. Cf. *Is.* 5:1 ff.; *Ps.* 79:8–12 (EVV 80). For the pagan world the vine is the symbol of immortality: cf. LEONARDI, *Ampelos*, pp. 60 ff.

72. *Psalms of Solomon* 17, 18.

73. CERFAUX, 'La première communauté chrétienne à Jérusalem', *Rec. Luc. Cerf.*, II, p. 141. In this connection we may quote *Acts* 4:27; *I Clem.* LIX, 2. It is remarkable that the term $\pi\alpha\hat{\iota}s\ \theta\epsilon o\hat{v}$ is applied in the *Acts* both to David (4:25) and to Jesus, as in the *Didache*.

74. Cf. PETERSON, *op. cit.*, pp. 6–8.

The second prayer begins: 'We give Thee thanks, O Our Father for the life and knowledge (ζωή καὶ γνῶσις) which Thou didst make known unto us through Thy servant Jesus' (IX, 3). Now this is a Jewish Christian theme:

> The giving of thanks for having obtained knowledge is a theme that Christian euchology owes to the Jewish; and this observation enables us to crystallise in a particular example the continuity that existed between the prayer of the Church and that of the Synagogue. The Jewish inspiration of the ancient Christian prayer explains the great part played by gnosis in the liturgical parts of *I Clement*. Thus it is that the gnosis theme finds its way into the Eucharistic anaphora of *Didache* IX, 3.[75]

Then comes the celebrated passage: 'As this broken bread was scattered upon the mountains and being gathered together became one, so may Thy Church gather together from the ends of the earth into Thy kingdom, for Thine is the glory and the power through Jesus Christ for ever and ever' (IX, 4). The prayer for the 'gathering together' stems from *Is.* 18:3 by way of the tenth of the Shemoneh Esreh, the Eighteen Benedictions recited every Sabbath. The word κλάσμα, used to denote a piece of bread, is an expression also found in the New Testament (*Jn.* 6:12; *Mk.* 8:8) and is archaic in character.[76] Finally, the image of the corn on the hills seems especially to suit the land of Judah, with its hills covered with wheatfields.[77] The prayers of the *Didache* may be regarded as 'a few fragments which have survived of the Eucharistic devotions of the Christians of the Mother Church of Jerusalem'.[78]

The third prayer begins with these words: 'We give Thee thanks, Holy Father, for Thy holy Name which Thou hast made to tabernacle in our hearts. . . . Thou, Almighty Master, didst create all things for Thy Name's sake' (X, 2-3). This is perhaps the most decisive passage of all. The divine 'Name'—that specifically Jewish expression—occurs twice,[79] and is, moreover, linked with 'tabernacling', which is also a Jewish expression. In Judaism the two ideas are associated: the *Book of Judith* speaks of 'the

75. DUPONT, *Gnosis. La connaissance religieuse dans les Epîtres de Saint Paul*, pp. 33–34.
76. Cf. H. J. GIBBINS, 'The Problems of the Liturgical Section of the Didache', *JTS*, XXXVI, 1935, p. 377. Gibbins' views have been contested by REICKE, 'Das Brot von den Bergen', *Erani*, LIV, pp. 142–150.
77. Cf. GIBBINS, *op. cit.*, p. 380.   78. Cf. GIBBINS, *op. cit.*, p. 386.
79. Cf. also *I Clem.* LIX, 2, 3.

Tabernacle where the Name resteth' (9:8). It only remains to add that here is the probable origin of the Eucharistic epiclesis. The very term signifies 'calling upon' the Name; it is an appeal to the Name to come and dwell, and only has meaning if the Name stands for God Himself.[80]

The closing words of the prayer are as follows: 'May grace come and may this world pass away. Hosanna to the God of David. If any man is holy, let him come. Maranatha, Amen.' Three expressions in this passage are remains from the Aramaic liturgy of the primitive Church. The first, *Hosanna*, is a liturgical acclamation that comes from the Jewish worship in the Temple. It occurs in *Ps.* 117:24 ff. (EVV 118), the psalm of the solemn Feast of Tabernacles: 'This is the day which the Lord has made, let us exult and rejoice in it. O Yahweh, save now (*hoshi'a na*)! . . . Blessed is he that cometh in the Name of the Lord.' The same expression comes in the Gospels at the Triumphal Entry into Jerusalem, and is evidence of the Messianic character of the scene. The Christian liturgy has continued to use it, together with the next verse of the Psalm, after the Trisagion of the Mass.

The second expression is the *Maranatha*. This is an Aramaic phrase, and should be regarded as the Church's oldest liturgical prayer. Its meaning has been debated. Theodoret translates it: 'The Lord has come', breaking it up into *Maran atha*, which makes it an affirmation of the coming of the Messiah; but it seems more likely that it ought to be divided *Marana tha*, and translated: 'Come, Lord.' In *Revelation* (22:20) the expression Ἐρχοῦ, Κύριε Ἰησοῦ certainly looks like a Greek translation of this phrase,[81] and the Aramaic form appears in *I Cor.* 16:22. It voices the strongly eschatological attitude of the Jewish Christian community.

Of more immediate concern, however, is its liturgical significance, and it is for this that its appearance in the *Didache* is precious. On this subject the following words can hardly be bettered:

> The *Didache* tells us that the *Maranatha* was also pronounced during the Last Supper within the framework of the Eucharistic liturgy. It must therefore have played a very important part in primitive worship, since Paul quotes it in Aramaic in an Epistle written in Greek. By

80. OESTERLEY (*The Jewish Background of the Christian Liturgy*, pp. 204–230) and DIX (*op. cit.*, pp. 220 ff.) both saw this point clearly. PETERSON goes further and thinks that the Name here stands for Christ: 'The Name of God pronounced over the bread has a sanctifying power. I would regard this as the origin of the epiclesis in the Oriental liturgy' (*op. cit.*, pp. 219 f.).

81. Cf. F. DÖLGER, *Sol salutis*, 2nd edn., 1925, pp. 198–211.

contrast with other Eucharistic prayers in the *Didache*, which often recall Jewish prayers even in their wording, in the *Maranatha* we have a specifically Christian element of the primitive liturgical prayers, a very close link with the Resurrection of Christ that was celebrated every Sunday; since it was on this day that Jesus appeared to the disciples while they were at their meal, he was asked to reappear during the Supper . . .; and as this spiritual presence of Christ in his Church is the pledge of his glorious return at the end of time, this ancient prayer is both a recalling of his appearance on the day of the Resurrection, and an appeal for its renewal at the moment of the holy Supper, and an announcement of his final Parousia, which is also to take place in the setting of the Messianic feast.[82]

The last of the three expressions is the *Amen*. This is a Hebrew word and marks 'the affirmation of faith in the divine truth and fidelity'.[83] It expresses the fulfilment of the promise; but whereas this fulfilment was still awaited by the Jews, for the Christians it had already been realised.[84] This is why the word is one of the names of Christ in two remarkable passages: 'These things saith the Amen, the faithful and true witness' (*Rev.* 3:14), where it will be observed that the expression following Amen is really a translation of it; and again in *II Cor.* 1:20: 'For all the promises of God in him are Yea, and in him Amen, unto the glory of God by us.'

In the Jewish liturgy the *Amen* was the response of the people to the blessings. The practice goes back to the liturgy of the Temple, and that is why *Amen* is found in the *Psalms* (41:13, etc.); but it was also used in the liturgy of the synagogue.[85] It played the same role in the Christian Eucharistic liturgy. The prayer of the *Didache* should probably be regarded as a dialogue. The minister says: 'If any man is holy let him come; if any man is not, let him repent. *Maranatha*.' And the people answer 'Amen' (X, 6).[86] This particular *Amen* is represented in our present liturgy first at the end of the prayer of consecration, and then again before the communion; but the place of these two was probably taken by one in the primitive liturgy, in which the prayer of consecration concluded with the

---

82. CULLMANN, *Early Christian Worship*, pp. 13–14.
83. SCHLIER, art. 'Ἀμήν, *TWNT*, I, p. 341.
84. Cf. DIX, *The Shape of the Liturgy*, p. 341.
85. Cf. OESTERLEY, *op. cit.*, p. 71.
86. The *Maranatha* and *Amen* are juxtaposed in *Rev.* 22:20.

12—T.J.C.

communion. There are some early witnesses to this *Amen*. Thus in Justin, for example:

> Having ended the prayers, we salute one another with a kiss. There is then brought to the president of the brethren bread and a cup of wine mixed with water, and he taking them, gives praise and glory to the Father of the Universe . . . and offers thanks . . . for our being counted worthy to receive these things at His hands. When he has finished the prayers and the Eucharist, all the people present utter the cry Amen.[87]

The Liturgy of Saint Cyril of Jerusalem in the fourth century describes the *Amen* before the communion in terms very similar to those of the *Didache*: 'The priest says: Holy things to the Holy, and the faithful receive the consecrated bread in their hands and say: Amen.'[88]

The study of these various expressions does in truth take us back to the primitive Jewish Christian liturgy. It has been well said: 'The language is clearly archaic; Christ is the Name of God and the Vine of David. The people cry *Hosannah* to the Son of David; they expect the second Parousia (*marana tha*), which will probably be in Palestine, hoping that the faithful of the Diaspora will join the faithful of the Synagogue in the Kingdom.'[89]

87. *I Apol.* LXV, 3-4.
88. *PG*, XXXIII, 1124B; cf. AMBROSE, *PG*, XVI, 444C, AUGUSTINE, *PL*, XXXVIII, 1247.
89. PETERSON, *op. cit.*, p. 13.

CHAPTER TWELVE

THE ORGANISATION OF THE COMMUNITY

T HE previous chapter examined Christian initiation as it appears to have been practised in Jewish Christian communities. Now it is necessary to consider the pattern of life of the community. This falls under three headings. First to be considered are the liturgical structure of the day, the week and the year. It is well known how important were 'times', καιροί, in Judaism at the time of Christ. The fixing of these times is one of the principal objects of *I Enoch* and the *Rule of the Community*, and it would, therefore, be only to be expected that they should be equally important in Jewish Christianity.[1] Two further sections will deal with the questions of hierarchical organisation, and the discipline of penance and reconciliation.

There used to be a common tendency to regard primitive Christianity as a spiritual, mystical or eschatological movement in which the development of an organic form was only of secondary moment; but more recent knowledge of Jewish society of the period shows how improbable is this view. On the contrary it seems as if Christianity adopted from the beginning the forms of contemporary Judaism. It is only later, when it comes into contact with the Greek world, that hesitation and retreat become noticeable. For many of these forms did not fit in with the new society in which Christianity was seeking expression, and this brought about the abandonment of certain practices, while others survived. It is, therefore, necessary to try to re-discover the structure of this first Christianity, in respect both of what has survived and of what has disappeared.

THE LITURGICAL YEAR

The ritual of the *Didache* prescribes prayer 'three times a day' (VIII, 3), but it does not state what are the hours of prayer. It might be supposed

1. Cf. *I Clement* XL, 1–2: 'The master hath commanded us to perform the offerings (προσφοράς) and ministrations at fixed times (καιροῖς) and seasons (ὥραις).'

that the three hours for going up to the Temple were intended, namely the third, the sixth and the ninth.[2] There is, however, another, more likely hypothesis.[3] In the *Rule of the Community* it says that the Essenes prayed three times a day, 'at the beginning of light and when it is in the middle of its course and when it retires into the abode which has been appointed for it' (X, 1). It is probable that the Christians preserved the Essene practice. Indeed this is stated explicitly in *II Enoch*: 'In the morning, at noon and in the evening of the day it is good to go into the House of the Lord to give glory to the Lord of all things' (LI, 4).[4]

For the *Didache* this threefold daily act of prayer consists of the Lord's Prayer with, be it noted, the ending: 'For Thine is the power and the glory for ever and ever' (VIII, 2), which is certainly a Jewish Christian addition. Another feature that merits attention is the practice of praying towards the East. This is not mentioned in the *Didache* but its use is very ancient, and according to Basil it goes back to Apostolic traditions,[5] which means, as has often been remarked already, traditions dating from the Palestinian Jewish Christian community. This might at first seem surprising since it is not the Jewish practice to pray towards the East; indeed, as may be seen from *Ezekiel* (8:16), it was associated with the pagan practice of sun-worship; but it was in fact done by the Essenes (JOSEPHUS, *Bell.* II, 8:5 [128]), and may indeed have originated with them.[6]

Another explanation has, however, been suggested.[7] Is the Christian practice an imitation of the Jewish custom of praying turned towards Jerusalem? This practice must have arisen after the fall of Jerusalem and would be related to the Jewish expectation of a messianic restoration of the city. It is found among the Ebionites, and therefore existed by the beginning of the second century; it was, moreover, counted as a mark of Judaism in these heterodox Jewish Christians, as Irenaeus mentions in his accusation against them.[8] The Christian practice of praying towards the

2. This is Oesterley's suggestion: *The Jewish background of the Christian Liturgy*, p. 125.
3. Cf. JUNGMANN, 'Altchristliche Gebetsordnung im Lichte des Regelbuches von En Feshka', *ZKT*, LXXV, 1953, pp. 315-316.
4. It is also, perhaps, worth remembering that synagogue prayers at these times are attested from an early period: cf. EPIPHANIUS, *Panarion* XXIX, 9: 2; also *DSD* X, 10, 14.
5. *De Spir. Sanct.* 27.
6. As F. J. DÖLGER has observed: *Sol Salutis*, p. 44.
7. PETERSON: 'Die geschichtliche Bedeutung der jüdischen Gebetsrichtung', *TZ*, III, 1947, pp. 1-15; 'La croce e la preghiera verso l'oriente', *EphL*, LIX, 1945, pp. 52-61.
8. *Adv. haer.* I, 26:2.

East would be a copy of this Jewish practice, and would therefore appear at the same period.[9] The connection between the practice of praying towards the East and the expectation of the Parousia seems to be well founded. It takes the custom back to a very early period, putting it in the context of the polemic against that Jewish and Jewish Christian millenarianism, with its expectation of a restoration of the earthly Jerusalem, which characterised the beginning of the second century.

This does not, however, explain why Christians expected Christ's return in the East. The explanations given by the Fathers—based on *Zec.* 6:12 or *Ps.* 67:5 (LXX : EVV 68: 4)—are of secondary importance; Christ's word is more decisive: 'As the lightning cometh forth from the east, and is seen even unto the west; so shall be the coming of the Son of Man' (*Mt.* 24:27), though this saying itself belongs to a particular context and that a Jewish one, and so points back to the Essenes. However, the statement in Josephus does not imply that prayer *ad orientem* had for them an eschatological meaning. Care is required in interpreting Josephus. He was addressing himself to the Greeks, and excelled in translating Jewish practices in terms of their imagery. Now it is a striking fact that the Jewish practice of praying towards Jerusalem was associated with the star of *Num.* 24:17.[10] This text is a favourite theme with the Essenes, and it may therefore be asked whether the prayer *ad orientem* may not have had a Messianic significance for them.

On the other hand, it should be noted that the star theme reappears in primitive Christianity. The star of the Magi appears 'in the east' (*Mt.* 2:2). It seems, therefore, that the origin of Christian prayer towards the East was not in the first place merely a reaction against the practice of the Jewish *qibla* towards Jerusalem, but is explained by a prior Essene custom, namely the expectation of the coming of the Messiah in the East in connection with the sun, the star or lightning.[11] One may indeed agree that these data provided no more than a basis for imaginative speculation, and that the practice of prayer towards the East in worship dates only from the beginning of the second century; but even so it still arises out of a Jewish community, and from controversies between Jewish Christians of a millenarist tendency and those of an Essene tradition.

Another feature has already been examined,[12] namely the connection

9. PETERSON, *loc. cit.*, p. 7.
10. Cf. PETERSON, *op. cit.*
11. Cf. W. BROWNLEE, 'Messianic Motifs of Qumran and the New Testament', *NTS*, III, 1957, p. 207.
12. Cf. pp. 268 ff. above.

between prayer towards the East and another Jewish Christian theme, the Cross of Glory. It looks very much as if in Jewish Christian symbolism the star of *Numbers* was transformed into the Cross of light.[13] Thus, to pursue the question of the practice of praying towards the East is to find oneself surrounded by a whole group of specifically Jewish Christian ideas: the Cross of Glory and the expectation of the Parousia, which confirm the Jewish Christian origin of this particular theme.

Beside the hours of prayer during the day Christianity exhibits from the first the practice of nocturnal prayer in the form of a watch or vigil lasting till dawn (cf. *Acts* 20:7–12). The same feature reappears in the Clementines; for example, in the *Recognitions*: 'Peter, rising at the crowing of the cock and wishing to rouse us, found us awake, the evening light still burning' (III, 1; cf. also II, 1; IV, 3). This too may be Essene in origin. In the Qumran community 'the Many watch in common for a third of the nights of the year to study the Law and bless God' (*DSD* VI, 7). Neither case refers to unusual vigils, but to a custom that for some people was a normal one.[14] It will be observed that the *Apostolic Tradition* mentions the practice of rising 'at midnight' to pray and adds: 'Men of holy memory (elders), who handed on the Tradition to us, taught us thus' (35). The mention of the Elders here seems to be another allusion to the παράδοσις, i.e. to Jewish Christian practices.[15]

The liturgy of the week raises few problems. The institution of Sunday goes back to the very first community and is a purely Christian creation. It is attested by the *Didache* as follows: 'And on the Lord's own Day gather yourselves together and break bread and give thanks' (XIV, 1). Similarly *Barnabas* has: 'We keep the eighth day for rejoicing, in the which also Jesus rose from the dead' (XV, 9). At first in a Jewish environment, the Sunday existed side by side with the social observance of the Sabbath. According to Epiphanius this practice was kept up by the Nazarenes, together with circumcision (*Pan.* XXIX, 8:5), and of course it is found

---

13. 'For it (the star of the magi) was not a star like the other stars, but was a great star in the form of a wheel, its appearance being like a cross' (F. ROBINSON, *Coptic Apocryphal Gospels*, p. 165); for the Cross as a wheel cf. again *Od. Sal.* XXIII.

14. CLEMENT OF ALEXANDRIA, mentioning this custom, adds that 'they who watch (by night) . . . make themselves like the angels (*Paed.* II, 9:79) whom we call "watchers"'. . . . . 'Watchers' is one of the characteristic names of the angels in Jewish Christianity (*II Enoch* XVIII). The dual association with praise and with the nature of the angels suggests a Jewish Christian context.

15. Cf. A. BAUMSTARK, *Nocturna laus*, Münster, 1957, pp. 18–21.

among the Ebionites. However, as Ignatius of Antioch records, it was rejected in Syriac Christianity: 'Those who had walked in ancient practices attained unto newness of hope, no longer observing sabbaths, but living lives in keeping with the Lord's Day (μηκέτι σαββατίζοντες ἀλλὰ κατὰ κυριακὴν ζῶντες': *Magn.*: IX, 1).

However, another feature of the weekly liturgy requires further attention. The *Didache* contrasts the Christian fast-days, Wednesday and Friday, with the Jewish ones, Monday and Thursday (VIII, 1). The choice of these days cannot be explained by a connection with a specifically Christian reality as in the case of Sunday, although later attempts were made to justify them in this way. How then did they originate? It has been noticed that these two days had a special importance in the priestly calendar used at Qumran.[16] Moreover, it is known from other evidence—to which reference will be made later—that this calendar was probably followed by the first Christian community. It is therefore very probable that the choice of these two days as days of fast and assembly for worship is of Essene origin. There are good grounds for the following judgment: 'It is understandable that the little group of disciples would be predisposed to adopt these already venerable liturgical days, while giving them a new significance.'[17]

In the matter of the annual liturgy the problems are much more complex, for there is no clear contrast between Christian and Jewish observances.[18] Judaism possessed a highly organised liturgical framework with its principal feasts of the Passover, of Weeks and of Tabernacles. The oldest Christian documents, on the other hand, make no reference to any calendrical data, though the Jewish liturgical year did clearly hold an important place in their eyes. The New Testament records the life of Christ in the setting of the Jewish feasts, and the importance attributed to this setting leads one to suppose that it still had some meaning for the communities to which the Gospels were addressed. This raises several questions. Did the Jewish Christians retain the Jewish feasts while giving them a new meaning, or did they reject them, as they rejected the Sabbath and circumcision? And if they did retain them, what calendar did they follow in observing them?

The first problem is that of Easter. The question whether the feast was retained from Judaism obviously does not arise, for it is purely a celebration

16. A. JAUBERT, *La date de la dernière Cène, RHR*, CXLVI, 1954, pp. 168–169.
17. A. JAUBERT, *op. cit.*, p. 169.
18. Cf. J. VAN GOUDOEVER, *Biblical Calendars*, Leiden, 1959, pp. 151–275.

of the anniversary of Christ's Passion and Resurrection. The real problem concerns the date of Easter. From the second century onward there were two opposing opinions, that of the Asiatics who followed the Jewish calendar and fixed Easter on the 14th Nisan, and the other which placed Easter on the Sunday following the Spring equinox.[19]

Now this difference of opinion seems in fact to go back to Judaism, which at the time of Christ had two calendars, the official one, based on the lunar month, and the archaic priestly calendar. The Asiatic Christian use seems to correspond to the official Jewish calendar, in which the celebration of Passover always fell on the evening of the 14th Nisan. Here is a tradition, certainly one of the oldest, which definitely goes back to Jewish Christianity; but the other tradition, which was finally to oust the first, and which placed Easter always on a Sunday, also has venerable authority. Eusebius sees in it an Apostolic tradition (*HE* V, 23:1). It represents the immemorial practice of Palestine, Alexandria and Rome, and appears to be related to the priestly calendar, which always began the celebration of the Feast of Weeks on the Sunday after the Passover.[20]

Whatever discussion there may be about the date, there is no doubt that Passover time was observed by Jewish Christians as the Feast of Christ's Resurrection. This probably implied from the beginning the celebration of the fifty days following, the Pentecost, in imitation of Judaism. In the light of this it may be asked what was the position with regard to the Feast of Tabernacles. No trace of its celebration is found in any document, unless there be an allusion to it in a passage in *Hermas* which reflects the practices of the feast (*Sim.* VIII, 2:1–4). On the other hand, just as with Pentecost, it seems unlikely that the feast should leave no trace at all. Study of this question has shown that traces of the Feast of Tabernacles are in fact to be found, but attached to other times of the year.[21] In the first place Palm Sunday seems to be an anticipation of the feast at Passover time[22]; secondly, it is the source of many features in the observance of Epiphany.[23]

---

19. Cf. C. SCHMIDT, *Gespräche Jesu mit seinen Jüngern*, pp. 577–726.
20. Cf. A. JAUBERT, *op. cit.*, p. 170; VAN GOUDOEVER, *op. cit.*, pp. 164, 182–194.
21. Cf. DANIÉLOU, 'Les Quatre-temps de septembre et la Fête des Tabernacles', *Maison-Dieu*, XLVI, 1956, pp. 114–136: also VAN GOUDOEVER, *op. cit.*, pp. 261–271.
22. As T. W. MANSON has shown: 'The Cleansing of the Temple', *BJRL*, XXXIII, 1951, pp. 271–282.
23. Cf. E. G. SELWYN: 'The Feast of Tabernacles, Epiphany and Baptism', *JTS*, XII, 1911, pp. 225–236.

It appears, therefore, that before being displaced, for reasons which will be explained presently, the Feast of Tabernacles was certainly kept in the month of September by Jewish Christianity as by the Jews. This may have left a trace in the *Gospel of Mark*, if it is accepted that this book constitutes a series of lessons for a liturgical year, beginning in September and ending with the Palm Sunday lesson, the Passion lesson being separate.[24] This would synchronise the Feast of Tabernacles with the lection relating the Baptism of Christ; and it should be noted incidentally that in the Fourth Gospel the feast is expressly linked with Baptism (*Jn.* 7:37–39). Possibly, being the feast of the beginning of the year, and the annual commemoration of Christ's own Baptism, it included the celebration of Christian baptisms.[25]

It now remains to enquire why the feast did not disappear but was transferred. The connection with Palm Sunday and the borrowings by Epiphany respectively seem to call for different explanations. The former seems to be typical of the *Gospel of John*, and is connected with an Asiatic setting. Here two reasons militated in favour of a transfer of the Feast of Tabernacles to Eastertide. One factor was that the beginning of the year, which in the priestly calendar fell on the first of Tishri, came on the first of Nisan in the official calendar. Since John followed this in the case of Easter, he probably adhered to it for the beginning of the year also. If this were so, the lessons on the Baptism of Jesus which begin the year and those of Palm Sunday which end it should both fall near Easter; and this is exactly confirmed by Oriental practice. 'The Sunday after Easter served as the beginning of the year and the readings from the Gospel of John on the Baptism of Christ were then begun.'[26] Moreover, it is in the East that the Feast of Palms first appears on the Sunday before Easter. The interval of a fortnight was filled by the special lectionary of the Passion.

Another factor may have assisted in Asiatic communities, and at the end of the first century, in severing the connection between the Feast of Tabernacles and September, namely that in contemporary Judaism the feast was associated with Messianic hopes in their more temporal form. This temporal Messianism had a strong influence on Christians in the form of millenarianism, which had its centre in the Asiatic environment to which

24. Cf. P. CARRINGTON, *The Primitive Christian Calendar*, 1952, pp. 32–41.
25. E. G. SELWYN has shown that the *Odes of Solomon*, which have a marked baptismal character, are full of allusions to the Feast of Tabernacles: *op. cit.*, pp. 231 ff. On the subject of the Mandaeans, cf. A. ADAM, *Die Psalmen des Thomas*, Berlin, 1959, p. 79.
26. BAUMSTARK, *Liturgie comparée*, pp. 133 f.

both Papias[27] and Cerinthus belonged. This Messianic agitation was connected with the mystique of festivity,[28] which belonged essentially to the Feast of Tabernacles. The total suppression of the September feast in the Gospel of *John* may, therefore, be regarded as a sign of an anti-millenarian polemic.[29] The Feast of Tabernacles plays an important part in the *Revelation*, but it is transferred to the eschatological plane, and is amalgamated with the Paschal liturgy of the Lamb.

There still remains the connection of Tabernacles with the Epiphany. The change just examined arose out of internal conflicts in Jewish Christianity, whereas this one is the result of Christianity's moving into a Greek environment, in which it was impossible to avoid conformity with the official calendar. The Julian calendar began on the first of January, so that it would be natural to begin the liturgical year on that date with the account of the Baptism. But in Jewish Christianity this account had been so closely associated with the Feast of Tabernacles that some of the themes of the latter were transferred with the other to the beginning of January. In origin, therefore, Epiphany would seem to be a practice developed by Christianity in a pagan setting, but inheriting a certain number of elements from the Jewish Christian Feast of Tabernacles.

PRESBYTERS AND PROPHETS

The problem of the hierarchy in the primitive Christian community is one of the most obscure in the history of Christian origins. It is not proposed to deal with it in its entirety,[30] but it will be necessary to consider what elements in the hierarchy, according to our documents, originate in Jewish Christianity. The discoveries at Qumran have yielded some valuable information on this matter. Whereas the hierarchy used often to be re-

27. It will be remembered that the crucial text quoted by Papias on the subject of the millenarianism of the Presbyters relates to the fruitfulness of the vine, which would seem to suggest the month of September (PREUSCHEN, p. 96).
28. As REICKE has shown: *Diakonie, Festfreude und Zelos*, pp. 174–227.
29. Cf. DANIÉLOU, *op. cit.*, pp. 123–124. It should be noted, however, that AILEEN GUILDING thinks that there may have been a connection in Jewish Christianity between the Feast of Tabernacles and the Nativity of Christ, celebrated in September (*The Fourth Gospel and Jewish Worship*, London 1960, pp. 98–104).
30. On the subject in general, cf. G. DIX, 'The Ministry in the Early Church', *The Apostolic Ministry*, London, 1946, pp. 183–304; H. VON CAMPENHAUSEN, *Kirchliches Amt und geistliche Vollmacht in den ersten drei Jahrhunderten*, Tübingen, 1953; J. COLSON, *Les fonctions ecclésiales aux deux premiers siècles*, Paris, 1956.

garded as belonging to the second stage of a Christianity which had at first been simply a mystical movement, these texts, revealing as they do highly organised Jewish communities at the very time when Christianity appeared, make it more likely that the hierarchy of the Christian community dates from very early times.[31] It may be as well to add that it is not the ultimate origin of this hierarchical organisation, which like that of the sacraments goes back to Christ himself, that is at issue here, but rather the particular development which that organisation underwent in the Jewish Christian period.

One of the first features to be noted is the institution of the ἐπίσκοποι. The word is already found in the New Testament (*I Tim.* 3:2), synonymous with πρεσβύτεροι (*Tit.* 1:5). It designates one who is responsible for a local community. Paul recommends Titus to 'appoint Elders (πρεσβυτέρους) in every city . . . a bishop must be irreproachable as being God's steward' (*Tit.* 1:5–7). The description in *I Timothy* is on the same lines. Each of the presbyters or episcopi is responsible for a definite community. It will be observed that they are on an entirely different plane from Titus or Timothy. The latter are St. Paul's successors and mandatories endowed with full powers, and the appointment of heads of local communities falls to them.[32]

This is the state of affairs presented in Jewish Christian documents, and it reflects one definite feature of the organisation of the primitive community. The *Didache* writes: 'Appoint for yourselves therefore bishops (ἐπισκόπους) and deacons worthy of the Lord, men who are meek and not lovers of money, but true and tested (δεδοκιμασμένους); for unto you they also perform the service of the prophets and teachers' (XV, 1). In this text the details describing the bishop should be noted: he must above all be 'a tested man', a phrase which will be met with again. Also he fulfils the functions of prophet and teacher. This seems to indicate that these activities are not the ones which directly constitute the episcopate, the latter being primarily a governmental function.[33] Side by side with it there seems to exist another type of priesthood, that of the prophets and teachers —a point to which it will be necessary to return later—but the episcopate may also assume these functions.

The *Epistle of Clement* describes the origins of the institution along

31. Cf. J. DANIÉLOU, 'La communauté de Qumran et l'organisation de l'Église ancienne', *La Bible et l'Orient*, pp. 110–113.   32. Cf. DIX, *op. cit.*, pp. 72–73.
33. Cf. VON CAMPENHAUSEN, *op. cit.*, p. 99.

exactly the same lines as the *Epistle to Titus*: '(The Apostles), preaching everywhere in country and town, appointed their first-fruits, when they had proved (δοκιμάσαντες) them by the Spirit, to be bishops and deacons unto them that should believe' (XLII, 4). And again later:

> (The Apostles) appointed the aforesaid persons, and afterwards they provided a continuance, that if these should fall asleep other approved (δεδοκιμασμένοι) men should succeed to their ministration. Those therefore who were appointed by them, or afterward by other men of repute (ἐλλογίμων) with the consent of the whole Church . . . these men we consider to be unjustly thrust out from their ministration (XLIV, 2–3).

Especially significant in this text is the fact that the Apostles have as their successors men of repute (ἐλλόγιμοι), who have a mandate to appoint the bishops of local communities. This corresponds to the evidence of Paul in regard to Titus and Timothy, and clearly distinguishes the successors of the Apostles from the heads of local communities.

The *Shepherd* gives a description in agreement with this. There is a clear distinction between 'the apostles and the teachers' on the one hand (*Sim.* IX, 25:2) and the 'episcopi' (IX, 27:2) on the other. The description of the latter agrees fully with that given in the Pastoral Epistles. Bishops are praised mainly for their hospitality and for their ministrations to the needy and the widows. This recalls *I Tim.* 3:2, where similar functions are obviously being described. Another passage lists together the three kinds of function to be found in the Jewish Christian community: 'The stones that are squared and white, and that fit together in their joints, these are the apostles and bishops and teachers and deacons, who walked after the holiness of God' (*Vis.* III, 5:1). All texts attest the existence of deacons, the other two functions being that of the episcopus and the apostle-doctor-prophet, to which further reference will have to be made.

The institution of the presbyter or episcopus, the head of the local community, is therefore one of the clearest data from the oldest stratum of Christianity. It appears to be of Apostolic institution as is shown by the Pastoral Epistles; but the important point is that in their dividing up of the community the Apostles seem to have been almost certainly inspired by the Essene organisation, with one *mebaqqer* (inspector) who presided over gatherings, and another responsible for communal property (*DSD* VI, 12–14). The Greek name for this official is ἐπιμελετής, which is reminiscent of ἐπίσκοπος. There is such a close likeness between the two offices that the one must almost certainly be inspired by the other.[34] This is one of the features in which the Jewish Christian community most resembles that of Qumran. Furthermore, its presence in the Pastoral Epistles is evidence that it was a characteristic of the first Palestinian community, from which Paul must have received it.

The institution of the ἐπίσκοποι under the inspiration of the Qumran community probably brought with it some of the elements that were associated with it at Qumran. Among these might be included especially the discipline of penance, with its temporary or permanent exclusions, which played a large part at Qumran, and the importance of which in Christianity is shown by *Hermas*. Another characteristic feature was the administration of the property of the community. Finally it seems as if with the ἐπίσκοπος can be associated the organisation of baptism with its preparatory novitiate catechesis and fasts which, as already remarked, are directly inspired by Qumran.[35] Moreover, in this incorporation of new members all traditions reserve the preponderating role to the ἐπίσκοπος.

Beside ἐπίσκοποι Jewish Christian texts give evidence of other offices in the community. The deacons, whose origin is recounted in the New Testament and who do not seem to have any Jewish counterpart,[36] may be left aside. The other group is more important. It has been given various titles which seem to be equivalent to one another. The *Didache* speaks of prophets (XIII, 4), prophets and teachers (XV, 2), and apostles and prophets (XI, 3), and treats them as similar to one another. *Hermas* mentions 'Apostles and teachers who preached unto the whole world' (*Sim.* IX, 25:2; cf. also *Vis.* III, 5:1; *Sim.* IX, 15:4), and also speaks of prophets in similar terms to those of the *Didache* (*Mand.* XI, 7, 12, 15, 16). This all constitutes a coherent whole, but what it means remains to be determined.[37]

34. REICKE, JEREMIAS, BENOIT and KUHN are in agreement over this, and SCHMIDT writes: 'The Qumran institution of the *mebaqqer* is manifestly a parallel one to the Christian ἐπίσκοπος. The parallel is complete and exclusive, for not only are there no other examples in the various currents of contemporary Judaism, but it covers every aspect of the respective offices' ('Sacerdoce judaïque et hiérarchie', *RevSR*, XXIX, 1955, p. 257).
35. Cf. CAMPENHAUSEN, *op. cit.*, p. 92.
36. REICKE, however, connects them with the institution of the *agape*, the repast for the poor which originally accompanied the Eucharist. This would make them a specifically Jewish Christian institution (*Diakonie, Festfreude und Zelos*, p. 30).
37. The various theories that have been suggested are sufficiently well known. HARNACK

What then is the distinction between the two groups? In the opinion of the present writer the distinction here is between a stable priesthood, that of the presbyters and bishops, and a missionary priesthood, that of the ἀπόστολοι. The various roles assigned to these ἀπόστολοι are all related to this primary and distinct vocation. They are essentially preachers, and this aspect of their ministry is indicated by the terms prophet and didascalos. As prophets they announce the Kerygma to the pagans; as didascaloi they prepare those pagans who have decided to receive baptism.[38]

From this point of view it is easy to understand the phrase in the *Didache* about the bishops: 'Unto you they also perform the service of the prophets and teachers' (XV, 1). It simply expresses the establishment of a local hierarchy to take the place of the itinerant missionaries. This is indeed a law of the Church's development. It also explains the recommendation 'despise them not' (XV, 2), for the bishops come from the community which elects them (XV, 1). They are a native clergy, whereas the teachers are foreigners and have the privileges of strangers. The members of the community must therefore be taught to respect the man they have appointed from among themselves.

This missionary clergy exhibits other characteristic features. The *Didache* and *Hermas* give numerous and very curious indications on the point: 'Let every apostle when he cometh to you, be received as the Lord.'

---

38. It will be noted that they celebrate the Eucharist in the same way as bishops (*Didache* X, 7). Similarly they are 'high priests' (XIII, 3). All this clearly indicates their priestly character.

---

saw that they were itinerant missionaries, but he held that their ministry was of charismatic origin, rather than the result of priestly institution. Dix goes still further by denying the apostles, teachers and prophets any ministerial character, and by regarding them as private persons acting under the impulse of the Spirit, as opposed to the institutional priesthood of the presbyters and episcopi. Colson is obliged to recognise that the didascaloi represent in some cases the same reality as the presbyters (*op. cit.*, p. 130 but he nevertheless devotes a whole chapter to the prophets as pure charismatics (pp. 354–367).

The error of Dix and Colson is their refusal to grant to the body of apostles and didascaloi the character of a true ministry. In consequence of this they are obliged to set aside the authority of the *Didache* upon one pretext or another. But in this matter the *Didache* is the vital document, and it forces us to accept the institutional character of these functions in the Jewish Christian setting. This archaic feature was preserved in Ebionism, in which the didascaloi were ordained by the Apostles and their successors (*Diamartyrion*, 1). It is not a case of charisma on one side and institution on the other, but rather that prophets and presbyters, didascaloi and episcopi, are all both ministries and charismata. Cf. Campenhausen, *op. cit.*, p. 195; also Audet, *La Didachè*, p. 206.

He should not remain more than two days and at his departure he is to be given bread only (*Didache* XI, 4–6). The prophet speaks in the Spirit, but whether or not he is a true prophet may be discerned from his conduct. If he 'order a table' he should abstain from eating of it (XI, 9). Every true prophet that establishes himself in a country deserves his food, 'for they are your chief priests (ἀρχιερεῖς)' (XIII, 3). *Hermas* confirms these data. The true prophet is known by his life. He speaks in the Spirit, and leads the prayer in the assemblies (*Mand.* XI, 7–10).

Leaving aside the itinerant character of the teaching mission, the striking thing here is the practice of the evangelical counsels. The prophets and teachers seem to continue the role of the 'disciples', the missionaries sent out by Christ during his earthly life, who were commanded by him to combine with their ministry the practice of the evangelical counsels.[39] The prophet has no possessions and lives on alms, and in addition he seems to preserve virginity. This seems to be the meaning of a passage in the *Didache* not so far considered: 'And every prophet approved and found true, if he doeth ought as a cosmic mystery of the Church, and yet teacheth not others to do all that he himself doeth, shall not be judged by you' (XI, 11). This passage about 'the cosmic mystery of the Church' is an enigma; but there are data which may well throw light on it.

The expression 'cosmic mystery of the Church' seems to stand in opposition to a 'heavenly mystery of the Church'. This heavenly mystery is the celestial marriage of Christ to the Church, which also finds its expression in this world. The allusion in this passage would therefore seem to be to those spiritual unions which existed in Jewish Christianity between prophet-apostles and a sister.[40] Hermas also appears to allude to this custom (*Sim.* IX, 10:6–11:8), while a similar reference may underlie *I Cor.* 7:36 ff. The custom endured in the institution of Virgins. The relation of these unions to their heavenly ideal is explicitly stated by the Gnostics: 'Some of them prepare a nuptial couch and perform a sort of mystic rite (μυσταγωγία) . . . affirming that what is performed by them is a spiritual marriage after the likeness of the unions (συζυγιῶν) above' (*Adv. haer.* I, 21:3).

The mention of *Hermas* and the *Didache* points to Jewish Christianity;

39. The relevant N.T. passages are *Mt.* 9:35–10:23; *Lk.* 10:1–16, with which may be compared *Mk.* 6:7–13. In the light of the present discussion the terminology of *Mt.* 10:1 and 10:2 provides an interesting conjunction. (*Ed.*)

40. Cf. ADAM, 'Erwägungen zur Herkunft der Didache', *ZKG*, LXVIII, 1957, pp. 1–47; SCHLIER, *Untersuchungen*, p. 92.

but to find the ultimate context it is almost certainly necessary to go back to the Essenes and the Therapeutae, for that is the only setting in which are to be found both the ideal of virginity, and at the same time ascetics and virgins in neighbouring communities. Moreover, it is known that the Qumran ascetics practised complete poverty, and that on a journey they took nothing with them, so that they were a charge to those who received them (*Bell.* II, 8:4 [125]). This recalls Christ's precepts to the disciples when he sent them on their mission. It is hard to believe that the ascetic ideal of Qumran was not at least partially continued in the Christian community. Finally it should be added that Qumran was the only society in which prophecy was practised at that date.

Thus the prophets of the *Didache* seem to carry on the tradition of the spirituals of Qumran. But it is important to notice a vital difference, namely that the Qumran ascetics were solitaries, whereas the prophets of the *Didache* are Apostles, a genuinely Christian feature which seems to have been instituted by Christ himself, when he sent his disciples on their mission. This mission invested them with a function, a truly ecclesial function, a priesthood. Otherwise their manner of life is that of the prophets and is a continuation of the Qumran ascetic tradition. There does not, therefore, appear to have been a Christian monachism to succeed to that of Qumran; the direct connection is with the way of life of the prophet-missionaries.[41] The influence of the Essene ideal on the founding of Christian monachism came later through literary channels, the texts of Philo and Josephus.

This quasi-monastic conception of the priesthood seems to have been too closely bound up with Jewish Christianity to be able to survive. Its characteristics rendered it impracticable in a Hellenistic society. Spiritual marriages, possible among the pious Essenes, gave rise to abuses no less than did the sacred meals which, it will be remembered, it was one of the duties of the prophet to organise as occasions both of prayer and of charitable relief of the poorer brethren. This practice fell into disuse and only the *agape* of pure charity was preserved. Prophecy itself also led to such abuses in Greek society (*I Cor.* 14:1–19), that it too was bound to dis-

---

41. EUSEBIUS was so struck with these resemblances that he saw in the account which Philo gives of the Essenes a description of the earliest Christian community. After mentioning the functions of the deacons and bishops he concludes: 'That when Philo wrote thus he was thinking of the first heralds of the Gospel teaching, and of the customs handed down from the beginning by the Apostles, is obvious to all' (*HE* II, 17:23–24).

appear.[42] The same considerations may explain the prohibition of women from speaking in Christian assemblies. In a Jewish Christian setting they could perform the function of prophets, as, for example, the case of the daughters of the Hellenist Philip (EUSEBIUS, *HE* III, 31:4)[43]; and this practice continued in Montanism.

The link between the ascetic ideal and the priesthood is not the only distinguishing feature of the Jewish Christian community. It would seem that in this community the priesthood was associated also with the idea of the possession and handing on, together with the rule of faith, of a higher teaching—that in fact which has been studied in all the earlier part of this book. The priesthood stands at the junction of the two conceptions of tradition remarked hitherto, the strictly Christian conception of the handing on of revelation in the proper sense of the word, and the Jewish conception of the handing on of higher speculations. The former was to gain the upper hand in the Great Church, and the latter in Gnosticism. It was the peculiar role of the Jewish Christian priesthood to unite them.

This link between the priesthood and Jewish Christian gnosis manifests itself in various ways. The passage in *Heb.* 5:11–14 which contrasts the νήπιοι who need the milk of the catechesis with the τέλειοι who are able to receive higher teaching has already been mentioned. It is remarkable that this higher teaching should be concerned with speculations on Melchizedek which constituted one of the favourite themes of Jewish and Jewish Christian gnosis, as can be seen in *II Enoch*. The writer also contrasts the νήπιοι with the διδάσκαλοι—a second appearance of the class of teachers, surmised above to have been priests.[44]

The Epistle is set, therefore, in a Jewish Christian context of converts from Essenism. More precisely, they were people who could be addressed as didascaloi. The entire context indicates that they were priests of a Jewish Christian community, but with Ebionite tendencies and still viewing

---

42. The *Ascension of Isaiah* laments this disappearance (III, 27). It will be noted how hard this work is on the 'presbyters', i.e. the episcopi—an example, no doubt, of the attitude which the *Didache* has in mind when it urges believers not to 'despise' them. It is an expression of nostalgia for the prophetic priesthood in the face of episcopal priesthood.

43. Cf. also *I Cor.* 11:5: what is referred to is not preaching, but praying in public.

44. On the other hand, P. BRAUN believes that the letter was addressed to convert Zadokite priests who found it hard to accept the idea of a Messiah who was not descended from Aaron.

things from an Essene standpoint, regarding Christ as an angel. These priests must have been capable of receiving a higher teaching—they were indeed didascaloi, but owing to their errors they were not worthy of this title. This all seems to point to a connection between the priesthood and Jewish Christian speculation in a setting that was still close to that of Qumran.

The question of the presbyters is usually explained from the same angle. The term πρεσβύτεροι has been encountered twice in the present work. In the first place there were the Elders spoken of by Papias, Irenaeus and Clement, who were Jewish Christians, who elaborated the theology we have been considering, and whose tradition it was which these writers preserved. On the other hand, πρεσβύτεροι also denotes the priests of the Jewish Christian community. There is no reason why the same word should stand for two different classes of people,[45] and it is therefore justifiable to affirm that those entrusted with the Jewish Christian gnosis were the priests of the early Christian community.

This is of the first importance if the didascaloi are to be identified with the Jewish Christian priesthood, for this constitutes a formal declaration that the presbyters are the guardians of the tradition of gnosis. Vice versa these presbyter-theologians are clearly the didascaloi, the Jewish Christian teachers. The fact that they are designated by the term presbyter attests their priestly character, and also shows that the boundary between the missionary priesthood and the local priesthood was not very well defined. The gnostic tradition, like the ascetic ideal, seems to be as characteristic of presbyters and episcopi as of apostles and teachers.

This seems, therefore, to have been the situation in Jewish Christianity, which preserved something of the Essene esotericism side by side with the public revelation of the Gospel. In a Hellenistic environment such a confusion was seen to be fraught with danger. The gnosis came to be regarded as the essential matter, while the common teaching took second place. This situation developed in Gnosticism and is apparent also in Ebionism—an indication that these movements are a corrupt form of Jewish Christianity. The crisis shows itself clearly in *I–II Corinthians*. Apollos is seen as the typical representative of missionaries of a Gnostic tendency. His speculations dazzle the Corinthians, and this leads Paul to show, without denying the gnosis, that it is secondary. In this Paul was responsible for a further

45. Cf. D'ALÈS, 'Le *ΠΡΕΣΒΥΤΗΣ* de Saint Irénée', *REG*, XLII, 1929, pp. 398–405; CAMPENHAUSEN, *op. cit.*, p. 86.

step in freeing the Christian priesthood from its Jewish Christian attachments.

Attention has been drawn several times to the mention of a degree higher than both episcopi and prophets. These are the ἐλλόγιμοι ἄνδρες of *I Clement*, men such as Titus and Timothy, who appoint the bishops. They must clearly be regarded as the heirs of the Twelve and constitute a different group from those discussed so far. This institution plainly derives from Christ himself. However, as with the Eucharist, it may be a case of a framework borrowed from Judaism. It has in fact been observed that beside the overseers of local communities the Qumran community provides evidence of a council with twelve members which presides over the whole community.[46] The *Rule of the Community* describes them in terms somewhat reminiscent of the Twelve: they are the foundation on which the community is built.[47] This conception may, therefore, derive from an Essene context.

This, however, is a New Testament problem. What is of immediate concern is the later development of the Twelve in the Jewish Christian period. Their role seems to have been above all missionary in the fullest sense of the word. They are founders of the Church, but they do not seem to be connected with any particular church. The local hierarchy seems to have been a lower degree and is represented by the episcopi or presbyters. This is the situation in all the texts studied so far. There is, however, one important exception, namely the Church of Jerusalem. Here the figure of James was prominent at a very early date in consequence of his being head of this Church. Moreover, Hegesippus records that James, who was a cousin of the Lord, was succeeded by other members of Christ's family.[48]

This position of James and his successors seems to have been something special, connected with Jerusalem and its metropolitical character. In this case there seems to be a transformation in the institution of the episcopate. Above the number of episcopi or presbyters, each responsible for one group of the community, was apparently established a higher local authority of the same rank as the Apostles. This gave the Church of Jerusalem a unique character during the period up to A.D. 70. This

46. REICKE, 'Die Verfassung der Urgemeinde im Lichte jüdischer Dokumente', *TZ*, x, 1954, pp. 106–107; DANIÉLOU, *op. cit.*, pp. 111–112.
47. Cf. DANIÉLOU, *Les manuscrits de la Mer Morte et les origines du christianisme*, Paris 1957, pp. 29–30.
48. This is what STAUFFER has called a caliphate: cf. 'Zum Kalifat des Jacobus', *ZRGG*, IV, 1952, pp. 193 ff.

character would explain Paul's collection for Jerusalem which was intended to show that he was in communion with the Mother Church.[49]

In A.D. 70, however, this predominance came to an end, and like the Jews the Jewish Christians were dispersed. A small group remained, probably in Transjordan, clinging to the successor of James, who at that time was probably Simeon (*HE* IV, 22:4), and these were to form the group of the Nazarenes. But the majority went elsewhere to Syria,[50] Antioch then becoming the centre of Jewish Christianity. There the most important Jewish Christian body, the Judaeo-Syriac was formed. It was paramount not only in the sphere of creative theology—at Antioch was developed, for instance as was seen earlier, the theology of the *katabasis* and *anabasis*—but also in the sphere of authority. A hierarchy grew up in Antioch on the model of the one in Jerusalem, and claiming to be its successor. Possibly it already based its authority on that of Peter, and made his sojourn there the basis of a claim to a primacy in authority. However that may be, it seems to be the first local Church after Jerusalem to show a hierarchy with two ranks and to have at its head a successor of the Apostles.

Such is the situation at the time of Ignatius of Antioch. There is a strictly ordered hierarchy with a bishop, presbyterate and deacons. The texts relating to this are too numerous and too well known to be quoted. This organisation is seen to be typically Jewish Christian in that it takes its inspiration from what had previously existed at Jerusalem only; but starting from Antioch the pattern of a two-level hierarchy, from being purely local, was to develop and spread by degrees to the whole Church.[51]

It is now possible to form a fairly comprehensive picture of the Jewish Christian hierarchy. There is first of all a higher degree, that of the successors of the Apostles, who are not yet called bishops, but are founders of the Church. At first itinerant, they gradually acquire fixed headquarters. The lower rank of the ministry includes two groups. On the one hand, there is a missionary priesthood, apostles, prophets and teachers, who are a continuation of the group of 'disciples of Christ', and who have others, men and women, as their associates, who do not have the priestly character; on the other, a local priesthood consisting of presbyters and episcopi, who replace the missionaries once the Churches are organised.

49. Many authors, and especially BRANDON, have pointed out this predominance of the Church of Jerusalem throughout the early period of the life of the Church.
50. Not to Alexandria as BRANDON says.
51. In particular it seems to have been unknown in communities of Pauline foundation, so that CAMPENHAUSEN is right in contrasting the latter with the Palestinian type of church; but he is mistaken in seeing the contrast as one between a charismatic and an institutional church. They were simply two different institutional organisations.

Chapter Thirteen

PERSONAL HOLINESS

S OME of the features of Jewish Christian spirituality have already been encountered a number of times in this book. The theory of preparation for Baptism will have made familiar enough the conception of the two spirits, while the study of the hierarchy has revealed the importance of ascetical tendencies in Jewish Christian society, and especially that of virginity. However, the gnosis, the speculative content of which has been the object of study in the greater part of this work, also has a spiritual side; and it will therefore be necessary to take up again the main themes already considered, this time in order to extract from them any material relevant to this spiritual aspect, which has so far been ignored.

THE TWO SPIRITS

There are many who uphold a kind of evangelical spirituality, which is claimed to be the pure expression of Christ's teaching, in opposition to a more ascetic, speculative spirituality, the product, it is said, of Stoic or Platonist influences in later Hellenistic Christianity. It is indeed true that in Greek society Christianity adopted many forms of expression belonging to the Hellenistic φιλοσοφία; ἀπάθεια and θεωρία were among the Greek expressions that were to be Christianised. As in the case of theology or the hierarchy, however, it would be a mistake to suppose that this Hellenistic form of expression replaced a purely evangelical attitude. In reality, from the very first, Christianity made use of the ascetical conceptions of Judaism; and Jewish Christianity was the more profoundly influenced by these ascetic tendencies from the fact that they were so pronounced in the environment in which it appeared.

One of the most important features that Jewish Christianity received from Judaism, and more particularly from Essene circles, was the doctrine of the Two Spirits. This has already been examined in its cosmological aspect and in its place in the catechesis, and now it must be considered from the point of view of spirituality. Essentially it expresses the existence of a dual orientation in the human soul. This is sometimes seen as a conflict between two tendencies, and is similar to the doctrine of the two *yeṣerim*, which existed in Judaism at the time of Christ and was to endure in the rabbinic tradition.[1] The doctrine may be studied in *II (4) Esdras*, where it is particularly prominent. The place of the *yeṣer* is the heart, and the evil *yeṣer* was in the heart of Adam from the beginning (4:30). It is not sin, but a propensity to sin, and for this reason its origin can be attributed to God. Adam's consenting to it established its domination over him and his descendants.

It may be that this doctrine of the two *yeṣerim* is to be found in *Saint Paul*.[2] It certainly appears in a developed form in Jewish Christian writers, as, for example, in the following passage from the *Testaments of the Twelve Patriarchs*: 'Two ways (ὁδοί) hath God given to the sons of men, and two inclinations (διαβούλια), and two kinds of action . . . and two issues' (*Test. Asher* I, 3). It should be noted that the Hebrew *yeṣer* is translated by διαβούλιον.[3] This specifically Jewish Christian word, which appears frequently in the *Testaments* (*Test. Reuben* IV, 9; *Test. Simeon* IV, 8, etc.), was later to be replaced by the term λογισμός, which is of Stoic origin, occurs in the Clementine *Homilies* (IX, 12), and was used by Origen, Gregory of Nyssa and Evagrius in their psychology of temptation.

The specifically Jewish Christian trait, however, was to associate these inclinations with the action of two spirits, the angels of light and of darkness. This feature is characteristic of Essenism, and is developed at length in the *Rule of the Community*. From the Prince of Light come all good inspirations (IV, 2–8); but 'to the spirit of perversity belong greed, and slackness in the service of righteousness, wickedness and falsehood, pride, haughtiness, lying and deceit . . . abominable works in a spirit of fornication' (IV, 9–10). As was remarked earlier, this feature reappears in the catechism of the Two Ways (*Epistle of Barnabas* XVIII, 1–2), and it is found also in the *Testaments*: 'Two spirits wait upon man—the spirit of truth and the spirit of deceit' (*Test. Jud.* XX, 1), in *Hermas*: 'There are two angels with a man, one of righteousness and one of wickedness' (*Mand.* VI, 2:1), and in the Clementines (*Hom.* XX, 2–3). Gregory

1. Cf. G. F. MOORE, *Judaism*, I, pp. 479–492.
2. Cf. DAVIES, *Paul and Rabbinic Judaism*, p. 27.
3. Cf. *Ecclus.* 15:14.

of Nyssa was to mention it[4] as a παράδοσις, that is to say, a teaching going back to Apostolic times.

On the other hand, there is a further aspect of the question, by which the doctrine is definitely linked with Jewish Christianity, namely the conception of a special devil presiding over each vice and an angel over each virtue. This doctrine appears in the *Testaments*, but one cannot say definitely whether it comes from a Jewish source or whether it is Jewish Christian The *Testaments* speak of the spirit of anger (πνεῦμα τοῦ θυμοῦ) (*Dan* I, 8), the spirit of envy (πνεῦμα τοῦ φθόνου) (*Sim.* IV, 7), the spirit of jealousy and vainglory (*Dan* I, 7), the spirit of lust (πνεῦμα ἐπιθυμίας) (*Jud.* XVI, 1). Above all, the *Testament of Reuben* connects seven principal vices with seven devils (III, 3–6), the seven spirits of falsehood (II, 1–2). This passage was to have a considerable influence on Origen. It is hard to avoid seeing an allusion to this doctrine in the mention of the seven devils driven out of the sinful woman of Magdala (*Lk.* 8:2) and still more so in the seven spirits (πνεύματα) which the unclean spirit, after being driven out of a man, brings back with him (*Mat.* 12:45). This is almost certainly the origin of the idea of the Seven Deadly Sins, with the refinement that in Jewish Christianity seven devils were believed to preside over them.[5]

Before Origen, however, this doctrine is found in another Jewish Christian text, the *Shepherd*. Thus 'slander ... is a restless spirit' (δαιμό-νιον) (*Mand.* II, 3), 'a mighty demon (δαιμόνιον) is stubbornness and vain confidence' (*Sim.* IX, 22:3), 'angry temper, the most evil of evil spirits (πνεῦμα)' (*Mand.* V, 2:8), 'double-mindedness (διψυχία) is an earthy spirit from the devil' (*Mand.* IX, 11), 'sorrowfulness (λύπη) is the most malignant of all spirits' (*Mand.* X, 1:2).[6]

Sim. IX contrasts twelve virgins, the twelve spirits (πνεύματα) of the virtues, with twelve women clothed in black, who are the twelve demons of the vices. Among the latter are included sadness, back-biting and anger (IX, 15:3). A little before this occurs a list of twelve virgins who are figures of the spirits of the virtues (IX, 15:2).

It will be observed that Hermas uses side by side with πνεῦμα the term

4. *Life of Moses*, II, 45. On the Hellenistic parallels cf. P. BOYANCE, 'Les deux démons personnels', *RP*, LIX, 1935, pp. 8 ff.
5. Cf. J. DANIÉLOU, art. 'Démons', *Dict. Spir.*, IV, cols. 169–170.
6. Sorrowfulness here surely denotes St. Paul's 'sorrow of the world that worketh death', or the black mood which a long line of spiritual writers have included in the sin of accidie or acedia. Cf. also with the list here given 'the angel (ἄγγελος) of self-indulgence and of deceit' (*Sim.* VI, 2:1).

δαιμόνιον, the expression employed in the Judaism of the time to designate evil spirits. It occurs in the LXX (*Deut.* 32:17) and in the New Testament (*Mt.* 7:22; 9:33, etc.). There is an interesting passage in Josephus: 'Various kinds of passions (πάθη) and devils (δαιμόνια) used to smother Saul, afflicting him with suffocation and strangling' (*Ant.* VI, 8:2 [166]). The equivalence of πάθος and δαιμόνιον will be noted. It is also of interest that the demons in *Hermas* are said to number twelve, a detail in which he parts company with the *Testaments*, though the same number does occur in the Hermetica.[7]

In those New Testament texts that speak of seven devils, the latter are described as making their abode in man, who thus becomes the object of genuine possession. This doctrine appears frequently in Jewish Christianity. As early as the *Testament of Reuben*, seven demons were described as taking up their abode each in an organ of the body (III, 3-6). The *Epistle of Barnabas* shows the soul before Baptism inhabited by devils: 'Before we believed on God, the abode of our heart was . . . full of idolatry and was a house of demons' (XVI, 7). The same feature reappears in *Hermas*, in the case of the baptised man who gives way to temptation: 'When all these spirits dwell in one vessel where the Holy Spirit also dwelleth the vessel cannot contain them but overfloweth . . . when (the delicate spirit) hath removed from that man (he is) filled with the evil spirits' (*Mand.* V, 2:5-7).

This conception of the indwelling of devils in man was to undergo strange developments in the various heterodox traditions. The Clementine *Homilies* describe the demons as 'delighting to enter into men's bodies', because, although they are spirits, they have 'desires after meats and drinks and sexual pleasures' (IX, 10). Once men have allowed them to enter into themselves, 'they become blended with the soul' (IX, 9). Lurking in the soul they suggest to it evil thoughts, 'whence many, not knowing how they are influenced, consent . . . as if they were the reasonings (λογισμοί) of their own souls' (IX, 12).[8] The last point is a polemic against those who only see in temptations a psychological fact, a *yeṣer*. The Gnostic doctrine was along the same lines,[9] Basilides holding that 'man embraces in one body a host of . . . different spirits' (CLEM. ALEX., *Strom.* II, 20: 113), and

7. XIII, 7: NOCK-FESTUGIÈRE, II, p. 203. In *Hermas* this may therefore be a trace of Hellenistic influence, or alternatively, the passage in which it comes may belong to a later version, and the number seven associated with the virtues be part of the original stratum.
8. Cf. SCHOEPS, *Aus frühchristlicher Zeit*, pp. 56-58.
9. Cf. DANIÉLOU, 'Démons', in *Dict. Spir.*, IV, cols. 170-172.

Valentinus that 'so long as the soul remains impure, it serves as an abode (οἰκητήριον) for many demons (δαίμονες)' (*Strom.* II, 20: 114).[10]

There is an interesting point here which was to be developed by Hermas —the incompatibility of the two spirits:

If thou art long-suffering the Holy Spirit which abideth in thee shall be pure, not being darkened by another evil spirit, but dwelling in a large room shall rejoice and be glad with the vessel in which he dwelleth. . . . But if any angry temper approach, forthwith the Holy Spirit, being delicate, is straitened . . . and seeketh to retire from the place; for he is being choked by the evil spirit. . . . For the Lord dwelleth in long-suffering, but the devil in angry temper. Thus that both the spirits then should be dwelling together is inconvenient and evil (*Mand.* V, 1:2–4; cf. also 2:5).

It will be observed that the Devil, the prince of the evil spirits, is no longer opposed to another prince, but to the Holy Spirit, in whom is to be seen the Third Person of the Trinity.[11]

There is another quite remarkable feature in the teaching of the *Shepherd*: the discernment (διάκρισις) of spirits according to their effects on the soul.

How then... shall I know their workings, seeing that both angels dwell in me?—Hear, saith he, The angel of righteousness is delicate and bashful and gentle and tranquil. When then this one enters into thy heart, forthwith he speaketh to thee of righteousness, of purity, of holiness, and of contentment, of every righteous deed. . . . When all these things enter into thy heart, know that the angel of righteousness is with thee. . . . Now see the works of the angel of wickedness also. First of all he is quick-tempered and bitter and senseless, and his works are evil, overthrowing the servants of God. . . . Whenever a fit of angry temper or bitterness comes upon thee, know that he is in thee (*Mand.* VI, 2:2–5).

This is the first expression of a doctrine that was to be taken up again in the fourth century by Athanasius in his *Life of Anthony*, and was to remain a classic doctrine in spiritual theology.

The spiritual life is thus seen first as a fight against the demons. They are

10. Cf. HERACLEON, *Frag.* in BROOKE, p. 77; also HIPPOLYTUS, *Elench.* VI, 34, in which the word κατοικητήριον appears.

11. Contra AUDET, 'Affinités littéraires et doctrinales du Manuel de discipline', *RB*, LX, 1953, p. 63: also chapter 4, pp. 142 ff. above, where the opposition of Christ and the Spirit to the Devil was seen to have been substituted for that between the latter and the Prince of the Angels.

indeed driven out by Baptism—this is affirmed by the *Epistle of Barnabas* (XVI, 7–8) and by the Clementine *Homilies* (IX, 19)—but they may re-enter a soul if it allows itself to be won over by their suggestion, their ἐνθύμησις (*Mand.* VI, 2:7). It is important, therefore, to strive against them; and the weapons in this struggle are principally prayer (*Hom.* IX, 10) and fasting (*ibid.*). Fasting plays a most important part in the *Shepherd* (*Vis.* II, 2:1; III, 1:2, etc.), and it has already been remarked that the pre-baptismal fast had the force of an exorcism.

Furthermore, there is no need to be afraid of the devil, for he has no power where he comes up against true faith. Hermas often emphasises this aspect: 'Fear not the devil; for if thou fear the Lord thou shalt be master over the devil, for there is no power in him' (*Mand.* VII, 2). Again he writes: 'Do thou trust the Spirit that cometh from God, and hath power; but in the earthly and empty spirit put no trust at all; for in it there is no power, for it cometh from the devil' (*Mand.* XI, 17). The 'angel of repentance' has Hermas truly in his power (*Mand.* XII, 4:7), and from henceforward 'the devil can do no more than frighten, but the fear he inspires is ineffectual' (*ibid.*). It will be observed how different this is from the pessimism of *II* (4) *Esdras* in which the domination of the *yeṣer-ha-ra'* was ineluctable. In Jewish Christianity everything is changed because the devil has been overcome by Christ. The concepts come from Judaism, but the outlook is quite different.

Ἁπλότης AND Γνῶσις

Another characteristic of Jewish Christian spirituality is the ideal it sets before men, which, although it is inspired by the Gospel, is strongly coloured by contemporary Jewish ascetisicm, and especially by Ebionism. This colouring is already apparent in some passages of the New Testament, but is still more marked in Jewish Christian works; and again the chief texts are the *Testaments* and *Hermas*. It has been noted earlier that these writings showed more marked Essene influences than the rest, and it is this influence which must chiefly be taken into account. Moreover, these are the texts which have probably had the most influence on the history of Christian spirituality, especially through Origen who uses them frequently and explicitly. This is, therefore, one of the branches of theology in which Jewish Christianity has exerted the greatest influence.

One of the most striking features of these texts is the importance in them of ἁπλότης, the essential disposition of the faithful Christian, and the opposite of διψυχία.[12] The concept of ἁπλότης was developing in Biblical Greek contemporaneously with the beginnings of Christianity. In that language it denoted an intention of seeking only the will of God, and translated the Hebrew *tam*; but in Jewish Christianity it began to occupy a more important place, and to take on a more technical meaning. This may be seen first of all in the *Testaments*.[13] Men are to walk in 'singleness of heart' (ἐν ἁπλότητι τῆς καρδίας) (*Reub.* IV, 1); ἁπλότης is associated with the gifts of God (*Sim.* IV, 5) and the fear of God (*Levi* XIII, 1); it represents wholeness, rectitude. It is the opposite of duplicity: 'The works of Beliar are double (διπλᾶ) and there is no singleness (ἁπλότης) in them' (*Benj.* VI, 7), and in this sense is related to the doctrine of the Two Spirits; the double man is he who remains divided between God and Beliar (*Benj.* VI, 7, according to the reading of MS A).

The *Testament of Issachar* is devoted entirely to a eulogy of ἁπλότης. 'My father blessed me, for he saw that I walked in rectitude (ἁπλότης) before him' (III, 2). 'Απλότης means both the love of God and of one's neighbour: 'On all poor and oppressed I bestowed the good things of the earth in the singleness of my heart' (III, 8). It is also associated with innocence (ἀκακία) (V, 1), and takes no account of the opinion of the world (IV, 6). It characterises the attitude of the man who rules his conduct in accordance with the Law of God alone, without making any account of the judgment of the world, and seeks to please God only, without seeking personal advantages.

It will be observed that the concept of ἁπλότης is linked both with the doctrine of the Two Ways and with the fundamental precepts of the good life, the love of God and one's neighbour. This recalls the fact that the catechesis began with precisely these two points; and it is not, therefore, altogether surprising to find that in *Barnabas* mention of them is

---

12. The concept has recently been studied by C. EDLUND (*Das Auge der Einfalt*, 1952) who has shown that the word is rare in the LXX, but takes on a greater importance in the deutero-canonical books (*I Macc.* 2:37; *Wisd.* 1:1). It occurs frequently in Aquila and Symmachus (*op. cit.*, p. 61), and in the New Testament, especially in St. Paul, who uses it to express the absence of any ulterior motive in serving our neighbour (pp. 83, 98). 'Απλοῦς is synonymous with τέλειος (p. 81). In *Mt.* 6:22 and *Lk.* 11:34 it means that sincerity of the will which seeks to accomplish what God wills; in *Eph.* 6:5 and *Col.* 3:22, it stands for obedience to masters for the sole motive of fulfilling the will of God (p. 97). Of great significance is the expression ἡ ἁπλότης ἡ εἰς χριστόν (*II Cor.* 11:3), transferring to Christ what the Old Testament said of the Law.

13. Cf. A. CAUSSE, 'L'idéal ébionitique dans les Testaments des XII Patriarches', *Jub. Alf. Loisy*, I, pp. 54.

immediately followed by 'Be simple (ἁπλοῦς) in heart and rich in spirit (πνεῦμα). Thou shalt not cleave to those who walk in the way (ὁδός) of death' (XIX, 2). The substantival form ἁπλότης occurs in (XVII, 1) and later there is a condemnation of its opposite, διψυχία (XIX, 5). This condemnation is also found in the *Didache* (IV, 4), but here its Essene colouring is less marked than in *Barnabas*.

In an important passage *I Clement* contrasts ἁπλότης and διψυχία: 'The Father bestoweth His favours on them that draw nigh unto Him with a single mind (ἁπλῇ διανοίᾳ). Wherefore let us not be double-minded (διψυχῶμεν)' (XXIII, 1–2). In order to justify this affirmation the author quotes a text which he represents as Scripture: 'Wretched are the double-minded (δίψυχοι), which doubt (διστάζοντες) in their soul and say: We have heard that these things were said to our fathers also, . . . and nothing has happened' (XXIII, 3).[14] This certainly belongs to a Jewish Christian apocryphon; it recalls *II Pet.* 3:4 which has a markedly Jewish Christian flavour, and may depend on the same source. The only New Testament text in which δίψυχος appears is *Jam.* 1:8, which also uses ἁπλῶς (1:5), and is markedly Jewish Christian in character.

It is not surprising, therefore, to find these themes again in *Hermas*. He appears, however, to use ἁπλότης only of one's duty to one's neighbour, though in this sense he does employ it frequently. It is associated with innocence (ἀκακία) (*Vis.* I, 2:4), with innocence, understanding and piety (σεμνότης) (*Vis.* III, 8:5), and is included among the seven principal virtues (*Vis.* III, 8:2). The *Second Mandate* is devoted to it, linking it with refraining from slander (2–3), with piety (4), and also with alms-giving: 'Give . . . freely, not questioning to whom thou shalt give, and to whom thou shalt not give' (4). In the *Ninth Similitude* it is associated with the spirit of childlikeness (νηπιότης) (IX, 24:3). Thus in *Hermas* simplicity means above all the simplicity of a charity which only seeks good, and this anticipates the definition of it which Clement of Alexandria was to give: 'that tenderness and directness (ἁπλότης) of intention in human relationships which is innocence (ἀκακία)' (*Paed.* I, 5:14).

The other aspect of ἁπλότης, which concerns fidelity to the Law of God, is often referred to in *Hermas*, but in a negative form by the condemnation of διψυχία.[15] Διψυχία shows a lack of firmness in the adherence

14. Cf. also *I Clem.* XI, 2 (δίψυχοι); *II Clem.* II, 2 (ἁπλῶς) of prayer with right intention; XIX, 2, where διψυχία is linked with ἀπιστία.
15. Cf. O. J. SEITZ, 'Antecedents and Significations of the Term δίψυχος', *JBL*, LXVI, 1947, pp. 211–219. The author relates the term to the two *yeserim*.

of the will to God (*Vis.* IV, 2:6: cf. II, 2:4; III, 2:2), lack of faith in the word of revelation (*Vis.* III, 3:4; 4:3), failure to resist denials and contradictions (*Vis.* III, 7:1), a readiness to be over-awed by the attacks of the demon (*Vis.* IV, 1:4–7),1 ack of confidence in the efficaciousness of prayer (*Mand.* IX, 1; 5; 7; 8; 9; 10; 11; 12). In this *Mandate*, which is entirely devoted to it, διψυχία is shown as a demon, whose opposite is πίστις, which seems in *Hermas* to replace ἁπλότης in the sense of confidence in God and as the contrary of διψυχία.[16]

Another characteristic feature of Jewish Christianity is the importance of γνῶσις. The expression occurs in Saint Paul, and attempts have been made to regard this as a 'Gnostic' element in him. Gnosis in Saint Paul, however, is the knowledge of eschatological secrets, of the μυστήριον which is revealed in Christ[17]; and this, as has often been remarked already, is a specifically Jewish conception, being indeed an essential factor in apocalyptic writing, which consists in the revelation of eschatological secrets and of the heavenly world, and is the true speculative theology of Judaism at the time of Christ. Far from this being an effect of 'Gnosticism', the facts are rather that Gnosticism adopted the expression, and interpreted it both in its content and meaning in a heterodox manner, combining it with foreign, oriental or Hellenistic conceptions.

The discoveries at Qumran have confirmed this view decisively, for gnosis as the knowledge of divine secrets plays a very important part in them.[18] Thus the *Rule of the Community* speaks of 'mysteries of gnosis' (*DSD* IV, 6). This 'true gnosis' (*DSD* IX, 17) must only be communicated to those 'who have chosen the way',[19] and who will be instructed in the 'true and wonderful mysteries' (*DSD* IX, 18). God alone is the source of this gnosis (*DSD* X, 12; XI, 3); it is 'a wisdom hidden from men, a gnosis and a thought (hidden) from the sons of men' (*DSD* XI, 6), and only God 'opens the heart of his servant to this gnosis' (*DSD* XI, 15–16). It will be seen that gnosis is closely linked with 'the Way', being only communicated to those who have chosen the latter. Finally, its subject matter

16. It is possible that this too derives from a Jewish background, if πίστις can on occasion in the NT denote not 'faith', but the 'faithfulness' or 'truth' (ʾemunah) of God: HEBERT, 'The meaning of πίστις', Theology, LXVI, 2, 1956, pp. 277 ff.; but cf. the critique by BARR, Semantics, pp. 160–166. Cf. also II Clem. XI, 1–2.

17. As DUPONT has shown: Gnosis, La connaissance religieuse dans les Épîtres de Saint Paul, p. 38.

18. Cf. W. D. DAVIES, 'Knowledge in the DSS and Mt. 11:25–30', HTR, XLVI, 1953, pp. 113–141.

19. Cf. also DSD X, 24.

is the imminence of the eschatological events announced by the prophets (*DSH* VI1, 1–7).

Gnosis in Jewish Christian writings belongs to the same complex of ideas. It is the knowledge of eschatological secrets, with an especial emphasis, already examined, on the exegesis of Cosmic mysteries in the opening of *Genesis*; but it is also more than this, it is the knowledge of the fulfilment of these eschatological events in Christ. The general conception is still in the tradition of the *Midrash of Habakkuk*, but now the events in question have been accomplished, and with Christ the eschatological tale is complete. Consequently gnosis at once takes on a new character. It becomes itself a part of the eschatological good things; it is a return here and now to Paradise, a realisation of the Kingdom. From being prophetic it now becomes mystical, and so the way is opened to the distortions which were to be associated with Gnosticism, according to which gnosis was to be regarded as actual salvation, and not merely as the knowledge of the saving event.

The *Testaments*, which are a transitional work between Essenism and Jewish Christianity, describe gnosis as communicated by the Messiah: 'The light of knowledge ($\varphi \hat{\omega}\varsigma$ $\gamma\nu\omega\sigma\epsilon\omega\varsigma$) shalt thou (the Messiah, son of Levi) light up in Jacob and as the sun shalt thou be to all the seed of Israel' (*Levi* IV, 3). This is especially apparent in the great Christological passage: 'A star shall arise in heaven, like that of a king, shedding forth ($\varphi\omega\tau\iota\zeta\omega\nu$) the light of knowledge as the sun the day' (*Levi* XVIII, 3). Noteworthy here is the connection between gnosis and enlightenment which had already been a feature of the *Rule of the Community*, and was to reappear in the interpretation of Baptism as $\varphi\omega\tau\iota\sigma\mu\acute{o}\varsigma$. This gnosis is to shine on all the peoples: 'In his priesthood the Gentiles shall be multiplied in knowledge upon the earth, and enlightened through the grace of the Lord' (*Levi* XVIII, 9). The Christian character of the doctrine is seen in a final passage: 'And there shall arise in the latter days, one Beloved of the Lord, of the tribe of Judah and Levi, . . . with new knowledge ($\kappa\alpha\iota\nu\grave{\eta}$ $\gamma\nu\hat{\omega}\sigma\iota\varsigma$) enlightening the Gentiles' (*Benj.* XI, 2).

The *Didache* contains allusions to gnosis which are all the more precious because they come in the ancient Eucharistic prayers. 'We give thee thanks, O our Father, for the life and knowledge which Thou didst make known unto us through Thy Son Jesus' (IX, 3). There is a close resemblance to the *Testament of Benjamin*, in which gnosis is communicated by the 'Beloved'. Christians confess Christ alone as the source of the true gnosis.

A later passage reads: "We give Thee thanks, Holy Father . . . for the knowledge and faith and immortality, which Thou hast made known unto us through Thy Son Jesus' (X, 2), of which it has been said: 'Christian euchology is indebted to the Jewish euchology for the theme of thanksgiving for the obtaining of knowledge. This remark is a precise indication of the continuity that existed between the prayer of the Church and that of the Synagogue, and by this route the gnosis theme entered into the Eucharistic anaphora of the *Didache*.'[20]

The *First Epistle of Clement* has a doctrine of gnosis deriving from the same source.[21] The gnosis of the Corinthians is praised (I, 2); it is through Christ that 'the Master willed that we should taste of the immortal gnosis' (XXXVI, 2),[22] all of which is in harmony with the thanksgivings in the *Didache*. Gnosis is concerned with the deep things (βάθη) of God (XL, 1), a point that was to be taken up by the Gnostics.[23] This knowledge implies certain responsibilities (XLI, 4). Gnosis is seen as a charisma, which is able 'to expound a deep saying' (XLVIII, 5). It should be added that the verb γινώσκειν occupies an important place in the liturgical prayer which concludes the *Epistle*. First, there is mention of the acknowledgment (ἐπίγνωσις) of the glory of the Name (LIX, 2), and then the text continues: 'Grant us that we may . . . open the eyes of our hearts, that we may know Thee (γινώσκειν)' (LIX, 3).

For the *Epistle of Barnabas* gnosis means the knowledge of the fulfilment of prophecy in Christ, and of the spiritual worship which in him is to replace external worship. This conception is still fundamentally similar to that of the gnosis of the *Midrash of Habakkuk*, which sought to show how prophecy had been fulfilled in the foundation of the Qumran community and in the mission of the Teacher of Righteousness; but for *Barnabas* this fulfilment is the coming of Christ and the foundation of the Church, and it is the knowledge of this reality which is the true gnosis. The object of *Barnabas* is in fact to explain the true sense of the Old Testament, the whole of which is nothing but one great prophecy whose meaning remained hidden until it was manifested in Christ.

The author declares: '(I write to you) that along with your faith (πίστις)

---

20. Dupont, *op. cit.*, pp. 38–39.   21. Dupont, *op. cit.*, p. 39.

22. As Benoit notes (*Le baptême chrétien au Second Siècle*, p. 85) this passage seems to be connected with the baptismal φωτισμός; but this does not imply a Hellenistic influence, as the author affirms (p. 94).

23. Cf. Irenaeus, *Adv. haer.* II, 22:3.

ye might have your knowledge also perfect' (I, 5). Faith is the means of introduction to the community; gnosis, the perfect knowledge of the secrets of the Kingdom will be given to the faithful. Gnosis is associated with wisdom (σοφία), understanding (σύνεσις), knowledge (ἐπιστήμη) (II, 3).[24] It is related, as it was in the *Testaments*, to the Two Ways: 'A man shall justly perish, who having knowledge (γνῶσις) of the way of righteousness (ὁδὸς δικαιοσύνης) forceth himself into the way of darkness' (V, 4).[25] To cite concrete examples, the knowledge which gnosis imparts is the hidden meaning of the land flowing with milk and honey, mankind re-created in the flesh of Christ (VI, 9–16); it is the understanding (γνῶσις) of the symbolism of the 318 servants of Abraham (IX, 8), the knowledge of the figurative meaning of the OT dietary laws (X, 10).

The *Odes of Solomon* afford a further example of the liturgical thanksgiving for gnosis, such as that found in the *Didache*. The gnosis theme recurs constantly: 'The Lord has multiplied the knowledge of Himself and is zealous that those things should be known which by His grace have been given to us' (VI, 5). Thus gnosis is the knowledge of the eschatological gifts given in Christ, and it is Christ himself who reveals them: 'Ignorance hath been destroyed because the knowledge of the Lord hath arrived' (VII, 24). Gnosis is here contrasted with previous ignorance. Furthermore, it makes possible the true praise (VII, 28), a detail which recalls the *Rule of the Community*. This 'knowledge of the Most High' is a secret and is only given to those who recognise Christ (VIII, 9–11).[26] Thus gnosis perfects faith.

Gnosis in the *Odes* is linked with Baptism. A baptismal hymn begins: 'I acquired His knowledge' (XI, 4), and through this knowledge the baptised 'forsook the folly which is spread throughout the earth' (XI, 9). It is knowledge of the way of light: 'The thought of knowledge hath been mine . . . through Him. The way of error I have left and have walked towards Him' (XV, 5–6),[27] but this knowledge, 'given abundantly' (XII, 3), is meant to be communicated: 'The Lord hath directed my mouth by His word: and He hath opened my heart by His light . . . and granted me to speak the fruit of His peace, to convert the souls of them who are willing

24. Cf. also XXI, 5.   25. Cf. also XVIII, 1; XIX, 1.
26. This was a characteristic of the Essene gnosis, which was communicated only to the initiate.
27. BERNARD (*op. cit.*, p. 62) compares this with CLEM. ALEX., *Paed.* I, 6:29: 'The illumination that we receive is knowledge (γνῶσις) . . . which makes ignorance disappear.'

to come to Him' (X, 1–3). This link between gnosis and praise is very reminiscent of the Qumran *Psalms of Thanksgiving*, and especially of the ending of the *Rule of the Community* (*DSD* X, 12–15). The *Odes* are simply a thanksgiving for the true gnosis which is the knowledge of the gifts of salvation.

Two conclusions may be drawn from this enquiry. First, Jewish Christian texts exhibit the two principal meanings of gnosis in the Qumran manuscripts, namely, the knowledge of the fulfilment of the Scriptures, and the knowledge of the secrets of the kingdom, a motif derived from Apocalyptic. Secondly, the *Odes of Solomon* present the possession of the gnosis in a threefold light, as knowledge, teaching and enthusiasm; and these are the three aspects which, according to Clement and Origen, should characterise the true gnostic, who is to be a theologian, a teacher and a mystic. Moreover, this gnosis is connected with Baptism; it is the entering into possession of the eschatological good things, which are already present realities. All these features show that Christian gnosis was a development of the Essene gnosis through the medium of Jewish Christianity.

This Jewish Christian gnosis was adopted by Gnosticism which drew its inspiration from it, but at the same time modified it profoundly. The Gnostics separated it from Baptism, and connected it with a new revelation, changing its characteristic of being reserved to Christians into deliberate esotericism. They gave it a more speculative and less eschatological sense, and made knowledge itself the condition of salvation. Above all they profoundly changed its content, making it the vehicle of a dualist worldview, which they claimed to discover from an allegorical exegesis of the Old Testament. It is noticeable that all these features at once recall and distort the gnosis of Jewish Christianity. It would be possible to make a study of Gnosticism from this point of view, but it would involve immense labour, and it is sufficient for the purposes of the present work to have pointed out the connection that exists between Jewish Christian and Gnostic gnosis, and to have rejected the claim of those who try to maintain that the former was indebted to the latter.

ENCRATISM[28]

There is another feature of Jewish Christianity which must be considered, namely a certain encratism. By this term is not to be understood

28. Cf. Glossary s.v.

13—T.J.C.

that common asceticism which is found in every religion, and which Christianity also demands, nor at the other extreme that condemnation of the flesh which results from a dualistic metaphysic. Rather does it refer to a whole series of restrictions in the use of material good things, which seems to be bound up neither with the essence of Christianity nor with Gnostic influence, but simply with the fact that the first Christians belonged to a Jewish environment. Here again it seems as if Jewish Christianity owed these tendencies to Essene influences. They are to be found both in orthodox Jewish Christians, and in others who take them to extremes and base them on dubious speculations.[29]

Of the several heads under which this topic may be considered the first relates to food. Here Hegesippus provides a valuable text, which speaks of James, the head of the Jewish Christian church of Jerusalem in the following terms: 'Now he was holy from his mother's womb, drank no wine nor strong drink, nor ate anything which had been alive; no razor came upon his head, he anointed himself not with oil, and used no bath' (EUSEBIUS, *HE* II, 23:5). The interpretation of this text is disputed. Is it a historical picture or an ideal portrait, and if the latter might it not be the product of a heterodox group? But in that case to which group would it belong?—for taken collectively the ideas given in the text do not fit in with any known group. For that reason there does not appear to be any ground for calling in question the historical validity of the text.

Of the two details given regarding food, the abstention from wine and intoxicating drink is clearly reminiscent of St. Luke's text on John the Baptist: 'He shall drink neither wine nor strong drink' (1:15). This must have been a feature of the asceticism of certain Jews. The Essenes did not exclude the use of wine, for there is mention of the blessing of a cup in the *Rule of the Community* (VI, 4–5). However, it will be noticed that the text takes for granted a blessing of bread, but adds only: 'If any drink wine . . .' (*DSD* VI, 3–4), which may suggest that some abstained from wine.[30] In his account of an Essene meal Josephus speaks only of bread and one dish (*Bell.* II, 8:5 [130]),[31] and represents the novitiate as a time of 'practice

---

29. Cf. PETERSON, 'L'origine dell' ascesi cristiana', *Euntes docete*, I, 1948, pp. 195–204: reprinted and expanded in *Frühkirche, Judentum und Gnosis*.

30. Cf. VERMÈS, *Les manuscrits du désert de Juda*, 1953, pp. 60–61. Jerome praises the Essenes for abstaining from wine (*Adv. Jov.* II, 14).

31. Philo, on the other hand, explicitly mentions the abstention from wine in the case of the Therapeutae (*Vit. Cont.* 37, 73).

in asceticism' (πεῖρα ἐγκρατείας) (*Bell.* II, 8:7 [138]).[32] All this is a clear indication of the ascetical tendencies of the Essene community.

An argument suggesting abstinence from wine among the more pious Jews may also be found in the fact that Christ causes surprise by being a drinker of wine (οἰνοπότης) (*Lk.* 7:34); but the chief significance of the incident is that Christ here breaks with the food prohibitions, and it is therefore all the more remarkable to find them observed by James. Abstinence from wine should therefore be regarded not as a Christian feature, but as a survival of Jewish pietism. Moreover, in James this is accompanied by other features of Jewish origin, such as that of not allowing a razor to touch his head, which was also a feature of the *nazorim*, those who had made a vow. The abstention from baths, quite the opposite of Essene practice, would here point also towards the practices of the Nazirite, rather than to a strictly Essene setting.

Whatever may be its origin, the proscription of wine was to remain a feature of certain Jewish Christian groups with heterodox tendencies. Hippolytus records it as a mark of the Encratites (*Elench.* VIII, 27), and it was also typical of the Ebionites, who did not use wine even for the Eucharist, but acknowledged only a cup of water: '(The Ebionites) reject the commixture of the heavenly wine, and wish only the water of this world' (IRENAEUS, *Adv. haer.* V, 1:3).[33] The same custom was to be found among the Gnostics. Thus in the *Acts of Thomas*, the Apostle refuses the wine Mygdonia brings him for the Eucharist: 'He brake bread and took a cup of water...' (121).[34]

Secondly, according to Hegesippus, James abstained from all animal flesh. Here again rigorist tendencies appear. The Jewish Law forbade the eating of the blood of animals, and consequently of 'strangled' (πνικτά) meat; and the *Acts of the Apostles* relates how insistent James was that this precept should be preserved in the Church (15:29). It was certainly the common practice of Jewish Christians, and not merely of the Nazarenes of strict observance who also retained circumcision and the sabbath. In Ebionite circles, however, this tendency was extended to the use of all

32. The same is true of the Therapeutae (*Vit. Cont.* 34).
33. The words 'heavenly' and 'of this world' are an allusion to the mixture as a symbol of the union of the divinity and humanity in Christ: cf. H. J. SCHOEPS, *Theologie und Geschichte des Judenchristentums*, p. 194.
34. Clement of Alexandria speaks of heretics who use 'bread and water in the oblation, in contravention of the rule of the Church. There are even some who celebrate the Eucharist with mere water' (*Strom.* I, 19: 96); cf. also *Acts of Peter* 2.

meat, involving a rigorous vegetarianism.[35] The *Clementine Homilies* describe Peter as using 'only bread and olives, and rarely vegetables' (XII, 6). Clement records a tradition, which is certainly Jewish Christian, according to which Matthew 'partook of seeds, and fruits, and vegetables, without flesh' (*Paed.* II, 1:16).

These views led the Ebionites to modify Scripture to fit in with their theory, according to the doctrine of the false pericopes.[36] Thus Epiphanius records that they regarded as an interpolation the passage which says that 'Abraham offered a calf with milk to the angels' (*Pan.* XXX, 18:7). In the same way they altered the Gospel story: John did not live on locusts (ἀκρίδας), which Clement of Alexandria regarded as already 'carrying temperance to the extreme' (ὑπερτείνας τὴν ἐγκράτειαν) (*Paed.* II, 1:16), but on girdle-cake (ἐγκρίδα) (*Pan.* XXX, 13:5); to the Apostles' question: 'Where wilt thou that we eat the Passover?', Jesus answers: 'Do you think I have desired to eat flesh at the Passover with you?' (XXX, 22:4), an answer intended to rule out the idea that Christ could have eaten the Paschal lamb. Epiphanius states that 'they abstain from all meat and from every kind of flesh' (XXX, 15:3). In this case also precedents can be found in Essenism.[37]

There is one more feature of Ebionism that calls for examination: the daily use of baths of purification. Epiphanius records it in his account of them (XXX, 16:1), and it is mentioned also in the *Clementines*, where Peter, the ideal of the ascetic, apparently bathes morning and evening (*Hom.* IX, 23; X, 1; X, 26). These writings seem to distinguish two forms of purificatory bath, quite apart from Baptism.[38] One is the bath required after sexual intercourse, an expression of the duties connected with the sexual life. This bath is obligatory, belonging to the traditional Jewish elements upheld by the Council of Jerusalem, and it was a feature of the life of every Jewish Christian. The other, which consisted of daily ablutions, characterised the devout man, the ascetic. This use of the daily bath was a feature of Qumran, and may be regarded as also of Essene origin.

35. MOLLAND has shown clearly the distinction between the general obligation of abstaining from πνικτά and the ascetics' ideal of 'vegetarianism': 'La circoncision, le baptême et l'autorité du décret apostolique', *ST*, IX, 1955, p. 32.
36. Cf. pp. 57 ff., 60 f. above.
37. JOSEPHUS, *Bell.* II, 8, 5[133]; PHILO, *Vit. Cont.* 37, 73. Satornil abstained from meat through false asceticism (continentiam = ἐγκράτειαν: IRENAEUS, *Adv. haer.* I, 24:2).
38. MOLLAND, *op. cit.*, p. 35; cf. also STRECKER *Das Judenchristentum in den Pseudo-klementinen*, pp. 208–209; PETERSON, *Frühkirche, Judentum und Gnosis*, pp. 235, 288.

Whatever, therefore, may have been the case with regard to the obligatory prescriptions of the Law, these features indicate that in Jewish Christianity an ideal of encratism survived which involved abstention from wine and from meat, and frequent purifications. This ideal seems to be connected with a Jewish pietist and more particularly an Essene milieu, and to have been adopted by John the Baptist. Although it was set aside by Christ, there is evidence that it persisted in the Jerusalem community, and especially in the person of its bishop James. Later it was to be found in Ebionism (together with distinctly heterodox features such as the suppression of wine in the Eucharist), while the Jewish Christians of the *Clementines* regarded such practices as the normal accompaniment of the life of the perfect ascetic, without however making them of obligation.

Similar problems are presented with regard to virginity. It was remarked in the previous chapter that in some cases virgins seem to have occupied a special position in the community. It is quite certain that virginity itself, as an ideal set before particular individuals, was part of the Christian message, Saint Paul for one being quite explicit on this point; but this does not mean that the way in which virginity was regarded in Jewish Christianity did not owe something to the Jewish environment.

The evidence, indeed, suggests that it did, for although the ordinary Jewish tradition exalted marriage, it is possible, at least in the case of the Essenes, to see the ideal of virginity emerging in Judaism at the time of Christ. The question is, however, a complicated one. Philo seems to say that celibacy was the normal state of Essenes, and Josephus says the same, nevertheless pointing out that some of them were married. The Qumran documents assume marriage as the normal state of the Zadokites,[39] and female bones have been found in the cemetery at Qumran.

There is no denying that there is here a degree of contradiction. It may have been a case of gradual evolution, but the real solution seems to lie in another direction. Philo describes the life of the monks of Qumran. These were not, however, the entire body of Essenes, but rather the elite of the community; and there may, therefore, have been two categories of Essenes: the perfect, vowed to contemplation and observing celibacy, and the main body of the community, who led a normal life and practised no special asceticism.

It is worth noting that something similar to this is found in Jewish

39. Cf. VERMÈS, 'Quelques traditions de la communauté de Qumran', *Cah. Sioniens*, VIII, 1955, pp. 42–44.

Christianity. Marriage is not condemned, but appears to be to a certain extent looked down upon, and this difference at the ascetic level seems moreover to correspond to a higher and lower level of initiation into the knowledge of mysteries. Here already is the union of gnosis and apatheia which was to mark the 'gnostics' of Clement of Alexandria, and far from being a Greek innovation this is on the contrary a traditional feature.

Such a tradition was preserved for a long time in the Syrian community[40]; but the same thing is also found among the Ebionites. They had two stages of initiation[41]: the body of the faithful had to observe the Noachic[42] precepts, but some practised a higher asceticism. The *Diamartyrion* (1) shows that the latter were admitted after a long initiation to receive closely-guarded teachings which they were required to keep secret.

The same pattern is observable in their attitude to virginity. The Clementine *Homilies* do not condemn marriage; they exhort young people to marry in order to avoid the disorders of fornication (III, 68). Elsewhere the statement is found: the true prophet made marriage a law, but allowed continence. The account in Epiphanius which describes a later stage of the community states: 'Nowadays virginity and continence are forbidden among them, as in the other sects like them. But formerly they held virginity in esteem, probably because of James, the brother of the Lord, to whom they attribute the writings to the presbyters and virgins' (XXX, 2:6).

This exaltation of celibacy and the privileged position of virgins in the community seem to have led, partly no doubt as a result of outside influences, to two kinds of exaggeration, which indicate the strength of these tendencies in Jewish Christianity. These exaggerations are characteristic in particular of certain Gnostic groups. The first is a tendency to depreciate the importance of membership of the general community, and of Baptism by which people are introduced into it, and to hold that the true community is that of the faithful of the second degree, who call themselves Gnostics.

The second exaggeration is, however, the more important in this context, since it condemns marriage. As might be expected, it appears among the Syrians, Satornil regarding marriage as diabolical (*Adv. haer.* I, 24:2), and Tatian condemning it and founding the sect of the Encratites (*Adv. haer.* I, 28:1). But the same excesses crop up in other places: in Asia Minor Marcion is hostile to marriage, while in Egypt the same tendency is found

40. Cf. Vööbus, *op. cit.*, pp. 20–25.
41. As Molland has rightly emphasised, *op. cit.*, pp. 10–11.
42. Cf. Glossary s.v.

in the *Gospel of the Egyptians*, quoted by Clement of Alexandria (*Strom.* III, 5: 45; III, 9: 66). At the end of the second century Julius Cassian published his treatise *On continence* (περὶ ἐγκρατείας) or *On the Life of the Eunuch*, which entirely condemns sexuality (*Strom.* III, 13: 91).

One aspect of this hostility to marriage may be seen in apocryphal Acts influenced by Gnosticism, namely the invitation to spouses to separate. This feature too derives from Jewish Christianity. Thus in the *Acts of John*, Andronicus at John's direction lives henceforward with Drusiana as a brother with a sister (63).[43]

It may be asked whether similar tendencies did not appear in orthodox circles. Such a tendency does indeed seem to have developed in Syria, to judge from the *Odes of Solomon*,[44] and in the *Shepherd* the angel advises Hermas to live with his wife henceforward as with a sister (ἀδελφή) (*Vis.* II, 2:3), which recalls John's advice to Andronicus. *II Clement* shows a similar tendency (XII, 2–6), the author quoting the *Gospel of the Egyptians* in support of his thesis.[45]

There is evidence, therefore, of several different attitudes. On the one hand there is the Christian teaching of virginity as an ideal recommended to some, a doctrine found notably in *St. Paul*; at the other extreme there is the radical condemnation of marriage which characterised circles affected by Gnostic dualism. Between the two is the Jewish Christian community, which was influenced by Essenism and in which, without there being any condemnation of marriage, there was nevertheless a pronounced Encratite tendency. Finally, in certain Judaising groups like the Elkesaites, a condemnation of virginity and an obligation of marriage can be observed.

The spiritual vigour of primitive Christianity found its expression in forms borrowed from the practices of the Jewish community and markedly Essene in character. Some of these features seem almost to distort the Christian message, but by and large they are simply a particular mode in which it found expression. In a Hellenistic environment the idea of the sage was to play a similar role. In both cases there is a working out of that general law by which the Gospel message is grafted on to the forms of asceticism current in the environment in which it develops.

43. Cf. also *Acts of Peter* 34. Marcion's position is the same (EUSEBIUS, *HE* V, 18:2).
44. Cf. PETERSON, 'L'origine dell' ascesi cristiana', pp. 198–200.
45. H. KÖSTER (*op. cit.*, pp. 102–105) considers, however, that the two texts have a common source.

CHAPTER FOURTEEN

MILLENARIANISM

ILLENARIANISM, the belief that there will be an earthly reign of the Messiah before the end of time, is the Jewish Christian doctrine which has aroused and continues to arouse more argument than any other. The reason for this, however, is probably a failure to distinguish clearly between the various elements of the doctrine. On the one hand, it seems hard to deny that it contains a truth which is a part of the common stock of Christian teaching, and which occurs in the New Testament in *I-II Thessalonians*, in *I Corinthians* and in the *Revelation* of John. This truth is that of the Parousia, Christ's return to this earth at the end of time to establish his kingdom, a belief which was attacked by Marcion, and which Tertullian rightly defended against him.[1] It implies no more than that there is to be a period of time, the duration of which is unknown to men, and which in the last days will cover the return of Christ, the resurrection of the saints, the general Judgment and the inauguration of the New Creation.[2]

In *Revelation* and in Jewish Christian theology this doctrine is expressed in symbolism borrowed from Jewish apocalyptic. The conception of a Messianic reign preceding the Last Judgment and the New Creation is to be found as early as *Ezekiel*, and this made it possible to attach the two types of eschatological prophecy in Scripture, namely that relating to an earthly triumph of the Messiah, and that speaking of a New Creation, to two successive stages in Time. This conception took on a more precise form in the non-canonical apocalypses. It appears in *I Enoch* and *II* (4) *Esdras* 6:20-28, and *II Baruch* describes the Messianic reign in the imagery of Paradise (XXIX, 4-8). The *Revelation* of John made use of the same material to describe the times of the Parousia.

It must be added, however, that Jewish Christian authors, following

1. *Adv. Marc.* III, 24. Cf. H. BIETENHARD, 'The Millennial Hope in the Early Church', *SJT*, VI, 1953, pp. 15-17.
2. Cf. O. CULLMANN, *Königsherrschaft Christi und Kirche im NT*, Basle 1941, p. 14.

Jewish influences, added other more dubious elements. Old Testament prophecies or those of Christ regarding the world to come were applied to the reign of the Messiah. Moreover, the promises made to Israel were taken literally, and some saw the millennium as the triumph of the Chosen People. It is easy to understand that Christians coming from Hellenism would find such notions 'mythical' or 'Judaic'. But these Hellenist converts, not knowing how to distinguish what was valid in such conceptions, rejected the millenarian doctrine *in toto*, either impugning the canonicity of the *Revelation*, like Gaios, or condemning literal interpretation of the text, like Origen, or like Tyconius and many moderns, seeing the millennium as the time of the Church.

JEWISH CHRISTIAN ESCHATOLOGY

Millenarianism is the form in which Jewish Christianity expressed the doctrine of the Parousia. An early witness to this is the *Ascension of Isaiah*, which after describing the reign of Antichrist, who is identified with Beliar, goes on to say:

And after 1332 days the Lord will come with His angels and with the armies of the holy ones from the seventh heaven, with the glory of the seventh heaven, and He will drag Beliar and his armies into Gehenna. And He will give rest to the godly whom He shall find in the body in this world. . . . But the saints will come with the Lord with their garments which are stored up on high in the seventh heaven: with the Lord they will come, those whose spirits have been re-clothed; they will descend and be present in the world; and He will establish those who have been found in the body, with the saints, in the garments of the saints; and the Lord will minister to those who have kept watch in this world. And afterwards they will be transformed in their garments on high, and their bodies will be left in the world (IV, 14–17).

This text belongs to a very primitive stage of the Christian faith. The context is the same as that of *Thessalonians* and *Corinthians*, and the doctrine appears in the standard form, making use of apocalyptic imagery. Christ's Parousia involves first the victory over Antichrist (cf. *Rev.* 19:19), when Beliar is cast into the lake of fire (cf. *Rev.* 19:20; 20:10; *II Thes.* 1:8 f.), then the resurrection of the saints who are already dead (cf. *Rev.* 20:4; *I Cor.* 15:23; *I Thes.* 4:16). Next the saints who are still living are transfigured (cf. *I Cor.* 15:51 f.; *I Thes.* 4:17), and all reign on the earth with Christ (cf. *Rev.* 20:4). This is called the Time of Rest (*II Thes.* 1:7) or the millennium (cf. *Rev.* 20:4), and after it comes the Last Judgment, the resurrection of the wicked for punishment, and the transfiguration of the righteous, which is a second resurrection and an entry into incorruptible life (cf. *I Cor.* 15:25 ff., 53 ff.; *I Thes.* 4:17; *Rev.* 20:11–15).

This form of millenarianism, which the *Ascension* shows to have been present in the Syro-Palestinian area, is an early type, representing a common basic belief, and not connected with any one particular group. *I–II Thessalonians* show that it was the belief of Christians in Greece, since Paul is content merely to add some precision in detail, and assumes that his correspondents were expecting this earthly reign of Christ.[3] Moreover, the doctrine underlies the various developments to be found in the *Revelation* of John. The essential affirmation is of an intermediate stage in which the risen saints are still on earth and have not yet entered into their final state. Nothing, however, is said about the nature or duration of this stage, for this is one of the aspects of the mystery of the last days which has as yet to be revealed.

At the opposite extreme to the conception shown in the *Ascension of Isaiah* is Ebionite messianism,[4] which is a continuation of Jewish temporal messianism, and corresponds to the 'Judaic' tendency that was to be condemned by the Fathers of the Church. Its main feature is the very material character of the expected messianic kingdom. Saint Jerome alludes to this kind of millenarianism when he writes: 'The Jews and the Ebionites, heirs of the Jewish error, who have taken the name of the "poor" through humility, understand all the delights of the thousand years in a literal sense.'[5] Here Jerome underlines two important features: first, the influence exerted upon this school by Jewish messianism—a point which must be referred to later—and secondly, the literal interpretation of the prophecies.

Jerome's evidence seems to be confirmed by an earlier witness to which attention does not appear so far to have been drawn, namely that of the *Clementine Recognitions*. Here Caiaphas is presented as conducting the trial of orthodox Christianity, which for the author means of course Ebionism:

Caiaphas attempted to impugn the teaching of Jesus, saying that He affirmed things that were inconsistent (*vana*); for he had said that the

3. Cf. J. DUPONT, 'Ev Χριστῷ, Louvain 1952, pp. 40–45.
4. Cf. H. J. SCHOEPS, *Theologie und Geschichte des Judenchristentums*, pp. 82–87.
5. *Com. Jer.* LXVI, 20.

poor were blessed, and yet had promised earthly rewards, and had placed the source of reward in an earthly inheritance, and had promised that those who should fulfil righteousness should be satisfied with meat and drink.[6]

There are striking affinities between this text and that of Jerome. Both speak of the poor, who are the Ebionites; and although the emphasis is here placed not on Christ's return and His reign, but on the material rewards of the righteous, yet in both cases this hope is based on a literal exegesis. On this point, moreover, the text of the *Recognitions* supplies an important piece of information, in the shape of a clear allusion to the Beatitudes. Another passage which is called to mind is *Mk.* 10:29–30: 'No one hath left home or brothers, or sisters, or mother, or father, or children, or lands for my sake and for the sake of the gospel, but shall receive a hundred-fold *now in this present time.*' The presumption is that there existed among the Ebionites a millenarian exegesis of the New Testament, which was to find a parallel in orthodox writers like Irenaeus.

True millenarianism lies between these two conceptions. It is charac-terised by the elaboration which it was able to give to the ordinary teaching on the Return and Reign of Christ by making use of the symbolism of Jewish apocalyptic. It is this elaboration which constitutes the Jewish Christian theology of millenarianism proper, and the primary document for it is the *Revelation* of John. There is no need to study in detail here chapters 19:11 to 21; all that is necessary is to note that they contain three elements. First, there are the Christian themes of the Parousia, of the resurrection of the saints, and of the reign of Christ, which have also been noted above in Saint Paul.[7] Secondly, John is inspired by Ezekiel 36–48, as is shown conclusively by the allusion to Gog and Magog (*Ez.* 38:2; *Rev.* 20:8). Finally there is the allusion to the thousand years, which occurs six times (20:2–7) and is connected with Jewish apocalyptic. It will be necessary to enquire into the origin and meaning of this conception.

The earliest and most conclusive witness to this millenarianism comes from the same Asiatic background as the *Revelation*, namely Papias, the contemporary of Polycarp, who records older traditions going back to

6. *Rec. clem.* I, 61.
7. Cf. H. BIETENHARD, *Das Tausendjährige Reich*, Zurich 1955, pp 60–62; A. WICKEN-HAUSER, 'Das Problem des tausendjährigen Reiches in der Johannes-Apokalypse', *RQ*, XL, 1932, pp. 13–27.

Apostolic times. In the section which he devotes to Papias, Eusebius makes an explicit allusion to this doctrine:

> The same writer (sc. Papias) has quoted . . . certain strange parables of the Saviour and teachings of His and some other things of a rather mythical character as coming to him from unwritten tradition. And among these is his statement that there will be a certain period of a thousand years (χιλιάς) after the resurrection from the dead, when the kingdom of Christ must be set up in a material order on this earth (*HE* III, 39:11–12).

This passage is quite in harmony with the *Ascension of Isaiah*, envisaging as it does an earthly reign of Christ surrounded by the risen righteous before the Judgment.

These elements from Papias were to be developed still further in Irenaeus:

> (The blessing of Isaac) refers unquestionably to the times of the (messianic) kingdom when the righteous shall bear rule upon their rising from the dead; when also the Creation, having been renovated and set free, shall bring forth an abundance of all kinds of food (simply) from the dew of heaven, and from the fertility of the earth. The Elders who saw John, the disciple of the Lord, related that they had heard from him what the Lord used to teach in regard to these times, saying: The days will come in which vines shall grow each having ten thousand branches, and in each branch ten thousand twigs, and in each twig ten thousand shoots, and in each one of the shoots ten thousand clusters, and on every one of the clusters ten thousand grapes, and every grape when pressed will give five and twenty measures of wine. And when any one of the saints shall lay hold of a cluster, another shall cry out: 'I am a better cluster, take me; bless the Lord through me' (*Adv. haer.* V, 33:3).

Irenaeus goes on to declare that it will be the same with corn and the other fruits of the earth, and then adds: 'All the animals, feeding only on the produce of the earth, shall in those days live in peaceful harmony together, and be in perfect subjection to Man. And these things are attested in writing by Papias, the disciple of John, and a companion of Polycarp, a man of ancient time, in his fourth book, for there were five books compiled by him. And he says also: These things are credible to those who believe. And the traitor Judas did not believe, and said: How shall such prophecies be fulfilled by the Lord? And the Lord replied: They who shall come to those times shall see' (V, 33:3–4).

The new element here is the renewal of the earth. It will produce without any need of tilth or sowing, and will display extraordinary fecundity. This of course implies that during the earthly reign of the Messiah those risen from the dead will continue to take material nourishment, and, in quoting Papias, Maximus the Confessor emphasises this detail: 'In his fourth volume Papias spoke of the pleasure of food at the time of the resurrection.'[8] This fits in well with the evidence of the *Ascension of Isaiah*, which stresses the fact that it is only after the earthly reign that men will cast off their flesh. That is why there will be a first resurrection in which the just will have a transfigured body, but it will still be earthly and will be followed by a second more complete transformation.

This view is developed explicitly by another, later, author who is, with Irenaeus, a vital witness to the Asiatic tradition of millenarianism. Methodius of Olympus writes:

> Just as the Jews, after the repose of the Feast of Tabernacles, arrived at the Promised Land, so I too, following Jesus who has passed into the heavens, shall attain to Heaven, no longer living in tabernacles, or rather my own tabernacle no longer remaining as it was, but being transformed after the millennium ($\chi\iota\lambda\iota o\nu\tau\alpha\epsilon\tau\eta\rho\iota s$) from a human and corruptible form into angelic greatness and beauty (*Conv.* IX, 5).

Here Methodius sees the time spent by the Jews in tabernacles in the desert before they entered the Promised Land as a type of what he had earlier called 'the thousand years of rest' and 'the resurrection'. The 'tabernacles' represent the bodies of the risen men who still keep their earthly form during the millennium.[9]

It will have been observed that with the idea of the spontaneous and marvellous fecundity of nature Papias associates that of the reconciliation of the animals to one another and their submission to Man. This is a traditional feature of the description of messianic times, being found in *Isaiah* (11:6–9; 65:25), as Irenaeus himself remarks in commenting on Papias (V, 33:4). The conception reappears in apocalyptic (cf. *II Baruch*

---

8. *Schol. in Eccl. Hier.* 7.
9. It will be observed that the body remains corruptible. In the millennium it has in fact only an exceptional longevity, viz. that of Adam in Paradise, which was precisely a thousand years. The gift of incorruptibility is only given after the thousand years, as Tertullian states; cf. below p. 389.

LXXIII, 6). Similarly, the idea that in messianic times the earth will produce its fruits without any need of man's labour, and that its fruitfulness will be unparalleled, also has its origin in the Prophets (*Amos* 9:13), and in Apocalyptic acquires the actual form which Papias uses: 'For all the seed which is sown thereon each measure shall bear a thousand' (*I Enoch* X, 19).

In the Prophets and in Apocalyptic however these descriptions refer to the future world in general, which is conceived as a transfiguration of the earth. The originality of the tradition witnessed to by Papias consists in its application of these paradisal descriptions to earthly reign of the Messiah. The only Jewish parallel is in *II Baruch*, and even this is concerned only with the fruitfulness of the earth, not with peace between the animals (XXIX, 5–8).[10] Moreover, in the *Revelation* the unheard-of fertility of the trees is not a feature of the millennium, but of the new creation.[11]

These facts help to bring out one of the characteristic features of Asiatic millenarianism, namely that it applies to the reign of the Messiah certain prophecies of the Old Testament which properly relate to the world to come, though it is of course true that in the Prophets themselves these two kinds of prophecy are not distinguished. It was such prophecies about the reconciliation of the animals (*Is.* 11:6–9; 65:25), the increased splendour of the sun and the moon (*Is.* 30:26), and the unprecedented fertility of nature (*Am.* 9:13), that gave millenarianism the 'mythical' character which so shocked Eusebius, and which is not to be found in the *Revelation* of John.

It remains to observe that these conceptions seem to have been current in a fairly widespread circle. Irenaeus attributes them in the first place to the Elders, and then adds that they are also to be found in Papias. They are not, therefore, restricted to the latter. Moreover, according to Papias, the Elders claimed to have received them from John, who in his turn said that he had had them from the Lord. This ascription is a still unsolved mystery. There can be no question of attributing these teachings in fact to Christ; but they must at least go back to the very first Christian community, and this accounts for the respect in which they were held by a man of the stature of Irenaeus.

Besides the evidence of Papias there are other indications of the presence of millenarian conceptions in the Asiatic community, namely those provided by heterodox writers such as Cerinthus, who according to Irenaeus

10. The same is true of *Or. Sib.* VII, 146–149.
11. Cf. also *Visio Pauli* 21–22: JAMES, *Apocr. Anec.*, pp. 22–23.

was known to the Apostle John (*Adv. haer*. III, 3:4).[12] Caius, quoted by Eusebius, sums up his doctrine thus: 'He says that after the resurrection the Kingdom of Christ will be on earth, and that the flesh, dwelling at Jerusalem, will once more serve lusts and pleasures. And, enemy that he is of God's Scriptures, he asserts that there will be a period of a thousand years (χιλιονταετία) to be spent in nuptial feasting.'[13] Dionysius of Alexandria attributed the same views to Cerinthus,[14] adding the detail that Cerinthus believed in the restoration of animal sacrifices,[15] a feature that was to reappear in the millenarianism of Apollinarius in the fourth century. It is strange that in his account of Cerinthus Irenaeus makes no mention of millenarianism, and one can only conclude that he did not regard him as heretical on this point.

This evidence as to Cerinthus' views is interesting in two respects. First, it provides information on millenarianism complementary to that of Papias, and attests the archaic character of certain themes found in Irenaeus. A number of these features have already been noted, among them the period of one thousand years which seems to be the most characteristic tenet of Asiatic millenarianism. As for the belief in material nourishment during the millennium, since the intermediate state was one of a risen, but not transfigured body, this question was bound to arise. A new ingredient, however, is the restoration of the earthly Jerusalem. This formed no part of the *Revelation*, which knew only of a heavenly Jerusalem after the new creation, but it was to reappear in Irenaeus.

Secondly, however, although these features link Cerinthus with the Asiatic group which had included Papias and John, he nevertheless interprets them in a materialistic sense which betrays Jewish influences. It will be noted how he emphasises the sensuous pleasures of the millennium; and even if Eusebius exaggerates this materialist aspect, there can be no doubt that it did form part of the general position of Cerinthus. Again, the statement that there is marriage during the millennium is important; this feature was to reappear in Commodian,[16] and was to be one of the central points of later arguments on millenarianism. Finally, the restoration of the earthly Jerusalem is thought of as accompanied by a renewal of the Temple

12. W. Bauer explicitly connects the millenarianism of Cerinthus with Jewish Christian influences (art. 'Chiliasmus' *RAC*, II, col. 1076).
13. Eusebius, *HE* III, 28:2.
14. *Ibid*. III, 28:3-4.   15. *Ibid*. III, 28:5.
16. *Inst*. II, 3. Cf. H. Bietenhard, 'The Millennial Hope in the Early Church', *SJT*, VI, 1953, pp. 24-25.

sacrifices. This is a specifically Jewish trait.[17] Marcion was probably attacking a millenarianism of this kind when, according to Tertullian, he criticised those who expected a restoration of the Jews in Palestine during the thousand years,[18] nor should it be forgotten that Marcion was himself an Asiatic.

These details are of special interest in that they help to put Cerinthus in his proper setting. They provide evidence of Asiatic Jewish Christian groups in which Jewish messianism was especially virulent, even going so far as to look for the restoration of the power of Jerusalem and the Temple worship. This should be related to the fact that there was a very strong Jewish element in Asia, which influenced the Christian communities and kept alive, even among Jews converted to Christianity, the hope of a temporal reign of the Messiah.[19] This messianic fever was never so lively as between A.D. 50 and 70, that is to say, at the period when the influences which shaped Cerinthus were active, and its special intensity in Asia (elsewhere it was not so strong) is probably connected to some extent with the fact that whereas at Alexandria and Rome Judaism was obliged to exercise prudence, in Asia it was less threatened and could be more virulent.[20]

THE FIRST RESURRECTION

It will by now be clear that the doctrine of the earthly reign of Christ persisted above all in the Asiatic Jewish Christian community, though it does not appear to have endured in orthodox Jewish Christianity as a whole. Indeed, after having expounded the millenarian interpretation of the prophecy of Isaiah on the peace between the animals, Irenaeus adds: 'I am quite aware that some persons endeavour to refer these words (regarding the animals) to the case of believers of various nations and customs, who when they have believed act in harmony with the righteous' (*Adv. haer.* V, 33:4). Thus the prophecy of Isaiah is here applied to the times of the Church.

This appears to have been the standpoint adopted in particular by the Jewish Christian community in Rome. The *Epistles of Peter*, which accord an important place to eschatology, make no reference to millenarianism. On the contrary, *II Peter* 3:8 quotes the classic text of the millenarians:

17. Cf. COMMODIAN, *Carm. Ap.* 941–946.   18. *Adv. Marc.* III, 24.
19. Cf. REICKE, *Diakonie, Festfreude und Zelos*, pp. 283–287.
20. Cf. G. DIX, *Jew and Greek*, pp. 53–62.

'With the Lord one day is as a thousand years' (*Ps.* 89:4: EVV 90) only to apply it to the period between the Incarnation and the final catastrophe, which would seem to be an actual instance of understanding the millennial reign as relating to the times of the Church. It is easy to see how this conception, which was later connected with the doctrine of the seven millennia, provided a basis for expecting the end of the world in the year A.D. 1000, the seventh and last millennium having been inaugurated by the coming of Christ. It is worthy of note that neither Clement of Rome nor Hermas make any allusion to millenarianism—indeed, with the latter the emphasis is placed on the times of the Church as immediately preceding the final judgment.

Irenaeus does not exclude this exegesis in terms of the period of the Church, acknowledging that it is legitimate to apply the prophecy of the reconciliation of the animals to the union of the nations in the Christian body (V, 33:4).[21] But he affirms that this allegorical interpretation does not exhaust the meaning of the prophecy, for God is rich in all things (V, 33:4), nor would the ecclesiological interpretation account for the whole prophecy (V, 35:1). His real target, however, is not this typology of the Church, but the allegorism of the Gnostics, which emptied the prophecy of its historical content by transferring it to the timeless world of the Pleroma. When Paul speaks of Jerusalem which is our mother, 'he does not say this with any thought of a wandering Aeon, or of any other power which was separated from the Pleroma' (V, 35:2).

It was primarily in order to combat this Gnostic exegesis, and only secondarily to defend Asiatic millenarianism, that Irenaeus devoted to the question those chapters of the *Adversus haereses* in which he recounts and confirms the Asiatic tradition of millenarianism. In these pages there are elements which belong to his own theology, and therefore are not relevant here, but there is also a whole mass of traditional material which makes these chapters the most important source of information on Asiatic millenarianism. His quotations from Papias and the Elders have already been cited, but his work also contains a complete collection of Biblical *testimonia*, which throw great light on these particular Jewish Christian beliefs. The next task must be to assess the value of this information.

In the first place Irenaeus explains how 'the righteous must first receive the inheritance which God promised to the fathers, and reign there, when they rise again in the renewal of this creation, which is to take place at the

21. Cf. also JUSTIN, *Dial.* LXXXI, 1 ff.

appearing of God; and all this will come to pass before the Judgment' (*Adv. haer.* V, 32:1). The first reason for this, based on *Rom.* 8:19–21, is that 'the creation itself, restored to its primal state, must be without restraint at the service of the righteous'. He then points out that only thus can the promises made to the Patriarchs be fulfilled,[22] giving on this point a list of texts relating to these promises. Next comes the evidence from the New Testament. Christ says to his Apostles at the Last Supper: 'I will not drink henceforth of this fruit of the vine, until that day when I drink it new with you in my Father's kingdom' (*Mt.* 26:29). Irenaeus comments on this: 'He cannot by any means be understood as drinking of the fruit of the vine when established with His disciples in a super-celestial place; nor, again, can those who drink it be devoid of flesh' (V, 33:1).

Irenaeus also applies to 'the times of the kingdom' the saying about the hundredfold promised 'in this world' (*Mk.* 10:30). He has the following comment to make:

> What are the hundredfold rewards of this world, the feasts to which the poor are invited, the banquets given as a reward? These are to take place in the times of the kingdom, that is upon the seventh day, which has been sanctified, in which God rested from all his works, the true sabbath of the righteous, in which they shall not be engaged in any earthly occupation, but shall have a table at hand, prepared for them by God, supplying them with all sorts of dishes (V, 33:2).

It is in connection with this that Irenaeus adduces the evidence of Papias and the Elders regarding the marvellous abundance of the earth without any toil. The reference to the seventh day and sabbath rest may be left aside for the moment, since it does not appear to belong to the original Asiatic millenarianism, but it will be necessary to return to it later.

After this Irenaeus goes on to consider the prophetical texts. The most important of these is *Isaiah* 65:20–25 which he quotes twice and which has already been indicated as the basic text of Asiatic millenarianism. It is interesting to note that in the LXX this passage contains the verse: 'As the days of the tree of life shall be the days of my people' (V, 34:4). Irenaeus has no special comment to make on this, but it should not be forgotten that earlier he had recalled that the days of the tree of life were

---

22. Cf. A. HOUSSIAU, *La christologie de Saint Irénée*, pp. 129–135.

a thousand years (V, 23:2). By contrast he emphasises the reconciliation of the animals. The return to Paradise presupposes the reversion of the animals to their paradisal food, which was vegetable; and this must imply a luxuriant vegetation: 'If the lion feeds upon straw, of what a quality must the wheat itself be, of which the straw shall suffice as food for lions?' (V, 33:4).

Secondly, there is an important group of prophecies devoted to the New Jerusalem, which includes *Is.* 31:9; 54:11; 65:18; *Bar.* 5:1 ff. With regard to the last of these Irenaeus writes: 'Such things cannot be understood of the heavenly world, for it is written: God will show to the whole earth that is under heaven thy glory (*Bar.* 5:3). But they will take place in the times of the kingdom, after the earth has been renewed by the Lord and Jerusalem rebuilt after the pattern of the Jerusalem above' (V, 35:2). Then, quoting *Rev.* 21:2, Irenaeus shows that the Apostle John is speaking of the heavenly Jerusalem, which only appears after the new earth and the new heaven: 'It is after these things have taken place on earth that John, the Apostle of the Lord, says that the new Jerusalem from above shall descend. Of that Jerusalem the image is the city which was on earth before (her descent), and in which the righteous were trained for incorruption' (V, 35:2).

Thus Irenaeus makes an explicit distinction between the earthly rebuilding of Jerusalem during the millennial reign and the manifestation of the heavenly Jerusalem after the Judgment and the New Creation. In this respect his exegesis of the *Revelation* is coherent. The mention of the rebuilding of Jerusalem is important for it shows to what extent the ideas expressed here by Irenaeus were those of the Asiatic millenarianism of Cerinthus and Montanus, for whom the Jerusalem theme was of the first importance. At the same time he reveals the sources of this theme by showing that it is connected with the prophecies of Isaiah, understood in their literal sense. The feature peculiar to Irenaeus in this passage is the idea of the millennium as a first familiarisation with incorruptibility, a conception to which he returns later: 'Man will truly rise, and be truly trained for incorruption, and grow and become strong during the times of the kingdom, in order that he may be capable of receiving the glory of God' (V, 35:2).

There is one other feature by which Irenaeus here reveals his connection with the original millenarianism, namely the emphasis on those whom the advent of the millennial reign will find still alive, and who will continue to live on earth: 'All these and other words were unquestionably spoken in reference to the resurrection of the just, which takes place after the coming of Antichrist, . . . and to those whom the Lord shall find in the flesh, awaiting Him from heaven, and who have suffered tribulation' (V, 35:1). In this particular, millenarianism is still linked with the original messianic expectation, which for the Jews involved an intervention of God on earth to triumph over his enemies, and to deliver the persecuted righteous. The resurrection is simply a means of associating in this triumph the righteous who are already dead, and constitutes strictly speaking a resuscitation, a restoration of the dead to a better earthly condition—not as yet a transference into the city of God.

Irenaeus therefore testifies to the persistence of millenarianism in the Great Church at the end of the second century: and with him may be associated Melito of Sardis.[23] There was, however, also a heterodox movement which testifies to the presence of millenarianism in Asia at this period, namely Montanism. The affinities of the latter with the Johannine circle and Irenaeus are obvious, especially in the importance accorded to the Paraclete. Montanism appears to have been a conservative movement which at the end of the second century reverted to the fervent eschatological expectation which had existed in the primitive Asiatic community, and especially to its millenarianism. For this reason it supplies evidence of archaic doctrines, and information about a state of affairs identical with the Asiatic background of Papias or of Cerinthus, with which it may have been connected although itself of a later date.[24]

Tertullian is the great source of information on the millenarianism of Montanus.[25] In one passage he declares:

> We confess that a kingdom is promised to us upon the earth, before (the entry into) heaven and in a different state of existence; but after the resurrection, and for a period of a thousand years in the divinely-built city of Jerusalem, a kingdom come down from heaven. And the word of the new prophecy (= Montanism) which is part of our faith bears witness to this Jerusalem, telling us even that there will be a vision of the city as a sign before its actual coming (*Adv. Marc.* III, 24).

23. Cf. L. GRY, *Le millénarisme*, Paris 1904, pp. 81–82.
24. Cf. K. ALAND, 'Der Montanismus und die kleinasiatische Theologie', *ZNW*, LIV, 1955, pp. 113–114.
25. J. H. WASZINK has collected the principal relevant passages in his edition of the *De Anima*, pp. 591–593.

It will be observed how in his concise style Tertullian gathers together all the features of Asiatic millenarianism: the earthly kingdom of a thousand years following the resurrection and preceding heaven, and implying a state of body different from that of heaven[26]—all of which recalls the *Ascension of Isaiah* and Methodius of Olympus.[27] The most interesting feature is the place given to Jerusalem. Whereas the millenarianism of Papias belongs to the tradition of prophecies of the new Paradise, that of Montanus derives from those of the New Jerusalem. This is not the heavenly Jerusalem, but the restored earthly Jerusalem, as Irenaeus was careful to distinguish. This feature links the millenarianism of Montanus with that of Cerinthus, and anticipates the theories of Apollinarius.

The Thousand Years

The expression 'millennium' has occurred several times applied to the reign of the Messiah, but it is not always associated with it. It is not found for instance, in the Jewish texts which speak of the intermediate reign, and seems to be a stranger even to the earliest stratum of Christianity, to judge from the evidence of the *Ascension of Isaiah*. It appears in fact within a definite group, that of Papias and the Elders, of Cerinthus and of the *Revelation*. Various hypotheses have been suggested with regard to its origin, and in particular it has been associated with the doctrine of the cosmic week made up of seven millennia. While, however, it is true that it was connected with that doctrine, it is not there that its origin must be sought; for the latter also appears in the *Epistle of Barnabas*, which belongs to the Jewish Christian gnosis of Egypt and to a completely different environment from that of Asiatic messianism.

On closer examination it will be observed that in Papias the conception of one thousand years appears to have had some connection with the paradisal colouring given to millenarianism[28] and this raises the question whether there may not be a connection between the fertility of the earth, the reconciliation of the animals, and the thousand years? It is only neces-

26. 'After the reign of a thousand years, which includes the resurrection of the saints, and once the final Judgment is accomplished, changed in a moment into the nature of angels by the vesture of incorruption, we shall be translated into the heavenly Kingdom' (III, 24).
27. Cf. *De Resurr.* 25.
28. This is also true of the *Visio Pauli* 21–22; cf. JAMES, *Apocrypha anecdota*, pp. 22–23.

sary to go to the texts of the Prophets and Apocalypses to see that one of the features of the messianic reign was an extraordinary longevity. Thus the LXX of *Isaiah* 65, which has already been quoted with regard to the reconciliation of the animals, reads:

> Neither shall there be any more a child that dies untimely,
> or an old man who shall not complete his time;
> For the youth shall be a hundred years old . . .
> For as the days of the tree of life shall be the days of my people
> (65:20–22).

Similarly in *I Enoch*, longevity is associated with the fertility of the earth as a feature of messianic times (X, 17).

But there is more to be said. In the *Book of Jubilees*, in a passage of vital importance, we are told that in paradisal times Man should have lived for a thousand years, but that this span was cut short for Adam because of his sin, so that according to *Genesis* he died at the age of 930 years: 'Adam died seventy years before attaining a thousand years, for one thousand years are as one day (*Ps.* 89:4: EVV 90) in heaven; and this was because of that which is written concerning the Tree of Knowledge: On the day that ye eat thereof ye shall die. For this reason he died before completing the years of this day' (*Jub.* IV, 29–30). Here there is an exegesis of *Gn.* 2:17 in terms of *Ps.* 89:4: Adam dies on the day on which he eats the forbidden fruit; but in this context a day means a thousand years, and therefore Adam dies before completing a thousand years.

Irenaeus provides explicit evidence that this tradition of *Jubilees* was known in the Asiatic community. Commenting on *Gn.* 2:17 he writes:

> The Lord, therefore, recapitulating in Himself this day, underwent His sufferings on the day preceding the Sabbath, that is, the sixth day of the creation, the day on which man was created. . . . Some, again, link the death of Adam with the period of a thousand years; for since, they say, A day with the Lord is as a thousand years, he did not exceed the thousand years, but died within them, thus fulfilling the sentence passed on his transgression (*Adv. haer.* V, 23:2).

Irenaeus therefore confirms that there existed before him in Asia a tradition, identical with that of *Jubilees*, in which the span of life in Paradise is a thousand years.[29]

29. Cf. also *Clem. Rec.* IV, 9.

Since the Asiatics, following the lead of apocalyptic, regarded the messianic reign as a return to Paradise, it was natural that in it the length of life should be the same as Adam's ought to have been (cf. *Jub.* XXIII, 27). Now this is precisely how Justin develops the idea, with an explicit reference to the text of *Jubilees*, in a passage in which he defends millenarianism in the name of the primitive tradition against the spiritual interpretations of the Gnostics, both orthodox and heretical. It will be remembered that the *Dialogue with Trypho* in which this passage occurs, takes place at Ephesus, and therefore in the context of Asiatic Judaism. In this respect Justin is probably connected with the Asiatic millenarian circle, and is simply re-echoing its ideas—an assessment which seems all the more certain when it is remembered that the same developments appear in Irenaeus without in any way implying his dependence on Justin.

One text is of prime importance: 'I, and all other entirely orthodox Christians, know that there will be a resurrection of the flesh for a period of a thousand years in a Jerusalem rebuilt, adorned and enlarged, as the prophets Ezekiel and Isaiah, and others affirm' (*Dial.* LXXX, 4). This is exactly the same type of millenarianism as that of Cerinthus and Montanus, as the allusion to Jerusalem indicates. Justin continues: 'For thus saith Isaiah concerning this period of a thousand years ($\chi\iota\lambda\iota o\nu\tau\alpha\epsilon\tau\eta\rho\iota\varsigma$)', and then quotes *Is.* 65:17–25, in the LXX version. Certain passages only need be noted: 'For, behold I make Jerusalem gladness . . . and there shall not be there one of untimely days any more, nor an aged man who does not fill out his time . . . for according to the days of the tree of life shall be the days of my people. . . . Then wolves and lambs shall feed together' (LXXXI, 1–2).

The interest of this quotation lies in the fact that it reveals the point at which all the themes of Asiatic millenarianism converge. Here are the themes of the New Jerusalem, that of the reconciliation of the animals and that of longevity. It seems as though the essential characteristic of Asiatic millenarianism lies in its applying to the doctrine of the first resurrection the predictions of this chapter from *Isaiah*. The only element which is missing is the logion on the fruitfulness of the vine; and since this is a Jewish apocalyptic tradition, it is possible that it was associated with the chapter from *Isaiah* by certain Jewish messianist groups in Asia, and that the Christians took over the whole complex, and applied it to the intermediate kingdom. Nevertheless, the millennium in the strict sense of the word does not appear in this passage, though Justin does assert that Isaiah foretold the reign of a thousand years. The justification for this statement becomes apparent later, when he connects it with verse 22, where the LXX reads: 'As the days of the tree of life shall be the days of my people.' The introduction of the tree of life here is, of course, a speculative interpretation by the LXX and does not appear in the Hebrew; and it may, therefore, even at that time have constituted an allusion to the paradisal millennium.

Justin, who is here a witness to an earlier tradition, goes on to make the allusion more definite:

> Now we are of opinion . . . that by these words: For according to the days of the tree shall be the days of my people . . . he signifies a thousand years in a mystery. For in accordance with that which was said to Adam, that in the day in which he should eat of the tree, in that day he should die (*Gn.* 2:17), we know that he did not fill up a thousand years. We understand also that the saying: A day of the Lord is as a thousand years, accords with this. And, further, a man among us named John, one of the Apostles of Christ, prophesied in the *Revelation* that they who have believed on our Christ will spend a thousand years in Jerusalem, after which will come to pass the universal, and, in a word, eternal resurrection of all at once, followed by the judgment. And this too our Lord said: They shall neither marry, nor be given in marriage, but shall be as the angels, being children of the God of the resurrection (*Dial.* LXXXI, 3–4).[30]

Here in one passage are all the documentation and all the argumentation connected with the millennium, comprising *Ps.* 89:4, which appears in *Jubilees* and in *II Peter*, *Gn.* 2:17 and *Is.* 65:22 in the LXX version. Basing himself on *Jubilees* Justin shows that life in Paradise is for a thousand years; and since *Isaiah* makes the span of life in messianic times equal to that of life in Paradise, it is clear that the length of life in the messianic kingdom will be a thousand years. This he explicitly associates with the millennium of *Revelation*. It is clear, however, that in this context of ideas the chronological aspect of the millennium is secondary; what matters is that it points to a paradisal state of existence. Hence Asiatic millenarianism may be said to derive exclusively from speculation on the paradisal character of the messianic age, and to signify that after the first resurrection the just will live a thousand years in a new earth, but after an earthly manner.

30. On the text of this last verse, cf. REITZENSTEIN, 'Eine frühchristliche Schrift von den dreierlei Früchten', *ZNW*, xv, 1914, pp. 70–71.

Then, following the judgment, they will be translated to heaven, and become like angels.

This last point may perhaps throw light on an important feature of millenarianism, and distinguish in it two tendencies. One of the stumbling blocks of the belief was the sexual licence which it appeared to admit during messianic times. The Jewish apocalyptic tradition had linked with the exceptional fecundity of Nature that of men also: 'The righteous shall live till they have begotten a thousand children' (*I Enoch* X, 17). According to Dionysius of Alexandria, Cerinthus interpreted messianic times as a time of enjoyment of all kinds, and according to Caius made it 'a nuptial festival'.

This very materialistic conception persisted in later Christianity, occurring in Commodian and in Lactantius, who refers directly to *Isaiah* and the Jewish Apocalypses:

> After the resurrection the Son of the Most High . . . will reign among men a thousand years, and will rule them with most just command. Then they who shall be alive in their bodies shall not die, but during those thousand years shall beget an infinite multitude. As for those who shall be raised from the dead, they shall preside over the living as judges. The sun will become seven times brighter than it now is; and the earth will display its fruitfulness, and bring forth abundant harvests. Beasts shall no longer feed on blood (*Div. Inst.* VII, 24).

The begetting of many children is here seen as a feature of the millennial reign.

This conception seems to be the one assumed by Justin, since he associates Christ's saying: 'They neither marry nor are given in marriage', only with the eschatological kingdom after the messianic age. By contrast, neither the Elders, nor Papias, nor Irenaeus, nor Montanus make any reference to the continuance of procreation during the messianic reign; and indeed, if what has been said so far is correct, this is the only conception which is consistent with the application of the Adamic millennium to messianic times, for the Adamic millennium would apply to a single generation which would cover the entire thousand years, and would not, therefore, allow of the birth of children.

In the third century this second view finds a supporter against the materialistic conception of Lactantius in Methodius of Olympus:

> For now, at this very moment, the earth still yields its fruits, the waters are gathered together, the light is still severed from darkness and the

allotted number of men is not yet complete. But when the times have reached their goal, and God ceases to work on this creation, in the seventh month, on the great day of the Resurrection, the Feast of our Tabernacles shall be proclaimed by the Lord. . . . Then, in the seventh thousand of years, the fruits of the earth shall all come to an end, men shall no longer beget nor be begotten, and God shall rest from the creation of the world (*Conv.* IX, 1).

Leaving aside for the moment what the text has to say regarding the conception of the seventh millennium and its parallel with the seventh day, this is simply a clear statement of the cessation of procreation during messianic times.

It will be observed that Methodius also denies the fecundity of the earth at this period, and in this he goes a good deal further than Irenaeus. This may be a reaction and an effort to save millenarianism by spiritualising it; but it is not impossible that it may be a development of the old millenarian tradition along the lines of a typology of the repose of the seventh day, uncontaminated by the apocalyptic contribution found in Papias, which Irenaeus also used and which Lactantius was to carry to its logical conclusion. Methodius makes it clear that he is here attacking the Jews, who 'believe that the Law and the Prophets have explained everything in a material manner, and who only aspire to the good things of this world' (IX, 1). A similar polemic against the Jews on the subject of millenarianism occurs in Saint Jerome.[31]

Now it happens that there is extant an early witness which agrees exactly with the conception of Methodius, namely, the Jewish Christian *Sibylline Oracles*. The passage describing the last epoch of the world reads: 'Then thy race shall cease to be as it was before; none shall cut the deep furrow with the rounded plough; there shall be neither vine-branch nor ear of corn, but all alike shall eat of the manna from heaven with their white teeth' (VII, 145–149). Here is the same conception as that of Methodius, a cessation of the production of life, and a kind of repose of the Creation. Moreover, the text seems to be speaking of the terrestrial reign and not of the world beyond. It will be noted that the repose theme is the same as the one found in *I Thessalonians* and the *Ascension of Isaiah*, but that Methodius has related this primitive element to the theme of the cosmic week and the seventh day.

31. *Com. Zach. III*, 14.

All this suggests three distinct schools of thought in Asiatic millenarianism. The most radical one, that of Cerinthus, conceives the millennial reign as a time of material pleasures in which procreation continues, together with the fruitfulness of the earth; the moderate group, that of Papias and Irenaeus, admits material pleasures and the fruitfulness of the earth, but not the continuance of human procreation (of the three this view seems to be most in keeping with the idea of Adam's thousand years); and the third school, that of Methodius, assumes a cessation not only of human procreation, but of the fruitfulness of the earth as well. The latter viewpoint seems to be connected with a new theme, that of the millennium as the seventh day of the cosmic week, during which God ceases to carry out the work of Creation. This raises a final aspect of the question.

The Seventh Millennium

Allusions have already been noted in Irenaeus and Methodius to the millennium as the seventh day, a designation which is connected with speculations on the cosmic week. Some authors see in these speculations the origins of millenarianism,[32] a view which to the present writer seems highly debatable. Asiatic millenarianism is connected with messianist Jewish Christian circles, and the background of Jewish tradition from which they drew their inspiration knew nothing of any division of world-history into seven millennia. The conceptions of the world epochs to be found in *I Enoch* or in *Jubilees* are quite different. The idea of the seven millennia, like that of the seven heavens, was born in Hellenistic Judaism,[33] and forms no part of primitive Asiatic millenarianism. It is, therefore, hardly surprising that the earliest evidence for it occurs elsewhere.

The first work in which the doctrine of the seventh millennium is found is the *Epistle of Barnabas*. He writes:

Of the sabbath he speaketh in the beginning of creation: And God made the works of his hands in six days, and he ended on the seventh day, and rested on it. Give heed, children to these words: He ended in six days. He meaneth this, that in six thousand years the Lord shall bring all things to an end, for with him a day is as a thousand years; and this He Himself beareth me witness, saying: Behold, the day of

32. Cf. M. Werner, *Die Entstehung des christlichen Dogmas*, pp. 83–84.
33. There is evidence for it among the Samaritans, together with the messianic conception of the seventh millennium (Bauer, art. 'Chiliasmus', *RAC*, ii, 1075).

the Lord shall be as a thousand years. Therefore, children, in six days, that is in six thousand years, everything shall come to an end. And, He rested on the seventh day, meaneth this; when His Son shall come, and shall abolish the time of the Lawless One, and shall judge the ungodly, and shall change the sun and the moon and the stars, then shall He rest gloriously on the seventh day. Ye see what is His meaning; He says to the Jews, It is not your present sabbaths that are acceptable (unto Me), but the Sabbath which I have made, in the which, when I have set all things at rest, I will make the beginning of the eighth day which is the beginning of another world (XV, 3–8).

It is important to try to distinguish the principal elements in this passage. First, a relationship is established between the eschatological repose and the sabbath. This does not as yet imply any millenarianism. There is a whole tradition, to which Origen in particular is a witness, which understands the sabbath as signifying eternal life (*Hom. Num.* XXIII, 3).[34] All that is involved here is a typology of the week in which the six days of creation represent the time of this world, and the seventh day the world to come. This belongs to Jewish tradition, and was adapted by Philo.

By contrast, the conception of the ages of the world as a series of millennia seems to be an idea foreign to Judaism. The division is not necessarily sevenfold, but it takes this form in the circles of 'hellenised Magi', where it is combined with a conception, Babylonian in origin, which sees the seven cosmic periods as each dominated by a planet. Thus a system is arrived at in which seven millennia constitute the total time of the world, a scheme quite foreign to Judaism, where the duration of the world is *six* days, the seventh day representing eternal life. Hence there is no evidence of it among them at an early date.[35]

So far then there is a Jewish contribution: the repose on the seventh day, and a Hellenistic one: the seven millennia. In the passage in *Barnabas* a third element intervenes—the eighth day. Attempts have been made to find Hellenistic origins for this component. It is certain that the ogdoad plays some part in the Pythagorean number-mysticism, to which Philo is indebted, but it is not an important one; on the other hand, in Gnosticism it is of the highest importance. However, like most of the material used by

34. Cf. Daniélou, *Bible et Liturgie*, pp. 326–328.
35. It occurs in the *Prayer of Moses* (James, *Apocr. Anec.*, p. 172), and in the *Vision of Kenaz* (*ibid.*, p. 179).

the Gnostics it is borrowed from other sources. It was Christianity that gave the eighth day its importance [36]; Christ rose on the day after the sabbath, and thenceforward the eighth day is the day of the Resurrection, the Sunday, which distinguishes Christians from Jews. [37]

Into this elaborate complex of ideas the author of the *Epistle of Barnabas* introduces the archaic doctrine of the earthly reign of Christ. He does not seem to have derived it from Asiatic circles, since the characteristic of material fecundity, which it acquires with Papias, is lacking. On the contrary the *Epistle* recalls to a remarkable degree the *Ascension of Isaiah* with its idea of repose, except that in the *Ascension* this repose was not associated with speculations about the week—a detail which simply confirms the evaluation made earlier of the *Ascension of Isaiah* as a witness to the primitive stratum, earlier than the developments which the doctrine was to receive independently and in different directions from Papias and Barnabas, Asiatics and Alexandrians alike. In Barnabas, however, there is already a millenarian feature which did not appear in the *Ascension*, namely the quotation from *Ps.* 89:4. The absence of any earthly messianism seems, as has already been remarked, to be connected with the more difficult situation of Jews and Jewish Christians in Egypt.

It will be seen that the originality of *Barnabas* lies in his relating the primitive data of the eschatological repose to the speculations on the cosmic week inherited from Judaism as well as from Hellenism and Christianity. *Barnabas* was to retain both the Hellenist notion of the seven millennia as constituting the sum of history, the Jewish idea of the privileged character of the seventh day as a time of rest, and, from Christianity, the conception of the eighth day as eternal life. Here millenarianism appears rather as an answer to the speculative problem of the passage from the hebdomad to the ogdoad than as a concrete hope, while the millennium itself is conceived simply as rest. Augustine was to defend this kind of millenarianism for a long time, although condemning the Asiatic type.

Side by side with the orthodox gnosis of *Barnabas* there is further evidence of the presence of speculations on the hebdomad and the ogdoad in heretical Gnosticism. It is interesting to compare the solution provided by *Barnabas*, based on his view of the history of salvation, with that of the Gnostic Mark. In transferring these speculations to the world of Gnosticism Mark first considers the hebdomad, which is the fallen world. The problem

36. Cf. SCHMIDT, *Gespräche Jesu mit seinen Jüngern*, p. 279.
37. Cf. DANIÉLOU, *Bible et Liturgie*, pp. 329–354.

is the restoration of the hebdomad into an ogdoad, and this is achieved through the intervention of Jesus. The name 'Ιησοῦς consists of six letters; and the number six is represented by the letter *waw*, which has disappeared from the alphabet. Its re-introduction into the series of vowels changes the latter from a hebdomad into an ogdoad.[38] The analogy with the *Epistle of Barnabas* will be apparent.

The text of *Barnabas*, then, introduces a type of speculation on millenarianism which is quite different from that of the Asiatics. In it the emphasis is placed on the seven millennia followed by the eighth day, rather than on millenarianism in the strict sense. There is still a trace of this conception in Clement of Alexandria who speaks of 'time which, through the seven ages of the world, effects the restoration (ἀποκαθιστάς) of the perfect rest' (i.e. the ogdoad) (*Strom.* IV, 25:159). The Alexandrian gnosis, however, both orthodox and heretical, was to abandon this historical view for a cosmological one, in which the hebdomad signified the terrestrial world ruled by the seven planets, and the ogdoad the celestial city. This view occurs both in the Valentinians[39] and in Clement.[40]

Nevertheless, this speculation of *Barnabas* was to be combined with Asiatic millenarianism, and by none other than Irenaeus, who made a synthesis of the Asiatic tradition of the paradisal millennium and of the Gnostic tradition of the seventh millennium as a time of rest. On the latter point he seems to be dependent on *Barnabas*:

> In as many days as this world was made, in so many thousand years shall it be concluded. And for this reason the Scripture says: And God finished upon the sixth day the works that He had made, and rested the seventh day from all His works. This is at once an account of things past and a prophecy of things to come. For if 'the day of the Lord is as a thousand years', and 'in six days all created things were completed', it is plain that this completion will come to pass at the end of six thousand years (*Adv. haer.* V, 28:3).

Here are the same ingredients and the same quotations as in the passage in *Barnabas*, and it is hard to deny direct literary dependence. This confirms the hypothesis put forward earlier that the conception of the seven millennia is foreign to the old Asiatic tradition, and suggests that it was

38. *Adv. haer.* I, 14:4–7.
39. IRENAEUS, *Adv. haer.* I, 5:3; CLEM. ALEX., *Excerpta* 63.
40. *Strom.* VI, 14; 7, 10.

associated with it only by Irenaeus. Moreover, this conception of the cosmic week fitted in well with the theology of Irenaeus, and other allusions to it are therefore to be found in his works. There is an especially interesting passage which exactly identifies the seventh millennium with the messianic kingdom:

> When this Antichrist shall have devastated all things in this world, he will reign for three years and six months, and then the Lord will come from heaven in the clouds, sending this man and those who follow him into the lake of fire, but bringing in for the righteous the times of the kingdom, that is, the rest, the hallowed seventh day (*Adv. haer.* V, 30:4).

This line of thought was to be continued by Lactantius.

The strict conception of *Barnabas*, that which elaborates the original doctrine of the 'repose' of the righteous in a speculation on the seven millennia, without any reference to Asiatic apocalyptic millenarianism, is also found in Methodius of Olympus and Victorinus of Pettau at the end of the third century. The former has already been quoted. The latter writes:

> Isaiah and his colleagues broke the sabbath, in order that it might be the true and righteous sabbath which should be observed in the seventh millennium, according as the Lord made seven thousand years to correspond to the seven days. For thus it is written: In thine eyes, O Lord, a thousand years are as one day; wherefore, as I have narrated, that is the true sabbath, in which Christ shall reign with his elect.[41]

This millenarianism, less materialistic then that of Irenaeus, was the one which endured in the West, in Hilary, Gregory of Elvira and others, down to Augustine.

It may still be asked, however, whether *Barnabas* was the source of this conception, for it seems to be foreign to Egyptian gnosis and unrelated to the main theme of the Epistle. Therefore the ultimate origin must be sought elsewhere, in fact in a Syriac setting. It was here in the second century, inspired by the Irano-Babylonian speculations of the followers of the Magi on the cosmic years, that there appeared the first calculations of Christian chronographers aimed at determining the time of the Parousia.[42]

41. *De fabrica mundi* 6.
42. Cf. DANIÉLOU, 'La typologie millénariste de la semaine', *VC*, II, 1948, pp. 1–5.

The seven millennia taken in a literal sense provided a convenient frame-work for the history of the world. These speculations seem to be indigenous to the Jewish Christian environment, where the question of the Parousia was of exceptional interest.

The earliest important evidence comes in Theophilus of Antioch. He was one of the first Christian writers to take an interest in the theology of history, and was to influence Irenaeus in this direction. In his recapitulation of the chronology of world history he fixes the birth of Christ in the year 5,500.[43] He makes no direct allusion either to the seven millennia nor to millenarianism; but this figure shows quite definitely that in his view Christ was born in the middle of the sixth millennium, and this implies that the year 6,000 will begin the messianic reign which is to fill the seventh millennium, and that the year 7,000 will be the end of the world and the founding of the heavenly city.

The validity of these deductions, moreover, finds fresh support in the evidence of an author whose millenarianism was certainly that of the Syrian community, whether or not he can be identified with the Roman priest Hippolytus.[44] The *Commentary on Daniel* contains the following passage:

> And six thousand years must needs be accomplished, before the Sabbath can come, the rest, the holy day on which God rested from all His work. For the Sabbath is the type and emblem of the future kingdom of the saints, when they shall reign with Christ, when He comes from heaven, as John says in the Apocalypse. For a day with the Lord is as a thousand years. Since, then, in six days God made all things, it follows that six thousand years must be fulfilled. And they are not yet fulfilled, as John says: five are fallen; one is, the other is not yet come (*Rev.* 17:10). Moreover, in speaking of the other he specifies the seventh, in which there shall be rest (*Comm. Dan.* IV, 23).

The tradition is the same as that of *Barnabas*, with the seven millennia, the typology of the sabbath as the messianic rest, the quotation from *Ps.* 89:4 and the absence of Asiatic features. But Hippolytus adds chronological details which agree with Theophilus. The quotation from the *Revelation* is taken to mean that five millennia have passed, the sixth is now

---

43. *Ad Autolycum* III, 28.
44. NAUTIN believes he was a Syrian bishop, and not a Roman priest (*Hippolyte et Josippe*, Paris 1947, pp. 87 ff.).

14—T.J.C.

in progress, and the seventh is awaited. This is made more explicit by an allegory:

> The things that took place of old in the wilderness, under Moses, in the matter of the Tabernacle, were ordained as types and emblems of spiritual mysteries in order that, when the truth came in Christ in these last days, you might be able to perceive that these things were fulfilled. Now the ark was five cubits and a half in length, and these are the 5,500 years at the end of which the Lord came. From his birth, then, 500 years have still to pass to make up the 6,000, and then shall be the end (*Comm. Dan.* IV, 24).

Beside Theophilus, Bardaisan also attests the importance of these speculations in the Syriac community in the second century. According to George the Arab, Bardaisan held that the world would last six thousand years, and supported this by calculations on the revolutions of the planets.[45] Now this seems to imply that there is to be a seventh millennium, a conclusion confirmed by the fact that George adds to his own evidence that of Hippolytus; for the extant version of the *Didascalia of the Apostles*, which dates from the third century, but contains older elements and derives from Syria, presents the same view: 'The Sabbath is a symbol which was ordained for a season. It is a symbol of the (final) rest, and predicts the seventh millennium' (VI, 18: CONNOLLY, p. 238). The sobriety of all these texts on the subject of the millennial reign, which is associated purely with the idea of rest, should be noted.

With the same school must be associated the third century Palestinian Julius Africanus, the chief chronographer of the period. He makes the seven millennia the basis of his universal chronicle, distinguishing six periods of a thousand years, three up to the death of Peleg, when the Tower of Babel episode and the dispersion of the peoples occurred, and three up to the end of the world. He too places the Incarnation of Christ in the middle of the sixth millennium in the 5,500th year of the world.[46] Apart from the evidence of Hippolytus and Julius Africanus this era of 5,500 years, which is of millenarian origin, is confirmed by the efforts of the chronological calculators to make their reckonings coincide with it as nearly as possible.[47]

45. *PS*, II, 613–614.
46. Cf. BAUER, *Ursprung und Fortwirken der christlichen Weltchronik*, Graz 1910, p. 14.
47. Cf. RICHARD, 'Comput et chronographie chez Saint Hippolyte', *MSR*, VII, 1950, p. 239.

From this analysis may be determined the primitive developments of Jewish Christian millenarianism. The oldest element is the conception of an earthly reign of the Messiah which comes before the new creation and constitutes the 'repose of the saints'. This element is developed in a distinctive manner in Asia and in Syria. In Asia, in the world in which the *Revelation of John* was written, and for which Papias is our informant, this earthly kingdom was painted in the paradisal colours used by the Old Testament and the Apocalypses to describe the messianic age: the reconciliation of the animals, the extraordinary fecundity of the earth, and a human life-span of a thousand years. This is the millenarianism of Papias, Cerinthus, Montanus and Tertullian.

Along a different line of development in Syria and Egypt the messianic reign was related to the calculations of the astrologers on the cosmic week consisting of seven millennia. The seventh millennium is seen as corresponding to the seventh day of creation, on which God rested, and is associated with the messianic reign regarded as the 'repose of the saints'. This view differs profoundly from the Asiatic conception in that it implies the cessation of God's creative action, whereas in the Asiatic view this was intensified. This second view was held by Bardaisan, Theophilus of Antioch, Hippolytus, the *Sibylline Oracles* and Methodius of Olympus. Through the medium of Theophilus it became known to Irenaeus, who fused it with the Asiatic conception.[48]

Millenarianism had no place in the Alexandrian world, whether orthodox or Gnostic. It is true that it does appear in the beginnings of Christian Alexandrianism in *Barnabas*, but only as a foreign importation which, according to the evidence, must be connected with a Syriac influence. The true Alexandrian typology of the week of creation is the one found in Philo, Clement, Origen and the Valentinians, which contrasts the hebdomad as the world of time with the ogdoad as the world of eternity. The messianic reign is entirely absent from it. There is, however, an equivalent of this reign in Gnosticism, the conception of an intermediate place between the earthly Kenoma and the heavenly Pleroma.

48. Cf. V. ERMONI, 'Les phases successives de l'erreur millénaire', *RQH*, LXX, 1901, p. 369. It may be worth remarking that of these two millenarian traditions the first ultimately rests on an exegesis of the Paradise story in *Gn*. 2-3, and the second constitutes a speculation on the Hexaemeron, that is, on *Gn*. 1. Once again it is impossible to escape the fact which has loomed so large throughout this investigation, namely that Jewish Christian theology was to a great extent developed on the basis of a Jewish gnosis of the opening chapters of *Genesis*.

Millenarianism is equally a stranger in the Church of Rome, but for different reasons. The evidence of Hermas shows that there interest was concentrated on the building up of the Church, the completion of which is the condition for the coming of the heavenly kingdom, and the Messianic age seems therefore to be identified with the times of the Church, which themselves constitute the seventh millennium. *II Peter* supports this interpretation by applying the words of the Psalm, 'One day with the Lord is like a thousand years', the leit-motif of millenarianism, to the time separating the Incarnation from the final cataclysm. On this view Christ would have been born not in the year 5,500, but in 6,000, and calculations aimed at discovering the end of the world would therefore place this event a thousand years later, in the year A.D. 1,000. The Middle Ages have left behind an echo of these calculations, which seem to be a continuation of the Western current of speculation.

CONCLUSION

THE task which we set ourselves at the beginning of this volume was to examine the documents which have come down to us from the Jewish Christian period of the Early Church in order to draw, at least in outline, a picture of the theology of Jewish Christianity. That this theology did indeed exist as a distinct entity will by now, it may be hoped, have been established to the reader's satisfaction; but how may the character of this complex and unfamiliar material be summed up?

At every point of the investigation three concepts have constantly recurred: cosmos, apocalypse, gnosis. The subject with which Jewish Christian theology conceives itself to be dealing is essentially history, but not simply that small section of history constituted by the recorded affairs of nations, and acted out within the horizons of terrestrial sea and land. Its concern is with cosmic history, from the Beginning of things to the End of time, and from the great abyss, through Sheol, earth, firmament, planets, stars to the last infinite Heaven of God. The axis pinning together this immeasurable sphere of things and events is the Incarnation, the tabernacling in human flesh and season of the concealed glory of the Son. The source from which Jewish Christian theology is presented as deriving is apocalypse—the unveiling of the mysteries to the eyes of the servants of God, so that for the first time they see and understand the truth about the created order and the divine plan for its consummation; and this revelation is naturally enough presented in the imagery which the Jewish literature of revelation *par excellence*, that is, apocalyptic, had made its own. The result of this apocalypse is gnosis—the saving knowledge of what the divine action proclaimed in the Gospel message has effected for all men and all creatures for all time, and of the divinely appointed means of arriving at this knowledge in the esoteric exegesis of the Scriptures.

Within this framework it is possible to find an intelligible setting for many details. A first striking feature of Jewish Christian doctrine is the parallelism between Creation and Eschatology, the correspondence between *Urzeit* and *Endzeit* which the researches of Gunkel and Dahl had already shown to be a characteristic of the Semitic world-view. It is in this light that we are to understand the fondness of Jewish Christians for the various titles of the Son as Beginning, borrowed from the opening of *Genesis*; the parallelism between the function of the Name as bearer of the first Creation, and of the Cross as bearer of the second—a relation symbolised by, and perhaps even deduced from, the fact that the sign of the Cross, or *tau*, at first signified the Name; the conception of the Church, pre-existent before the Aeons, and yet waiting to be manifested in the last days, and of the waters sanctified at the beginning of the world as a foreshadowing of their sanctification by the Spirit in Baptism; and lastly, the restoration of Paradise at the end of time seen as a regaining of the Paradise that had been Man's original home.

This symmetry accords well with another central preoccupation of Jewish Christianity, that of demonstrating the events in the life of Christ and of the Church as the realisation of God's eternal Grand Design. As in Jewish apocalyptic, the eschatological realities have pre-existed in God, and before Time was the heavenly Book contained the realities only manifested at the moment when Time ceases to be. Thus the divine plan stands out in all its logic and coherence, and Man's anxious fears of being at the mercy of contingent circumstance vanish in the inner certainty created by knowledge of this plan, and by the rational and comprehensive vision which it gives him of the history of the world.

This concern with the inherence of the End in the Beginning is also of a piece with that passion for the speculative exegesis of the first chapters of *Genesis* which it is one of the major results of our investigation to have brought to light. Almost every theme of Jewish Christian teaching is linked in some way with this exegesis. The theology of the Trinity draws its inspiration from the symbolism of the three days and the seven, that of the Word from the *bereshith* and the light that is called Day, that of the Church from the creation of the cosmos and of woman, eschatology from the account of Paradise. This one feature of the Judaism of the time seems to have suggested to Jewish Christian theologians an inexhaustible variety of applications.

Indeed, in their Biblical exegesis in general, the main interest of these writers seems to have centred on the parallels to be drawn between the first and second creations. Typology, the exposition of the foreshadowings of Christ in the history of Israel, was for them more a subject of elementary catechesis; the higher speculations were directed to the knowledge of the First and Last Things, and sought principally to set the biblical data within the framework of a total world-view. Hence the value to them of angelological imagery in their teaching on the Incarnation and Redemption. For them redemption was a cosmic matter; the action of the Word extended through every region of the spiritual universe, from Sheol to the seventh heaven, and touched every creature. The Cross, the instrument of redemption, is not merely the historical and material gibbet used by God as the creative pivot of history, marvellous though that may be; it is also the double axis of the universe, transcending Space by stretching out its arms to unite all nations of men and by reaching up its head to join heaven and earth, the angelic hierarchies and the spirits of them that sleep, and transcending Time by descending as a living being into the lower parts of the earth to preach salvation to the righteous who died before Christ, and by coming in the East as the glorious herald of the Saviour's final Return.

Lastly, side by side with these advanced theological mysteries, the Jewish Christian Church had its own pattern of elementary instruction, again distinctive in character, closely connected with the processes of initiation. Here the teachings of the Two Ways, the two great commandments, the Angel of Light and the Prince of Darkness, the spirits of the virtues and the demons of the vices, and the exhortations to steadfast singleness of mind confronted the baptizand with the overwhelming reality of a clear, hard exercise of the moral will to choose, before admitting him to the sacramental world where the fire of Christ descended into the waters to destroy the demon, and the grains of God's wheat gathered from the mountains to await the Coming of the Lord.

Many of these patterns and details will find their counterparts in the more hellenised theology of the next generations; but so far as this part of our whole work is concerned it may be of value to conclude with some brief reflections on two aspects of general interest.

First, it will by now have become clear that when the language of this, the most archaic form of Christian theology, is correctly interpreted, it becomes even less possible than it was to consider the complexities of orthodox doctrine, the teaching of the great Church, as a superstructure added to some simple basic Gospel by later centuries. Here, so early as in some instances even to go behind the New Testament, we find still the divine pre-existent Christ—Name, Son and Word—his divinity attested all the more forcefully by the strange distortions to which the figure of Michael, or the great Angel, is subjected when compelled to act as the vehicle of such a visitant. We find the divine Person of the Holy Ghost, the

fact of His true personhood again made undeniable by the angelic symbolism; we find the *virginitas in partu* of the Mother of God. Even more
striking, in view of some theories that have been held, there is the clear
evidence of an elaborate doctrine of the Church as an indispensable
element in the eternal plan of God for His Creation; of a full-scale ministry,
both missionary and indigenous; and of a developed sacramental procedure,
understood as the effectual realisation of the mysteries which it signifies.
These, and other instances which it would be tedious to recapitulate, leave
little room to doubt that in all major features the Christian faith in its most
archaic expression was even then what it always has been.

Nevertheless, this unchanging faith has in every generation brought
forth things new and old out of its treasures to meet human need; and the
second service which the study of Jewish Christianity can perform for us
is to remind us of truths and resources in the Christian faith which our
own age has forgotten or underemphasised. For once again Man feels
himself imperilled by two main enemies: the demonic forces of evil within
the individual and the mass psyche, and the forces of matter and chance in
the universe around him. Of all gifts he perhaps craves most those of single-
mindedness, proceeding from an ordering and purifying of the enemies
within, and knowledge, the comprehension at last of the rationale of his
infinite and infinitely complex environment.

If, therefore, we would in this age bring to troubled mankind the salvation which only Christ can give, we could do worse than ponder the vision
of Jewish Christianity, for which saving faith meant the knowledge that
there was indeed wisdom in things, the certainty of the fulfilment of God's
Grand Design ordained from the foundation of the world; for which Christ
was Lord not only of the heart but of the heavens; for which Baptism was a
partaking in the cosmic conquest of evil; and for which the ultimate hope
was to follow the Son into the heavenly places and to hear the Thrones and
Dominations cry, 'Lift up your heads, O ye gates: and the King of Glory
shall come in.'

BIBLIOGRAPHY

BIBLIOGRAPHY

ABRAHAMS, I., *Studies in Pharisaism and the Gospels*, Cambridge 1917.
ADAM, A., *Die Psalmen des Thomas und das Perlenlied als Zeugnisse vorchristlicher Gnosis* (BZNW 24), Berlin 1959.
ADAM, A., 'Erwägungen zur Herkunft der Didache', *ZKG*, LXVIII, 1957, pp. 1–47.
ALAND, K., 'Das Montanismus und die kleinasiatische Theologie', *ZNW*, XLVI, 1955, pp. 109–116.
ALÈS, A. D', 'Le *ΠΡΕΣΒΥΤΗΣ* de Saint Irénée', *REG*, XLII, 1929, pp. 398–410.
ALLEGRO, J. M., 'Further light on the history of the Qumran sect', *JBL*, LXXV, 1956, pp. 89–95.
ALLEGRO, J. M., 'Further Messianic references in Qumran literature', *JBL*, LXXV, 1956, pp. 174–187.
ALLEGRO, J. M., *The Dead Sea Scrolls*, London 1956.
ALLGEIER, A., 'Vidi aquam', *RQ*, XXXIX, 1931, pp. 23–41.
ANDRESEN, C., *Logos und Nomos*, Berlin 1955.
ASSEMANUS, S. E., *Acta martyrum*, Rome 1748–   .
AUDET, J. P., 'Affinités littéraires et doctrinales du Manuel de Discipline', *RB*, LIX, 1952, pp. 219–238, and LX, 1953, pp. 41–82.
AUDET, J. P., *La Didachè, Instructions des Apôtres*, Paris 1958.

BAKKER, A., 'Christ an Angel?', *ZNW*, XXXII, 1933, pp. 255–265.
BANNARD, L. W., 'The Epistle of Barnabas and the Tannaitic Catechism', *ATR*, XLI, 1959, pp. 177–190.
BARBEL, J., *Christos Angelos*, Bonn 1941.
BARDY, G., 'Cérinthe', *RB*, XXX, 1921, pp. 344–373.
BARDY, G., *La théologie de l'Église de Saint Clément de Rome à Saint Irénée*, Paris 1945.
BARDY, G., 'Expressions stoïciennes dans la Prima Clementis', *RSR*, XII, 1922, pp. 73–85.
BARR, J., *Semantics of Biblical Language*, London, 1961.
BARTHÉLEMY, D., 'Redécouverte d'un chaînon manquant de l'histoire des LXX', *RB*, LX, 1953, pp. 18–29.
BARTHÉLEMY, D. and MILIK, J. T., *Discoveries in the Judaean Desert I : Qumran Cave I*, London 1955.
BARTHOULOT, J. and TIXERONT, J., *Démonstration de la prédication apostolique (PO XII)*, Paris 1919.
BATIFFOL, P. and LABOURT, J., *Odes de Salomon*, Paris 1911.
BAUER, W., 'Chiliasmus', *RAC* II, cols. 1073–1078.
BAUER, W., *Das Leben Jesu im Zeitalter des neutestamentlichen Apocryphen*, Tübingen 1909.
BAUER, W., *Rechtgläubigkeit und Ketzerei im ältesten Christentum*, Tübingen 1934.
BAUER, W., *Ursprung und Fortwirken der christlichen Weltchronik*, Graz 1910.
BAUMGARTEN, J. M., 'Sacrifice and Worship among the Jewish sectarians of DSS', *HTR*, XLVI, 1953, pp. 141–159.
BAUMSTARK, A., 'Die Zitate des Mt.-Evangeliums aus dem Zwölfprophetenbuch', *Biblica*, XXXVII, 1956, pp. 296–313.
BAUMSTARK, A., *Liturgie comparée*, Chevetogne 1939.
BAUMSTARK, A., *Nocturna laus*, Münster 1957.
BELL, H. I. and SKEAT, T. C., *Fragments of an Unknown Gospel and other early Christian papyri*, London 1935.

BENOIT, A., *Le baptême chrétien au second siècle*, Paris 1953.
BENOIT, P., 'L'Ascension', *RB*, LVI, 1949, pp. 161–203.
BERNARD, J. H., *The Odes of Solomon (Texts and Studies* 8), Cambridge 1912.
BERTRAM, G., 'Der religionsgeschichtliche Hintergrund der Erhöhung', *ZAW*, LXVIII (N.F.27), 1956, pp. 57–71.
BETTENCOURT, E., *Doctrina ascetica Origenis*, Rome 1945.
BEUMER, J., 'Die altchristliche Idee einer präexistierenden Kirche und ihre theologische Auswertung', *WW*, IX, 1942, pp. 13–22.
BIDEZ, J. and CUMONT, F., *Les mages hellénisés* (2 vols.), Paris 1938.
BIEDER, W., *Die Vorstellung von der Höllenfahrt Jesu Christi*, Zurich 1949.
BIETENHARD, H., *Das tausendjährige Reich*, 2nd edn., Zurich 1955.
BIETENHARD, H., *Die himmlische Welt im Urchristentum und Spätjudentum*, Tübingen 1951.
BIETENHARD, H., "Ονομα, *TWNT*, V, pp. 242–283.
BIETENHARD, H., 'The millennial hope in the Early Church', *SJT*, VI, 1953, pp. 12–30.
BOISMARD, M.E., 'Une liturgie baptismale dans la Prima Petri', *RB*, LXIII, 1956, pp. 182–208.
BONNER, C., 'Two Problems in Melito's Homily', *HTR*, XXXI, 1938, pp. 175–190.
BONSIRVEN, J., *Le Judaïsme palestinien au temps de Jésus-Christ : sa théologie* (2 vols.), Paris 1934.
BOTTARIUS, J. G., *Sculture e pitture della . . . Roma Sotteranea* (3 vols.), Rome 1737–1754.
BOUSSET, W., *Hauptprobleme der Gnosis*, Göttingen 1907.
BOUSSET, W., *Jüdisch-christlicher Schulbetrieb in Alexandria und Rom*, Göttingen 1915.
BOUSSET, W., 'Platos Weltseele und das Kreuz Christi', *ZNW*, XIV, 1913, pp. 273–285.
BOUYER, L., *La Bible et l'Évangile (Lectio Divina* 8), Paris 1951 [ET: *The meaning of sacred Scripture*, tr. by M. P. Ryan, London 1960].
BOYANCE, P., 'Les deux démons personnels', *RP*, LIX, 1935, pp. 8 ff.
BRANDON, S. G., *The Fall of Jerusalem and the Christian Church*, London 1951.
BRAUN, F. M., 'Les Testaments des Douze Patriarches et le problème de leur origine', *RB*, LXVII, 1960, pp. 516–549.
BRETON, V., 'Jésus au Cénacle. Une hypothèse exégétique', *EL* II, 2, 1953, pp. 263–278.
BROWNLEE, W. H., 'Messianic motifs of Qumran and the New Testament', *NTS*, III, 1, 1956, pp. 12–30.
BÜCHLER, E., 'La Fête des Tabernacles chez Tacite et Plutarque', *REJ*, XXXVII, 1898, pp. 189–197.
BUGGE, C. A., 'Das Gesetz und Christus', *ZNW*, IV, 1903, pp. 89–110.
BULTMANN, R., 'Bekenntnis- und Liedfragmente im I Pt.', *Conjectanea neotestamentica*, XI (in honorem A. J. Fridrichsen), Uppsala, 1947, pp. 1 ff.
BURNEY, C. F., 'Christ as the 'Αρχή of Creation', *JTS*, XXVII, 1926, pp. 160–177.
BURROWS, E., *The Oracles of Jacob and Balaam*, London 1938.

CABANISS, A., 'The Harrowing of Hell, Psalm 24 and Pliny the Younger', *VC*, VII, 1953, pp. 65–74.
CABANISS, A., 'Wisdom, XVIII, 14: an early Christmas text', *VC*, X, 1956, pp. 97–102.
CADIOU, R., 'Origène et les écrits pseudo-clémentines" *RSR*, XX, 1930, pp. 506–515.
CALDER, W. M., 'Epigraphy of Anatolian heresies', *Anatolian Studies in honour of Sir W. M. Ramsay*, London 1923, pp. 76 ff.
CAMELOT, P., *Ignace d'Antioche : Lettres* (Sources chrétiennes, vol. 10), Paris 1954.
CAMPENHAUSEN, H. VON, *Kirchliches Amt und geistliche Vollmacht in den ersten drei Jahrhunderten*, Tübingen 1953.
CARCOPINO, J., *De Pythagore aux Apôtres*, Paris 1956.
CARCOPINO, J., *Le mystère d'un symbole chrétien*, Paris 1955.
CARRINGTON, P., *The primitive Christian calendar*, Cambridge 1952.
CASEY, R. P., *The Excerpta ex Theodoto*, London 1934.

CAUSSE, A., 'L'idéal ébionitique dans les Testaments des Douze Patriarches', *Jub. Alfred Loisy* I, pp. 54 ff., Paris, N.D.

CERFAUX, L., 'Citations scripturaires et tradition textuelle dans les Actes des Apôtres', *Recueil Lucien Cerfaux* II (Bibl. Ephem. theol. Lovan., Vol. 7), Gembloux 1954, pp. 93–103.

CERFAUX, L., 'La première communauté chrétienne à Jérusalem', *Recueil L. Cerfaux* II, Gembloux 1954, pp. 125–157.

CERFAUX, L., *La théologie de l'Église suivant Saint Paul*, Paris 1942; 2nd rev. edn., 1948 [E.T. by G. Webb and A. Walker, *The Church in the Theology of Saint Paul*, New York 1959].

CERFAUX, L., 'Un chapitre du Livre des Testimonia (Pap. Ryl. Gr. 460)', *Recueil L Cerfaux* II, Gembloux 1954, pp. 219–226.

CHADWICK, H., *Origen: Contra Celsum*, Cambridge 1954.

CHADWICK, H., 'The authorship of Papyrus Egerton no. 3', *HTR*, XLIX, 1956, pp. 145–151.

CHADWICK, H., 'The silence of bishops in Ignatius', *HTR*, XLIII, 1950, pp. 169–172.

CHARLES, R. H., *Apocrypha and Pseudepigrapha of the Old Testament* I–II, Oxford 1913.

CHARLES, R. H., *Ascension of Isaiah*, London 1900.

CHAVOUTIER, L., 'Querelle origéniste et controverses trinitaires', *VC*, XIV, 1960 pp. 9–14.

COLLOMP, P., 'Une source de Clément d'Alexandrie et des Homélies pseudo-clémentines', *RP*, XXXVII, 1913, pp. 19 ff.

COLSON, J., *Les fonctions ecclésiales aux premiers siècles*, Paris 1956.

CONNOLLY, R. H., *Didascalia Apostolorum*, Oxford 1929.

CULLMANN, O., *Baptism in the New Testament*, London 1950 [E.T. of *Die Tauflehre des N.T.*, Zurich 1948].

CULLMANN, O., *Die Christologie des Neuen Testaments*, Zürich 1957 [E.T. by S. C. Guthrie and C. A. M. Hall, *The Christology of the N.T.*, London 1959].

CULLMANN, O., 'Die neuentdeckten Qumrantexte und das Judenchristentum der Pseudo-Klementinen', *Neutestamentliche Studien für R. Bultmann* (*BZNW* 21), Berlin 1954, pp. 35–51.

CULLMANN, O., *Dieu et César*, Paris 1956.

CULLMANN, O., *Early Christian Worship*, London 1953.

CULLMANN, O., *Königsherrschaft Christi und Kirche im Neuen Testament*, Basle 1941.

CULLMANN, O., *Le problème littéraire et historique du roman pseudo-clémentin*, Paris 1930.

CULLMANN, O., ' Ὁ ὀπίσω μου ἐρχόμενος', *Conjectanea neotestamentica*, XI (in honorem A. J. Fridrichsen), Uppsala 1947, pp. 26–32.

CULLMANN, O., 'The significance of the Qumran texts for research into the beginnings of Christianity', *JBL*, LXXIV, 1955, pp. 213–226.

CUMONT, F., 'Les vents et les anges psychopompes', *Pisciculi* (*Festschrift F. J. Dölger*), Münster 1939, pp. 70–75.

DAHL, N. A., 'Christ, Creation and the Church', *The Background of the N.T. and its Eschatology* (*in honour of C. H. Dodd*), ed. W. D. Davies and D. Daube, Cambridge 1956, pp. 422–443.

DAHL, N. A., 'La terre où coulent le lait et le miel selon Barnabé VI, 8–19', *Aux Sources de la Tradition chrétienne* (*Mélanges M. Goguel*), Neuchâtel 1950, pp. 62–70.

DAIN, A., 'Note sur le texte de Clément de Rome', *Mélanges Jules Lebreton* I (=*RSR*, XXXIX, 1951), pp. 353–362.

DANIÉLOU, J., *Bible et Liturgie*, Paris 1950 [E.T.: *The Bible and the Liturgy*, London 1960].

DANIÉLOU, J., 'Bulletin d'histoire des origines chrétiennes', *RSR*, XLII, 1954, pp. 585–627.

DANIÉLOU, J., 'Catéchèse pascale et retour au Paradis', *Maison-Dieu* 43, 1955, pp. 99–120.

DANIÉLOU, J., 'Christos Kyrios: une citation des Lamentations de Jérémie dans les Testimonia', *Mélanges Jules Lebreton* I (=*RSR*, XXXIX, 1951), pp. 338–352.

DANIÉLOU, J., 'Das Leben das am Holze hängt', *Kirche und Überlieferung* (*Festgabe Geiselmann*), Freiburg 1960, pp. 22–34.

DANIÉLOU, J., 'Démons', *Dictionnaire de Spiritualité* III, cols. 152–189, Paris 1957–

DANIÉLOU, J., 'Eschatologie chrétienne et eschatologie sadocite'. *Les Manuscrits de la Mer Morte* (*Colloque de Strasbourg, 25–27 mai, 1955*), 1957, pp. 118–125.

DANIÉLOU, J., 'La charrue symbole de la Croix', *RSR*, XLII, 1954, pp. 193–203.

DANIÉLOU, J., 'La communauté de Qumrân et l'organisation de l'Église ancienne', *La Bible et l'Orient*, 1955, pp. 105 ff.

DANIÉLOU, J., 'La typologie millénariste de la semaine', *VC*, II, 1948, pp. 1–16.

DANIÉLOU, J., 'Le Bon Samaritain'. *Mélanges Robert*, Paris–Tournai 1957, pp. 457–465.

DANIÉLOU, J., 'Le psaume 21 dans la catéchèse patristique', *Maison-Dieu*, XLIX, 1957, pp. 17–34.

DANIÉLOU, J., *Les anges et leur mission d'après les pères de l'Église*, 2nd edn., Chevetogne 1953.

DANIÉLOU, J., 'Les démons de l'air dans la Vie d'Antoine', *Antonius Magnus Eremita* (*Stud. Anselm.*, XXXVIII), Rome 1956, pp. 136–147.

DANIÉLOU, J., *Les manuscrits de la mer Morte et les origines du christianisme*, Paris 1957.

DANIÉLOU, J., 'Les Quatre-Temps de Septembre et la Fête des Tabernacles', *Maison-Dieu*, XLVI, 1956, pp. 114–137.

DANIÉLOU, J., *Les saints païens de l'Ancien Testament*, Paris 1956 [E.T. by F. Faber: *Holy pagans of the O.T.*, London 1957].

DANIÉLOU, J., 'Les sources juives de la doctrine des anges des nations chez Origène', *RSR*, XXXVIII, 1951, pp. 132–137.

DANIÉLOU, J., 'L'étoile de Jacob et la mission chrétienne à Damas', *VC*, XI, 1957, pp. 121–138.

DANIÉLOU, J., *Sacramentum futuri: Étude sur les origines de la typologie biblique*, Paris 1950 [E.T. by W. Hibberd, *From Shadows to Reality*, London 1960].

DANIÉLOU, J., 'Une ancienne liturgie judéo-chrétienne', *Cahiers Sioniens*, LII, 1950, pp. 1–11.

DANIÉLOU, J., 'Une source de la spiritualité judéo-chrétienne: la doctrine des deux esprits', *Dieu vivant*, XXV, 1953, pp. 127–136.

D'ALVERNY, M. T., 'Les Anges et les Jours', *CA*, IX, 1957, pp. 271–300.

DAUBE, D., *The New Testament and Rabbinic Judaism*, London 1956.

DAVIES, W. D., *Paul and Rabbinic Judaism*, London 1948.

DAVIES, W. D., '"Knowledge" in the Dead Sea Scrolls and Mt. 11, 25–30', *HTR*, XLVI, 1953, pp. 113–139.

DELLING, G., Ἡμέρα (im N.T.), *TWNT* II, pp. 950–956.

DIETSCHE, W., *Didymus von Alexandrien als Verfasser der Schrift über die Seraphenvision*, Frieburg 1942.

DINKLER, E., 'Jesu Wort vom Kreuztragen', *Neutestamentliche Studien für R. Bultmann* (*BZNW* 21), Berlin 1954, pp. 110–129.

DINKLER, E., 'Zur Geschichte des Kreuzsymbols', *ZTK*, XLVIII, 1951, pp. 148–172.

DIX, G., *Jew and Greek*, London 1953.

DIX, G., 'The Ministry in the Early Church', *The Apostolic Ministry*, London 1946, pp. 183–303.

DIX, G., 'The Seal in the Second Century', *Theology*, LI, 1948, pp. 7–12.

DIX, G., *The Shape of the Liturgy*, London 1945.

DOBSCHÜTZ, E. VON, *Probleme des apostolischen Zeitalters*, Leipzig 1904.

DODD, C. H., *The Bible and the Greeks*, London 1935.

DODD, C. H., *The Interpretation of the Fourth Gospel*, Cambridge 1953.

DOIGNON, J., 'Le salut par le fer et le bois chez Irénée', *RSR*, XLIII, 1955, pp. 535–544.

DÖLGER, F. J., 'Die eigenartige Marienverehrung der Philomarianiten oder Kollyridianer in Arabien', *Antike und Christentum I*, Münster 1929.

DÖLGER, F. J., *Ἰχθύς: das Fisch-Symbol in frühchristlicher Zeit*, 2nd edn., Münster 1928.

DÖLGER, F., *Sol Salutis*, 2nd edn., Münster 1925.

DORESSE, J., *L'Évangile selon Thomas et les Paroles de Jésus*, Paris 1959.

DORESSE, J., *Les livres secrets des gnostiques d'Égypte*, Paris 1959 [E.T. by P. Mairet, *The secret books of the Egyptian Gnostics*, London 1960].

DORESSE, J. and MINA, T., 'Nouveaux textes gnostiques coptes découverts en Haute-Égypte', *VC*, III, 1949, pp. 129–141.

DUMÉRY, H., *Philosophie de la Religion*, Paris 1957.

DUPONT, J., *Ἐν Χριστῷ*, Louvain 1952.

DUPONT, J., *Gnosis. La connaissance religieuse dans les Épîtres de Saint Paul*, Louvain 1949.

DUPONT-SOMMER, A., 'Adam père du monde', *RHR*, CXII, 1939, pp. 182–196.

DUPONT-SOMMER, A., *Le quatrième Livre des Macchabées*, Paris 1939.

DUPONT-SOMMER, A., *La doctrine mystique de la lettre Waw*, Paris 1946.

DUPONT-SOMMER, A., *The Jewish Sect of Qumran and the Essenes* (tr. by R. D. Barnett), London 1954.

EDLUND, C., *Das Auge der Einfalt*, Uppsala 1952.

EDSMAN, C. M., *Le baptême de feu*, Uppsala 1940.

ELLIS, E. EARLE, *Paul's Use of the Old Testament*, Edinburgh 1957.

EPPELT, R., 'Les tables de la Loi et les tables célestes', *RT*, 1937, pp. 1–12.

ERMONI, V., 'Les phases successives de l'erreur millénariste', *RQH*, LXX, 1901, pp. 353–389.

EVANS, E., *Tertullianus: adversus Praxean*, London 1948.

FABBRI, E., 'El bautismo de Jesús en el Evangelio de los Hebreos y en el de los Ebionitas', *RevT*, VI, 1956, pp. 36–55.

FABBRI, E., 'El bautismo de Jesús y el Reposo del Espiritu en la teologia de Ireneo', *Ciencia y Fé*, XII, 1956, pp. 38–63.

FABBRI, E., 'El bautismo de Jesús y la unción del Espiritu', *Ciencia y Fé*, XII, 1956, pp. 1–27.

FESTUGIÈRE, A.-M. J., *La révélation d'Hermès Trismégiste*, Paris 1944– .

FEUILLET, A., 'L'Église plerôme du Christ d'après Eph. I, 23', *NRT*, LXXVIII, 1956, p. 462.

FISHER, B., 'Le Christ dans les Psaumes', *Maison-Dieu*, XXVII, 1951, pp. 86–113.

FRIEDLÄNDER, M., *Der vorchristliche jüdische Gnosticismus*, Göttingen 1898.

FROIDEVAUX, L., 'Sur trois textes cités par Saint Irénée, *RSR*, XLIV, 1956, pp. 408–421.

GCS, *Die griechischen christlichen Schriftsteller der ersten drei Jahrhunderte*, herausgegeben von der Kirchenväter-Commission der Königl. Preuss. Akademie, I– , Berlin 1897– .

GEFFCKEN, J., *Komposition und Entstehungszeit der Oracula Sibyllina (Texte und Untersuchungen)*, Leipzig 1902.

GIBBINS, H. J., 'The problem of the liturgical section of the Didache', *JTS*, XXXVI, 1935, pp. 373-386.

GIET, S., 'La Guerre des Juifs de Flavius Josèphe et quelques énigmes de l'Apocalypse', *Rev SR*, XXVI, 1952, pp. 1-29.

GOODENOUGH, E., *By Light Light*, London 1935.

GOODENOUGH, E., *Jewish Symbols in the Greco-Roman Period* (6 vols.), New York 1953-1956.

GOPPELT, L., *Christentum und Judentum*, Gütersloh 1954.

GOUDOEVER, J. VAN, *Biblical Calendars*, Leiden 1959.

GOULDER, M. D. and SANDERSON, M. L., 'St. Luke's Genesis', *JTS* (NS), VIII, 1957, pp. 12-30.

GRANT, R. M., *Gnosticism and Early Christianity*, New York 1959.

GRANT, R. M., 'The Bible of Theophilus of Antioch', *JBL*, LXVI, 1947, pp. 173-196.

GRANT, R. M., 'The Odes of Solomon and the Church of Antioch', *JBL*, LXIII, 1944, pp. 363-377.

GRANT, R. M., 'Theophilus of Antioch to Autolycus', *HTR*, XL, 1947, pp. 227-256.

GRANT, R. M., 'The problem of Theophilus of Antioch', *HTR*, XLIII, 1950, pp. 179-196.

GRANT, R. M., *The Secret Sayings of Jesus according to the Gospel of Thomas*, London 1960.

GRÉBAUT, S., *Apocalypse de Pierre* (Ethiopic text and French translation), *ROC*, XV, 1910, pp. 198-214; 307-323; 425-439.

GRÉGOIRE, H., 'Un nom mystique du Christ', *Byzantion*, II, 1925, pp. 449-453.

GREIFF, A., 'Das älteste Pascharituale der Kirche, Did. 1-10, und das Johannesevangelium', *Johanneische Studien*, Paderborn 1929- .

GRILLMEIER, A., *Der Logos am Kreuz*, München 1956.

GRY, L., 'La création en sept jours d'après les Apocryphes de l'Ancien Testament', *RSPT*, II, 1908, pp. 277-293.

GRY, L., *Le millénarisme*, Paris 1904.

GRY, L., 'Séjours et habitats divins d'après les apocryphes de l'Ancien Testament', *RSPT*, IV, 1910, pp. 694-722.

GUILDING, A., *The Fourth Gospel and Jewish Worship*, London 1960.

GUILLAUMONT, A., 'Sémitismes dans les Logia de Jésus retrouvés à Nag Hammadi', *JA*, 1958, pp. 113-123.

GUILLAUMONT, A. and others, *The Gospel of Thomas*, Leiden etc. 1959.

GUTWENGER, E., 'Papias. Eine chronologische Studie', *ZKT*, LXIX, 1947, pp. 385-416.

HAENCHEN, E., 'Aufbau und Theologie des Poimandres', *ZTK*, LIII, 1956, pp. 170-175.

HANSON, R. P. C., *Origen's Doctrine of Tradition*, London 1954.

HARNACK, A. VON, *Die Mission und Ausbreitung des Christentums in den ersten drei Jahrhunderten*, 4th edn., Leipzig 1924.

HARRIS, J. RENDEL, *Testimonies*, Cambridge 1916.

HARRIS, J. RENDEL, *The Odes and Psalms of Solomon*, Cambridge 1909; 2nd edn. 1911.

HAUTECOEUR, L., *Mystique et architecture. Symbolisme du cercle et de la coupole*, Paris 1954.

HEITMÜLLER, W., *Im Namen Jesu*, Göttingen 1903.

HEMMER, H., *Clément de Rome: Épître aux Corinthiens* (text and French translation), Paris 1909.

HEMMER, H., *II Clément* (text and French translation), Paris 1909.

HEMMER, H., *Épître de Barnabé* (text and French translation), Paris 1907.

HEMMERDINGER, B., 'Trois nouveaux fragments grecs du Livre III de Saint Irénée', *Scriptorium*, X, 1956, pp. 268 f.

HENNECKE, E. and SCHNEEMELCHER, W., *Neutestamentliche Apokryphen in deutscher Übersetzung*, 3rd edn., Tübingen 1959.

HILGENFELD, A., *Die Ketzergeschichte des Urchristentums*, Leipzig 1884.

HILGENFELD, A., *Judentum und Judenchristentum*, Leipzig 1886.
HOENNICKE, G., *Das Judenchristentum im ersten und zweiten Jahrhundert*, Berlin 1908.
HOUSSIAU, A., *La christologie de Saint Irénée*, Louvain 1954.

IMSCHOOT, P. VAN, 'Baptême de feu et baptême d'Esprit Saint', *ETL*, XIII, 1936, pp. 653–666.
IMSCHOOT, P. VAN, *Théologie de l'Ancien Testament* I, Paris 1954.

JAMES, M. R., *Apocrypha Anecdota* (*Texts and Studies* II, 3; V, 1), Cambridge 1893; 1897.
JAMES, M. R., *The Apocryphal New Testament*, corr. edn, Oxford 1953.
JAMES, M. R., *The lost apocrypha of the Old Testament*, London 1920.
JAUBERT, A., 'La date de la dernière Cène', *RHR*, CXLVI, 1954, pp. 140–173.
JEREMIAS, J., 'In Pap. Oxyr. V, 840, l. 27', *Conjectanea neotestamentica*, XI (in honorem A. J. Fridrichsen), Uppsala 1947, pp. 103 f.
JEREMIAS, J., *Unbekannte Worte Jesu*, Zürich 1948.
JONGE, M. DE, *The Testaments of the Twelve Patriarchs*, Assen 1953.
JUNGMANN, J., 'Altchristliche Gebetsordnung im Lichte des Regelbuches von En-Feschka', *ZKT*, LXXV, 1953, pp. 215–219.

KAHLE, P., *Die hebräischen Handschriften aus der Höhle*, Stuttgart 1951.
KELLY, J. N. D., *Early Christian Creeds*, London 1950.
KILPATRICK, G. D., *The Origin of the Gospel according to Matthew*, Oxford 1946.
KITTEL, G., *Die Probleme des palästinischen Spätjudentums und das Urchristentum* (BWANT III, 1), Stuttgart 1926.
KLAUSER, T., 'Taufet im lebendigen Wasser! Zum religions- und kulturgeschichtlichen Verständnis von Didache VII, 1–13', *Pisciculi* (*Festschrift F. J. Dölger*), Münster 1939, pp. 157–165.
KOEP, L., *Das himmlische Buch in Antike und Christentum*, Bonn 1952.
KÖSTER, H., *Synoptische Überlieferung bei den Apostolischen Vätern*, Berlin 1957.
KRAELING, C. H., *The Excavations of Dura-Europos: Final Report*, New Haven 1956.
KRAFT, R. A., 'Barnabas' Isaiah text and the Testimony Book hypothesis', *JBL*, LXXIX, 1960, pp. 336–350.
KRETSCHMAR, G., 'Himmelfahrt und Pfingsten', *ZKG*, LXVI, 1955, pp. 209–253.
KRETSCHMAR, G., *Studien zur frühchristlichen Trinitätstheologie*, Tübingen 1956.
KRÜGER, P., 'Gehenna und Scheol in dem Schrifttum unter dem Namen des Isaak von Antiochien', *OS*, II, 1953, pp. 270–279.
KUHN, H. B., 'The angelology of the non-canonical Jewish Apocalypses', *JBL*, LXVII, 1948, pp. 217–232.

LAMPE, G. W. H., *The Seal of the Spirit*, London 1951.
LANNE, E., 'Chérubim et Séraphim', *RSR*, XLIII, 1955, pp. 524–535.
LARRANAGA, V., *L'Ascension de Notre Sauveur*, Rome 1938.
LEBRETON, J., *Histoire du dogme de la Trinité*, Paris 1937.
LECLERCQ, H., 'Anges', *Dictionnaire d'archéologie chrétienne et de liturgie* (ed. F. Cabrol and H. Leclercq) I, cols. 2080–2161, Paris 1903–
LEONARDI, C., *Ampelos*, Rome 1947.
LIGHTFOOT, J. B., *The Apostolic Fathers*, London 1891.

LINDESKOG, G., *Studien zum neutestamentlichen Schöpfungsgedanken*, Uppsala 1952.
LIPSIUS, R. A. and BONNET, M., *Actes apocryphes des Apôtres*, Leipzig 1891– .
LOHMEYER, E., *Die Offenbarung des Johannes (HNT* 16), 2nd edn., Tübingen 1953.
LUECKEN, W., *Michael*, Göttingen 1898.
LUNDBERG, P., *La typologie baptismale dans l'Ancienne Église*, Uppsala 1942.

MALININE, M., PUECH, H. C. and QUISPEL, G., *Evangelium Veritatis*, Zürich 1956.
MANSON, T. W., 'Miscellanea Apocalyptica III', *JTS*, XLVIII, 1947, pp. 59–61.
MANSON, T. W., 'The argument from Prophecy', *JTS*, XLVI, 1945, pp. 129–136.
MANSON, T. W., 'The Cleansing of the Temple', *BJRL*, XXXIII, 2, 1951, pp. 271–282.
MARMORSTEIN, A., 'Jüdische Parallelen zur Petrusapokalypse', *ZNW*, X, 1909, pp. 297–300.
MARTIMORT, A. G., 'L'iconographie des catacombes et la catéchèse antique', *Riv AC*, XXV, 1949, pp. 105–114.
MASSAUX, É., *L'influence de l'Évangile de Saint Matthieu sur la littérature chrétienne avant Saint Irénée*, Louvain 1950.
MEINHOLD, P., 'Geschichte und Exegese im Barnabasbrief', *ZKG*, LXIV, 1940, pp. 255–303.
MEINHOLD, P., 'Schweigende Bischöfe', *Festgabe Lortz*, Baden-Baden 1957, pp. 467–490.
MICHAELIS, W., 'Zeichen, Siegel, Kreuz', *TZ*, XII, 1956, pp. 505–526.
MICHAELIS, W., *Zur Engelchristologie im Urchristentum*, Basle 1942.
MIGNE, J. P., *Patrologiae graecae cursus completus*, Paris 1857– .
MIGNE, J. P., *Patrologiae latinae cursus completus*, Paris 1844– .
MILIK, J. T., 'Fragments d'un midrash de Michée dans les manuscrits de Qumrân', *RB*, LIX, 1952, pp. 412–418.
MILIK, J. T., 'Le Testament de Lévi en araméen', *RB*, LXII, 1955, pp. 398–406.
MOFFATT, J., 'An approach to Ignatius', *HTR*, XXIX, 1936, pp. 1–38.
MOLIN, G., 'Qumran, Apocalyptic, Essenism', *Saeculum*, VI, 1955, pp. 244–281.
MOLLAND, E., 'La circoncision, le baptême et l'autorité du décret apostolique (Act. XV, 28 sqq.) dans les milieux judéo-chrétiens des Pseudo-Clémentines', *ST*, IX, 1955, pp. 1–39.
MOLLAND, E., 'The Heretics combatted by Ignatius of Antioch', *JEH*, V, 1954, pp. 1–6.
MOORE, G. F., *Judaism in the first centuries of the Christian era* (3 vols.), Cambridge, Mass. (U.S.A.) 1927.
MORIN, G., 'Hieronymus de Monogrammate', *RBen*, XX, 1903, pp. 225–236.
MORIN, G., *Tractatus contra Originem de visione Isaiae (Anecdota Maredsolana III*, 3), Oxford 1903.
MÜLLER, A., *Ecclesia-Maria: die Einheit Mariens und der Kirche*, Freiburg-i-d-Schweiz 1951.
MUNCK, J., *Untersuchungen über Klemens von Alexandrie*, Stuttgart 1933.
MUSURILLO, H., 'The problem of ascetical fasting in the Greek Patristic writers', *Traditio*, XII, 1956, pp. 1–64.

NAUTIN, P., *Hippolyte et Josipe*, Paris 1947.
NOCK, A. D. and FESTUGIÈRE, A.-M. J., *Corpus Hermeticum* I– , Paris 1945– .

OESTERLEY, W. O. E., *The Jewish background of the Christian liturgy*, Oxford 1925.
ORBE, A., 'Cristo y la Iglesia en su matrimonio anterior a los siglos', *EE*, XXIX, 1955, pp. 299–344.

ORBE, A., 'En los albores de la exegesis johannea', *Estudios valentinianos* II, Rome 1955.
ORBE, A., 'Los primeros herejes ante la persecución', *Estudios valentinianos* V, Rome 1957.
ORBE, A., 'Teologia bautismal de Clemente Alejandrino', *Gregorianum*, XXXVI, 1955, pp. 410–448.

PETERSON, E., 'Beiträge zur Interpretation der Visionen im Pastor Hermae', *OCP*, XIII, 1947, pp. 624–635.
PETERSON, E., 'Das Amulet von Akra', *Aegyptus*, XXXIII, 1953, pp. 172–178.
PETERSON, E., 'Das Praescriptum des I Clemens-Briefes'. *Pro Regno Pro Sanctuario* (in honour of G. van de Leeuw), pp. 351–354.
PETERSON, E., 'Das Schiff als Symbol der Kirche', *TZ*, VI, 1950, pp. 77–79.
PETERSON, E., 'Didache cap. 9 e 10', *Eph L*, LVIII, 1944, pp. 3–13.
PETERSON, E., 'Die Begegnung mit dem Ungeheuer: Hermas Visio IV', *VC*, VIII, 1954, pp. 52–71.
PETERSON, E., 'Die geschichtliche Bedeutung der jüdischen Gebetsrichtung', *TZ*, III, 1947, pp. 1–15.
PETERSON, E., 'Die Spiritualität des griechischen Physiologos', *BZ*, XLVII, 1954, pp. 60–72.
PETERSON, E., *Frühkirche, Christentum und Gnosis*, Rome 1959.
PETERSON, E., 'La Croce e la preghiera verso l'oriente', *Eph L*, LIX, 1945, pp. 52–68.
PETERSON, E., 'La libération d'Adam de l'Anankè', *RB*, LV, 1948, pp. 199–214.
PETERSON, E., 'Le traitement de la rage par les Elkasaïtes', *RSR*, XXXIV, 1947, pp. 232–238.
PETERSON, E., 'L'origine dell' ascesi cristiana', *Euntes Docete*, I, 1948, pp. 195–204.
PETERSON, E., 'Über einige Probleme der Didache-Überlieferung', *Riv AC*, XXVII, 1951, pp. 37–68.
PHILONENKO, M., 'La notice du Josèphe slave sur les Esséniens', *Semitica*, VI, 1956, p. 69–73.
PHILONENKO, M., *Les interpolations chrétiennes des Testaments des Douze Patriarches et les manuscrits de Qumrân*, Paris 1960.
PITRA, J. B., *Spicilegium Solesmense* (4 vols.), Paris 1852–1858.
PLUMPE, H. J., 'Some little-known early witnesses to Mary's virginitas in partu', *TS*, IX, 1948, pp. 567–577.
PO, *Patrologia orientalis* I– , ed. R. Graffin and F. Nau, Paris 1903– .
PREISIGKE, K. F., *Wörterbuch der greichischen Papyrusurkunden*, Heidelberg 1924– .
PREUSCHEN, E., *Antilegomena*, 2nd edn., Giessen 1905.
PUECH, H. C. and QUISPEL, G., 'Le quatrième écrit gnostique du Codex Jung', *VC*, IX, 1955, pp. 65–102.
PUECH, H. C. and QUISPEL, G., 'Les écrits gnostiques du Codex Jung', *VC*, VIII, 1954, pp. 1–51.
PUECH, H. C., QUISPEL, G. and VAN UNNIK, W. C., *The Jung Codex*, London 1955.

QUISPEL, G., 'Christliche Gnosis und jüdische Heterodoxie', *ET*, XIV, 1954, pp. 1–11.
QUISPEL, G., 'L'Évangile selon Thomas et le texte occidental du Nouveau Testament', *VC*, XIV, 1960, pp. 204–215.
QUISPEL, G., 'L'inscription de Flavia Sophè', *Mélanges de Ghellinck*, Gembloux 1951, pp. 201–214.
QUISPEL, G., 'The Gospel of Thomas and the New Testament', *VC*, XI, 1957, pp. 189–207.

RAHNER, H., 'Das Kreuz als Mastbaum und Antenne', *ZKT*, LXXV, 1953, pp. 129–173.
RAHNER, H., 'Das Meer der Welt', *ZKT*, LXVI, pp. 89–118.

RAHNER, H., 'Das mystische Tau', *ZKT*, LXXV, 1953, pp. 385–410.

RAHNER, H., *Griechische Mythen in christlicher Deutung*, Zürich 1945.

REAGAN, J. N., *The Preaching of Peter*, Chicago 1923.

REICKE, B., *Diakonie, Festfreude und Zelos*, Uppsala 1951.

REICKE, B., 'Die Verfassung der Urgemeinde im Lichte jüdischer Dokumente', *TZ*, X, 1954, pp. 106 ff.

REICKE, B., *The disobedient spirits and Christian baptism*, Copenhagen 1945.

REITZENSTEIN, R., *De centesima sexagesima tricesima*, cf. below, 'Eine frühchristliche Schrift'.

REITZENSTEIN, R., 'Eine frühchristliche Schrift von den dreierlei Früchten', *ZNW*, XV, 1914, pp. 60–90.

REITZENSTEIN, R., *Poimandres*, Leipzig 1904.

RESCH, A., *Agrapha (Texte und Untersuchungen* N.F. 15, 3–4), Leipzig 1906.

RICHARD, M., *Asterii sophistae commentariorum in Psalmos quae supersunt*, Oslo 1956.

RICHARD, M., 'Comput et chronographie chez Saint Hippolyte', *MSR*, VII, 1950, pp. 237–268.

RIESENFELD, H., 'Ignatius såsom hellenist', *Religion och Bibel*, XII, 1953, pp. 1–18.

RIESENFELD, H., *Jésus transfiguré*, Copenhagen 1947.

RIESENFELD, H., 'La signification sacramentaire du baptême johannique', *Dieu vivant*, XIII, 1949, pp. 29–37.

RIST, M., 'Additional parallels to the Rending of the Veil in Melito's Homily on the Passion', *HTR*, XXXI, 1938, pp. 249–250.

ROBERTS, B. J., *The Old Testament Text and Versions*, Cardiff 1951.

ROBINSON, F., *Coptic apocryphal gospels*, Cambridge 1896.

ROLLER, O., 'Das Buch mit sieben Siegeln', *ZNW*, XXXVI, 1937, pp. 98–113.

ROUSSEAU, O., 'La descente aux enfers fondement du baptême chrétien', *Mélanges Jules Lebreton* II (=*RSR*, XL, 1–2, 1952), pp. 273–297.

ROUTH, M. J., *Reliquiae Sacrae* (5 vols), Oxford, 1846–8.

ROWLEY, H. H., *The Relevance of Apocalyptic*, 2nd edn., London 1947.

RUDOLPH, K., *Die Mandäer* I– , Göttingen 1960– .

SAGNARD, F. M., *Clément d'Alexandrie: Extraits de Théodote*, Paris 1948.

SAGNARD, F. M., *La gnose valentinienne et le témoignage de Saint Irénée*, Paris 1947.

SAHLIN, H., *Der Messias und das Gottesvolk*, Uppsala 1945.

SANDERS, L., *L'hellénisme de Saint Clément de Rome et le paulinisme*, Louvain 1943.

SCHENKE, H. M., 'Das Evangelium nach Philippus', *TL*, LXXXIV, 1959, pp. 1–12.

SCHENKE, H. M., *Die Herkunft des sogenannten Evangelium Veritatis*, Göttingen 1959.

SCHERER, J., *Le commentaire d'Origène sur Rom.*, III, 5–V, 7, Cairo 1957.

SCHILLE, G., 'Katechese und Taufliturgie', *ZNW*, LI, 1960, pp. 112–131.

SCHILLE, G., 'Zur urchristlichen Tauflehre. Stylistische Beobachtungen am Barnabas-brief', *ZNW*, XLIX, 1958, pp. 31–52.

SCHLIER, H., 'Ἀμήν, *TWNT* I, pp. 339–342.

SCHLIER, H., 'Ἀνατολή, *TWNT* I, pp. 354–355.

SCHLIER, H., *Christus und die Kirche im Epheserbrief*, Tübingen 1930.

SCHLIER, H., *Religionsgeschichtliche Untersuchungen zur den Ignatiusbriefen*, Giessen 1929.

SCHMID, J., 'Didache', *RAC* III, cols. 1009–1013, Stuttgart 1950– .

SCHMIDT, C., 'Das koptische Didache-Fragment des British Museum', *ZNW*, XXIV, 1925, pp. 81–99.

SCHMIDT, C., *Gespräche Jesu mit seinen Jüngern nach der Auferstehung*, Leipzig 1919.

SCHMIDT, R., 'Aetates mundi: die Weltalter als Gliederungsprinzip der Geschichte' *ZKG*, LXVII, 1955–6, pp. 288–317.

SCHMITT, J., 'Sacerdoce judaïque et hiérarchie ecclésiale', *RevSR*, XXIX, 1955, pp. 250–261.

SCHNEIDER, T., 'Das prophetische Agraphon der Epistola Apostolorum', *ZNW*, XXIV, 1925, pp. 151–154.

SCHNEIDER, T., 'Der Engel Jakob bei Mani', *ZNW*, XXXIII, 1934, pp. 218–219.
SCHOEDEL, W. R., 'Naassene themes in the Coptic Gospel of Thomas', *VC*, XIV, 1960, pp. 225–234.
SCHOEPS, H. J., *Aus frühchristlicher Zeit*, Tübingen 1950.
SCHOEPS, H. J., 'Handelt es sich wirklich um ebionitische Dokumente?', *ZRGG*, III, 1951, pp. 322–336.
SCHOEPS, H. J., *Theologie und Geschichte des Judenchristentums*, Tübingen 1949.
SCHOEPS, H. J., *Urgemeinde, Judenchristentum, Gnosis*, Tübingen 1956.
SCHOLEM, G., *Major Trends in Jewish Mysticism*, 2nd rev. edn., New York 1946; French edn. (*Les grands courants de la mystique juive*), Paris 1950; 3rd edn., London 1955.
SCHRENK, G., Βιβλίον, *TWNT* I, pp. 615–620.
SEGELBERG, E., *Masbūtā : studies in the ritual of the Mandaean baptism*, Uppsala 1958.
SEITZ, O. J., 'Antecedents and signification of the term δίψυχος', *JBL*, LXVI, 1947, pp. 211–219.
SELWYN, E. C., 'The Feast of Tabernacles, Epiphany and Baptism', *JTS*, XIII, 1912, pp. 225–249.
SELWYN, E. G., *The First Epistle of Saint Peter*, London 1947.
SIMON, M., 'Les sectes juives chez les Pères', *Stud Patr*, I, 1956, pp. 526–540.
SIMON, M., *Verus Israel*, Paris 1948.
SIMONIN, H. D., 'Le doute (διψυχία) d'après les Pères Apostoliques', *VS*, LI, 1937, pp. 165–178.
SMITH, J. P., 'Hebrew Christian midrash in Irenaeus (*Dem.* 43)', *Biblica*, XXXVIII, 1957, pp. 24–34.
SMITH, J. P., *Proof of the Apostolic Preaching* (ACW 16), London 1952; Westminster, Md. (U.S.A.) 1953.
SOURY, G., *La démonologie de Plutarque*, Paris 1942.
STAUFFER, E., 'Zum Khalifat des Jacobus', *ZRGG*, IV, 1952, pp. 193–214.
STEFFES, J. P., *Das Wesen des Gnostizismus und sein Verhältnis zum katholischen Dogma*, Paderborn 1932.
STENDAHL, K., *The School of St. Matthew*, Uppsala 1954.
STOMMEL, E., Σημεῖον ἐκπετάσεως, *RQ*, XLVIII, 1953, pp. 21–42.
STRACK, H. K. and BILLERBECK, P., *Kommentar zum Neuen Testament aus Talmud und Midrasch* (5 vols. in 6), Munich 1922–1956.
STRECKER, G., *Das Judenchristentum in den Pseudoklementinen*, Berlin 1958.
SULZBERGER, M., 'Le symbole de la Croix', *Byzantion*, II, 1925, pp. 356–383.

TAYLOR, V., *The Names of Jesus*, London 1953.
TEICHER, J. L., 'The Christian interpretation of the sign X in the Isaiah Scroll', *VT*, V, 1955, pp. 189–198.
TEICHER, J. L., 'The Dead Sea Scrolls: Documents of the Jewish Christian sect of Ebionites', *JJS*, II, 1951, pp. 67–99.
THOMAS, J., *Le mouvement baptiste en Palestine et Syrie*, Gembloux 1935.
THYEN, H., *Der Stil der jüdisch-hellenistischen Homilie*, Göttingen 1955.
TILL, W. C., *Apocryphon of John*, cf. *Die gnostischen Schriften* below.
TILL, W. C., *Die gnostischen Schriften des koptischen Papyrus Beroliniensis 8502 (Texte und Untersuchungen)*, Berlin 1955.
TISSERANT, E., *Ascension d'Isaïe*, Paris 1909.
TURNER, H. E. W., *The Pattern of Christian Truth*, London 1954.

UNNIK, W. C. VAN, 'Is I Clement 20 purely Stoic?', *VC*, IV, 1950, pp. 181–189.
UNNIK, W. C. VAN, 'The origin of the recently discovered Apocryphon Jacobi', *VC*, X, 1956, pp. 149–156.
USENER, K., *Kleine Schriften* (4 vols.), Leipzig 1912– .

VAGANAY, L., *Évangile de Pierre*, Paris 1930.

VAILLANT, A., *Le Livre des secrets d'Hénoch*, Paris 1952.

VERMÈS, G., 'A propos des commentaires bibliques découverts à Qumrân', *La Bible et l'Orient* (*Congrès d'archéologie et d'orientalisme biblique de Saint-Cloud*), 1955, pp. 95–104.

VERMÈS, G., 'La secte juive de la Nouvelle Alliance', *Cahiers Sioniens*, Sept. 1950, pp. 18–21.

VERMÈS, G., *Les manuscrits du désert de Juda*, Tournai 1953.

VERMÈS, G., 'Quelques traditions de la communauté de Qumrân', *Cahiers Sioniens*, VIII, 1955, pp. 42–44.

VILLETTE, J., *La résurrection du Christ dans l'art chrétien du Ier au VIe siècle*, Paris 1957.

VOKES, F. E., *The Riddle of the Didache*, London 1938.

VÖÖBUS, A., *Celibacy, a requirement for admission to Baptism in the Early Christian Church*, Stockholm 1951.

WAITZ, H., *Die Pseudo-Klementinen* (*Texte und Untersuchungen* N.F. 10, 4), Leipzig 1904.

WASZINK, J. H., *Tertullianus: De anima*, Amsterdam 1947.

WERNER, M., *Die Entstehung des christlichen Dogmas*, Leipzig 1941.

WIKENHAUSER, A., 'Das Problem des tausendjährigen Reiches in der Johannes-Apokalypse', *RQ*, XL, 1932, pp. 13–25.

WIDENGREN, G., *The Ascension of the Apostle and the Heavenly Book*, Uppsala 1950.

WILPERT, G., *I sarcofagi cristiani antichi* I–II, Rome, 1930–2.

WILSON, R. McL., 'Gnostic origins', *VC*, IX, 1955, pp. 193–211.

WILSON, R. McL., 'Gnostic origins again', *VC*, XI, 1957, pp. 93–110.

WILSON, R. McL., 'Simon, Dositheus and the DSS', *ZRGG*, IX, 1957, pp. 21–30.

WILSON, R. McL., *Studies in the Gospel of Thomas*, London 1960.

WILSON, R. McL., 'The Early History of the Exegesis of Gen.I, 26', *Stud. Patr.*, II, 1957, pp. 420–437.

WINTER, P., 'Zadokite fragments IV, 20–21, and the exegesis of Gen. 1:27 in Later Judaism', *ZAW* LXVIII (N.F. 27), 1956, pp. 71–84.

ZAHN, T., *Marcellus von Ancyra*, Gotha 1867.

ZELLER, H., 'Corpora sanctorum', *ZKT*, LXXI, 1949, pp. 385–465.

ZWAAN, J. DE, 'The Edessene origin of the Odes of Solomon', *Quantulacumque: Studies presented to Kirsopp Lake*, London 1937, pp. 285–302.

INDEXES

TEXTUAL INDEXES

OLD TESTAMENT

APOCRYPHA (Biblical)

NEW TESTAMENT

JEWISH WRITINGS

JEWISH CHRISTIAN WRITINGS

APOCRYPHAL ACTS

GNOSTIC WRITINGS

FATHERS OF THE CHURCH

MISCELLANEOUS WRITINGS

DE LICENTIA SUPERIORUM ORDINIS. NIHIL OBSTAT: HUBERTUS RICHARDS, S.T.L., L.S.S., CENSOR DEPUTATUS. IMPRIMATUR: ✠ GEORGIUS L. CRAVEN, EPUS SEBASTOPOLIS, VIC. GEN. WESTMONASTERII, DIE 13A JANUARIUS 1964. THE NIHIL OBSTAT AND IMPRIMATUR ARE A DECLARATION THAT A BOOK OR PAMPHLET IS CONSIDERED TO BE FREE FROM DOCTRINAL OR MORAL ERROR. IT IS NOT IMPLIED THAT THOSE WHO HAVE GRANTED THE NIHIL OBSTAT AND IMPRIMATUR AGREE WITH THE CONTENTS, OPINIONS OR STATEMENTS EXPRESSED.